DANCE WITH DEMONS

DANCE WITH DEMONS

"If I go to hell, I will not be afraid of the devil. Because I have worked with Jerome Robbins."

—MEL TOMLINSON, former soloist,
New York City Ballet

nowitz and, finally, *The Poppa Piece.* While Robbins struggled to create scenes directly from the emotionally charged raw material of his memories, the performers never knew what to expect from one day to the next. They were often given newly scripted pages at the last minute and could never be sure if they would be called in on a particular day or not.

As the rehearsals progressed, one of the actors, Jace Alexander, sensed Robbins' frustration. "As we began to get closer to stuff that would touch on HUAC, which all of us always felt like he was dancing around—all of us felt like he wanted to go there, like he finally wanted to go to this place. It was very therapeutic, the whole thing, but every time he came close to it, that's when the rehearsal would end and the scripts would change."

Finally, without any formal announcement, Robbins simply gave up on the project. He couldn't go through with it.

"I think it was too hard," another cast member, Ron Rifkin, speculated. "I think Jerry was too old. I think he had too many losses. I think it brought up too much shit for him."

Dancer Joey McKneely agreed. "He would have had to go to a deeper place, a darker place, where he might not have wanted people to see."

Dance with Demons is the story that Robbins was unable to tell. It is based on years of research; done with the help of dozens of Robbins' friends, family members and colleagues; and meant to be the full measure of both the artist and the man. While many of the great and near-great move through its pages—names such as Balanchine, Bernstein, de Mille, Kazan, Clift, Mostel—it is Robbins himself who stands at the center, a figure of towering achievement and tortured complexity—a searching portrait of light and dark.

It was also all bound up for Robbins with his turbulent relationship with his father, the man he never seemed to be able to please. "His father had imbued him with the sense," says lyricist Sheldon Harnick, "that because he was Jewish and because he wasn't that talented, but particularly because he was Jewish, no matter what he accomplished in his life, no matter what prizes he won, no matter what money he made, ultimately everything would be taken away from him. And so he said that to go up before the Committee that was like his worst nightmare."

For the rest of his life, it would all be hopelessly tangled, his creative genius and his demons. His attitude toward his sexuality would remain so conflicted that it would be his relationships, engagements and near-engagements with women that he would present to the world, while his affairs with men remained as clandestine as possible. His father's attitude toward his early dancing career, says Bob Silverman, basically would have been, "My son's a fag—how can I talk to him?" His driving fear of failure produced work of stunning achievement, but also led him to a perfectionism that many felt bordered on the sadistic (one day, his dancers simply watched as he backed up until he fell down into an open orchestra pit—said one eyewitness, "Nobody said, 'Watch it!' Nope. Off he went").

All of these spectres came together for Robbins when he was confronted by the threat of exposure. He never did convince Sullivan to put him on his show. And when HUAC did indeed call him to testify three years later, he quickly caved in, giving them the names of eight Party members of his acquaintance. "It won't be for years until I know whether I did the right thing," he confided to playwright Arthur Laurents.

"Oh, I can tell you now," said Laurents. "You were a shit."

In fact, his conscience was already bleeding. While his career and artistry flourished to ever-greater heights, he lost many friends, and the memory of his decision to inform haunted him until his death. He refused to let anyone write his biography, intent on concealing everything that was most precious in his life, except for the art that was his legacy.

Only once did he seriously attempt to deal with his demons publicly. In 1991, at the age of seventy-two, he decided to stage an autobiographical drama, called variously *The Jew Piece, The Home Play, Rabinowitz by Robbins, Robbins by Rabi-*

Preface

In the spring of 1950, Jerome Robbins should have been on top of the world.

At the age of thirty-one, he was already a commanding creative force. On Broadway, he had choreographed five musicals, including the groundbreaking *On the Town*, and his work with Ballet Theatre and the New York City Ballet had established him as an artist of astonishing diversity. In the decades to come, he would transform Broadway, as both a choreographer and a director, with such shows as *West Side Story, The King and I, Gypsy, Peter Pan, A Funny Thing Happened on the Way to the Forum, Fiddler on the Roof* and *Jerome Robbins' Broadway*. In ballet, he would create more than sixty works that became the cutting edge to a homegrown revolution; dances, as he put it, "paced with an American tempo," airy sylphs and enchanted princesses banished in favor of earthly themes and a language of movement all his own. For all this, he would win five Tony Awards, two Academy Awards, a Kennedy Center Honor, the National Medal of the Arts and the French Legion of Honor.

But in the spring of 1950, Robbins felt it all slipping away.

His reputation as an up-and-coming new star had won him a coveted invitation from Ed Sullivan to appear on his television show that Easter Sunday—but now Sullivan had canceled him. In the Senate, Joseph McCarthy held sway, and Sullivan's sponsor, the Ford Motor Company, had instructed him to clear all of his guests with a right-wing publication called *Counterattack: The Newsletter of Facts to Combat Communism* before allowing anyone on the air. And *Counterattack* had just named Robbins as a suspected Communist.

Robbins' agent desperately arranged a meeting with Sullivan to try to get him to change his mind, and the night before, Robbins had dinner with his cousin Bob Silverman.

"Jerry said, 'I got a call from Ed Sullivan, and he wants me to come to his office tomorrow morning. He said he wanted me to give him the names of the people who were at that party—you remember the party at my place that Lena Horne gave?' I said, 'Of course.' That party was a benefit for Soviet-American friendship. Jerry says, 'Do you remember who was there?' I said, 'Sure. I remember who was there.' He said, 'Shhh! Don't talk so loud.' He was in a panic, looking around. I mean he was really paranoid. He was looking at the waiter who was coming by at that point. Jerry said, 'I don't know what to do. What would you do?' I said, 'I wouldn't give 'em the time of day. You can't give them names, Jerry. You can't tell on your friends.' He said, 'Right.'

"So we finished dinner and went our ways. He had an appointment in the morning with a lawyer before he met with Sullivan. But you know what Sullivan told him? I heard Sullivan told him that if Jerry didn't give the names [of fellow Communists] that he [Sullivan] was going to run items in his newspaper column about Jerry being homosexual. You have to know what that means. In those days, that was death. That was death in your own family, first of all . . . because that was not what good Jewish American boys did. So that had to be a real terror for him. That's why I thought about it all these years. God, what he had to go through, the pressure they put on him."

The terror was further compounded by Robbins' certainty that Sullivan was only the beginning—he was sure to be called before the House Committee on Un-American Activities (HUAC)—and he didn't know what he would say to them. He couldn't afford to let his sexuality be known (although as one of his colleagues, actor James Mitchell, later pointed out, "He was living in some kind of dream world. Who didn't know?"). But if he didn't cooperate with the Committee, then the details of his sex life would be spread out all over the newspapers.

ALSO BY GREG LAWRENCE

Dancing on My Grave (with Gelsey Kirkland)

The Shape of Love (with Gelsey Kirkland)

The Little Ballerina & Her Dancing Horse (with Gelsey Kirkland)

DANCE with DEMONS

THE LIFE OF JEROME ROBBINS

Greg Lawrence

G. P. PUTNAM'S SONS   NEW YORK

G. P. Putnam's Sons
Publishers Since 1838
a member of
Penguin Putnam Inc.
375 Hudson Street
New York, NY 10014

The author gratefully acknowledges permission to quote the following:

Writings by Leonard Bernstein © Amberson Holdings, LLC. Used by permission.
Lyrics from "A Puzzlement" and "Something Wonderful" by Richard Rodgers and
Oscar Hammerstein II. Copyright © 1951 (Renewed) by Richard Rodgers and Oscar
Hammerstein II. Williamson Music owner of publications and allied rights throughout the
world. International copyright secured. All rights reserved. Reprinted by permission.
Excerpts from Arthur Laurents' *Original Story By*. Copyright © 2000 by Arthur
Laurents. Reprinted by permission of Alfred A. Knopf, a Division of Random House, Inc.
Excerpts from *Stephen Sondheim: A Life* by Meryle Secrest. Copyright © 1998 by Meryle
Secrest. Reprinted by permission of Alfred A. Knopf, a Division of Random House, Inc.
Excerpts from *Bird's Eye View: Dancing with Martha Graham and on Broadway* by Dorothy
Bird. © 1997 by Dorothy Bird and Joyce Greenberg. Reprinted by permission of University
of Pittsburgh Press.
The author is likewise grateful to the estates of Marc Blitzstein, Agnes de Mille and
Leland Hayward for permission to quote from material in their control, and to the
Kennedy Center Oral History Project.

Library of Congress Cataloging-in-Publication Data

Lawrence, Greg.
Dance with demons : the life of Jerome Robbins / Greg Lawrence.
p.   cm.
ISBN 0-399-14652-0
1. Robbins, Jerome. 2. Choreographers—United States—Biography.
3. United States—History—20th century. I. Title.
GV1785.R52 L39   2001   00-047065
792.8'2'092—dc21
[B]

Printed in the United States of America
1   3   5   7   9   10   8   6   4   2

This book is printed on acid-free paper. ∞

For my sister,
Paula Stricklin

Contents

ONE

The Making of a Gypsy

He was born Jerome Wilson Rabinowitz on October 11, 1918, exactly one month before the end of World War I. He came into the world at the Jewish Maternity Hospital (later incorporated into Beth Israel Hospital) at 270 East Broadway, in the heart of Manhattan's Lower East Side immigrant neighborhood. At the time, the Rabinowitz family lived in a large apartment house at 51 East Ninety-seventh Street, at the northeast corner of Madison Avenue. The birth could have taken place at nearby Mt. Sinai Hospital, but Jerome's mother and father, Lena and Harry Rabinowitz, favored a Jewish hospital that provided kosher food and Yiddish-speaking doctors.

From his earliest days, Jerome was called "Jerry" by family and friends, and according to his sister, Sonia, his middle name, Wilson, reflected their parents' patriotic enthusiasm for the current President. The family name meant literally "son of a rabbi" and was never one that Jerry liked; it marked him as the son of Jewish immigrants, a stigma that he resented in his youth and which he identified with his parents, especially with his father, who retained a thick Yiddish accent and the habits of the Old World.

Harry (originally Chane) Rabinowitz was born September 11, 1888, and emigrated from his native Russia in 1904 while still a teenager, traveling first to England and then to America. His departure had required subterfuge in order to avoid serving as cannon fodder in the Russian army. Robbins' sister recalled that their father "managed to escape the draft in Russia by being declared dead . . . which he would have been if he had been drafted." Harry's father, Nathan Mayer Rabinowitz, made his living as a baker, a trade that he passed on to his children. His wife, Sara Luniansky Rabinowitz, had apparently died relatively young. As an elderly widower, Harry's father remained behind in the village of Rozanka, a tiny rural community in the province of Vilna near the shifting Russian-Polish border. As was common for such impoverished Jewish families, the Rabinowitz clan emigrated one at a time. The first to leave was Harry's oldest brother, Julius, who established himself in Manhattan and later arranged passage for the others—first Harry, and eventually two more brothers, Samuel and Theodore, and their sister, Ruth.

The Rabinowitz siblings were part of the great wave of Jewish immigrants who came to this country to escape the pogroms and outbreaks of anti-Semitic violence that were occurring throughout Eastern Europe. The world of the *shtetl* was one of privation and miseries endured. A familiar adage of the *shtetl* was the heartfelt lament, "If God lived here, His windows would be broken." For a poverty-stricken community increasingly under siege religious faith served as both a solace and essential bond. But in the New World, faith was coupled with a practical ambition for material success, a dream now at least within reach for the uprooted Rabinowitz family.

Harry soon went into business with his brothers, opening a Kosher delicatessen on the same block as their East Ninety-seventh Street apartment house. One of Jerry's young cousins, Jack Davenport, retains fond memories of the deli and its proprietors. "Uncle Harry used to tell me that he kept my mother on the cutting table. . . . She could cut turkey [and] tongue so that you could read a newspaper through it. . . . Harry was the family practical joker and neighborhood ass-pincher and project supervisor. . . . [He] never lost his dialect, [which was] hard to understand, and in later years turned off his hearing aid—conveniently. . . . Lena was the head of the household and super smart, very organized." The neighborhood at the edge of Carnegie Hill and what is now Spanish Harlem was then largely Jewish. More than fifty other families lived in the building, all of them immigrants representing the strati-

fied Jewish world of Europe, with Germans at the top and Russians, Poles and
Hungarians at the bottom. Harry's younger siblings, Samuel and Ruth, also
lived in the apartment and worked in the deli, as would Harry's future wife,
Lena, and her sister, Jean. Harry would prove himself an able provider, but by
the time Jerome was born, the inherited dream of success had magnified beyond anything his lower middle-class father might have imagined. Like many
of his generation, Jerry would embrace the idea of putting as much social distance as possible between himself and his origins.

At the age of twenty-four, Harry Rabinowitz had married Lena Rips,
who lived just across the river in Jersey City. The nuptials took place on February 9, 1911. Cousin Viola Zousmer recalled, "Lena was my mother's best
friend and introduced her to Harry. My mother's name was Honey Zousmer.
My mother and Jerry's father were first cousins." Lena, the bride, was two years
younger than her husband, and, according to relatives, she soon proved herself
opinionated and outspoken on all domestic matters. She was also ahead of her
husband in education, having graduated from high school and spent two years
at a college in Des Moines, Iowa, and unlike her husband, she spoke English
with perfect diction. On June twenty-seventh of the following year, Lena gave
birth to their first child, Sonia.

The marriage made for a large extended family with strong ties to the Old
World and the old ways. The Rips clan had immigrated from Minsk in the
early 1890s and settled in the largely Jewish, Hudson City district of Jersey
City, an area known as "the Heights." The family was devoutly Orthodox.
Lena's father, Aaron Rips, worked as a cutter in the garment trade and later
owned a candy store. He was also a founder of the local synagogue, Congre-
gation Mt. Sinai. Lena's mother, Ida, helped establish the first Hebrew school
in the district. She was a member of Hadassah and first director of the Hebrew Home for Orphans and Aged. Jerry's cousin, Jack Davenport, recalled
that Ida "was one of the driving forces and founders of the Sherman Avenue
Talmud Torah. Grandma Ida Rips was the energy and drive in the Jewish community in Jersey City."

Another cousin, Jean Handy, would later dance as a teenager in Jerry's first
Broadway show, *On the Town*. She remembered that, at the age of seventy-three,
Ida moved in with Harry and Lena after Aaron died in 1931, just months be-

fore Jerry's bar mitzvah. "Grandma was a great influence, a great thing for Jerry, much more so than I ever knew because she died [in 1941] when I was quite young. . . . Jerry always told the story about how [Grandma Ida] would come into the room and ask for his change. And the change went into the fund for the neighborhood, because as old as she was she was still out in the neighborhood seeing to families. She always collected money for them, and she collected it from Jerry, too."

Like Ida, Jerry's parents devoted themselves to civic and charitable causes. Lena was active with the local chapter of the National Council of Jewish Women and belonged to such organizations as the Unity Link and the Order of the Golden Chain, of which Harry had been a founder and patron. Staunch in their shared commitment to faith and community, Harry and Lena undoubtedly expected their son to follow in their footsteps, but they would be disappointed. As Jerry later succinctly put it, "As a child, I went to Hebrew school and hated it. It had nothing to do with the rest of my life. I went through a Bar Mitzvah and then said 'that's it' to the whole business."

According to friends and family, he made no secret early on that he deplored being Jewish and poor and from what he saw as the wrong side of the tracks, although his family never descended to poverty even in the depths of the Depression. Many decades later, in one scene of his autobiographical *Poppa Piece*, Robbins depicted himself mocking his Hebrew tutor behind his back. Like many of his peers, he was caught between two worlds, that of the largely conservative Jewish community and that of mainstream America with all of its lures and temptations. Though the latter would win, he would still feel the conflict keenly for the rest of his life.

With the boom of prosperity that came early in the 1920s, Harry and his brothers sold the deli. Julius went on to head the kosher division of HyGrade Foods, while Harry moved his family to Weehawken, New Jersey, by way of Jersey City, where Lena's parents lived. Weehawken was then a town of 14,000 nestled on the cliffs of the Palisades, and familiar to most New Yorkers only as the other end of a short ferry ride. Ten years before the Rabinowitzes moved to Weehawken, Fred and Adele Astaire had lived there briefly as children only a block away from one of Jerry's boyhood homes.

During an interview in the 1940s, Robbins remembered the town as "about three blocks deep and nine wide . . . grubby, ugly and uninspiring." His opinion softened with the nostalgic hindsight of later years. Looking east from 57 Hudson Place, where his parents rented an apartment, the skyline of Manhattan was visible. At night, the lights would beckon, exciting his imagination. Family lore includes affectionate tales of him dancing on the rooftop and giving puppet shows in the front windows of the apartment. "We were the same age," said Viola Zousmer. "We were brought up together. At seven years old, we went up on the roof, two kids, and Jerry climbed on the edge of the roof and said, 'Come on, join me. I'm a bird.' I said, 'Oh no, not me.' Seven years old, and he was a daredevil."

Not long after moving to Weehawken, Harry Rabinowitz and one of Jerry's uncles, Benjamin Goldenberg, went into business together operating a corset factory in nearby Union City. Like the delicatessen, the factory became a family enterprise, this time involving Lena's relatives. The original 1928 deed for the land indicates that Harry's father-in-law helped him acquire the site. Lena worked with Harry in the business just as she had worked with him behind the counter in the deli. In later years, Robbins mounted the original sign that read COMFORT CORSET COMPANY on a wall in his office. As a boy, he and his young cousins often visited the factory. "When we were taken there," Jack Davenport reminisced, "we played, mainly shooting corset stays at each other. . . . They were made of steel and you bent them and let them snap out of your fingers."

His mother's side of the family represented an ideal of conventional family ties that would remain absent in Robbins' life. Aaron and Ida Rips had raised seven children. Lena had five sisters, Anna, Mary, Jean, Gertrude and Francis, and a brother, Jacob, the eldest, who died of appendicitis in 1926, leaving behind a wife and two children. A second brother was said to have died in infancy back in Minsk. The three eldest sisters, Anna, Lena and Mary, and their brothers had been born in Russia. All of the sisters married and raised families of their own. None of them ever divorced (though two were widowed and remarried). Together, they were an aggressive, formidable matriarchal force. Their tight-knit stability and mutual support were later a source of pride and fascination shared by all of their children, including Jerry. Like their parents during hard times, they took in less fortunate family members and loaned them money, with generosity felt as an obligation. They celebrated holidays together and had seder at each other's homes—though they also marked Christmas with an exchange of gifts, perhaps feeling that doing so would help them assimilate into the non-Jewish world.

Jerry's cousin, Bob Silverman, pointed out one area where the sisters may have been lacking. "None of them had a sense of humor. . . . You can't say any one of them was witty or verbal. They were all very middle-class Jewish women, busy raising their families, living extremely conventional lives, as the second-generation children often had to do."

Of the six sisters, Lena was the dominant one. She ruled the roost in her own household and usually prevailed over the others with her strong will and practical intelligence. Sonia suggested that her mother played the role of family martiarch "very much like Ida Rips," and remembered that "in our culture, women had to be strong." According to Silverman, who later became a successful composer and publisher, "Jerry often talked about writing a book or play about the six sisters. . . . Lena was the man in the family. She wore the pants, she made the decisions. When some decision had to be made and the sisters got together, that would have been Lena organizing things like that. When the family got together, it was often at Lena and Harry's place out in Jersey. They had the largest apartment, and they were seemingly making a bit more than the rest of us during those years."

Jerry's large circle of relatives—he had twenty-eight first cousins—provided a number of theatrical and show-business influences. Bob Silverman described some of the other dancers in the family. "My father, Jack Silverman, was a professional ballroom dancer and met my mother at Roseland, when it was a big social place where young people went for ballroom dancing, and they paid ten cents, something like that, for a partner. My Aunt Jean [Davenport] used to go there all the time, and Jean was probably the best dancer of the six sisters. My father—don't ask me how it all came about—found himself as a young man living with two other guys, Bing Crosby and George Raft. Now you gotta get this picture. These three were among the shortest men ever born, like Edward G. Robinson, who was also related to the family. The three, Bing Crosby, George Raft and my father, started out as ballroom dancers. Ten cents a dance. . . . So there was this dancing gift, if you will. And Jerry, of course, knew all about this stuff."

In fact, Edward G. Robinson had been born Emanuel Goldenberg and was indeed related to Jerry's uncle Benjamin Goldenberg, who had married Lena's sister, Mary, before going into the corset business with Harry. At least one of Jerry's aunts, Jean Davenport, visited with Robinson when he was filming one of his early movies along the Palisades. Jean also played the piano for the silent movie houses in and around Jersey City. But she was the only one of the sisters who displayed such musical talent.

Another show-business connection came from Jerry's uncle Daniel Davenport, who ran a successful chain of vaudeville and later burlesque theaters, including the Apollo Theatre on 125th Street. According to Daniel's son, Jack Davenport, the original family enterprise—billed as Hurtig and Seamon—had competed with the Shuberts early in the century. Daniel Davenport's father, Louis Cohn, and his brother, Vic, performed on the vaudeville circuit as an acrobat-comedy team known as the Davenport Brothers. One of their playbills from the 1890s boasted "acts of posturing, ground and lofty tumbling, acrobatic display . . . and mirth-provoking encounters."

The Davenport Brothers had been a featured act with the Barnum and Bailey Circus, and as a novelty attraction, their show sometimes included Wonder, a two-legged horse. They frequently performed on stage with Fanny Brice before the turn of the century. Lou's son, Daniel, had followed him into the business as a theater manager. With his white shoes and spats and refined manner, Daniel Davenport was an uncle who surely caught Jerry's eye at family gatherings, when the tale was told of how Uncle Dan had accumulated a small fortune from his theaters, only to lose it all in the darkest days of the Depression. This branch of the family contributed to Jerry's enthusiasm for the rough and tumble of vaudevillian comedy. Years later, Uncle Dan's surviving son, Jack Davenport, would bequeath his father's collection of vaudeville and burlesque scripts to his famous cousin.

Although neither of his parents exhibited any remarkable artistic gifts, they made sure that Jerry and his sister were exposed to the arts. "Their concern, I think, was purely a Jewish cultural thing. . . . And it saved my life," said

Robbins. "When I was a child, art seemed like a tunnel to me. At the end of that tunnel, I could see light where the world opened up, waiting for me."

Both Rabinowitz children were recognized early on as prodigies and pushed toward the stage by their mother. Sonia was given dancing lessons and Jerry studied music. At three and a half, he was already composing pieces for the piano and found himself performing his first recital at a children's concert at Manhattan's Aeolian Hall. "Mother told me that I got through it very well," he later remarked, his words hinting at a need for maternal approval that would manifest itself in other ways later in life.

His music teacher, Miss Effa Ellis Perfield, delighted in the boy and faithfully collected his early compositions, as one journalist observed, "like a squirrel hoarding nuts." Sonia also studied with Perfield and remembered, "She had this great method of teaching harmony especially, a system that she had established, with major, minor, diminished and augmented chords. It was a very quick system for the piano based on the number of sharps and flats. Her studio was at 33 East Thirty-sixth Street. There were other people in her classes and we had competitions to see how fast we could play the major and minor chords at the piano. Jerry had a perfect ear, everything was easy for him. I had to study and learn it, but he would hear it. He did everything by ear."

A family friend, Dorothy Gilbert, said, "My parents' home was within walking distance of where Jerry and Sonia lived. He would walk over usually on Friday evenings, and he had a little violin with two strings, a broken down fiddle. And he would join us for Friday night dinner and get to our piano and play the violin tucked under his chin with one hand while playing the piano with the other hand. My mother and father just sat there in amazement at this little fellow. I will never forget it."

Jerry also took violin lessons, wrote poetry and exhibited a range of talents, any one of which might have served as the imaginary gateway for him to escape the constraints of what he identified as his parents' corseted world. "I painted. I wrote. I played music," he later said. "I spent time with a toy puppet theater. The only world that was really exciting for me was the world in which I could make believe that things were not the way they were."

Those last words betray Robbins' real feelings about his childhood. For all their parents' diligence about exposing them to culture, Jerry and Sonia did not grow up happy. It wasn't just Jerry's dread of growing up a self-described "poor Jew." There were huge conflicts at home—and huge gaps as well. Sonia sums it up this way: "Both Jerry and I were taken care [of] as well as they knew how, but we both missed the nourishing feeling of love that children need. We did not really know family. We didn't touch, we didn't hug. Our parents only did the mundane with the kids. They dressed us and put us in the right clothes, and made sure we were in the right place at the right time. It was without passion. They just had to love us and they didn't. Oh sure, they cared about us, but the caring was making sure the clothes were clean and we had the right shoes. It was mechanical. It was the facade of being a good American parent and being patriotic and all the crap that goes with it. There was no empathy, or no understanding of what we felt. There was no feeling in it all, and we were not allowed to express any. The only feelings we expressed were being angry and hysterical when we were growing up. Jerry got out very quickly and got into his own life with whatever he wanted to do."

Jerry was left with wounds and a volatile pool of anger, especially concerning his father, that he would carry with him into adulthood. As far as most people knew, Harry was an affable man who was usually content to follow his wife's lead with regard to raising the children. Family members saw him as the henpecked husband who deferred to Lena and was powerless in the face of her maternal authority. Although he went along with his wife's interest in the arts, Harry was the type who preferred playing pinochle with his cronies. His daughter remembered him as "a man of humor, fun, almost awful with his practical jokes." Bob Silverman said, "Jerry's father was a very funny man, and Jerry's humor came from him. That twinkle that was in Jerry's eye when he created a dance came directly from his father."

But there was a destructive edge to Harry's humor as well, especially when it came to his son's dancing. "Harry was sarcastic," said Silverman. "I think it runs in the family. He had a cruel streak, I mean, a sarcastic streak, a non-gentle side behind the facade of 'I'm being funny.' I think that what happened with Jerry as a boy—and you know this is much more important than if an adult hits a child—was that Harry said some cruel, terrible things to Jerry. . . . Harry's attitude about Jerry being a dancer would have been he's not an all-American boy. 'What am I gonna do, go out and throw a baseball with a kid that would rather be lifting his legs in a dance studio?' That was totally out of Harry's vision."

In the face of such paternal resistance, Sonia was her brother's only ally at home. She said, "We had fights, my father and myself. We had terrible fights in regard to Jerry. I knew he was really terrific and that was what he really wanted to do—he was driving passionately to be a dancer. My father said to me he should be a shoemaker. 'Better he should be a shoemaker!' I always remember him saying that."

Viola Zousmer also recalled Harry's harsh opposition to his son. "To his father it didn't make sense for a boy to be a dancer. 'That's it!' Many times he said it when Jerry was very young. 'Where does a *boy* come into this!'"

Sheldon Harnick recalls another story that Robbins told him when they were preparing *The Poppa Piece*. "What I remember is he described his father as the kind of person [who] as soon as there were guests in the house . . . was on and became a wonderful entertainer filled with good humor and comedy . . . the life of the party. And as soon as everybody left, then up went his newspaper, out came the cigar, and he was just not interested in the family. The other thing he [Jerry] said was that his father did things to get laughs and also did things which made him not trust his father.

"For instance, one Christmas, his father dressed up as Santa Claus. He [Jerry] was very little. . . . There were guests in the house and Jerry was thrilled when Santa Claus gave him a toy, a little train. . . . So he was playing with it, and at bedtime he became a little difficult because he didn't want to put the toy away. He just wanted to keep playing with it. The mother couldn't get him to give up the toy. So what the father did was to dress up as Santa Claus and come back and tell him that because he had been a bad boy, he didn't get to keep his toy. He took the toy away from him, and Jerry said he was in tears and he couldn't understand why all the guests in the house were laughing. Finally, the father took off the Santa Claus beard and [Jerry] realized that it was his father. He said it was just so humiliating. It just made him feel so unwanted, and so, like nothing. It was a bad relationship."

In time Robbins would also learn to wield his humor as a derisive weapon just as his father had. And though they would reconcile later in life, Jerry would never forgive him for what he regarded as his betrayals.

Robbins' mother, on the other hand, was the one who actively encouraged Jerry toward the arts, even if she, too, initially discouraged the idea of her son being a dancer. Less abrasive in manner than her husband, she was no less insistent about instilling her goals and values in her children. When Jerry was six, Lena and Harry's cousin Honey Zousmer took Jerry and Sonia and Honey's son, Jesse, on a trip back to the Old World, to Poland, whose borders now claimed the *shtetl* where the Rabinowitz family had its roots. "You have to imagine in those days," said Viola Zousmer, "for two women on their own to take their children across the ocean . . . that took courage." Although Robbins later remembered very little of this childhood journey, he would nevertheless recall it with much sentiment to his collaborators on *Fiddler on the Roof,* noting that his family's village, Rozanka, had been decimated during World War II.

But Robbins' relationship with his mother, too, had a dark side. Robbins kept a note, a lifelong keepsake that he had written to his mother around the time they made their trip to Poland. In later years, one of his assistants ran across this childhood memento and was struck by its implications. "I think it was a very six-year-old-boy kind of note. It said, 'Dear Mommy, you're beautiful, I love you, when I grow up I want to marry you.' But what was interesting about the note was that someone—and I presume it was his mother—had corrected it in red pencil. I said, 'Oh, I get it.' And his mother was—you've probably seen the photographs—a very beautiful woman. So that was the thing, and I found it very early on, and I just felt like it was a key to who he was. . . . I think he was afraid of his mother. Afraid is maybe too strong a term, but I think his mother was the power in the house. She was the power. And that was why I always found it enormously interesting that he surrounded himself with very strong, powerful women."

Sonia, too, had an incident with her mother when she was very young, one she recalled vividly more than eighty years later. "When I was five years old I had spilt boiling milk on my chest. Pot on the stove. I remember screaming. My father rushed in and pulled the front of my dress away from my chest. I was scheduled to dance at the school that morning. My mother mended the dress with a piece of material in the front. . . . After the performance my mother took me to a doctor. I had a huge blister and for many years a scar."

Thereafter, Sonia mistrusted her mother's priorities. Though she would later say, "As I grew up and matured, I understood and loved and cared about her very much," her other words speak louder: "As a kid, I hated my mother."

It was Sonia who would open the way for her brother in the world of dance, freeing him from inhibitions with her own exemplary passion and early accomplishments. Closely guided by her mother, Sonia had already embarked on a professional career by the age of four. She was a child star in the Charles D. Isaacson *Herald Tribune* concert series and danced everywhere from Carnegie Hall and the Hippodrome Theatre to Sing-Sing Prison. In the early 1920s, she toured America and went to Cuba with Irma Duncan. Irma was one of Isadora Duncan's six adopted daughters, who were known affectionately as the "Isadorables," three of whom, including Irma, established their own dance companies. Like her famous mother, Irma drew her inspiration from Greek art and classical music, performing many of the same highly emotive, interpretive dances that expressed Duncan's utopian vision of the body and the art form itself. An iconoclast and revolutionary, Isadora was the antithesis of the frivolous twenties flapper. She had rebelled against the toe shoes and technical strictures of classical ballet, and in so doing, inspired a movement based on her celebrity mystique that was both a creed and an aesthetic.

As spiritual disciples, Duncan dancers studied with a kind of religious fervor, while their dances lent themselves to any number of avant-garde social and political agendas. Sonia absorbed her lessons with zeal and brought them home, sharing them with her brother, enchanting him with her adventures and the promise of magical worlds that existed far from Weehawken. Jerry often tagged along with his sister to the dance studio and attended her performances. Years later, after Robbins staged his ballet *Dances at a Gathering*, with its Chopin score, he would say, "That music I feel I am very identified with and always have been. It may go all the way back to my sister's dancing days as a Duncan dancer. I think a lot of that's in there."

Jerry grew up all but concealed in his sister's shadow. Six years older than her brother, Sonia was the one who was the dancer, setting the stage for a protracted sibling rivalry even as she taught her brother his first steps and enticed him to follow her. According to Bob Silverman, "Sonia showed the early talent and she got all the early attention. Jerry was kind of neglected. Being the first child, Sonia was a very aggressive, dominating sister. . . . Sonia had to be an extremely difficult child, a demanding, type A, aggressive little girl. And grabbing all the spotlight. And along comes Jerry, and at first Jerry's no challenge to Sonia. But when Jerry starts to move into Sonia's world, which was not the world of anybody else in the family, he became a threat in a way. So there had to be rivalry."

Disagreeing with her cousin, Sonia did not think of herself as being difficult, though she did admit to some early jealousy, noting that Jerry "was thin and small and Mom felt he [needed] nourishment and care, which he got. That care I was jealous of." If there were a rivalry between Jerry and his sister as dancers, Sonia saw the contest as one-sided. "I think Jerry was very competitive about me. He didn't want to be near me. He didn't want to dance with me. He just wanted to be himself. I don't think I ever challenged him very much. I think he thought he was much better than I was from the very beginning. He was a better dancer—that was Jerry—and I'm not competitive. By the time I danced onstage with Jerry, I had been dancing for fifteen years already. I was getting heavy, and not having had the training was a great disappointment for me. A shocking disappointment. I had to fake everything. I could fake a tap dance. I could fake a Spanish dance. I could fake everything. But I had never been trained. And when Jerry started, I knew it was too late for me to learn."

At first, dancing was a secret pastime Jerry shared with Sonia and kept from his male peers, most of whom were far more intent on trying to perfect their baseball swing. Although he did make a mark with swimming and horseback riding, Jerry had set himself apart with his pursuit of the arts. In the face of parental opposition, as his infatuation with dance grew, it would take the form of an illicit and forbidden love.

Jerry went to Weehawken's public schools and attended Woodrow Wilson High School, where he joined the math and debating clubs and the Lambda Theta Gamma Dramatic Club. He appeared in school plays with titles like *Forward Pass* and *A Table Set for Himself*. He loved Shakespeare and credited his high school English teacher, Miss Margaret McArdle, with having "cut his imagination loose." Although the adult Robbins would recall mostly the bleakness and psychic injuries of his childhood, there was also evidence of happier times. The line in his high school yearbook reads, "With his eyes in floods of laughter."

In the same year that Jerry entered high school, his father's corset factory went bankrupt, and Harry reorganized the business without his partner, Benjamin Goldenberg. Evidently, there were no hard feelings between the two men, as Harry supported Goldenberg on his next venture. Uncle Ben and his wife Mary, turned a family lodge into a popular children's camp called Kittatinny, tucked away in the hills of New Jersey about seventy-five miles from Manhattan. Jerry and his cousins went to the camp during the summers of the Depression years. Family members pitched in and received a discount on the fee, which was $150 for nine weeks. The camp's special attraction for Jerry was its small theater and the chance to perform in several Gilbert and Sullivan musicals.

Jerry performed the comic leads in *HMS Pinafore* and *The Mikado*, and in *Pirates of Penzance*, he snared the role of Major General Stanley. One of his fellow campers, James Jacobs, who played the Sergeant of Police in *Pirates*, would never forget Jerry's uncanny talent for creating comic bits in these amateur forays. "Jerry had a tremendous sense of humor in everything that he did. He invented little shticks. When he used to sing in [*The Mikado*], he gave me a triangle to hit at a precise moment when he would have a piece of business that he invented. But he did no dancing whatsoever. He kept that a deep secret."

Of course, such a secret was bound to come out sooner or later. Sonia's friend Dorothy Gilbert remembered one of his earliest solo performances at the camp. "I was a teenager and I was helping with the horses. Now, on Parents' Day—that was one weekend I will never forget—the campers were displaying their talents, and little Jerry (I mean he was little!) came out in a long black coat. It probably was someone's jacket that fit him as a coat. And on a Ping-Pong table he did a dance, an old European dance. I don't think there were too many people without tears in their eyes among the adults who were watching this. I don't know where it came from. I just know he could dance. And my parents happened to be there, and forty years after that they talked about it. This was a big audience, and he was completely uninhibited. I don't even remember what he used for music. There was a Victrola or something. It was an Hasidic dance, and very European, and I don't know where that came from either except they did have an elderly grandma [Ida] living with them."

While he may have been encouraged by his sister in these early endeavors, Jerry also had to endure his father's caustic resistance to his dancing. Another fellow camper, Arnie Walton, once found himself caught between father and son when the issue erupted. "Jerry never liked me. Since we were little kids, he didn't like me, and Sonia's . . . one of my dearest, oldest friends. It was a family thing. I'd gone to the summer camp that his family owned, Kittatinny. I was a kid actor and fairly successful, I guess. He had an argument with his father, who said, 'What is dancing! Why can't you be a mensch like Arnie?' Well, that's all Jerry had to hear—for the rest of his life!"

Once he found his way into the dance studio a few years later, Jerry returned to Camp Kittatinny and performed for the younger generation of campers. His cousin Jean was also an aspiring dancer at the time. "Jerry gave an impromptu dance on one of the hills," she said, calling up a cherished memory. "I can still see him flitting around on that hill, up and down that hill, with his black outfit on . . . a *danse macabre*. It's just one of those visual things you keep."

Viola Zousmer also spent summers at Kittatinny, and she remembered that at least one adult in the family failed to recognize Jerry's talent. "We were in a show together called *The Monkey's Paw*. I was the mother. Jerry was the father. Jack Davenport's father [Daniel], who was a talent scout in the theater, was in the audience. He saw the show and he called my mother and said, 'Honey, you gotta do something for Viola—she is sensational! She's gonna make it.' Mother said, 'What about Jerry?' He said, 'That kid, I'm afraid, hasn't got it.'"

Having first taken classes informally from Sonia, Jerry went on to study with her teacher Alyce Bentley, who taught interpretive dance in a small studio at Carnegie Hall. On occasion, Bentley had rented out the space to Irma Duncan, who was a kindred spirit of the barefoot school. Modern dance, as it developed in the 1930s, held sway over ballet, as the former seemed more in keeping with the prevailing intellectual and critical temper of the Depression years, when the arts across the board were expected to exhibit a commitment to social struggle and to reflect the stark realities of the times. While ballet stars like Pavlova, Fokine, Mordkin and Nijinsky, as well as Diaghilev's Ballets Russes, had toured America with some success over the previous two decades, modern dance appeared to lend itself more readily to a climate of harsh realism and combative political activism.

In the years to come, through the eyes of his sister, Jerry would witness some of the early pioneering experiments by the likes of Martha Graham, Charles Weidman and Doris Humphrey. Other modern choreographers like Helen Tamiris and Anna Sokolow, with whom Jerry maintained a lifelong friendship, emerged from the radical settlement-house movement that included large numbers of Russian-Jewish immigrants whose customs and beliefs were in the throes of upheaval. Much of this ferment in the dance world would be absorbed by Jerry as a teenager from a unique vantage afforded by Sonia.

A crucial turning point came in 1932, when Jerry accompanied his sister into New York and saw her onstage at the Dance Center, a small studio theater located over a garage at 105 West Fifty-sixth Street, off Sixth Avenue. The tiny performance space had been built on the third floor of a narrow brownstone and provided only enough room for about a dozen rows of audience seats, which rose steeply on an incline toward the ceiling in back. Lit by a few overhanging spotlights, the stage, with its cramped wings, was no wider than the building itself. The curtains and walls were black and the atmosphere deliberately austere, yet full of allure for a boy of fourteen. Given the timing and the personalities involved, his seduction into this world could not have happened under more fortunate circumstances. Jerry might have found his calling elsewhere, but this theater would provide him with the direction that would one day make him arguably the most distinctly American of choreographers.

The Dance Center group was one of the first ballet companies to win a foothold and achieve a measure of critical recognition in New York City (before George Balanchine's arrival in 1933). Comprised of dancers with widely varied backgrounds and individual styles, the fledgling troupe was run by Senia Gluck Sandor and his wife, Felicia Sorel, a pair of charismatic innovators. They were fusing ballet and modern dance (and later Stanislavski's acting techniques imported from the Group Theatre) in a series of highly theatrical, stylized productions. The country's first dance critic, John Martin of the *New York Times*, lauded the Dance Center's 1932 season, which saw 113 performances, many of them staged in the concert hall of the Barbizon-Plaza Hotel.

Using the stage name "Sonya Robyns," Jerry's sister appeared in several of these ballets, including *Dream Phobias* and *Tempo*. The latter dramatized a story about Depression-era marathon dancing, in this case, nine teams of dancers in a 1,032-hour contest. The designs were by Reginald Marsh, and the performances were well received. John Martin wrote of Gluck Sandor, who not only directed and choreographed most of the productions but danced in them as well: "He will undoubtedly prove himself a genius. Though he has the most extravagant flights of fancy, he has also a compensatory practicality which makes him unusually adaptable. He is able to utilize various techniques, to harmonize all sorts of influences, and out of them to produce something which, no matter what it may lack in other directions, never fails to exhibit an extraordinary flair for what is effective in the theater. In the entire American field he is unique."

This was the singular artist Jerome Robbins would call his "guru." He was born Samuel Gluck in Harlem in 1899, of Jewish immigrant parents who had come over from Hungary and Poland. He studied dance with Louis Chalif and with Blanche Talmud at the Neighborhood Playhouse before embarking on a mercurial career, making his professional debut in 1918 at the Metropolitan Opera in Adolph Bolm's ballet *Le Coq d'Or*. Bolm was a Russian premier dancer and choreographer who, like Michel Fokine and George Balanchine, had come to America via the Maryinsky Theatre and Diaghilev's company. Under the name Senia Gluckoff, Sandor toured with Bolm's company, Ballet Intime; and later—most significantly perhaps—he danced in Fokine's *Thunderbird* at the old Hippodrome, a long-vanished arena that once drew crowds to Sixth Avenue and Forty-third Street. Sandor stepped in to replace Fokine himself, who would in the not-so-distant future play an essential role in Robbins' career as well, one of those momentous liaisons in which tradition is passed along by a fortuitous crossing of paths.

During the 1920s, Sandor worked in vaudeville and on Broadway, for several years producing the overtures and opening-act numbers at the Paramount Theater, and then creating dances for such venues as Earl Carrol's Vanities revue and the Minsky Brothers' Burlesque. With his salary from the latter, Sandor, as impresario and producer, was able to finance the Dance Center; and he was also able to experiment with choreography while on the job, although his dances for Minsky's showgirls always had to conclude with the standard burlesque routine.

A visionary and spiritual sage of dance, Sandor also painted hauntingly vivid, Expressionist works. Surviving photographs of his ballets suggest that he had an astonishing eye for stage gesture—a gift that Sandor claimed he had learned from studying his mother's beautiful hands. With the slightest turn of the head, diverted gaze or nuance of gesture, he knew how to win and control the rapt attention of his audience—a lesson that would not be lost on young Jerry, who years afterward reflected, "We dancers were taught to perform with the concentration of an actor." While Sandor never established his own school or specialized system of training, he did provide a spiritual and philosophical orientation.

One of the young dancers who would later join Sandor's company was another modern trailblazer, José Limón, who offered a portrait of the choreographer: "He was a dynamo. Not a bundle, but a bale of nerves, restless, bold and completely unafraid. . . . Sammy was a martinet, a tyrant, impatient, tempestuous and explosive. He was also lovable, warm and human, with an irresistible sense of humor. But above all else, he was an artist. When the curtain went up, there was magic."

Sandor's repertory included his own interpretations of *Afternoon of a Faun* and *Prodigal Son*, after Nijinsky and Balanchine respectively. According to Limón, *Salome* was Sandor's masterpiece, with Constructivist designs by Vincente Minnelli, who was working at Radio City at the time. Owing to connections that Sandor cultivated with the Group Theatre and the WPA Federal Dance Project, Elia Kazan would one day play the role of Herod. Under the leadership of Lee Strasberg, Harold Clurman and Cheryl Crawford, the Group Theatre developed a marvelous ensemble with talents like Kazan, Robert Lewis, Lee J. Cobb, Karl Malden, Irwin Shaw and Clifford Odets.

While much of the work was based on Stanislavski's acting techniques, the Group was a hotbed of radical idealism and attempted to dramatize the political, social and economic struggles of the day. Like Anna Sokolow, Sandor was invited to teach dance at the Group Theatre, and a number of the actors in turn participated in productions at the Dance Center. John Garfield would appear on the scene, and a newcomer named Montgomery Clift would later attend rehearsals with Sandor and his wife, taking photographs of the dancers.

Sandor also choreographed a new *Petrouchka,* performing the title role himself and winning critical accolades. Departing from Fokine's approach, Sandor staged the ballet in the style of Aubrey Beardsley, while retaining Stravinsky's score and the familiar bittersweet story of the puppet brought to life. This was a ballet both Jerry and his future mentor took deeply to heart. Indeed, Petrouchka was a role that Robbins, who had a passion for puppets, would one day make his own.

Another dancer, Anzia Kubicek, recalled that Sandor "was very much led by the music. He was very musical and the music dictated to him how he treated the drama. He preferred to do things with a story line. Sometimes it was a very abstract kind of story. His imagination would just go a mile a minute, and he worked with the bodies that he had to work with, which sometimes were limited. So he had to perform miracles with the dancers he had, sometimes even very young teenagers." Many years later, Robbins lauded Sandor's versatility to Paris Opéra ballerina Ghislaine Thesmar, who recalled, "This adaptability to all the occasions was the thing. It was phenomenal, Jerry said. He spoke about this man with great affection."

During his high school years, Jerry was limited to admiring Sandor from a distance while his sister continued to perform at the Dance Center. Whenever he could, he would follow his sister into the studio and watch rehearsals. The dream of dancing had taken hold, and the boy no doubt felt the absence deeply when Sandor disappeared for two years to live in Europe, where the choreographer studied with Mary Wigman and the so-called German school. At home, Robbins was compelled to turn his attention toward more practical concerns, as his parents pressed him with their demands that he pursue a college education.

After graduating from high school in 1935, Jerry went on to New York

University, where he spent his freshman year majoring in chemistry, with his father's blessing and financial assistance. But the corset business hit another skid and Harry's funds ran low the next year. Jerry was soon forced to work shifts at his father's factory. He now desperately wanted to drop out of school in order to devote himself full-time to dance. His prospects were bleak, and he sensed his theatrical dreams slipping away. But in 1936, with his sister's help, Jerry arranged to audition for Sandor, who had recently returned to New York to reestablish his company.

Dressed in coat and tie, with his hair neatly combed, Jerry took the ferry into Manhattan and presented himself to the choreographer at the Dance Center. As an eighteen-year-old, Jerry was hardly an imposing figure. He had not yet reached his adult height of five-eight, and he could still pass for twelve getting into movie theaters. After looking the boy over and leading him through some warmup exercises, Sandor instructed him to get up on the stage under the spotlights and improvise as Shiva, the Hindu deity responsible for destruction and creation. Overcoming the fear and insecurities that he would bring with him to the stage for the rest of his life, Jerry complied and quickly invented a short dance. He remembered it years later as a spontaneous performance that was alternately destructive and creative in mood and execution. Perhaps in that moment of truth he was unknowingly drawing on two warring sides of his personality. In any event, Sandor was impressed with his shy intensity and ardor.

After repeating the performance, Jerry accompanied Sandor and his petite, chain-smoking wife, Felicia Sorel—"Miss Sorel," as Sandor addressed her formally—into a nearby bar for a meal. Coincidentally, the bar was named "Jerry's" and stood at the corner of Fifty-fourth Street and Sixth Avenue. The future dancer would never forget his visit to the men's room with Sandor, when the older man washed in front of him, bending over the sink. Trying to protect Sandor from hitting his head, Jerry accidentally dispensed soap into Sandor's unusually long hair. After discovering what had happened, Sandor suddenly turned on the boy and stared at him.

In the awkwardness of the moment, Jerry was sure that he had given up his chance to dance with Sandor's company. There may have been some veiled sexual tension in this encounter, or it may simply have been that Jerry was abashed at facing his idol under such circumstances. Sandor's protégé and adopted son, Philip Lanza Sandor, speculated in retrospect that Jerry harbored a secret infatuation, which came out over time in the form of dreams, like those of a smitten schoolboy, that Jerry tried on occasion to relate to his mentor. "Jerry would say, 'I had a dream about you last night,' and Sandor would say, 'Go tell Miss Sorel, please. I'm very busy.'"

Whatever the dreams he dreamed, Jerry was invited to join the company, and Sandor agreed to help him win over his parents. "He had what you call a photographic memory," Sandor recalled a few years before he died in 1978. "Once he saw something, he could do it backward. Before I would do a thing, he had it. He could anticipate what was to come. He was sensitive and he was musical. I spoke to his parents and said, 'Why not let the boy become a dancer? If he doesn't like it, OK. But it might be good for him.' He was kind of slender and frail then, and very gentle. So they agreed, and he stopped school and plunged into it."

Prophetically, Sandor advised the young dancer, "Study ballet. It will come back."

"I took his advice," Jerry remembered, "even though I thought I didn't like the ballet. I didn't understand it then." In spite of his resistance to what he viewed as stodgy and artificial, Jerry took classes with Ella Daganova ("Miss Daggy," as Robbins later nicknamed her), a refined American teacher who had performed with Anna Pavlova's company. "I pushed him into Daganova," Sonia recalled. I said, 'Enough of interpreting those falling leaves, get to the barre.'" Daganova taught ballet at the New Dance League, and Jerry paid for three classes a week by mopping the floor and washing her Venetian blinds. He also studied Spanish dancing with José Greco's teacher, Helene Veola, and Oriental dance with the highly regarded Yeichi Nimura. At the New Dance Group, he took classes in choreography, referred to as "composition," with Bessie Schoenberg, another fountainhead of the era who had studied with Martha Graham. Describing Schoenberg's influence, Robbins said, "It was like an angel putting her hand on my shoulder and giving me a nudge and saying, 'Go on with it.'"

Jerry was impassioned about his initial preference for the modern school. "I used to get into fights with the other dancers because I thought modern dance was much better than ballet." He was won over to ballet later after seeing Russian ballerina Alexandra Danilova perform on tour with the Ballets Russes. Her alluring stage virtuosity convinced him that Sandor was right, that ballet offered more possibilities than Jerry had previously imagined.

Aside from dance technique, Robbins was also exposed to a heady atmosphere of radical politics. Before he dropped out of school, Martha Graham announced her decision to boycott the 1936 Olympics in Germany. Galvanized by the events taking place in Europe before the war, dancers were becoming political. The New Dance Group, where Jerry first studied choreography, was a left-wing dance collective that made use of the parlor floor of a tenement building on West Eighteenth Street near Fifth Avenue. Union Square at Fourteenth Street was the popular hub of Communist Party organizing activities, with headquarters overlooking the square in 1930. During the decade, much of the modern dance movement was politicized on the left and located in the downtown neighborhoods, along with the union halls, workers' cafeterias and bookstores. There were rallies, dances and benefit concerts to support a wide range of causes from the labor movement to civil rights. With its appeal to social conscience and worldly concerns, this was an area that would attract Sonia before it would her brother, though both would eventually be drawn into the political fray.

Within months of his audition, Jerry developed enough technique and stage presence to make his first professional appearance. Acting on Sandor's advice, he adopted various stage names to mask his Jewish identity. He was first Robin Gerald, and then Jerry Robyns after his sister, and later Gerald Robbins, finally settling on Jerome Robbins. The name stuck when Sandor happened to introduce Jerry to John Martin at a rehearsal one afternoon. Sandor told the influential critic to remember the name because it would be "big someday." But no one would have guessed such a future, to judge by Robbins' first paid sally onto the boards.

He made his debut on September 20, 1937, with a one-line walk-on in a play called *The Brothers Ashkenazi* at the Yiddish Art Theater. Sandor had been hired to oversee the choreography. Jerry's sister remembered dancing with her brother in the production and recalled that the show ran for almost a year.

One night Albert Einstein attended a performance and afterward visited with the cast.

"Because I looked four years younger than I actually was," recalled Robbins, "I was called in to play the part of the brothers' father as a child. I didn't really know Yiddish—my parents only used the language when they didn't want me to understand something. But all I had to say was, 'yuh, Tata,' meaning 'yes, Father.'" The two words were delivered in answer to the question of whether he had been a good boy. Robbins' Yiddish was so poor that the other actors would cough mischievously or pinch his cheek to cover him during each performance. Even his mother, sitting in the audience on opening night, failed to hear his line. "The whole thing was a wonderful experience for me, though," said Robbins. "Those actors—this was a Maurice Schwartz show—were fantastic. When we stopped general rehearsals and went into dress rehearsal, the art of makeup was so extraordinary that I literally didn't recognize anyone."

Robbins continued, "It was an enormously long show, I remember. I only had to appear in the first and third scenes of Act One, and that left me to take a walk in the park, have lunch, go to the zoo, and still come back in plenty of time to make the opening of the second act. Oh yeah, we also had a strike. The actors played every night of the week and twice on Saturdays and Sundays, for which we got ten dollars. So we struck, and they made it fifteen dollars."

An acclaimed actor of the day, Maurice Schwartz, directed the show. Jerry's name was second on the program, and a critic for the *New York Daily Mirror* used it in his review, noting some of the actors as they appeared in order in the cast list: "Others outstanding in the unusually large cast are Julius Adler, Jerome Robbins . . ." Robbins recalled, "Next day when the notice came out, all the other actors were furious with me. They said 'he doesn't do anything— he goes onstage and gets a notice! What I couldn't do with that notice if I'd gotten it.' They said they could go into any agent's office with it and ask for parts. Oh, they just muttered around."

During the show's run, Jerry gave himself barre exercises at a dressing-room sink, much to the amused horror of the veteran Yiddish actors. Sonia recalled, "He was so concentrated—I can't tell you the focus he had on his work. We did a ballroom dance together. I danced with him like I would dance with anybody."

One of their fellow performers was an aspiring actress named Elizabeth Shub. Years later, she looked back on the experience of working with Jerry with wistful pangs of nostalgia. "There was a dancing scene, ballroom dancing, and he danced. As a matter of fact, he never got off his toes—he was always dancing! Backstage he'd walk into the girls' dressing room and visit, still on his toes. Once he gave me a delightful marionette as a present, yes. He just walked into the dressing room and said, 'Here's something for you.' He was terribly sweet. When we were in the show, I do remember for some reason or other, I don't know why, going to his home with his sister. He opened the door on his toes. Truthfully, at that time I thought he was very gifted and I liked him. It never occurred to me that he would become a great dancer. The only thing that might have indicated [it] was his total obsession."

With Sandor's encouragement, in November of 1937, Robbins danced with Russian ballerina Lisa Parnova in a free concert at the YMHA. In terms of size and age, the partnership was a mismatch. Parnova was a Fokine-trained ballerina who created her own eclectic repertory and had been touring for years. Jerry was again dancing under the name of Gerald Robbins when the concert was reviewed by Anatole Chujoy, who wrote, "Robbins' partnering hinders rather than helps the performance." It was one notice that the young dancer would save the rest of his life.

His sister remembered, "Gluck Sandor also directed the *9 o'Clock Revue* at the Barbizon-Plaza on Sunday nights, [and] Jerry and I worked in that show." Sandor also cast him as the Assistant Eunoch in *Schéhérazade*, which was staged in a large outdoor arena at Jones Beach. In the fertile atmosphere of the Dance Center, he absorbed every scene, every experience, from sewing costumes to building sets. He spent hours in classes trying to make up for having had such a late start with his training as a dancer. Like his sister, Jerry was now living and breathing dance and threw himself into Sandor's repertory, performing roles in *Prince Igor, Isabella Andreini* and *El Amor Brujo*. Set to a score by Manuel de Falla, *El Amor Brujo* was a Spanish production that told the story of a dead lover coming back to possess the spirit of a living person (a theme that Robbins would take up himself when he later staged *The Dybbuk* with Leonard Bernstein).

His father attended a performance of *El Amor Brujo* in which Jerry had been given a featured Spanish dance. But afterward, Harry offered his son neither criticism nor encouragement. It was not until shortly before Harry's death in 1977 that Jerry would hear his father's review. Harry had retired and was living in Florida when Jerry visited and tried to talk about his career as a dancer. Harry reminded his son of that long-ago performance of *El Amor Brujo* and the fact that the critic John Martin had been in the audience. Robbins later related the story to a friend, actor Barry Primus, who recalled, "Jerry said, 'I asked my dad, didn't you ever worry about me being a dancer?' And his father said, 'Do you remember that critic who was there?' And Jerry said, 'Yeah, you mean John Martin?' His father said, 'Well, while you were dancing I walked over to him and I said, *You see that boy over there, that boy Jerry? What do you think of him?* And John Martin said, *Who, him? I wouldn't worry about him.*' And his father said to Jerry, 'I never worried about you after that.'" Apparently, Harry had needed only the word of the expert to assure him that his dancing son would make good. Yet, at the time, he withheld any fatherly assurance from Jerry.

After two years spent immersed in studying, rehearsing and performing at the Dance Center, Jerry sensed it was time to move on. Sandor was too much of an artist, too puritanical in his ambitions to have ever been commercially oriented. There was little money for his company, and like many struggling dancers, Jerry was auditioning for the Broadway chorus lines. Although he would remain a lifelong disciple, his days with Sandor had been numbered all along. Robbins later recalled that it was difficult to find the courage to break away from his mentor. In the dance world, to leave a teacher or director was often an emotional drama that carried implications of betrayal. Robbins was understandably conscience-stricken when he faced his mentor and announced his departure. But without any outward display of bitterness, Sandor simply advised him to do his best and let him go. Even with the graceful parting of ways, issues of artistic integrity and loyalty would remain flashpoints of contention between them each time their paths crossed again in the theater.

For the next several years, Jerry lived at his family home in Weehawken and commuted into Manhattan for auditions. If not quite independent, he was a full-fledged hoofer, a gypsy, going to dance classes, grabbing cheap meals at Horn & Hardart automats and trying out for shows, though usually unsuccessfully. At least he was on his own, and if he wanted, he could rent a room for five dollars a week, and sometimes he did. But most of the time he took the ferry ride back to Weehawken. It cost a nickel when he was growing up, and it gave him the chance to dream about his future.

"I used to come to New York and audition for shows," he remembered, "and not get them, and go back to Jersey and look back from the Palisades and say, 'Well, I'll be back tomorrow . . .'"

During the next six years, momentous opportunities were to come his way. A man still in his early twenties, he would create two of his most enduring works, *Fancy Free* and *On the Town*, one a ballet and the other a Broadway musical. By the time those fateful curtains rose, he had conquered the two worlds that he would inhabit the rest of his life. If there was any disappointment in his early glory, it was Sandor, who would turn down the invitation to attend Robbins' first triumphant opening night.

TWO

Fancy Free

Not long after Robbins made his stage debut with *The Brothers Ashkenazi* in the fall of 1937, Leonard Bernstein, then a nineteen-year-old Harvard undergraduate, was making one of his early forays into New York City. Bernstein had been invited to composer Aaron Copland's birthday party at his loft on West Sixty-third Street, where Lincoln Center's State Theater now stands. The gathering was a salon party for Manhattan's intellectual elite and included a number of gay and bisexual artists such as Paul Bowles and Virgil Thomson. When Copland heard that Bernstein was a fan who knew the composer's *Piano Variations*, he dared the college boy to play them. Bernstein said, "Well, it'll ruin your party." But Copland assured him, "Not *this* party."

According to Bernstein, Copland and his guests were soon "drop-jawed," captivated by his impromptu performance at the piano. Bernstein's biographer Humphrey Burton described that evening's experience as one of extreme "culture shock" for the young musician, whose ultimate artistic and sexual orientations were yet to be decided. It was just such a shock that would be waiting for Robbins when he arrived on the scene, and when he did, it would be in spectacular fashion, in the company of the same Leonard Bernstein.

Remembering his days as a struggling Broadway gypsy, Robbins said, "It was a rough period. . . . My parents were footing a lot of my bills because I wasn't making enough money. It's very hard to fight that. But as soon as I began to earn my own living, the battle was over. Then I learned that I had really been fighting to break away from the family. I was late in growing up in every way."

At nineteen, he remained at odds with his father over his career ambitions. Naturally, there were clashes about money and living expenses under Harry's roof, and the always-nagging reminder that Jerry had dropped out of college. Though unemployed, he was now the dancer in the family, as his sister had recently retired from the stage. Having gained weight and filled out with maturity, Sonia did not fit the svelte image of the female dancer that was coming into vogue. She taught dance intermittently, and for a time she worked in a dry-cleaning business. While she was still living at home, her free-spirited, independent lifestyle caused further domestic discord. "As I remember her in the early years," said Bob Silverman, "by the standards of the time, Sonia was totally liberated. We wouldn't say anything about it today. In those days, if she didn't have a steady boyfriend, if every time she would come to our house it was with a different guy, I'd hear remarks from my mother and father. There would be muttering about the fact that she was morally loose."

In retrospect, Sonia rejected "the stereotype label" that "Communist equals free love." She explained that during her early life of touring and working in the theater, "the sleeping here, there, with anyone, did not matter because sleep was the only priority and sex was last if not least." Lena's disapproval of her daughter's emancipated ways undoubtedly contributed to Sonia's early antipathy for her mother. At the same time, Sonia's outspoken political views clashed with her father's "rock-ribbed Republicanism." As a small businessman, Harry had little patience for Sonia's growing interest in the trade union movement and in social issues. According to Silverman, "Everybody in the family knew that Sonia was red, because she was very verbal about it. She was kind of proselytizing like it was her religion. But Jerry wasn't verbal." Jerry may have sympathized with his sister's left-wing views, but others in the family characterized him as politically naive and disinterested at the time. "His enthusiasm was strictly for theater and dance," said Bob Silverman's brother, Saul.

Because of the implicit sexual stereotype, the idea of Jerry being a dancer surely raised other unsettling questions that no one in the family could easily have articulated. This was an area that was never discussed, not even in later years, when unpleasant revelations threatened to surface. "I cannot recall that any member of the family, any of the sisters, any of the husbands, certainly not the kids, ever mentioned Jerry's homosexuality," said Bob Silverman. "It was—you don't talk about it. It's all in the family. Keep it quiet. It was not a conversational topic." According to Jerry's sister, his bisexuality was apparent to her during his adolescence, and by the age of sixteen, he was leaving home for periods of time and staying in Manhattan. "It was such a hard road he chose for himself," said Sonia. "Very difficult being a young boy, being Jewish, and being a homosexual—what else can you have!" Yet Jerry also brought one of his young female companions home to live with his family for a brief period that lasted until his mother vetoed the arrangement. Sonia recalled that her parents engaged in a form of denial over the years, never admitting to the gay side of their son's lifestyle, his heterosexual romantic adventures allowing them to maintain their one-sided view.

Jerry's sexual uncertainties would become a source of enormous confusion and guilt as he tried to fulfill his parents' expectations with regard to his sexual preference and their presumption that he would one day marry and settle down. "I think that he felt that his role was to get married," said Silverman. "That was the way to go. Back in the early days, we all thought Jerry was going to get married."

Viola Zousmer also expected Jerry to pursue the conventional matrimonial path. She remembered his boyhood infatuations at Camp Kittatinny and later in life never accepted rumors that he might be gay. "I knew him at camp when we were kids together, and he always had a crush on a girl."

Given the widespread homophobia during the years that Jerry was coming of age, there was no language available for polite social discourse regarding homosexuality or bisexuality. The word "homosexual" rarely found its way into print, and when it did, according to author Charles Kaiser, it was associated in the media with lurid connotations. A 1943 article in the *Herald Tribune* sought to explain homosexuality with words like "vice," "unnatural," "moral leper," "monster," "pervert," "degenerate," "evil" and "sinister." While the psychiatric community at the time viewed homosexual behavior as mental illness, the law treated homosexual acts as criminal. Undercover police in Manhattan routinely exposed themselves in public restrooms in order to entrap gay men, a practice that continued into the sixties. In such an adverse atmosphere, the theater, with its tolerance for unconventional lifestyles and sexual orientations, undoubtedly represented a haven for Robbins, as well as the means by which he might free himself from financial dependence on his father.

H is first break came when choreographer William Dollar cast him in the chorus of *Great Lady*, a Broadway musical that was quite lavish by the standards of the day, with a large ensemble, period costumes, and elaborate designs that incorporated a revolving stage. George Balanchine arranged some of the dances, and the show opened on December 1, 1938, at the Majestic Theatre. This was Robbins' debut on the Great White Way, and even if his name was not yet up in lights, at least he could tell himself and his family that he was following his dream and being paid for it. The star was French soubrette Irene Bordoni, and aside from Robbins, other notable dancers in the chorus included Nora Kaye, Annabelle Lyon, Alicia Alonso, Leda Anchutina and André Eglevsky. According to Alonso, Jerry contributed steps to the show. "He would say to me, 'Do this step, do this step,' and he would make me do it and try it out on stage. Then the choreographer came and said, 'I like that,' and put it in the show. This was for Nora Kaye and myself and Fernando Alonso. So Jerry started from the beginning to choreograph."

Unfortunately for Jerry, *Great Lady* closed before Christmas after only twenty performances, and he suffered at least one embarrassing reversal during the run. He played an assistant tailor in a Napoleonic period shop, and his big scene was a dressmaker's ballet that ranged from a stately minuet to farce. The set consisted of male and female dressing rooms that were separated by a dividing wall. The audience watched as the courtly gentlemen and ladies fit their evening clothes on opposite sides of the stage. According to the script, a fight ensued over the wardrobe, and the scuffle among the men was to become so violent that they would break through the wall. That part of the wall was made of paper, and each of the improvising dancers tried not to be the first to go through, if only because the others were directed to pile on top of him. One night Jerry happened to be the first, but instead of hitting the paper spot, he banged into the wood and stood frozen in place. After the others crashed through, the stage revolved and he was thrown off unceremoniously into the wings.

Undeterred, Robbins soon joined the chorus of *Stars in Your Eyes*, a more rewarding musical comedy romp directed by Joshua Logan. J. P. McEvoy's book had originally been intended as a spoof on the left-wing politics of certain wealthy Hollywood filmmakers, but the script was revised to meet Logan's suggestion: "Let's throw all the unfunny Communist stuff out the window and just do a show about the crazy way Hollywood people mix sex and movies." Featuring Jimmy Durante and Ethel Merman, the show opened at the Majestic Theatre on February 9, 1939, and managed a run of 127 performances. Logan rated the musical a modest success. "*Stars in Your Eyes* had everything in it but the M-G-M lion. . . . One scene was the wildest I've ever tried. It had Merman and Durante singing a duet of a good song, 'It's All Yours.' In the middle of each chorus, with the music still going, Durante would stop singing and do one of his notorious jokes. He'd grab a phone from the footlights and shout, 'Hello, is dis de meat market? Well, meet my wife at six o'clock!' Then he'd throw the phone on the floor and continue the song, with Merman never missing a beat."

This was the sort of thirties musical comedy fare that Robbins would eventually master and later seek to transform. "Musicals tend to be facetious," he said later. "No one has ever used them as a medium to depict deep personal struggle, and I think this can be done." Before he could act on such aspirations, however, Robbins had a long way to go to escape the anonymity of the chorus line. Logan recalled, "During the out-of-town tryouts, we had trouble with the dances. There was talk of changing the choreographer. We should have looked right into the ranks of our own chorus, which included the soon-to-be-famous Nora Kaye, Alicia Alonso, Maria Karnilova, and a very shy kid named Jerome Robbins."

His shyness in those days did not strike everyone as entirely innocent. "He was the boy who put snakes in the girls' beds," said dancer-choreographer Ruthanna Boris, referring to a vaguely recalled prank that Robbins carried off later that summer at Camp Tamiment. Situated in the idyllic Poconos about ninety miles from New York, Tamiment was a Borscht-belt resort that served as a unique training ground for aspiring dancers, choreographers, musicians, actors and comedians. Each summer, the camp presented a series of ambitious performances in its large social hall, which lent itself to stage productions and cabaret floor shows.

Robbins later remembered, "I was part of the entertainment staff, along with Anita Alvarez, Ruthanna Boris, and people from the Graham company, and we formed sort of a team for a while. We did three shows a week—a big Saturday night revue, a vaudeville-style revue and one night club thing. We just kept throwing dances on, so if we had an idea for a dance, we were usually allowed to do it. This is where I started little choreographic sketches."

Talent for Tamiment's theater was recruited by Max Liebman, who would go on to produce *Your Show of Shows*, a groundbreaking television variety show that aired live on NBC during the early fifties and established Liebman as the "Ziegfeld of television." The show featured the talents of Imogene Coca, Sid Caesar, Carl Reiner, Howard Morris and choreographer James Starbuck. As the director of Tamiment's entertainment program, Liebman developed a revue formula, striving for Broadway-quality productions that were written, rehearsed and staged within a single week. The camp was owned by the Rand School for Social Research, which had been founded by the Socialist Party in 1906 and remained committed to the ideals of political reform championed by Eugene V. Debs. The goal of the camp was to provide recreation and cultural enrichment, traditionally the exclusive province of wealth and privilege, to working-class families. The Rand School's Manhattan headquarters, located at 7 East Fifteenth Street, was called "The People's House," and that was where Boris first encountered Robbins, after the two boarded a bus that would deliver them to Tamiment that season.

A Balanchine-trained dancer still in her teens, Boris had ambitions to be a choreographer and had recently danced on Broadway for Agnes de Mille in *Hooray for What!* Boris took a seat on the bus behind two dark-haired boys. One of them turned around to break the ice, saying cheerfully, "Hi. I'm Eddie Gilbert. I'm the set designer."

Following suit, Boris introduced herself. "Hi. I'm Ruthanna Boris. I'm the choreographer."

Hearing her claim, the other boy cut in, saying pointedly, "I'm Jerome Robbins, and *I'm* the choreographer."

So began a friendly competition that was not without its tense moments. Robbins and Boris first worked together during the second of five summers (1937–1941) that he spent honing his craft at Tamiment. She remembered a sketch that they choreographed for Danny Kaye, who was also learning the show-biz ropes at Tamiment, along with Imogene Coca and Kaye's future wife, Sylvia Fine. "Danny wanted to do a kind of Jewish or Hebraic piece in a show with a dance, and he wanted to chant Kol Nidre. He asked Jerry and me to stage it for him, but neither of us really had an idea of what to do. So we went down the hill to the ILGWU camp. We both learned from the people at the other camp. They were all very religious, and we picked up some Talmudic gestures and this and that. Danny was dying to be a cantor . . . and he had a wonderful voice. Jerry and I collaborated, and we both danced it as two boys. I had to strap my boobs down. That's one thing we did together, and he didn't fight me."

Boris also sensed Robbins' discomfort with "things Jewish." She saw him as standoffish and even somewhat malicious when he carried out his school-boy stunt of putting garter snakes in the beds of the bunkhouse that she shared with three roommates. Over the years, she came to suspect that Jerry harbored some secret emotional anguish that he vented in the theater. Boris speculated that much of his inner conflict traced to his parents, as she put it, "because they were immigrants and Jews, and there's a very special kind of shame that goes with that." She also recalled, "I felt very sorry for him. I'm vulnerable. When people are hurting, I can feel it a mile away."

One of Boris' roommates, Dorothy Bird, a Graham-trained modern dancer, offered a very different impression of Jerry, who was to inspire such contrary opinions throughout his life. Bird recalled him as a "young man with laughing eyes" whose nickname at camp was "Mr. Happy." She wrote in her memoir, *Bird's Eye View*, "As the summer progressed, it became apparent not only that Jerry was a very talented performer but also that he wanted to become a serious choreographer. Max [Liebman] . . . provided rehearsal space and scheduled time for Jerry to work with the dancers. Thus Jerry had the opportunity to create his first ballet. Albia Kavan, a former soloist in Ballet Caravan and dedicated Balanchine dancer from the School of American Ballet, was in the company. She, Ruthanna, and I along with a few other dancers took a ballet barre together religiously every morning. All of us were seriously motivated to dance and were prepared to be quiet and respectful at Jerry's rehearsals. There we saw him become a different person—resolute and purposeful.

"Jerry was the moving force spirit behind a hornpipe trio danced by Anita Alvarez, Jerry and me. We put it together quite spontaneously using a couple of steps from the traditional hornpipe I had learned . . . plus some new steps Jerry devised. It climaxed with split jumps that brought down the house. I sometimes wonder if our little hornpipe trio was the seed of an idea that Jerry first developed into *Fancy Free* and then later into *On the Town.*"

The third member of the trio, Anita Alvarez, had also been trained by Martha Graham. At this time, Robbins still considered himself primarily a modern dancer, though he would soon make his conversion to ballet. Alvarez said of him, "He was very inventive even then, and he had a great sense of humor. He had his limitations as a dancer. He was very lightweight at that time. He was also very straight then. He was in love with Albia Kavan, who was a ballet dancer." Encouraging his interest in classical dance, Albia Kavan was a ballerina from Chicago who had danced with Jerry in the chorus of *Great Lady*. She eventually joined Ballet Theatre (later called American Ballet Theatre) and married Rex Cooper, who played the bartender in the original cast of *Fancy Free*.

While engaging in the innocent rituals of summer romance, Jerry also created several short dances that touched on serious political themes. With Alvarez, he performed a duet to Billie Holiday's recording of "Strange Fruit." Bird extolled this dramatized tale of a lynching. "In the middle of the dimly lit stage stood a very tall ladder. Jerry was costumed aristocratically in a dark outfit, with his throat and wrists accented by white that caught the light. In marked contrast, Anita wore a plain, perhaps even torn, shift of nondescript color. They danced with great intensity. Toward the end, Jerry slowly mounted the ladder. Anita stood motionless. When Jerry approached the top of the ladder, he stopped and looked down. We then became aware that Anita seemed to be hanging, suspended by her neck. It appeared to snap slightly, as her head toppled over to the side. The moment was understated. *Strange Fruit* was one of the most dramatic and heart-breaking dances I have ever seen—a masterpiece."

A similarly haunting romantic tragedy was created by Alvarez and Robbins to the folk song "Frankie and Johnny," and both dances were subsequently performed in Manhattan at the Ninety-second Street YMHA, under the auspices of TAC, the Theatrical Arts Committee, a performing arts magazine that sometimes sponsored concerts. Robbins received a favorable notice from a leftist dance critic, Edna Ocko, with whom he cultivated an acquaintanceship, as he was then trying to use radical politics to win critical recognition for his dances. Ocko's name would reenter his life some years later during his most challenging personal crisis with the HUAC investigation. The stage was already being set for Robbins' entrapment in this ideological inquisition, as the House Special Committee on Un-American Activities under Congressman Martin Dies had emerged in 1938 as the forerunner of HUAC. Robbins was waiting in the wings along with many other artists involved with the left, although his activities at this point appear to have been nothing more than a flirtation that served his choreographic ambitions.

In a dance entitled *Incident in Harlem,* Jerry told the story of a group of whites who went "slumming" in an uptown dive and instigated a tense racial incident. He recalled that the audience "laughed at all the serious moments. I guess I compressed it too much. It was only seven minutes long." In 1939, he created a short sketch called *Death of a Loyalist* about the Spanish Civil War. In this piece, he danced the role of the Prisoner. His subject may have been suggested by personalities and events at home. Jerry's sister became romantically involved with a veteran of the Abraham Lincoln Brigade, George Cullinen, who was a member of the maritime union and an impassioned Communist. Sonia would soon marry him, with her brother serving as best man. Jerry may not yet have voiced the radical views espoused by Sonia and George, but he was surely affected by their strong opinions, if only as topical ideas that might be absorbed into gripping choreographic pictures. Five years later, however, he would take a more active stance, and lend his name to a *New York Times* advertisement advocating that the United States break its ties with Franco's Spain.

While at Tamiment, Robbins also choreographed *Lazy Day*, which he suggested was based on the "fence painting incident from Tom Sawyer," and *A La Russe*, which he described as "a French farce as done by a Russian ballet company." As a dancer and fledgling choreographer, Jerry overcame his shyness onstage and achieved a degree of freedom that was otherwise lacking in his life. Bird credited him with spellbinding virtuosity as a cabaret performer. "He was mysteriously confident and outwardly carefree, even casual, about every aspect of his solo work. . . . He choreographed startling, dazzling entrances for himself, certain to capture everyone's attention. . . . He moved improvisationally from table to table, reaching out to people, before suddenly spinning, leaping and sliding across the floor to another table. . . . As he heard the climactic moment approaching in the music, he readied himself to execute the most theatrical exit imaginable. He disappeared to thunderous applause, then laughingly returned to bow, always at ease but in total control. Jerry openly loved being in intimate touch with his audience. . . . His youthful confidence and zeal were infectious. Everyone shared in the fun."

Not everyone, however, held such a sanguine view, and even Bird admitted to feeling maligned by Jerry's humor when he invented a dance that caricatured her as a stripper. "Jerry did one thing during the last show that summer that tarnished my own self-image . . . Jerry did a takeoff on me. . . . He had captured just enough of my qualities—juxtaposed with insinuating, earthy ingredients—that the audience recognized it was me. They laughed uproariously. . . . Instead of feeling flattered that Jerry would choose to imitate me, I felt cheapened and distinctly soiled. He could not possibly have known how his imitation would inhibit me, causing me to shrink back into my shell."

The passions that fired Jerry's creativity already seemed to divide his personality onstage and off. In the theater, he was unrelenting in his approach to the work, and at times, even in these earliest years, came across as excessive with his demands, possessed as he was with a single-minded need to test his ideas and fulfill his vision. His most frequent partner at camp, Alvarez, would later work with him on Broadway. She recalled, "In personal relationships, he wasn't mean. It was just when he was working. It was his drivenness, his seeking for perfection or whatever. If he couldn't get what he wanted, he was murder. He got disgusted with me because I didn't see it as the end of the world and I wouldn't rehearse as much as he wanted to. This was at Tamiment, so it goes way back."

Tamiment led Robbins back to Broadway in the fall of 1939 with a musical entitled *Straw Hat Revue,* which featured the soon-to-be-famous Danny Kaye and Imogene Coca. The show had originated from sketches that were performed at the camp during that summer. Liebman arranged a backers' audition and managed to sell the idea to the Shuberts by not including any politically controversial or ethnic material in the show. The war in Europe had broken out and newspaper headlines carried dire reports of the hostilities. In this increasingly grim atmosphere, the producers believed that the mood of the audience would not tolerate anything but the lightest musical comedy fare. Before the opening, Liebman waged a public relations campaign to disassociate the show from the Rand School and the camp's reputed socialist orientation. He was compelled to announce on behalf of the Shuberts that *Straw Hat Revue* "has no social significance" and "does not rely on newspaper headlines for material."

When the material for the show was finally selected, several of Robbins' political numbers were passed over in favor of his less provocative pieces. He had collaborated on a sketch called "Piano and Lute," which was deemed worthy of inclusion, as its central conflict came down to nothing more contentious than a spirited competition between modern and ballet dancers. Another of Jerry's sketches, this one a dance to James Shelton's song "Hometown," was incorporated in the show as a group number entitled "Our Town." The cast of ten included Jerry, Bird and Boris, but the staging was taken over by the Shuberts' aggressive representative, Harry Kaufman, who used his power to usurp Liebman's position as director. "It was pretty much out of Max's hands," Bird reported. "He let them do what they wanted—he was just so happy to have a show." At one rehearsal, Bird became incensed when Kaufman, who had a reputation for being overbearing and crude, sharply criticized her performance and offered what she took to be inept stage direction. She recalled, "I could not understand why Jerry did not stand up to defend me and his choreography. Self-conscious and confused, I began to feel the stage was no longer such a safe place for me to be."

Jerry would learn his own bitter lesson from the experience. Although he and Boris had provided much of the choreography for *Straw Hat Revue*, the sole credit went to Jerome Andrews, who was considered a name at the time and had been brought in by the Shuberts to supervise the dancing. In the theater, of course, credit is serious business often involving extensive negotiations, especially to the artists whose careers may be on the line depending on whose name appears on the marquee. Broadway lore has always included its share of behind-the-scenes backstabbing. In this case, the motley group of Tamiment players had no legal protection. For Jerry not to have received proper billing and recognition for his creative work was a stinging blow to his ego, as well as an insult to his sense of justice. He would never allow it to happen again.

Straw Hat Revue opened on September 29, 1939, at the Ambassador Theatre and lasted seventy-five performances, a fair run in light of the stiff competition from two major musicals that season, *Hellzapoppin* (which had been at the Winter Garden for a year) and Rodgers and Hart's new offering, *Too Many Girls*. Straight plays such as *The Philadelphia Story, The Man Who Came to Dinner, Key Largo* and *Life with Father* were also attracting audiences that fall, as was *Tobacco Road*, then in its seventh year. At the time, Broadway ticket prices were usually under five dollars for the best seats in the house.

If the numbers were low by today's inflationary standards, the rules and stakes of the game were much the same then as now, and Robbins would learn them with the same thoroughgoing dedication that he brought into his dances. Over time, his ability to read his audience and know exactly what would work on stage would be matched by his equally shrewd commercial instincts. If his father had instilled a fear that his livelihood might be taken away from him in the non-Jewish world, Jerry would master the business, hire the best lawyers and adopt a certain highhanded ruthlessness in protecting his interests. While the theater offered a personal refuge from his family and shielded him to some extent from social intolerance, the harsh realities of show business were quickly leading him into a life of combat.

Robbins' last appearance as a Broadway gypsy took place in the spring of 1940, when he danced in the chorus of *Keep off the Grass*, a short-lived musical flop that starred Ray Bolger, Jimmy Durante, Jackie Gleason and Ilka Chase. The show was choreographed by George Balanchine, who during these early years was moonlighting both on Broadway and in Hollywood. Robbins had first encountered Balanchine during rehearsals for *Great Lady*. The versatile Russian choreographer already possessed a reputation and following among ballet cognoscenti thanks to his early work with Serge Diaghilev's original Ballets Russes, and later, with Colonel de Basil's Ballet Russe de Monte Carlo. He had since devoted his talents to his School of American Ballet and to the struggling American Ballet Company, which for several years had been unsuccessfully associated with the Metropolitan Opera.

A few years earlier, Jerry had tried to apply for a scholarship at Balanchine's school, only to be turned away by a secretary. Robbins later counted himself fortunate that he had not fallen into Balanchine's orbit too early, before having had the chance to develop his own individual style of choreography, which initially took the form of storytelling through the dance, as in his Tamiment sketches, rather than Balanchine's more abstract and often plotless approach. Robbins described Balanchine as "such a god of the dance, so overwhelming an influence, that I don't see how any young dancer who has gone through the School of American Ballet . . . and then wants to choreograph can possibly retain his own identity."

Robbins' exposure to Balanchine in *Keep off the Grass* was limited to learning steps with the rest of the chorus, though the young dancer was singled out for some special attention along the way, however slight a nod it may have been. "Balanchine came to do some dances," Robbins recalled, "and he asked me to understudy José Limón," whom Jerry had idolized since first meeting him at the Dance Center. Limón remembered that Balanchine spent most of his time "trying to conceal his infinite boredom with the assignment. He had very little with which to work." Like most of the cast and the rest of the country, Limón was troubled by events in Europe during "that spring of nightmares," when France capitulated to the Nazis. "At the theater we went through the motions of performing," said Limón, "but everything was empty and meaningless."

An asthmatic condition would keep Robbins out of military service. He later looked back on the war years after seeing the film *Schindler's List*, recalling that he was distracted from those distant events and remained uninformed about the horrors of the concentration camps. "I was not aware of what was going on in Europe," said Robbins. "From 1939 to 1944, I was trying to be a dancer, and all that was somewhere else." The statement is surprising in light of his subsequent political activities and the fact that he would soon create a ballet that he described as "World War II as it appeared in the streets of New York." But at the time of *Keep off the Grass*, Robbins' obsessive concern, as with so many young performers, was the advancement of his career, even if this musical would not further his cause. Limón called the show "a dismal and well-deserved failure," though the fault was not Balanchine's, whose "hands had been tied behind him." The Shuberts' hired gun, Harry Kaufman, had overseen the fiasco and heaped abuse on the choreographer during rehearsals.

Balanchine had come to this country in 1933 as the prize of Lincoln Kirstein, then an aspiring impresario and scholar fresh out of Harvard. Jewish, gentrified and quixotic, Kirstein was heir to the Filene's department store fortune. A brilliant aesthete and self-proclaimed Renaissance man, he would establish himself at the center of New York's elite intellectual and cultural circles and remain there for more than fifty years. Like others in his milieu, Kirstein delighted in the visual spectacle and sheer physical beauty that ballet and its glamorous practitioners had to offer. He had been an ardent balletomane since adolescence and was long enthralled by the mystique of Nijinsky and the lore of Diaghilev's company. He used his wealth and social connections to bring Balanchine to America with the grand scheme of founding an indigenous theater on the order of the greatest national ballet companies that existed in Europe. From its inception, it was nothing if not an ambitious dream, one in which Robbins would eventually come to play a crucial role, but only after first making his own indelible mark elsewhere.

Kirstein and Balanchine were not the only ones trying to realize such dreams in New York. The competition included a man who shared Kirstein's pedigree and his fervor for ballet. Princeton architect and entrepreneur Richard Pleasant was soon to become a founder of Ballet Theatre, and he was just as determined as Kirstein to promote the art in America. The enterprise grew out of former Bolshoi star Mikhail Mordkin's recital troupe, the Mordkin Ballet, which included in its ranks a wealthy New England widow, Lucia Chase, whose money came from the Waterbury Clock Company (rather than the Chase National Bank, as many supposed). Her short-lived marriage to Robert Ewing had left her a sizable inheritance, and this young socialite ballerina bankrolled the new company and also performed in its early productions. Over the years, Chase invested more than $40 million of her fortune in Ballet Theatre, in effect purchasing the ultimate decision-making authority for herself. A New York businessman and theater devotee, Rudolf Orthwine, initially served as president, while Pleasant, as managing director, took the lead in setting the company's commercial and artistic policies. Pleasant's stated goal was a theater "international in scope and American in spirit."

In the early going, the aging Russian émigré Mordkin was deemed expendable and forced to step down from his position of artistic leadership by the triumvirate of Pleasant, Chase and Orthwine. This was the sort of conspiratorial ballet intrigue that Robbins would later satirize in his show *Look, Ma, I'm Dancin'!* One of the original members of Ballet Theatre, Maria Karnilova, who would later work extensively with Robbins on Broadway, recounted Mordkin's plight to Antony Tudor's biographer Donna Perlmutter. "I felt sorry for him," said Karnilova, recalling "how badly they treated him. But he never protested. He used to bring a windup Mickey Mouse to class and shoot it with a toy gun he would pull out. 'Gangsters, gangsters,' he hollered. Everyone thought him mad, but not so. This was his way of telling us they were all gangsters who were robbing him."

Unlike Kirstein, who was to bet all of his chips on Balanchine, the founders of Ballet Theatre recruited a number of eminent choreographers and set out to develop an eclectic repertory reflecting Russian, English and American influences. The company was bureaucratically divided into two stylistic wings, one devoted to traditional European works, which included the white tutu ballets like *Giselle,* and the other committed to modern ballets, which were further subdivided by nationality into American and British. Among those staging productions during the company's early years were Michel Fokine, Léonide Massine, Adolph Bolm, Anton Dolin, Eugene Loring, Bronislava Nijinska, Antony Tudor and Agnes de Mille. Balanchine turned down an early offer to join them, even as the new company paid top dollar and lured talents like Loring and William Dollar from Kirstein's Ballet Caravan.

Ballet Theatre's first performance was given on January 11, 1940, at Rockefeller Center's enormous Center Theatre. The three-week season had been announced with sensational fanfare. One advertisement boasted, "The Greatest Ballets of All Time Staged by the Greatest Collaborators in Ballet History." The company went a long way toward living up to its hype, on many nights selling out the 3,500-seat house with both traditional and newly created works. The eighty-five original dancers included well-known European stars as well as up-and-coming, homegrown talent. The only drawback was the budget, as big-time ballet carried a hefty price tag. The expensive overhead and short three-week season brought about a reported loss of $200,000. Nevertheless, according to most accounts, the inaugural season was an auspicious success. *Times* critic John Martin called it "the beginning of a new era."

One of the early supporters of Ballet Theatre was Dwight Deere Wiman, who had produced both *Great Lady* and *Stars in Your Eyes*. Thanks to Wiman, many of the chorus dancers from both Broadway shows joined Ballet Theatre to open its first season. Robbins, however, missed the opportunity and was then temporarily sidetracked with *Keep off the Grass*. In the summer of 1940, with the help of his friend, David Nillo, whom he knew from dance classes, Jerry was finally able to audition. Nillo was already in the company, and remembered, "We were very great friends at the beginning. I got him into Ballet Theatre. I went to Anton Dolin and said, 'This is a good dancer.' There weren't too many men around in those days. I said, 'Let him audition.' I was a friend of Dolin's and he said, 'Okay. Bring him around.' So Jerry got in. But we drifted away from each other after a while."

Nillo was one of a number of friends Jerry left behind or estranged over the years when his ambitions called for a shift of personal allegiances. With regard to dance, those ambitions had already gathered the force of an inspired mission, and Ballet Theatre was a much coveted entrée with its promise of a diverse repertory and more-or-less steady employment. Even with a salary of forty dollars a week, if there were a possibility of his staging a ballet for a major company one day, this was an opportunity he could not pass up. And there was an additional incentive for Jerry—for the first time in his life, he would be on his own. Traveling on the road with the troupe for much of the year would finally enable him to establish his independence from his family, although he continued to live with his parents at their Weehawken apartment and observed the religious holidays with the Rabinowitz clan whenever he was in town, however detached from such obligatory family rituals he may have felt. As one of his relatives remarked, "He didn't really want anything to do with the family, because it was not his family anymore. The dancers became his family."

Anton Dolin, a British premier danseur and choreographer, was regisseur for the company's classical wing. He recounted his part in bringing Robbins into Ballet Theatre. "We auditioned dancers in both Philadelphia and New York. Sixty or seventy applicants turned up. We needed two boys and two girls. We selected Jerry Robbins and Johnny Kriza. The girls we chose were Muriel Bentley and Alicia Alonso. . . . I knew right away that these four were going to emerge as particularly important in the history of American ballet. Of course, I was absolutely right. I usually am!"

Alonso soon became one of the company's leading prima ballerinas, years later returning to her homeland to direct the Ballet Nacional de Cuba. She described Ballet Theatre's early corps de ballet as unique in character and talent, singling out Robbins, Nora Kaye, Muriel Bentley, Donald Saddler, David Nillo and future Broadway choreographer Michael Kidd. "We were so good and so proud of being Ballet Theatre dancers," recalled Alonso. "We had discipline within ourselves—such discipline! I think that was the beginning of Ballet Theatre, that was the beauty of it. We were not just *hired* dancers in a company, we *were* the company."

Another original member of the corps, Miriam Golden, recalled the fun-loving spirit of the group, as well as their dedication in the face of financial adversity. "All I can say is we were a bunch of personalities. We were crazy. They don't make 'em like that anymore. And we were getting paid almost nothing. If we asked for a two-dollar raise, we almost got fired. That's what happened with Alonso. She asked Lucia for a two-dollar raise and Lucia almost fired her. Can you imagine?"

Alonso recalled that it was Robbins who first encouraged the dancers to unionize, another early indication of his disposition toward social activism. In this instance, self-interest agreed with conscience when he proselytized for the union cause. "He spoke to a small group of us," said Alonso. "Nora [Kaye] was in the group, but she was not close to him at this time. We were working very hard in the company with many choreographers, and sometimes we didn't have time for lunch or dinner or anything, and our feet were so swollen that we could hardly walk. We sat in chairs with our feet up. Jerry said, 'This is no good. Dancers should belong to a union.' So he really was the man in the company who pushed ballet dancers to join the union."

The company's first headquarters had been established at the A. C. Blumenthal mansion on Fifty-fourth Street at Sixth Avenue, where both the executive offices and rehearsal studios were located. The war brought an influx of foreigners, including a number of stellar figures who regularly taught classes and rehearsed the dancers. The young Americans were more than impressed by the talent they encountered. Golden recalled, "We were in awe. They looked at us and we looked at them. There was no familiarity. They were trying to assess us. We were trying to impress them. But we were scared, because we knew these classes with Fokine and Dolin and Tudor and Loring were like auditions and we wanted to be chosen for their ballets."

The stylistic range and diversity of the choreographers assembled at Ballet Theatre made it an ideal finishing school for Robbins. With the demands of the repertory, being a dancer at this time meant not only mastering ballet technique but also the craft of acting. Sono Osato, who joined Ballet Theatre in its first season and later starred in *On the Town*, emphasized that in those days, dancers were required to think in terms of drama and theatricality. "We did ballets by everybody—we did Fokine, Massine and Tudor. We were different characters every night and every matinee. You couldn't just come onstage and dance the steps—it would be dead, no good. Our generation was trained to express feelings. We had to act and dance."

All of the dancers faced hardships maintaining the rigorous physical discipline required for performance, as the troupe embarked on a hectic touring schedule that continued throughout the war years. Michael Kidd recounted how he and Robbins and the other dancers took over train cars to accommodate themselves traveling between engagements. "We didn't usually have sleeping cars because they were too expensive, and we had to make long trips after one-night stands to go to the next town. Nobody had much sleep. We had it down to a system. The old railroad cars had seats where you could pull the backs out. You brought a small suitcase, which you laid between the two seats at just the right height, so you pulled the back off, laid it across the suitcase and stretched out there. When you came onto a train after not having much sleep the night before, you immediately stripped the car. I remember the look of astonishment on the conductor when he walked in and saw this whole car virtually demolished and everyone stretched out asleep."

Once the American troop buildup was under way, train travel was fraught with uncertainty. Dancers were often bumped off trains and stranded to make way for soldiers being transported between bases. Jerry's friend John Taras remembered how the troop movements played havoc with the company's performance schedule. "There were times when we couldn't get on the train when we were scheduled to go because of the troops. For an eight o'clock performance, we might get to the theater at eight-thirty or nine, and Mr. Dolin, who was performing that night, would come out in his dressing gown and talk to the audience, trying to keep them calm while we were getting ready. That's often the way it was." Taras also recalled that Lucia Chase, while controlling the company's purse strings, danced on the tours and tried to conceal her position of authority. "Lucia always traveled with us and insisted on being one of the girls. She didn't want anyone to know that she was paying for the company."

Chase's budget was never generous when it came to providing for the corps. Robbins described a con game that he and the others used to save money checking into hotels. "In those days we played the army game together. Because there were no rooms on tour and because we got paid so little—for instance, we'd get to Bloomington, Indiana, and this company of eighty people would descend on the hotel lobby, and the desk clerk would go berserk with all this signing-in and registration, and then the lobby'd be cleared and they'd look down and find that there were only maybe twenty people registered. And we would double up, of course, in rooms, and take mattresses off the beds and sleep four in a room that was registered for one."

Not long after joining Ballet Theatre, Robbins danced in the corps at New York's Lewisohn Stadium, Philadelphia's Robin Hood Dell and later with the Chicago Civic Opera. Among the ballets in which he appeared was Antony Tudor's *Goya Pastoral,* a piquant Spanish fable that John Martin called "a lighthearted little ballet." That Robbins had been chosen for this particular offering was significant, even if it was one of its creator's lesser works. Tudor was the iconoclastic British choreographer who many would come to regard as a genius for his probing psychological dramas. Combining natural gesture and the idiom of classical ballet, he forged a language of movement remarkable in its meticulous subtlety and expressive power—a lesson in the art of dance and storytelling that would serve Robbins well.

Tudor had worked in London for the Ballet Rambert and had already staged such acclaimed works as *Jardin aux Lilas* and *Dark Elegies.* Robbins' friend and fellow corps member Donald Saddler said, "We knew Tudor was an exciting choreographer and we felt very fortunate when chosen to work for him." Indeed, it was considered an honor in the company to be recognized as a Tudor dancer. He attracted a cultlike following that included Robbins, who faithfully attended his classes and recalled "hanging around on the off chance of getting into a Tudor ballet." Two years later, both Saddler and Robbins would dance in the corps as "Lovers-in-Experience" in Tudor's first American masterpiece, *Pillar of Fire;* and the following year, Robbins was particularly delighted to be cast as Benvolio in Tudor's *Romeo and Juliet,* later dancing the part of Mercutio as well. Shakespeare's tragedy of forbidden love held a fascination for Robbins that would eventually lead to *West Side Story,* and Tudor's treatment of the tale inspired Robbins to talk with other dancers at the time about his own ideas for staging the drama.

Tudor's rehearsals often took on the tense atmosphere of psychodrama, as in his own idiosyncratic fashion he utilized Stanislavski's acting techniques as well as Freudian analytical insights. Tudor used these tools manipulatively to explore the psyches of his dancers as well as the emotional lives of the characters that inhabited his ballets. While other choreographers were interested in steps and decorative movement, Tudor was devoted to examining human passions and relationships. In the process of creating his ballets, he exhibited a rapier wit that some characterized as unnecessarily cruel and demeaning. Dancers were often reduced to tears by acerbic barbs that crossed the line between artistic criticism and personal attack. The same abrasive style and uncompromising, messianic perfectionism would one day be attributed to Robbins, and no doubt there was some degree of emulation. Although inhibited at first by youthful insecurities, Robbins eventually came to enjoy the sparring matches with Tudor, whose methods and artistry made him an especially engaging challenge as well as a role model.

"I think Tudor had the greatest influence on Jerry," said Alonso, "even with the Broadway shows. Jerry admired him very much." Tudor would launch Nora Kaye to overnight stardom when she portrayed the dramatic lead, Hagar, in *Pillar of Fire*, the story of a lonely spinster overcoming her Victorian reticence and self-doubt to embrace love. Kaye, who became Tudor's principal muse, was short and dark-haired, with gifts of intellect that were sometimes masked by her brashness and high, nasal New York accent. Though not a classic beauty, she possessed a remarkable ability to project emotion and character onstage. Kaye described the kind of preparation that Tudor demanded even of those, like Robbins, dancing minor roles. "When Tudor started *Pillar*, we knew all about the town where it takes place. We knew what wallpaper was in the house, what photos were in the bedroom the audience doesn't see. Tudor talked. It was part of the Stanislavski method. Every character knew who he or she was."

Kaye and Robbins would eventually share a strong artistic and emotional bond, but initially Jerry was limited to the periphery of her all-consuming relationship with Tudor, which was the center of an exclusive social clique. "Jerry was more interested in Nora than any other member of the company that I could see," recalled ballerina Mimi Gomber. "I think he respected her talent. She was competitive like him, and conniving so you couldn't really trust her. But I think their relationship was a pretty honest one, Jerry and Nora. I guess she made Jerry feel like he was in the inner circle with Tudor and Hugh."

Tudor's tempestuous romantic affair with the flamboyant West Indian dancer Hugh Laing was well known, though never flaunted in the theater, where varying degrees of discretion were exercised by gay and bisexual artists.

Jerry was personally reticent in that regard, and struggling to find his way, which can only have made the task of creating himself as an artist all the more problematic. In a sense, he was already living a double life, split between the conformity of the outside world and the sheltered world of the company, which was really a touring caravan of one-night stands, both in terms of its performance schedule and the casualness of its amorous affairs. Gomber described the atmosphere on one of the early train rides. "I remember on the first sleeper tour that we took, there were people running from berth to berth, all the Russians and French and international dancers. I mean they found their own sex lives—all night long they were going from berth to berth!"

Lacking maturity and experience, Robbins appears to have been more at ease with the camaraderie of the men than in the company of women, as he created entirely different impressions with his male and female fellow travelers. John Taras remembered him as high-spirited and mischievous with his humor. "Jerry and I were what he used to call 'bunkies' because we used to share a room on tour. I didn't think he was inhibited at all. He was outgoing. He cut up at parties and also at rehearsals."

Janet Reed, on the other hand, an original in the cast of *Fancy Free*, characterized Robbins as a very private person who held back socially. "I remember the first time I met him, thinking, Little Boy Lost. He was naive, and he had a lot of fear early on. He was afraid of failure. He was driven and very unsure of himself sexually and in every way. There was a kind of intimacy when we toured, but Jerry stayed off to the side. He showed up at parties, but he wasn't the last to leave." Reed noticed the difficulties that he had in adjusting to life on the road. "You get closer to other people when you tour, and you're cut off from other connections. But I don't think Jerry was especially happy touring. He needed his own space, and he liked to be free of all those personal relationships that are established in a touring company. You know, you sit on trains hour after hour. In one way, you develop relationships and it's good; in another way, it's too close. He needed the freedom and deserved it."

Maria Karnilova, known as Marusia to her friends, was one of a select few who became close to Jerry when they toured together. "He was innocent, totally innocent when I first met him," she remembered. "He was a very young, inexperienced boy. He didn't have many friends and didn't seem to fit in with the group. He was sort of alienated. He hadn't yet decided whether he was gay or not. He didn't know what he was. He was experimenting. This is just my observation. We spent many hours talking on the train rides, and I got the feeling that he was a tortured human being. Even then, he was unable to face things, or if he loved someone, particularly women, he couldn't deal with it. I think way back it had something to do with his father and mother. We all have our problems from childhood and we carry them with us. We drag them along. He was not a pretty boy, and he had this beautiful sister and a father who was very handsome. I think all these things played on his insecurity.

"We did a lot of talking and I got to know him quite well, but he would always withdraw and stay to himself, as if he were embarrassed by the relationship or had made himself too vulnerable. For instance, we would spend a night in the train speaking and being young and looking out the window and telling each other our dreams, and then in the morning he would pass me in the dining room as if he didn't know me. He was like that. Yet he did love some people. I know he loved and respected me. But it was very difficult for me to deal with him, because he became so inarticulate and uncomfortable. I could never feel comfortable with him, for all the years I knew him and all the many times I worked for him."

Karnilova was to have featured roles in such Robbins shows as *Gypsy* and *Fiddler on the Roof*. While acknowledging his artistic gifts and his support for her career, she sounded a note of criticism about his Jekyll-and-Hyde temperament that would be echoed by many of those who worked with him in the future. "He was a contradiction. A strange man. He wasn't a lovely man. He was cruel. I saw his soft vulnerable side only very early in Ballet Theatre. When he was vulnerable and had a particular relationship with someone, as I understand, perhaps he could be loving or whatever. Every human being has a side that is loving. But much of the time he was just mean . . . sometimes even evil. He was very difficult to work with for some people. I got along with him because I stayed above it all. I didn't get involved with him anymore personally after the early years of Ballet Theatre. I was just an employee and he treated me as such."

Karnilova's friend Mimi Gomber recalled that in the early years, "Jerry was sort of a loner, even though he was a part of everything. He never really let anybody into his life. He didn't make close connections with people. I think he had a lot to hide. He was pleasant, he was funny, he was all these things. But everything was on the surface. There were parts of him that he just didn't share with anybody." Janet Reed recalled that while Jerry participated socially, "he withdrew and spent a lot of time alone. I think he had to dream and contemplate."

Alonso believed that in his own way Robbins was gathering material as an artist and working on choreographic ideas all along. "Jerry was an observer," she said. "He didn't talk too much. He studied people. Always with his eyes very shiny and alive. He would look and look and look all the time. You can be sure from the beginning when we worked with him, he was making up steps. He'd be more relaxed outside the studio, but he was always thinking about dancing."

Robbins may have been somewhat ill at ease socially, especially with the opposite sex, but by all accounts he was never lacking in drive and motivation, as both a dancer and choreographer. Indeed, he was nothing if not determined to make a major career for himself. "He really worked his way up," said Gomber. "He was ambitious, and he knew what he wanted and worked towards that end. He wasn't necessarily considerate of anybody else's feelings or thoughts. I mean, he knew where he was going and, of course, the talent came out."

Another corps dancer, Hubert Bland, suspected that Jerry had his own private agenda from the beginning. "He used to read a lot of books. I remember one book was *What Makes Sammy Run?* He was ambitious, though not always showing it. But we could see that he was doing things, in his head working on things for the future. We could sense it. When he and Don [Saddler] and David [Nillo] and a bunch of them rehearsed, they used to kid around together. And they would do sort of silly things at a party, make up steps and have fun. Then Jerry stepped out and did a few comedy things in the ballets. That was when he started to take off."

R obbins first distinguished himself with a brief solo in Agnes de Mille's allegorical farce *Three Virgins and a Devil*, which critic Edwin Denby lauded as a "little satire on virginal vanity." Jerry played the insouciant Youth in red who lured The Lustful Virgin, danced by Annabelle Lyon, to her agreeable destruction. His role called for him to cross the stage twice, which took up only a thirty-two-bar passage in Ottorino Respighi's score. Yet de Mille explained that she chose Jerry for the part because of his musicality. "I wanted a boy who could do a most intricate jazzy kind of counting out in the music, and none of the Ballet Theatre boys could. But they said there was this boy Robbins who could count anything. And so I made an appointment and he didn't show up. He came though, the next time, and he learned what I had to teach him in twelve and a half minutes. And he said, 'What more?' I said, 'There isn't any more,' and he said, 'Oh well.' And he stopped the show."

"He was excellent," recalled Lyon. "It was just two crossovers, but he was right for it." Lucia Chase and de Mille danced the parts of the other two virginal damsels. Sono Osato was struck by how much the qualities Jerry brought into his performance contrasted with his personality. "Offstage he was reserved and seemed rather melancholy, particularly on tour. But his audacious sense of humor shone on stage, most brilliantly in Agnes' *Three Virgins and a Devil*. In one passage, Jerry walked jauntily to center stage and paused to admire one of the virgins, while twirling a flower nonchalantly in his hand. He gave the chaste girl a knowing nod, tipped his hat, and sauntered offstage again with a bobbing gait. With just those few gestures, he never failed to make an audience chuckle or titter with glee." Osato remembered "laughing out loud" when she first saw him in the part. The premiere took place at the Majestic Theatre, February 11, 1941, and Robbins received a favorable one-line notice in the *Times*, with John Martin asserting that he and the rest of the cast were deserving of "high praise."

Later that year, Robbins was promoted to soloist—though he would continue to put in time with the corps, in the next three years dancing in virtually all of the ballets in the company's repertory. He also gladly served as an offstage "catcher"—which meant waiting in the wings to catch prima ballerina Alicia Markova when she made her exit from the graveyard in *Giselle*. Robbins provided a brief, handwritten portrait of himself when he filled out a questionnaire for the company's publicity department. He described his favorite food as ham and eggs, and mentioned Mahler's *Dark Elegies* as his most thrilling musical experience. He also wrote, "Negro, Jazz and Blues—I like." He said his hobby was collecting pictures and that he enjoyed swimming and riding.

His favorite actors were Bette Davis and Paul Muni, and he admitted to the superstitious ritual of knocking on wood and touching his forehead before each performance. In every way he projected the wholesome image of an all-American boy, although curiously, he chose not to answer the question of whether or not he wanted his children to follow in his footsteps.

Robbins' working relationship with Agnes de Mille led him further into the study of acting. De Mille introduced him to her longtime friend Mary Hunter, who had recently founded a small theater and ensemble group, the American Actors Company. One of the first female directors to work on Broadway, Hunter was teaching and producing plays at the Provincetown Playhouse in Greenwich Village. Her original group included de Mille and playwrights Horton Foote and Tennessee Williams. Foote recalled, "I met Jerry at the same time that Mary did. He was bright and intelligent and obviously very talented. Jerry got interested in the company and we became friendly and saw each other quite a bit. I went out and met his family later, and I think we had a seder one time with them. He certainly was interested in my ideas and work, and I admired him a lot. We always stayed in touch."

Hunter was to become one of Robbins' closest lifelong friends in the theater, and together they would later collaborate on *Peter Pan*. During the spring of 1941, he sat in on rehearsals of her *American Legend*, an exuberant celebration of Americana that included a one-act play by Foote and also featured de Mille dancing as a pioneer girl in a hoedown. By the time the show closed, Robbins was studying with Hunter in earnest. "We were already good friends," she recalled. "He didn't quite understand what improvisation meant. I said, 'Come and see, and you'll learn how it can be very useful.' He did that and then used it in his work."

Janet Reed also studied with Hunter and remembered, "There was a period when Jerry and I went to her classes together. A lot of people had an influence on Jerry, but Mary Hunter was quite important during that time. We did a lot of improvisations in her class, and you get to know a person well with improvisation. Mary Hunter was very sympathetic and I know that she helped him a great deal. One of the improvisations that we did was based on *Romeo and Juliet*, in which Jerry was a Jewish boy and I was a Catholic girl. So this was really a modern version of the play. I remember talking with him about it on the subway. I think that's where he might have first come up with the idea for *West Side Story*. It was already on his mind."

With his training as an actor, Robbins developed a dramatic flair on stage that enabled him to compensate for his limitations as a classical dancer. He had come to ballet too late in his career to have achieved the technical virtuosity of a *premier danseur*. According to Karnilova, "Jerry was not trained properly balletically. Quite a few of the men were trained with strong classical technique. Jerry never had that technique. He was rather a naughty boy onstage when he was young. You would never think that he would grow up to be such a disciplinarian. In *Helen of Troy*, he would blow bubbles while I was doing my most difficult variation. With pink bubble gum! Oh, my God, that kind of improvised thing was never permitted once he started working as a director or choreographer himself."

Yet his improvisational approach to the role of Hermes in *Helen of Troy* would later win accolades. "It was not much of a role," said Robbins. "So I added a little of this and that." The ballet, depicting a comic version of the Trojan Wars, was started by Fokine before his death in 1942 and was then taken over by David Lichine, who received the final credit as choreographer (though Balanchine also tinkered with it). Edwin Denby wrote that Robbins "does it beautifully. It is a part in straight American—real Third Avenue, in fact. One of the interesting things about it is that, where everyone else dances with a particular vivacity, he moves with an American deliberateness. The difference is as striking as it used to be in peace time abroad, when a stray American youth appeared in a bustling French street, and the slow rhythm of his walk gave the effect of a sovereign unconcern. So Robbins on the stage, by being very natural, looks different enough to be a god; and that a god should be just like someone you see any day on the street is a nice joke."

It was exactly this kind of joke that Robbins would perfect and carry off again and again as a performer. But he remained his own worst critic, even with applause and recognition. Like many dancers, male and female alike, he was haunted by what he saw in the mirror, dissatisfied with both his lack of technical prowess and his physical appearance. "Jerry had an image problem," said Richard Thomas. "He was in a company at a time when one young man was prettier than the next, and Jerry was this little scrawny Jewish kid with all the talent who hated the way that he looked." Alonso danced with Robbins during their first year in such Spanish-flavored works as *Capriccio Espagnol* and *Goyescas,* and while she greatly admired Jerry's dancing, she also sensed his self-doubts. "He was not sure that he was a good dancer. I have the feeling that he always thought someone else was better and he kept looking at them."

But on the stage, Robbins managed to conceal any sense of inferiority. He turned in another memorable performance in Mexico City in the fall of 1941, appearing as a troubadour—the Spanish Lover—in Fokine's *Bluebeard,* the comic ballet set to the Offenbach operetta and given at the Palacio de Bellas Artes. Annabelle Lyon remembered, "Jerry, of course, was not a classical dancer but he did a lot of character roles like *Bluebeard.* In that ballet he moved on stage like he was playing a guitar and singing. He did that very well, and Fokine used to always sit there and smile when Jerry did it."

The company returned to Mexico City for an extended engagement that began in the summer of the following year, and Jerry wholeheartedly immersed himself in the adventure of exploring this foreign culture. Karnilova said, "We were all put into a hideous pensione. It was like being in a convent, packed together in this pensione with connecting gardens. So some of us took off to make our own arrangements. I remember that Donald Saddler and Jerry Robbins and I all moved to the Hotel Hunter, which was on the big avenue that went down to Chapultepec Park. It was a charming hotel that was reasonable and served breakfast. At that time it was heaven."

When he first arrived in Mexico, Robbins wrote to his cousin Jean Handy, suggesting that life for the dancer was all work and no play, with ballet class at nine in the morning, rehearsals in the afternoon, and Spanish dancing classes until ten at night. Still, he had Sundays off and did his share of sight-seeing. In addition to stage performances, Robbins and the company also took part in the filming of two Mexican movies, one of which featured the country's comic icon, Cantinflas, who was romancing one of the American ballerinas at the time. The evening performances at the Bellas Artes theater attracted the fashionable cultural elite and avant garde of Mexican society. Karnilova recalled, "We had a wonderful opportunity to meet Diego Rivera and his wife [Frida Kahlo], who was also a painter. A gorgeous woman. Almost savage-looking. Jerry and several of us who were interested in art went to see their work and were entertained by them."

Jerry was himself an avid painter, and his enthusiasm for the visual arts took him to galleries, museums and churches all over the city. He was introduced to Marc Chagall on the set of Massine's *Aleko*, as the Russian artist designed the production. While Jerry danced only the bit part of a gypsy in this ballet, Fokine also offered him the much sought-after title role of the puppet brought to life in *Petrouchka*, which would be the greatest challenge and opportunity of his early career. Robbins set about learning the ballet, knowing that his characterization would require painstaking attention to the details of mimetic gesture. Describing his preparation for the role, he recalled, "I looked at the pictures of Petrouchka and decided he was painted as badly as he was because he probably wouldn't see very well, hear well, and generally had a hard time focusing; so the studies I did were all about how he would physically relate to everything. I would go into the puppet booth and try to imagine the first time he found his consciousness there—trying to go at it as an actor, so that I knew everything I could about him. I was very intense about it in those days!"

Robbins also remembered, "Fokine encouraged me tremendously. . . . He taught me Petrouchka—although, in all fairness, I must say that I was the third Petrouchka in the rehearsal line of Petrouchkas when he first taught it to Ballet Theatre; but I was there through rehearsals, and he was very inspiring to work with." Robbins performed the role the first time on September 9, 1942, at the Bellas Artes theater and then danced it in New York the following month at the Metropolitan Opera House. For many in the audience, his performance was a revelation, one that would not be equaled until Baryshnikov came on the scene. In 1990, Clive Barnes recalled the impression made by Robbins' interpretation. "No one who ever saw his Petrouchka could ever forget it—it had a forlorn, sawdust agony I can still vividly summon to memory after more than forty years."

With this role, Robbins established himself as one of the company's leading dancers, and yet he was anything but content with his position. "Dancing is an awful life," he said. "There's the physical strain and financial insecurity. And very few top dancers have been able to maintain their ground." Robbins was also disenchanted by the distinctly Russian direction the company had taken with its repertory since his arrival. Richard Pleasant had been unable to sustain budgetary support for his eclectic standards of taste, and he had resigned just before Ballet Theatre's third season. The company's booking and publicity had been taken over by impresario Sol Hurok, with his associate, German Sevastianov, assuming the role of managing director. Chase gave these two assertive men free reign, and they undertook an all-out Russification campaign that went so far as to advertise "The Greatest in Russian Ballet by Ballet Theatre." The American and English camps were put on the defensive, afforded less and less in the way of support for their productions. "I was in a company that dealt exclusively with Russian folklore," said Robbins. "One whole year, I was a gypsy. Another, I was a sheaf of wheat and got reaped every night. I began to feel pretty rebellious about babushkas and boots."

Robbins' rebellion was to be political as well as artistic. At the end of 1943, he joined the Communist Party. In private testimony that Robbins later offered the FBI, he explained that he felt discriminated against at Ballet Theatre because he was Jewish, and that he was attracted to the Communist Party because of what he initially saw as its commitment to fighting anti-Semitism. In his testimony before HUAC, he stated that he had experienced "several instances of very painful moments because of minority prejudice," and that the Communist Party "had been presented to me as an organization which was very much for minorities and for advancing their causes." While he may have misread the Communists, his sense of discriminatory bias in the company was probably justified at the time. Reputedly anti-Semitic and anti-American, Sevastianov had taken control of promoting and demoting dancers within the company, and under his direction, Jewish dancers like Robbins, Nora Kaye, Muriel Bentley, Miriam Golden, David Nillo and others found themselves in some jeopardy.

Robbins' involvement with the left was surely becoming something more than flirtation by now, but he rarely communicated his convictions to his friends, most of whom believed that he was non-political even when he later publicly lent his name to various left-wing causes. Mary Hunter recalled that she tried to discourage Robbins' interest in the Communist Party. "I remember going to a Communist cell meeting by invitation and saying to Jerry, 'You know, this is just an attempt to get you involved, and you don't really belong here. Why don't you just get out?' And he was only on the fringes of the movement, really on the fringes. And it was too bad, because he was the most unpolitical creative artist I ever knew, totally unpolitical in every sense of the word."

For the most part, Robbins appears to have kept his politics under wraps socially, in the same way that he practiced the utmost discretion with regard to the gay side of his lifestyle. His political sympathies were hardly surprising, given the intellectual climate of the times, with both the liberal and radical left attracting support from any number of artists concerned with issues of social justice. Jerry's cousin Bob Silverman was recruited into the Communist Party in the early forties by one of his piano teachers at Juilliard, though he stayed involved for only a few months. In addition to Robbins, there were several other dancers at Ballet Theatre who were for a time politically active on the left, including Nora Kaye and Sono Osato. According to playwright Arthur Laurents, who first met Robbins and Kaye shortly after the premiere of Tudor's *Pillar of Fire* in 1942, Kaye was known in some circles as the "Red Ballerina," though she was never a member of the Party. Sono Osato would later be named by *Red Channels*, the publication that promoted blacklisting in television by exposing show-business figures suspected of having Communist associations.

Kirsten Valbor, a ballerina who danced for Robbins in *Call Me Madam*, recalled that he once tried to rally support for the cause at Ballet Theatre. "At one point, Jerry and another dancer wanted us to do a free performance for the Communist Party. He wanted us to do that as a fund-raiser. I had little patience for causes, and we didn't do it, because there were a lot of people like me who wouldn't go along."

Actress Madeline Gilford, who was Madeline Lee at the time and later married actor Jack Gilford, remembered meeting Robbins at a union benefit. A passionately committed activist, she resembled in her way the Barbra Streisand character in the film *The Way We Were*, written by Arthur Laurents. At the time that Gilford encountered Robbins, she was organizing a political campaign with Broadway actress Lois Wheeler, who would later marry author Edgar Snow. Gilford recalled, "Lois and I were given lists of Equity members and petitions for them to sign. We had this Jerome Robbins on our list. We didn't know who he was, just that he was a dancer and he was in Equity. So at this benefit down on Astor Place where 1199 used to be, this guy taps me on the shoulder. This was at a dance with a band in a big hall, and I was a pretty good Lindy-hopper—still am—and he tapped me on the shoulder and said, 'My name is Jerome Robbins, and I'm doing a dance about three sailors for Ballet Theatre. I've been on the road since I was a teenager with the ballet, so I don't know many street dances. Would you teach me?'

"So then I did teach him the Lindy-hop, and we became very close friends. He was adorable. Not only was he cute, but he laughed all the time and he was funny and charming, and we had, I would say, a very serious flirtation. And yes, he was a left-wing person who did Russian war relief and was in and around our left-wing circles. You have to know the Communist Party was not only legal then, but was in the forefront of a very large cultural movement, especially in New York. In those days between the May Day Parade and many other causes, the artists were pitching in. There was the movement for bread-and-butter issues in the union—for pension funds, for hospitalization and unemployment benefits—and there was the campaign to end Jim Crow and the poll tax. Jerry was a part of all of this."

Gilford and her friend Lois Wheeler, who later became romantically involved with Robbins, were at first unaware of his bisexuality. "We didn't even know about anybody who was bisexual," said Gilford. "Truthfully, we knew gay people, but they were really in the closet mostly. Any of the more conservative ones, like Hiram Sherman, were just people who were adorable but never getting married. And those who were overtly gay, who were flamboyant, they were in the choruses, and they began to talk about Fire Island and Cherry Grove early on, about how many mosquitos there were there and everything. That was the level on which we knew it."

Robbins never discussed the details of his bisexual lifestyle with her, but Gilford heard stories and was later confronted by a journalist about her relationship with Robbins. "I was in *Embezzled Heaven* with Ethel Barrymore, and we were rehearsing at the gorgeous mansion that the Theatre Guild had near the Museum of Modern Art. There was a double round staircase in front, and on my way out one day, this reporter from the *Journal-American* stopped me. I thought he was going to ask me some things about the show, about working with Ethel Barrymore. The *Journal-American* was a ratty newspaper in those days, a real Hearst paper. The reporter said, 'Are you Madeline Lee?' And I said, 'Yes.' And he said, 'Don't you go out with that fag, Jerry Robbins?' I said, 'What are you talking about?' Then I just got irate and left."

At this point, rumors that circulated about Robbins' personal life were nothing more than idle gossip and had no bearing on his rising career at Ballet Theatre. Following the lead of de Mille, he was about to launch his own insurrection against the company's Russian-dominated repertory. Robbins' idea for a ballet about three sailors was one of several proposals that he offered to the company's management, gamely presenting himself as choreographer. The proposals took the form of written librettos, including one for a full-length, four-act Americana ballet, and another for a psychological drama based on the Cain and Abel story. But these two early scenarios were rejected as being too ambitious and too expensive.

The sailors' story, which eventually became *Fancy Free*, had a circuitous genesis that began with an offhand suggestion to try a low-budget approach. Robbins said, "I had been propagandizing Ballet Theatre to do my ballets for some time. . . . I think it was Anatole Chujoy, the editor of *Dance News*, who said to me, 'Why don't you get together a small ballet with a few people?'" Robbins took the advice and turned to Mary Hunter for help. "She suggested that I should base a ballet on a picture, maybe *The Fleet's In*," said Robbins. "So I looked at *The Fleet's In* and thought, well, that's an idea."

The 1934 painting was part of Paul Cadmus' controversial *Sailor Trilogy* that was removed from a Public Works of Art Project exhibition at Washington's Corcoran because of the explicit homosexual content in its treatment of American sailors. Tame by today's standards, the painting depicted a sidewalk scene of debauching sailors ashore and included one apparently gay man with wavy hair offering a tough-looking marine a cigarette. Mary Hunter recalled taking Robbins to see the painting in New York. "I was enchanted with Cadmus' treatment of the current scene. I thought it was wonderful. I said, 'Jerry, why don't you just use this material? It will be wonderful.' He thought about it and didn't say anything at first. He thought it was too risqué, but he used it."

Robbins later met Cadmus, whose sister, Fidelma, married Lincoln

Kirstein, a longtime friend and patron to the painter. Cadmus said that he could not recall Robbins ever personally acknowledging that his paintings had played a part in the creation of the ballet. "I would see him at parties," said Cadmus. "He was very reclusive and didn't have many friends. I was never alone with him, and I don't think he ever said anything to me about my paintings influencing his work. If he did, I can't remember. He told somebody and my friends told me about it."

Distancing himself from any identification with the gay element in Cadmus' work, Robbins said in an interview with the *Christian Science Monitor*, "After seeing . . . *Fleet's In*, which I inwardly rejected though it gave me the idea of doing the ballet, I watched sailors, and girls, too, all over town." Robbins added, "I wanted to show that the boys in the service are healthy, vital boys: there is nothing sordid or morbid about them." Self-protection may have called for a certain amount of public posturing to bolster his heterosexual image for the mainstream audience, but his inward rejection of the painting's gay sailors and brazen sensuality also undoubtedly reflected his ongoing turmoil about his own sexual identity. However torn he was by his conflicted inclinations, Robbins certainly knew the direction in which he had to go with his ballet in order to have the widest commercial appeal. He would simply eliminate Cadmus' gay imagery and tell the story of three happy-go-lucky sailors chasing girls.

There was no shortage of raw material in his life for a story ballet about roving sailors on shore leave. Manhattan was teeming with soldiers of all stripes during the war, and Robbins drew from the scenes he saw around him, incorporating the popular social dances of the day like the Lindy-hop, boogie-woogie and Shorty George. "At that time," Robbins said, "we were dancing at the old Metropolitan Opera House, which was situated at Thirty-ninth to Fortieth Street and Broadway, and Times Square was right there and that was bubbling out over us. We saw it everywhere we looked—the kind of incident, the kind of people, the kind of kids that were dancing then."

On tour, Robbins applied himself to the choreography during every free moment, absorbing ideas and images on the road, working with his small cast in out-of-the-way nightclubs, ballrooms and theater basements. Janet Reed recalled how Robbins sometimes spontaneously created steps for the dancers wherever they happened to be, even on the sidewalk. "We were in Blooming-ton, Indiana, and we were walking to the theater, carrying our bags. And Jerry said, 'What if you did this . . .' And I stood there, and he walked a little bit ahead, and I said, 'You mean like this . . .' And I ran and threw myself, and he dropped his bag and caught me. And that indeed is in the choreography."

The libretto for *Fancy Free* was originally submitted to Lucia Chase and John Alden Talbot, who had replaced Sevastianov as managing director in May of 1943. Robbins won approval later that year only after another commis-sioned ballet was withdrawn and had to be replaced on the schedule at the last minute. His first collaborator on the project was Oliver Smith, who had re-cently designed de Mille's *Rodeo* and was soon to become one of the company's artistic directors. "I remember my first meeting with Oliver very vividly," said Robbins. "I was in the Ballet Theatre chorus then, and was rehearsing *Fair at Sorochinsk*. We were riding broomsticks or carrying hay when the door opened and a long thin body appeared and asked where was Jerome Robbins. I told him, and I guess he was surprised. He introduced himself and asked if I would look at some of his designs for sets."

So began a warm friendship and a working relationship that was to re-ward both artists many times in the years ahead. In addition to his talent and steady, unflappable equanimity, Smith offered the choreographer access to a vibrant social scene that included a number of notable artists and at least a few colorfully eccentric personalities. At the time that he met Robbins, Smith was living in a Brooklyn Heights boardinghouse, a four-story brownstone that had been renovated and converted into a successful Bohemian experiment in communal living. The arrangement had initially been organized by Lincoln Kirstein and *Harper's Bazaar* editor George Davis, who was the landlord. Some of Smith's fellow boarders over time were Paul and Jane Bowles, Richard and Ellen Wright, W. H. Auden, Benjamin Britten, Carson McCullers and Gypsy Rose Lee, along with an animal trainer who kept a seal on the premises. Smith and Paul Bowles were distant cousins, and their relationship eventually led to collaborative efforts between Robbins and Bowles, who was then primarily known as a composer. More important, the connection to Bowles enabled Smith to lead Robbins to the composer for the score of *Fancy Free*.

Bowles and Leonard Bernstein had been friends since the late thirties when they met at Aaron Copland's apartment. Smith, in turn, knew Bernstein through Bowles. When Robbins began his hunt for a composer, Bernstein's name was suggested by Morton Gould and Vincent Persichetti, both of whom Robbins had tried to interest in doing the score for the ballet. "He had been told," Gould recalled, "that he could choreograph a work on spec. He said he had an idea about three sailors and asked if I would compose the music. I told him I couldn't do that. I was paying alimony and had children to support." Likewise Persichetti turned Jerry down, but for a different reason. "Robbins came down to Philadelphia," Persichetti remembered, "and spent four hours with me. He described his idea for *Fancy Free*. I thought it needed jazz. I like jazz, but I don't get involved with it as a composer. So I suggested Lenny."

Later recalling that Persichetti gave him an address for Bernstein, Robbins said, "I went to the address when I came back to New York and it was an empty lot on Fifty-second Street. So I could not find Lenny. By chance I mentioned it to Oliver, and he said, 'Oh, I know Lenny. He lives at Carnegie Hall. I'll give a call and see if we can go up there.' So we did."

Smith and Robbins arrived at Bernstein's door late that evening. Robbins pitched his idea to Bernstein and asked the composer if they might hear some of his music. "Funny you should ask," Bernstein recalled saying, "because this afternoon in the Russian Tea Room I got this tune in my head and I wrote it down on a napkin." Bernstein sang the melody for them. "Jerry went through the ceiling. He said, 'That's it, that's what I had in mind!' We went crazy. I began developing the theme right there in his presence. . . . Thus the ballet was born."

It was not an easy collaboration to arrange, as all three of the principals were soon separated, traveling in different parts of the world—Robbins was touring, Smith was off to Mexico, and Bernstein was conducting between New York, Boston and Pittsburgh. They stayed in touch by phone; and over time, Bernstein mailed Robbins installments of notated copy and recordings of the yet-to-be-orchestrated score—piano renditions that were performed by the composer and by his friend and mentor, Aaron Copland. "If I had a problem," said Robbins, "I would call or write [Lenny] from out of town. I remember we had differences over the second variation . . . which I didn't understand; didn't get it. So in a case like that he would explain it more, and

say what he felt about it, and then I'd start to see the light of it. . . . And th.
kind of work went on, backwards and forwards this way, until I was able t(
come to New York."

At the time that Bernstein first came into the picture, his *Jeremiah* symphony had not yet been performed and he was not to have his debut conducting the New York Philharmonic until later that fall. Like Robbins, he was still
relatively unknown, and the two men had a great deal more in common. They
were the same age and shared the same Russian-Polish and Jewish heritage.
Both had fathers who had disapproved of their chosen careers. Both were am-
bivalent sexually. In the minds of many of those who later worked with them,
the fact that as artists they were both so enormously ego-driven ruled out any
sort of romantic affair between them, with neither willing to risk a collaboration that was at various times central to both their lives.

But others who knew them well disagreed. "They went to bed together,"
said Oliver Smith's longtime companion, Richard D'Arcy, who danced in *On
the Town*. "They a had a kind of brief encounter, an affair just in that early period when they were doing *Fancy Free*, at the beginning when the score was
being written." Gore Vidal offered a recollection that may be credible in light
of what D'Arcy and other well-placed sources recalled. "When Bernstein was
here just before he died," Vidal wrote, "he said that he had been in bed with
the entire original cast of *Fancy Free*." The entire cast meant Robbins, Johnny
Kriza and Harold Lang. Vidal told of his own liaisons with two of the three,
Kriza and Lang, in his memoir, *Palimpsest*. The original women in the ballet—
Muriel Bentley, Janet Reed and Shirley Eckl—were, according to Reed, not included in Bernstein's trail of amorous conquests. "He meant the men," said
Reed, after hearing about the composer's claim.

Reed worked with Robbins and Bernstein in the studio when they returned to New York. The composer often sat at the piano in rehearsals and
improvised to meet the immediate practical needs of Robbins, who was creating his own Latin-flavored role in the ballet, drawing in part on a Mexican
dance (a *danzón*) similar to the rumba. He specified to Bernstein exactly what
he wanted in the score, from mood and tempi to the number of bars of music
necessary to cover the dancing and the action onstage. In rehearsing the *pas de
deux* with Reed, the trio spent long hours together, sometimes becoming so ex-

hausted at the end of their sessions that all three collapsed on the floor in fits of hysterics.

Though Bernstein and Robbins sometimes disagreed over the music and sparred with each other, the rapport between them was infused with heady excitement and mutual respect. Bernstein usually acquiesced to Robbins' demands, avoiding any confrontation. There was certainly a natural attraction between them, but Reed doubted that any romantic intimacy between Robbins and Bernstein could ever have gone anywhere. "They were both so ambitious and hellbent on their careers that they would have gotten in each other's way."

The other two men in the cast, Kriza and Lang, were thought at times by many of their friends to have had affairs with Robbins, if only because close friendships between male dancers led those around them to draw such conclusions, and in this instance, both Kriza and Lang were uninhibited about their ambiguous sexuality. According to Reed, "Johnny Kriza and Harold Lang were more open about being gay than Jerry was. Harold was also bisexual. He had a girlfriend in the San Francisco Ballet. It was hard to know with Harold. He was very ambitious, and it seemed to me that any homosexual relationship he had was for getting ahead. But Jerry didn't have anything to gain, whereas they had everything to gain from him."

The friendship between Kriza and Robbins was one of special affection. According to dancer Shaun O'Brien, "The real love of Jerry's life then was Johnny Kriza. It was sort of common knowledge that he truly loved Johnny." The popular Kriza, with his manly good looks and humor, had charmed almost everyone in his path after arriving at Ballet Theatre from his home in Illinois. "He and Jerry were very good, close friends when I met them during the war, and remained so," Arthur Laurents related. "They may well have gone to bed together, but that was par for the course at Ballet Theatre. Jerry really adored and consequently idealized Johnny [and gave him] his solo in *Fancy Free*."

Like Robbins, Muriel Bentley was fond of Kriza, and she described how the choreographer had tailored the part for him in *Fancy Free*. "Jerry really caught Johnny in that role—the sailor who always paid the check," said Bentley. "Somehow Johnny always picked up the check. Johnny was the sweet one. Johnny was the good one. The one who just loved to dance, loved going to par-

ties, loved driving his car out on tour, loved people. . . . He was not a brilliant dancer. He was a terrific performer. He gave a lot of himself. He didn't care how much money he made as long as he could get out on the stage and dance. He was kind. He was simple. He was generous. How do I describe Johnny Kriza? I'm very partial. I was madly in love with him. He was loved by a lot of people. There isn't another one like him." Robbins would dedicate the ballet to his friend some years later, after Kriza had married another dancer and fallen victim to alcohol, one day tragically drowning on a swim in the Gulf of Mexico.

Bentley had known Robbins since 1938, when the two had appeared in *Prince Igor* at the New York World's Fair. The first time they met, she had taunted him. Her longtime friend Betty Farrel recalled, "Muriel told the story frequently of how, when the dancers first gathered and were standing in line, she turned around and saw this young man behind her. And she looked at him—now Muriel would have been maybe five feet and a hundred pounds at the most, because she was very tiny—and she said, 'Little boy, do you think you're going to be able to lift me?' And that was Jerome Robbins."

As with each of the other members of the *Fancy Free* cast, Robbins gave Bentley exact instructions about the character she was portraying. Her costume called for her to wear patent-leather shoes with ankle straps, and this detail found its way into his description of the part. Bentley recalled that he told her that her role was to be like "patent leather," meaning that "the character was to be sleek, shiny, bright and to the point."

Touring with the company, the two sometimes flirted and cuddled during train rides, but regardless of his personal feelings for Bentley, Robbins was merciless with his demands on her in rehearsals, often driving her to tears and causing her to question his motives. "It was just six to eight months of sheer torture for me," said Bentley. "Jerry picked on me constantly. I was the patsy. [Harold] came in for it a little bit maybe, but Johnny and Janet—they had it easy, they were the golden ones. He adored them, and maybe he knew he couldn't get away with that kind of thing with them. But not me. Anytime Jerry was unhappy with me, he really let me have it. I took it all. I never answered him back. I didn't have it in me. It was hell. I cried a lot, I can tell you, working on that ballet."

It was not unusual for a ballerina to consider herself the instrument for a choreographer, selflessly serving his imagination rather than seeing herself as a creative or even interpretive artist in her own right, and there may have been some degree of sadomasochism in such a relationship. Yet Bentley proved herself to be as resilient as her character. In spite of the grief she endured, she suggested that the ends justified the means, accepting Robbins' behavior with the idea that allowances had to be made for genius. After all, he was the one who shaped her performance. "You know something, everything Jerry did for me was right for me," said Bentley. "Now, looking back, I think he felt [that] in badgering and belittling me, he could make me perform better. I never agreed with his tactics, but I really think that's what he meant to do."

Robbins explained that he pushed Bentley only because her performance "had to be exact." His methods were deliberate and, however harsh, they were also effective. He was creating his ballet for dancers who were not stars, but rather those most appropriate for the roles because of the particular qualities and talents that they had to offer; and he used his familiarity with each in the group to advantage within his choreography. Bentley said, "He took six people and really made a ballet around our personalities." Robbins knew these dancers intimately and fashioned their roles in ways that were highly personal, yet consistent with the fictional characters that he had first described in his libretto, which the ballet was to follow virtually to the letter.

The time was "the present, a hot summer night" and the place "New York City, a side street," Robbins wrote. "It is a jazz ballet, light in mood, running about 15 minutes." All of the months of work would in the end come down to a ballet that was to run just under a half hour. Bernstein summarized the action and described Smith's set in a program note: "The curtain rises on a street corner with a lamp post, a side street bar and New York skyscrapers pricked out with a crazy pattern of lights, making a dizzying back drop. Three sailors explode on the stage. They are on a 24-hour shore leave in the city and on the prowl for girls. The tale of how they first meet one, then a second girl, and how they fight over them, lose them, and in the end take off after still a third, is the story of the ballet."

Fancy Free premiered April 18, 1944, on a long program that included

Swan Lake, Tudor's *Gala Performance* and the *pas de deux* from *The Nutcracker.* It was a night of almost disastrous mishaps avoided only by luck and speedy recoveries. Before the performance, Robbins was in the wings still revising his solo when he broke a zipper on his sailor pants and had to make a hasty, last-minute repair with needle and thread. Meanwhile, it had escaped everyone's notice that there was no phonograph onstage to provide the opening music for the barroom jukebox. Bernstein was to conduct that night, and two of his friends, Betty Comden and Adolph Green, happened to be seated in the audience before the show. The situation became one of "sudden hysteria," according to Comden, but she and Green quickly came to the rescue, as if unknowingly acting to ensure their roles as future collaborators in *On the Town.* Green recalled, "I rushed uptown with Betty to her apartment, and we got a portable record player, and put it on stage just in time for the first performance."

The audience was taken by surprise from the first moments when the curtain rose with the sound of a blues song apparently coming from the jukebox. This effect was so outlandish at the time that some in the audience at first thought a radio had been left on in one of the dressing rooms. The number, "Big Stuff," had been written by Bernstein for Billie Holiday, but when she turned out to be too expensive for Robbins' shoestring budget, a recording was made with Bernstein's sister, Shirley, supplying the vocals. Her deep voice set the scene. Then Robbins and his two sailor mates made their dazzling entrance, cartwheeling onto the stage to the sound of rim shots on a snare drum. There was yet another near calamity later in the performance, when the rung of a barstool split under Robbins' weight as he was leaping to the floor during his solo. He had the quick reflexes to pull through in that split-second without losing his balance, and the rest of the ballet went off without a hitch.

The outcome was beyond anything the cast expected. The audience demanded an encore of Harold Lang's bravura solo, and there were at least two dozen curtain calls that night. Agnes de Mille described how shaken Robbins was by the experience. "While the audience gave itself to applause, I rushed backstage and discovered Robbins sweating and startled, leaning against a wall. His eyes moved about almost in terror. His mouth was open. He kept giggling in short mirthless gasps. I didn't think he could have taken in what I said, but I kept talking anyhow. I held him tight. I told him he was safe and need never be frightened again, because with such humor and tenderness, with such a grasp of form, he could do whatever he intended to."

De Mille called it "the finest first work she had ever seen in the theatre," and many of the critics agreed. *Cue* magazine compared the ballet to de Mille's *Rodeo,* but credited Robbins with being "louder and funnier." John Martin wrote in the *Times,* "To come right to the point without any ifs, ands and buts, Jerome Robbins' *Fancy Free* . . . is a smash hit. This is young Robbins's first go at choreography, and the only thing he has to worry about in that direction is how in the world he is going to make his second one any better. He has managed to get into this lighthearted little piece of American genre the same quality of humor which has always characterized his personal dancing, the same excellent actor's sense of the theatre."

Robbins was thrilled by the audience response, which he had anticipated moment by moment in the ballet. He described a recording that Bernstein made of the opening night: "It is really terrific from the very start. You can hear the audience gasp right after Bernstein raises his baton, and jukebox music comes from the stage. You can hear them giggling and laughing out loud and applauding and cheering at all the places where I hoped they would when we were working on it."

This was not the first ballet to treat a contemporary American subject, but the ingenious way that Robbins combined classical technique with popular social dances, acrobatics and natural gesture enabled him to tell his story with a flair and simplicity that uniquely captured the spirit of the age. As he wed cartwheels and pirouettes, his sense of comic pacing was brilliant. The audience was enthralled to see familiar, vernacular images incorporated into this highbrow art form, as when the three sailors split a piece of gum and later flipped a coin to see who would pay for the drinks. The solo variations with which they tried to win the girls perfectly reflected their three individual characters. Through them, Robbins brought to life the elusive rapture of young love as he had experienced it during the war years. Indeed, he was revealing himself, or at least one side of himself, through the dance.

That first night, Jerry attended a celebration party at the apartment of Nora Kaye, and for the next several days, according to de Mille, the Rabinowitz family held High Holiday. She recalled, "The doors of his home stood open and his mother and sister and aunts never left the stove. Everyone in the apartment house came and stayed; everyone in the street went in and out at will. It was too much. Robbins ran away, and very quietly in humility and terror in the arms of friends sought privacy and a chance for revaluation and peace."

Suddenly inundated with offers from Broadway and Hollywood, Jerry found himself in such demand that he told friends he was distressed and frightened by his change of fortune. The day after the premiere, he shared his impressions in a letter to his cousin Bob Silverman, who recalled, "I was lying in a hospital in England. I was in the service and had been wounded in combat, and this letter came at that time. My mother kept it, so I had occasion to read it again after the war. As I remember, Jerry said in the letter, 'Yesterday I was just a schnook from Weehawken, and if I went to see a producer, his secretary would ask me, *What's it about?* And I would say, *I want to talk to him about doing the dances for his next show.* And the secretary would give me some excuse, and I would be shown out of the office. This morning, twelve producers have called me. Was I any more talented last night than I was a week ago? Look at how one small ballet has changed my life.'"

Robbins was bewildered at being thrust into the limelight. "It was a shocking change," he said. "From nothing to—to everything. And I wasn't prepared for it. I think really what happened was . . . that somewhere in my early life I had thought that all my career and personal problems would change once I was a success. Well, here I was a success, and although there was much more opportunity and attention, none of my personal problems changed. I realized I had to look somewhere else rather than to being well-known and accomplished, to straighten myself out inside of myself."

There was little time to reflect on such personal concerns. Attendance at the Metropolitan Opera House broke box-office records. The 3,300-seat house sold out within hours when Sol Hurok extended the run at the Met over the following weekend. There were, in all, two dozen performances in New York that spring. The ballet was added to the repertory for Ballet Theatre's national tour and quickly became the company's signature piece across the country. In the next year, *Fancy Free* was performed 162 times. According to the terms of his contract with Chase, for each performance of the ballet,

Robbins received only a ten-dollar royalty, an agreement which was to remain in effect for more than thirty years.

But his circumstances were soon to change even more drastically, as Oliver Smith prevailed upon him and Leonard Bernstein, despite their initial resistance, to turn the ballet into a Broadway show. Smith said, "They wanted to do something more serious. I tried to persuade them as hard as I could, and at a certain point they said, 'OK, let's go.'"

Of this new project, Robbins remembered, "I didn't realize how deep the water was going to be and I waded right in, arms flailing"—flailing, perhaps, but with the world now at his command. He had proven himself in one night, and there was surely no reason for Robbins to suspect at the time that his political views or personal life could in any way jeopardize such phenomenal success. "Heavens knows, I'm full of ideas and ambition," he said. "All I need is for the ideas to be valid and the ambition to continue. Oh, and some luck and a few other things, and maybe everything will be all right."

THREE

New York, New York

"Sex and art don't mix. If they did, I'd have gone right to the top."

—MADAME DILLY,
On the Town

"We were all novices," said Robbins, describing the *On the Town* creative team, most of them twenty-something, brimming with naive, youthful enthusiasm. "We didn't know a goddamn thing about doing a show. But we were a good bunch, a nice package together." *On the Town* was to be Robbins' first taste of the rough-and-tumble of Broadway collaboration, and he would have to prove himself in record time. He later marveled that the show was written, rehearsed and mounted in little more than six months. "We wrote *On the Town* that summer and got it on at the end of the year. How could we do that? We didn't know any better."

The most elegant and reserved member of this group of energetic youngsters, Oliver Smith, produced the show with Bernstein's Carnegie studio roommate, Paul Feigay, the team's go-getter point man. In the spring of 1944, Smith and Feigay managed to raise $25,000. After being turned down by Elia Kazan, they secured the services and considerable clout of veteran Broadway director George Abbott later in the year. With Abbott onboard, Metro-Goldwyn-Mayer provided another $250,000. This was the first time a film company bought the movie rights for a show before it opened, and the investment represented a substantial gamble on talents that were for the most part unknown and untested.

One exception was Ballet Theatre's Sono Osato, who had recently made a name for herself dancing on Broadway in *One Touch of Venus* and was cast in *On the Town* as Miss Turnstiles. Osato recalled the pressure that Robbins was under from the start. "With *On the Town,* he was scared. That's the way I would put it. He'd had a big hit with *Fancy Free.* Now he had to achieve a similar success or a greater success [with] his first musical, which he had never done in his life, and that's a terrible pressure. . . . The strain, I think, was just very, very hard on him. And also he had never worked with so many people, because *Fancy Free* was something like three men, three girls and a bartender. Here he was with a musical, a whole [cast] of dancers and singers and so forth. Today they have dance captains and swing dancers, they have all kinds of help. But he had no assistants at all. That's the way it was. All I can say is that it was very tense and very hard, and everything was on his shoulders."

While Robbins carried the burden of choreographing all of the dances, the give-and-take of the collaborative process demanded that he compromise his original vision and relinquish much of the creative control that he had enjoyed with *Fancy Free.* Bernstein pointed out that the musical was not simply an expansion of the ballet either in terms of the story or score. "There was not a note of *Fancy Free* music in *On the Town.* . . . We started from Square One with a totally new series of conceptions . . . different plot ideas, different scenarios, which we had great fun bouncing off each other's brains and souls. . . . *On the Town* was not about three sailors competing. It was about three sailors with twenty-four hours' shore leave in New York, period."

The book and lyrics were written by Bernstein's friends Betty Comden and Adolph Green, who were part of a Greenwich Village nightclub act, the Revuers, which for a time also included Judy Holliday. Bernstein had dedicated the score of *Fancy Free* to Green, and the composer later recommended his two club friends for the musical. Robbins and Smith, who had been in favor of lyricist John Latouche and playwright Arthur Laurents, saw Comden and Green perform their satirical revue one night at the Blue Angel and were quickly won over, an indication of their talent as well as the respect commanded by Bernstein within the group. As Comden noted, this was a collection of "roaring egos." Yet Bernstein and Robbins managed to yield to each other during moments of contention and held the team together through the early going. Once George Abbott joined the show, the revered director exercised absolute authority. Abbott would have the final word on every aspect of the production. His regard for the choreographer was later reflected in his habit of signing memos to Jerry, "Your assistant, Abbott."

As it happened, both Bernstein and Green were scheduled to have minor surgery just after the project got under way—Lenny for a deviated septum and Adolph to have his tonsils removed. On June 13, 1944, while newspapers were tracking the Normandy invasion and the fall of Rome, gossip columnist Leonard Lyons reported in the *New York Post* that "Leonard Bernstein and Adolph Green will be operated upon on the same day by the same doctor." The two shared a hospital room and continued to work between games of gin rummy, visits from friends and the ministrations of nurses. This hospital scene was as riotous as the show they were creating. At various times the sounds of laughter, boisterous arguments and numbers from the score being belted out in full voice could be heard in the hallway outside their room. One of the harried nurses said of Bernstein, "He may be God's gift to music, but I'd hate to tell you where he gives me a pain."

In August, Robbins and Bernstein traveled with Ballet Theatre on the company's California tour, teaming up again for performances of *Fancy Free*, with Lenny conducting. They were joined in Los Angeles by Comden and Green, and for several weeks the *On the Town* team resided in a "dream of a Spanish villa" on Watsonia Terrace in the Hollywood Hills. Robbins was temporarily smitten with Nancy Walker, the Broadway comedienne who was to perform the role of the feisty cab-driver, Hildy. Walker had been working on a three-picture deal for M-G-M after appearing the year before in another George Abbott production, *Best Foot Forward*. Dancer Todd Bolender recalled, "Jerry had a big thing with Nancy Walker. I was with Ballet Theatre for one season and we were out on the West Coast. Jerry was dating Nancy a great deal at that time." Robbins was apparently not the only one to fall for Walker's charms. Cris Alexander, who played Ossie, said of her, "Nancy went after every queen in reaching distance. All she had to do was catch sight of an attractive gay man and she wanted to fuck him. She had an appalling number of conquests." Of the Walker-Robbins relationship, Alexander added, "Oh, they would absolutely crack each other up."

Robbins managed to carry on an increasingly active social life despite the workload. Among the pleasant distractions that he and his cohorts encountered along the way was Bernstein's twenty-sixth birthday, with Lenny conducting a concert at the Hollywood Bowl. Afterward, there was a gala party attended by such vintage Tinseltown celebrities as Tallulah Bankhead. In a letter to Aaron Copland, Bernstein wrote, "Hollywood is exactly what I expected, only worse. . . . Agents, agents, blood, money. But a pretty place. . . . We're getting a show done by leaps and bounds. It's amazing how hard it is—such an unwieldy thing to juggle."

Initially skeptical about using the three sailors for the book, Comden and Green transformed the ballet's characters and turned the story into a full-blown farce, writing two of the central roles, Claire de Loone and Ozzie, for themselves. Instead of the competitive antics of the *Fancy Free* buddies, *On the Town* presented three sailors who, through their affectionate camaraderie, supported and humored each other as loyal friends. Comden, whose own husband was called away by the war, later wrote a *New York Times* article with Green and described their conception of the characters: "The main thing was that having decided on three sailors, we wanted them to come off as people. No matter how extravagantly treated, we wanted them to possess the qualities and attitudes of the servicemen we had seen coming into the city for the first time and at least touch on the frantic search for gaiety and love, and the terrific pressure of time that war brings."

Likewise, the show's three women were fleshed out and given much greater emphasis than their counterparts in the ballet. *On the Town*'s evenly matched relationships illustrate the way that female roles and gender balance had altered during wartime. The innocent sailor, Chip, is pursued by the pushy, irascible taxi-driver, Hildy. Ozzie, the make-out champ, is paired off with the daffy, sex-crazed anthropologist, Claire de Loone. The through-line of the story is provided by Gabey (played by John Battles, after Kirk Douglas bowed out), the romantic dreamer who falls under the spell of a subway promotional poster of "Miss Turnstiles for June," Ivy Smith, a student who pays for her art and music classes by working as a Coney Island hootchy-kootchy dancer.

Unified by its central romantic quest, the musical was a picaresque adventure that captured both the jazzy, hard-edged reality of New York City and the jingoistic mood of America at war. The sailors' journey would take the audience on a rollicking tour of the city, featuring a dozen backdrops that ran from the Brooklyn Navy Yard and Times Square to Central Park, Carnegie Hall and Coney Island, where a subway train suddenly came apart and a roller coaster appeared, its lights sparkling in the night. With all of the action packed into one madcap day, the tale was zany and surreal, yet always tender and sentimental in its embrace of life and love. At the heart of the show, masked by all of the slapstick onstage, was a poignant vulnerability that the audience was to understand as a given—that these three sailors were entering the lives of three women they might never see again once the boys returned to active duty.

Costume designer Alvin Colt sensed from the beginning how innovative the show was in every department. "There'd never been anything like it before. There'd never been a score like that, there'd never been an idea like that. It had a certain realistic quality about it which was unusual for a musical then. I remember when I was taking sketches around for bids, they would say, 'Where are the sets?'—meaning the set of costumes, the sixteen [chorus] girls alike. There wasn't anything like that in *On the Town*."

With Bernstein's classically sophisticated pop score—"that Prokofyef stuff," Abbott called it—and the ingenuity of Smith's mobile designs, the team set the stage for symphonic hoofing the like of which had not been seen on Broadway before. In the end there would be almost thirty minutes of dancing in the show, far more than had been offered either in *Oklahoma!* or in *Carousel*. There were fifteen musical numbers in Act I—including "New York, New York," the city's anthem "that made swing almost classical"—and ten numbers in Act II. Bernstein observed, "I believe this is the first Broadway show ever to have as many as seven or eight dance episodes in the space of two acts; and as a result, the essence of the whole production is contained in these dances." In Robbins' hands, the dances would become the key to meshing the elements of book, score and design. Sono Osato recalled the "Times Square Ballet" that closed the first act, and her description might be aptly applied to Robbins' dances as a whole: "Jerry's choreography was a carousel of racing, meandering, meeting, and parting of the throbbing, never-ending crowds of a New York that never sleeps."

Allyn Ann McLerie, who was engaged to marry Adolph Green at the time and would eventually step into Osato's role, recalled Robbins at the first rehearsal that fall. "I remember him coming in and saying, 'My name is Jerry—not Mr. Robbins—and I'm allowed to be late, but you're not.' And Lenny waltzed in with his coat draped over his shoulders and sat down at the piano and played the 'Times Square Ballet.' We were all just in love with everybody. We had a great time at all the rehearsals, and Jerry liked me very much. At one point he said, 'Oh, Allyn Ann, if there were only ten like you.' I was pleased because sometimes he'd pick out somebody not to like, but it wasn't me."

Cris Alexander remembered one performer who Robbins singled out for special treatment. "During *On the Town* there was this wonderful old character actress, Susan Steell, who was obviously not a dancer. She was the original Madame Dilly, and Jerry tried to put her into a lot of movement, which of course she couldn't do. And I've never seen anybody being so vicious with just no reason whatsoever. She was in tears all the time." Osato saw little of Robbins' abrasiveness but later heard some of the stories. She explained, "He was an extremely nervous person . . . not a placid man. He was very high-strung. I'm sure he didn't set out in the morning saying, 'Well now, today I'm really going to yell.' But something would trigger it."

Robbins' friend and colleague Mary Hunter remembered, "Jerry had a reputation, which I think was unfortunate, in the theater that he was difficult and demanding, and [it was] alleged that he picked out somebody in the company whose work he particularly disliked and that person got pretty rough treatment. . . . I think it was a kind of instinctive self-protection. Rather than have your hostility bubbling through the whole work, you plant it on one person."

Throughout his career, one or two performers in each production would indeed become sacrificial victims for Robbins who, according to many who danced for him, would release himself from a block in the choreography by venting his frustration and rage. In this way his emotional tantrums, which could be quite frightening for those dancers he targeted, became a kind of vicious circle that was increasingly integral to his creative process. Janet Reed, who worked for Jerry on Broadway and on his ballets, speculated that his behavior stemmed from his own "driving fear of failure." Reed explained, "About that business of his losing his temper, actually, I don't think it was the case that he would get angry because he thought the dancers were not taking the work seriously, but sometimes he made the dancers so nervous that they behaved in a very strange fashion. They might giggle hysterically, and Jerry didn't realize how nervous and frightened he made them. He fastened on to particular people who were already so intimidated by him, and that made him angrier still. Knowing how full of fear he was, I just thought, oh well, he sees his own fear and it makes him angry."

Robbins' cousin Jean Handy, who was just out of high school when she joined the cast of *On the Town*, recalled a more moderate tactic that he used. "I know that when someone didn't seem to be getting what he needed, there sort of was a quiet time, and then he would talk one-on-one with that person. Generally after that, they understood and something new came out of it. . . . He was always very adamant about what he wanted." Royce Wallace, who also danced in the show, recalled, "You didn't know what you could do and what you couldn't do, and he'd say, 'Well, try it! Go over to the corner and practice.' He wanted it done, and what he wanted, he got. He really made an art of keeping people on their toes by demanding that they work as hard as he did. He'd say, 'I'm working hard. I want you to work hard, too. I want this to be the best you've ever done!' Everybody knew that he wanted it to be perfection. But he could produce a phobia in you."

The methods Robbins brought to rehearsal were much the same as those he utilized when working on his ballets. One of his techniques traced back to Gluck Sandor, who often asked his dancers to learn and retain a number of distinct versions of a particular dance variation or sequence of movement. As Robbins made his way through the choreography with characteristic fits and starts, he would call for any one of a number of versions designated by numbers or letters, placing added pressure on his dancers to recall all of the alternative options that had been tried out in previous rehearsals. Robbins typically waited until the last minute before finally deciding which version he wanted to use onstage. Between his unpredictable temper and meticulous perfectionism, dancers were caught in a kind of psychological vise and many of them were in this way desperately driven to win his approval, if only to avoid the perils of suffering his displeasure.

"He was intense," Dorothy McNichols remembered. "We had versions. Number one, number three, number five or ten. And you were supposed to re-member all these versions. . . . So I used to practice in the subway, on the plat-form waiting for my train. Da-da-da-ta, da-da-da-ta! You had to dream it, you had to sleep it, you had to eat it, you know. You were aware of it all the time."

Richard D'Arcy, who was to prove an able partner in the "Lonely Town" number, believed like many that working with Robbins was an education. "As far as dance was concerned, I was actually an idiot. I had no sense of what I was doing. To me, you got up on stage and smiled a lot and did a lot of steps. But Jerry treated me with kid gloves, which was very unusual. He told me later that he didn't dare attack me because I would just clam up. But he literally taught me how to dance. I never knew how to dance, and he made me a dancer. Oh, he got a performance out of me, I must say. He said, 'You will thank me one day.' He was right."

Looking back at the age of seventy, Robbins reflected on his early emo-tional turmoil in the theater and offered what was for him a rare admission. "I thought, there's so much joy in this work and so much happiness. And I don't think I was particularly a person you wanted to be around to have kicks and joys and laughs. I remember having so many problems, so many difficulties getting my life and insights adjusted. . . . I know I was quite driven and all the worst stories about me were probably coming out about then."

The controversial stories and rumors would continue to circulate for years. His reputation as a fierce and sometimes vicious taskmaster had already been established at Ballet Theatre, and with *On the Town*, word of Robbins' fe-rocity soon spread on Broadway. Other choreographers in the dance world—for instance, Jack Cole, Antony Tudor and even Agnes de Mille—were known for their toughness and cruelty at times, but Robbins would surpass them in the folklore of the age. This was an era when dance teachers sometimes used canes to discipline their students, and in many ways, Robbins' approach simply represented a refinement of traditional heavy-handed methods that could be justified by the results achieved onstage.

The more lurid excesses of Robbins' combative style were usually restrained in the presence of George Abbott, whom Jerry idolized as a mentor. The choreographer bowed to the director even when it came to staging the dances. Robbins described working with Abbott during *On the Town*: "I liked the work I had done in rehearsal very much, but found it didn't work in the context of the show. This threw me. Mr. Abbott was clear and helpful in editing and suggesting cuts, in clipping a ballet in half and putting it in two places in the show. He was very skillful and very helpful, and decisive."

At Abbott's insistence, the script had to be rewritten. Robbins and his colleagues spent at least one long weekend in Bradley Beach, New Jersey, where Jerry's parents had a summer home. Robbins hired his teenage cousin Saul Silverman as a gofer for the occasion. Silverman recalled, "They had a great time together. There're always issues in something like that, but there was a lot of fun going on there at the same time. They would take off and bike around as they were rewriting the whole thing."

Along the way, Robbins put his own personal stamp on the story. While Comden and Green had eliminated the sailors' competitiveness and invented the wild twists and turns of the plot line, Robbins conceived the final *pas de deux* as a confrontation between Gabey and his dream girl that was to be staged in a boxing ring, with Miss Turnstiles leashing the sailor with her red turban scarf and forcing him into submission. If Robbins, at the age of twenty-six, was inclined to see love between men and women as a kind of slapstick combat, an amorous prizefight defying convention, he might have been forecasting, however unwittingly, what was to come in the years ahead with his own romantic adventures, with both sexes.

The script underwent a number of revisions before winning Abbott's approval. In his memoir *Mister Abbott*, the director recalled, "I liked *On the Town* but I thought some things were wrong, and it seemed best to say so early in the game. For instance, there were many long and involved interruptions of the main plot by a judge and an old lady, two characters I thought unnecessary." Abbott recollected that his young collaborators resisted his proposed changes

until he gave them an ultimatum. "I said, 'You'll have to take your choice between me and the old lady.' They chose me, and we used the old lady simply
as a crossover."

By the time the show traveled to Boston for its only out-of-town tryout,
the production was beset with difficulties. Abbott remembered, "The inexperienced managers had allowed only two weeks for the tryout in Boston. This
was much too brief by all normal standards, and the problem was further ag-
gravated by the snowstorm which delayed the scenery's arrival. In actual fact,
we were to have but ten days in which to get the show ready for Broadway."
Further complications ensued when it was discovered that Smith's sets, which
had been designed for New York's Adelphi, would not fit Boston's Colonial
Theater. Abbott requested that the critics not review the premiere because of
"delays in changing scenery which had not yet been properly hung."

The night of the opening, which Bernstein conducted despite the set
problems, Robbins cracked under the strain. The next morning he disappeared, leaving behind a panic-stricken cast. "It was very frightening," Richard
D'Arcy recalled. "The nerves got to him and he just ran. Everyone was hunting for him, and George Abbott said the show goes on as far as he's concerned.
He said, 'Bring someone else in.' I think they brought in a girl called Alice
Dudley. . . . She was going to take over the choreography. But Oliver [Smith]
said, "No, we're not going to do this. Jerry is who we're going with. He'll come
back. We're going to get him back.'"

According to dancer Duncan Noble, "Jerry went back to New York to see
his analyst." In fact, some months earlier Mary Hunter had referred him to her
Park Avenue psychoanalyst, Dr. Frances Arkin. Hunter said that Robbins had
been "very upset" and she advised him to "see my analyst just to get acquainted." Robbins later stated that he was being treated for what was called
"a neurotic condition." So began a lifelong involvement with Freudian analysis. Aside from attempting to deal with emotional depression and the tribulations of the show, he was trying to come to grips with his increasingly
anguished sexual confusion. Actress Lois Wheeler, with whom Jerry would seriously consider marriage a short time later, said, "About Jerry's problem sexually, it was such a different time, you know, nothing was as it is—nothing was
really acknowledged and it was all considered something pretty terrible. And

Jerry was involved with psychiatrists and trying to grapple with the problem, and it wasn't an easy thing for anybody to do at the time."

Dr. Arkin was apparently of a Freudian persuasion similar to that of Tennessee Williams' analyst, Lawrence Kubie, as her advice to Robbins essentially involved repressing his gay lifestyle and finding a suitable woman to marry. Ironically, in 1937, Freud had written, "Homosexuality is assuredly no advantage, but it is nothing to be ashamed of, no vice, no degradation, it cannot be classified as an illness." But Freud was inconsistent on the subject, and the prevailing attitude of the American psychiatric profession and its vocal practitioners like Kubie reflected and reinforced the homophobic bias of society at large. As such, Robbins' experience in analysis in those early years was likely to have taken a toll on his self-image and self-esteem.

If homosexuality was seen as a mental illness, then it was something to be cured, which was the position taken by Arkin, whose therapy entailed some degree of meddling in her patient's life. Of this misguided campaign to set Jerry straight, Hunter said simply, "That was a lost cause." Sono Osato agreed, noting, "He must have been at times very lonely, because if he didn't have a friend or had separated from a friend, he would be really all alone. But I don't think it would have worked out, his being with a woman. Because then he'd be attracted to some boy or some man and then off he would go. That wouldn't have been good at all."

Osato remembered that Robbins returned to Boston after two days, just in time to finish work on her solo variation and carry out the final changes called for by Abbott. The Boston reviews were favorable, though restrained. *Variety* suggested that *On the Town* "could develop into a wham if properly developed up here." Abbott "froze" the show just before it closed its brief out-of-town run. As Robbins and the cast headed to New York, expectations were mixed, if only because the Adelphi Theatre was not a house where anyone would have expected to stage a hit that year. *On the Town* had been relegated to the Adelphi due to heavy show traffic on Broadway—*One Touch of Venus, Oklahoma!, Mexican Hayride, Follow the Girls* and *Carmen Jones* were already running, and they were joined that season by newcomers that included *Bloomer Girl, Rhapsody, Song of Norway, The Seven Lively Arts, Laffing Room Only* and *Sing Out, Sweet Land!* Moving into such an out-of-the-way theater at Fifty-fourth Street and Seventh

Avenue, Robbins was justified in having misgivings. Bernstein had written to Copland, "Maybe it will be a great hit, and maybe it will lay the great EGG of all time."

On the Town opened December 28, 1944. Osato remembered, "Standing in the wings to watch the three hilarious nightclub scenes that opened Act Two, I sensed we might just have a hit from the sound of the audience's roars of laughter." At the end of the act, "the boys ran back to the ship, with their girls waving goodbye, just in time for the next group of sailors to rush down the gangplank for their twenty-four-hour leave, and a rousing reprise of 'New York, New York.' . . . The final curtain fell, and we stood bowing to an ecstatic crowd. Their applause took on the sound of a force of nature. . . .'"

The reviews gave the show the push that it needed to run 463 performances over the next thirteen and a half months. *On the Town* eventually moved to the Martin Beck Theatre and grossed more than $2 million. Lewis Nichols announced in the *New York Times* that it was "the freshest and most-engaging musical show to come this way since the golden day of *Oklahoma!*" Jack O'Brien of the Associated Press enthused that "a reviewer gets an opportunity to heave his hat into the stratosphere, send up rockets and in general start the sort of journalistic drooling over a musical comedy that puts an end to all adequate usage of superlatives." In the *Journal American*, Robert Garland extolled Robbins' dances as "ingenious." Louis Kronenberger wrote in *PM* that like Bernstein's score, "Mr. Robbins' choreography is also unhackneyed without being high brow. It is crisp, humorous and fast; once or twice it is exciting; only in the Coney Island dream sequence does it sometimes seem arty." Kronenberger concluded, "This show . . . should put Broadway—the Broadway of tasteless lavishness, of stale gags and stupid smut, of tired formulas and meaningless furbelows—in its place."

Robbins and Bernstein had succeeded in combining high and lowbrow elements—classical and commercial entertainment—in a way that was to define all of their future collaborations. The following year, Robbins would contribute an article to the *New York Times Magazine* that was in reality a manifesto announcing his aesthetic intentions. Written at a time when Robbins was secretly attending Communist Party cell meetings and reading the *Daily Worker,* the piece was entitled, "Ballet Puts on Dungarees" and elaborated his view of what he called "the ballet revolution." Offering historical and social analysis of theatrical dancing and sounding like one of the left-wing, populist critics of his day, Robbins described how ballet was becoming a "people's entertainment." As an elitist, classical art form imported from Europe, ballet was to become accessible to the masses, he argued, by embracing American culture and absorbing popular music and social dances. At the same time, according to Robbins, the traditional American musical as light entertainment was destined to incorporate more serious subject matter and classical aesthetic principles. It was to be a two-pronged revolution, and he placed himself at the vanguard.

Robbins concluded the *Times* piece by offering an ideal perspective on dance that he would embrace in the theater for the next fifty years. "A choreographer can justifiably look to the ballet as a medium in which he can say pertinent things about ourselves and our world, no less than a playwright or a novelist or a movie scenarist. For its part, the audience will come to expect as much of ballet as it does of a play, a novel or a film. And as the ballet and the theater draw closer to each other, an exciting prospect opens in which not only musicals, but theater pieces with vital ideas, will combine drama, dance and music, to the benefit of all three." The prospect of a fully unified work combining dance, music, story and design—like the Wagnerian ideal of the *Gesamtkunstwerk*, a totally integrated theatrical experience—had already been seized upon by Robbins as a personal credo and quest even with his first show.

Robbins' zeal surely had its effect on Bernstein, whose mentor, Boston Symphony conductor Serge Koussevitzky, was critical of this excursion onto Broadway and held the musical in very low esteem. It was Robbins who saw the potential to revolutionize the form and impressed his ideas on Lenny, although the composer would wait ten years before returning to Broadway to work with Jerry again. In the meantime, they started and later abandoned a sequel to *Fancy Free* entitled *Bye Bye Jackie*, a vignette about a Brooklyn boy who leaves his family and girlfriend behind when he enlists in the Navy. The concept was apparently not compelling enough to satisfy either collaborator. Paul Bowles later offered testimony that Robbins exerted a strong, high-minded influence on Bernstein at the time. "Jerry and Lenny saw a great deal of one another and I can only surmise that Jerry persuaded Lenny that I had been a pernicious influence with my cynical and frivolous attitude towards existence." Bowles added, "Jerry was in analysis and inclined to be what seemed to me over-serious about everything, not in a merry state of mind. . . ."

More and more, Robbins' serious concerns extended to political and social issues, and the same was true for Bernstein, who had served as guest of honor for a dinner given by the Anti-Fascist League during *On the Town*'s tryout run in Boston. Consistent with Robbins' support for minorities and the civil rights movement, the show broke new ground on the racial front. In light of the country's wartime hostility toward Japan, Sono Osato was more than justified when she observed, "It was amazing to me that, at the height of a world war fought over the most vital political, moral and racial issues, a Broadway musical should feature, and have audiences unquestionably accept, a half-Japanese as an All-American Girl. This is probably the most indelible impression I have had of the magic of the theater. I could never have been accepted as Ivy Smith in films, or later, on television. Only the power of illusion created between performers and audiences across the footlights can transcend political preference, moral attitudes and racial prejudice."

On the Town also broke through the color barrier as the first completely integrated Broadway show. The cast included six African-American performers, and the press reported that "Negroes and whites" could be seen dancing together onstage, although one interracial number had been cut as potentially too provocative. Dorothy McNichols, who had studied with Martha Graham, remembered Robbins' support when the show went out of town the following year. "We had trouble all over the road, being the first integrated show. We left New York and went to Baltimore, Maryland, and they wouldn't let me in backstage to work. They said we weren't in the show, and my picture was out front! Oh, and then we had to send for Jerry, and Jerry gave them a few choice words, you know, swore at them. He said, 'If you keep any of my people out of this theater, you're gonna lose your jobs.' There were all sorts of stories. In Pittsburgh, they wouldn't serve us between shows for dinner. In Chicago, we were put out of a hotel. They said all of the sudden they had a convention. It was terrible. Jerry had a conscience, you see, because he had to struggle because of the prejudices."

"That's right," said Royce Wallace, McNichols' longtime friend in the cast. "Jerry wouldn't put up with it. He said, 'This is *my* show!'"

"He lives by his work," Oliver Smith later observed. "His work is Jerry Robbins. It may seem ruthless, but it isn't because that's what he's about. He is more involved in his work than in his human relationships." Yet Robbins was to have more than his share of passionate involvements and heartfelt intimacies. At a party during the casting period of *On the Town*, Robbins had introduced Smith to Richard D'Arcy, who was to become the designer's lifelong companion. D'Arcy recalled his own brief flirtation with Robbins and characterized Jerry's clandestine relationships with men at the time. "It was very strange," said D'Arcy. "You see, he was interested in me when I first met him, but his whole idea of a relationship was that he would want you to go live in a room where he could come and visit when he pleased, and that was a great big dark mystery. You were supposed to run around wearing veils or something, not to have anyone see you or know you. He was that hidden about his homosexuality in those days. When he was with the dancers and there was a party, he was a hoot and everything was very funny, but there was a privacy he maintained. He kept trying to hide it."

In spite of the fears and anxieties that went along with leading a double life in the erotic underworld of the theater, the gay aspect of his lifestyle may also have afforded Robbins certain advantages as an artist. Playwright Jean-Claude van Itallie met Robbins and Bernstein one night in 1966 when his show *America Hurrah* was being produced at LaMama. "If you were a gay man," van Itallie observed, referring to his own younger generation, "you knew about the gay world, but you could also 'pass' in the straight world. You knew how to communicate to a straight audience what it was like to live dangerously, what it was like to be on the outside. That knowledge of a double reality was tremendously creative. It was about living on the edge."

Van Itallie suggested that Robbins and Bernstein and their generation "in a sense had to conform more" but nevertheless derived special insights from "living in two worlds simultaneously, therefore being able to see into both and being able to translate for the audience." In a similar vein, author Charles

Kaiser speculated, "One reason that lesbians and gay men often make great artists may be that being gay and creating art both require similar strengths: the ability to create an original world of one's own, and a willingness to jettison the conventional wisdom in favor of one's own convictions."

Robbins had moved into Manhattan during preparations for *On the Town*, renting a small apartment in Greenwich Village at 34 West Eleventh Street. Early in 1945, he moved to 24 West Tenth Street, two doors from where Smith had recently taken an apartment with Paul and Jane Bowles, whose salon scene continued to flourish. In that circle Robbins became involved with pianist Robert Fizdale, who had studied at Juilliard and was a partner in a successful piano duo with Arthur Gold. Gold and Fizdale, as they were known, made their New York debut recital in 1944 at the New School for Social Research with an evening of music by John Cage. The early affair between Robbins and Fizdale led to a lifelong friendship. Fizdale's friend Harold Talbott remembered, "They were extremely fast friends and they came from the same background, namely Russian-Jewish parents who had come to the States. They absolutely spoke the same language from the incubator, though Bobby grew up in Chicago and his parents were Communists."

Intent on concealing his unorthodox lifestyle, Robbins appears not to have lived with any of his male lovers during these early years. D'Arcy pointed out the necessity at the time for gay couples to maintain separate addresses. "Oliver lived on Tenth Street. I lived on Tenth Street, but my address was Fifty-seventh Street. You didn't live in the same apartment because people would put two and two together that way. Some things were very undercover. Jerry did the same. That was the reason. You didn't flaunt things like that. It was the times."

Another reason for Robbins' discretion on the home front was the fact that he reportedly gave his mother keys to his apartment. Lena often visited and cooked meals for her busy son, whose success was now a matter of immense pride for both his parents, who with their son legally changed their surname to Robbins in November of 1944. Harry attended all of Jerry's opening nights and stationed himself in the lobby during intermissions to overhear comments from the audience. Robbins' sister kept his scrapbook for him. His change of fortune enabled him to deal with his family for the first time on his own terms, and this included a growing appreciation of his Jewish roots. In

1989, Robbins described a moment of realization that he experienced at the age of twenty-five in the home of his father's brother, Theodore Rabinowitz. "I was invited to a family seder in the Bronx and I went. It was held in the basement of a house because my family is so big. Everyone sat around a huge U-shaped table. I walked into that basement and looked around at that crowd and thought, 'My God, they're all mine!' It gave me a kind of pride. Well, I've had no problems about being Jewish since, although I am not observant in a religious sense." Robbins apparently had an easier time coming to terms with being Jewish than reckoning with his conflicted sexuality. Sono Osato observed, "I think that his sexuality was more of a problem than his Jewishness because in the theater who cares? Race doesn't count in the theater. But if he was troubled by sexuality, that's something else. That he would have to resolve himself. Going to Israel would not help that."

Robbins' renewed interest in his family and heritage was encouraged by Dr. Arkin as part of her effort to lead him into a conventional lifestyle. Robbins, like Bernstein, wanted to be "cured" of being gay. Jerry would make repeated efforts throughout his life to establish an enduring relationship with a woman. Bernstein, too, spent much of his life in analysis. He later married actress Felicia Montealegre and fathered two children. Stephen Sondheim described the composer's strong commitment to his family: "The idea of family was deeply rooted: patriarchy. It had nothing to do with pretending to be heterosexual or anything like that." Given the conflict between family values and gay promiscuity, Bernstein sometimes referred to his homosexual inclination as his "demon." Robbins undoubtedly shared this view early on, torn as he was by his own bisexuality. Arthur Laurents suggested another reason that Robbins may have turned to the psychiatrist: "I think he went into analysis to go straight because he thought that would get him full acceptance. He often did things to get accepted and then blew it because he had to prove he could do whatever he wanted. I went once to a party he gave for his family—Mary Hunter and I were the only outsiders. I had a good time, Jerry had a terrible time. 'Why did you give the party?' 'Because my analyst told me to.' He wanted his analyst's acceptance."

Robbins continued his relationship with Arkin until the mid-1950s when, according to Laurents, Jerry "dumped the analyst." He eventually turned to Dr. Shervert Frazier, who was for a time associated with McLean's Hospital and also served as a director of the National Institute of Mental Health. During the later years of his life, Robbins continued therapy with New York psychiatrist Dr. Robert Michels. Ironically, Robbins' long experience with the self-probing discipline of Freudian thought would prepare him to perform the role of Freud in Robert Wilson's 1969 production, *The Life and Times of Sigmund Freud,* just a few years before the American Psychoanalytic Association finally removed homosexuality from its list of psychiatric disorders.

During the winter of 1945, Robbins befriended his cousin Bob Silverman, who had recently returned to New York to find his way in the music world. Silverman later composed the score for Robert Joffrey's ballet *Persephone* (1952) and eventually became the longtime publisher of *The Piano Quarterly.* That the two were of different sexual persuasions in no way inhibited their friendship. "I came out of the army having gone through a pretty terrible experience," said Silverman. "I was just released from an army hospital. Jerry went out of his way to introduce me to the whole theatrical world that he was part of. He brought me into that world and helped me make the transition back to civilian life. I have often thought how kind that was." Taken under wing by Jerry, Silverman became part of an ever-widening social circle that included Bernstein, Smith and Laurents—three of Jerry's future collaborators on *West Side Story,* all of whom were gay or bisexual. Silverman said, "I didn't care or think about Jerry in terms of gayness. I knew many of his friends were gay, but even knowing that didn't mean a damn thing to me. Nobody ever made a play for me. Jerry did not act gay. There was never any indication, never at any of the parties, never in any of the social gatherings when it was just a handful of people. There were girlfriends going on, and he was trying to keep up a facade."

Ina Kurland was one of the dancers that Robbins saw socially in his early Broadway years, and she recalled his effort to spare her feelings when it became clear to both that a romance was not in the cards. "I auditioned for the road company of *On the Town* when I was about seventeen or eighteen. It was love at first sight. I was in love with Jerry, but I knew that was not possible. He would take me out. He took me to parties. He would just love to walk with me. . . . I remember we were in Boston . . . and we had a snowstorm. And then when that subsided after the show, he wanted to take a walk. I didn't have boots, I didn't have anything. We walked through a park, and I'm not kidding when I tell you the snow was almost up to my knees. But I was with him and all I knew was I didn't care. I didn't feel pain from being frozen, nothing. As I say, I was in love with him. He just liked me a lot. He liked being with me. That's all I can say. Richard [D'Arcy] told me a long time ago that Jerry told him how he felt about me, but Jerry said he didn't want to hurt me."

Like the characters in *On the Town*, Kurland visited Coney Island's amusement park with Robbins. "He used to love to go on the roller coaster, where you sit and feel like you're coming out of your seat. He wanted to sit in the front car. I was scared to death. We sat in the front car, and I thought I was going to die. After it was over, we got out and he said, 'Now we're going to sit in the back, the last car.' He loved those rides. He was like a little kid, and he had a funny little laugh. It was wonderful to see him that way." Kurland, who was later cast by Robbins in *Look, Ma, I'm Dancin'!*, added, "But I saw the things that he did in the theater. One girl, a dancer, always wore long skirts, and he would say to her, 'I know why you're wearing that long skirt, because you have big fat ugly legs.' . . . He was wonderful to me all the years that I knew him, except for one time. We were on the road and he was picking on me all week, just little things during rehearsal. Towards the end of the week, there was a crossover between myself and another dancer, and one went upstage and one went downstage, and I just felt I was right. But he started yelling at me. I went up to him and I shook my finger in his face. I said, 'Don't you ever yell at me again,' and I walked out of rehearsal. We were very close, and I guess I was brazen.

"So I went to the theater that night and put my makeup on, and someone said, 'Jerry's been looking for you.' I said, 'Well, just let him keep looking.' I went down to the basement for my costume, and I heard him calling my name. He was so sweet. He apologized to me, hugged me, kissed me, got me a little book called *Stuart Little* about a little mouse who's born into a normal family. Jerry couldn't have been sweeter. My dealings with him were really good. He felt some kind of feeling for me."

Kurland was part of a small group of dancers who worked consistently with Robbins on a number of his shows and were often called in for "pre-rehearsals." These were actually unofficial work sessions that Robbins, like Agnes de Mille, undertook to start preparing the choreography on a show without paying for rehearsal time, a practice that continued during the 1940s until the unions finally imposed stricter rules. In addition to Kurland, Robbins' group included Helen Gallagher, Donald Saddler, Arthur Partington and Jacqueline Dodge. Gallagher recalled, "He had so many sides to his personality. He was a difficult man to be around because you had to have a certain kind of very outgoing nature to be around him, because he could not initiate. He was reticent with parts of himself, and he was looking for people to liberate him in a way. Of course, when I'd be around him, though I was part of his group in those early years—we'd all go to the beach together and have lots of fun—I was always on the outside because I was very reticent. . . . I loved him dearly, believe me, I would have walked on coals for him, and he was very fond of me. He initiated my career in a way. But at the same time, personality-wise, I didn't do good things for him and he didn't do good things for me. We inhibited each other rather than freeing up each other, so I never remained longtime friends with him because of that.

"We used to go to Coney Island and Jones Beach and [have] cookouts and things like that. We all loved him. When kids today complain about how difficult he was, he was more difficult with himself than he was with anybody. The people that loved him would sit around and think, 'Oh God, let him scream at somebody so we get out of this torturous period we're in.' It was so oppressive when he'd get stuck, because he [was] going down underneath the mind and the ego. It was like a black cloud came over everything. The minute he would explode, then the work would come. So you knew that and you thought, 'Oh, anything, just anything, let him scream at me.' That's why he always had a scapegoat—it was a process for him. I think people recognized that, the people that loved him."

Having made his mark on Broadway with *On the Town*, Robbins continued his association with Ballet Theatre as a dancer and choreographer and soon became a member of the company's Artistic Advisory Committee, which included Aaron Copland, Antony Tudor, Oliver Smith, Agnes de Mille, Henry

Clifford and Lucia Chase. According to the company's archivist, Charles Payne, Robbins would later complain "that the system under which Ballet Theatre operated was not motivated by a desire to pursue excellence in art but was controlled by considerations of finance (he did not go so far as to use the inappropriate words 'profit motive')." A pattern was established early, with Robbins typically asking for more rehearsal hours for his ballets than the management, Lucia Chase in particular, wanted to provide. The sparring between them, though sometimes rancorous, was not without affection and was moderated by an element of mutual self-interest, as Chase also reportedly invested in Robbins' early Broadway shows. Lucia Chase's son, Alex Ewing, recollected, "I saw Jerry Robbins all my life, and it wasn't such a bad relationship between them [Lucia and Jerry]. It's that they were on slightly different tracks. . . . When he was rehearsing for Ballet Theatre, there was always a fight over the studio and the cast. He often got his way." Robbins was promoted from soloist to principal dancer by Chase in 1945.

As a featured performer, Robbins continued studying ballet intensively, taking classes with teachers such as Helene Platova and Ninette Charisse. Glen Tetley joined the cast of *On the Town* after the show opened. He recalled being berated by Jerry after a rehearsal for not having sufficient training to carry out the dancing in one of the scenes. "The moment came for me to go on," said Tetley, "and I had to do this very light, jaunty tap dance across the stage. I was so nervous that I wet my pants. At the end, Jerry thundered backstage and glared at me. He said, 'You get your ass in here in the morning, and I will give you something you can do.' I was frightened out of my head, but I came in. I had heard stories about Jerry in the show, what a monster he could be. But he was actually very kind . . . and said, 'Look, you have tremendous talent, but you have to have training. I think you should go to my [ballet] teacher,' who at the time was a Russian émigré named Helene Platova. It was a wonderful thing for him to do. And she was a great choice, because she was . . . quite a philosophical person and she saw deep spiritual meanings in movement. She was an ardent vegetarian. Jerry was in class, too, and I remember we had cats in the studio all the time that were winding through our legs while we were taking class."

Like a concerned parent, Robbins kept tabs on his dancers and made sure they attended classes regularly. Ninette Charisse had a large following of Rob-

bins dancers, including Robert Tucker, whom she later married and who became one of Robbins' most trusted associates. He remembered, "Jerry would
call up and say, 'Is Helen Gallagher in class today?' He was getting ready to do
a show and he wanted to know. 'Is this person in class? Is that person?'"

To organize his personal and business affairs, Robbins hired a secretary,
Edith Weissman, who would serve him faithfully for more than thirty years.
Eventually, she had a buzzer installed by her bed so that he could beckon her
at all hours. According to many observers, she was a paragon of strength and
efficiency who devoted her life to her endlessly demanding employer. Robbins
was also represented by a number of theatrical agents over the years. His first
agents were Dick Dorso and Jane Deacy. Deacy later handled clients like James
Dean and George C. Scott. Dorso also represented Janet Reed, who remembered him as "suave and sophisticated . . . and really a nifty dresser." Arthur
Laurents recalled, "Dorso was very attractive and ended up where he belonged—with a fancy men's shop in Beverly Hills."

Robbins' next ballet, *Interplay*, was first performed as part of Billy Rose's
Concert Varieties at the Ziegfeld Theatre on June 1, 1945, and entered Ballet
Theatre's repertory in October. The cast included Robbins and his *Fancy Free*
cohorts, John Kriza, Muriel Bentley and Janet Reed (along with Michael
Kidd, Bettina Rosay, Erik Kristen and Roszika Sabo). Robbins had started the
collaboration with Paul Bowles, who recalled in his memoir, *Without Stopping*,
"At one point Oliver [Smith], who had just become a director of the Ballet
Theatre, thought that Jerry Robbins and I ought to collaborate on a ballet.
Jerry was elaborating one in his mind; it was to be called *Interplay*. He would
come down to Tenth Street in the afternoons and talk about it. He worked in
a different way from the choreographers with whom I had previously collaborated. To me everything he said had the air of being supremely subjective, almost to the point of being hermetic. For Jerry it was somehow connected with
the psychoanalysis he was undergoing at the time. We never managed to get
anything decided during our discussions, and finally we gave up the project.
Later Morton Gould wrote the score."

Gould contributed a jazzy, blues-tinctured concoction, *American Concertette*.
Robbins' ballet was inspired by children's games and sketched scenes of lighthearted competition. Kriza and Reed danced a romantic *pas de deux*. Edwin

Denby wrote in the *Herald Tribune,* " 'Interplay' looks like a brief entertainment, a little athletic fun. . . . You see four boys come out and then four girls and all eight join in improvised games (such as follow-the-leader) done in dance terms. . . . The characters of 'Interplay' seem to be urban middle-class young people having a good time who know each other well and like being together but have no particular personal emotions about each other and no special keenness of response. They know about sex as a jive joke or as a general blues sentiment; they don't know it as an individual focus of passion."

In a sense, Robbins may have been drawing from personal experience, but he was also proving himself an acute observer of social relationships, even in this ostensibly plotless work. Writing in *PM,* Robert Hague noted that this ballet's "contemporary idiom, high spirits and distinctly American flavor" were presented in "a more formalized, abstract composition" than Robbins had offered in *Fancy Free.* Robbins' departure into a more abstract style may have reflected the earliest influence of George Balanchine. In 1961, Robbins recalled a brief encounter with the Russian choreographer: "I think I learned more from Balanchine just sitting in a train from Nantucket to New York not long after I had done *Fancy Free* than I have learnt in all the years since then. I barely knew him at that time but we sat and I listened. He wasn't trying to teach me anything, he was just talking about how he felt about dance." While Robbins credited Balanchine with ultimately determining his own approach to "form, construction and the use of music," Balanchine's "pure" neoclassical style had not yet significantly altered Robbins' essentially dramatic orientation to dance.

Janet Reed remembered that Balanchine, "Mr. B" as he was often called, was delighted to bring *Interplay* into the repertory of his New York City Ballet in 1952. She said, "Balanchine liked that ballet, and if he was interested in developing a dancer, he would cast them in *Interplay,* with Jerry's permission, because that ballet demanded a lot of speed. And Balanchine liked speed. He was trying to get away from the romantic European style. He liked dancers that moved like greased lightning, and Jerry did it in that ballet. *Interplay* was hard-driving and required a lot of speed and endurance. It was a technical tour de force."

Just before *Interplay* opened, Robbins found himself embroiled in a public squabble with New York City's Mayor Fiorello La Guardia. The point of contention, though presented in lighthearted journalistic terms, was the sexual stereotype associated with male dancers. The *Daily News* reported on May 25, 1945, that at a corporate meeting of the City Center, the Mayor had asserted, "I'm so prejudiced against ballet. I can't be fair about it. It's the male dancers I can't stand." Robbins was described as "terribly exercised over the whole matter." He threatened to take up the issue with the dancers' union, AGMA, and laid down the gauntlet to the Mayor, saying, "Hizzoner says he can't tell the difference between a tour jeté . . . and a pas de deux . . . but he doesn't like the ballet. Seems to me the Mayor's taking an entrechat in the dark."

Robbins continued his protest, adopting an aggressive, masculine pose. "The Mayor's chief complaint . . . directed against male ballet dancers in particular, really baffles me. The ballet is a universally recognized and loved art form. You don't have to be an authority on the ballet—you can be as uninformed as Mayor La Guardia and still see it would be somewhat less appealing if ballerinas had other ballerinas for partners. . . . What's wrong with male dancers? Ballet is one of the most strenuous forms of endeavor a man can undertake. . . . Looks to me like the Mayor hasn't a leg to stand or dance on." The article concluded with Robbins' taunting offer "to dance alone for the Mayor or to put on as big a ballet as La Guardia could desire."

During the same period, Robbins' name began appearing repeatedly in the *Daily Worker* for his support of various Communist Party front groups. Robbins' FBI file reported that "the DAILY WORKER of 5/7/45 . . . carried an article stating that the INDEPENDENT CITIZENS COMMITTEE of the ARTS, SCIENCES and PROFESSIONS had issued a statement approving [the] Bretton Woods Agreement. JEROME ROBBINS was one of the signers.

"The DAILY WORKER of 9/25/45 . . . carried an announcement that PAUL ROBESON as Chairman had announced the formation of a group of 1,000 artists and professional people for the reelection of BENJAMIN J. DAVIS, Jr. One of the sponsors was listed as JEROME ROBBINS.

"The DAILY WORKER of 9/30/45 . . . announced the formation of the Arts, Writers and Professional Division of the DAVIS Non Partisan Committee and listed JEROME ROBBINS as one of the sponsors.

"The DAILY WORKER of 10/18/45 . . . stated that a cabaret show had been held entitled 'BROADWAY FOR BEN DAVIS' . . . at the PENT HOUSE, 13 Astor Place. This party was headed by PAUL ROBESON and JEROME ROBBINS was listed as a sponsor."

Benjamin Davis was a New York City councilman who was also a member of the Communist Party. Aside from the Davis reelection campaign, Robbins also supported the May Day Parade and an ongoing civil lawsuit to allow the Communist Party to appear on the New York state election ballot. The *Daily Worker* was, of course, part of the public record. While Robbins could allow his name to be associated with various left-wing causes, he was compelled to conceal his membership in the Communist Party in order to protect his career. If his sexuality had forced him into one double life, his politics demanded still another. Yet there was an additional complication for Robbins, because at the time the Communist Party was not a bastion of tolerance as far as homosexuality was concerned. The idea of gay liberation was decades away from being embraced as a cause by the left. Gay Communists usually stayed in the closet, as did gay Democrats and gay Republicans. The stigma attached to being a homosexual was as great as or greater than the stigma associated with being a Communist, and at this point, Robbins was living in serious double jeopardy.

Bob Silverman recalled his cousin's brooding intensity and moodiness on a ten-day trip they made to Cape Cod. Silverman was studying at Juilliard at the time. He and Jerry rented a car for the occasion and shared the drive, taking off in high spirits. "We talked about a lot of things," said Silverman, "about projects and music and whatever. We had a wonderful time going up there. We sang together for hours, mostly making up fugues. I can tell you, I'm a trained musician, and Jerry was easily my equal. We went through the Bach preludes and fugues. Then we get to this motel. It was off-season and beautifully quiet. We didn't even have a reservation. We signed in at the desk and then we went to the room. The clerk had given me the key just because I was walking in front.

"So I had the key, and I opened the door. There were two double beds. And as I walked in, I threw my bag down on the first bed. Jerry was right behind me. You gotta get this picture. We have spent hours and hours together having an absolutely fun time, and we're highly stimulated at that point and relaxed and happy. And he said to me, 'Why did you take that bed, Bobby?' I turned and I said, 'What do you mean, Jerry?' He said, 'Didn't you think I might want that bed?' I said, 'You want this bed? I'll take the other bed.' 'No,' he said. 'You put your bag on there and that was selfish of you. I'll take the other bed.' I told him, 'Jerry, I don't give a damn which bed I take.'

"Now we spent ten days from that moment, and a screen came down between us. Everything on my part felt strained when I talked to him. It was as if you pulled a see-through screen down. There he was, but it wasn't quite him, and the joy was gone. We relaxed a little more as the days went on, but it was still tense. We used to take long walks out on the beach. So one day we're going out on the beach and we're walking along all by ourselves through miles of sand dunes, and I stumble across a piece of driftwood. So I dug it out of the sand, and it's a piece of wood approximately a foot and a half by ten inches in diameter. I figured out a little later it was part of a spar of a boat. And it was burned, and the sand and the water had gotten at it for years and created all kinds of remarkable designs. I've never seen a piece of wood anywhere resembling anything like it. So I grab it and I put it on my shoulder. We look at it together, and Jerry doesn't say anything.

"Then when we get back to the room he says to me, 'Bobby, can I have that piece of wood? I'd like to have it.' I said, 'I don't think so, Jerry. I like it.' I'm usually a generous person, but with his attitude and the tensions between us, I just wasn't going to be so generous. So no more was said. I go back to New York, and I had a one-room place up near Juilliard. One day, Jerry calls me and he says, 'Bobby, you know that piece of wood?' We'd been out to dinner and done other things. I had seen him many times since the trip. Out of the blue, he says, 'You know that piece of wood you found up there in Cape Cod?' I said, 'Yes.' He says, 'If I gave you a thousand dollars, would you give it to me?' And I said, 'No, it's not for sale.'"

Despite such minor frictions, the friendship between the two cousins continued without interruption for the rest of the decade. Many years later, after a long period of estrangement, the piece of driftwood would reappear as a reminder for Silverman of their youthful adventure together, of the choices that each had made in life—choices that would ultimately drive them apart. In the meantime, there were the salon parties, the Broadway openings, the ballet rehearsals that Silverman attended with his cousin. The young musician always remembered the walks they took together in Manhattan. "Jerry had an artist's eyes," said Silverman. "He could see things no one else could see. We'd walk along the street at night and he'd see shadows from the buildings, subtle details. His visual sense was so strong. He was looking at everything. He'd say, 'Look,' and he'd describe what he saw, like a vivid scene in the theater, and I'd look at it and I'd see what he saw. There were endless moments like that between us."

When the first moment of truth and panic arrived for Robbins with regard to the tangled issues of politics, sexuality and career, Silverman was one of the trusted few to whom Jerry would confide.

For his next venture on Broadway, *Billion Dollar Baby*, Robbins once again teamed up with producers Smith and Feigay. Comden and Green provided the book and lyrics, and Abbott directed. But instead of Bernstein, who had reservations about working on Broadway again, Morton Gould composed and orchestrated the music—an undistinguished pop score that one reviewer later called "stunty without being melodic." Indeed, none of the songs from this show was ever going to click on the hit parade. If Robbins was going to make the dances succeed, he would have to do so without great music to back him up.

As far as the script, Comden and Green chose to pursue new directions in this show rather than repeat what they had done in *On the Town*. They started writing *Billion Dollar Baby* during the summer while still performing their *On the Town* stage roles. Comden remembered, "We could see the first scene and the last—the little gold digger in Staten Island starting out to get what she wants in the boom of the 1920s, and winding up with her wedding just as Wall Street crashes. . . . The first title we chose was 'Here We Go Again.' 'Nostalgia' was what some of the critics called our show, but, believe me, we had no nostalgia for the twenties. It was a dreadful decade. We'd been thinking, though, of the speakeasies, the gangsters and the inflation as wonderful material for satire."

Green expressed the point of view that he and Comden shared with Robbins. "Integration. That's what we aimed at. . . . Everything in the piece must have something to do with the plot and characters. For instance, we won't throw in a whale of a tap dance, just because it will bring down the house." The plot revolved around the scheming gold-digger, Maribelle Jones, played by Joan McCracken, a plucky dance-actress who had won acclaim in *Oklahoma!* and *Bloomer Girl.* She was joined by former Hollywood child star Mitzi Green, who specialized in comic impressions and appeared as Georgia Motley, a take-off on the outrageous real-life figure of Texas Guinan.

The character of Maribelle was outlandish at the time as a heroine without endearing virtues. A Staten Island bathing beauty in the era of flappers and bathtub gin, she was portrayed as ruthless and conniving, going through a string of expendable men that included a marathon dance champion, a celebrity gangster and his bodyguard, and finally a billionaire Wall Street tycoon. Virginia Gibson understudied McCracken and later stepped into the role. "That show was very strange because it was anti," said Gibson. "It was before we did anti-hero and anti-heroine roles." Unlike the innocent young female characters that audiences were accustomed to seeing, Maribelle "was a horrible little girl in that show. She clawed her way to the top. And Joanie had a very unusual look. I think that's what Jerry liked. He sensed that she could be used for that part, because it wasn't your typical little ingenue and Joanie wasn't a glamorous girl. . . . I remember doing that song—she says, oh, money doesn't interest her, and then she says, it's the things you can buy with it. And then she has the gangster, and in the ballet, he got shot. Jimmy [Mitchell] was playing the young lead, the dance part, and she got him shot. It was a very unusual show—it was, I think, way ahead of its time. And the [gangster's] funeral that Jerry did was hysterical. It was really wonderful, with bumps and grinds, and everybody was in black. That was the guy that she had done in. So it was not a typical musical and not a typical character."

The casting of Mitchell and McCracken caused a temporary strain between Robbins and Agnes de Mille, who was Jerry's friendly competition on Broadway and at Ballet Theatre. Mitchell, McCracken and two other dancers had left de Mille's *Bloomer Girl* to go into *Billion Dollar Baby,* and de Mille charged that Robbins had "raided" her show. In a letter posted to Robbins from London, where she was working at the time, de Mille wrote that she understood that Mitchell's move would help his career, "but I don't think it is quite ethical to tease the chorus boys away at a time when they are so dreadfully difficult to replace, and when I am far from the scene. . . . I cannot bear to think of you and me playing at this cut-throat game, and caring not a damn what hurt we do to one another's works or reputations. Out of friendship and mutual respect I think we should not raid one another's shows unless we can better the lot of the individual dancer. . . . I do burn up to learn that a good piece of my chorus has skipped out to join your chorus. . . ." Yet de Mille also wrote, "In spite of the foregoing you know that I wish with all my heart for your success in the new show," and closed her letter, "affectionately."

De Mille was easy enough for Robbins to handle from a distance, but there were other conflicts closer to home on this show. Mitchell danced the role of the gangster's bodyguard, Rocky, in the elaborate funeral ballet that opened Act Two. He recalled the histrionics during rehearsals that came about because of McCracken's apparent infatuation with the choreographer. "Jerry couldn't have been more charming socially. Everybody was in love with him. Everybody wanted to marry him or go to bed with him, men and women. . . . Joan was married to Jack Dunphy, and she was madly in love with Jerry, sobbing, sobbing, not going on, sobbing and running around and wailing all over the theater. It was very tense. I guess Jerry finally said, 'I want nothing to do with you.'" Jack Dunphy was away in the service at the time. In a world where sexual identities often changed overnight, Dunphy eventually became Truman Capote's lover and lifetime companion. McCracken later married choreographer Bob Fosse and went on to a short film career, starring in MGM's remake of *Good News!* in 1947. Despite any unrequited feelings she may have harbored for Robbins during *Billion Dollar Baby* and despite the fact that Abbott thought McCracken had been miscast, she turned in a performance that was to receive many favorable notices. Lewis Nichols wrote in the *New York Times*, "Miss McCracken is practically a musical comedy in herself."

Robbins had researched the period thoroughly. At the Museum of Modern Art, he reportedly sat through an early Joan Crawford movie, *Our Dancing Daughters*, fourteen times. He also read F. Scott Fitzgerald and Elinor Glyn, and consulted with his sister about the fine points of dances like the Black Bottom and the Charleston. Trude Rittmann worked as a rehearsal pianist on the show and later arranged the music on *Look, Ma, I'm Dancin'!* She encouraged Robbins to get further musical education. "I could see that he was innately deeply musical and [had a] very talented ear . . . but he couldn't read music . . . he couldn't see where he was in the music. Terrible. I said, 'Jerry, that's just inexcusable' . . . So he really listened, and first took up the recorder." Rittmann attributed Robbins' personal angst to his "search for the truth within himself," and recalled the challenges of working with such an uncompromising artist. "In the beginning he was just murder . . . not that he did it to me, but he did it to the kids and to himself. . . . This man constantly murdered himself. He was so high-strung and so self-tormented."

Robbins' assistant on *Billion Dollar Baby* was Anita Alvarez, who recalled, "I learned a lot about how he worked, and it was rough. He was very involved in what he was doing. If he didn't get the kind of response he wanted from certain dancers, he was brutal. There was one dancer who broke a leg because Jerry kept working on him to do something and couldn't get it the way he wanted it. It was that rough. But he got along well with the stars. And he did a lot of wonderful numbers because he had a wonderful sense of humor." Robbins was helped on one tap number by dancer-choreographer Danny Daniels, who performed the role of the marathon dance champ, Watson. "I had created a dance with a drum in the army, and I auditioned with the drum dance . . . and Jerry was intrigued with it and decided to put it in the show. Jerry was very supportive. He let me stage it with the girl, a song-and-dance number . . . 'I've Got a One-Track Mind.' He was busy doing his big [funeral] ballet in the second act and his Charleston ballet."

On Broadway at the time, the term *ballet* could refer to any long dance that used a large group of dancers, whether the dancing involved jazz, classical, tap, acrobatics or other forms. In the case of the comic ballet called "Charleston," Robbins utilized the social dance to bring the period to life, even though Gould's music offered little in the way of twenties chromatics or tempi. One of the dancers, Maria Harriton, was astonished that Robbins was still revising the number on opening night. "We were standing behind the curtain. The orchestra had started the overture, and Jerry was changing counts in the Charleston number. Now that is perfectionism!" Harriton added, "Jerry was quite an adventure. He scared more people than anyone I think that ever lived. If necessary, he'd grind you up. He didn't just try to correct you, he demolished you. *Billion Dollar Baby* was his second show. and he hadn't solidified any real success yet in his estimation. He had to go with his own gut feelings, I guess, but he was just horrendous, and I think we all would have happily let him fall into the pit and break his head."

Harriton referred to an incident that was witnessed by others in the cast. At one point while giving the dancers corrections onstage with his typical General Patton style, Robbins backed up over the edge and took a dangerous fall into the orchestra pit. The story of his fall would be repeated over the years, with each generation of dancers attributing it to different Robbins shows. In this way, the tale took on the apocryphal uncertainty of legend, most often erroneously included in the lore of *West Side Story.* James Mitchell recalled, "It is not legend, it is absolutely true. I was there. Everyone stood around in a combination of absolute amazement and delight. [Jerry was] talking, talking, talking, edging closer and closer. Nobody said, 'Watch it!' Nope. Off he went. He could have killed himself. I think he fell into the bass drums. Nobody went to his rescue, not for quite a while."

Arthur Partington was one of the other dancers onstage at the time, and he also remembered that the drums broke Robbins' fall. Could his dancers have been so full of enmity that they would have allowed him to fall without warning him? Were they simply too intimidated to interrupt him? Helen Gallagher did not think the dancers failed to warn Jerry out of any sort of malice, but rather that he fell before any of them had the chance to say anything. She said, "Everybody tells the story like we let him drop into the pit, but I remember it being like one of those moments [when] something is going to happen and you're frozen in time. That's kind of what happened."

Although Betty Comden had no recollection of the fall, she said, "I think probably the cast was mad at him. . . . Jerry did get people very angry. He drove them and drove them very mercilessly. A lot of people who worked for him as dancers didn't like him particularly." Still, however disliked he may have been in the heat of the moment, it seems unlikely that this group of dancers would have actually wished him serious injury. In any event, the story would soon take on a life of its own. Years later, when Robbins was rehearsing *Jerome Robbins' Broadway*, one of his young dancers, Joey McKneely, took a similar fall into the pit. The star of the show, Jason Alexander, and several other by-standers remembered Robbins looking on and saying only, "That happened to me once."

Billion Dollar Baby opened at the Alvin Theatre on December 21, 1945, and for the most part received glowing reviews, despite some critical misgivings about the score and book. *PM's* Louis Kronenberger called Robbins "the hero of the evening." The *New York Sun's* Ward Morehouse pointed out that *Billion Dollar Baby* "is by no means up to *On the Town*, but it comes forth as a professional job with enough all-around values to make it go." The show would survive 220 performances over six months. Director Abbott called it "a passable success," complaining after the fact that the "principal ballet was too long, making the second act drag." But for Jerry, the show secured his place on Broadway as well as his relationship with Abbott, with whom he would work on his next two musical productions. The choreography for *Billion Dollar Baby* earned Robbins his first Donaldson Award later that year.

O n May 25, 1946, Robbins appeared at a dance benefit organized by the Greater New York Committee for Russian Relief. The event took place at the Brooklyn Academy of Music and featured modern dance and ballet performers such as Michael Kidd, Janet Reed, Martha Graham, Charles Weidman, Katherine Dunham and Dorothy Bird. Robbins staged a short concert work for himself and Nora Kaye, set to Stravinsky's *Five Easy Pieces* for duet piano. This was the first pairing of Robbins as choreographer and Kaye as muse, in what was to be a deeply complex personal and professional relationship that would span the years until her death in 1987.

Of Russian-Jewish parentage, Kaye had been born Nora Koreff in 1920 in New York City. Her parents had named her Nora after the heroine of Ibsen's *A Doll's House*. She changed her surname early in her career because she felt that "an American dancer ought to have an American name." As a child, Nora was trained by Michel Fokine and Margaret Curtis at the Metropolitan Opera Ballet School, and later she joined Balanchine's American Ballet during its tenure at the Met. Her father, Gregory Koreff, had studied with Stanislavski at the Moscow Art Theater, and Nora recalled, "I was brought up in the Stanislavski method of acting." She had a long romantic history that started as a teenager when she endured an abusive marriage to *Studs Lonigan* author James T. Farrell that was later quietly dissolved. Other marriages included Isaac Stern and a great grandson of President Martin Van Buren. Of her time with the violinist, Nora remarked to Gore Vidal that she "couldn't stand it" because of "that squeak, squeak, squeak all day when he practiced." Given her savage wit and thespian gifts, Robbins had more than met his match, and Kaye now figured prominently into his plans.

One perspective on Kaye is offered by Arthur Laurents, who, like Robbins, later had an affair with Kaye. In his memoir, *Original Story By*, Laurents wrote of her, "Like most ballerinas, she walked like a duck; unlike most, she had slightly nasal New York speech and was wickedly funny camp. She lived on Fifty-second Street in a walk-up over a jazz club across from the old Tony's (its bar was largely gay), which was a hangout where she loved to drink and laugh and listen to Mabel Mercer; or to Tony singing while standing on his head; or, on occasion, to a loaded Anna May Wong doing comic monologues in Chinese. It floored me to see how much Nora could drink, how much all the dancers could drink and still dance brilliantly the next night—until I learned most of them were on amphetamines to get through the season. Nora was so connected to Tudor and Hugh Laing, Tudor's strikingly handsome lover and her partner in Tudor ballets, that when Hugh walked into Tony's one night with a mynah bird on his shoulder, someone called out, 'Now what have you done to Nora Kaye?' Her nickname for Hugh was 'Hugh Wang'; before going onstage, she touched it for luck."

On June 20, 1946, Robbins and Ballet Theatre's troupe of fifty dancers sailed to London on the *Queen Mary.* "The dancers, accustomed to rail-coach travel under wartime conditions," wrote Charles Payne, "enjoyed the six-day passage as though it were a luxury cruise." When they arrived for their engagement at Covent Garden's Royal Opera House, they checked into the Savoy Hotel and found a postwar London suffering from food shortages and other material deprivations. The trip was no holiday for Jerry. With only a week to rehearse until the opening on July 4, he was described by dancers as suffering from a severe case of nerves. Rehearsals for his ballets were especially punishing, as he was feeling the dual pressure of facing the British audience for the first time as performer and choreographer.

Payne wrote that *Fancy Free*, "though acclaimed, was labeled as 'music hall'" by the British. Still, the London audiences responded with ovations. One British critic recalled that Robbins "tasted the triumph of London's first view of *Fancy Free* and *Interplay*, in both of which he danced, appeared in Fokine's *Helen of Troy* as Hermes, and in Agnes de Mille's *Three Virgins and a Devil*, with what devastation we know, and disappeared quietly by the end of the second week." After performing the title role of Petrouchka, Robbins abruptly returned to New York before the end of the tour. He was embroiled in a conflict with management over rehearsal time for two ballets that the company had recently commissioned from him. The first was an abstract ballet set to music by Vivaldi that Robbins had started rehearsing but later canceled, protesting that Ballet Theatre had not provided him with sufficient hours in the studio. The second work involved a new collaboration with Bernstein.

In August, Robbins spent five days with Bernstein in Stockbridge, Massachusetts, working on the story concept for a highly dramatic ballet, *Facsimile*, scheduled to premiere October 18. The premise of the ballet derived from medical researcher Santiago Ramón y Cajal, who had offered an observation that intrigued Robbins and gave him a starting point for discussions with Bernstein: "Small inward treasure does he possess who, to feel alive, needs every hour the tumult of the street, the emotion of the theater, and the small talk of society."

According to Humphrey Burton, the ballet represented the outcome of "the somewhat bitter fruits of the psychoanalysis sessions both Robbins and Bernstein had been undertaking. . . ." Burton also related that "for a time Bernstein went to a woman analyst recommended to him by Robbins, who had heard about her from Martha Graham." Burton may have been referring to Dr. Arkin, as Robbins' social relationship with Graham had only recently been established when Agnes de Mille brought her to a dinner hosted by Robbins at his apartment. In any case, *Facsimile* undoubtedly reflected the analytical experiences shared by the two collaborators and also called to mind the territory staked out by Tudor with his psychological explorations in ballets like *Pillar of Fire* and *Undertow*. Years later, Robbins admitted that *Facsimile* "came out of a situation in my own life—I found myself involved with two other people and what was going on sort of interested me. I tried to make a ballet out of it."

For this nineteen-minute piece, Robbins cast Nora Kaye, Johnny Kriza and Hugh Laing, but Robbins himself danced the Laing role on opening night. To the extent that the ballet derived from a particular romantic triangle in Jerry's personal life, there may have been a certain deliberate irony in his casting choices. Janet Reed surmised, "He was mad about Johnny Kriza. And Nora and Jerry were later going to get married. So there was the triangle right there."

Rehearsals were grueling. Robbins discarded a *corps* of eighteen dancers along the way and subjected the principals to 138 hours in the studio. "Not since the creation of *L'apres-Midi D'un Faun* by Vaslav Nijinsky," Charles Payne wrote, "had so many hours been devoted to the rehearsal of so few dancers in so short a ballet." Payne characterized the intensity and duration of Robbins' rehearsal process as "what a Prevention Society would term Cruelty to Dancers." At a meeting of the company's Artistic Advisory Committee in September, Robbins contended that his ballet was under-rehearsed and requested that the opening be postponed until the following season. He received only a week's delay. In that short space of time, "Robbins instructed Bernstein to rewrite the mezzo-soprano's role so that it could be performed instead by a horn. . . ." The composer complied, dedicating the score to Robbins, and the ballet opened October 24, 1946.

When *Facsimile* was later adapted for the concert hall, Bernstein offered a program note in which he stated, "The inspiration of [Robbins'] scenario, with its profoundly moving psychological implications, had entered into this music in a degree which, I believe, produced what one might almost call a 'neurotic music,' mirroring the neuroses of the characters involved. The action of the ballet is concerned with three lonely people—a woman and two men—who are desperately and vainly searching for real interpersonal relationships. They meet for the first time, develop quick and passionate connections, and, inevitably, find themselves left in a state of ennui and resentment: inevitably, because they are unintegrated personalities with little if any capacity for real relations." Describing the unsettling climax of the stage action when all three characters perceive the futility of their passions, Bernstein wrote, "This point is accomplished in the ballet by the desperate cry of 'Stop!' from the woman, followed by a minute of silence in which only her sobbing is heard. The men stand by abashed and motionless."

The word uttered aloud onstage in the ballet was calculated by Robbins for its shock value. Oliver Smith designed the set, conceived as "a lonely place," which was an empty, Daliesque beach. The day before the opening, Robbins gave an interview to *PM* in which he said that his characters "in fright . . . take on false manners and politeness. You have seen people doing this at cocktail parties. You put three people together acting roles like this and it results in disaster. Finally, they realize that they must go off alone." Robbins announced his intention in presenting a ballet that was such a marked departure from the comic material seen in his previous work: "I don't want to stick to being the great American 'yak' choreographer." He also commented somewhat defiantly, "I'm trying to rip off the facetiousness that everyone indulges in. . . . As someone said in a rehearsal, 'It's like probing under an everyday occurrance' [sic]. I think it packs a dramatic punch and it's a step forward for me whether it comes out successfully or not."

Walter Terry was one critic who agreed, writing in the *Herald Tribune* that "Jerome Robbins with four smash comedy hits behind him . . . endangered his not yet rooted success as a designer of gay dances by creating the bitter and not-pap-for-the-audience *Facsimile*. . . ." Terry suggested that Robbins' new direction indicated "contrived shadows of past successes could not hope to rival the fresh substance of a new creation." The rest of the critics were divided. Edwin Denby declared, "Of Robbins's choreographic genius, after his new *Facsimile* there can be no doubt." John Martin thought the ballet "worthy of respect," but complained it was "an ugly work about ugly people. . . . Its theme is trite—a silly woman plays with two equally silly men and ends nowhere; its people are lay figures conceived with only surface observation. It never gets under the cuticle."

Time magazine was even less sympathetic, perhaps indicating that Jerry had touched the nerve he intended with his theme: "To a frantic score by Leonard Bernstein, three insecure people . . . rolled on the floor, kissed indiscriminately, tussled. Then the two men tossed Nora Kaye back and forth like a shuttlecock until she fell sobbing on the floor. . . . At this point, ballerina Kaye cried out 'Stop!' One unkind critic felt she had said everything that needed saying." The unkind critic was Robert Sylvester of the *World-Telegram,* who offered scathing ridicule in his summary of the action: "Robbins kisses Nora's hand. He kisses her on the kisser. She kisses back. He kisses her knee. She jumps around and falls down. He kisses her foot. She gets coy. He sulks. She kisses the back of his neck. Then they both fall down and play dead for a while. . . . In comes John Kriza, in red underwear. Everybody gets all mixed up, kissing Nora some more, until at one point Kriza nearly kisses Robbins."

According to Jerry's sister, after watching the ballet on one occasion, his mother said somewhat cryptically, "So, it was all Nora's fault." Her comment might have indicated that Lena knew or suspected more about what was going on in her son's personal life than she ever let on to others in the family, although it appears unlikely that she ever admitted the full truth to herself. Apparently, Lena blamed Nora for the failed romance rather than her son. Of his relationship to Nora, one of her roommates, Ruth Ann Koesun, said, "It was a difficult relationship, but they did adore each other, they really did, not just personally but artistically. The ballets he did for her may have had something to do with the personal relationship because *Facsimile* and [later] *The Cage* were not exactly complimentary to women. They were wonderful roles for Nora, but as [depictions of women] they were not very flattering concepts. . . . [*Facsimile*] wasn't complimentary toward the male dancers either, but that was Jerry. He was a very complex person."

Nora later characterized Jerry as "a demon worker," and explained, "He knows exactly what needs fixing and how to fix it. His eye for what is wrong is fabulous. But *his* idea always comes first. He molds the dancer to his way, and sometimes it can be painful. He was never easy to work with. . . . He has always expected the most. Why should he settle for less?"

The following year, Robbins offered a revised version of the work that was toned down, and according to John Martin, "less sardonic than satirical." Jerry was not one to cast a deaf ear to his critics. Nevertheless, the ballet soon fell out of the repertory, and the acrobatic complexities of the choreography were lost forever, as no record of the work was kept either in notation or on film.

As if to placate his audience, Robbins returned to lightweight subject matter. In the spring of 1947, he staged *Pas de Trois* for Ballet Theatre luminaries Alicia Markova, Anton Dolin and André Eglevsky. Illness forced Markova to withdraw at the last minute, and she was replaced by Rosella Hightower when the ballet opened at the Metropolitan Opera House on March 26 under the auspices of Sol Hurok and the Original Ballet Russe. With music from Berlioz' *Damnation of Faust,* the ballet gently satirized the vanity and egos of ballet stars, like those in the cast. John Martin lauded it as "a witty little piece." Robbins was again taking advantage of the idiosyncrasies of his performers. Eglevsky, for instance, was famous at the time for the extraordinary number of pirouettes he was able to execute. Martin wrote, "Every spectator will probably choose a different moment to find most hilarious, but for this one the high point is Mr. Eglevsky's tremendous preparation (accompanied by impressive noises from the orchestra) to accomplish a single turn."

On May 13, Robbins took part in a benefit program at New York's City Center sponsored by the American-Soviet Music Society, which had been founded the year before by Koussevitsky. The theme of the evening was "theatre music of two lands," and for the occasion, Robbins staged *Summer Day* to Prokofiev's *Music for Children.* With this dance, Robbins parodied classical ballet by looking at it through the eyes of children. The choreographer portrayed a pair of child dancers breaking away from their barre exercises to investigate a box of wigs and props. Their ensuing imitations of adults allowed Robbins to lampoon the classic European tradition with what Martin of the *Times* called, "the most apparently guileless of dead-pan ribbing." Robbins danced with Annabelle Lyon, and they were accompanied onstage by pianist Ray Lev, yet another artist who was also active in the Communist Party. By all accounts, *Summer Day* was the hit of the evening, and the ballet was added to Ballet Theatre's repertory in December, with Ruth Ann Koesun replacing Lyon as Robbins' partner.

"I liked Jerry very much," said Koesun. "We had our tiffs . . . but I think everybody did with Jerry, especially when you've worked so hard. He demanded it and we wanted to do it. And then, at the last minute, he'd change the cast, and you've come into the theater and you weren't dancing. But that was

Jerry, what could you do? I never really fought with him face to face. I used to tell Oliver Smith, but I said, 'You know, Jerry is smarter than I am.'" Koesun also recalled the vibrant social scenes that would repeatedly lead Robbins into fruitful exchanges with other creative artists. "There was a lot of socializing. It was really quite remarkable, the people we were able to meet, other artists and writers and literary folks. It was a wonderful period in ballet, because what happened in dance after the Second World War was like what happened for artists and writers after the First World War—it was such an enriching time."

Crossing back to Broadway, Robbins undertook his next show, *High Button Shoes*, after signing with agent Howard Hoyt, who was packaging a project based on Stephen Longstreet's novel *The Sisters Liked Them Handsome*. Longstreet's Beverly Hills neighbor was composer Jule Styne. The two brought the *High Button Shoes* script and their friends, lyricist Sammy Cahn and comedian Phil Silvers, to Hoyt. The agent, in turn, brought in Jerry, along with set designer Oliver Smith and costume designer Miles White. Meanwhile, Silvers recruited his friend, Copacabana owner Monte Proser, to ante up the seed money and produce. To help with the financing, Proser turned to his pal, Joe Kipness, "an exuberant, decent bull of a man," according to Silvers. Nanette Fabray, who would star in the show, described Kipness as "very colorful. Joe was a very, very sentimental, emotional man, and a mobster. At nineteen he was head of the trucking association in New York, so you knew he was really involved. Joe, either as a cover or because he could no longer be in the mob . . . was in the garment business, which many of them went into. He had suits and coats and whatever downtown."

While Proser and Kipness acted mainly as cash cows and absentee producers as far as the actual business of creating the show, Fabray recalled Kipness being on hand for the three-week out-of-town run in Philadelphia's Forrest Theater, where the show premiered on September 15, 1947. "One of my fondest, most loving memories, is the opening—getting ready to open out of town—and our costumes aren't ready, because there were so many last-minute changes, and my soft-shoe costume wasn't ready. It was a multilayered soft skirt which hung straight but it could turn and flare out when I danced—it had to have some pretty movement to it. The machine that they were using to hem all of the costumes was being used . . . and nobody was there hemming my [costume]. And I went downstairs and there's Joe Kipness . . . hemming my skirt. He said, 'I have to do something!' I don't know if he knew how to sew or not, but he wanted to be part of the show. And Joe had a face—a round gangster face and little tiny eyes, big flat nose. He looked like a mobster, his big fat hands sewing up my skirt. There were so many things like that going on in that show."

Like many of those who worked for Robbins, Fabray was for the most part unaware of his sexual orientation in the theater. "You never saw anything of him being homosexual. It wasn't displayed in any way, as it was with some of the dancers or some of the other actors or performers—and I have no feeling about that one way or another. What's the old joke—'some of my best friends . . .'? In our business, who cares? But you could sometimes, even though somebody would be cautious, you could tell. You didn't care, but you just knew. But I never saw anything with Jerry that would give a clue to any of that one way or the other. From my point of view, he was completely divorced from showing favoritism or interest in anybody in the show."

Robbins hired his former mentor, Gluck Sandor, as his assistant on the choreography. Sandor's adopted son, Philip, claims that Jerry turned to Sandor in desperation early on. "Jerry said, 'I'm in trouble. I have to start all the production numbers.' So Sandor started about nine or ten of them. He used to walk Jerry home, and they [would sit] on the stoop. . . . and Jerry was very unhappy. He said, 'I'm not doing anything beautiful.'" Robbins' comment may have been intended entirely for Sandor's benefit, as the elder choreographer continued to represent a kind of artistic conscience for Jerry, who was pursuing a more commercial direction with his Broadway career than Sandor might have wished. Sandor suggested that Robbins choreograph a duet, and Jerry obliged with several numbers in the show, one of which, a brief sequence in what he called his "Picnic Ballet," would carry heartfelt significance for the young dance-maker.

Robbins started the show with Mary Hunter slated as director. Hunter, however, was soon replaced by George Abbott, as the producers apparently thought his name would help win backing from the Shubert organization. The show did eventually open at the Shuberts' Century Theatre. A subsequent lawsuit brought by Hunter against the producers established a contractual precedent for stage directors, protecting them from arbitrary dismissal, and introduced Robbins to two of his future high-powered attorneys, William Fitelson and Floria Lasky. Hunter recalled, "Floria became Jerry's lawyer. He had admired her work for me in this case. She won hands-down and established the position on which the Society for Stage Directors and Choreographers was built—which was that you were a private person [as a director] and you could contract as an individual, [having] all the rights of whatever your employment contract was."

There were almost as many conflicts among members of the production team as there were in the script. In his memoir, *The Laugh Is on Me: The Phil Silvers Story*, the comedian recounted his coming to the aid of Kipness. "With Mr. Abbott involved, we had a guaranteed hit. The money flowed in and a faction grew, convinced that we didn't need Joe Kipness anymore. He looked like an uncouth slugger and he still mangled the English language. All he'd done was keep the show alive. The anti-Kipness faction held a meeting at Sardi's at Mr. Abbott's table. When I walked in, I spotted Joe sitting all alone. I sat down with Joe and made it clear to the others: If you want me, you'll have to keep Joe. So Joe became co-producer. . . ."

The script for *High Button Shoes* was rewritten by Abbott and Silvers, with Abbott receiving a percentage of author's royalties from the producers. With his book being rewritten, Stephen Longstreet withdrew from the show in righteous protest. Staying clear of the production conflicts, Robbins set about to research his subject. Part of the play was set in "Atlantic City, circa 1913," and Robbins visited the Museum of Modern Art, where he studied the silent-movie classics of Charlie Chaplin and Mack Sennett's *Tillie's Punctured Romance* and *The Surf Girl.* The latter contained a simple chase scene that Robbins expanded into almost ten minutes of breakneck stage lunacy that came to be known as "The Mack Sennett Ballet." Robbins' idea for the dancing drove the narrative, with a diabolical cops-and-robbers chase that included eight bathing beauties, seven iron-hatted Keystone Kops, three robbers, two pairs of male and female twins, fourteen singers, a lifeguard and a gorilla. All of them were to be seen racing on the boardwalk and in and out of seven bathhouses, their dizzily accelerating progress marked by slamming doors and all manner of orchestrated mayhem.

Helen Gallagher recalled rehearsing the scene with Robbins. "He was just so much fun. I always remember him standing at those doors laughing his head off. . . . We were all killing each other backstage, because when he first staged that ballet we didn't have any doors until we got out of town and got a set. So people were crashing into it, because we had certain counts that we had to go through those doors, and people were killing each other, literally killing each other to get to their door on a count." Dancer Sondra Lee was knocked out cold behind one of the doors during a run-through, and Gallagher recalled, "We all just jumped over her, literally went through the door over her body." So one day in rehearsal, we said, 'Jerry, we're killing ourselves backstage.' He said, 'Oh, okay, well, do it one more time and I'll come up with some solution.' And what he did was he stood where he could see downstage and upstage of the doors from the wings—laughing his head off. He *laughed*, he was just rolling with what we were doing. And the next day at rehearsal, he said, 'Keep to the right.' So he knew the solution all along, but he wanted to see what was happening."

Robbins recounted working on the music for his Mack Sennett Ballet with composer Jule Styne and Genevieve Pitot, who arranged the music for the dances. "I asked Jule for themes, this kind of music; that kind. I said things like, 'Give me chase music here, give me fill-in music there. . . .' Then the dance arranger took it and made it into the ballet, with my needs in mind." While much of the music for the scene was original, it also drew from such disparate sources as Liszt's *Second Hungarian Rhapsody* and Offenbach's can-can theme from *Orpheus in the Underworld*. Part of the initial difficulty in staging the chase scene was apparently caused by Silvers, as the comedian was confused by the musical counts. Fabray recalled, "Phil learned to count, but he didn't know that you don't go past a single count. So Phil was going ten-two-three-four, eleven-two-three-four, a hundred and twenty-two-three-four . . . and of course, he's going through the door where he *thinks* he's supposed to go. . . . Bit by bit, we're all getting killed because Phil is going through the wrong door and knocking it down. . . . "

Virginia Gibson recollected some tense moments when Robbins chose one of the dancers as his whipping boy in the scene. "Poor Joe Landis!" said Gibson. "Jerry would find somebody to let it all out on. One day he said to Joe, 'I want you to move faster! If you don't, I'll take a firecracker and shove it up your ass, and then you'll move.' This guy was shaking, shaking, shaking in his boots. That's how angry Jerry was, because Joe wasn't moving as fast as he could. Jerry was using people to get his results." Another dancer who later joined the show, Ralph Linn, summarized the process in the rehearsal studio that would become increasingly calculated and effective for Robbins. "Jerry's forte was to destroy you, and then he would try to remake you the way that he wanted you. He used his method of destroying and rebuilding for what he wanted dance-wise."

Even Fabray recoiled from Robbins at times when he savaged his dancers. "He would push me to do more, but never mock me or make fun of me as he did with the chorus. Boy, if they couldn't do it, he would chew them up one side, down the other. I would walk away in horror at this person—I'm looking at Jekyll and Hyde." Yet Fabray largely recalled the gentle side of Jerry's nature, which was especially apparent when he demonstrated and discussed what he wanted in the dance. "To watch Jerry was to watch magic, because he was a great dancer. And to see him do these ballet steps, your heart would swell. . . . And he could be a man or a woman when he danced." In the soft-shoe number, "he wanted the man to be virile but soft. How do you do that? Well, he got this performance out of Jack [McCauley], who was a sweet, sweet man. But [Jerry] said, 'No, you're not sweet. You're virile, but you're soft. We had these conversations. . . . And that number stopped the show cold. People told me that they would walk into the theater just to see it. They'd come in to see the Mack Sennett Ballet and then they'd go off across the street to Sardi's and have a drink, and then come back and watch this soft-shoe because it was such a beautiful number."

Robbins explained his approach to the show's particular brand of madcap, nostalgia comedy and period dances, saying, "First, I had to get the style and then I had to distort it. If I had done it exactly as it had been done, then it might look tame, might even be boring. It's like furniture. You don't furnish your home exactly as the Victorians did, for instance. You combine it with modern stuff to spike it up and give it emphasis. . . . I had to make a comment on those dances, relate them to modern times, give them some punch that we would understand and make points about certain things. Otherwise, they wouldn't seem funny. The costumes of *High Button Shoes* are a good example— they're authentic, but they are also exaggerated in order to bring out a point." The exaggeration of the costume designs was not accomplished without struggle. Designer Miles White recalled that Robbins was "a terror as always. . . . We'd finally get to dress rehearsal and he'd tear up costumes or rip things off or change them around. . . . Jerry was a very witty, sweet person socially, but working with him was just hell."

The show was a tailor-made vehicle for comedian Silvers, who played the smarmy con man, Harrison Floy (before going on to Sgt. Bilko in the television series *You'll Never Get Rich*). The plot tracked the shenanigans of Floy and his sidekick-shill, Mr. Pontdue, performed by Silver's fellow burlesque comic, Joey Faye, as they set up a phony real-estate deal in the suburban college town of New Brunswick. An offstage Rutgers-Princeton football game served as a backdrop for one of the scenes, with Floy wagering against Rutgers and then trying to collect on his bet by maiming the team's quarterback during halftime. There was to be plenty of Americana in the confection, from a vintage Model T Ford to a pastorale of lady bird-watchers. The crooks would carry out their nefarious real-estate scheme at the expense of the Longstreet family, loosely based on the characters in Stephen Longstreet's book. The mother, Sara Longstreet, was a twenty-five-year-old Fabray, and the father, Henry Longstreet, was played by veteran Broadway actor Jack McCauley, who was in reality more than twenty years older than his ingenue "wife."

For Fabray, the role of Mama Longstreet was an opportunity to stretch her talents and break out of the ingenue mold. The actress appreciated Robbins' complexities as an artist and treasured her experience working with him. "The thing that I really loved about Jerry was if you did the best you could, then he was one hundred and one percent for you, and he knew what your limitations were. . . . I was a good dancer, but I wasn't a marvelous dancer like the other cast members. I did the best I could and so he was very gentle and very kind to me—not because I was a leading lady but because of my efforts. He was not kind to Phil because Phil used his voice as an excuse. Phil was always looking for some excuse for why he couldn't sing well today or he couldn't do this. He was very insecure and Jerry was very hard on him.

"One clue as to the genius of Jerry and how secure he was in his talent was that he wasn't afraid to admit that he didn't know something. For instance, the big hit song of the show, 'Poppa, Won't You Dance with Me?' was not supposed to be a polka—it was a Castle Walk. . . . In the song they say, "I love the polka" [and] we did the polka at the end of the dance. . . . But Jerry said it had to be a Castle Walk, and he said, 'I don't know anything about it.' So he found the three surviving teams that knew how to do the Castle Walk that were left alive. And [he] brought them in and paid them to teach him everything about what the Castle Walk looked like. . . . We learned that with the Castle Walk, when a woman has her hands on the man's arm and shoulder, you don't put your hand on his shoulder, you put the *back* of your hand on his shoulder; you don't put your hand on his hand, you put your hand on his sleeve. In other words, you don't touch skin to skin—[it's] very delicate, you keep a distance and it's mostly feet. And we discovered that you bow quite formally, like the old Edwardian bows were. In the dance, you didn't jiggle the body, you bowed and moved formally. This is what the Castle Walk was . . . a formal dance between the Edwardian period and the turn of the century. More daring dances like the polka and things like that were more loose-bodied. My God, in the waltz, you *touched* each other. But this was Jerry's concept, that it was to have that elegant walk, and that is what he did for [the number].

"Once I sang the song 'Poppa, Won't You Dance with Me?' and sat on his lap, and got him to stand up. And Jerry says, 'And then what? Once you've got him to dance, what do you do with it? . . . Well, we'll do the Castle Walk, but we'll do one chorus of it, and then you both sit down and that's the end of the number'—because the number was written for a [picnic] scene at this place out in the woods. [It] was just a little song meant to have everybody stand around and watch us . . . and then Phil would go into his big number . . . Well, 'Poppa, Won't You Dance with Me?' stopped the show cold. We had no encores, no nothing. Phil came on and started to try to do his number and had to back off the stage. Jerry and Sammy went out into the lobby and said we have to work on another chorus on this, we have to do something else. The next day, we came in and rehearsed encores to do with the show. That's the way things worked in those days, you could just go out in the hall, go into the ladies' room, or the men's room, and invent another chorus."

Jule Styne remembered that working for both Robbins and Abbott was a daunting experience. "Not so much physically, but in terms of their personalities, I felt like a grape between two pieces of steel. Both Abbott and Robbins could chill you with a single look." According to Styne, there were several dances, including the polka and a soft-shoe routine ("I Still Get Jealous"), that Robbins delayed working on until Abbott goaded him by having another choreographer, Sammy White, initially set the numbers. Helen Gallagher recalled that Robbins kept putting off the tango that he was to stage for her and Paul Godkin. "Jerry wasn't that interested in doing that tango. It was cut and then finally had to go back in for some reason. And Abbott came up from the bowels of the theater where he was rehearsing and said, 'Jerry, have you finished that number yet?' And Jerry said, 'No, I haven't had time.' Abbott said, 'Well, you better put it in because it goes in tonight, and if you don't do it, I'll do it.' That's the way Abbott handled everything. He didn't brook any disagreement or anything like that. . . . very authoritarian. He'd listen to anybody—he'd listen to a chorus person for an idea—but he made the decisions."

The show opened in Philadelphia to lackluster reviews, though it played to sold-out houses. One critic panned the book and suggested, "Substitution of more spontaneous and funnier material, rather than cutting, is the need." Silvers despaired that reports from Philadelphia predicted a flop: "The word on our show flew around New York—*High Button Shoes* is sick." The show was indeed in trouble, but the three-week Philadelphia run gave Abbott and Robbins time to make adjustments and allowed Silvers to bring his antic burlesque style into his role as pitchman. "I informed Mr. Abbott that I would be ad-libbing from now on," the comedian recalled, "but always within the context of the story and the period. He gave me his blessing. And Jerry Robbins joined me in revising and changing the scenes." Arthur Partington, who danced in several Abbott-Robbins musicals, recalled, "They just built the whole show out of town. *High Button Shoes* was a big surprise to everybody because it was a completely different show than we went out of town with."

The musical opened on Broadway on October 9, 1947, and most of the critics heaped accolades on Robbins' choreography and Fabray's performance. Richard Watts, Jr., wrote in the *Post*, "I hasten to report that the hero of the evening is Jerome Robbins. . . . There is more humor and unconventional inventiveness and less stuffiness in Mr. Robbins than in most directors of the pirouette. . . ." In the *Daily News*, John Chapman declared, "It is a Jerome Robbins night. . . ." *Time* magazine called his "Mack Sennett Ballet" "a masterpiece of controlled pandemonium," and Louis Kronenberger deemed it "one of the comic glories of the age."

Regarding the musical as a whole, however, there were a number of critics who had serious reservations. Even Kronenberger suggested, "What I think *High Button Shoes* most needed was more time, rather than more talent: some things in it are straight-out lousy, but others look as if they just weren't allowed to come to a boil . . . but the show's worth seeing." Fabray explained how the show survived: "We got very mixed reviews, but in those days you could cheat [with the ads]. You could say, 'I loved the show,' and not add on, '. . . . but it really didn't work.' You could just say, 'I loved the show,' and use that quote. You can't do that anymore with reviews. So they did this big ad about Jerome Robbins' ballet and we played to half-empty houses the first three months, until word of mouth got around and it caught on, and then it became a big hit."

High Button Shoes ran 727 performances over the next two years, moving to the Shubert Theatre and finally closing July 2, 1949, outlasting Rodgers and Hammerstein's *Allegro*, which had opened the same week. For Robbins, who would win his second Donaldson and first Tony on this outing, the dance highlight of the show that was his personal favorite was not the pyrotechnical "Mack Sennett Ballet," but the whimsical picnic interlude, with its sentimental depiction of a young man losing at love. "Everyone has had a beautiful girl sometime or other and been turned down by her," said Robbins, while the show was still running. "It's an experience, a familiar one. Perhaps if it hasn't been a girl, it's been something very lovely he has wanted very much and wasn't able to have. . . . What I'm driving at is the 'Picnic Ballet' is a number that everyone understands because they've experienced the same thing. It's real. It has meaning."

Robbins' grasp of such poignant universals informed his vision as a dramatist as well as a choreographer, and established the crucial emotional link to his audience that he would maintain throughout his career. As Abbott's wunderkind protégé, Jerry possessed ambition in the theater that already transcended the making of dances. On the heels of his Broadway success, he told the press, "I haven't found my right forte. I'm now typecast as a comic choreographer. But I want to try serious ballet. And I want to act and direct. Right now, I'm studying over at Elia Kazan's acting school. I'm not going to let success go to *my* head. Not me."

FOUR

Are You Now or
Have You Ever Been?

In May 1946, Robbins had moved from Greenwich Village to a four-flight walk-up apartment at 421 Park Avenue on the corner of Fifty-fifth Street, previously the home of photographer Georges Platt Lynes. Jerry would reside in this five-room flat through the next decade. His Broadway success gave him six-figure contracts and a steady flow of royalties, yet he was neither extravagant nor ostentatious in his lifestyle. The Depression years had inspired a steadfast frugality and he allowed himself few indulgences. He decorated with Victorian antiques, hired a maid named Murtie and acquired a Brussels griffon—"Jerry was an intense dog-lover," said Bob Silverman. The producers of *High Button Shoes*, Proser and Kipness, expressed their gratitude to Jerry with gifts that included a baby grand piano and a cream-colored 1947 Dodge. According to his friend Robert Tucker, Jerry exhibited the same aggressive attitude behind the wheel of his car as he did in the dance studio. "He was a maniac driver," said Tucker. "One of those, if there was bad traffic, he would drive on the shoulder. Then he'd waltz the car down the road in time to the music."

One of Jerry's neighbors on East Fifty-fifth Street and a fellow student at the Actors Studio was Montgomery Clift. The actor was two years younger than Robbins and had already established himself on the New York stage, having won acclaim in such plays as Thornton Wilder's *Our Town* and *The Skin of Our Teeth*, Lillian Hellman's *The Searching Wind*, and Tennessee Williams' *You Touched Me!* In their youth, Monty and Jerry shared a certain wildness of spirit and all-consuming love for the theater. Later, of course, Clift would be remembered as the smoldering screen idol who suffered a disfiguring car accident in 1956 and died tragically ten years later at the age of forty-five. Clift's acting coach and close friend, Russian émigré Mira Rostova, recalled that she and Monty sometimes met Jerry on the street when he was walking his dog. Rostova was jealously protective of Clift and apparently unaware of the emotional attachment that developed between Monty and Jerry. "They were acquaintances," said Rostova. "I don't know how friendly they were."

In fact, they were more than friendly, as Clift's biographer Patricia Bosworth discovered when researching her book about the ill-fated star. Bosworth attempted to interview Robbins about Clift, but found that Jerry was extremely guarded on the subject. "He didn't want to get into it at all," said Bosworth. She subsequently refrained from naming Robbins as Clift's lover when the biography was published in 1978. Instead, she wrote cryptically about the furtive life that Monty shared with a certain choreographer. "For Monty . . . his sexual ambiguity was a private torture. He lived in New York between pictures so he could conduct his complicated private life without too much publicity. . . . He always made it clear to reporters that he disliked discussing romance: 'I have no time—no time!' . . . For the record, he was dating Terry Moore; for the record, he escorted Mira Rostova to parties and dinners. Off the record, he had been until recently emotionally committed to a Broadway choreographer—a 'theatrical genius,' Monty called him early in their affair."

With a memory vague on details, Rostova recently recalled that she and Monty attended a dinner party together at Jerry's apartment. Bosworth described how that evening came about just after Monty's friendly competition, a young Marlon Brando, opened in *A Streetcar Named Desire* in 1947. "Mira Rostova confided in Monty that she wanted to meet him [Brando], but she was too shy to go backstage. She talked about Brando so much that Monty finally arranged to have Jerry Robbins give a dinner at his apartment, to which

Brando and Mira were both invited." According to another Clift biographer, Robert La Guardia, Brando and Clift "kept their distance at first" that evening but eventually left Jerry's party together. "Marlon walked up to Monty and asked him if he would like to go for a ride on his motorcycle. It was the big happening of the party. As they zoomed off together, Jerome Robbins half-jested to the others, 'If anything happens to them, we've just lost the shining lights of the American theater.'"

All three shining lights—Brando, Clift and Robbins—joined the Actors Studio and attended its first classes, along with such talents as Maureen Stapleton, Julie Harris, Kevin McCarthy, Tom Ewell, Eli Wallach, E. G. Marshall, David Wayne, Patricia Neal, Karl Malden, Lois Wheeler and Sidney Lumet. Dedicated to Stanislavski's system, the studio was founded by Group Theatre veterans Elia Kazan, Robert Lewis and Cheryl Crawford. Robbins, Brando and Clift took class three times a week with Bobby Lewis, first at an abandoned church on West Forty-eighth Street, and later at 1697 Broadway in the heart of the theater district. Stressing Stanislavski's inner psychological approach to acting, teachers like Kazan, Lewis and later Lee Strasberg each offered various, sometimes conflicting interpretations of Stanislavski's training techniques. In his memoir, *Slings and Arrows*, Lewis described how his classes differed from those being taught by Kazan, who went by the nickname Gadget or Gadge: "Gadget concentrated on technique exercises with his group: sensory recall, imagination, improvisation, etc. I delivered the downbeat of my class with a talk on the nature and importance of Intention. Scenes were then chosen. We analyzed the complete plays, described the character elements of the parts being studied, broke down the chosen scenes into sections, and staged them."

Lewis had great reservations about Lee Strasberg's doctrinaire codification of the so-called Method, especially the particular emphasis that Strasberg placed on concepts such as Sense Memory and Private Moments. These were exercises aimed at releasing the actor's emotions, often by having him conjure deeply felt personal memories. To Lewis' way of thinking, this type of work only enabled an actor to portray various versions of himself rather than the character. Similar criticisms were voiced by Clift. Robbins may have been sympathetic privately, but over the years he stayed clear of the factional disputes between Stanislavski's exponents and maintained friendly associations with both Lewis and Strasberg. According to many performers and directors who worked with Jerry, he was fascinated by Stanislavski's system, as he struggled with varying degrees of success to find an effective language for communicating his vision to actors as well as to dancers.

Lewis recalled Jerry's earliest work in class: "Jerry's performing experience was rooted in a sense of form. He was a superb young dancer, now wishing to explore what the difference was in the source of expression for acting as opposed to dancing. We chose a completely realistic scene for him from Odets' *Waiting for Lefty*, with Jerry playing the young Jewish intern, a victim of anti-Semitism in a large hospital. I still remember the look on the future choreographer's face when, in my critical remarks after the scene, I complained that, fine as his emotional quality was, his physical movement was a bit awkward." Evidently, Robbins was able to accept such criticism without taking it personally, unlike some of the performers on the receiving end of his own more harshly critical barbs.

After Lewis had a falling-out with Kazan in 1948, he withdrew from Actors Studio and his class was taken over by David Pressman. Pressman recalled, "I do remember that Jerry did some wonderful exercises, strictly acting exercises, because he was so interested in the class as related to his choreography. . . . [In one exercise] he gave himself a problem—that he had to reach the other side of the stage and the place was full of water. . . . He did an improvisation—he built himself a bridge. This was more than fifty years ago, but I do remember his intensity and how he did it with such high quality. . . . The acting of it was quite remarkable."

Like others in the early Actors Studio classes, neither Maureen Stapleton nor Patricia Neal recalled being aware of any special relationship between Jerry and Monty. Monty's longtime friend Kevin McCarthy said that he was unaware of Clift's borderline sexuality for many years. Brando stated in his memoir that he never knew about the gay side of Clift's lifestyle. "I do know," said Brando, "he carried around a heavy emotional burden and never learned how to bear it." At one point, Brando encouraged Clift to go into therapy to deal with his increasingly obvious problems with alcohol and drugs. Like most heterosexual friends and colleagues, Brando, too, was evidently unaware of Monty's ongoing affair with Jerry. Cris Alexander once saw them together holding hands in Central Park, but such overt displays of affection were rare indeed in their closeted world. Richard D'Arcy knew about the relationship and remembered, "It got to the point where [Monty] was often there with Jerry, and he was rather strange. He always stood in the shadows. You'd be at a party and he would not be in the middle of it. He'd be in the hallway, in very dark areas."

At times Clift would appear on the scene falling-down drunk, and some believe that Monty's lurid excesses reinforced Jerry's instincts toward self-control. In these early years, neither risked frequenting the city's gay cruising scenes. As highly visible Manhattan celebrities, they were under the scrutiny of gossip columnists like Hedda Hopper, Walter Winchell, Ed Sullivan and Dorothy Kilgallen. But Monty would eventually become quite reckless about public exposure with his excursions into the Lower East Side bathhouses and the uptown gay bars near Third Avenue—which were known as the "bird-circuit," with names like the Blue Parrot, the Golden Pheasant and the Swan. D'Arcy recalled that Jerry usually avoided the bars, but found himself pulled into the volatile social world that Monty shared with torch singer Libby Holman. While not a trained actress, Holman had appeared with Clift in Robert Lewis' production of *Mexican Mural* in 1942. She was a perpetually tan and emaciated femme fatale with a fondness for Jungle Gardenia perfume, amphetamines and marijuana. A decade earlier, she had been charged with the murder of her husband, Zachary Smith Reynolds, an heir to the tobacco fortune. Though the charges against her were dropped for lack of evidence, Libby never escaped the haunting stigma of her dark past, which was undoubtedly part of the fascination for Clift.

"Monty was a very confused person himself, extremely so," said D'Arcy. "Then he got hold of Libby. . . . He was great friends with her. It was a disaster. She was the hard-luck girl. Everything happened to her. . . . Everything she touched was a tragedy." D'Arcy's companion, Oliver Smith, was one who privately disapproved of Monty, especially when the actor was in the presence of Holman, who for a time also lured Smith's cousin, Paul Bowles, into her web.

Smith said simply, "Monty acted like a spoiled brat around Libby—I couldn't stand him."

Like Jerry, Monty cultivated brief, yet often extravagant passions for men and women. Clift once said to his friend, Bill Le Massena, "I love men in bed, but I really love women." Rostova explained to Bosworth, "Monty was totally split sexually. . . . That was the core of his tragedy, because he never stopped being conflicted and he never stopped feeling guilty about being conflicted. . . . He wanted to have a lasting relationship with someone . . . but he was unable to." As Monty slipped more and more under the sway of self-destructive demons, Jerry appears to have played the role of caretaker, nursing his friend through bouts of dissipation. Ina Kurland recalled, "The Monty Clift thing—I was supposed to have dinner with him [Jerry] at his apartment, and he called me and had to break it off because he said a friend of his was there and was very sick. And it turned out to be Montgomery Clift." While unaware of the Robbins-Clift romance, Bob Silverman recalled seeing Monty at Jerry's apartment on occasion and was struck by the physical resemblance. "Jerry looked like Montgomery Clift and also like Richard Avedon and me. We were all small, dark and thin in those days. We all could have been brothers. It was just a physicality thing, but it almost bordered on more than coincidental."

Clift was about to make the transition to Hollywood with his first movie roles in *The Search* and *Red River*. During this period, he may have contributed to the genesis of Robbins' future collaboration on *West Side Story*. Although the story is denied by Rostova, Monty was apparently working on a scene from *Romeo and Juliet* and discussed the play with Jerry. At some point, the two came up with the idea of interpreting Shakespeare's tale in modern terms. Most likely at this stage, the story would have taken the form of Jewish-Catholic strife, as it had in the improvisation that Jerry worked on with Janet Reed and Mary Hunter. In 1984, Robbins told John Percival of the *London Times*, "It began because Montgomery Clift, who was a friend of mine, was going to play Romeo. He said to me, "I don't know how to play that character, he's so passive." That made me read the play again, and I was wondering how I would try to make him interesting. Trying to relate him to something in life today, the idea came to me of a *Romeo and Juliet* among the gangs of New York. Originally, it was to be set on the Lower East Side, among the Italians and Irish, and while we were working on it, things suddenly blew up in the city, and my collaborators Arthur Laurents and Leonard Bernstein had the idea to change it to the Puerto Ricans on the West Side."

Russ Tamblyn, who played Riff in the *West Side Story* film, remembered Jerry reminiscing about Monty when the movie was being made. "I was on the set one day," said Tamblyn, "and we were on a break and sitting around the piano. Jerry told us then, he told several people including myself, that Montgomery Clift—and he could have made this up—but he said that actually the original idea came from Monty Clift . . . at a party on Fire Island. Jerry said, 'It was such a simple concept.' I remember he used the word *concept* because I was thinking at the time that that's what Jerry got billing for, was *conceived* by. I remember him using that word, that Monty came up with this really simple concept, which was *Romeo and Juliet* as a musical but with gangs."

There is some disagreement as to whether Monty gave the idea to Jerry or vice versa, and Rostova claims that Monty never actually worked on the role of Romeo. "As far as Shakespeare goes," said Rostova, "Monty always thought he might work on Hamlet, but never on Romeo. And he never got around to Hamlet." Likewise, David Pressman had no recollection of Clift working on Romeo at Actors Studio. Still, Jerry confirmed to Leonard Bernstein's biographer Humphrey Burton that "Robbins' idea had been born when he was asked by his friend Montgomery Clift for guidance in playing Romeo in a contemporary way." As Robbins indicated to John Percival, the first incarnation of the project would appear in 1949 under the title *East Side Story*, and the plot involved an Easter-Passover conflict between Jewish and Irish families in New York City's slums—Romeo was Catholic, and Juliet was Jewish.

Monty and Jerry remained passionately involved at least until Clift went to Arizona to film *Red River* during the summer of 1947. In Monty's absence, Jerry again tried to act on his analyst's advice to pursue a lasting relationship with a woman, and once again, a triangle played itself out in the manner of his *Facsimile* psychodrama.

Jerry met Rose Tobias at a benefit for Spanish war relief that he attended with his sister at the Belasco Theatre. Sonia recalled that, from their seats, Jerry spotted a young beauty with long blond hair and announced that he simply had to meet her. Rose was an aspiring Jewish actress from the Bronx who later became a highly successful casting director. A whirlwind courtship ensued, and the couple spent the July Fourth weekend together at a Fire Island beach house shared with Gerald Kabat, an accountant who specialized in clients from the entertainment field. Kabat recalled that Jerry "just came for that weekend with Rose. And I remember it very clearly, because my sister-in-law got an asthma attack from sleeping on a dusty mattress that we pulled out of the closet, and she had to go to the beach at four in the morning to get rid of the asthma. I remember his sister came out to the beach, too. Jesus Christ, how do I remember that from fifty-two years ago? She came out there because he had told her about it, and Sonia came over to our house because she knew Rosie. Nobody thought of Jerry Robbins as being gay then. After all, he was Rosie's sort of boyfriend."

In time there was talk of marriage and children and at least an informal engagement. During the period that he was working on *High Button Shoes*, Jerry brought Rose out to Weehawken to meet his family. "He was going to marry her," said Arthur Partington, "but apparently he didn't." According to Sonia, Jerry never gave any of his fiancées engagement rings, an indication through the years that he was by nature unable to commit himself fully to the matrimonial path, even as he came closer and closer to taking the plunge. He planned to use his mother's treasured ring when he found the right partner, but the ring would remain under wraps as a family keepsake for more than fifty years. Dancer Mimi Gomber speculated, "The sexuality was never worked out at all. I don't think Jerry could ever give enough of himself to any relationship. I just don't feel Jerry had enough to give to another person where he would ever pin himself down and make a commitment of any kind. I think it was important for him to have relationships. He probably wanted it more than the people he became involved with because they had the capacity to give more."

Later in the year, Jerry asked Rose to live with him at his Park Avenue apartment and she moved in with the expectation of marriage at some point in the uncertain future. This domestic arrangement was to be short-lived. At the time, photographer Arnold Newman had been courting his future wife, Augusta Rubenstein, who moved into the bedroom that Rose had vacated in a West Forty-seventh Street apartment shared by several roommates. Newman recalled that soon after moving out to live with Jerry, Rose asked to move back, explaining to her roommates that things had not worked out.

In a recent letter, Rose recounted the story that she confided to her friends. "One night we [Jerry and I] were woken up by the bell and someone calling his name from the street. I think it must have been three or four a.m. It was a drunken Monty Clift, crying and vomiting. Then it all came out. He was devastated when Monty went to Hollywood, and his lady psychiatrist told him to find the most feminine woman/girl, and start a relationship, and I was it. . . . He desperately wanted to marry and have a family, he hated being homosexual. I may not have known at that time what I wanted out of life or a man, but I knew it was not a bisexual and certainly not a homosexual. My last words to him, before I left, were that he should be grateful that he's not a clerk at Lord and Taylor, that in his profession no one really cared about his sex life." Rose added, "He did love me in his way, and he was my first love."

Newman speculated about the breakup: "My impression was that Jerry really couldn't face living with a woman, and he would wander the streets at night. . . . That's why she [Rose] came home. She realized it wouldn't work out. . . . Monty coming in at that point probably was the trigger. She probably was getting rather frantic at that point." The following year, Jerry gave an interview to *The Boston Post,* which reported, "Lucky as Robbins has been in the theatre, he hasn't fared so well in love. Recently, he and his fiancée by mutual consent broke their engagement. Robbins is no heartsick swain, however. He is very sensible about the whole thing. 'It hurt for a while,' he admitted, 'but we both knew it was the best thing.' This turn of affairs leaves Jerry in a vulnerable spot. Good-looking, wealthy, successful and still a bachelor!"

The romance with Clift cooled as well, but their friendship continued until 1953, when Jerry testified before HUAC, at which point Monty told his brother, Brooks, that he had "lost all respect" for Robbins. Nevertheless, in 1966, Robbins attended the funeral services for Clift at St. James Episcopal Church. The actor had succumbed to heart failure. A select group of one hundred fifty were invited to pay their respects. Although other mutual friends like Nancy Walker and Lauren Bacall appeared among the mourners, Jerry reportedly sat alone. Years later, Robbins was said to have been discomfited

when one of his dancers innocently suggested to him that his gestures and facial expressions sometimes resembled those of Monty Clift.

In December 1947, during rehearsals for his Broadway musical, *Look, Ma, I'm
Dancin'!*, Robbins gave an interview in his Park Avenue apartment to Selma
Robinson of *PM*. Robinson noted that the living-room wallpaper was "dark
bottle-green, with carpet to match" and pointed out a "curious coffee table
made of driftwood with a glass top." The flat was full of nooks and alcoves.
One living-room wall was covered with photographs, and opposite, large windows overlooked the avenue. Jerry's mother was present at the beginning of
the interview and was described as "a warm, dignified woman in her fifties,
whose face ran over with pride when she chatted for a moment about Jerry."
Lena admitted that she had never expected her son to become a dancer—"a
pianist, maybe, but never a choreographer." As his mother excused herself to
"straighten up" and make tea, Jerry complained about the hours he was spend-
ing in the theater: "I'm away from home so much, now that I'm working so
hard on the show, I like to come back just to see if the living room is still
where I remember it."

As was typical of Robbins during interviews, he steered the conversation
toward work and away from personal matters, while admitting to the journalist that his new show was based on an original idea and suggested that it was
somewhat autobiographical. "The basic idea," said Jerry, "was to show a ballet company on tour. That opening scene is Grand Central Station with the
company just getting back to start another tour. There'll be railroad stations,
stage-door alleys, hotel rooms—really one big railroad station, hotel room
and alley-way all across the country, whether the name is Joplin or Des Moines
or Amarillo. The production is full of dances but there are only two large production numbers—don't call them ballets or you'll scare the critics.

"The gimmick is that these ballets are not just ballets," Robbins continued. "They grow out of the hero's personality and in that way they develop
the story. That first one is a kind of *Hellzapoppin* version of the ballet because
the hero at that time is a brash show-off, fresh out of vaudeville, and it's hectic because he has a need for success at any cost. He has put into it everything

he has learned on the borscht circuit. By the end of the second act, after he has had a chance to reexamine himself and his relationship to people, he does quite a different kind of ballet, more thoughtful and human."

With *Look, Ma, I'm Dancin'!*, Jerry created a revealing caricature of himself in the character of Eddie Winkler, for whom love was to teach a lesson in humility. Although the book was written by Jerome Lawrence and Robert E. Lee, Robbins provided many of the details for the characters and plot. Jerry wrote in his scenario, "This is a ballet about the yearnings and hopes and dreams of teenage kids, about all the things that combine to make a boy like Eddie obsessed with a desire for success . . . it's a commentary on the Sad Generation. It's the feeling, the music, the tempo of the kids who grew up in the Twenties and Thirties, and are becoming men and women in the Forties." According to Robbins, the generation of "war babies" who grew up between the Depression and World War II suffered through adversities that wounded them psychologically. "That's what makes Eddie seem obnoxious sometimes," Robbins explained in an interview. "He's got a feeling that he simply has to be a big success to make up for it."

The role of Eddie was performed by Harold Lang, who was romantically linked at the time to the show's female star, Nancy Walker. The comedienne, later known as Ida Morgenstern on *The Mary Tyler Moore Show* and *Rhoda*, played Lily Malloy, the daughter of a Milwaukee brewery tycoon who pays for the ballet troupe and insists on dancing in spite of her limited talent. This was Robbins' tongue-in-cheek sendup of Lucia Chase, and he included a Hurok-like impresario in the story as well. Hugh Martin contributed an uneven score, reaching its high points with his choral rendering of "Jazz" and his near-hit for Walker, "I'm Tired of Texas." The concept gave Robbins plenty of room to burlesque the world of classical ballet and to bring in dances like the Irish jig, the conga, the waltz and the square dance. Not only was he choreographing the show, he was now co-directing with George Abbott, who also produced. Robbins again hired Gluck Sandor to assist him, but Sandor squabbled with Abbott early on and was replaced by June Graham.

Abbott remembered, "Jerry started his dance rehearsals two weeks earlier than the rest of us in order to perfect a rather spectacular ballet he had planned. I kept away from these because I know from my own experience that it is no fun to have someone peering over your shoulder critically when you are in the formative stages of your work. But I kept getting word from my stage manager that progress seemed to be slow. One Sunday I was out in the country when a message came that Jerry wanted to see me immediately. I rushed into town, and he asked me to look at what he had done. It was not good; he knew it and he wanted to have it verified. We immediately jettisoned the whole ballet, and he started a new one. His two weeks' work later became a little fragment used as atmosphere in another scene. The best dance which Jerry did for this show was conceived and executed in two days while we were on the road. It was the 'Sleepwalker's Ballet,' and it required a lot of unusual techniques from the dancers because they had to stand erect on each other's shoulders and be carried around as though in a trance." For this scene, also called "The Pajama Dance," Jerry was drawing from memories of his Ballet Theatre tours as he depicted flirtatious, sleep-walking couples roaming from berth to berth in a Pullman sleeping car.

Full rehearsals commenced in mid-November. Richard D'Arcy recalled that he and Forrest Bonshire came up with a nickname for Jerry inspired by his black hair and dark eyes. "We used to call him the Crow, and when he lived on Park Avenue, we referred to it [his apartment] as the Crow's Nest. We'd say, 'There's a party at the Crow's Nest tonight.' " The dancers in the cast devised a signal to warn each other when Jerry came into the theater. Ninette Charisse, whose husband, Robert "Bobby" Tucker, danced in the show, remembered, "You know, Jerry was very stern. Sometimes the kids would [flap] their arms and say, 'The Black Crow's out there!' That was the sign." According to dancer Dody Goodman, the warning adopted by dancers in the next several Robbins musicals was "The Crow Flies!"

With his recent Stanislavski training in mind, Jerry tried to instill in his cast the cutthroat competitive attitude that he saw in the ballet world. D'Arcy recalled how the gypsy dancers in the musical resisted this type of manipulation. "He went at dance almost as if you were at the Actors Studio, that type of approach. . . . Jerry would like to create friction between the dancers— competition, I should say. Being from a ballet company, this is what ballet companies were about. . . . But these dancers all respected each other, and we were all different; so we'd just look and no one would compete. You'd realize you couldn't be the other person, they couldn't be you, so it just wouldn't work in that show. He thought that created a spark somehow if people tried to beat each other."

Robbins sometimes allowed his personal feelings to show in playing favorites with the dancers. He offered encouragement over the years to his friend Robert Tucker. Tucker's wife, Ninette Charisse, remembered her husband breaking his ankle when *Look, Ma, I'm Dancin'!* traveled out of town. "Jerry was very inspired when he did choreography," said Charisse, "and didn't think about the dancers that much sometimes. The curtain opened and Bob was in practice clothes sitting on the piano. Then he got off the piano and had to do twenty [*sissonnes*] cold. Then he ran and jumped over a wardrobe trunk and that did it." Tucker added, "And down I went. We were in Boston, and we'd been rehearsing all day and then doing the show at night so I was very tired." Richard D'Arcy recalled coming to Tucker's aid, only to be berated by the choreographer. "I picked him up and took him off the stage, and laid him out," said D'Arcy. "Jerry came walking out very upset and shouted, 'This should have happened to you. It should have been you!' I said, 'That's ridiculous,' but that's the way he was. He and Bobby [Tucker] were close then."

With his friends from Ballet Theatre, Janet Reed and Harold Lang, Robbins staged the *pas de deux* from the second act of *Swan Lake* in the second act of the musical. Reed played Ann Bruce, a chorus girl smitten with Jerry's ambitious alter ego, Eddie. Robbins encouraged Reed and Lang to improvise and invent dialogue for their scene. "I was not too happy with my part in the show," explained Reed, "but it was interesting work, as usual. . . . The scene takes place in the basement underneath the stage, and you hear the orchestra playing *Swan Lake* and you know the performance is going on up on stage. And down in the basement the girl and the aspiring choreographer are doing the *pas de deux* in practice clothes, and they're having dialogue about their feelings for each other. We improvised that completely . . . and Jerry had the writers put it in [the script]. It was a great way of working."

Look, Ma, I'm Dancin'! opened at the Adelphi Theatre on January 29, 1948. With its flimsy book and lackluster score, the show received mixed reviews, yet managed to limp through a run of almost six months. Brooks Atkinson writing in the *New York Times* called it "a good knockabout musical comedy," while

Louis Kronenberger in *PM* described it as "a fine might-have-been; possibly even a fine should-have-been. . . . But it's not a good show." The day after the opening, Robbins said of the critics, "They don't seem to agree about the show, but they're awful nice to me." Robbins' choreography was such a dominant element on the stage that some reviewers called this musical a "dansical." Nancy Walker's performance stole the show, but she was sidelined due to illness during much of the run, limiting its potential success.

According to Abbott, "It was almost a great show—but not quite. I don't think I can remember a funnier entrance than Nancy Walker coming down the New York Central platform with a gigantic wolfhound as tall as she was. My combination gardener and chauffeur, Lawrence Larry, had a chance to go on the stage as a redcap, and he was put in charge of the dog. One night, out of kindness, one of the stagehands brought the wolfhound a bone. When the time came for his entrance, the wolfhound didn't want to leave his bone; he became ferocious, and for a time it looked as though the dog would lose his entrance and the redcap would lose an arm. But Larry had a great way with animals, and he was able to drag the beast onstage just at the last minute, though the audience may have wondered why the dog was looking so longingly offstage right."

During the run, frictions between Robbins and the cast took a comic turn. Richard D'Arcy recalled, "He had been rather mean at rehearsals. So we all went up to the dressing room—the dressing room was across the alley and upstairs. We got up there and we decided to have a voodoo session and get Mr. Robbins. So we started with this voodoo. Forrest Bonshire had finger paint on the mirror, [as if] splashing 'blood' on it. I was in my dance belt and beating my side, and we were beating the tables in this rhythm, and everyone was going, 'Burst-ing appen-dix, burst-ing appen-dix!' Well, suddenly everything went out from underneath and [our voices] diminished until there was nothing happening—there was Jerry in the doorway. He had a great sense of humor. He just looked and said, 'Bread and water from now on!' But he was carried away the next day with appendicitis. [He] had an operation, yes."

Ina Kurland also remembered the appendicitis attack and explained, "They must have seen something coming on, because he wasn't feeling too good." She added that she did not lend her support to the voodoo ceremony.

"I was yelling at everybody. They knew how I felt [about Jerry]. In fact, I took care of Jerry's dog when he went into the hospital. Oh yeah, I was so upset."

After Robbins was released from the hospital, D'Arcy recalled, "He sent Forrest Bonshire a huge box of black candles with a note saying, 'Thought you might be running out of these.'" For Jerry's thirtieth birthday later that year, D'Arcy and Bonshire hunted for a special gift. "We found this antique, white snow owl in a glass dome. We figured it was very beautiful, it would fit in his apartment, a great gift. He hit the ceiling. For some reason it had some con-notation—I don't know what got into his mind. He said, 'How dare you give me this!' He saw some psychological meaning in this bird. He hated it."

R obbins' track record on the four shows that he had choreographed and his recent co-directing credit earned him the opportunity in the summer of 1948 to direct his first musical. Entitled *That's the Ticket*, the show was co-produced by Jerry's old friend Joe Kipness, the "gangland" impresario from *High Button Shoes*. Robbins defined his role strictly as director and hired Paul Godkin to choreograph. Oliver Smith designed the sets. The score was composed by Harold Rome, and the book was written by Julius and Philip Epstein.

The script was an outlandish political satire about a right-wing third party and a Presidential candidate recruited from a pond in Central Park—"Alfred the Average" was a character from the Middle Ages who had been turned into a frog by a medieval witch and, according to the authors, returned to human form in time for the national election. The political concept may have held some ironic appeal for Jerry, as he was supporting the campaign of the left-leaning third-party candidate, Henry A. Wallace, the former Vice President whose Progressive ticket was also supported by the Communist Party. In April, the *Daily Worker* reported that Robbins contributed material to a political cabaret show called *Show Time for Wallace.* Other participants included composer Marc Blitzstein, playwrights Jerome Chodorov and John Latouche, actor Jack Gilford, folksinger Pete Seeger and Robbins' collaborator on his new musical, Harold Rome. If Jerry thought political satire would find a re-ceptive audience on Broadway during an election year, he would soon change his mind.

That's the Ticket would be tested out of town, and Robbins' contract gave him approval on its anticipated Broadway run. The role of Alfred the Average was performed by Leif Erickson, who was joined in the cast by Jack Carter, Edna Skinner, Loring Smith, George Irving and newcomer Kaye Ballard. This was Ballard's first break in the theater, and she remembered, "That was his first directing job, and we both weren't ready for it. He wasn't ready to direct and I wasn't ready to star in a show. . . . I played Marsha LaRue, who was a sexpot. At the time I didn't even know what a proscenium was. I had no business being there. I had a raw talent that they saw, but I had never been in a show. [Jerry] would say, 'Keep your hands off the proscenium,' and I'd say to Maureen Stapleton who had come to watch me rehearse, 'Maureen, what is a proscenium?' I adored him [Jerry], but that's how I hurt my knee forever, you know, doing that show, because he would have me do a knee drop . . . and I was so young and stupid. He didn't say, 'Put on knee pads,' but I did adore him anyway. I thought he was the sexiest man I've ever seen. He had gorgeous legs."

Ballard continued, "I sang a song called 'Take Off the Coat.' Really it stopped the show. I had something but I didn't know what it was, and [Jerry] couldn't help me really because that was his first directing job, so he was terrified himself. I know a lot of dancers are crippled because of Jerry Robbins, but he was wonderful. . . . You must say that I adored him, even though he ruined my career for a while. . . . He did a lot of damage to me, because he said, 'You can't take direction.' He didn't know how to give direction. But he told some people, and consequently I couldn't get a job for a long time because he made that statement. . . . He was insecure about directing and yet he was a genius."

George Irving also used the "g" word to describe Robbins' talents, and acknowledged what a difficult character he could be. "People liked to dislike Jerry to varying degrees. . . . But when you're dealing with genius you have to be prepared to turn your collar around." Irving described how Jerry had to come to the aid of Paul Godkin, who was having some difficulty with the choreography in *That's the Ticket*. "I do remember at one point the choreographer got stuck. Jerry came in and helped him finish."

The show opened a day late on its out-of-town run at the Shubert Theatre in Philadelphia on September 24, 1948. Miles White, who designed the costumes, remembered, "There was a big sign on the Shubert at the time . . . and Jerry had a contract that said his name had to be bigger than George Abbott's had ever been." The reference to Abbott may be an exaggeration, but Robbins was indeed a stickler about his billing. Unfortunately, this musical would not help Robbins make a name for himself as director. The *Philadelphia Inquirer* reported that the show "probably looked good on paper. . . . On last night's stage, however, it produced mixed results—principally because the approach suggests nothing in modern politics more than the gait and grace of the animal that is the GOP symbol. . . . The music and lyrics by Harold Rome give the show what pungency and wit it has. But they are not in the best Roman tradition, and the direction of Jerome Robbins was not always sprightly. There is some bright choreography by Paul Godkin. . . ."

Isabel Brown, who danced in the show, was a close friend of Nora Kaye's and Kaye's future husband, film director Herbert Ross. Brown recently recalled that Robbins pulled the plug on the production after its week-long run in Philadelphia. "I was in Jerry's first flop . . . that was headed for Broadway. *That's the Ticket*. And Herbert Ross and I were in there, we were together dancing. And Herbert Ross, who is my best friend in the world, we talked about it the other day. Because . . . it was the very first show Jerry directed . . . and he was smart enough to know that it wasn't working. And rather than open on Broadway, he canceled the show. It was very brave because you don't do that with your first show. But that's how smart he was. That was the beginning of his Broadway career and he wasn't about to bring in a flop. I remember that very well. . . . I was very young, about twenty or something. I was stunned that he knew exactly what to do even though he was very young too." Brown added, "It wasn't a bad flop, it was good, but it wasn't good enough, he felt, to be brought to Broadway as a first show, so he nixed it."

Recalling his "first goof," Robbins later said, "It closed out of town, so quietly that no one ever heard of it. . . . I was too young to direct then; it was a step I took too soon."

Jerry turned his attention again to ballet and wrote a fan letter to George Balanchine, who, with Lincoln Kirstein, had recently set up residence for their fledgling company, the New York City Ballet (NYCB or City Ballet), at the City Center on Fifty-fifth Street. According to Robbins, "I saw a performance of [Balanchine's] *Symphony in C* . . . everyone was dancing so rapturously that I absolutely fell in love with it. Tanny Le Clercq made me cry when she fell backward at the end [of her adagio] and I thought 'Oh, boy! I want to work with that company!' So I wrote [Balanchine] a note and said ' . . . I'd like to work with you, I'll come as anything you need or anything you want. I can perform, I can choreograph, I can assist you.'—I got a note back saying 'Come on.'"

Robbins joined New York City Ballet in the fall of 1948 and was named an associate artistic director the following year. The company offered a number of attractions for Jerry, not the least of which was Balanchine himself. Robbins said of the Russian master, "He made me see that the work was more important than the success . . . that work in progress was what mattered most." Jerry told Balanchine's biographer Bernard Taper, "Balanchine wanted to get me to choreograph more. . . . He wanted to get me not to worry about making a masterpiece every time. 'Just keep making ballets,' he used to say, 'and every once in a while one will be a masterpiece.'"

While Jerry undoubtedly absorbed knowledge of his craft from Balanchine's example, the young choreographer also derived a kind of spiritual benefit by establishing his home with Balanchine's company. City Ballet was to become an invaluable refuge for Jerry in the years ahead. Unlike Ballet Theatre, City Ballet was not primarily a touring company. Many of the dancers in this troupe, like Tanaquil Le Clercq, were sleek, long-limbed creatures trained for speed at the School of American Ballet. While the early company was composed of a diverse group of performers with disparate backgrounds, over time Balanchine would establish a distinctive style and image for his dancers. "Ballet is woman" became his famous dictum, and he defined a standard for female beauty with the long necks and exotic line of his ballerinas. Detractors later called it the "pinhead" look, but this aesthetic and Balanchine's company would increasingly dominate American ballet for the rest of the century, helped along the way by substantial infusions of Ford Foundation funding.

As always, Robbins adapted himself to the particular talents and idiosyncratic qualities of dancers he had at his disposal. There were other Ballet Theatre defectors who joined the New York City Ballet during this early period, including Janet Reed, Nora Kaye, André Eglevsky, Hugh Laing, Diana Adams and Antony Tudor. Some, like Tudor and Kaye, would stay only temporarily. Reed remembered, "You see, by that time, we had all had it with the touring, the one-night stands and all that. And this was a ballet company that was in the City. I think I moved over [to City Ballet] first. Then Jerry came . . . then Nora came, and Tudor and Hugh and Diana came. In other words, I think that maybe, I don't know, maybe Balanchine raided the company. The thing is that he was building an audience at City Center. And Balanchine had worked with Ballet Theatre—he choreographed things for Ballet Theatre, so he knew all of us. But he needed to diversify his company and to build an audience. Later, after he built the audience, and [the company] moved from City Center to Lincoln Center, then he began to mold it more in his own vision. So you see, he had a very diverse group there with Tudor and Hugh and Diana and Nora and Jerry. These were not Balanchine dancers by a long shot."

Reed, who later served as ballet mistress at City Ballet, also pointed out that, as a gesture of support, Balanchine usually gave Jerry the courtesy of first choice in casting his ballets. To whatever extent Robbins may have been in Balanchine's shadow, both thrived in what was to be a lifelong association. "Balanchine gave Jerry a place to work where he had the freedom to fail," said Reed. "It was a place where he could work where it didn't have to be a smash. Balanchine said, 'This is our theater and we can do what we want.' He also gave Jerry the freedom to work elsewhere and then come back whenever he wanted to."

The first ballet that Robbins choreographed for City Ballet was *The Guests*, which was to have its premiere on January 20, 1949. Balanchine frequently attended Jerry's rehearsals and offered encouragement. "Sometimes," Robbins remembered, "he'd bring in some prop he'd found in a store that he thought would be of use to me. I was amazed. Here I was, just a young choreographer, and there was the great master of our age bringing in props to help me, as if he were some fourth assistant to the stage manager."

In fact, Balanchine visited a store and bought masks for the ballet. Balanchine's wife at the time, Maria Tallchief, was of Native American background, and she danced one of the leads in Jerry's ballet. "It was so funny because it was a lot of hard lifting," Tallchief recently recalled. "The *pas de deux* was all lifting. I probably never touched the ground. And so it was difficult for Nicky [Nicholas Magallanes], but Nicky didn't complain. Jerry said to us before

[one] rehearsal, 'Now, why don't you just mark this,' in other words, don't do it full out. So we didn't. We just walked through it and we didn't do any of the lifts. Afterwards, Jerry comes into my dressing room with this look on his face. [He said,]'What's the matter, are you and Nicky quarreling?' I said, 'Well, Jerry, you told us to mark it and that's what we did.' And he would keep changing it all the time. Finally—I'll never forget at the old City Center—I thought, if Jerry comes in here one more time wanting to change something, I'm going to kill him. But other than that, I had fun with Jerry. He was very funny and wonderful to be with. . . . I can remember going to the beach with Jerry. Sitting there, he said the only reason people go in the water is when they have to pee. I thought, oh criminy, is that the kind of water I'm swimming in? . . . He had a typical New York sense of humor."

Tallchief continued, "Jerry was sort of a contradiction. At times you thought he was, oh, one of those smart types, but I think he was very insecure, too. That's the reason why the constant changes in the choreography, the constant wanting to do better, thinking it could be better." Looking back, Tallchief also recollected that her *pas de deux* in *The Guests* was a source of special joy for Robbins. "Whenever I danced it, Jerry made sure to go out and sit in the audience. He just loved it. He always said that this was his favorite part for me, that *pas de deux*. It had a lot of character, shall we say." For his part, Robbins later said of Tallchief, "She is such an image in my mind of what a dancer should be."

The music for *The Guests* was composed by Jerry's friend Marc Blitzstein, who dedicated the score—jazzily symphonic and at times somewhat reminiscent of Prokofiev's *Romeo and Juliet*—to Lincoln Kirstein. Blitzstein was a gay artist and, like Jerry, a member of the Communist Party. Blitzstein's biographer, Eric A. Gordon, speculated that the theme of the ballet for both Blitzstein and Robbins was related to their political sympathies and sexual persuasions. "The treatment [of *The Guests*] is a protest," wrote Gordon, "albeit subdued, against prejudice. At the same time, it is another case—in a city where police arrested hundreds of homosexuals every year just for patronizing a bar or 'disturbing the peace' by dancing together, and in a society that gave open homosexuals little freedom of action—where two gay artists may have sublimated their own cries for justice into a slightly more acceptable Romeo and Juliet theme. That at least could be articulated publicly."

The dancers were divided into two groups—ten with stars on their foreheads marking them as a socially superior caste, and six others unmarked and recognized as inferior. According to the Robbins-Blitzstein scenario, the two groups come together to dance at the invitation of a host, who eventually gives them masks to cover the caste marks. A young man and woman dance a central *pas de deux,* and at the end of their dance, when the masks are removed, the romantic couple are revealed to be members of the opposing castes—the woman with the mark and the man without. Both are rejected by the two groups and forced to flee. Opting for a bittersweet and unresolved climax, Robbins chose not to specify whether the ostracized couple were to depart separately or together.

One of the original dancers, Rita Karlin, later recognized that Jerry's exploration of the Romeo and Juliet theme in *The Guests* was a precursor to *West Side Story.* After the *pas de deux* was performed by Tallchief and Magallanes, Karlin recalled, "Lo and behold, Nicky and Maria found each other. Everybody, of course, when we realized that they were in love, or they had some kind of thing going, looked in absolute horror. . . . That's why I'm saying it's a forerunner to *West Side Story.*"

On its opening night, *The Guests,* a twenty-minute work, was given between Balanchine's *Symphonie Concertante* and *Orpheus.* The reviews for Robbins were mixed. Noting that it was Jerry's first ballet in two years, John Martin called it "a very neatly contrived Romeo and Juliet romance," but added that it was "on the whole, a disappointing work." In the *Herald Tribune,* Walter Terry wrote, "It is a truly classic ballet, for all its contributory modernisms, and it is a ballet implicit with drama in spite of the absence of specific plot. If 'The Guests' in its current form, is not a great ballet, it is, nevertheless, an absorbing one which adds stature to its young choreographer and which augurs new directions for classic dance." Harriet Johnson in the *Post* preferred the score over the choreography, while Robert Sylvester in the *Daily News* suggested that Blitzstein "can turn out some of the strangest boiler factory sounds this side of bebop."

Blitzstein was apparently disappointed with Jerry's staging and wrote to Kirstein's sister, Mina Curtiss: "The ballet was fine from my point of view. I mean I think I did a good, direct, even beautiful job on the music. Jerry Robbins' visual plan was fine, but cloudy, not direct, and not *structural*; he muffed the climax, through prudish avoidance or his own 'immaturity' (a totally inadequate word), and concentrated on the *pas de deux*, a truly grand conception and execution. But a *pas de deux* isn't enough, you will grant; it was the crown of a work not sufficiently garbed, like the Emperor's new clothes which didn't exist."

While the music survived, the choreography was eventually lost. Tallchief remembered Robbins asking her about the ballet near the end of his life. "We were at the Ginger Man in New York . . . and he came up to me and asked me if I remembered *The Guests*. You know, we didn't dance it that much . . . and then it was out of the repertoire. I said, 'Oh, Jerry, I'm really sorry. I remember some of the variations, but I really don't remember it.' I thought later he was very disappointed that I hadn't remembered. That was the last time I saw him, unfortunately."

On March 24, 1949, Robbins and Blitzstein lent their support to the Cultural and Scientific Conference for World Peace, held at the Waldorf-Astoria. Lillian Hellman was probably the most visible American sponsor of the event, which divided the intellectual community over the issue of whether or not Americans should engage in dialogue with representatives of the Soviet Union. The Cold War was intensifying, and the HUAC probe was under way, with its mandate of purging subversives from the entertainment industry. When the peace conference began, the hotel was picketed by a group of anti-Communists led by Sidney Hook. Inside the hotel, Jerry joined Helen Tamiris and others at the choreographers' table and listened to Hellman and a parade of speakers address the several thousand delegates who assembled for the occasion. On his first visit to America, Dmitri Shostakovich was among the Soviet guests.

According to testimony that Robbins later gave to the FBI, he had at this point already withdrawn from active membership in the Communist Party.

His FBI file (which should not be read as literal truth by any means) indicated that Robbins attended the peace conference because "he had always desired to meet AARON COPLAND, whom he considered one of the foremost American composers, and that he had also desired greatly to meet DMITRI SHOSTAKOVICH. . . ." Of course, Robbins already knew Copland through Bernstein, but Jerry's desire to attend the conference because of the other distinguished participants is probably true to a large extent. At this point, he was retreating from left-wing activism and would have been drawn to the conference probably as much by the names of the artists involved as by the political cause.

The peace conference would be Jerry's last ostensibly political foray in public for almost fifty years. Even his public support for the Wallace campaign, with its central plank of "peaceful coexistence" with the Soviet Union, ceased in the months before the 1948 election. Jerry dated his break with the Communist Party as having taken place in the spring of 1947. He had been a member of what he called the "theatrical transient group," which was a part of the Party's cultural division. Under the leadership of Earl Browder, the name of the Party changed to Communist Political Association (CPA) while Robbins was a member. He later testified that he was dismayed when the name reverted and the Party became more secretive. He first told the FBI that he had attended only twelve meetings between 1944 and 1947, and later revised the number to twenty, admitting that at least one Communist Party gathering had taken place at his apartment and that he had paid approximately $200 to $300 in dues to the Party. He said he could not recall ever having a membership card, though he had made formal application for membership. While denying that he had read Marx and Engels, Robbins acknowledged that he had kept up with Party literature. Clearly he had more than a passing interest in certain issues raised by Party policy, as he indicated that he had been troubled by the so-called Albert Maltz letter. Robbins explained, "He [Maltz] had written an article why the artist should be free to write what he wants to write about and how he wants to write it. This was severely criticized in the *New Masses* and the *Daily Worker*, and finally Maltz retracted. This became the subject of many meetings and much discussion back and forth."

According to his HUAC testimony, Robbins' disillusionment with the

CP took place over time and for various reasons. He said that he disliked the secrecy enforced by the Party's leadership. But his concern about artistic issues appears to have been a crucial factor in leading him to disavow the Party line. Particularly unsettling for Jerry was the treatment of artists in the Soviet Union. "I could not understand how the Soviet musicians would be accused of writing—I think the word was—formalistic music and bourgeois music, having to repent publicly, and then get a benediction to move on and continue composing. I found this intolerable to an artist. I feel that they must be allowed to say what they want to say as they feel it, and that the minute they become subject to any dictum, they're being false."

While championing the proletariat and socialist realism in the arts, Soviet and American Communist Party criticism of so-called bourgeois formalism in dance would later include George Balanchine among its targets. Robbins testified that he was deeply disturbed when he heard about this type of criticism being leveled at an unnamed dancer whom he admired. "I attended one meeting in which someone reported to me that, the meeting before, a very great American dancer, not in the least Communist, had been called the Face of Fascism. I have the highest respect for this woman who was accused of portraying the Face of Fascism. This again floored me. I didn't understand what it was about, and it again brought forth this procedure to label things which did not conform as Fascistic, bourgeois, decadent, degenerate. Other things which did conform, whether they were artistic or not, were seemingly praised."

When asked by investigators if he believed that the "Communist Party is as anti-Semitic as the Nazi Party ever was," Robbins said, "It appears to be that way." But it is doubtful that he was aware of Soviet anti-Semitism when he left the party in 1947 (though Robbins may have been aware to some degree of Russian anti-Semitism in the dance world). Many American Communist activists were Jewish and sincerely committed to fighting anti-Semitism and Fascism. Many resisted believing the evidence of Stalin's anti-Semitism when it later surfaced, dismissing such reports as American propaganda and misinformation. Others, like Robbins, converted from Communist to liberal anti-Communist.

Writing for the *New York Times Magazine,* author Jacob Weisberg recently suggested, "The reason Communism was attractive to many Jews seems clear:

they thought they found in Marxist universalism both a response to persecution and a way out of the physical and psychic ghetto. For other Jews in the 1940s and 1950s, anti-Communism was a ticket to acceptance and assimilation, a way to demonstrate their loyalty and patriotism." To this day, even with the fall of the Soviet Union, the Jewish intellectual community remains deeply split over the issues raised by McCarthyism. While recent disclosures from KGB sources and files suggest as many as several hundred American Communists may have been paid agents of the Soviet Union, and while similar revelations appear to strengthen the cases against Alger Hiss and the Rosenbergs, it still appears likely that most Communists joined the Party for reasons involving social conscience. In Robbins' case, the Party may also have offered some career advantage through his exchanges with fellow artists on the left. Although they may have held radical political views, most of these artists were certainly not engaged in espionage, stealing atomic secrets or any other criminal acts.

Robbins testified that "the final straw" of disillusionment had come for him at his last Communist Party meeting when a dispute erupted over "parliamentary procedure, and everyone began arguing and yelling, and I suddenly realized I was in the midst of chaos, of an unorganized, frantic group." Robbins told the FBI that at that point in the meeting he saw the Communist Party as "a disorganized flock of misinformed introverts." While many of his friends remained involved with the Party and its various front organizations, Robbins made a choice to withdraw based on conviction, though he was perhaps also influenced by his growing fear of exposure. According to Nora Sayre, author of *Previous Convictions: A Journey Through the 1950s,* "In 1948 the Communist leadership told homosexual members they must leave the Party because they were likely targets for the police and could be pressured to testify against other Communists. . . . To gain a gay man's cooperation, the police could produce a couple of juveniles and talk about statutory rape. Therefore left-wing homosexuals were threatened with exposure and imprisonment on morals charges as well as with blacklisting." While it may have been a consideration for any gay leftist, no evidence has come to light that Robbins was ever threatened in this fashion.

In any event, Robbins' allegiance in the political sphere had shifted toward Zionism by the time Israel achieved statehood in May of 1948. According to one of Robbins' lawyers, R. Lawrence Siegel, one of the reasons Jerry initially joined the Communist Party was because he mistakenly believed that the Party at the time supported "restoration of Palestine to Jews."

Robbins later told investigators that his Communist experience involved painful memories that "he had hoped . . . to forget." Arthur Koestler went through a similar process of disenchantment, conversion and repudiation of the Communist faith. "As a rule our memories romanticize the past," wrote Koestler. "But when one has renounced a creed or been betrayed by a friend, the opposite mechanism sets to work. In light of that later knowledge, the original experience loses its innocence, becomes tainted and rancid in recollection. . . . Those who were caught in the great illusion of our time, and have lived through its moral and intellectual debauch, either give themselves up to a new addiction of the opposite type, or are condemned to pay with a lifelong hangover."

Jerry's psychic hangover was only beginning, and his personal trial would soon take the form of a Kafkaesque morality play. At one point, he told the FBI that he had turned to his analyst for counsel regarding his political uncertainties. According to his FBI file, Robbins "pointed out to the interviewing agents that he had discussed the matter of Communism with Dr. Arkin, who assured him that from the conversation had between the two that it would be impossible for him to be a Communist and that Robbins had no further fears along that line."

But there were deeper fears taking hold of Jerry. The Hollywood Ten had been cited for contempt by Congress in the fall of 1947 when each in this group, composed primarily of screenwriters, refused to give a yes or no answer to the infamous question: Are you now or have you ever been a member of the Communist Party? The era of the blacklist had arrived and thousands of lives would soon be affected. As recently as 1946, Robbins had offered his name as a sponsor to a group called Citizens United to Abolish the Wood-Rankin Committee. The Communist-hunting Committee during that year included a notorious anti-Semite, Mississippi Congressman John Rankin, and Georgia Representative John S. Wood. By the time HUAC hearings commenced the following year, Robbins had apparently decided against calling further attention to himself and withdrew his support from the protest movement.

Jerry's fears would be compounded when Congress expanded the scope of its investigations to include homosexuals as well as Communists. Author Charles Kaiser wrote, "The Communist witch-hunt conducted by McCarthy and his cohorts is the nightmare remembered by most liberals who lived through this period. But a parallel persecution of lesbians and gay men began in 1950, with devastating effects. . . . What one liberal columnist described (ironically) as Washington's 'homosexual panic' began after a State Department official shocked a congressional committee by disclosing that ninety-one employees had been dismissed between 1947 and 1949 because they were homosexual—far more than had been fired for being suspected Communists." By the time this story broke, Jerry had good reason to believe that he was being investigated, that in certain quarters he was under suspicion of being both a Communist and a homosexual.

In the spring of 1949, Robbins headed back to Broadway with a new musical that seemed to have everything going for it: music from Irving Berlin, direction by Moss Hart, and a book from Pulitzer Prize winner Robert Sherwood. Jerry described his reaction when he first learned about the project: "I heard that Moss Hart, Robert Sherwood and Irving Berlin were doing a show, and I said to my agent, 'Get me that.' It turned out to be *Miss Liberty*." Remembering that the show did not turn out as expected, Robbins asked, "In theater, why do so many conventional shows, the ones that aren't supposed to be risky, turn out to be flops?" The female lead was Allyn Ann McLerie, who had starred with Ray Bolger in *Where's Charley?* Her husband, actor George Gaynes, summarized *Miss Liberty* as the story of "how five geniuses can make one turkey." The fifth "genius" was the show's set designer, Oliver Smith. Motley contributed the costumes. As it happened, *Miss Liberty* was financed by Berlin, Sherwood and Hart to the tune of $175,000.

At the time, Robbins did not yet command the name recognition of those three fellow collaborators, though he surely enjoyed more celebrity status as choreographer than did his friend Oliver Smith, as set designer. Jerry complained lightheartedly to a reporter that he was able to walk down Fifth Avenue without causing any heads to turn. "But the payoff," Jerry said, "happened in

Philadelphia while *Miss Liberty* was trying out. One night I went to a nightclub with Irving Berlin, Moss Hart, Robert Sherwood and a few others from the show. The club owner heard we were there and he announced each of us to the audience.

"Everybody, of course, knew Berlin. They applauded him wildly. Then Sherwood and Hart were introduced. And the audience cheered them. But when my name was mentioned . . . all I heard around me was, 'what the devil is a choreographer?'"

For the book, Sherwood, who had also put in time as a speechwriter for FDR, contrived a story about the Statue of Liberty and a newspaper-circulation war between Joseph Pulitzer's *World* and James Gordon Bennett's *Herald*. The farcical premise centered on Monique Dupont, a French waif fraudulently presented as the model for Bartholdi's sculpture by a young photographer, Horace Miller, played by Eddie Albert. The plot turned on the machinations of the impostor model and the photographer as they foisted their hoax on the newspaper titan, Bennett. The photographer's girlfriend, Maisie Dell, played by Mary McCarty, added only gratuitous romantic complications to a book that otherwise went nowhere. Once the masquerade was finally exposed in Act Two, the tone changed in heavy-handed fashion and the show became a patriotic celebration of America as the welcoming haven for the world's oppressed, a syrupy commemoration of the statue's inscribed poem by Emma Lazarus.

Eddie Albert remembered his encounter with Robbins while rehearsing during the show's month-long out-of-town tryout in Philadelphia. "The play was in trouble and, of course, that meant trouble for Robbins. He was shouting at everyone. I didn't have much dancing in *Miss Liberty*, a lot of running around, stage business and comic routines. I was in the middle of one of my routines, and he shouted at me. So I stopped and walked over to him and said very quietly, 'If you do that again, I'm going to throw you up on the f—ing balcony.' I didn't have any trouble with him after that." The actor called the confrontation "a quiet talk," and said that it was a technique that he had learned from Edward G. Robinson for dealing with "rude directors." Albert added, "Robbins was rude, a little shit. But I would have done the same thing in his position, shouted at the dancers. I mean they were kids standing around picking their noses, and Jerry Robbins was a marvelous artist." Albert and his wife, Margo, though not Communists, suffered from blacklisting early in their careers, and he was sympathetic to Jerry's plight when he learned about it later. "He was under terrible pressure with having his sexuality exposed. Today no one would care," said Albert, though he was not a friend and had no direct knowledge of Robbins' situation as it evolved.

Allyn Ann McLerie, who also performed as a guest with Ballet Theatre, recalled some passing moments of friction with Jerry on *Miss Liberty* and speculated that he had more difficulty communicating with actors than with dancers. "I don't think he knew how to work with actors. . . . With dancers, he would get up and do it and then you would try to be him. You would imitate him. Acting doesn't work that way. [It's] more an indirect method. Dancing is very direct. . . . Ballet dancers, boy, they do what you tell them, if they can. But that's what they do. For somebody who has a big part in a show, like the leading lady, I think he had more trouble . . . because there's the character and maybe the credit accrues a little bit to the performer. He got in his own way, I think, so he was a little difficult." McLerie continued, "At one point he said, 'I don't know, you just take the starch out of me.' I take the starch out of Jerry Robbins! He thought I was criticizing. I said, 'No, what I was trying to do, I didn't do very well, that's all.' He got over it. We were fine at the end."

McLerie also recalled one show-stopping number that was finally taken out of the show: "'Mr. Monotony' was cut out. . . . It was a shame because it was wonderful. Everybody used to come to the wings to watch it. It was Tommy Rall and Bill Bradley, I think, and sort of a seduction thing. And Rodgers and Hammerstein came to Philadelphia, and they saw this number. It stopped the show. . . . I think it was Rodgers, maybe both of them, said to Berlin and Moss Hart and all those fancy people, 'You have to have the courage to cut out the showstopper because it's bad for the girl's character. Where does she get so sexy all of a sudden?' Since I didn't have a character, I was very miffed, because the book was dreadful. It was Robert Sherwood, who was drunk all the time. . . . Moss told me later, he said, 'You know, I gave up in Philadelphia because this is how the story conference would go. I would say, Bob, I don't like this scene. And he would say, I do. And that was the end of it.' So he [Sherwood] left us adrift."

Moss Hart's widow, Kitty Carlisle Hart, remembered that her director-husband was the one who informed Jerry that the "Mr. Monotony" number had to be cut. "Moss said to me, 'I'm going to have to tell Jerry it's out of the show.' And so I said, 'When are you going to do it?' He said, 'At the matinee.' So we went to the matinee, and I'm sitting nearby . . . and as Moss is about to tell [Jerry] this, 'Mr. Monotony' finishes, and it's the only number in the show that got thunderous applause. So I hear this . . . and I say to myself, 'What is Moss going to tell Jerry?' Moss said to him, 'Jerry, the number is out.' So Jerry looked up, and he said, 'That number is out!' And Moss said, 'Yes, it doesn't belong in the show.' And so Jerry took it out, and there was never a peep out of him. Can you imagine Jerry Robbins behaving that way? . . . He really loved Moss, he really did, and he admired him enormously."

Miss Liberty arrived at Broadway's Imperial Theatre on July 15, 1949. Irving Berlin's daughter, Mary Ellin Barrett, remembered that the show "got reviews that my father had never seen before: 'too much corn, not up to his standards.'" Brooks Atkinson in the *Times* called it "a disappointing musical comedy," but credited Robbins with having "improvised a tumultuous Paris masquerade for the first act, and a riotous policeman's ball for the second . . ." In the *New York Sun,* Ward Morehouse called *Miss Liberty* "gravely disappointing," primarily because of its book. "But the weakness in the story structure . . . didn't disturb the brilliant Robbins, nor did it particularly dismay Irving Berlin, who went heroically about the business of throwing out songs and putting in new ones during the frenzy of the try-out period. He has not written one of his best scores, but it is creditable. There are several good numbers, 'Let's Take an Old-Fashioned Walk,' 'Only for Americans,' and 'Homework' being three of them." The waltz, "Let's Take an Old-Fashioned Walk," became the show's only hit.

In spite of the decidedly icy critical reaction, *Miss Liberty* ran for 308 performances, thanks to the big names that drew heavy advance ticket sales. Writing with the advantage of hindsight, Ethan Mordden observed, "At this time, it seemed, Jerome Robbins could not put a foot wrong, not even when he followed 'A Little Fish in a Big Pond' with a dance using the corps costumed as sharks (mimicking the Pulitzer-Bennett war). Anything in Sherwood's stupid book inspired Robbins—Parisian lamplighters at dusk, a train tour (three dancers in rolling-stock getups played the train), the policeman's ball. But then, Robbins had a lot to work with: not in the story, but in the score, one that might have served a hit had the script been up to its level."

While *Miss Liberty* continued its run over the next eight months, Jerry applied himself as both dancer and choreographer at City Ballet. The first ballet in which Robbins performed was not a Balanchine work, but Todd Bolender's *Mother Goose Suite* in November 1949. Bolender recollected, "Janet Reed did the Young Girl and Jerry was Hop O' My Thumb. . . . Just before he did that, he danced on a program of my ballets at the 92nd Street YMHA, in *Comedia Balletica*. . . . All through that period, I was a great admirer of Robbins. I'd met him when we were ballet students. In the ballet world, everybody knew everybody—or did then. . . . Jerry left an indelible mark on every role he danced. . . ."

On December 1, 1949, Robbins danced in the premiere of Balanchine's stylish comic romp *Bourrée Fantasque*, set to a score of unrelated pieces from Emmanuel Chabrier. John Martin observed, "There is comedy not only in the unexpected distortions of classic movement and in the wonderfully amusing use of groups of three figures together in quietly outlandish design, but also in the relations of the individual dancers to each other." Jerry partnered Tanaquil Le Clercq, a twenty-year-old ballerina who was to become Balanchine's next wife at the end of 1952. The chemistry between Jerry and Tanny, as she was called, stirred rumors of romance early on. "I think that they had a thing going," said Janet Reed. "I think that they were in love, or he was in love with her. And then I don't know, she off and married Balanchine. . . . When I heard this was going on, I said to her, 'It's all right to be in love with a choreographer, but for God's sake don't marry one!' Did she pay attention to me? No."

Le Clercq had first met Robbins when she was a teenager and attended a Greenwich Village Christmas party with her mother. She remembered bobbing for apples with him and "getting drenched with water." Jerry and Tanny were an unusual pairing onstage, as Le Clercq in her pointe shoes appeared to tower over Robbins. The ballerina described the rapport that she and Jerry established while working on *Bourrée Fantasque*: ". . . Jerry and I danced together in the first movement. He was a good partner and great fun to dance with. The idea was a tall girl and a smallish man out together. It had elegant [Barbara] Karinska costumes, a chic hat for me, a beret for Jerry. Jerry always said, 'You are the French maid, walking her poodle.' I do not think Mr. B saw it like that. I never felt like a maid, but what was the harm? There is a great step where you swing your leg up behind you, knee bent, and lightly tap your partner on the back of the head. When I was mad at Jerry, I would whack him very hard on the head. Jerry would complain later, 'What are you *doing*? You'll knock my teeth out.'"

In the *Herald Tribune,* Walter Terry deemed their first appearance in *Bourrée Fantasque* "nothing short of triumphant." The critic wrote, "Miss Le Clercq's wide and innocent eyes and her long legs projected the wit of her sequences to perfection, and Mr. Robbins, agile as a leprechaun and twice as mischievous, created a character which must be classed with his immortal Hermes in *Helen of Troy.*" John Martin agreed in the *Times,* calling Robbins and Le Clercq "irresistibly funny."

Balanchine next cast Robbins with Maria Tallchief in the revival of *Prodigal Son* that was given at the City Center on February 23, 1950. Tallchief recalled the difficulties that she and Jerry encountered in the roles of the Prodigal and Siren that Balanchine had originally created for Serge Lifar and Felia Doubrovska. "The trouble was that even though I wasn't that tall, he [Jerry] was too short for me. Our first performance was, in a word, hilarious. During my solo, I tripped over my cape and became enmeshed in it; then in the *pas de deux,* because I wasn't tall enough I had trouble wrapping my legs around Jerry, which was essential for the partnering. Worse, I forgot an important piece of choreography. At one point the Prodigal sits on the floor and the Siren, straddling him, is supposed to lower herself onto his head. I just stood there doing nothing.

"'Maria!! . . . For God's sake, sit on my head,' Jerry hissed.

"I just froze. Seconds ticked by until, finally, I lowered myself onto him and we finished the dance."

Of Jerry in the title role, John Martin noted that it "is a demanding one technically, for it is by no means a matter of miming, and Mr. Robbins dances with power and brilliance." This was one of Balanchine's more dramatic works, and given Jerry's experience with method acting, he may have derived some advantage for his portrayal from his conflicted relationship to his own father. Critic Francis Mason recalled in 1988, "I watched Balanchine rehearse Robbins and Tallchief for the first staging of that ballet in America, and saw, I believe, every one of his performances of the rebellious youth. There has never been a more emotionally true homecoming for the Prodigal than Robbins'. Here, we were in the world of Joseph and his brothers, as Robbins gave us a kind of Biblical hero we haven't witnessed since in the role."

Mason added, "And as a classicist, it should not be forgotten, Robbins danced with character and distinction in the Mozart-Balanchine *Caracole . . .*" This was the first ballet that Balanchine staged to Mozart's Divertimento No. 15 in B flat major, and Robbins was again cast with Tallchief. The ballerina remembered, "Balanchine was anxious for Jerry to learn real classical dance, because as you know Jerry was more the Broadway type in the beginning with the three sailors and this and that . . . so George had him dance in the Mozart [*Caracole*], which is about as classical as anybody can be. . . . Jerry was one of three men, and he had on a tam with a feather in it." In her memoir, Tallchief wrote, "One evening Jerry's mother was in the house. At the end of the performance she came backstage and said the ballet was wonderful. She looked as if she had enjoyed herself, but it was obvious something was bothering her. She kept staring at Jerry and shaking her head. Finally she said, 'You know, Jerry, I really think you should take off that hat. If you saw what you look like, you'd agree. And maybe it's time you took off your dancing slippers, too.'" Tallchief recently noted, "That was the end of Jerry's dancing that kind of role."

Ruthanna Boris had seen Robbins before that same performance and remembered, "Opening night of that, I was standing downstairs backstage at the City Center waiting to go out front, and Jerry came down. . . . There was a big mirror in that lobby before you went on the stage. . . . He stood in front of the mirror. His costume was mauve tights, a white flowering poet's shirt with a black vest over it, and a velvet tam . . . tilted to one side. Very, very démodé and Parisian poet. He stood there and he looked, and he said, 'Well now I look exactly like my father thought I would when I told him I wanted to be a dancer.'"

Robbins choreographed his second ballet for the company, *Age of Anxiety,* to Bernstein's *Second Symphony,* based on the poem by W. H. Auden. Le Clercq recalled, "We rehearsed it to death and Jerry changed it all the time. Version A, Version B, Version C. He had four principals: himself, with Roy Tobias rehearsing the role, Todd Bolender, Frank Moncion, and me. He would keep us four after the rest of the cast had left and keep us at it until we got a little goofy from fatigue. We were rehearsing at the School of American Ballet on Fifty-ninth Street and Madison Avenue, on the fourth floor. There was no elevator service on weekends, when we were often rehearsing, so it seemed we were endlessly tramping up and down those stairs!"

"Those were horrendous rehearsals," said Todd Bolender, who had been given the nickname "Toddles," by Jerry. "This was the old days before unions and . . . we'd have a class in the late morning . . . then we'd have a rehearsal all afternoon, then we'd break for dinner, and then we'd come back and we'd work until eleven or twelve at night." Bolender continued, "But I must say, outside of the fact that Jerry was rather insistent upon everything, as he always has been, there was a wonderful relationship between the four of us. It worked like dynamite. I think back on those days with great pleasure because we were all so warm and friendly and it was so meaningful, our relationship." Bolender also recalled that Robbins was explicit in his choreographic demands and discussed the meaning of the work at length, although "he didn't go into any great depths about the Auden poem. I think we all knew that it was Auden, but it was Jerry's version of the thing. It always had to be his version."

Age of Anxiety opened February 26, 1950, to a sold-out house and received an ovation that *Newsweek* described as "probably not equalled since *Fancy Free.*" Auden disliked the ballet. Lincoln Kirstein reported that Robbins "took Bernstein's symphonic reading of Auden's 'Age of Anxiety' and, using ingenious photomontage by Oliver Smith, made a popular piece, although the poet prized it not at all." According to Eric Bentley, Robbins' treatment of the ballet grated against Auden's British aristocratic sensibility. Bentley recalled Auden saying, "I don't think Robbins ever got beyond the title. He's so vulgar, my dear." Bentley added that Auden had probably been disappointed in his expectation that Robbins would consult with the poet as to the meaning of the poem. Auden wasn't the only one disgruntled by the ballet. According to Philip Lanza Sandor, when Robbins' early mentor, Gluck Sandor saw the ballet, he was furious, believing that Robbins had stolen some of the choreography from Sandor's 1932 ballet, *Dream Phobias*. Sandor reportedly said, "Hey, those are my phobias!"

The three collaborators—Robbins, Bernstein and Smith—once again divided the critics, as they had six years earlier with *Facsimile*. Of the new work, Robbins said, "I would be surprised if it had been wholly intelligible on first performance since it is so complex." In the *Daily News*, Douglas Watt dismissed it as "a tiresomely sentimental piece of claptrap." But John Martin, by now as much zealous fan as critic, agreed with Robbins. Martin suggested the ballet should be seen more than once and offered a summation of the action to help those in the audience who might have been confused: "In the prologue we meet four people . . . who are deeply disturbed by life in their time. They discuss (for reasons which are probably clear to Mr. Auden) the seven ages of man, they embark on a series of dream journeys seeking some kind of answer to their unrest, they worship a superman who falls to pieces before their eyes, they take refuge in a false merriment and, in the epilogue, they part. In the poem there is a short peroration in which the poet seems to imply a return to mystical religion as the answer; in Mr. Bernstein's music comes the dawn in a kind of glorious Technicolor, and Mr. Robbins' four figures simply bow to each other with a new peace, which has come from nowhere discernible, and separate."

After seeing the ballet for the third time, Martin decided, "There can be no doubt after this that Robbins is one of our major artists." But four years later, the critic would change his mind about *Age of Anxiety*: "The work itself is one of Mr. Robbins' more experimental ones, and now that the ingenious scheme by which he has worked out its complex idea has become transparent with many seeings, it is perhaps a less intriguing piece than it was. Its content is sentimental and somewhat overwrought. . . ." Jerry might have contented himself that at least he was no longer regarded primarily as a "yak choreographer."

Within two weeks of the premiere of *Age of Anxiety*, Robbins finished his first collaboration with Balanchine on *Jones Beach*, set to Jurriaan Andriessen's *Berkshire Symphonies*. Although the two choreographers differed enormously in temperament and working styles, they enjoyed a fluid exchange, adding to and revising each other's contributions along the way. Robbins, who also danced in the ballet, told Balanchine biographer Bernard Taper that he felt honored by the invitation to collaborate with Balanchine, "though he [Robbins] also suspected that Balanchine might not have asked him if the music had been a score that had been closer to Balanchine's heart." At the time, one report suggested that Balanchine had "suffered a back injury while his new work was in rehearsal, and Robbins took over, contributed the amusing Third Movement, in which the sun-worshippers fight a 'War with Mosquitos' and a characteristic [Robbins] touch here and there in the first movement, 'Sunday.'"

Tanaquil Le Clercq credited Robbins with the Third Movement: "The scherzo is all Jerry's. He used three boys who are attacked by female mosquitos [on pointe]. The girls keep buzzing around, stinging, and the boys keep slapping at them. George choreographed the last movement for Jerry and Maria [Tallchief]. They came tearing on upstage left, made a diagonal, and performed a fast and jazzy number. Then they came way down to the orchestra pit and pretended to roast hot dogs. They wore shiny, zebra-striped bathing suits. All of us were in bathing suits by Jantzen—free costumes; there was no money in those days." Balanchine's first two movements offered a crowded "Sunday" beach scene and a slow-motion pantomime-adagio called "Rescue," during which Nicholas Magallanes saved a drowning Tanaquil Le Clercq.

The score had been commissioned from its Dutch composer by the government of the Netherlands, and on opening night, Lincoln Kirstein, ever the resourceful showman turning each City Ballet premiere into a publicity event, delivered a curtain speech dedicating the ballet to Serge Koussevitsky. The Dutch Consul General and members of the diplomatic staff were on hand for the opening, as was New York City Parks Department Commissioner Robert Moses. The critics received the joint Robbins-Balanchine effort warmly. In the *Herald Tribune,* Walter Terry enthused, "By its very nature—antic, gay, exuberant—*Jones Beach* is assured a position as a popular repertory favorite. Furthermore, it boasts some excellent choreography and this, of course, gives it real dance substance beyond its communicable air of brash good spirits." John

Martin called it "a piece of vivacious nonsense," complaining only that it was "too long for its content. . . ."

Blithe, carefree and as American as its beach scene, the ballet was perhaps a small harbinger of what was to come in a decade marked by omnivorous conformism in the arts and society at large. From a gay standpoint, Charles Kaiser aptly characterized the fifties: "Mass entertainment was careful to promote the values of what remained a remarkably puritan and (publicly) innocent place. Even after the loosening effects of World War II, sex and death remained unmentionable, abortion was illegal, divorce was difficult for anyone who couldn't afford a quick trip to Nevada, the segregation of public schools was still legal, and the Lord's Prayer was a morning staple in most of those public schools. The suburban family with three children, a barbecue, and a two-car garage was good for business—and almost no one was questioning the notion that whatever was good for General Motors was also good for the United States."

Television shows like *I Love Lucy, Father Knows Best* and *Ozzie and Harriet* would keep corporate sponsors happy through the decade by avoiding unpleasant or controversial topics like racism and sexuality. *The Ed Sullivan Show* (called *Toast of the Town* from 1948 to 1955) was already on its way to becoming a Sunday night institution. Sullivan, the host known for his promise of "a reeeallly big SHEW tonight," had parlayed his syndicated gossip column into the popular TV variety show that gave both up-and-coming and established acts national exposure, from Judy Garland, Elvis Presley and the Beatles to Bing Crosby, Topo Gigio and the Singing Nun. With Robbins' reputation on Broadway and in ballet now firmly established, he received an invitation from Sullivan to appear on the program on Easter Sunday of 1950.

Robbins' TV appearance was negotiated by his agent-manager, Howard Hoyt, remembered by Janet Reed as a small, red-haired man with a single-minded interest in making deals for his clients and collecting his percentage. The contract had already been signed when Hoyt received word from Sullivan that Robbins' appearance would have to be canceled, because Jerry had been named as a suspected Communist in *Counterattack* after he had recently agreed to appear at New York's Capitol Hotel at a benefit for the Arts, Sciences and

Professions Group of the Progressive Citizens of America (the same group that had organized the Waldorf-Astoria peace conference). For Sullivan's benefit, Robbins withdrew his name from the event. Like *Red Channels*, *Counterattack* served as a reference manual for enforcing the blacklist in radio and television. Sullivan informed Hoyt that he had been instructed by his sponsor, the Ford Motor Company, to clear all guests on his show with *Counterattack*, which was published by a right-wing former FBI agent, Theodore Kirkpatrick. As many observers pointed out, *Counterattack* and *Red Channels* were Red-baiting operations that frequently made no distinction between actual Communists and apparent Communists. Any number of fellow-travelers on the left who were not members of the Communist Party were victimized simply because the investigative procedures of these self-appointed watchdogs were shoddy at best. Such were the fear-driven excesses in the era of the Red Menace.

Of course, Robbins had been a Party member. His agent arranged meetings with Sullivan and later with Kirkpatrick to try to clear Jerry's name, and it was the day before the Sullivan meeting that Jerry had his panicked dinner with his cousin Bob Silverman, and Silverman told him not to give them the time of day.

One of the things that Sullivan was particularly interested in was the names of those who had attended a party at Robbins' apartment given by Lena Horne on behalf of Soviet-American friendship. According to her biographer James Haskins, Horne would eventually be named as a suspected Communist by *Red Channels*, and blacklisted until she was able to clear herself with the help of columnist George Sokolsky. In his book *Naming Names*, Victor Navasky reported that the *New York Journal-American* tried to have Horne canceled from a scheduled appearance on Ed Sullivan's show in 1951. Navasky wrote that "her manager, Robert Harris, announced that Miss Horne had 'made her peace' with *Counterattack* by conferring with ex-FBI agent Theodore Kirkpatrick, its publisher. The substance of what she told him was not revealed, only the purpose of the conversation: 'to clear up once and for all the propaganda emanating from *Counterattack* charging her with having been associated with 'subversive' causes and implying that she was therefore unfit to entertain Americans. . . .'"

Silverman, who would later break with his cousin over the issue of informing, was visited by the FBI. "One day I was at home and the doorbell rang," recalled Silverman. "It was in the afternoon, and it was two young men who identified themselves as FBI agents. I let them in. They were very polite. One of them said, 'We'd like to ask you some questions about a party that Lena Horne gave at the home of Jerome Robbins.' I simply said, 'I have nothing to say. Please leave.' And they did."

There were, of course, also the stories that circulated among Jerry's circle of friends that Sullivan had threatened to run pieces exposing Robbins as a homosexual in his gossip column. Silverman recalled, "I've said to myself, Would I have been able to withstand that kind of pressure? Of course, I'll never know. Nobody will ever know. Some people told them to get lost and some people caved in."

Silverman's brother, Saul, said of the alleged blackmail threat against his cousin, "I found out afterwards that it was one of his considerations. You have to realize that Ed Sullivan and Walter Winchell were very powerful people and very vicious in what they would do to people." Robbins repeated the Sullivan blackmail story to his sister and brother-in-law, George Cullinen. Sonia said, "Jerry talked to us and told us what was happening." Sonia and her husband were now raising two children, Robbin and Cydney Lou, and running a nursery school in Little Neck on Long Island. They continued to be active on the left, and they were also visited by the FBI. "Going after us had nothing to do with Jerry," said Sonia. "It had to do with us and what we were doing at that time when everybody was investigated and chased. George was known as a 'premature anti-Fascist' and had lost his passport. But we weren't intimidated. We weren't scared." Sonia and her husband were not cooperative with the FBI and refused to answer any questions. "George was very calm about this, and very nice," said Sonia. "But I was very angry. It was a most dreadful period of history."

As Sonia, Bob Silverman and others came to understand the purported threat from Sullivan, the gossip columnist was going to name names in revealing Jerry's homosexual affairs. If this were so, Robbins might have been confronted with the choice of naming his Communist friends or seeing his gay lovers exposed in Sullivan's column. Sonia recalled that Jerry was also terrified of going to prison. This fear may have stemmed from his awareness of the risks involved for those who were testifying as "unfriendly witnesses" before HUAC and risked being jailed for contempt (members of the Hollywood Ten had spent up to a year in prison). He may also have seen prison as a possible consequence of his gay lifestyle, perhaps envisioning that he would be charged with having crossed state lines for immoral purposes.

Robbins' meeting with Ed Sullivan and a subsequent meeting with *Counterattack* publisher Theodore Kirkpatrick are documented in the FBI files, though there is no evidence of any explicit threat being made by Sullivan to smear Robbins as a homosexual. Agent Edward Scheidt of the FBI's New York office drafted an eleven-page memo to J. Edgar Hoover reporting on Robbins. The memo was dated April 27, 1950, two days after Robbins, Hoyt and Hoyt's lawyer, Paul W. Williams, met with Scheidt and other FBI agents in Manhattan. Scheidt's memo stated that "the purpose of their visit was to furnish the FBI with information concerning their recent contact with COUNTER-ATTACK and possibly securing clearance from the FBI." Scheidt informed Robbins and the others that the FBI was "receptive to hearing any information they had to furnish us concerning the security of this country," but Scheidt also indicated to them "that the FBI does not clear anyone and . . . that the FBI would not be injected into a private dispute between them and any other party such as 'COUNTERATTACK.'"

According to Scheidt's memo, "As a result of ROBBINS' alleged Communist connections, SULLIVAN stated that he would allow HOYT to 'bow out' by sending him a telegram stating that ROBBINS was unable to appear on the show because of HOYT'S inability to clear the necessary music or some such excuse." Hoyt told the FBI that Sullivan had encouraged Robbins to meet with *Counterattack* publisher Kirkpatrick to clear himself, and Robbins had agreed to do so. According to Hoyt, he and Robbins met privately with Kirkpatrick during the first week of April. Kirkpatrick informed Robbins that in order to be cleared by *Counterattack,* Jerry would have to make a public statement "admitting his past Communist affiliations." The memo asserted that "Kirkpatrick had previously told ROBBINS that it was to his definite advantage that he straighten himself out as soon as possible for if an Atom Bomb were to be dropped the FBI would no doubt pick up ROBBINS among the first of those rounded up." At first, Robbins agreed to furnish the public statement that Kirkpatrick had requested, but then balked on the request, fearing that *Counterattack* would misuse the statement and that the adverse publicity would undermine his career.

Scheidt's memo detailed Robbins' political activities between 1944 and 1948, including Jerry's admissions about being a former member of the Communist Party. Scheidt wrote to Hoover, "The interviewing agents stated that they received a very poor impression of both ROBBINS and HOYT. It was their opinion that they are in the middle of a squeeze play between SULLIVAN and 'COUNTERATTACK' . . . that they had no interest in furnishing any information to the FBI of value but [were] merely trying to inject the FBI in a controversy where the FBI had no concern in the matter. Further it was obvious to the interviewing agents that ROBBINS was far from being honest in his answers in that he had a very convenient memory and that there was absolutely no indication from the conversation that ROBBINS is no longer a Communist. In fact, the interviewing agents feel that it is very possible that he still is sympathetic to the Communist cause."

The FBI's suspicions derived from Jerry's evasive manner and his attempt to withhold the details of his personal history in the Communist Party, especially his refusal to name others whom he had known in the Party. He told the FBI "that in 1943, he began touring the country with the ballet theatre as a chorus boy and that in connection with his activities in the ballet theatre he had met and had an affair with a girl whom he declined to name. . . . He stated that through this unnamed girl he had become interested in Communism since he understood that it was opposed to anti-Semitism . . ."

There were a number of female dancers who might have recruited Jerry into the Party, including modern dancer Katie O'Brien, with whom Jerry had a brief romantic affair. Richard D'Arcy called O'Brien "Jerry's connection to the Communists." O'Brien had arranged for D'Arcy to audition for *On the Town*, and she was active in the union effort to have dancers admitted to Equity. But the recruitment story may have been a fabrication, and other names would eventually surface in this regard. Arthur Laurents suggested, "I question the veracity of the quote from Hoover's agents. Jerry would have wanted them to believe he had an affair with a girl rather than a boy. Declining to name the girl prevented checking up on the story." Laurents also pointed out that Jerry's sister had been a Party member, but according to Sonia, she was never directly involved with Jerry in the Party. Indeed, they appear to have been traveling in different political circles, although Jerry was certainly aware of Sonia's activities during the period before he joined the Party. The identity of the woman in question, the "unnamed girl," would remain a mystery for several years.

Meanwhile, Robbins continued to dodge Kirkpatrick and Sullivan. At this point, however fearful he might been about Sullivan's alleged threat to publicize his private life, Jerry decided not to offer *Counterattack* any public statement. While there was surely some doubt about what Sullivan might or might not publish in his column, Robbins could imagine the career damage that might result from publicly identifying himself as an ex-Communist, given the political climate of that year. Cold War hysteria was at an all-time high with the onset of America's military involvement in Korea and with public awareness that the Soviet Union possessed the atom bomb. Yet, as far as the impact of blacklisting went, Robbins was not affected on Broadway. Because the theater didn't possess the corporate character of television and movies, the blacklist was much less of a factor there. With Hollywood under siege, many blacklisted writers, directors and performers eventually took refuge on the Great White Way.

During the summer and fall of 1950, Robbins was able to devote himself to a new musical, *Call Me Madam*, a savvy and warmhearted political satire directed by George Abbott and produced by Leland Hayward. Ethel Merman was the star, and Paul Lukas was her leading man. Irving Berlin composed the score, and Howard Lindsay and Russel Crouse contributed the book, which made for a three-hour evening in the theater. Merman's character, Sally Adams, was based on Perle Mesta, a Washington, D.C., party hostess who had been appointed ambassador to Luxembourg by her Democratic friends. Denying any real-life inspiration, the program stated, "The play is laid in two mythical countries. One is called Lichtenburg, the other the United States of America." The plot would provide plenty of raucous comedy and even a few touching moments for Merman as Adams, the brash and naive American who was to win over the tiny European country, along the way wooing and marrying Cosmo Constantine (Lukas), a suave, conservative Lichtenburg diplomat. The script was a perfect vehicle for Merman's scene-stealing gifts. At one point, trying on her gown for a royal reception, she quipped, "I don't mind the train, but did they have to give me the Super Chief?"

Abbott hired a recent University of Pennsylvania graduate, Hal Prince, to serve as assistant stage manager. This was to be Prince's first brief association with Robbins. In a recent letter, Prince characterized the relationship between Abbott and Robbins: "Jerry admired Mr. Abbott. I think he was a mite afraid of him and certainly extremely respectful of him. He behaved. I do believe that he deferred to Mr. Abbott's judgement, perhaps reluctantly on occasion. The only similarity between Abbott and Robbins is they were disciplined. But, Jerry was mercurial and often apprehensive. He would delay rehearsal dates, potentially costing the production money. He would delay casting decisions, well beyond anyone else I've ever known. I think Jerry was always afraid to commit himself to decisions, none of which applied to George Abbott, who made decisions quickly—sometimes the wrong ones—but swiftly. George Abbott was not a temperamental man, Jerry Robbins was. George Abbott was a man so secure in his talent that he was generous and encouraged hundreds of young people in their careers. Jerry Robbins was not generous. I think he was jealous (and protective) of every inch of turf he won and worried about billing, which as indicated above, George Abbott did not.

"Their directorial styles were very different. Abbott was very terse and had enormous verbal capacity; after all, he was a writer. Jerry did not possess those powers of articulation, and it could frustrate him. But of course, every time the decision came down to movement, he was extraordinarily quick. He had a fertile imagination and a desire to be intellectual, bordering on the pretentious. In my opinion, this is a good thing. Not to make this interview about me, but I've always felt that if at one point or another a project seemed a bit pretentious, that was a healthy sign."

Abbott recalled the first rehearsals for *Call Me Madam* in his memoir: "As was customary, Jerome Robbins started work first with his dances. He had conceived a big number about the wild men from the mountains coming down and dancing in the village. Eventually this number had to be jettisoned. Time and time again the ambitious dance effort will fail, whereas something conceived for practical purposes and on the spur of the moment will be a success. This is equally true of songs."

Abbott and Robbins doctored the show on the road, dropping numbers like "Mr. Monotony" (the same Berlin song earlier cut from *Miss Liberty*) and a Merman solo, "Free" (which would later be reworked for Rosemary Clooney as "Snow" in the movie, *White Christmas*), and adding the second act opener, "Something to Dance About." Abbott described the genesis of one of the show's hits. "During the tryout of *Call Me Madam* we discovered that we needed a new song to fill a certain spot in Act Two. I had been very much taken with one old song of Berlin's called ['Play a Simple Melody'], which was done in counterpoint and which had a revival of popularity at this time. When I urged him to contrive something along those lines for this spot, Irving went back to the hotel and disappeared for the day. Crouse had a room directly over Berlin's and he, therefore, would give us reports from time to time about the music which floated up to him. Two mornings later he hurried into the theatre with a big grin and said gleefully, 'I think he's got something. I keep hearing the same tune over and over.' Indeed, he had got something: that wonderful counterpoint melody called ['You're Just in Love'], with which Ethel Merman and Russell Nype stopped the show every night." Nype played Merman's idealistic young secretary in romantic pursuit of Lichtenburg's Princess Maria (Galina Talva).

Once again Jerry had his work cut out for him, with four of Berlin's thirteen songs calling for ensemble dances. These were more decorative than plot-driven dances, and Robbins exploited every opportunity to show off his stylistic virtuosity. In "Something to Dance About," Jerry exploited the Argentine Tango, the Charleston, rhumba, fox trot and waltz. For the dancers in the show, rehearsals were typically punishing. According to Kirsten Valbor, two dancers became favorite targets for Jerry. One of them was Muriel Bentley, who had first drawn his fire in *Fancy Free*. "Jerry was venomous with

Muriel," said Valbor. "He was cruel to her. The things he said were stunning, they were breathtaking, because you couldn't look at anybody or at her. She took it all and never said a word. I don't know what she said when they were alone, but it was painful." Valbor added, "Then there was another dancer named Billy Weslow. Jerry lacerated Billy. Billy was cute . . . really a fresh kid. But Jerry would nail him. Oh my!"

Some of his dancers, like Bentley, repeatedly forgave Jerry for his excesses. Others, like William Weslow, would not. Weslow also danced with Ballet Theatre and City Ballet, and he had earlier had a brief affair with Robbins. The embittered dancer recalled, "He should have been cut up in small pieces and burned in a microwave somewhere because he was so horrible to me. . . . I had an experience in *Call Me Madam*. The guy that Jerry adored was Tommy Rall. I was understudying Tommy. . . . I had a very good technique and I could probably match Tommy in the pirouettes and everything. We became very friendly because I had known him as a child and we studied together in Seattle. Jerry saw this, and he was mad about Tommy Rall, had the hots for him.

"So Tommy and I went out to eat a couple of times after rehearsal and Jerry turned dark when he saw this. Then we had a run-through and everybody was out front. Mary Martin and all the stars from all over were there for this big run-through of *Call Me Madam*. A gypsy run-through. Jerry said to me, 'Okay, now, you understudy Tommy. You're very good. You both do it differently, but you're wonderful. When Tommy comes out and does the number, I want you to come out in back of him and dance it full out in back of him.' I said, 'I can't do that. He's the star.' Jerry said, 'Do you want a job? Do you want your ass fired?' I said, 'No.' He said, 'Then do as I say. When Tommy comes out, I want you to come out and scream and yell . . . and do the whole number in back of him.' And Merman was out front and she saw him talking to me. I was very upset. She knew his sadistic bit, too, but didn't interfere.

"The number started and Tommy runs on with this big whip, and I had a whip, and I'm doing all this behind him, and he stops and says, 'Just a minute, stop the music.' He said to me, 'What the hell are you doing?' I said, 'Tommy, I didn't want to do this, but Jerry told me to do it full out in back of you.' . . . So he turns around to Jerry, who was in the pit, and says, 'Did you tell him to do this?' He said, 'No, I never told him to do that.' Then Jerry said to me, 'Get the hell off the stage! What the hell's the matter with you? You're only an understudy.' And later Merman said, 'Boy, I've never known anyone to do that.' When she spoke up for me, Jerry was even more sadistic. And of course, Tommy never spoke to me again. After what Jerry did to us, Tommy and I were never friendly again, and Jerry loved that."

Arthur Partington recalled that early on the indomitable Merman was somewhat condescending toward Robbins, as she had known him since he was a chorus boy in *Stars in Your Eyes*. "Paul Lukas was her leading man," said Partington, "and he asked her, 'Who is this choreographer?' And Ethel said, 'Oh, he used to be in one of my shows in the chorus.' That's how she referred to him to Paul Lukas, not as the number one choreographer in New York at the time. As far as Ethel was concerned, Jerry was just there to help out. But she was okay. She was a pro. She did her work and she worked full out, and you could never say that she wasn't ready for the job."

Robbins was friendly with Partington, and according to the latter, some dancers mistakenly assumed that they were lovers. Ralph Linn remembered, "When [Jerry] got into an argument with Arthur Partington, we would all pay for it. One time, Arthur was dancing with Pat Hammerlee in the opening number of the show, and [Arthur and Jerry] had an argument. I guess they had a disagreement, and all of a sudden Pat Hammerlee said to me, 'Come on, Ralph, we're doing it.' I said, 'What do you mean, we're doing it?' And the curtain went up. Of course, I understudied and I knew the part, so I did it. [Afterward] Jerry came back, and I blasted him, I called him every name in the book. He just turned his back and walked out to the audience. I'll be honest with you, he was a son of a bitch to work for, but I admired him. He was a bastard in many respects, but if he was alive today and I was young and dancing, I would be more than honored to work for him."

The show's producer, Leland Hayward, who was to be closely associated with Robbins over the next decade, later speculated about the familiar problems that many had working with him: "Jerry is a perfectionist, which doesn't make it easy. He also has a deep need to be wanted, needed and loved. Unless he feels that with anyone he's working with, Jerry gets obstreperous."

With decor from Raoul Pène du Bois and haute couture for Merman from Mainbocher, *Call Me Madam* opened on October 12, 1950, at the Imperial Theatre. Brooks Atkinson of the *Times* called it, "Quite an evening on the whole," and lauded "Jerome Robbins' festive ballets." In the *Post*, Richard Watts, Jr., wrote, "it richly deserves to be Broadway's latest hit. What else could it be with Miss Merman?" In the *Herald Tribune*, Howard Barnes joined the chorus of critical raves, labeling it, "A fetching, old-fashioned musical jamboree." Dwight Eisenhower, then President of Columbia University and being touted as a potential GOP candidate for the White House, was in the audience to hear the second-act jubilant campaign number, "They Like Ike."

George Abbott remembered, "Ethel Merman gave a beautiful performance on opening night and the show was a tremendous hit. Later on in the run, she got angry at Paul Lukas and wouldn't look at him. Night after night, I would have to go backstage and give her notes telling her that she ought to look at the leading man during the love scenes. She would agree blandly and would look at him for a couple of performances, but when I returned the next week, I'd find her standing there talking to the audience and leaving Lukas out on a limb all by himself. The audience didn't seem to mind, however; only the theatre-wise knew the difference."

Call Me Madam enjoyed a year-and-a-half run of 644 performances. The musical went on to be a hit in London, toured for a year after its Broadway run (with Elaine Stritch taking over Merman's part) and gave Merman a movie. If the success of the show put Robbins at the top of his field, it also defined how much he had to lose as his political and legal troubles continued to fester.

On March 21, 1951, almost a year after the cancelation of Jerry's appearance on Ed Sullivan's show, actor Larry Parks was called to testify on Capitol Hill as a witness before HUAC. Parks had achieved fame for his portrayal of the title role in *The Jolson Story* in 1946. The HUAC hearings were now resuming after all of the appeals by the Hollywood Ten had been exhausted. Parks admitted to the Committee that he had been a member of the Communist Party from 1941 to 1945. Unlike the unfriendly witnesses of the Hollywood Ten, Parks was willing to provide testimony about his personal history in the Communist Party, but he had reservations about naming others who had been active with him. "I would prefer, if you would allow me, not to mention other people's names," said Parks, adding that "to force a man to do this is not American Justice." Parks pleaded, "Don't present me with the choice of either being in contempt of this Committee and going to jail or forcing me to crawl through the mud to be an informer. For what purpose?"

There was and still is widespread moral prejudice against an informant, as indicated by such terms as "stool pigeon," "rat" and "snitch." As Victor Navasky pointed out, in a case where personal allegiances are torn between friendship and patriotism, many Americans would probably endorse E. M. Forster's famous pronouncement, "If I had to choose between betraying my country and betraying my friend, I hope I should have the guts to betray my country." In the same way that the Biblical Herod identified for Christians the image of informant as traitor, there was in the Jewish tradition severe censure for any Jew who informed to the non-Jewish world. The Minean curse warned, "And for the informer may there be no hope." Zero Mostel, who was an unfriendly witness, once said that "as a Jew, if I inform, I can't be buried on sacred ground." With regard to HUAC and McCarthy's Senate Permanent Subcommittee on Investigations, moral partisanship would give rise to endless controversy. While not dealing with Communism, the Elia Kazan-Budd Schulberg movie, *On the Waterfront*, directed and written by two artists who had named names, made a persuasive case in 1954 that under certain circumstances, as when a criminal act was involved, informing might be seen as the most honorable and ethically justified course of action.

HUAC ultimately rejected Parks' plea, insisting that the witness had to provide names to prove that he was willing to cooperate fully. In the opinion of those on the Committee, because Parks had testified about himself, he had waived his legal right to refuse to talk about others. Victor Navasky argued persuasively that the Committee already knew all of the names and already possessed the evidence that they were demanding from Parks. The Committee's chairman, John S. Wood, initially asked, "How can it be material to the purpose of this inquiry to have the names of people when we already know them?" But such misgivings were quickly overcome and the naming of names was adopted as the litmus test for witness credibility.

Navasky suggested that "the Committee was in essence serving as a kind of national parole board, whose job was to determine whether the 'criminals' had truly repented of their evil ways. Only by a witness's naming names and giving details, it was said, could the Committee be certain that his break with the past was genuine. The demand for names was not a quest for evidence; it was a test of character." The Congressional hearings were not courtroom trials, and the legal rights of witnesses were a matter of contention. "The purpose of the hearings, although they were not trials, was clearly punitive, yet the procedural safeguards appropriate to tribunals in the business of meting out punishment were absent. . . ."

After Parks made his futile plea, the Committee went into closed executive session, and two days later it was leaked to the media that he had offered up the names. The significance of Parks' testimony was not lost on Ed Sullivan. Nor had Sullivan forgotten about Robbins. On March twenty-third, just as the story was hitting the press that Parks had succumbed to the Committee, Sullivan published his own lengthy front-page article in the *Philadelphia Inquirer*. Sullivan's headline read: TIP TO RED PROBERS: SUBPENA [sic] JEROME ROBBINS.

"I accuse," Sullivan wrote. "I'd suggest that the House Un-American Activities Committee subpena [sic] ballet star and choreographer Jerome Robbins to fill out the picture sketched by Larry Parks.

"In my office not long ago, Robbins revealed that he had been a card-member of the Communist Party.

"Witness to that astonishing revelation was Ted Kirkpatrick, ex-FBI agent and one of the editors of Counter-Attack.

"Occasion of the disclosure was Robbins' eagerness to be purged of Commie-front associations. But despite that professed eagerness, Robbins never went through with it. He stalled and delayed but never came clean.

"The importance of Robbins is that he figured importantly in Broadway shows and Hollywood. Now that Parks has shown the way, Robbins may be willing to name his accomplices in the Communist apparatus designed to destroy America."

Sullivan offered some rather doubtful testimony from the chore-ographer. "'I became a Communist,' explained Robbins, 'because it meant advancement in my profession, via the Commie escalator sys-tem. I'd have joined the Girl Scouts just as readily, if they'd promised I'd get ahead as a dancer. The Commies kept their word. Their direc-tors of shows moved me from the second row to the first row; their newspaper and magazine sympathizers started giving me all sorts of publicity. Overnight I became a celebrity in my field.'

"'Who got you to join the party and what show business people did you meet?' asked Kirkpatrick.

"'I can't tell you that,' said Robbins, 'because it might interfere with my professional career. Suppose people booed my ballets?'

"'American boys are being killed for this country,' said Kirk-patrick. 'You must do this for your country.'

"Robbins and his manager promised to think this over, but we never heard from them again. Robbins had to go to Hollywood at that time to work on a film adaptation of one of his Broadway shows.

"A few days later I contacted Kirkpatrick.

"'As Americans,' I suggested, 'we are in the position of having heard a Broadway celebrity confess he was a card-carrying member of the Communist Party. It seems to me that we are placing ourselves in a particularly unenviable position by failing to turn this information over to some government agency. You, as an ex-FBI agent, know the ropes and I suggest that you inform the proper authorities that we so heard Robbins testify.'

"Kirkpatrick undoubtedly did."

Sullivan continued, "So the House Un-American Activities Committee should subpena [sic] Robbins. He knows Broadway and Hollywood members of the conspiracy. Despite his timidity I'm sure that he'd cooperate, now that Parks had [sic] demonstrated it can be done and should be done.

"The importance of Robbins in such an investigation is in direct ratio to the number of Commies in Broadway shows and in the classic ballet.

"Week after week, lining up my TV show, I've had to cancel contracts with ballet performers because they have an unhappy and unholy faculty of getting hooked up with Commie-front organizations. . . .

"Robbins can give the Committee backstage glimpses of the musical shows which have been jammed with performers sympathetic to the Commie cause. His dance arrangements have distinguished at least five Broadway shows. They were conspicuous, not only for his imagination, but for the undisputed fact that the casts were made up of performers who subscribed to the party line.

"Robbins, like Parks, attended many private parties given for the party faithful. He knows who were on our side and who were against us.

"You can be equally sure Robbins knows and can name Communists who are prominent as conductors and arrangers in concert music. He has a wide familiarity with Commies of all hues. In accusing him, I also call upon him as an American to aid the Government in identifying conspirators who hide behind the music racks, ballet bars [sic] and musical comedy billing.

"I believe Robbins will talk, as an American, to rid show business of an evil influence.

"If the House Committee wishes to have me repeat this testimony before it, when it resumes April 10, I will be happy to fly to Washington. It will be a small repayment to the boys I've seen in military hospitals, their arms and legs shot off by Russian guns."

Such fulminations hardly meshed with the public's image in later years of the avuncular Sunday night host. In light of Robbins' FBI file, Sullivan as a journalist was evidently capable of outright mendacity and was not beneath putting words in the mouth of his victim. In trying to portray Robbins as a Hollywood figure, Sullivan was stretching the truth. Robbins had received film offers from Hollywood ever since *On the Town* (which MGM had emasculated by dropping Robbins' choreography and most of Bernstein's score). The headline of a 1949 *New York World-Telegram* article suggested, "Famed Dancer Shuns Hollywood." Movie deals had fallen through on *High Button Shoes, Billion Dollar Baby* and *Look, Ma, I'm Dancin'!* But Jerry did spend two weeks in California discussing film projects during the spring of 1950, shortly after his separate meetings with Sullivan and Kirkpatrick. Yet nothing materialized as far as a movie, and Jerry admitted to having misgivings about Hollywood. Remembering his earliest encounter with Robbins, playwright-screenwriter Jerome Chodorov said, "I first met Robbins through Sam Goldwyn, strangely enough. We were going to do a movie, *Billion Dollar Baby* which never came to pass. He [Jerry] dropped out very quickly because he didn't want to be any part of a movie, of a flop. I shortly followed him."

Curiously, Sullivan chose not to include the Robbins story in his nationally syndicated column, and the story was not picked up by the major newspapers in New York City, including the *Daily News*, which regularly carried Sullivan's column. Nevertheless, word of the article spread quickly to theatrical circles in Manhattan. HUAC investigators were already aware of Jerry and a subpoena was forthcoming, though it had little immediate impact on Robbins' career. According to Arthur Laurents, "When Jerry Robbins was called, he was choreographing *The King and I.* They were still out of town [in Boston]. He went to the producers [Rodgers and Hammerstein] and they said, 'Do whatever you want.'"

According to Mary Hunter, Jerry received advice early on from his showbusiness lawyer, William Fitelson. Hunter recalled, "Bill Fitelson said to him, to my knowledge, that he'd have to make his own decision whether he would name names or not. But Bill said, 'I don't think it's necessary because they've got them anyway and you'll be giving them nothing but your own feelings.'" Fitelson, the epitome of the belligerent, bulldog theatrical attorney, represented David Merrick and Elia Kazan among others. Fitelson also happened to be a Trotskyite whose opinions on politics Kazan initially mistrusted when he had his own reckoning with HUAC. In his autobiography, Kazan wrote, "I had an energetic and devoted lawyer . . . Bill Fitelson, who'd done me and my family many services. I would almost always accept Bill's recommendations on business matters. But politics? That was something else. He was intensely caught up by the political infighting of that day and was the first person I knew who was left and also anti-Stalinist. He was called a Trotskyist. I didn't know what that meant, but the way it was said by my friends confirmed my untutored suspicion that it was something I didn't want to be."

Whatever misgivings Robbins may have harbored about his lawyer's political views, Fitelson's field was entertainment law and not civil rights. Jerry soon turned to attorney Morris Ernst, later revealed in an ACLU Freedom of Information Act lawsuit to be an FBI informant who referred to himself as "Hoover's lawyer." Jerry's sister recalled, "It was known by everybody that Morris Ernst was a pipeline to the FBI. Jerry was misled. We tried to discourage him, but somebody pushed him into Ernst's lap."

At this time, like Sonia and others who were close to him, Mary Hunter believed that Jerry was being terrorized, that he was threatened with public exposure of his sexuality. If Ed Sullivan had indeed made such a threat, however veiled, there would surely have been one question looming in Jerry's mind: Now that he had been subpoenaed, would Sullivan follow through and expose him if he failed to cooperate with HUAC? While there is no compelling proof that Sullivan ever actually suggested this nightmare scenario to Robbins, according to some of those to whom he confided, Jerry expressed his fears in this regard three years before he finally testified before the Committee. From that point, the story would take on a life of its own, eventually including an allegation that HUAC investigators had utilized this type of social blackmail to compel Robbins to testify as a friendly witness. But no evidence has emerged so far that either the FBI or HUAC ever subjected him to this type of coercion, and years later, Robbins himself would deny this version of the story. Nevertheless, fear of such exposure was undoubtedly a factor that would have weighed heavily on him throughout the investigation.

Noting that such fears would overcome the resistance of others confronting the inquisition, Dalton Trumbo, a member of the Hollywood Ten, later argued, "What are you to do, for example, about a homosexual caught by the FBI and given the choice of informing or being exposed—in a time when homosexuality was regarded differently than it is now? What were you going to say to that man? It's a choice I wouldn't have wanted to make, and I'm not prepared to damn him. Lillian Hellman once said, 'Forgiveness is God's job, not mine.' Well, so is vengeance, you know. . . . Hate is just a goddamned unhealthy thing." While concluding that some moral humility was in order, Trumbo also suggested pointedly, "The enemy was the goddamned Committee."

FIVE

Betrayals, Triumphs
and Fairy Dust

Between tours with New York City Ballet and Ballet Theatre in 1950, Robbins' personal life was complicated by another volatile romantic triangle, one that was played out while he was under the scrutiny of HUAC investigators, the FBI and Ed Sullivan. Robbins was now sharing his Park Avenue apartment with a gay lover, Broadway dancer Buzz Miller, with whom he lived intermittently over the next five years. Robbins reportedly told Miller early in their relationship, "I suppose you know I'm engaged to Nora Kaye." Like most of Robbins' gay friends, Miller simply let it go. Despite the ongoing romantic affair with Miller, a Robbins-Kaye engagement was announced to the press and a wedding date set for April 16, 1951.

Kaye's longtime friend, Isabel Brown, remembered, "Jerry was crazy about Nora. He really loved her. They had so much in common. They were both Jewish with similar backgrounds . . . and they shared an enormous sense of humor. They laughed like crazy. And they were both well-read. For a dancer who has so little time for anything else, Nora was extremely well-read. And that's what Jerry loved about her. They could discuss a lot of subjects that dancers don't think about. Nora knew everything about the arts, and that's what they talked about. At that time, Jerry was swinging both ways. He liked girls. Although he was gay, he loved women. Many of his ballets are about beauty and women and partnership. And the way she did his work was exactly what he envisioned. He fell in love with the artist along with the woman. Everyone thought it was a joke, because they knew he was living with a man. But you know, in those days a lot of that was hidden. They didn't come out with it. And he always felt funny about that aspect. But Nora was a free spirit. Those things never bothered her."

Kaye was one of those who was able to see through Robbins' prickly facade. Describing him in a 1961 interview, she said, "Though he is tough and shrewd, he is a little boy underneath. He doesn't dare show, nor does he want to show, how vulnerable he is."

Both of their families approved of the match. Dorothy Gilbert, a friend of Sonia's and Jerry's since adolescence, remembered, "Jerry's mother wanted them to get married, and so did Nora's mother. In fact, there was a silver shower for her. You could tell by the preparations the families were in sync. But it never happened. They went off to Paris at that time and they came back unengaged."

The trip to Paris was part of a four-month European tour undertaken by Ballet Theatre during the fall and winter of 1950. Because his early ballets were still in the repertory, Robbins maintained an association with the company. It was not until after this tour that Nora Kaye left Ballet Theatre and followed Robbins to City Ballet. In Paris, *Le Monde* reported, "Jerome Robbins and the Ballet Theatre have enabled us to get to know America." For Robbins, this was the beginning of a love affair with the city that would continue until the end of his life.

Allyn Ann McLerie toured with Ballet Theatre as a guest artist and often roomed with Kaye. McLerie recalled, "At that point Jerry and Nora were going to get married. She said to me one day, 'I'm going to marry Jerry.' I said, 'Oh.' She said, 'Don't say anything. . . . I'm not going to room with you this time.' So Jerry and Nora then roomed together and I was in an attic, a garret, at the top of the same hotel, the Quai Voltaire, and they were on the third floor with French windows looking over the Seine. Jerry and Nora and I toodled around Paris. We were a funny threesome. We went to Montmartre. We discovered Genevieve. She was nobody then. She had hair to her knees, beautiful, and she had a partner and lover, I guess, with a guitar. [She was] this beautiful Eurasian girl. There was this funny little joint [where she performed] at the top of Montmartre, and we sat there and we said, 'Wow, she's good!' "

McLerie continued, "So one day I went in the theater, Palais de Chaillot, which is a labyrinth backstage, and I went down the hall and I peeked into Nora's dressing room, and she was doing her face. I said, 'So, how's it going?' She looked up at me and she said, 'Very difficult, very difficult!' Then pretty soon they were not getting married anymore."

Isabel Brown was also dancing for Ballet Theatre at the time. She and Kaye were the two friends who later inspired the characters played by Shirley MacLaine and Anne Bancroft in the movie *The Turning Point*. Brown speculated about the breakup between Robbins and Kaye: "I think it was mutual. My feeling was that it was an understanding between them. In the heat of the moment they wanted to get engaged and then they thought about it. They were both highly intelligent, and I think they realized there was no future in it, that he was going to go off with men and she needed more than he could offer."

James Mitchell recalled working with Robbins and Kaye in Paris. Mitchell was cast in the part that Robbins had created for himself in *Facsimile*. "Jerry came to Paris before we opened and performed it the first time," said Mitchell. "We were in some terrible garret and rehearsed it as best we could, but it was always very sketchy. It was very underrehearsed, and it was difficult stuff. It was long and exhausting, and I don't think Jerry and Nora were getting on too well at that time. Nora spoke right up to him, but she was terrified of him. The night that we performed it, [after] the first ballet was done, we were there being nervous, the three of us. He walked up to me onstage before the curtain, of course, and said, 'Do a pirouette.' I said, 'Okay.' So I did a pirouette. He said, 'Do two.' I did two. And then he said, 'Do three.' Well, I was not a ballet dancer, and three pirouettes was an achievement for me, let me tell you, but facing that terror, I did three. He said, 'That's the way I want your hair!' And then he turned away, and I don't know if he spoke to Nora or not. Then he drew a stool up just within the proscenium arch where we could see him, to keep his eye on us, to terrorize us. He could have watched very well out front. That's mean, that's terrorizing. And that he practiced.

"But Jerry was an absolutely charming man," Mitchell added. "I've always said he was the most charming son of a bitch I've ever known. I spent a lot of time with him outside the theater. He could be funny and just great to be with. He touched everybody, no matter what anybody says. He certainly touched Nora. [That was] a very deep emotion."

Yet Mitchell regarded Robbins' effort to marry Kaye as an exercise in futility because of his conflicted sexuality. "I don't think he was bisexual at all. I think he was homosexual and that he experimented. I don't think he was ever serious about being married. Nora married some very peculiar people. . . . She was a strange character. She was carrying on with this one and that one. She got rid of them like that. Had she married Jerry it would have lasted a second, just a second." Janet Reed voiced a similar opinion of the ill-fated match, saying, "I shudder to think what would have happened if he'd married Nora."

After returning to New York that winter, Robbins resumed the romance with Buzz Miller. "They were great lovers," said William Weslow. "Buzz was wonderful. They were very close and Buzz was very devoted." Originally from Arizona, Miller was a decorated World War II infantry veteran. He danced for jazz choreographer Jack Cole and would later work with Robbins on *Two's Company*, *The Pajama Game* and *Funny Girl*. He also danced with Marilyn Monroe in the film *There's No Business Like Show Business*. Miller's talent was undoubtedly part of the attraction for Robbins. According to British ballerina Lynn Seymour, who was close to Miller in later years, "They were great buddies. They used to play cards together quite a bit. . . . I think there was respect on both sides, actually. I think they'd probably driven each other mad but there was still regard. It was rather sweet, and Buzz was a very special kind of guy, too. He did know how to deal with Jerry, and of course he inspired Jerry, because he was such a great dancer. He was an unbelievably sensual performer. He had such physicality and all the things that Jerry loved."

Robbins lived in fear that his relationship with Buzz Miller would be exposed during the HUAC investigation, which would drag on for another two years before Robbins faced the Committee. Shortly before his death in 1999, Miller told author Stanley Siegel that because of Robbins' terror of being discovered, they never slept in the same bed during the time they lived together. Robbins continually checked the locks on the doors and windows of the apartment, believing that he was under surveillance. Gene Gavin, who was in the original cast of *West Side Story* and later became a friend of Miller's, re-membered, "The first time I ever saw Buzz, he and Jerry came to a concert. I think everybody knew about Jerry's relationship, that he was homosexual. Nothing was ever discussed, but I think he was afraid of the exposure, that they'd have this on him, so he tried to be very careful."

Whatever concerns Robbins may have harbored about his domestic arrangement, he managed as always to immerse himself in work. Early in 1951, while preparing for *The King and I,* he took time to sit for a portrait by his friend Ninette Charisse. Her painting shows Robbins seated on a couch, studying a French book on Siamese dancing. Charisse said she suspected later that the sadness she saw in Robbins' eyes and tried to capture in her por-trait reflected his sorrow that he was unable to have a family. "He loved chil-dren, really loved them," said Charisse. "He'd get very emotional with tears in his eyes when he saw some woman looking at a child."

Of course, such vulnerability on Robbins' part was rarely displayed in the theater, where more often his dancers were the ones in tears. One exception in *The King and I* was Yuriko Kikuchi (known professionally as Yuriko), a Martha Graham dancer who performed the role of Eliza both onstage and in the 1956 movie. Yuriko recalled, "Everybody cried. He made everybody cry. He would find a weakness of a person and just go zoom, dagger into it. The closer we got to coming to New York, it intensified, and whatever he had in mind [to accomplish] in the ballet, he got tougher on the dancers. When everybody started crying, I just made up my mind I wasn't going to cry, he wasn't going to make me cry. He would give class at the ballet barre. So what I did in those classes was, I checked his mood to see where he was at, and that way I could protect myself. I was watching him. What mood is he in? Is he in Asian mood today? Is he in European mood today? Or is he in mixed mood today? You could tell. I'm very sensitive. I would adjust to protect myself."

The King and I posed a thorny stylistic challenge for the choreographer, as it required him to set Eastern dance forms on Western dancers. The project developed under the auspices of its leading female star, veteran British actress Gertrude Lawrence ("Gertie"), who prevailed upon composer Richard Rodgers and lyricist-librettist Oscar Hammerstein II to turn the 1946 Twentieth Century-Fox film *Anna and the King of Siam* into a musical, though the source was ultimately credited to Margaret Landon's book. The movie was a drama based on the remarkable adventures of the real-life British governess, Anna Leonowens, who was employed by King Mongkut of Siam (Thailand) during the 1860s. Lawrence had not appeared in a musical since starring with Danny Kaye in *Lady in the Dark* in 1941. Envisioning herself as Anna, she initially leaned toward Noel Coward as the King and hoped for a Cole Porter score. But neither Porter nor Coward was available. After seeing the movie, Rodgers and Hammerstein agreed to undertake the project, even though they had never written a show with a specific star in mind and were aware from the outset of Lawrence's limited vocal range.

With *Oklahoma!, Carousel* and *South Pacific,* the visionary writing team had redefined the musical form during the forties. Breaking away from the operetta and vaudevillian musical traditions, the Rodgers and Hammerstein revolution cohesively integrated book, music and dance in much the same way Robbins had been working all along. The three were natural collaborators. "They just meshed," said Yuriko. In his limited role as choreographer, Robbins was deferential toward the composers whose work he esteemed.

After Joshua Logan turned down an offer to direct, playwright John Van Druten accepted the assignment, having established a name for himself directing *Bell, Book and Candle* and *I Am a Camera.* Robert Russell Bennett did the orchestrations, and with Robbins' guidance, Trude Rittmann arranged the dance music. Rodgers and Hammerstein produced *The King and I,* and the budget eventually ballooned to $350,000, a record for them at the time, with extravagantly lavish sets and costumes from Jo Mielziner and Irene Sharaff respectively. Investors included Twentieth Century-Fox, Leland and Nancy Hayward, Mary Martin, Josh Logan, Billy Rose and the authors' families. Robbins was paid a weekly salary of $350, which was more than that received by the relatively unknown actor who was eventually cast as the male lead. Once the show opened and was playing along with *Call Me Madam,* Robbins was reportedly earning $700 per week in royalties.

After a renewed effort to interest Noel Coward in the role of the King failed, an offer went to Rex Harrison, who had starred with Irene Dunne in the film *Anna and the King of Siam*. Harrison turned down the show because of schedule conflicts. Yul Brynner, who was working successfully as a television director at the time, auditioned for the role on the advice of Mary Martin, with whom he had appeared in *Lute Song*. Martin reportedly encouraged Rodgers and Hammerstein "to kidnap him if necessary—you'll never find a better King." The balding, muscular Brynner, a former circus acrobat, soon proved himself a force to be reckoned with in this show, and indeed, his entire subsequent career can be measured through the recognition he won for his portrayal. When the musical first opened on Broadway, Gertrude Lawrence's name was alone above the title while his was placed below. In the film, five years later, he shared billing above the title with Deborah Kerr. With the Broadway (1977 and 1985) and London (1979) revivals, Brynner was featured alone above the title.

Early on, according to Rodgers' biographer William G. Hyland, Rodgers tried to discourage Brynner from reading the Landon book, explaining that the role of the King would be quite different from the historical personage of King Mongkut, on whom the character was based. Mongkut was in reality a powerful despot who wore false teeth made of redwood; however, he was relatively enlightened in his commitment to modernize his country and he did engage the services of the prim British widow to tutor his children. In the musical, he was to be portrayed with greater sensitivity than he possessed in the book. His fictional first wife, Lady Thiang (played by Dorothy Sarnoff), aptly characterizes him when she sings the lines, "This is a man who thinks with his heart / His heart is not always wise . . ." The autocrat's dilemma and prescience are deftly expressed in Hammerstein's lyrics for "A Puzzlement," the King's first-act solo:

> *When I was a boy*
> *World was better spot.*
> *What was so was so,*
> *What was not was not.*
> *Now I am a man—*
> *World have change a lot:*
> *Some things nearly so,*
> *Others nearly not.*

Brynner ignored Rodgers' advice and read the book. Then he began shaping the role to fit his unique talents and personality. His line, "Is a puzzlement!" became a classic in musical theater and the curtain call image of Brynner with his arms in the air symbolized his triumph. In a 1989 portrait of his father *Yul: The Man Who Would Be King*, Rock Brynner wrote, "Gradually, he took command of the overall production, not because his assertive nature demanded it, not because he alone could coax Gertie to rehearse, not because there was a power vacuum—though all that was true. He took command of the production because only Yul could imagine the King, without whom there was no play. This was a role in which he could 'lead with his cock.'" Of course, the musical continued to be mounted successfully even without Brynner. The King was later played by such performers as Farley Granger, Darren McGavin, Rudolf Nureyev, Stacey Keach and Lou Diamond Phillips.

The part was crucial when Brynner originated the role, as the King's character was to set off and illuminate Lawrence in her starring role. In the oral history *It Happened on Broadway*, press agent Susan L. Schulman recalled, "The story is that when Gertrude Lawrence and Yul Brynner were creating the characters, they were kind of floundering until Yul said, 'We have to play it as potential lovers. Otherwise the play is just about two cultures, and who cares?' The sexual undercurrent added an electrifying element." Such an interpretation was consistent with the script. Writing in the *New York Times* before the musical opened, Rodgers and Hammerstein suggested that the romantic undercurrents were intentional as they conceived Anna and the King: "The strength of their story lies in the violent changes they wrought in each other. Yet their life together bears unmistakable implications of deep mutual attraction—a man and a woman relationship so strong and real and well-founded that it seems in some ways more than a love affair, more than a marriage."

When rehearsals started, Lawrence was dying of leukemia, although neither she nor anyone else was yet aware of her condition. Her biographer, Sheridan Morley, wrote that her tantrums and temperamental indisposition were subject to two interpretations at the time: "Those who loved her took the view that for a woman of fifty-two to have to carry, as Anna does carry, an entire 3½ hour musical during the course of which she walked four miles around the stage at every performance and wore a total of seven massively heavy costumes, each weighing 75 lbs and complete with steel hoops which bruised her legs every time she tried to curtsy to the King, was simply asking too much of an actress brought up in a gentler pre-war tradition of British leading ladies. Those who did not love her, and there were a great many of them, too, took the not totally irreconcilable view that she was simply past it and masking her inability to sing and her jealousy of Brynner's success by a series of psychosomatic collapses."

Lawrence actually adored Brynner, and often he was the one who consoled and guided her through her crises behind the scenes. She was enormously insecure with both the physical challenge and musical complexity of her role. Morley noted, "Rodgers had been careful to write numbers for her in a limited vocal range ('I Whistle a Happy Tune,' 'Hello Young Lovers,' 'Shall We Dance?') while giving his more demanding songs ('Something Wonderful,' 'We Kiss in a Shadow') to the trained singers, Doretta Morrow and Dorothy Sarnoff." According to the composer's daughter, Mary Rodgers, Lawrence "sang flat all the time, which drove my father crazy."

Robbins was careful to maintain his rapport with the two leading actors, both of whom could be as intimidating as he was. As the musical numbers were beyond Van Druten's talents as director, Robbins took the lead, first staging the "March of the Siamese Children," the charming interlude that depicted the initial meeting between Anna and the King's children. Though Lawrence and Brynner were not strong dancers, Robbins patiently guided them through "Shall We Dance?" In this number, Anna taught the King how to polka, and the couple managed not to trip over Lawrence's unwieldy hooped skirt, which enveloped them as they created an illusion of effortless grace. This was the critical scene that Hammerstein believed came closest to revealing the repressed sexual desire between the principal characters.

Robbins' masterpiece in the show was his Siamese ballet based on *Uncle Tom's Cabin,* performed in Eastern theater style and entitled "The Small House of Uncle Thomas." Although criticized by some at the time as overly long, the dance perfectly captures the show's central theme, that love and reason might prevail over racism. Rodgers encouraged Robbins to pursue a comic approach with the ballet; and according to Yuriko, the composer told Robbins, "Use the Siamese movement, but don't become a slave to it." The ballet is a classic play-inside-the-play appropriately related in the script by Tuptim (Doretta Morrow), the King's fugitive concubine whose love for Lun Tha (Larry Douglas) vividly exposes the monarch's savage barbarism and the horror of slavery.

The ballet's chase scenes depicted Eliza (Yuriko) being pursued by Simon Legree and his dogs and archers. Yuriko recalled that Hammerstein at one point questioned Robbins about why he had strayed from the script by including the character of Lover George in the scene. "Without missing a beat," said Yuriko, "Jerry said to me, 'Oh! Yuriko! Improvise the three chases without George. . . . Just do it, so we can see it.' So I improvised. 'Oh, yes,' said Hammerstein. 'It's much better. It makes sense.' With that, 'The Chase' was kept in this improvised form." Commenting on how Robbins later invented George's grand entrance as an angel, Yuriko noted, "This really proved to me that he [Jerry] was a true magician."

The climax at the end of the second act provides one of the most memorable moments in musical theater, when Anna confronts the King as he is about to lash the captured slave with a bullwhip. With Anna pleading for the King to spare Tuptim, he bellows to the heavens, "Am I to be cuckold in my own palace?" Then, under Anna's fierce gaze, his vicious resolve is broken and he retreats in shame. Hammerstein was decisive in having the King die in the final scene, departing again from historical accuracy in order to serve the drama.

The action in the second act was so swift—moving from the polka through the whipping scene to the King's death—Brynner had to fortify himself in each performance with an oxygen tank in the wings. Ronnie Lee was a thirteen-year-old who played one of the royal children and was later cast by Robbins in *West Side Story*. In *It Happened on Broadway*, Lee recalled, "In the final scene of the *The King and I*, Yul Brynner would lie on the deathbed, and I would kneel beside him. The bed was toward stage left, I was to the left of the bed, and the traveler, the curtain that goes in one direction, would be moving stage right to open stage left. As that was happening, Yul would whisper dirty jokes to me. I was supposed to be weeping, but instead I would be shaking with hysterical laughter."

For the dancers, the rehearsal process was as brutal as the Siamese court. Gemze de Lappe performed the role of Simon Legree in the show and in the movie (though she was uncredited in the film due to a studio error). She recalled that Robbins "worked like a dog himself and expected everybody else to do so. . . . I think the main thing was that the material was so hard. We were on our knees all the time, and we were doing all this very painful Siamese technique. . . . Western bodies really aren't accustomed to that. We were working at the Broadhurst, I think. It had been dark for years, and the floor was dirty, and [during] the work-light period, it was doom and gloom. And it was wintertime. We would go in, and it was cold, and by lunchtime we'd be dirty, and we didn't have those nice nylons that you could just rinse out. You had to go home and rub them. They were like iron, those rayon things that we wore. . . . So it was a combination of all these things. It was just very raw [and] painful."

Trude Rittmann, who arranged the music for the dances, recalled working with Robbins and said, "There was a point it was very difficult, but it was an enormous challenge for both of us. And he got enormously involved with the costumes, with the masks. It was beautiful. He kept saying, 'We are like a very old couple going up a steep hill. One is pushing the other.'"

Yuriko described Robbins' obsessive approach to the work. "When Jerry was creating, he was in another world, immersed and involved in the instant, and far, far from all of us. He didn't notice us as human beings, but rather as material he could use and dispose of at will. . . . He didn't think, 'Am I hurting someone's feelings?' He was in too great a hurry to accomplish what was on his mind."

Yuriko's daughter, Susan, took over her mother's role decades later when the show was revived and in *Jerome Robbins' Broadway*. Yuriko remembered the gentle side of Robbins in the way that he related to her daughter as a child. "There was a lovely relationship between Jerry and Susan. He called her Susie. He adored her from the beginning when I had to bring her to the studio to take care of her." Susan recalled, "I worked with him much later in his life even though I saw him on the set of *The King and I*. That's like a childhood memory. He gave me my first Pluto dog. So I saw him like a grandfather type in a way, but not really realizing who he was. He took me to *Peter Pan*. Those early memories of seeing Broadway shows had a big effect on me in terms of my whole life."

During its out-of-town, pre-Broadway tour, *The King and I* went through a major overhaul. The show was running almost four hours. Four numbers were eventually cut, and three were added, including "Getting to Know You." This song came about when Lawrence realized before the New Haven run that after Anna sang, "I Whistle a Happy Tune" to her son, there was a long, heavy interval until her next number. To lighten the act and to fulfill audience expectations of her role as a leading lady, Lawrence suggested to Rodgers and Hammerstein that Anna might sing to the Siamese children. They obliged. Thanks to a timely suggestion from Mary Martin, they reworked a song ("Suddenly Lovely") they had discarded from *South Pacific,* and in this way one of *The King and I's* finest songs was born. But the show was still in deep trouble.

Suffering from laryngitis, Lawrence missed the final dress rehearsal in New Haven, and her singing was extremely shaky when the show opened there February 27, 1951. Brynner was struggling with his accent, and the running time was still well over three hours. Leland Hayward, who had invested $15,000 in the production, reportedly advised Rodgers to close out of town. The competition would be stiff on Broadway that season. *Call Me Madam, Kiss Me Kate, Out of This World, Guys and Dolls, Gentlemen Prefer Blondes* and *South Pacific* were all up and running. Still, advance sales and expectations were high for *The King and I.* Frank Sinatra was already in the studio recording several of the show's songs ("I Whistle a Happy Tune," "We Kiss in a Shadow" and "Hello, Young Lovers"). The producers decided to forge ahead despite considerable trepidation. By the time the show traveled to Boston, the climactic "Shall We Dance" sequence was polished, though there were still other scenes yet to be trimmed. Reviews were mixed, but the word-of-mouth was promising.

The premiere took place on March 29, 1951, at the St. James (the same theater where *Oklahoma!* had opened almost eight years before). It was a gala evening despite the frayed nerves of all involved and early downpours of rain that snarled traffic and delayed the arrival of limousines and taxis. The Truman Administration was in full swing, and the First Lady was in the audience, as were Kitty Carlisle and Moss Hart, Eleanor Holm and Billy Rose, George Kaufman, Mike Todd, Edna Ferber, Arthur Schwartz and Herbert Bayard Swope. Black tie and furs were much in evidence. As was now customary for

Robbins with each of his openings, he arranged for his mother and father and many relatives to attend.

Onstage that night, Brynner almost stole the show, but Lawrence rose to the occasion and matched him, as if to prove under extreme duress why she had been a star for almost three decades. The critics were unanimous with their praise. Robbins received a fair share of accolades, although the composers and stars outshone him to some extent. While quibbling that the new Rodgers and Hammerstein show was not a match for *South Pacific*, *New York Times* critic Brooks Atkinson wrote, "Strictly on its own terms, *The King and I* is an original and beautiful excursion into the rich splendors of the Far East, done with impeccable taste by two artists and brought to life with a warm romantic score, idiomatic lyrics and some exquisite dancing." He noted that Robbins "has put together a stunning ballet that seasons the liquid formalism of Eastern dancing with some American humor." In the *Post*, Richard Watts, Jr., enthused that "nothing could be much more enchanting than a scene in which Anna teaches the King to dance." The *Daily News* called Robbins' Siamese ballet "the visual highlight—and entertainment highlight" of the evening.

The show ran three years and 1,246 performances. Robbins collected another Donaldson Award, but he missed out on a Tony that year. While Rodgers and Hammerstein, Lawrence and Brynner, Jo Mielziner and Irene Sharaff all won in their respective categories, Robbins lost to choreographer Robert Alton for his work on the revival of *Pal Joey*. Nevertheless, Robbins' triumph with *The King and I* would lead to his first Hollywood break four years later and brought him that much closer at the age of thirty-two to realizing his most ambitious dreams on Broadway.

In failing health during the show's long run, Gertrude Lawrence was replaced by Celeste Holm, during a week-long vacation, and later by Constance Carpenter. Lawrence gave her last performance three weeks before her death on September 6, 1952. Robbins joined the mourners, including the show's cast, as five thousand people crowded the streets outside the Fifth Avenue Presbyterian Church at Fifty-fifth Street. Hammerstein delivered the oration and spoke of Gertie's "magic light." She was buried in the pale pink "Shall We Dance" gown that she wore in the second act of *The King and I*.

Robbins returned again to City Ballet in the spring of 1951, and by his own account applied some of the specialized technical work he had done on *The King and I* to a controversial ballet, *The Cage*. He explained that the hyper-extended Siamese movements and gestures that he had employed in the Broadway show "spilled over into" the ballet. Set to Stravinsky's eerie String Concerto in D, *The Cage* depicts female insects who ravish and then kill their mates. The program notes suggested a "race or cult," and according to Robbins, the idea initially involved mythological Amazons. But during the early rehearsals the concept evolved into praying mantis-like insects. He would also draw from spiders and from the violence of the animal kingdom to produce what he called "a phenomenon of nature."

Robbins first became interested in choreographing *The Cage* when he turned over a recording of Stravinsky's *Apollon Muscagete* and found the 1946 concerto on the other side. His reaction was, "What a dramatic work this is!" He described the music as "terribly driven, coerced, compelled" and conceived of the three movements as a dramatic structure that he incorporated in the ballet. Robbins layered the dance with countless ideas and images that he absorbed along the way, from the plastered-down look of Nora Kaye's wet hair as she stepped out of a shower to a caged tiger effortlessly whipping its tail. He suggested that he was also inspired by the specific youthful qualities that he gleaned in the dancing of Tanaquil Le Clercq, whom he likened to "a gauche young colt, soon to become a graceful thoroughbred." Of this imagistic absorption process, Robbins noted, "I had a very special eye out looking for material. This 'special eye' is typical of anyone working creatively, whether he be painter, playwright, poet, composer, or choreographer. The 'eye' becomes a sort of Geiger counter which starts to tick in the brain and emotions as you approach a subject of value to you."

In this case, the subject would raise eyebrows, as the ballet was deliberately lurid in its brutality. Summarizing the action, Robbins said, "It's about a tribe, a tribe of women. A young girl, a novice is to be initiated. She doesn't yet know her duties and capacities as a member of the tribe nor is she aware of her innate instincts. She falls in love with a man and mates with him. But the rules of the tribe demand his death. She refuses to kill him but she is again ordered to fulfill her duty [by the Queen of the tribe], and when his blood actually flows, her animal instincts are aroused and she rushes forward to complete the sacrifice. Her affection yields to her tribal instinct."

In fact, under the direction of the tribe's Queen (Yvonne Mounsey), two male Intruders (Nicholas Magallanes and Michael Maule) were dispatched one at a time, with the female dancers' arms and legs lashing out viciously. As *Fancy Free* stretched the classical idiom by combining pirouettes and somersaults, *The Cage* was to further extend the limits of the form in grotesque fashion. "I did not have to confine myself to human beings moving in a way that we know is human," Robbins recalled. "In the way their fingers worked, in the crouch of a body, or the thrust of an arm, I could let myself see what I wanted to imagine. Sometimes the arms, hands, and fingers became pincers, antennae, feelers."

The predatory femme fatale, The Novice, was originally performed by Nora Kaye. Some observers speculated that Robbins' gruesome attitude toward women as expressed in the ballet was somehow an oblique reflection of his failed romance with Kaye. Isabel Brown said of the work, "It's basically what he thought of women, as being the aggressor, that's all. It came right out in that ballet. Jerry had some really ironic twists in terms of what he thought about women taking advantage of men. *The Cage* brought out something in him in that period which may have had to do with Nora or whoever and unrequited love."

There was tension between Robbins and Kaye during the rehearsal period. Ruthanna Boris was choreographing *Cakewalk* for City Ballet at the same time Robbins was working on *The Cage*. Boris recalled visiting one of Robbins' rehearsals. "Jerry was walking around looking extremely withdrawn. He was very grim. I sat down on a bench . . . and he started in on Barbara Bocher. He said, 'You fat pig!' And it was obvious that he was very upset and taking it out on her. And she wasn't fat, she was just a little plump. Nora was standing in the middle of the room waiting for him to stop tormenting Barbara and get going. Finally, Nora couldn't stand it any longer. She said, 'You know, Jerry, sometimes you stink!'"

The ballet premiered at the City Center on June 14, 1951. Designer Jean Rosenthal lit a set that was a stark, weblike construction of ropes, and Ruth

Sobotka costumed the performers in provocative, spidery garb. At the beginning, the overhanging network of ropes tightened ominously, a touch that
Robbins added as if to offer a warning of what was to come. But this spectacle, lasting less than fifteen minutes, would quickly overwhelm audience expectations. Robbins had calculated the ballet's dramatic impact, although he
may not have anticipated his mother's reaction. "We were there the night *The
Cage* opened," recalled Dorothy Gilbert. "I remember sitting next to Lena. We
attended every ballet, every new project that Jerry worked on. And it [*The Cage*]
was a very, very difficult time for Lena. She excused herself and got up and
walked out of the performance. [She] waited in the back. His mother was visibly upset."

The critical reaction was clamorous, yet much of it in Robbins' favor.
John Martin wrote, "It is an angry, sparse, unsparing piece, decadent in its
concern with misogyny and its contempt for procreation. It dodges no issues,
but cuts to the heart of the matter with sharp and steely thrusts. Its characters
are insects, it is without heart or conscience, and its opinion of the human
race is not a high one. But in spite of the potency of its negations, it is a
tremendous little work, with the mark of genius upon it." In the *Herald Tribune,*
Walter Terry concluded that Robbins "has created a startling, unpleasant but
wholly absorbing theater piece." He added that Nora Kaye "dances the role of
the Novice with ferocious brilliance. Except for her moment of temptation,
she is frighteningly inhuman, provocative and glittering but coldly feral."

Clive Barnes later described *The Cage* as "a repulsive bit of misemployed
genius." As if to come to Robbins' defense against charges of misogyny, Lincoln Kirstein called it "a manifesto for Women's Lib, twenty years *avant la lettre* . . ." Edwin Denby was perhaps the only critic to see the gestural language
as "so literally that of the important Broadway people at parties and in offices." At the time, Robbins was stung by strident reactions to the ballet and
issued a disclaimer, "I don't see why some people are so shocked by *The Cage*.
If you observe closely you must realize that it is actually not more than the
second act of *Giselle* in a contemporary visualization." Though he later explained that he intended his point as irony, he was referring to the Wilis, the
vengeful female spirits who murderously set upon Hilarion and Albrecht in
Giselle's famous graveyard scene. But *The Cage* lacked any hint of the redeeming

power of love that enabled Giselle to save her unfaithful prince. Robbins' vision of the ballet was relentlessly dark and cold-blooded, such that both of his
male Intruders had to die, with their female assassin displaying no human
emotion whatsoever. This was consistent with advice that he received from
Balanchine who, according to biographer Bernard Taper, told Robbins after a
run-through, "Keep it antiseptic."

While Robbins insisted that he never consciously borrowed or copied
material from Balanchine, *The Cage* suggested his familiarity with Balanchine's
Apollo and *Orpheus*. Kirstein wrote, "While it is impossible to imagine *The Cage*
without a double image of the bacchantes' final fury in *Orpheus*, the metrical
division which Robbins gave his hive of horrid creatures is due as much to
Stravinsky's syncopation as to Balanchine's structure. . . . It is not alone from
Balanchine that Robbins has borrowed or digested, just as Balanchine himself
has rifled the whole range of gesture and movement from well-known repertory 'classics,' circus, music-hall, film, and memories of which only he can
identify the original source."

Kirstein credited Robbins with "the gift for shock," and the point was
driven home the following year when the Netherlands tried to ban *The Cage*,
which one Dutch critic described as "pornographic." New York City Ballet
was touring Europe, and Robbins threatened to withdraw all of his works
from the repertory if performances of *The Cage* were canceled. Lending him
support, Nora Kaye said she would refuse to dance in any other ballets if the
company gave in to government pressure. In the end, official efforts to censor
the work only succeeded in increasing its popularity.

Shortly after the opening of *The Cage*, Robbins underwent an emergency
appendectomy. Taking time off, he sailed to Europe, where he spent most of
the summer touring. Adolph Green remembered bumping into Robbins in
Rome. "Outside of working with Jerry," said Green, "for me the best experience I ever had was in Italy. . . . I was traveling alone in Italy. I was feeling very
lonely, and I had heard vaguely that Jerry was in Italy. I went into a big hotel
in Rome. I went into the lobby and there was no one around, and I was thinking of Jerry. I started walking out, and in through the front door came Jerry.
And he looked very stricken. He said he had been on the street and by instinct
he went into that hotel lobby. He didn't know why. He had no purpose in

going in. So then we took a trip together, maybe about ten days. Jerry rented a terrible little car and we went all over the hills. Jerry was really methodical. He had a guidebook with every place marked and all the facts about it. Siena. It was one of the greatest times I ever had. We had such fun together."

At one point during their travels, the two checked into an inn, left their bags in the room and headed out onto a terrace for coffee. Looking up from their table, they saw water trickling down from a window above. "What kinds of idiots would leave the water running?" they wondered. After returning to their room, they had their answer, as they saw their suitcases floating in front of them. Green recalled, "We both broke down in fits of laughter."

During this trip to Europe, Robbins also made his first extended visit to Israel. The *World Telegram* reported that "he was deeply impressed by the dancing he saw in Israel, particularly the folk dances of the Yemenites." He later told HUAC investigators that he "traveled to Israel to teach there and to give what aid I can to that country, as far as my talent is concerned." In fact, he had been engaged by the American Fund for Israel Institutions (later called the America-Israel Cultural Foundation, or A.-I.C.F.) as a kind of roaming talent scout and cultural ambassador. The organization was committed to finding and supporting a dance troupe that could represent and promote Israeli dancing in Europe and America. Robbins was asked to recruit an appropriate group of dancers and to oversee the development of their talents in order to ensure professional standards. His search would continue the following summer. His Jewish heritage was by now a recurrent source of inspiration in his life, albeit secular rather than religious.

Still dancing, although more intermittently, Robbins was next cast by Balanchine in the eleven-minute comic vignette *Tyl Ulenspiegel*, based on the fourteenth-century Flemish mischief-maker and set to Richard Strauss' evocative tone poem. Historically, Tyl was a Robin Hood figure who came to symbolize Flemish resistance to Spanish invaders led by the Duke of Alba. The title role performed by Robbins involved more mime than dancing, and he later recalled that Balanchine was a marvelous exemplar in rehearsal. Robbins told Bernard Taper, "As a dancer, I got some of the best notices of my career for the role of Tyl . . . but I never got anywhere near the gusto and earthiness that he [Balanchine] achieved when he was demonstrating it for me in rehearsal."

To supplement the brevity of the score, Balanchine added a drum roll and staged a short prologue depicting Tyl as a child playing chess on a giant board with the boy king, Philip II. The juvenile monarch unleashed an armada of toy ships, and Tyl retaliated, wielding a loaf of bread. A brief fight ensued that led into the Strauss score. The main action involved the grown-up Tyl in a rollicking series of tricks, chases, duels and impersonations that roused the Flemish peasantry to fight against the foreign invaders. Inspired by the paintings of Hieronymus Bosch, Esteban Francés designed the sets and costumes. The ballet opened at the City Center on November 14, 1951. John Martin described Robbins as "warm and diabolical, genial and merciless, a subtle actor and a unique mime." Martin called it "a one-man show," while Walter Terry suggested, "Jerome Robbins, the dancer, triumphed—if George Balanchine, the choreographer, did not" because the secondary characters "scarcely had dimension." Unfortunately, not long after *Tyl* entered the repertory, a fire destroyed the costumes and props, and it was never revived.

With his next ballet, *Pied Piper*, Robbins changed moods again, picking up where he left off with the lighthearted antics of *Interplay*. Tanaquil Le Clercq described *Pied Piper* as "a fun ballet with Benny Goodman playing Copland's *Clarinet Concerto* at the side of the stage." The stage was bare except for scattered props and radiators against the wall behind the dancers, who wore simple rehearsal outfits. The original piper was clarinetist Edmund Wall, who started the festivities, entering in a business suit and sitting casually on a stool, where he played Copland's jazzy confection. In her first Robbins ballet, Jillana [Zimmermann] recalled, "Roy Tobias and I entered through the very back door of the stage. . . . We did a short adagio facing upstage, dancing to the shadows cast by lights coming from the front. . . . After the adagio section, which included Diana [Adams] and her partner [Nicky Magallanes], all heck broke loose and the remainder of the ballet stayed very upbeat." Others in the cast included Le Clercq, Janet Reed, Todd Bolender, Melissa Hayden, Barbara Bocher, Herbert Bliss and Robbins himself. They danced individually, in couples and in groups to create what John Martin called a "mild madhouse," only vaguely suggesting the legendary piper of Hamelin and his rats.

The ballet premiered on December 4, 1951, and Walter Terry called it a "joyous, infectious, captivating ballet." Jillana recalled that "Mr. Balanchine once played the part of the Pied Piper, with Mr. Wall playing in the pit." Veteran City Ballet dancer Ed Bigelow pointed out Robbins' unusual flair for comedy in ballets like *Pied Piper* and later *The Concert*. "Jerry is the only one in my experience of dance who ever made a funny ballet," said Bigelow. "Nobody else did. Balanchine has lots of wit in his stuff, but he didn't make a funny ballet." In her book, *Dance in America*, Agnes de Mille lauded Robbins' comedic gifts. "His great contribution is humor, possibly the most incisive in the dance world, on a level with the best American humor in any field, particularly that of the great comedians of the early motion pictures. There has never been in dancing anything like his capacity to make audiences laugh. It is not warm comedy. It is zany and satiric. It involves a degree of exaggeration and tremendous physical technique. The timing of his jokes serves as a model for actors the world over."

Walter Terry explained how the comedy in a ballet like *Pied Piper* involved the element of surprise working between the music and the dancers' bodies: "The jokes are muscle jokes, reactions are muscle-reactions. . . . a note on the clarinet jabs a dancer into action, a rhythmic pattern jolts him into vibrating, an unexpected sound paralyzes him, a phrase tickles him. He dances not to the music but because of it." Terry called Robbins' method "kinetic pantomime" because the movement was not primarily representational as in traditional mime. The demands placed on the dancers to create such wicked havoc onstage lend added meaning to Adolph Green's observation about Robbins' sense of humor: "It was never easy laughter."

Robbins soon turned from the raucous physical comedy of *Pied Piper* to the piquant whimsicality of *Ballade*. But with this ballet he fell flat, utilizing Debussy's *Syrinx* and *Six Epigraphes Antiques* to create a mood piece with commedia dell'arte figures, falling snow and balloons on strings. At the start, a minstrel delivered the balloons that brought the puppet-like characters magically to life. Tanaquil Le Clercq recollected, "Janet Reed and Roy Tobias danced a pas de deux, Columbine and her suitor, where she was a limp sawdust doll. Nora Kaye had a solo as Harlequin in a Cleopatra wig where she had to do a somersault and kept missing it. As Pierrot I wore Jerry's wig from *Tyl Ulenspiegel* and had a tulle skirt about my neck." Near the end Le Clercq was to release her balloon, deliberately giving up the gift of life, a fate shared by the other characters when the minstrel returned and collected their balloons.

Janet Reed called *Ballade* "a very depressing piece, a downer." But Robert Barnett remembered, "I think the most incredible ballet experience that I ever had working with Jerry was *Ballade* . . . because that ballet was very special to him. It would make your hair stand on end because he was dealing with all kinds of spiritual things. He would get so involved . . . it was just incredible. It was so intimate that it worked in the studio. I remember people watching in the studio and just raving about it. But we got it into the theater, and it was so intimate and so special it never carried across the footlights. So it only lasted one season."

Todd Bolender rehearsed the ballet, but Robbins replaced him at the last minute. "I was doing two roles," said Bolender. "I was doing a role with Janet [Reed], and Tanny [Le Clercq] and I were doing another role together, but doing the same roles. Then he decided that Tanny was right for that role, and that I was wrong for the other role [with Reed]. So I never danced in any of it, but I did all of the rehearsals. But that was typical of Jerry. You could do the whole thing and suddenly you were out. Probably something happened to change his point of view . . . which I think is perfectly legitimate, but it's rather tough on the dancer." Bolender noted that questioning Robbins' decisions was futile. "That never worked. You never argued with Jerry. It would be impossible because he would go into almost a tantrum if you argued with him. It would always end up with him throwing you out of the ballet, throwing you out of the room."

Others in the cast included Brooks Jackson, John Mandia and Louis Johnson, who was an African-American dancer recruited by Robbins from the School of American Ballet, opening the way for Arthur Mitchell and others who followed. Although blocked from becoming a permanent member of the company by what he called "politics," Johnson went on to dance in Bob Fosse's *Damn Yankees* and later distinguished himself as a choreographer. Robbins offered encouragement, and for a time while struggling to make ends meet, Johnson worked as a housekeeper in Robbins' Park Avenue apartment. "I loved Jerry Robbins," the dancer recalled. "I was very young when I first came to New York City. I didn't know him that well, but he was so kind to me. . . . *Ballade* was quite a wonderful piece, and I was very honored to be a part of it. I think it was the first time [in a ballet] that he used a black dancer really doing a part."

Ballade had its first performance on February 14, 1952. Walter Terry called it "sweet and touching," while noting that it was "not a theatrical rouser." John Martin concluded, "It was pretty bad." Martin also reported that the helium-filled balloon released by Le Clercq remained fugitive in the flies during the intermission that followed, then floated down to "thunderous applause" during the next ballet, upstaging Maria Tallchief, Melissa Hayden and André Eglevsky in Balanchine's *Pas de Trois*. Le Clercq recalled that for the rest of the season a stage manager used a BB gun to burst the balloon after each performance.

Later that year while Robbins was performing the first movement of *Bourrée Fantasque* with Le Clercq, he reportedly "found himself silently asking . . . 'What am I doing up here cavorting like this at the age of thirty-four?'" Soon thereafter and without fanfare, he retired as a dancer (except for his later stage appearances in non-dancing character roles). In 1995, he said that no record was kept of exactly where and when his last performance had taken place, and he had no recollection of it.

In the winter of 1952, while still awaiting his date with HUAC, Robbins commenced rehearsals for a new musical, *Two's Company*, starring Bette Davis, who saw the show as a change of pace from her Hollywood career. Davis was waiting for the studio release of *The Star* when she decided to try her talent in a Broadway revue, with music by Vernon Duke and lyrics from Ogden Nash and Sammy Kahn. Robbins had been a Bette Davis fan for years. He later recalled, "I heard that Bette Davis was in something. I admired her extravagantly, and I said to my agent, 'Get me that.'" The show's director, Jules Dassin, recently called it "a very unhappy project," one that he preferred not remember, characterizing his relationship with Robbins as "love-hate." Politics may have influenced Dassin's opinion to some extent. After directing movies like *Brute Force* and *The Naked City* in the 1940s, he was eventually blacklisted and fled to Europe, where he married Melina Mercouri, with whom he made *Never On Sunday* and *Topkapi*.

During rehearsals for *Two's Company*, both Dassin and Robbins clashed with the show's temperamental star. According to costume designer Miles White, Robbins and Davis "started out on the wrong foot. When Bette came to New York she took an apartment on Beekman Place, [and] she had a party for all the production staff and backers. There was a separate dining room, and I remember Jerry brought in people to discuss business, what he wanted to do here, what he wanted to do there. And Bette was giving a party, and he made it into a business meeting in the dining room. He'd bring people in there and keep them talking. She wanted everybody to become friends, and she got pissed off that he was running a business meeting."

Lyricist Sheldon Harnick contributed a number satirizing Frank Lloyd Wright ("A Man's Home") for the show's comic emcee, Hiram Sherman. Harnick recalled watching one of the rehearsals. "I dropped around the theater one day, and not knowing Robbins really and not knowing his reputation and the mixed feelings that his dancers had about him, I was quite surprised. I was watching a rehearsal of a number, I think it was called "Sadie Thompson," featuring Bette. And Robbins gave her some very simple dance movement which she was having great trouble getting. So he went up on stage and, as far as I could tell, very gently and very patiently started to guide her through the step. She became so self-conscious about this—for all I know her relationship with Robbins may already have been frayed—but what happened was that suddenly she said, 'You're trying to make me look like a horse's ass!' And she just stormed offstage. The dancers, everybody was . . . trying to hide their laughter as Robbins stood there very embarrassed. The only way that the rehearsal could go on, apparently, he had to go offstage to her dressing room and apologize profusely to get her to come back. But what was so apparent was the enjoyment that the dancers were having in this."

Robbins cast both Nora Kaye and Buzz Miller. He dated another dancer in the show, Eleanor Boleyn, who had earlier appeared in the Fabray role in *High Button Shoes*. According to Boleyn's brother, designer Saul Bolasni, "Jerry was drawn to her. But Eleanor was too smart. She would never fall for a gay man."

Robbins was especially demanding of Kaye while rehearsing *Two's Company*. Miles White recalled that his behavior caught Davis' attention. "Bette told me she couldn't understand how mean Jerry was to Nora Kaye. 'Nora Kaye's a great star,' she said. 'I don't understand Jerry, because he treats her so mean on stage and makes her stay after everybody else.'" At a memorial service after Kaye's death in 1987, Robbins offered his own warm recollection of himself and Nora working on one of her dances during the show's pre-Broadway run in Detroit. Robbins remembered the two of them rehearsing until the wee hours and finally breaking up with shared laughter after Nora joked, "Well, just think of it this way. It's our dream. Here we are . . . backstage like Ruby Keeler in *42nd Street*."

For Kaye, Robbins created "Roundabout," set under chandeliers and reminiscent of *Interplay* in its use of children's games; and "Haunted Hot Spot," the story of how a nightclub became haunted after a young man (Bill Callahan) ended a torrid romance by killing his fickle lover (Kaye). For Buzz Miller, Maria Karnilova and David Burns, Robbins set "Esther," turning a south-of-the-border love triangle into a bawdy farce. Frances Herridge wrote that the number was "so risque that it would never have passed the censors had it been spoken instead of danced."

Bette Davis' sketches included takeoffs on herself and Tallulah Bankhead, parodies of Arthur Miller and Noël Coward, and a skit in which she appeared as a black-toothed, hillbilly choir leader. She made her first entrance for the show's second number, "Just Turn Me Loose on Broadway," and closed before the finale with a strained torch song, "Just Like a Man." The writing never rose above the line, "Men are like fires—they should be regularly poked." Throughout the tryouts out of town, the tempestuous star was in a state of extreme nervous fatigue, which she was combating with injections of Dexadrine. She was later diagnosed with osteomyelitis of the jaw, a noncancerous bone condition that nevertheless required surgery and eventually forced her to withdraw from the show.

George Irving remembered Davis' collapse on opening night in Detroit. "She passed out [during her first number]. Oh, that was scary. Nobody knew what to do, and finally Red . . . the stage carpenter just came out onstage, and I think he picked up one foot and dragged her off. She never did that number again. It was a charming [song]. But when she came back on, she said to the audience, 'Well, you cahn't say I didn't faaall for you!' Well, they screamed for five minutes."

Robbins asked his friend Josh Logan and playwright Paul Osborn to come to Detroit to work with Davis and doctor the show before it was too late. In *Movie Stars, Real People, and Me*, Logan recalled his visit to the theater: "The show started and continued, and I kept waiting for Bette Davis to appear. Finally, the first act was over and she had still not appeared onstage once, although in the program she had been listed at least six times. I couldn't decide whether I was more frustrated or infuriated. The trip from New York had been hard enough, but the trip through that first act was the Gobi Desert. I went to Jerry at intermission. He said, 'She won't come on. She says her first-act scenes aren't good enough, so she just told the stage manager to cut them tonight.'

"I said, 'But doesn't she have any sympathy for the audience? That they paid money to see her?' Jerry simply shrugged his shoulders.

"In the second act she appeared three times and was marvelous each time. She sang one song, making the points as expertly as a Bea Lillie might."

Davis refused assistance from Logan. In Boston, her former drama school coach, John Murray Anderson, was enlisted to work with her. City Ballet dancer Sean O'Brien remembered a conversation with Robbins about Davis at the time. "Jerry said, 'You can't believe what she's like. She's completely out of contact with her body. She has no coordination. . . .' There was something really wrong with her locomotion that gave her those peculiar characteristics on the screen."

Frustrated by Davis, Robbins redoubled his efforts with the dancers. "We were rehearsing and rehearsing," said Ralph Linn, "and we were tired. Our arms ached, everything ached. . . . We'd knocked ourselves out, and at the end he said, 'All right, now that you've done it, let's see you dance it!' Our bodies hurt so much, my God, we started to cry."

The curtain rose at the Alvin Theatre on December 15, 1952. The show played only ninety performances before Davis bowed out for surgery, closing the production. The reviews were mixed at best, with many critics chastising the screen goddess for being inadequately trained to carry off the music hall routines. Brooks Atkinson deemed her performance "colorless and monotonous." Nevertheless, Davis played to sold-out houses. Robbins and his dancers fared better with their notices. Atkinson commented, "Every now and then Jerome Robbins and Nora Kaye collaborate on a humorous or a macabre ballet, and then 'Two's Company' has the wizardry of first-rate revue art." In the *Herald Tribune*, Walter Kerr commented that the show "shoots off sparks when Jerome Robbins is in charge." The choreographer picked up his fourth Donaldson Award and perfected a wry Bette Davis imitation that he later performed for friends.

At the beginning of 1953, George Abbott, in some desperation, asked Robbins to lend a hand on *Wonderful Town*, a musical version of *My Sister Eileen* that had opened for tryouts in Boston with Rosalind Russell. Robbins had served in this capacity as uncredited "show doctor" on Abbott's *A Tree Grows in Brooklyn* and Josh Logan's *Wish You Were Here*. With *Wonderful Town*, he was reunited with Leonard Bernstein, Betty Comden and Adolph Green. The three had been recruited by Abbott just before the show went into rehearsals. But the writers, Joseph Fields and Jerome Chodorov, were distressed by the satirical direction the musical team was taking. Abbott wrote, "There was more hysterical debate, more acrimony, more tension and more screaming with this play than with any other show I was ever involved with."

Robbins came on at the eleventh hour to assist his friend, Donald Saddler, the show's choreographer, and declined to take credit for the work. Betty Comden said, "Jerry was wonderful for us. He saved the show." Comden and Green credited Robbins with enabling Rosalind Russell to make her stage comeback with *Wonderful Town*. Comden recalled Robbins' guiding the star through the final scene: "Instead of trying to get Rosalind to do things she couldn't do, he [Jerry] said to Rosalind, 'What would you do here?' So she started jumping around and throwing her right hand up into the air, and he said, 'Yeah, that's it!' so he taught the company what *she* did. That is a very good indication of somebody born to work in the theater, because you use what the star has to offer."

Set in Greenwich Village in 1935, *Wonderful Town*, like *My Sister Eileen*, told the story of Ruth Sherwood (played by Russell), wisecracking older sister of Eileen, the pretty actress (played by newcomer Edith Adams). The concept derived from Ruth McKenney's autobiographical *New Yorker* pieces. The musical adaptation took advantage of the heartfelt familiarity Comden, Green and Bernstein shared with regard to the Bohemian life of the West Village in the 1930s, when the Revuers performed at the Village Vanguard, which became the "Village Vortex" in the script. With a score that ranged from big-band swing to the conga, the show opened at the Winter Garden on February 25, 1953. Though Robbins' name did not appear in any of the notices, he and Saddler registered favorably with the choreography. After a preview, the *Times* called it an "acrobatic production," pointing out that when lifted into the air by a crowd of sailors, Miss Russell appeared to be "wallowing on nothing more tangible than the Good Neighbor Policy."

During the out-of-town tryouts of *Wonderful Town*, Robbins made a discreet trip to Washington, D.C., to give testimony in a private session conducted by HUAC. With his attorney, R. Lawrence Siegel (who had replaced Morris Ernst), Robbins had already decided on his course of action. His public hearing was scheduled to take place in New York that spring. Kirsten Valbor recalled that after Robbins returned from Washington, he invited her and dancer Dody Goodman to dinner. "I don't know why he chose me and Dody to go out with," said Valbor. "It seemed such an odd choice. But maybe it was because we could make him laugh." Neither dancer recalled Robbins ever discussing the subject of the hearing. According to Valbor, "We talked about people and work and stuff like that."

One of the writers of *Wonderful Town*, Jerome Chodorov, had good reason to remember the tryout period and the fact that Robbins was not forthcoming to his colleagues about his legal entanglement with HUAC. "Jerry came in and he was doing his job, and he did a very brilliant job staging the numbers. Jerry was talented, no question about it. We owed a lot to him. But he was very strange with me, and I couldn't figure out why. Then of course I found out very quickly why." Chodorov explained, "Jerry and I had a very short relationship. As a [Communist] Party member, I never really saw him. He was in and out, and I was in California most of the time when he was a Party member. But he named my brother [Edward Chodorov] and myself. . . . I never was bitter about Jerry, because I figured in those days a homosexual was very vulner-able." Chodorov added, "Jerry was a weakling, but he was a very talented weak-ling. And I don't think that he did it out of viciousness. He did it out of fear. That's my personal feeling. He didn't want to hurt anybody. He certainly didn't want to hurt himself."

Unlike some of the other friendly witnesses, Robbins gave no warning be-forehand to those he was naming; and prior to his hearing, he chose not to discuss his decision with those friends and family members who he knew would disapprove. One exception may have been Nora Kaye. According to Arthur Laurents, Robbins turned to Kaye for advice. Laurents recollected that he later said to Nora, "You told him not to, I hope." And Kaye told Laurents, "No. What for? He was going to do it anyway, so I said the sooner the better and save yourself the agony." His sister recalled quarreling with their father about whether or not Jerry should cooperate with the Committee. "I fought with my father a lot," said Sonia. "When the McCarthy thing came along, we had big fights and arguments. My father said, 'What's he gonna do if he doesn't talk? He can only be a dance teacher or something like that. He'll lose his whole career!' We had terrific fights about that."

Former actress Lois Wheeler, whose romantic involvement with Robbins ended some years before, remembered her brief encounter with him during this troubled time. She wrote, "The last time we met was soon before he tes-tified—though I did not know he was going to do that. We saw each other at Sneden's Landing where my husband [Edgar Snow] and I had moved soon after our son was born. Jerry was, as I recall, visiting Aaron Copland who was living up the road from the Captain John House where we were. Jerry walked over one afternoon to sit with me on the small terrace in front of our house. He seemed shy—it had been a long time since we'd seen each other—but sweet and funny as he always had been. He was very fond of my little dog, Molka, and welcomed him to joke and play with as we talked. Whatever was said had nothing to do with his intended appearance before the Committee; there was no mention of that. I did not know why Jerry suddenly came to see me that day but I thought of it afterwards as a moment he made for me, to re-member a past that was soon to be overshadowed by what he thought would be an unforgivable act. I feel enormously sorry for him."

Robbins was finally called to testify before HUAC at 3:20 p.m. on May 5, 1953, in Manhattan's Federal Courthouse. He was one of eight witnesses scheduled to appear that day, but he was the only one who had chosen to cooperate with the Committee. The courtroom was crowded with reporters covering what promised to be front-page news. As the hearing got under way, the Committee's chairman, Harold Velde of Illinois, asked the witness if he wanted "the lights to be turned off," referring to the television and newsreel lamps. Robbins agreed, desperate to minimize the damage such media exposure was bound to cause. This was not the sort of publicity he had ever imagined. *The King and I* was still selling out on Broadway and a much-anticipated ballet, *Afternoon of a Faun,* was scheduled to premiere with the New York City Ballet the following week. Yet here he was, facing infamy.

The spectacle of the hearing lasted less than an hour. Robbins had rehearsed his testimony with his attorney. Siegel was a prominent civil rights advocate who also represented *The Nation* magazine and celebrities such as Gloria Swanson. The Committee's chief counsel, Frank Tavenner, and several congressmen quizzed Robbins about his meteoric success as a choreographer and his political activities. Robbins summarily repudiated his three-year association with the Communist Party. Explaining his willingness to cooperate with the Committee, he asserted, "I did it according to my conscience."

Congressman Clyde Doyle of California asked him, "What is it in your conscience, or what was it in your experience, that makes you, certainly one of the top men in your profession, one who has reached the pinnacle in your art, willing to come here, in spite of the fact that you knew some other people, who claim to be artists or authors or musicians, would put you down as a stool pigeon, and voluntarily testify as you have today?"

Robbins replied, "I've examined myself. I think I made a great mistake before in entering the Communist Party, and I feel that I am doing the right thing as an American." This was Robbins seeking to appease his inquisitors. Much of his testimony had the hollow ring of prepared statements delivered under duress. In *Naming Names,* a history of the McCarthy period, Victor Navasky wrote that Robbins' "demeanor before HUAC was so compliant that his appearance had about it the aura of social blackmail." According to Walter Bernstein, who later wrote the Woody Allen–starring movie *The Front,* "In

Jerry's case, the Committee led him all the way. And he gave them what they wanted to hear."

After thanking Robbins for performing his patriotic duty, Congressman Gordon Scherer commented, "I am going to see *The King and I* tonight, and I will appreciate it much more." Before the hearing adjourned, Congressman Doyle advised Robbins, "You are in a wonderful place, through your art, your music, your talent, which God blessed you with, to perhaps be very vigorous and positive in promoting Americanism in contrast to Communism." Robbins pointed out that his work was "acclaimed for its American quality particularly," and Doyle suggested, "I realize that, but let me urge you to even put more of that in it, where you can appropriately."

In addition to the Chodorov brothers, Robbins named actress Madeline Lee (who was by this time married to actor Jack Gilford), filmmaker Lionel Berman, dance critic Edna Ocko, actors Elliot Sullivan and Lloyd Gough, and a secretary-stenographer, Lettie Stever, who worked for his former agent, Jane Deacy. Curiously, when asked about the profession of Edna Ocko, Robbins claimed not to know, though he did recall that Ocko had been present at the last contentious Party meeting that he attended. Nor did he explain how he knew Lettie Stever, who was identified the following day as Lettie Stevens in the *New York Times*. Robbins testified only that Stever recruited him into the Communist Party. According to Madeline Gilford and others, she was a left-wing activist who shared an apartment during the war years with a group of politicized women whose husbands were away in the military. It may well be that this was the woman who enlisted Robbins into the Party and with whom he had an affair, as he earlier told the FBI. But he may also have been lying or bending the truth to protect others like Katie O'Brien. There were many Communist friends, acquaintances and family members whom Robbins chose not to name. Deals with the Committee to spare family members were not uncommon, and it seems unlikely that the Committee would have been unaware of the activities of his sister and brother-in-law.

Because of Robbins' high profile, the hearing generated enormous publicity and all those he named were stigmatized in the press. Actor Elliot Sullivan had been named before the Committee by actor Martin Berkeley two years earlier. The Chodorov brothers had been named in *Counterattack* but not in the

HUAC proceedings. Most of the others on Robbins' list were new names, those under suspicion who had not been identified previously in the hearings. "They were only interested in new names," said Jerome Chodorov. "Jerry had his choice of a lot of people. They must have said to him, 'Look, we've got all those people. We need some new names.' That's the way they operated." Madeline Gilford agreed, commenting, "We were named to order."

In his testimony, Robbins stated that at one of his earliest Communist Party meetings Gilford had asked him to give a lecture on how "dialectical materialism had helped me make *Fancy Free.*" He told the Committee he thought the request was ludicrous, that Communism had not influenced his work on the ballet, which predated his membership in the Party. Gilford later denied ever asking him to give such a lecture, insisting she had not even known the meaning of dialectical materialism in the early days of her left-wing activities. Recalling how she first met Robbins before he created *Fancy Free,* Gilford said, "The only thing I ever did was teach him the Lindy hop." Gilford and her husband were subsequently blacklisted, and a short time later both were subpoenaed to testify before the Committee. In the end, neither of them would name names.

According to Jerome Chodorov, his brother, Edward, also a playwright, after learning that he had been named by Robbins, quipped, "Stabbed by the wicked fairy." Eric Bentley, the editor of *Thirty Years of Treason: Excerpts from Hearings before the House Committee on Un-American Activities, 1938-1968,* recalled that Edward Chodorov denied privately that he had ever been a member of the Communist Party. Chodorov contended to Bentley that Robbins had lied under the threat of having his homosexuality publicized. But Chodorov was quite active on the left as a fellow-traveler, and a member of his family suggested that his claim of not being a Communist was "fanciful." Robbins' cousin Bob Silverman knew the Chodorov brothers and assumed both were Party members, and it seems most likely that Robbins made the same assumption. Both brothers were subsequently blacklisted.

Elliot Sullivan was a tall Texas-born actor known for his gangster roles in movies and on television, as well as for his appearances on Broadway in *Brigadoon* and *Green Grow the Lilacs.* After suffering under the blacklist and the legal ordeal of his own hearing, he and his family eventually fled to London.

His widow, Norma Sullivan, recalled that her husband attended Robbins' hearing. "It was a great shock. Elliot had known him [Robbins] and he had been very fond of Elliot, came to him as a kind of mentor about all sorts of things. Elliot hadn't seen him in a long time, but he was still very friendly and admiring. . . . Elliot was in the courtroom. He was told to sit in one of the front rows during the hearing. . . . In fact, when they called Jerry he had to pass Elliot, and he said, 'Sorry, Elliot. Excuse me.' Little did he know there was a lot more to come to be excused."

Despite the hardships she and her husband endured, Norma Sullivan harbored little bitterness toward Robbins, as she, too, heard the story that he had been blackmailed into informing. She said, "I must say that of all the informers, the only one—and it was only in the last few years—that I felt sorry for in a way was Jerry Robbins, and that was because what they threatened him with was to tell his mother that he was homosexual. That is as appalling as almost anything else they've done." Mrs. Sullivan also pointed out, however, that other gay artists targeted by the inquisition, like Aaron Copland and Marc Blitzstein, did not name names. In that regard, both Copland and Blitzstein were somewhat less vulnerable than Robbins, as neither composer was likely to work in television or movies, though Copland had done film scores in the thirties and forties. Blitzstein, whose hearing was canceled before he had to testify, described Robbins' action as "miserably revolting" and broke off any further collaborative relationship. But Copland, who suffered considerable agony at the hands of McCarthy's Senate investigation, would not hesitate to work with Robbins again.

Arthur Laurents recalled that Robbins "never mentioned homosexuality when he told me he had informed. And he never mentioned informing again. He knew where I stood and didn't care: he would not be questioned." One of the Hollywood Ten, Ring Lardner, Jr., doubted that Robbins informed because of the alleged exposure threat. Lardner suggested to Victor Navasky, "I don't know whether it's true or not, but if you were Jerry Robbins, wouldn't you like to have people believe that's the reason you did it?" Lardner admitted that he didn't know Robbins well. The idea that he would have invented or encouraged the story appears highly unlikely, given his apparent terror after his first encounter with Ed Sullivan three years before the hearing and his lifelong effort to conceal his sexuality.

The considerations that led Robbins to become a friendly witness almost certainly resulted from fear overcoming conscience; however, there may have been other motivating factors as well. Arthur Laurents believed that Robbins, like Kazan, became an informant because he wanted to further his career. In a recent letter, Laurents stated, "Jerry's ambition made him what he was and was the reason he did what he did." In 1999, Laurents wrote a play called *Jolson Sings Again,* based on his experiences during the McCarthy era. For his drama, he created a character resembling Robbins, as well as Kazan. Of the former, Laurents told the *New York Times,* "He was my friend. What I found out later, as it says in the play, was, 'You're not evil because you informed; you informed because you're evil.'"

Eric Bentley disagreed, even as the statement might apply to Kazan. "I don't think being an informer does reflect radical evil. I think in many cases it reflects a certain weakness, conformity, going along with what is being done, and in other cases it's semi-justified, as in the case of Kazan, because Kazan held opinions about Communism which we may not agree with but had some plausibility. Since the Communist Party had a policy of secrecy, and many of them pretended to be great Jeffersonian liberals when they were in fact slaves of Stalin, the policy of total disclosure was defensible. That was Kazan's position. I didn't share it but I respected it."

Kazan would make his case in dramatic terms the following year with *On the Waterfront.* Laurents suggested that Robbins disclosed names because he, too, was anticipating a movie career. "Not that he said that was his reason," wrote Laurents. "He gave several, dancing from one to the other—he'd been duped into joining the Party, he was scared, the Communists were a threat, Russia was anti-Semitic—but even Nora believed movies were the real reason." While Robbins never voiced any great enthusiasm for a film career (he was actually able to make more money with his most successful Broadway shows), he did choreograph the film version of *The King and I* two years later. His only other movie credit was *West Side Story.*

In May of 1953, he had a more immediate cause for concern about blacklisting, aside from any movie ambitions or exaggerated fears he may have had about his Broadway stage career. Thanks to Leland Hayward, Robbins had already contracted to choreograph the *Ford 50ᵗʰ Anniversary Show*, a television special that was scheduled to air the following month with Mary Martin and Ethel Merman. This was to be a two-hour live broadcast on two networks (NBC and CBS), a spectacular event by the standards of the day, with appearances by Frank Sinatra, Bing Crosby, Eddie Fisher, Rudy Vallee, Oscar Hammerstein and Edward R. Murrow. With Ford Motors as the sponsor, blacklisting would be enforced, although Ford would become the first major company to break from the policy with the broadcast of a concert by Leonard Bernstein (who was blacklisted though never called by HUAC).

One of the show's producers, Lawrence White, recalled that Leland Hayward exerted a great influence on Robbins. "We had our problems with Jerry during that period," said White. "I sat with him and Leland for hours and hours, because we had two things, one was Jerry and the other was the show. The show had to go on. To get him to organize it was a very traumatic experience for all of us, because we're doing a show, and we have to keep him in line all the time. . . . Leland calmed him down. . . . Otherwise he was ready to go out the window. We were up on Madison Avenue in the penthouse, Leland's office at that time, and boy, you could hardly contain him. He actually came back to see us right after the experience [in the hearing]."

White recalled the difficulties that arose with one network when the producers "went to a certain guy at NBC and they queered the whole thing saying Jerry was a Red. That was terrible." Even though Robbins' position with the show was in some jeopardy, White believed that fear of exposure was a deciding factor in Robbins' choice to cooperate with HUAC. "You must realize, he's like a finely tuned watch, you know, and he was vibrating all the time at a point of explosion."

Arthur Laurents recalled that there was turmoil for Robbins on the homefront as well. "He kicked Buzz Miller out of the apartment because he didn't want Leland and Slim Hayward—the gentile parents he wished he had—to know Buzz lived there, and because he wanted the freedom to trick." Nevertheless, the romance and live-in arrangement with Miller continued sporadically over the next couple of years, though Miller had his own East Side apartment.

While Robbins' career continued to flourish in the aftermath of the hearing, he lost many friends, and he was bewildered by his family's reaction. After he testified, Bob Silverman refused to have any contact with his cousin for more than twenty years. Robbins and his sister also had an anguished falling-out. Sonia and her husband were still active on the left, and within those circles, they were now looked upon with mistrust. "Jerry and I didn't talk for a long time," said Sonia. "We met a couple of times, but I was very angry and upset. The FBI didn't bother George and me so much as our friends, because it was guilt by association. . . . It was a big mistake Jerry made. It was not forgivable, but it was understandable."

Dorothy Gilbert maintained her friendship with both Sonia and Jerry. "It was something that was very difficult to understand," said Gilbert. "I tried to put myself in her place and I just couldn't. Jerry really loved his sister and I'm sure that she loved him. But there came a time when she sort of sat back and looked at the whole picture and she didn't like it. . . . Those were more than lost years. Jerry was heartbroken. I remember Lena, his mother, took it most seriously and there was very little she could do about it. The damage was done. I think it was most difficult to have two children who were not on speaking terms with each other at that time. I had hoped that we would someday see some ballet that might cover this."

In later years, Robbins never made any public statements about his HUAC experience and carefully avoided the subject during interviews, which he aggressively sought to control, often intimidating journalists by tape-recording them and demanding the right to edit and approve final copy. Unlike Kazan, who defended his decision to inform on political grounds in an ad in the *New York Times* and later in his autobiography, Robbins chose silence. Arthur Laurents recalled that on one occasion Robbins became righteously indignant when Kazan invited him to dinner. But in the early seventies, Robbins lent his tacit support to Kazan by attending a reception for the embattled director when he received New York City's prestigious Handel Medallion. Arranged by publisher Sol Stein, the gathering was held at the New York Public Library and was attended by Budd Schulberg, Abe Burrows and others who had cooperated with HUAC.

Prior to the publication of *Naming Names* in 1980, Navasky, editor and future publisher of *The Nation*, wrote a letter to Robbins that included the following inquiry: "The theme of my book has to do with what happens to a society when the state puts pressure on individuals to betray their principles. Your own experience as a witness before the House Committee is particularly relevant because of two stories surrounding it which have become a part of the folklore of the period. I write to you now to ask whether they are accurate and if not, in what respect.

"First, it is said that one of the factors which led you to appear as a cooperative witness before HUAC was your fear that if you failed to go along, the Committee would embarrass you by giving publicity to your sex life at a time when homosexuality was generally regarded as a stigma. Second, I was told that after you testified, a member of the HUAC staff made sexual advances towards you."

Navasky had interviewed Robbins' lawyer, Lawrence Siegel, prior to his death in 1981, and Siegel claimed that he filed a written protest on behalf of his client with the chairman of the Committee regarding the alleged harassment incident, although no record of such a protest has ever come to light. Robbins offered only a terse reply to Navasky, stating that he had never heard either story before, a rather incredible assertion given the wide circulation of the blackmail allegation. Robbins further insisted that both stories were entirely false. He made no admission whatsoever about his sexuality. As far as the gay side of his lifestyle, he remained steadfastly in the closet. Robbins was soon to become a Kennedy Center Honoree and was the focus of widespread adulation for a lifetime of achievement that was still far from over. He was not about to allow his private life to be invaded and marred by scandal. His personal affairs were strictly off-limits to inquiring journalists. Closing off the possibility of any further exchange with Navasky, Robbins indicated that he planned to deal with the subject of HUAC in his memoirs.

Robbins' attorney, Siegel, also represented writer-producer Sydney Buchman, an unfriendly witness who, like Elliot Sullivan, used the First Amendment to fight the Committee. In one of Navasky's interviews with Siegel, the lawyer claimed: "I was probably the major influence on him [Robbins]." Siegel remembered that in prevailing upon Robbins to name names, "HUAC told him [Robbins] . . . that people he admired and respected had testified—cooperated—secretly." The lawyer did not reveal who those people were, and he would only describe the sexual harassment incident by saying that "some members of the Committee staff—fags—approached him socially." Siegel's use of the epithet raises some doubt as to his ability to represent his client fairly in the first place.

Robbins would see things very differently in retrospect than he had at the time of the hearing. In later years, he once confided about his HUAC experience to his friend Michael Koessel, a philosophy Ph.D. now working on Wall Street. The conversation stuck in Koessel's mind because it was such an unusual subject for Robbins to bring up. "I just let him talk," said Koessel, "because I could tell that it was something that he would probably never talk to me about again, and I knew lots of people who had known him for a long time, and they said he'd never spoken about it."

Robbins indicated to his friend that no threat of exposure had been made regarding his sexuality. "He said, 'I wasn't threatened with that,'" Koessel recalled. "But he did say that he was completely motivated by fear, and he was very afraid, and he thought he got very, very bad advice from lawyers, which is part of the reason he's never liked lawyers since." Koessel speculated that the possibility of exposure was "probably something that fed into his fear. And I also asked him, 'Do you think your career would have been hurt by it?' And he said, 'In retrospect, no, not given where I worked and what I did ultimately.'"

With hindsight, Robbins was probably right. His career on Broadway and in ballet would most likely not have been seriously damaged by public exposure of his sexuality or by the blacklist had he resisted HUAC as others did by invoking his Fifth or First Amendment rights. He also must have realized after the fact that any threat that might have been made early on by Ed Sullivan would more than likely never have been carried out, if only because of the possible legal actions that might have ensued. Journalists, even those with the scruples of Sullivan or Winchell, knew they had to be cautious about libel. Liberace, for example, sued and won a case against a British publication that labeled him a homosexual in the 1950s. Robbins' reticence and lack of candor about his folly with HUAC are not surprising when, looking back, he could see that he had been victimized by fears that turned out to be unfounded in so many ways.

Koessel recalled that Robbins "implied that he felt very betrayed when he came out of it. He mentioned . . . that the first thing his sister said when he came out of the hearings [was] . . . 'What will I tell our children?' I felt like he also felt somewhat betrayed that people didn't show much of an understanding towards him and what he had done. But I didn't get the sense that he acted for political reasons, like some people did, that he felt Communism was so terrible and had to be fought at any cost."

Koessel added, "I always thought that he never completely recovered from whatever happened then. I felt that every night of his life and probably every day of his life that's something that plagued him."

Many of Robbins' relationships in the theater were strained with the fallout from HUAC. Leonard Bernstein, with his left-leaning political sympathies, disapproved but, like many, remained conciliatory toward Robbins for the sake of future collaborations. Nora Kaye was hard-pressed to maintain her friendship with Robbins. According to Isabel Brown, "Nora was never thrilled with what he did with the McCarthy thing. She kind of in a way never really forgave him. . . . She was a liberal, always was, and she was very upset. . . . But Jerry's life was his work, and if he was threatened in any way with that, his creative powers, he was going to do anything he could to save that. He always lived with enormous guilt about that."

Todd Bolender, who shared a dressing room with Robbins during the early years at City Ballet, believed that his personality was deeply affected by HUAC. "From 1953 on, working with him was always very difficult," said Bolender. "Jerry started changing pretty drastically. He developed a sort of a shell and a hardness that you couldn't break through at times." Bolender also speculated about Robbins and others who were investigated by the FBI. "I think [J. Edgar] Hoover had a vendetta against all people in the theater."

In fact, at the end of 1953, the New York office of the FBI recommended that the Robbins case should be closed since he had cooperated with HUAC; but a memo was soon forthcoming from Hoover's office that stated, ". . . you are instructed to continue your efforts to interview the subject and the results should be promptly submitted to the Bureau." Hoover later personally advised his agents, "In conducting this interview you should be most discreet. . . ." Robbins was interviewed on November 8, 1954, and the FBI continued to track Robbins' movements at least through the sixties, regularly notifying the CIA and Interpol about his trips abroad.

After his HUAC hearing, Robbins returned to his sanctuary at the New York City Ballet and continued rehearsals for *Afternoon of a Faun*, which traced back to the Diaghilev era and Nijinsky's celebrated ballet of 1912. Robbins utilized Debussy's score, but transformed Nijinsky's fauns and nymphs into a pair of ballet students in the studio. Departing from the American flavor of much of his previous work, Robbins chose European music and labored to achieve a subtle touch within the traditional confines of the classical form. There would be no rumbas or circus acrobatics, but rather a boy and girl in practice clothes relating to each other's reflections in the studio mirror. Instead of mimicking Nijinsky's portrait of self-gratification, Robbins created the picture of a shy, ten-minute courtship, with its restrained eroticism casting a wry and revealing light on the inherently narcissistic world of dancers.

The original dancers were Tanaquil Le Clercq and Francisco Moncion. Jerry also considered Buzz Miller and Louis Johnson for the male role, but was apparently unable to get approval for casting either of them, the latter perhaps because of 1953 reservations about casting an interracial couple to dance such a romantic *pas de deux* at the all-white City Ballet. Johnson recalled, "I was supposed to do it. . . . I had one rehearsal. . . . But I think Balanchine didn't want to have me . . . because that ballet would have put me permanently into the company."

According to Edward Villella, the City Ballet star who danced the role some years later, Robbins credited him for initially inspiring the ballet, which would, of course, go through the same imagistic layering process as all of Robbins' works. In his memoir, *Prodigal Son*, Villella wrote, "I learned that I had actually been Jerry's inspiration for *Afternoon of a Faun* when he had seen me as a teenage student work at SAB [the School of American Ballet] on Madison Avenue. Studios there had huge windows, and sunlight often poured in through them. One afternoon, I was standing in the fading light daydreaming and leaned against the barre, yawning and stretching absentmindedly. Watching me, Jerry was struck by an idea for the ballet." Robbins later recounted that he was impressed that afternoon by how "animalistic" Villella was as a young dancer still finding his way.

Another moment in the genesis of the ballet came one day when Robbins watched dancers, including Louis Johnson, rehearsing the *Swan Lake* adagio and was struck by the contradiction between the passionate intimacy of the choreography and the dancers' typically self-conscious concerns about correct technique, those studied rituals of ballet executed over countless hours in front of the mirror. Robbins himself was resistant to the idea of narcissism as it was eventually applied by critics to his ballet. He pointed out, "The mirror is the dancer's work tool."

Tanaquil Le Clercq recalled that Robbins' only difficulty with the ballet was deciding which way the dancers should face to establish the mirror, finally solving the problem by having them turn to the audience, as if the mirror covered that "fourth wall" of the stage space. Le Clercq also noted that Robbins incorporated into the ballet many of her natural gestures in rehearsal. "I'd complain about the heat and tug at my tunic and he would say, 'Great. Keep it in.'" Of Le Clercq in the role, Robbins wrote, "She understood the unconscious pleasures of the piece and possessed a subdued sensuality. She was totally innocent. Yet, the possibility that she just might conceivably be willing to have a love affair hovered about her like a faint perfume."

The idea of this piece is deceptively simple—that is, a simplicity engendered by the weight of Robbins' assiduously crafted details. The girl enters after the boy has warmed up and decided on a nap. The two soon partner each other in a *pas de deux* practiced before the mirror. After the boy spontaneously kisses her on the cheek, the girl slowly places her hand there in a kind of startled wonderment and withdraws. Robbins uses fleeting moments to convey his meaning, as when the girl is first lifted by her partner and allows her head to fall in the opposite direction of the lift, her gaze freed for an instant from the hold of the mirror and thereby revealing a blush of inner feelings. In the same way, the boy shudders just as the girl steps by him, with Robbins allowing him to convey the inward emotion appropriate to the romance, at the same time mirroring in homage a similarly impassioned shudder that appeared in Nijinsky's choreography.

In conception, to some extent, Robbins was influenced by Mallarmé's 1876 poem that had originally inspired the Debussy score. Francisco Moncion recalled, "Jerry had been looking around for a mood piece; he had already done *Ballade* to Debussy, but didn't feel he had finished with the idea. The languor of the people was his; he read Mallarmé, and the gestures he used were evocative of Mallarmé's faun—such as pushing through the reeds on a hot, humid afternoon."

The lighting and decor were essential to create the particular diaphanous atmosphere in which Robbins' enchanted interlude would take place. He showed designer Jean Rosenthal a Paul Cadmus drawing of dancers in a studio, and Rosenthal conceived of the set's china silk walls. Robbins recalled, "She made the silkiness of the set the counterpart to the whiteness of the paper." The effect of the integrated whole—dance, music and design—was captured by Adolph Green's observation about Robbins' vision in general: "Things that might at first seem ordinary, he made it seem that you had never seen them before."

The ballet premiered on May 14, 1953 (and became a mainstay in the repertory). While generally praising the ballet, Walter Terry wrote, "Not many years ago, Nijinsky's *Faun* shocked American audiences, for although the participants lived only in myth, they behaved with considerable physical candor. The Robbins *Faun* is not shocking in the same way at all, but it does invite shock of a different sort, for whether Mr. Robbins intended it or not, his ballet suggests that the dancer is, or tends to be, in love with himself."

The critics noted Robbins' departure from Nijinsky, and he later defended his contemporary *Faun*, oddly enough, as though it were performed by two male dancers (which may have been a Freudian slip or simply an error in translation). In a 1959 article in *World Theatre*, Robbins argued, "People said that this ballet showed disrespect to a work entirely governed by a poem, a musical prelude, perhaps even a choreography. But is it right to say that a work, complete in itself, is no longer able to suggest new forms, sensations and states of mind. For me the sensations of a faun may be felt on a beach, in a wood, in a street, in the heat of summer, now or in the future. Why not in a dance studio where two young men are exercising their bodies, where the music awakens in them the pleasurable sensations of their physical pursuits, where they are thus living a ballet in spirit while evoking it. And why not while recreating it?" Robbins added, "I try not to impose but to propose a subject and leave its interpretation to the audience."

After *Faun* premiered, Robbins managed to devote himself simultaneously to the *Ford 50th Anniversary Show* and to another ballet, *Fanfare*, set to Benjamin Britten's *The Young Person's Guide to the Orchestra* (based on a theme from the Baroque composer Henry Purcell). The ballet opened June 2, 1953, as part of the celebration on this side of the Atlantic for the coronation of Queen Elizabeth II. Appropriate for the occasion at City Center, there was much pageantry and indeed fanfare, replete with colorful banners and processions. Robbins devised a festive, didactic piece, giving each dancer an instrument to portray, creating visual counterparts onstage for the orchestra. The thirty-four dancers were divided into groups representing the various sections in the pit. For instance, dancers representing horns were costumed in brassy yellow (by Irene Sharaff) and Robbins gave them a series of staccato movements cleverly reflecting stridency in the music.

John Martin was less than enthusiastic and described *Fanfare* as "a combination of *Card Party* and *Peter and the Wolf.*" In the *Herald Tribune*, Walter Terry called it "a gay and frolicsome work." Terry singled out "the easy bravado of Edward Bigelow's tuba." Bigelow, who would later become one of the troupe's managers, described the esteem and concern that Balanchine expressed about Robbins. "Balanchine didn't respect very many choreographers, but he had respect for Jerry. Balanchine would say, 'I don't have to do that, let Jerry do that,' and that was a measure of his regard for Jerry. Balanchine complained to me sometimes about Jerry because he thought Jerry was asking dancers to do things that he [Balanchine] didn't think were proper for them to do physically. Balanchine said, 'I'm very worried about that because they're going to hurt themselves. They're going to get hurt. . . . It's not right. Jerry shouldn't do that.' But [Balanchine] didn't tell Jerry."

Robbins remembered that Balanchine came on to finish a section in the finale of *Fanfare* when he was unable to make it to a rehearsal. With Balanchine's blessing, he continued to divide his time between City Ballet and Broadway, and now the new frontier of television. Robbins spent several hectic weeks shuttling back and forth between the ballet studio and the TV studios where he was rehearsing the Ford anniversary show.

In her memoir, *My Heart Belongs,* Mary Martin recalled, "From the beginning rehearsals, Ethel [Merman] and I got on like gangbusters. Anything she didn't think of, I did. But the genius of Jerry Robbins really made the show possible. It was his idea that we do a number sitting on high stools, side by side, on an empty stage doing songs of our different roles. That got us both going. . . . It was Ethel's idea that we do the 'I' songs, songs like 'I Cried for You,' 'I Can't Give You Anything but Love, Baby'—all songs beginning with 'I.' But the stools were Jerry's idea, just rehearsal tools. 'Let's not clutter up,' he said. Wow! Did it ever start a trend."

This was the first time that Martin and Merman worked together. Producer Lawrence White did not recall their rapport being as harmonious as Martin reported. White said, "Oh, they hardly spoke to each other. Jerry and I and Leland concocted a solution, because when it came to the billing of these two women we had our problems. They both wanted top billing of the whole show. . . . The way it worked was the following: The advertisements in the papers for the show had a big circle, and way on the top of the circle you'd have Merman and Martin, so they had top billing there. However, one wanted to be in front of the other, so we had it like this, one day Merman, one day Martin."

Lawrence recalled that Robbins was uncertain about his first television venture. "He didn't know television," said Lawrence. "He wasn't sure whether he liked it or not, but we kibbutzed him into liking it a lot, and he did some creative work. At this point he didn't understand television, and he wanted a floor that would shine, and so somehow we had it oiled. And the next day the dancers came and slipped all over the place, and I had to spend the whole day cleaning up oil so Jerry could work. He gets this funny look on his face which was quizzical. . . . Any time he was in the wrong—when I say in the wrong, he wasn't in the wrong very many times—but when he was in the wrong, he'd get this innocence on his face, you know, which said, 'I don't understand this.'"

Staged at the old Center Theatre at Rockefeller Center, the show aired on June 15, 1953, with Henry Ford sitting in the audience. Martin recalled,

"Everything went perfectly and the showstopper—if you can call it that, because you can't stop a television show—was Ethel's and my duet, sitting on our stools." Robbins was honored with a Sylvania Award for his efforts, but it would be another two years before he returned to television, and he would always have serious misgivings about the medium, especially when it came to televising his ballets.

Later in the year, Robbins invited his longtime friend Anna Sokolow to oversee the mission that he had undertaken for the America-Israel Cultural Foundation—to develop an indigenous Israeli dance troupe that would tour internationally. Robbins had selected the Inbal Dance Theater, a company devoted to traditional Yemenite dancing under the direction of composer-choreographer Sara Levi Tanai. Sokolow and Robbins made the twenty-seven-hour flight to Israel in December, with Sokolow not yet decided whether or not she would accept the assignment. While sympathetic to the left and although Communist-hunting investigators once tried to question her, Sokolow never wavered in her affection for Robbins. This was her first trip to the Promised Land, and she recalled, "I certainly didn't expect to be affected so deeply, but the minute the plane landed I was overwhelmed with an indescribable feeling about being there. I didn't have any kind of strong Zionist background, but going there changed my point of view." After watching the Inbal group perform, Sokolow accepted the offer from Robbins and the A-ICF to introduce the Israeli dancers to modern theatrical styles and production techniques. Robbins maintained his association with the A-ICF until the end of his life.

Returning to New York, Robbins contributed some of the final touches to a touring folk concert, *Musical Americana*, which was produced and directed by Mary Hunter. Meanwhile, back at City Ballet, he commenced rehearsals for *Quartet*, a short ballet set to Prokofiev's String Quartet No. 2. The score drew from Caucasian folk songs that Prokofiev wove into the classical form, and in his own way Robbins followed suit. "As I went along I saw it more classical . . . but George [Balanchine] came in somewhere along the middle and said it had to be Caucasian. Once he put that idea into my head, the ballet started to go that way more and more. Although I had been to Israel recently (some of the critics knew this), it's not true that there was Israeli material in the ballet."

The original cast included three couples, Patricia Wilde and Herbert Bliss, Jillana and Jacques d'Amboise, Yvonne Mounsey and Todd Bolender. Wilde recalled, "I knew all of the things that people went through [with Jerry]. . . . but when we were working on *Quartet* it was quite pleasant."

Richard Thomas also rehearsed for the ballet, but he remembered, "We rehearsed endlessly. It went on forever. There was a lot of scandal. Jerry had Nicholas Kopeikine [the company's rehearsal pianist] playing this Prokofiev endless hours, and Kopeikine had to play a concerto or something and said that [Jerry] had to have another pianist. Jerry said, 'No Kopeikine, no ballet!' Kopeikine came to rehearsal and had every finger in Band-Aids. The other scandal with the ballet . . . when it came time to do the costumes, and Jerry and Karinska got together, he insisted on some incredibly expensive, beautiful silk from Siam or someplace. There was a terrible scene about the price of the silk for the bloody costumes. But he did what he wanted."

"We had gorgeous dresses," said Wilde. "We all wanted them. They were wonderful silk cocktail dresses." She added, "The ballet actually didn't last very long. We only did it one season. I know that the costumes were lost in a flood."

Quartet opened February 18, 1954, but reviews were delayed because critics were attending the opening of a group of touring Kabuki dancers. John Martin said it was "charmingly composed, with its accent chiefly on ensemble formations." Walter Terry called it a "non-nervous" work and explained, "The impatience of jazz is absent, the fear of conflict is missing, sudden anger and frightened innocence are not to be seen. In place there is serenity." Robbins may have intended to continue in a serene balletic vein, but he was again distracted by the commercial lures of Broadway and also by a brief excursion into opera. He would not create another ballet for two years.

Early in 1954, Aaron Copland invited Robbins to direct *The Tender Land*, the composer's first full-length opera, which was being produced by the New York City Opera Company at the City Center. Copland's work was initially inspired by the journey of James Agee and photographer Walker Evans in creating the book *Let Us Now Praise Famous Men*, documenting the lives of southern sharecroppers. Copland admired the book and suggested it to his friend Erik Johns as a starting point for the opera's libretto. Johns turned the story into a drama about a rural, Midwestern family, the Mosses, whose lives are altered by two drifters who pass through and are falsely accused of having molested young girls in the area.

Johns explained why the drama held special meaning for Copland in light of recent events: "The most dramatic scene was when the drifters are falsely accused, and then a few minutes later discovered to be not guilty. Aaron had just been through the McCarthy business and we were definitely influenced by that. When Grandpa Moss says to the boys, 'You're guilty all the same,' we were thinking about all the false McCarthy accusations and the effect they had on innocent people." Copland had faced McCarthy's Senate Committee in a private session on May 26, 1953, and testified that he had never been a Communist. Under interrogation, he explained with pride and acerbic humor that his support of various suspected Communist front organizations was always in the interest of promoting music. While Copland's case was altogether different from that of Robbins, the two artists undoubtedly shared an indignant view of how their lives had been invaded by what Navasky aptly called the "degradation ceremony" of the hearings.

Copland did not attend rehearsals for the opera. He wrote, "Jerry Robbins . . . thought it was very 'cool' of me not to go to rehearsals, but the fact was I didn't have time!" Delayed by other projects, Copland delivered the finished composition in March, and the first performance took place on April 1, 1954. Oliver Smith designed the sets, with lighting by Jean Rosenthal. John Butler choreographed, and Thomas Schippers conducted. *The Tender Land* ran only an hour and a half, and the evening was filled out with a performance of Gian Carlo Menotti's popular short opera *Amahl and the Night Visitors*. Most of the reviews were unfavorable. In the *New York Times*, Olin Downes criticized the libretto and second-act dramatic resolution as "inconclusive and unconvincing." Downes noted, however, that "the dramatic direction of Jerome Robbins was usually effective. . . ." The opera was revised and presented at Tanglewood in August, but Robbins was by then heading back to Broadway. He would never direct another opera.

At the beginning of April, Robbins' mother was hospitalized with breast cancer, and he dropped everything to be with her. "That was a very painful time," said Mary Hunter. "His mother was dying and it was very difficult [for him] to deal with that, very difficult." His sister remembered, "Jerry was in the hospital with my father at the time my mother was dying, and we were to-gether with my mom then, and when she was buried. . . . She was alive and kicking two weeks before she died. It happened very quickly. She must have had a lot of pain but you never heard anything about it. Very stoical lady. Two breast amputations."

Lena Robbins died on April 12, 1954, and was buried in the family plot at Riverside Cemetery in Saddle Brook, New Jersey. Her will stated, "It is my fervent hope and prayer that my beloved children shall take care of my beloved husband and that my children will continue to always assist each other in every possible manner and will keep in constant contact with each other."

According to Sonia, the reconciliation with Jerry that was her mother's wish took place at this time. Sonia recalled, "I wrote to Jerry before she died and Jerry said it was the best letter he ever received. I wrote out of my under-standing [his predicament with HUAC] and coming to the conclusion I could not be the judge of his actions and thinking how would I do in that situation."

In spite of any ill feelings that Robbins may have harbored toward his fa-ther, he supported Harry through the crisis. Dorothy Gilbert recalled, "Jerry, after his mother passed away, took his father to Israel with him. . . . He wouldn't permit his father to be alone. This tells you something about Jerry's character." Four years later, in memory of his mother, Jerry established the Lena Robbins Foundation, which was mandated to assist young choreogra-phers and to develop a film library dedicated to the preservation of dance.

With choreography credits for eight Broadway shows behind him, Rob-bins' ambition now focused on directing. After the Ford anniversary show, Mary Martin proposed that Robbins direct a new production of *Peter Pan*, a play which she had wanted to do for a number of years. The project was being produced by Leland Hayward, Edward Lester of the Civic Light Opera and Martin's husband, Richard Halliday. The book and score were still being written early in 1954, when George Abbott asked Robbins to choreograph his new show, *The Pajama Game*. At sixty-five, Abbott showed no sign of slowing down. Robbins turned down the offer, but suggested that Abbott might con-sider using a young choreographer named Bob Fosse.

Buzz Miller, who danced in the show, told Fosse biographer Kevin Grubb, "I don't mean to take credit for Bob getting the job, but I did suggest to Jerry that he go see *Kiss Me, Kate,* which had that fabulous 'From This Moment On' number in it." Fosse had staged the forty-eight-second number for himself and Carol Haney in the MGM movie. Trained in tap and vaudeville rather than ballet, he had also created a number gently satirizing Robbins and Agnes de Mille in the stage managers' benefit, *Stage 52,* a talent showcase that both Abbott and Robbins had seen. According to Gwen Verdon, who later married Fosse, "Jerry felt that Bob had a future."

Fosse's wife at the time, Joan McCracken, also encouraged Abbott on behalf of her husband, whose limited credits were not impressive enough to make him a serious candidate to choreograph a major Broadway musical. Abbott trusted the advice he received and was ready to give Fosse his shot. The producers of the show included Robert Griffith and Harold Prince, who had previously worked as Abbott's stage managers. In a recent letter, Prince wrote, "I remember George Abbott's suggestion that we take Bob Fosse, an unknown choreographer, who had worked in Hollywood as a young leading man and who had danced with Carol Haney in the film version of *Kiss Me, Kate.* . . . I recall that I, while agreeing to give Bob Fosse the contract, insisted that we have a protective backup—in this case, Jerry Robbins. Abbott agreed; and so did Jerry, who wanted to become a director and divined that if he insisted on co-directing credit, the word would be out in the field. I did not think that George Abbott should give him such credit, but Abbott replied to my objections: 'It doesn't matter; everyone will know who directed the show.' And so, the direction billing read: 'by George Abbott and Jerome Robbins.' And, indeed, Jerry's intentions were announced in an extremely successful show." In the same way, Abbott and Prince had Frank Loesser standing by to provide backup support for the show's young composers, Richard Adler and Jerry Ross.

Based on Richard Bissell's novel *7½ Cents,* the plot of the show turned on a labor dispute in a pajama factory. A story about striking factory workers at first seemed unlikely material for a Broadway musical, and to sell the concept at backers' auditions, Prince called it *"Romeo and Juliet* in the Midwest." The primary love interest of *The Pajama Game* involves the romance between a factory superintendent (John Raitt) and the head of the grievance committee (Janis Paige), thus labor and management replacing the Capulets and Montagues. The union conflict resolves itself when the superintendent takes advantage of the manager's secretary (Carol Haney) and discovers that the shady factory manager has already budgeted the 7½ cent raise the workers are demanding. The musical's secondary romance matches Haney's daffy character with a jealous efficiency expert (played by vaudevillian Eddie Foy, Jr.). Abbott teamed up with Bissell on the writing, and the two managed to put together a fast-paced comic gem, with Abbott always the stickler at making sure the songs and dances advanced the action. All in all, there was more humor than economics. The score's pop tunes from Adler and Ross included "Hernando's Hideaway," "Once a Year Day" and the hit "Hey There."

The show's most memorable number was "Steam Heat," with its syncopated rhythms inspired by the sound of hissing radiators and clanging pipes. To replace a ballet that opened the second act, Abbott asked Fosse for "an amateur entertainment that the union can put on at its meeting." Fosse used three dancers, Carol Haney, Buzz Miller and Peter Gennaro, outfitted in black suits. Scuffling and sliding and tossing their hats, they looked like they were doing a Chaplinesque music hall routine, with the spread hands that eventually became known as "Fosse hands." Haney and Miller were Jack Cole dancers, and the number bears Cole's stylistic imprint, with a nod to Fred Astaire. When "Steam Heat" became a showstopper during the New Haven tryout, Abbott decided the number should be cut because it slowed the action. Robbins reportedly told him, "Look, the number is just too good. You can't throw it out." Robbins prevailed, and the show traveled on to Boston, where it won early raves. Robbins later acknowledged Fosse's emergence with "Steam Heat," saying, "It isn't surprising that Fosse's style was there at the very start. Either you have a statement to make, and you make it, or you don't. He had a quality that was Bob Fosse's quality and nobody else's."

Hal Prince described the exchange between Robbins and Fosse on *The Pajama Game:* "I do not believe there was much of a collaboration between Bob Fosse and Jerry. Point of fact, Jerry came in and saw what Bob did, made a few suggestions, adding a rolling table to 'I'm Not at All in Love,' and totally restaged 'There Once Was a Man.' Ultimately, I insisted he [Jerry] do a new bow, which he did reluctantly the final day of rehearsal in Boston, before we returned to New York. What we had prior to that seemed cute and revue-ish and incompatible with the rest of the show."

Prior to the Broadway opening, as a good luck gesture, Robbins gave Fosse one of his father's gold cuff links and started a ritual between them. Gwen Verdon remembered, "There was a pair of cuff links that they both liked, and when the show opened, they split the cuff links and Jerry had one; Bob had the other. So [each time] Jerry had a new show opening, Bob would send it to Jerry, or if it was Bob, Jerry would send it to Bob. They were beautiful cuff links."

The Pajama Game opened at the St. James Theatre on May 13, 1954, and the critics were unanimous. Walter Kerr called it "bright, brassy, and jubilantly sassy." Brooks Atkinson announced, "The last new musical of the season is the best." The *Journal-American* declared, "This is a whale of an evening in anybody's auditorium." Carol Haney, who later moved into the Park Avenue apartment with Robbins and Miller, was singled out as the newcomer bound for stardom. But on the show's second night, Haney injured a ligament while warming up and had to be replaced by her understudy, an unknown chorus dancer named Shirley MacLaine.

Buzz Miller said, "Of course, Shirley made mistakes. . . . She'd hardly learned the part from Carol before she had to go on. I don't even think there had been a full rehearsal with Shirley. But she went out there and did it like there was no tomorrow. . . ." MacLaine had arrived at the theater that night intending to quit the show, discouraged into thinking that she would understudy forever. Recalling her unexpected performance, she said, "Somehow I did it. I remember thinking that the cast knows what I'm doing wrong, but the audience doesn't. The only thing on my mind was that I would drop the hat during 'Steam Heat.' I was thinking about the frigging hat, which is what you do when you're a dancer, and dropped it. I muttered 'shit!,' picked it up, and went on."

MacLaine's Hollywood career subsequently took off, thanks to film producers Hal Wallis and Bob Goldstein, who were in the audience that night, hoping to see Carol Haney in the part. But Wallis was so impressed by MacLaine that he offered the dazzling red-headed dancer a screen test. After

MacLaine left for Hollywood a short time later, Haney resumed the role, and
The Pajama Game ran for more than two years (1,063 performances).

The show established Fosse's style, both as a choreographer and in terms
of his famous erotic predilections. Buzz Miller told Kevin Grubb, "According
to Carol . . . the night she was injured, he [Fosse] came up to her dressing
room and had intimate relations with her, and it's my impression this was not
an isolated incident. . . . I think he carried on with the chorus girls from all of
his shows; this is not supposition so much as theater folklore." Unlike Robbins, Fosse was never reticent about making his sexual escapades public, later
chronicling his adventures in his movie *All That Jazz*.

Fosse won a Tony for *The Pajama Game* (as did Carol Haney and the show's
producers), while Robbins took home his fifth Donaldson Award. The two remained on friendly terms and would co-choreograph *Bells Are Ringing* two years
later. Gwen Verdon remembered visiting Robbins with her husband at Miller's
East Side apartment: "When Jerry and Buzz Miller were together, we'd go to
the apartment—a cold water flat which wasn't cold water. The bathtub was in
the kitchen, which I loved. I just sat down and said 'Great!' Buzz and I had
worked together and we were good friends. And Buzz cooked. I took a bath.
Jerry and Bob talked, and I don't know what they discussed." She added, "Bob
always said there are only two choreographers that can do both ballets and
stage, and they were Balanchine and Jerry."

In a 1984 interview for *Rolling Stone*, Fosse paid tribute to his friend's
artistry, suggesting that "[Robbins] talks to God. When I call God, he's out to
lunch."

By the time *The Pajama Game* opened, *Peter Pan* was almost ready to go into
rehearsals. The new show was set to open at the Curran in San Francisco
on July 19, 1954, with Robbins for the first time assuming the dual role of director-choreographer (as de Mille had with *Allegro* in 1947, and Balanchine
with his 1940 director credit on *Cabin in the Sky*). Robbins would command
this production as an omnipotent auteur, starting with its conception; yet he
would be compelled to compromise along the way with Mary Martin and the
producers (Hayward, Halliday and Lester). He also had to rely on his team of

collaborators, but it was Robbins calling the shots, with Mary Hunter as his associate director.

"Jerry's creativity was very individual and everything came from him," said Hunter. "There's no possibility of saying that other people who worked with him contributed much of anything really truly creative." Robbins was more modest, saying in reference to his experience on *Peter Pan,* "You depend totally on your collaborators. A show is only as good as what the talents will produce, no matter what your ideas are. You can come up with some wonderful ideas, and if your collaborators cannot achieve them, they do you no good."

Hunter remembered that one early stumbling block for Robbins was Martin's desire to cast her young daughter, Heller Halliday. "I really had to say, 'Jerry, if you don't want to have a rotten summer and an angry actress, you've got to do this one thing for Mary,'" said Hunter. "Jerry had a fit. He said, 'That's not right. I don't want anybody in the theater to think of Mary's private life at all for any reason whatever. It's inartistic, it's a rotten idea.' I said, 'Jerry, you'll spend one of the worst summers you've ever had in your life if you don't do this.' So finally he gave in and he gave in quite handsomely. He said, 'Well, I guess you're right and I guess the audience will be delighted.' And they were. So this tiny little scene, casting Mary's daughter as the maid, was accomplished. . . . And Mary loved playing the scene, and she did it beautifully, and she didn't try to cover the fact that she was playing with her daughter. I had to agree that Jerry was right artistically, but I was right in sparing us all a helluva rotten summer."

The play had gone through various incarnations, all based on Sir James M. Barrie's original fairy tale script. The three-act book for the musical was adapted by Robbins (without credit) from four previous versions as well as Barrie's story "Peter and Wendy," about the boy who wouldn't grow up and his adventures in Neverland (as Barrie called it). Robbins explained, "Of the scripts—one for Maude Adams, one for Eva Le Gallienne, one for Jean Arthur, and the other . . . standard Barrie version—I'd say that Maude Adams' was the most interesting." Robbins added that while cobbling the book together from these sources, ". . . I just said a prayer and hoped I wouldn't be hanged for monkeying around too much." Ultimately, Robbins Americanized the show, removing the story from its British quasi-Shakespearean mode, while preserving the essence of Barrie's script.

In later years, Robbins suggested that the ending—as he saw it, "Peter comes back and Wendy's grown up"—had been critical in his concept. "I thought, well, that's going to be a wonderful thing, to make a circle of the play, in that he [Peter] flies off again with the new Wendy. I tried to think a bit of the world as children saw it, especially Never-Never Land, and I thought, oh, that's wonderful because the Indians could be other children. Their opponents are the pirates, where Captain Hook equals Papa, in a way."

Robbins envisioned exactly which parts of the story lent themselves to musical adaptation. "When I was reading the play, I could see that every so often [Captain] Hook would get an idea to poison this person, to kill that one, or steal the children, and I thought it would be wonderful to musicalize that. That gave me the idea of him being supported by three or four pirate musicians, who then would play the music and he would hatch these plots. And this became a theme for the show." Mary Hunter added, "It was Jerry's idea to use children as the pirates, and I thought it was a wonderful idea, and still do think it was one of his most creative ideas because it changed the whole show."

The score started with numbers from Moose Charlap and Carolyn Leigh, including "I've Gotta Crow," "I'm Flying," "Tender Shepherd" and "I Won't Grow Up." Robbins decided their work had to be supplemented when the show was panned after its opening in San Francisco. Robert Tucker, Robbins' first assistant, recalled, "He gave a terrible time to Moose Charlap, who wrote 'I'm Flying.' He was a strange little guy and Jerry didn't feel comfortable working with him. He had written other things, but suddenly Jerry didn't like anything except 'I'm Flying.' So they hired Betty [Comden] and Adolph [Green] and Jule [Styne] to come into the show. Jerry felt very comfortable with them. He could tell them yes, he could tell them no. He didn't have to pull any punches at all."

Comden and Green recollected that they along with Styne were called in by Leland Hayward and Robbins because *Peter Pan* was in such disarray that the producers were considering closing out of town. The show lacked a theme song, and there was yet no character song for its prancing Captain Hook, played by Australian actor Cyril Ritchard. Nor did Hook and Peter have a duet—Styne reportedly told Hayward and Robbins, "You've got two big stars [Martin and Ritchard] and they never sing together. That's appalling." Green recalled, "We wrote about eight numbers and also with Jerry we discussed many aspects of the show. We changed the focus of the show. It became really a musical comedy, which it hadn't been." Comden added, "That's when we wrote 'Neverland,' and it tied the whole show together." The demands of musical phrasing led to the revised name and title, "Never-Never Land." Other Comden-Green-Styne numbers included "Wendy," "Distant Melody," "Captain Hook's Waltz," "Ugg-a-Wugg" and the coloratura soprano duet, "Oh, Mysterious Lady."

"Jerry did enchanting things in Never-Never Land," said Trude Rittmann. "But you know we simply couldn't get together on that, to this day it's without music. It's that aga-aga-wan. The Tiger Lily, the thing with her kids. . . . Well, it goes without music. . . . It couldn't be done. We had a thousand versions for this dance, as it sometimes goes. And Jerry was very very nervous at the time, and highly strung is a mild understatement, I must say. He was just beside himself."

Mary Hunter recounted how the show's star, Martin, stood up to pressure from friends who visited her in San Francisco and warned that the show would "ruin her career." Hunter said, "It was one of the most extraordinary and devastating experiences that could happen to a person who is responsible, as a star must be, to the success and final result of the show. Mary and Richard [Halliday] smiled sweetly, took those people out to dinner, got them plastered, and put them back on the train. And that was that. There was never any question but that she was going to do the show and eventually bring it to New York."

Martin recalled that she "was determined . . . to fly all over the place" and brought Peter Foy from London to serve as her flying instructor. "I wanted to fly at least sixty feet across the stage, up to the top of the wings in the back of the theater, in and out the window, everywhere. I also wanted a flying ballet with Peter and the children, Wendy, Michael and John, all sailing around together. . . . Peter Foy sort of gulped, but he agreed to try. Jerry Robbins and

Richard [Halliday] were almost as excited as I. . . . There is no secret about how it was done: it was all piano wires, harnesses, ropes and expert rope-pullers." Martin continued, "I wish I could express in words the joy I felt flying. I loved it so. The freedom of spirit—the thing Peter always felt—was suddenly there for me."

During a performance in San Francisco, the wire dropped Martin thirty feet and left her dangling perilously. She wrote, "The audience thought it was all part of the show. . . . the shock had jammed every nerve and muscle in my back so painfully that for months I had to have deadening shots up and down my spine to ease the pain enough for me to get into the harness. Richard, Ed Lester, [and] Jerry Robbins were all beside themselves because I wouldn't stop flying." There were other mishaps recalled by Robbins. "There's a projector just behind the top of the proscenium arch that throws the light that represents Tinker Bell . . . and one time the lens fell off and missed Mary by a foot. Another time, it damned near eliminated Kathy Nolan, who plays Wendy. As for my problems with the Lost Boys, we've actually lost one or two of them on occasion, and had to frisk the theatre to find them."

For Robbins, looking back, the problems with projecting Tinker Bell's light brought to mind the challenge of realizing his vision as director. "We had a lot of trouble with her [Tinker Bell], and once we had to have an understudy because the beam didn't work. . . . There is no way to communicate to you the five hundred details that have to be taken care of, day to day, moment to moment, that help make or break a show. I used to say that the life of a show was going to depend on whether the drummer's brother-in-law got out of jail that night, because otherwise he wouldn't be there to play that cue you need to make the number work."

The sets, created by Peter Larkin, were state of the art at the time. Motley designed the costumes for the show's youthful cast. Robbins noted, "There wasn't much dancing in the show, because I knew I was going to use kids, the pirates were mostly singers, and I tried to scale it down to what they were all capable of doing."

One of Robbins' imaginative touches was to open the first scene in Never-Never Land with three pantomime animals—the crocodile, kangaroo and ostrich. The ostrich was played by Joan Tewkesbury, who would one day write the Robert Altman movie *Nashville* and later became a director herself. Tewkesbury described Robbins as a mentor and recalled how she and others in the cast tried to counter his dark moods. "I went to New York when I was seventeen, and it was my first Broadway show, and [dancer] Billy Sumner was like my mother. He would always say, 'If Jerry's wearing black just avoid him.' [Billy] would run down this litany of things, that if [Jerry] was doing this today that was okay, but if he was doing this other thing, just stay away. And I was so stupid that I usually approached on the wrong day. . . . It was fascinating to see it happen because it was like this black thing would descend on him. His eyes would get blacker. . . . and Billy would say, 'Aw, here it comes.' It was like the bad wind. Now it's very funny, but as a young dancer it was utterly terrifying, and you were so immobilized for two days that you couldn't count, you couldn't do anything except go absolutely dumb, rigid, and do everything wrong. And then you'd get yelled at again."

Tewkesbury continued, "He was a tremendous influence on me, shithead that he was. And his sense of humor! I have never ever laughed so hard in my life as when he and Billy and Sondra [Lee] would start in on anything. They could do the phone book and it would be funny. But it was like one of those really bad dysfunctional families with the alcoholic father—you never know what he's going to do next. . . . The two things that would absolutely change any hideousness that was going on were if Buzz [Miller] walked into the theater or if those children ran down, crying, 'Jerry, Jerry!' There was something transformative about the personality of that man and those little kids, or anybody's children—it got his circuits all sorted out and he plugged in light somehow."

Tewkesbury pointed out that Robbins was loyal to those dancers like Sumner and Sondra Lee (who performed the role of Tiger Lily). Jerry hired them in show after show, and they often knew how to bring out his comic instincts. "I probably learned as much from Sondra Lee about comedy as any single soul I've ever known because her sense of timing was so precise," said Tewkesbury. "You could watch [her] and Jerry work through these conundrums over the beat, where it would fall, and it was nothing that was spoken, but it was all about what he would do, how she would respond. And the quickness of her response.

"And then there was always the complexity of Jerry's sexuality and who he liked and didn't like, and if you liked him, too, it was really big problems. Your part would get smaller. And Billy kept saying, 'Stop looking at that guy.' It was ridiculous, it was really silly. . . . I knew all about the complexities of people's sexuality. I had certainly danced my whole life and knew all about that, but I'd never known it used quite in that schoolyard way. We only did that in grammar school. So it was pretty funny." Describing Robbins' disciplinary fanaticism, Tewkesbury concluded, "He was hideous . . . but it really gets down to if you can't stand the heat, get out of the kitchen. As sick as it sounds, I would have gone back to that kitchen every opportunity I had, because every time I went back to it there was one more piece of fuel that would fuel me as an artist to create."

After tryouts in San Francisco and Los Angeles, *Peter Pan* opened at the Winter Garden Theatre on October 20, 1954. Brooks Atkinson called it "vastly amusing," suggesting that Robbins "has directed this phantasmagoria with inventiveness and delight." In the *Herald Tribune*, Walter Kerr wrote, "It's the way *Peter Pan* always should have been, and wasn't." Of Martin's flying, Kerr reported, "It's been choreographed by director Jerome Robbins. Result: it's not so much a nervous stunt as a rapturous lyrical experience, and you're going to be popeyed with happy disbelief. . . ."

The show ran fifty weeks on Broadway (152 performances), closing in February of 1955. Martin recalled that after each performance, she welcomed children backstage. ". . . I made a point of never getting out of my costume until they had all left the theater. So many of them came back, and it would have been too awful for them to see plain old Mary Martin standing in the dressing room, instead of Peter Pan. . . . We used to give them all fairy dust; we must have dispensed tons of it. We started out with tiny gold beads, but came down to little gold stars."

In March of 1955 and again in January of 1956, *Peter Pan* was broadcast live on NBC with Martin and most of the original cast. "We performed it out in the studio in Queens," Robbins recalled. "All the sets were in one studio; we had to do it continuously. We had a wonderful camera director, Clark Jones, who was terrific and a wonderful person to work with. I think we had about a week's rehearsal, but no more, and then we went out to the studio and had three days to do it."

Robbins directed only the first Emmy-winning broadcast, which was narrated by Lynn Fontanne. The *New York Times* called the show "perhaps television's happiest hour," and it drew a record number of viewers at the time. On that night, when Peter asked the audience watching at home to clap if they believed in fairies, an entire generation of children responded, and it was Robbins and Martin who inspired their innocent belief.

SIX

Switchblades, Strippers
and Insane Love

During the first half of 1955, Robbins diverted himself with show-doctoring, putting in brief stints on three musicals—*Silk Stockings, Ankles Aweigh* and *Seventh Heaven.* Of these, only the first responded to his eleventh-hour ministrations. "If a show is really sick, then nothing can help it," he said. "I've never seen a bad show turned into a good one by doctoring. Bad shows have been turned into hits but they still weren't good shows." *Silk Stockings,* with its Cole Porter score, became a hit on the order of *Can-Can,* while *Ankles Aweigh* quickly bowed into oblivion. *Seventh Heaven,* which opened in May to mixed reviews, was choreographed by Peter Gennaro (one of the era's leading specialty dancers) and featured the explosive high kicks of Chita Rivera. Two years later, Robbins would recruit both Gennaro and Rivera into the ongoing saga of *West Side Story.*

Leonard Bernstein published a log of *West Side Story*'s gestation in *Playbill* just before the show opened. Although not entirely reliable as a chronology, the log dated the inception of the project, January 6, 1949, when Robbins was rehearsing his ballet *The Guests.* Bernstein wrote, "Jerry R. called today with a noble idea: a modern version of *Romeo and Juliet* set in the slums at the coincidence of Easter-Passover celebrations. Feelings run high between Jews and

Catholics. . . . Jerry suggests Arthur Laurents for the book. I don't know him, but I do know *Home of the Brave,* at which I cried like a baby. He sounds just right." On January 27, the *Herald Tribune* reported, "The production is scheduled for next year. . . . This is an idea that Mr. Robbins has had for some time." Nora Kaye reportedly scoffed at the idea, calling it "the dance of the garbage cans." She also predicted that Robbins, Bernstein and Laurents would never deliver on the project. "You'll never write it," Kaye told them. "Your three temperaments in one room, and the walls will come down."

The early collaboration between Robbins, Bernstein and Laurents led to the Catholic-Jewish scenario, *East Side Story,* which languished for five years because of Bernstein's schedule and Laurents' initial lack of enthusiasm. The playwright had no desire to be credited for the libretto of what he feared would turn into a Bernstein opera. Laurents recently recalled that the collaboration "fell apart" because "Lenny was constantly on the road and I thought the idea was *Abie's Irish Rose* set to music." The project was revived in August of 1955, when Laurents and Bernstein chanced to run into each other at the pool of the Beverly Hills Hotel. Bernstein was conducting at the Hollywood Bowl, and Laurents was writing the movie *Summertime* (based on his play *The Time of the Cuckoo*). Laurents recalled, "Lenny and I happened to be in Hollywood at the same time. Juvenile gangs had come into existence and the morning's headlines were Chicano gang warfare. Lenny liked the idea of being able to use Latin rhythms but, since I knew little about L.A., I suggested New York, Spanish Harlem, etc. instead. Jerry loved the idea—he had been pushing all those years for us to write the show anyway."

Bernstein dated Robbins' endorsement of "our gang idea" as September 6, 1955, and wrote, "A second solemn pact has been sworn. Here we go, God bless us!" It soon became clear that this show would indeed require divine intervention to bring the collaboration to fruition and to secure financing. The initial producers were Group Theatre alumna Cheryl Crawford and her partner, Roger Stevens. Further postponements were inevitable, as the idea of a tragic musical comedy with such topical subject matter was not easy to sell. Broadway was still tied in many ways to the old leggs-and-laffs tradition. The project would be shelved again the following year when Bernstein was sidetracked with *Candide,* Lillian Hellman's adaptation of Voltaire's satire.

With the fate of *West Side Story* hanging in the balance, Robbins went to Hollywood late in the summer of 1955 to choreograph "The Small House of Uncle Thomas" for the movie version of *The King and I*. While retaining Yuriko, Gemze de Lappe and Michiko Iseri from the original Broadway cast, Robbins hired forty-five dancers on the West Coast and quickly put them through the paces. Yuriko recalled how Robbins overcame initial skepticism on the part of the film's producers and crew. "When he appeared at Twentieth Century-Fox Studios, everybody there had the attitude of 'Who the hell is he? He never made a movie! . . .' The crew's attitude was polite but hostile. Later, I learned that they had decided to allow Jerry 'to feel [his way] around' for two or three days, with the understanding that they . . . would take over. They had no confidence in him at all. Yet after the second day of shooting, the atmosphere began to change. They had seen the rushes, and they were amazed at the fine result. By the end of the week, Jerry could do no wrong. Whatever he wanted was done—and pronto."

The film was budgeted at $6.5 million, with a half million going to Robbins' fifteen-minute dance sequence. A hefty portion of the budget went to Irene Sharaff's lavish costumes, masks and headdresses. The makeup department provided a daily delivery of four dozen sets of handmade gold fingernails. The settings for the ballet were minimal, utilizing props and figurative cutouts to represent Uncle Tom's house, mountains, rivers and the ladder to Heaven. For one scene, at the choreographer's insistence, "rain" was imported from Japan in the form of traditional rice-paper spider webs.

The ballet sequence required seven days of rehearsal and two weeks of filming. According to Yuriko, because of the time constraint, Robbins was more lenient with the dancers in the movie than he had been with his gypsies in the show. There was, however, one exception. "He didn't hate this girl," said Yuriko, "but she wasn't a good dancer. She was Asian. And he was making fun of her." Referring to the long, spider-web streamers of rain that stretched across the stage, "he said to her, 'Go roll that up.' You know, on a tiny round lead! It was impossible. And she bent down, and he turned around and said, 'You see, she'll do *anything* I ask her to do.' That, I felt, was not necessary, to humiliate her."

Rita Moreno was cast in the role of Tuptim. Yuriko described how Robbins integrated Moreno's pivotal role as storyteller with the dancers, musicians and singers for the ballet sequence. "Jerry was with Moreno and the principal dancers in studio #1, which functioned as a command center, with three movie screens in it, each showing the projection of a separate camera. One screen showed the orchestra in studio #2, whose conductor was watching both Jerry in studio #1 and the singers in studio #3. Meanwhile, the singers were watching both Jerry in #1 and the orchestra in #2.

"In our studio, #1, Jerry sat facing the dancers, who were directed to move quietly. As he watched us, he mouthed our gestures. Moreno sat on a very high chair with a microphone. She spoke into the mike as she watched Jerry mouthing the words. And so the dancing, the singing, the orchestra, and Tuptim were synchronized quite literally through the person of the choreographer."

Already sensitive to the requirements of film versus stage, Robbins instructed the dancer, "Yuriko, remember, the camera comes to you. You don't have to project out to the audience as you would when you dance on stage. Facial expressions, body gestures should all be down, down, down."

Robbins' painstaking approach to filming the dance won him a Box Office Blue Ribbon Award and further national recognition when the movie was released the next year. He later suggested that he would have had a different career if he had truly been interested in film, but he mistrusted the high-stakes collaboration that movies entailed, "where there are scores of people you will never see who have something to do with what you're doing." Still, he would seize the next offer from Hollywood when it came his way, and it would prove to be both a blessing and a curse.

Early in 1956, Robbins returned to the New York City Ballet to create his incisive comic masterpiece, *The Concert (or The Perils of Everybody)*. While recovering from a bout of hepatitis, Robbins reportedly came up with the idea of spoofing a Chopin piano recital, but the satiric edge and universal insights of his humor went beyond the concert setting and its cast of bumbling, fantasy-driven characters. In his program notes, Robbins called the piece a "charade," and noted that "one of the pleasures of attending a concert is the freedom to lose onself in listening to the music."

Impelled by the music and circumstance, his characters gave themselves up to the most outlandish reveries. Tanaquil Le Clercq portrayed the ultimate, gushing music lover with an enormous floppy hat (like Garbo's in the movie *Camille*). She literally embraced the piano and became so carried away by the music that she failed to notice her chair had been stolen out from under her. Todd Bolender played a bored husband dreaming up Thurber-like schemes for murdering his wife. Swarms of angry butterflies (wearing derbies and sport caps) made charming mayhem out of the "Butterfly Etude." Robert Barnett literally raced through the "Minute Waltz" to beat an umpire's clock. Wielding umbrellas, the eccentric ensemble unfurled their pretenses and foibles for the "Raindrop Prelude." The "Mistake Waltz" featured eight dancers making the kinds of out-of-sync mistakes that only dancers can make. Much of the comic nonsense defied literal translation. Robbins' jokes relied on movement, vivid characterization and pinpoint timing, with the humor paced and leavened along the way by several lyrical passages (including a poignant mazurka for Le Clercq that was later cut).

Among those in the original cast, Richard Thomas recalled, "That was the most fun ballet in the world. Jerry was angry at me before he did that ballet because I blasted him one day in a rehearsal. I was twenty-eight years old. He came down on me and I said, 'Wait a minute, buster, one more word and I'll knock you flat on your ass.' After the rehearsal, he went to Vida Brown [the ballet mistress] and said, 'Take him out of every ballet.' But the next season, I was back. I did them all. In *The Concert*, I did the 'Shy Boy' with Tanaquil Le Clercq. You know, we all drew those characters ourselves. It was a wonderful thing. I wasn't crazy about the ballet, but it was wonderful because those characters came out of the individuals that he was working with. . . . He was very happy at the time."

Vida Brown had fond recollections of working with Robbins during this period. "I did enjoy watching him. . . . He was tireless in rechoreographing everything. He had several versions . . . and he'd say, 'Okay, let's do this version.' And he changes, changes constantly, so it was very tiring, but it was exciting because he got so much out of everyone. . . . The kids loved working with him, they loved him. There are a lot of people who say, 'Oh, to work with him, my God! It's so difficult.' But they liked him still, they really did. They respected him tremendously. To dance in his ballets was marvelous."

Robert Barnett suggested that Robbins' humor was more obvious to the audience than to the dancers during rehearsals. "It's not a ha-ha humor, it was a working humor. Jerry never liked humor for humor's sake. It was funny, but the cast never got it, the audience got it. That's the way it worked. Probably more than with any other ballet, there [were] individual rehearsals, because there were so many segments to it." Todd Bolender, who played the henpecked, homicidal husband, recalled that Robbins revised his scene repeatedly. "There were a lot of versions, believe me. He changed it several times, but I think the one that he finally ended up with was that I stabbed myself." Robbins noted, "Sometimes, as was the case with *The Concert,* I know that the ending is bad, but I don't know what to do about it at the time. Then I must rework it later."

With sets by Jean Rosenthal and costumes by Irene Sharaff, the ballet opened on March 6 to generally favorable reviews, though some of the critics seemed stodgily reluctant to admit their laughter (perhaps because it came at the expense of Chopin and lampooned pretenses that were close to home for some in the audience). John Martin called it "a completely lunatic fantasy," while complaining that "many of the jokes are corny." Walter Terry suggested that "in spite of its empty episodes, *The Concert* . . . is certainly worth salvaging, for its best scenes are as funny as anything to be found in the theater of dance." *The Concert* was later reworked for revivals with Robbins' Ballets U.S.A. in 1958 (with new drops by Saul Steinberg) and at City Ballet in 1971.

It's always dangerous to try to explain a joke, but in answer to his critics, Robbins made a supreme effort. "*The Concert* goes back to my childhood," said Robbins, "when a musical piece was briefly explained to me or when I was given its title which explained it all: 'Butterflies,' 'Raindrops' and so on. . . . It also goes back to my attendance at dancing classes, where only too often to the platitudes of musical interpretation were added the equally well-worn platitudes of its choreographic interpretation. People say that I have been guilty of a lack of respect towards Chopin's music? I do not think so. Fortunately, people also say that *The Concert* was a reinstatement of that same music. I allowed myself to introduce into it my own personal touch of madness, but it conceals a deeper meaning which I only discovered when I had finished composing it: in the short anecdotes I have outlined, there are no victors. Through the music, all the characters abandon their everyday selves. Whether they move up or down, they all try to do something extraordinary but they are all defeated by circumstances which inevitably bring them back to earth. If that expresses a certain danger (for each one of us) peculiar to our times, it is for the public to decide."

In the spring of 1956, Robbins made a brief visit to Copenhagen to stage *Fanfare* for the Royal Danish Ballet. He wrote several letters to Leland Hayward's wife, Slim, from the Hotel d'Angleterre. A leading society figure of the day, Slim had earlier been married to film director Howard Hawks, and first became acquainted with Robbins through Leland in 1950. This was to be an intimate friendship, and Slim, who was ten years older, became increasingly important to Jerry over the years. In her 1990 memoir, *Slim: Memories of a Rich and Imperfect Life*, Slim recalled that she and Robbins "saw a lot of each other when Leland was producing *Call Me Madam*, and as time went on we became good friends and then close friends. To this day, he is closer to me than any man or woman in my life." When asked by her friend Shervert Frazier (who happened to be Robbins' psychiatrist) if she trusted "anyone in the world," Slim answered, "Jerome Robbins. I would trust him to the end of the earth."

The Haywards were members of an elite and diverse social circle that over time included Ernest Hemingway, Lauren Bacall, Claudette Colbert, William Paley, Truman Capote and a host of colorful luminaries who fit into one compartment of Robbins' expanding social world. Slim's daughter, Kitty Hawks, was a child when she first met Robbins and recently recalled, "I was two when [my mother] married Leland [in 1948], so I knew Jerry from as early as I can remember. He never treated me like a child. I think there was an element of childishness and childlikeness . . . that was really easy for him to get to because of the playfulness in himself. I remember him giving me a ballet lesson on the lawn. I was dressed in a striped bathing suit and a straw hat and twirling around and jumping around, and Jerry giggling and loving every minute of it. On that level you never felt as though you were with somebody who was the adult looking down on you. . . . I think just based on Jerry's humor, my mother would have gone nuts for him, which she did. And based on her intellect and appreciation for music and for ballet and for everything else, they really had a very firm bond." During this period, Leland's nickname for Jerry was "Gypsy," and their relationship remained on solid ground personally and professionally.

Writing to Slim from Denmark in 1956, Robbins complained that the trip was all toil and no play, that he felt he might as well have been visiting China. He mentioned that he had toured Elsinor and the famous aquarium and that he was living on fish and beer. Robbins also observed that there was no gay scene or nightlife in Copenhagen comparable to New York (though he rated the Danish city superior to Paris in that regard). He complained to Slim that he needed more rehearsal time, and later in an article for *Theater Arts*, he expanded on his problems as a guest artist working with the "tradition-bound" Danish company (renowned for preserving the nineteenth-century repertory of Auguste Bournonville). At the same time, Robbins lauded Denmark's state-supported theater for providing lifelong security for the company's dancers and musicians, versus "the status of the dancer in America, winging it free-lance style." Robbins added, "The Danish dancer is considered a valuable contributor to the artistic life of the country, and therefore everything is done to enable him to develop—physically, spiritually and artistically—to the full extent of his potential."

Robbins and his extended New York City Ballet family experienced a stunning reversal later in the year. In Copenhagen, where the company was touring, Tanaquil Le Clercq was stricken by polio. Ironically, a decade earlier, Balanchine had cast the fifteen-year-old Le Clercq as the lead in a short Mozart ballet benefiting the March of Dimes. Balanchine himself had appeared in a black costume as a character identified as the "Threat of Polio," and Le Clercq had collapsed onstage at his touch. Balanchine later called it "an omen," and in some mystical sense blamed himself for the real infirmity that was to confine Le Clercq to a wheelchair for the rest of her life.

Former City Ballet board member Robert Gottlieb assessed the impact of the tragedy: "That so uniquely gifted and charming a person was so afflicted was terrible enough; that she was Balanchine's wife, a dancer central to the repertory and on whom he had created so many important roles (the most famous being the doomed girl who dances with Death in *La Valse*), was a devastating blow to the entire enterprise and to its followers. Balanchine stayed with his wife in Denmark until she was well enough to be brought home, and didn't return to the company on a regular basis for a year—a time of grief and uncertainty for everyone."

Robbins, who adored Le Clercq, was of course crushed by the news. He had not been with the troupe on tour and received word of her condition in New York. The company's longtime manager, Betty Cage, was with Robbins at the City Ballet offices when he telephoned Balanchine to offer his help. Cage was close socially and professionally to Le Clercq and to Robbins, whom she first met when he was creating *The Guests.* Jerry's friendship with Cage had been strained by his HUAC testimony and was to be further tested in the present crisis. As Balanchine's day-to-day confidante, Cage remembered, "Jerry called Balanchine and said, 'What can I do? I'll do anything to help.' George was still in Copenhagen with Tanny. . . . He said, 'Well, maybe you could come and take charge of the company because I can't be here. The only thing I'm worried about is there's nobody to run the company.' And Jerry said, 'Oh George, I'm so sorry, I'm just too tired, I have to go and have a vacation.' I couldn't believe it. He was Tanny's dear friend . . . and the one thing that Balanchine asked, he said, oh, he was just too tired. How could he do this? Why did he call at all? And the funny thing is that at that time and probably many times during the history of the company, Jerry was the only one that Balanchine would have trusted. What we finally did, whoever was there, we kept going. . . . Maybe I'm being too harsh, but certain things I find difficult to forgive."

Still, Cage stayed on relatively good terms with Robbins over the years. "I sometimes felt so sorry for Jerry," said Cage. "There was one point where he was screaming at me for some reason. We were standing in the corridor upstairs in the office, and he was really letting me have it. Then he turned and walked away, and as he was walking, I called and said, 'Jerry, be careful, you're going to have a heart attack or something. Don't let anything get you that upset. It's dangerous, really. It's not good for you.' He later told Tanny that he couldn't believe that we were having this terrible fight and I stopped him to tell him to look after his health. But I mean he was frightful because he was so out of control. I really thought he was going to have a stroke or something.

"But we knew each other for years. There were a couple of board members who used to take me for lunch every year for my birthday. Jerry was always invited . . . and he wouldn't think of not coming. It was the sort of friendship that I considered a real friendship because I think it was all Jerry was capable of giving, especially since I was in an adversarial position professionally. I think it was more than I should have expected, because we did get along. We got along very well if we weren't fighting over a rehearsal. . . . He could be so unreasonable."

Le Clercq remembered that Robbins sent her letters and gifts while she was in Copenhagen. She wrote, "He loved the [comic strip *Peanuts*]. I used to call him Charlie Brown and he called me Lucy. He sent me at the hospital an enormous stuffed Snoopy. When I came back to the States and went to the Warm Springs Foundation in Georgia, Jerry came down for a visit and arranged a luscious picnic with white wine." Jerry remained a loyal and devoted friend to Tanny. He undoubtedly had practical reasons (other than needing a vacation) for begging off from Balanchine's request to run the company. In fact, Broadway and other pursuits would keep Robbins away from City Ballet for more than twelve years. During this prolonged leave of absence, he stayed on cordial terms with Balanchine. Their relationship was always grounded in mutual respect and pragmatism. Robbins later admitted that it was some years before he and Balanchine were on a first-name basis, and the two never really became "bosom pals," though there was certainly a long-standing bond of affection.

During the fall of 1956, when Le Clercq became ill, Robbins was already immersed in preparations for *Bells Are Ringing*, a musical that he was slated to direct and co-choreograph with Bob Fosse. The idea, based on a telephone answering service, originated with Betty Comden and Adolph Green, who wanted to create a vehicle for their friend and Revuers-alumnus Judy Holliday. The effervescent Holliday had recently won an Academy Award for *Born Yesterday*, and this Broadway venture was to be her first musical. Composer Jule Styne agreed to provide the score, and with the obvious prospect of a hit, Armina Marshall and Lawrence Langner of the Theatre Guild signed on to produce. Even with everything going for it, the show turned into a contentious soap opera of infighting between the collaborators.

Conflicts first erupted over the casting. Holliday was onboard as the meddling phone-service switchboard-operator, Ella Peterson. Adolph Green pushed his friend Sydney Chaplin for the leading role of Jeff Moss, a playwright whose writer's block was to be remedied by his romantic entanglement with the benevolent phone operator. Sydney Chaplin, the handsome son of Charles Chaplin, was not blessed with singing talent, and Robbins fought against casting him. The situation became even more complicated when Holliday fell in love with Chaplin, just as her character did in the script. Holliday demanded that Chaplin play the part, and Robbins soon became the object of the star's outspoken enmity. Nevertheless, Jerry stood his ground, and an uneasy compromise was hammered out whereby Chaplin was to be tested for five days when the show opened for tryouts in New Haven.

There were more battles yet to come, because Chaplin was unable to handle several numbers and they had to be jettisoned, much to the chagrin of the composing team. Six weeks before rehearsals, Robbins told the composers, "I'm locking you in my house, then I'll know you're writing. I'll serve you lunch and you can go home at the end of each day." The disgruntled trio—Comden, Green and Styne—did exactly that. Comden said simply, "We had a pretty stormy time on that show."

Jean Stapleton, who played Holliday's boss at the answering service, recalled that she and the other actors actually had little contact with Robbins, who delegated many of his directorial responsibilities to his assistant, Gerald Freedman. Stapleton described Robbins as "inscrutable" in their working relationship (which later also included *Funny Girl*) and suggested, "I found the sweet, kind Jerry in my experience with him, but then these horrid tales [I heard] otherwise colored that more darkly."

Gerald Freedman worked with Robbins on a number of shows (including *West Side Story*) as a kind of interpreter and troubleshooter. "I went around repairing Jerry's damage with actors. I don't mean that in a negative way. It was just because he didn't know how to talk with them." Freedman continued, "Jerry understood character and relationship. . . . He *was* a director-choreographer. He didn't have the language, but he absolutely thought in terms of relationships and motivation. And he could . . . edit, know when it wasn't good. . . . He was wonderful that way, about the truth of a situation or relationship."

Robbins explained the problem of communicating with actors as opposed to dancers, saying, "The variety of approaches to work and performance is enormous among actors. There is no basic common technique or language to communicate with. The situation is much more disciplined with dancers, all of whom have, or should have, approximately similar training and direction."

Freedman recalled one of his early assignments on *Bells Are Ringing* that was carried out in the ballroom of the Theatre Guild headquarters. "Jerry set the charming routine for 'Just in Time' on me. He figured if I had enough physical coordination to do it, he could teach it to Sydney Chaplin, playing opposite Judy. It was simple and direct and based on relationship, which was the basis for all his work—in the ballet as well as the theater." Freedman described an early turning point in his relationship with Robbins when he stood up to his boss: "He [Jerry] turned on me in a very ferocious way like a terrier. It was really something. The adrenaline starts coming and I was frightened as hell. . . . But I said, 'Jerry, you can't talk to me like this' . . . and after that, I somehow won his respect. . . . I don't think he would respect sass, but if you had integrity or something on your side, I think it was easy to get his respect. . . ." Freedman added, "He had an unerring instinct for going for someone who was vulnerable. He would go after them. And I don't think . . . out of maliciousness, but [in pursuit of] perfection."

One of the actors who resisted taking direction from Robbins was vaudevillian comic Eddie Lawrence. "Jerry gave me some notes. I was just going on and he gave me some notes. I said, 'Will you stop this? Get out of here!' It was just unnerving me. I had to go over lines and stuff. So he said, 'I give Judy notes. Can I slip them under your door?' I said, 'Notes, notes! No notes!' I told him. 'No notes. It's not Chekhov!' He didn't treat me any differently even though I yelled at him."

Robbins had recently called it quits with Buzz Miller (though Miller later claimed to be the one who broke off the affair) and moved into more fashionable quarters at 154 East Seventy-fourth Street. One night during rehearsals, Robbins threw a party attended by Holliday, the composers and the musical director Milton Rosenstock. The cocktail chatter turned to the subject of a song to close the first act. Styne perused the libretto and suddenly announced, "Listen to this line. Listen. *I knew you before I knew you . . .*" He took a seat at the piano and began to improvise, then broke off and turned around to his audience. Holliday cried, "Don't stop! Don't stop!" Styne continued with Comden and Green chiming in with dummy lyrics. The song "Long Before I Knew You" was quickly added to the show.

The work didn't proceed quite as smoothly in rehearsals, and tempers flared during the out-of-town run. Comden explained to Howard Kissel of the *Daily News* how Robbins disarmed her during one of their creative disputes. "We had such a dreadful fight that we weren't even speaking that night when we arrived at the theater. We sat across the aisle looking at each other. . . . I had my two kids with me. I put Alan, who was two, on my lap. But Susannah, who was seven, sat next to me. She couldn't see. I took my coat off and folded it under her. She said, 'Mommy, I still can't see.' Suddenly, I saw Jerry's arm stretched out. 'Give her to me,' he said. She watched the show from his lap."

Bob Fosse was already set to move on to Hollywood with *Pajama Game* and *Damn Yankees.* Dancer Frank Derbas, who had earlier had a brief affair with Jerry, characterized the Robbins-Fosse relationship: "Bobby was dominated by Jerry. It was his [Fosse's] second show and it wasn't his best. You couldn't blame him because it's pretty tough to be a choreographer and have Jerry looking over your shoulder. I never saw Jerry do anything nasty to him. He changed some stuff after he [Fosse] left, but then it wasn't malicious, it was just stuff that didn't work."

Actor George Irving recalled, "The redoubtable Fosse got stuck. It was the subway number ['Hello, Hello, There!']. Jerry announced rehearsal at ten o'clock the next morning. *He* would set it. Everybody who was ambulatory showed up in practice clothes. They wanted to be in the number that Jerry was going to choreograph. And he set it instantaneously. Astonishing!" Derbas explained how Robbins doctored Fosse's work: "Bobby had us all shaking hands on the subway, and Jerry would have us reach out and put our hands way over our heads in a big circle [and] bring them down to shake hands. When you've got thirty people [onstage] that's what you need to see. So it really worked. . . .

Jerry changed one number, which was a pretty bad number. Girls were shaking their heads with ponytails until their hair was falling out. And so Bobby came to see the show, and the minute that number came on, he got up and walked out. A couple of weeks later, we told Jerry about it, so Jerry came and saw the show. And he was sitting in the audience, and at the same spot he got up and walked out. He was very funny."

The New Haven run posed yet another stumbling block for Robbins when, despite Sydney Chaplin's unimpressive singing, the actor became an instant hit as a matinee idol. His sex appeal enabled him to outshine Holliday, who delivered an ultimatum to Robbins three days before the show traveled into New York: she would not open unless she was given an 'eleven-o'clock' number, a big song that would close the second act and swing the balance back her way. Robbins turned to the composing team in desperation, and by opening night Holliday was mollified with her final number, "I'm Going Back." The show also spawned two huge Comden-Green-Styne pop hits, "Just in Time" and "The Party's Over."

With decor from Raoul Pène du Bois, *Bells Are Ringing* opened at the Shubert on November 29, 1956. The reviews, like the show itself, were all Judy Holliday. Brooks Atkinson admitted his "disenchantment" with the vaudevillian book, while noting that "Miss Holliday is a fantastic entertainer . . ." He added, "Trust Mr. Robbins and Mr. Fosse to provide the regulation good ballet numbers—notably a sort of fandango in a subway . . ." Walter Kerr called it "a sweetheart of a show." The *Journal-American* suggested, "The whole thing seems to be a happy union of Miss Holliday's unique talents . . . the intelligent scripting of Betty Comden and Adolph Green, the engaging music of Jule Styne, and the swift and sure direction of Jerome Robbins."

The show enjoyed a run of almost two and a half years and 924 performances (grossing more than $5 million on a $360,000 budget). Both Holliday and Chaplin garnered Tony Awards, and she would go on to co-star with Dean Martin in the 1960 MGM movie (without the Robbins-Fosse choreography and therefore fatally deficient). Curiously, the original billing on Broadway read, "Staged by Jerome Robbins; Choreography by Bob Fosse." Jean Stapleton recalled, "Jerry didn't take credit. It didn't say, 'Directed by' . . . and I thought, Well, that's very fair, because Gerry [Freedman] did the [scene] work and Bob [Fosse] did the dancing. Jerry didn't claim that directing credit, which is interesting. It's very honest."

Over time, perhaps in light of his next tour de force in the dual role, Robbins was credited as both director and choreographer. At the end of 1956, he told *Dance Magazine*, "I am influenced by all our great directors—Kazan, Logan, etc. As a choreographer-director, I am enormously impressed by Tyrone Guthrie." When Robbins was asked if he planned to leave choreography behind in favor of directing, he said, "Maybe—but not yet. Maybe later, when I'm too ancient to choreograph." In fact, the following year Robbins would attempt to bow out of choreographing *West Side Story*, which he hoped to direct without having to stage the dances.

According to Robbins, the motivating creative challenge of the *West Side Story* collaboration was to bring highbrow artistry into the commercial theater. "The aim in the mid-fifties," he said, "was to see if all of us—Lenny [Bernstein] who wrote 'long-hair' music, Arthur [Laurents] who wrote serious plays, myself who did serious ballets, Oliver Smith who was a serious painter—could bring our acts together and do a work on the popular stage. . . . The idea was to make the poetry of the piece come out of our best attempts as serious artists; that was the major thrust." *West Side Story* was surely a daring, innovative experiment, seemingly ahead of its time; yet the show also represented the culmination of the integrated concept musical that traced back to *Oklahoma!* Under the driving, authoritarian force of Robbins' direction, all the elements of book, score, choreography and design would be woven seamlessly to support what he defined as the show's central theme: "the futility of intolerance." There was to be more music and more dancing than ever before, with a lean, gritty book that borrowed more plot than poetry from Shakespeare's tragedy.

As the script and score were being written, there were frequent exchanges and clashes between Robbins, Laurents and Bernstein, and later, Hammerstein-protégé Stephen Sondheim, who came on as the team's junior member and was eventually credited for the lyrics. Laurents recalled an early discussion of the balcony scene with Robbins and Bernstein, during which the three envisioned "a gossamer fire escape; the language lifted above modern street level until it soared into song at the moment the lovers first kissed. And at that moment the surrounding buildings would disappear, leaving the lovers in space, in their own world." The image of the tenement fire escape was retained in the libretto, as Shakespeare's Verona was transported into an urban underworld of switchblades, zip guns and seething ethnic and racial hostilities.

Where *Romeo and Juliet* explores the amorous passion of the star-crossed lovers and their feuding family houses, Laurents' script shifts the focus to its warring gangs, the white-ethnic Jets and Puerto Rican Sharks, with Tony and Maria as demotic counterparts for Shakespeare's hero and heroine. The parallels and intersections of the two plots are numerous. Like Juliet, Maria has a nurse-like confidante, Anita, and a Paris-like suitor, Chino. Like Romeo, Tony has his Mercutio-like best friend, Riff (bonded, as they say, "womb to tomb" and "sperm to worm"), and a Friar Laurence-like ally, Doc, with the apothecary turned into a drugstore. The Capulets' ball where the lovers first meet becomes the high school gym dance, with Shakespeare's masks replaced by the gangs' dress colors. Most significant, Laurents' book borrows Shakespeare's central plot device that sets the tragedy into motion: After Tybalt kills Mercutio, Romeo takes revenge by killing Tybalt; and in the same way, events spin out of control for Tony when Bernardo kills Riff in the first-act Rumble scene, and a vengeful Tony in turn kills Bernardo, Maria's brother.

The two storylines differ crucially with their respective endings: Juliet dies, but Maria lives. Sensing perhaps what a musical might or might not be able to bear and still play to a popular audience, Arthur Laurents portrayed Maria in his script as a young woman "too strong to kill herself for love." There was to be no double suicide, but as in Shakespeare's play, a final processional brings the two families together thanks to the transcendent power of love. In this case, a mournful reconciliation is precipitated by Maria when she picks up the gun lying beside Tony's body and challenges the two gangs with the lines, "WE ALL KILLED HIM; and my brother and Riff. I, too. I CAN KILL NOW BECAUSE I HATE NOW." After hurling the gun away and breaking down into tears, she draws the two gangs into a secular ritual at least vaguely reminiscent of Shakespeare's "glooming peace." If the musical tilts toward melodrama rather than tragedy, it may simply be the result of the collaborators' efforts to replace poetry with song and dance. Laurents invented artful street slang ("cracko jacko," "frabbajabba") for his inarticulate teenage characters, but the language was never going to compete with Shakespeare's soaring lyricism.

Working with Bernstein on the lyrics, Sondheim sought "to bring the language down to the level of real simplicity." According to Bernstein, the key to his edgy, feverish music was the tritone interval, as was apparent in the melody of "Maria" and throughout the score ". . . in that the three notes pervade the entire piece, inverted, done backwards. I didn't do all this on purpose. It seemed to come out in 'Cool' and as the gang whistle [in the 'Prologue']. The same three notes." Bernstein suggested that while he and Sondheim were working on music and lyrics, "We raped Arthur's play-writing. I've never seen anyone so encouraging, let alone generous, urging us, 'Yes, take it, take it, make it a song.'" This was certainly the case with Tony's first-act song, "Something's Coming," which lifted its title from Laurents' scenario and incorporated his lines, "it may be around the corner, whistling down the river, twitching at the dance—who knows?" Links between songs underscored the fervent passion of the lovers, as with the strain of woodwinds connecting "Tonight" and "Somewhere." Bernstein also borrowed, or cannibalized in his fashion, unused music from his work on *Candide,* including "Gee, Officer Krupke" and "One Hand, One Heart."

Throughout their collaboration, Robbins was determined to realize his singular vision of the show and to retain primary authorship. He would ultimately insist on being credited for the conception, the direction and the choreography, with a contractual clause guaranteeing that his billing appear highlighted in a special "box." While respecting Robbins' artistry, Sondheim explained his heavy-handed tactics in getting his way: "I think the reason for Jerry's success at intimidation with everyone was that he had a knack for spotting essential weaknesses in people almost instantly on meeting them, and he would file the knowledge away in his memory for future use. One of his most effective ploys, which worked with Lenny as well as me, was public humiliation—that is to say, brazen criticism in front of one's own colleagues. . . . Jerry's artistic ruthlessness was combined with real sadism. Also, he always felt intimidated by anybody educated, so people like Lenny were prime targets. To my knowledge, the only two men who were never afraid of him were Arthur and Jule Styne. . . . In fact, Arthur and Jule were the only ones I ever saw tell Jerry off."

Bernstein appears to have shared this view to some extent. He repeatedly acquiesced to Robbins' demands, avoiding confrontation, on one occasion retreating to a bar and downing several scotches when Robbins changed the orchestration for "Somewhere." Bernstein wrote to his wife, Felicia, "Jerry continues to be—well, Jerry: moody, demanding, hurting. But vastly talented." According to Bernstein's longtime friend Sid Ramin, Robbins announced at an early cast meeting: "I know I'm difficult. I know I'm going to hurt your feelings. But that's the way I am."

During his ongoing exchange with Bernstein, however, there were many moments of creative breakthrough and shared exhilaration. Bernstein said, "I remember all of my collaborations with Jerry in terms of one tactile bodily feeling: composing with his hands on my shoulders. . . . I can feel him standing behind me saying, 'Four more beats there,' or 'No, that's too many,' or 'Yeah, that's it!'" Looking back after Bernstein's death in 1990, Robbins noted with regard to *West Side Story,* "The continual flow between us was an enormous excitement."

Despite the high-minded ambitions and high-profile names of those involved in the project, *West Side Story* nearly foundered in the spring of 1957 (when, as a joke, it was titled *Gangway*). Robbins and his team had been casting the show for months, but the financing was not yet in place. Many producers, including George Abbott, Rodgers and Hammerstein, and Leland Hayward, had passed on the project. A backer's audition was arranged by Cheryl Crawford, but not a penny was raised at the audition, with rehearsals scheduled to start in six weeks. Robbins' assistant director, Gerald Freedman, remembered that Elia Kazan discouraged Crawford. "Kazan said to Cheryl, 'It isn't realistic enough. How can you do gangs in this context?'"

On the morning of April 22, Crawford called the team into her office and announced she was pulling out. Suddenly the show had only one producer, Roger Stevens. The collaborators were crestfallen, but thanks to an appeal from Sondheim, Harold (Hal) Prince and Robert Griffith soon agreed to come onboard even though they had earlier declined. Prince recalled, "Bobby

Griffith and I took it over from Cheryl Crawford when she decided she couldn't raise the money and didn't want to take the big chance that it presented. . . ." In a week, Prince and Griffith raised $300,000. Even with the money secured, there were further delays when Robbins ordered Oliver Smith to redesign the sets. Under duress, Smith came up with the mobile scenic design for "Somewhere," having the suffocating tenement walls whirl away at the onset of the lovers' dream ballet, revealing a luminous "would-be world" of "space, air and sun."

No one denied the fact that *West Side Story* was a risky show with limited commercial prospects. Freedman surmised, "My understanding of it from everybody, from Jerry, Steve, Arthur, and Bobby Griffith and Hal—I don't know what was in the back of their minds, these guys were so career-driven— but nobody thought it was going to be a hit. They weren't working for a hit. They knew this was some strange animal, so that they could pour themselves into it, and it was only about excellence. Again, there were all these intramural clashes, sibling clashes if you will, but the bottom line, I thought, was that Bobby and Hal needed an arty success after *Pajama Game* and *Damn Yankees*— two hugely successful [shows]—but they wanted to do something more artistically elevated. So there was a wonderful commitment to the work and not to the audience, which was, I think, very special." There was undoubtedly some healthy idealism at work on this show, and it was surely something unusual for Broadway, though at one point Bernstein complained to his wife, "They're all so scared and commercial success means so much to them. To me, too, I suppose—but I still insist it can be achieved with pride."

To his biographer Meryle Secrest, Sondheim recalled the emergency negotiations that took place when Robbins tried to withdraw as choreographer: "About a week before rehearsals—they'd already got the capitalization and posted bonds, they had spent money, and a week before rehearsals Jerry called a meeting in Hal's office and announced to us that it was too much work for him to choreograph and direct as well. He just wanted to direct. He wanted Herbert Ross to do the choreography. And there was a shocked silence around the room. I didn't know about this; Lenny didn't know about this; it was just announced.

"Hal Prince, then thirty years old, who had just had a not-successful show open [*New Girl in Town*] and already, I am sure, had put in many thousands of dollars, said, 'I'll tell you what, Jerry. One of the reasons Bobby and I wanted to do this show, if not the main reason, was because of your genius as a choreographer, and if you don't want to do the choreography, I'm not sure we want to do the show. Let's all think about it, and come back here tomorrow.' And Jerry was turning bright red. A meeting took place the next day and it was wonderful. Jerry sat in Hal's seat at the desk and Hal had to stand, and Jerry was in a rage. But there was nothing he could do about it. And so he said, 'All right! I'll do the choreography *and* the directing. But I want an assistant choreographer.' Hal said, 'Fine,' and he [Jerry] said, 'I want eight weeks' rehearsal.' Now, these were the days when you never had more than four. Eight is doubling the cost. And Hal said, 'I think that will be okay,' and he [Jerry] said, 'I want three pianists.' Hal said, 'Why?' 'Well, I want one for the songs and one for the dance, and I just want to have another one around.' And Hal said, 'Well, why not wait and see?' In other words, Hal was that cool."

Confirming Sondheim's story about Robbins' effort to recruit Herbert Ross, Prince commented, "Certainly, Jerry tried, since it seemed he wanted to turn his back on choreography at that point and emphasize directing."

Sondheim recalled, "Peter Gennaro staged 'America,' and what's interesting, a wonderful lesson, is that we went to the rehearsal and it just didn't work. Moment by moment it worked, but something didn't come together. And then Jerry got his hands on it and reshaped it all and—suddenly, the number worked. He's a master artist." The satirical number "America" retained Gennaro's essential Latin style in its dancing and became the consistent showstopper.

While battling with all of his collaborators, including costume designer Irene Sharaff and lighting mastermind Jean Rosenthal, Robbins brought Method acting techniques into the auditions and rehearsals. Breaking with the traditional chorus/principal composition of musicals, the show required an ensemble of forty performers who would all act, sing and dance. With a cast of young, mostly unknown, raw talents, Robbins had his work cut out for him. Prince recollected, ". . . of course Jerry had more difficulty communicating with actors (vocabulary again) than dancers and, of course, he could be cruel and insensitive. Despite all of this, there is no question that the young people in *West Side* worshiped Jerry, and that he did give them an extraordinary foundation. After all, most of them were gypsies, and many of them learned to act, even more important, to take seriously the text they were assigned. Jerry believed in exercises that may have emanated at The Actors Studio. I can't be certain, but I do know that the *West Side Story* Sharks and Jets never mixed socially; they never had lunch [together] during the break. There was an antagonistic wall built up between them so that they could commit to the project heart and soul. And they did. I think, though, for such young, inexperienced actors, it was a good idea. And I've borrowed the technique myself since. Jerry knew how to create commitment in performers to a project."

The cast nicknamed the thirty-eight-year-old Robbins "Big Daddy," which communicated a measure of affection as well as fear and respect for his authority. Chita Rivera, who played the feisty Shark, Anita, recalled, "We were still at an age where we needed a father." Grover Dale performed the role of Snowboy and later became a Robbins protégé. Dale remembered, "We did homework. We had to write who, where, what our families were like. Who was in trouble? Who was kicked out of the house? Who took care of whom? Our real family was our gang buddies. We created our entire life's background. He wanted us to bring that onto the stage. He knew it would matter."

Dale continued, "He encouraged us to keep the war going offstage as well as on. During a rehearsal lunch break, a couple of the Jets found a large piece of cardboard in the alley by the stagedoor entrance. We got an idea. Within ten minutes, we climbed the ladder to the fly floor above the stage with a giant shark cutout stuffed with newspaper. We knew Jerry was onstage promptly. No one ever dared to be late for a Robbins rehearsal! Sure enough, at two p.m., the stage was occupied by a full contingency of Sharks standing there, like, Aren't we good boys! Jets were nowhere in sight. Jerry paced furiously, demanding an explanation from the stage manager, Ruth Mitchell, why the Jets weren't onstage. Perfect. Without a word, we tossed the cardboard shark onto the stage. It landed inches from Jerry's feet. Plop. He loved it."

Tony Mordente played A-rab, and he had personal reason to recall how the cast responded to Robbins' efforts to foment antagonism. "I started to date Chita [Rivera], and the Jets didn't talk to me for about a week," said Mordente. "That's how serious it was. He created the schism between us because he felt that it was a necessary way to work. And I'll tell you it worked. . . . It brought unity to each gang." Mordente and Rivera married during the run of the show, and she recalled, "I must say Mordente got away with murder. That's the truth. Jerry was mad, mad, mad for Mordente. He'll always have a favorite and he was crazy for Mordente."

Robbins was unrelenting with his effort to manipulate and incite the cast. While Mordente may have received special treatment and acknowledged that he was one of Robbins' "pets," he pointed out, "Jerry not only attacked you, he attacked your family, your background, where you lived, how you lived, who you studied with. He never stopped. David Winters [who played Baby John] and I used to sit down together and watch. We knew when Jerry was getting angry because he'd start kicking cigarette butts and moving his chair around. Once he started kicking cigarette butts, David and I would say, 'It's time to move to the back of the stage.' We would see it coming, and there was Michael [Callan] in the middle taking his lumps."

Michael Callan, who went by Mickey at the time, was cast as Riff and quickly became Robbins' favorite whipping boy. One of the Sharks, Jay Norman, remembered the abuse directed at Callan, but argued like many that Robbins' harsh methods brought results. "I was so proud that he [Callan] didn't come in one day with a gun and kill the man. I just wouldn't have been able to take what he took. It would have killed me. I wouldn't have had a career. What I saw happen was . . . when we started rehearsals, Mickey Callan was not Riff. He was a nice-looking guy, not a bad tap dancer, but couldn't dance as well as the rest of us as far as the other stuff. Jerry tore him apart . . . just totally dissected him. But Jerry put him back together. Perhaps I'm wrong, perhaps Mickey pulled himself back together, but when he came back together, he was Riff, and he was a damn good Riff. By that time, Mickey understood what Jerry wanted. In that sense, it was wonderful, but to watch it happen as a fellow human being was horrible. I would go home really despising Jerry for that. . . . It was amazing. Mickey couldn't even click in tempo. Jerry had him so rattled . . . in 'Cool,' his mouth was in time to the music and his hand was out of time. Now figure that. . . . But when the two of them were finished, when rehearsals finally came to performances, we had a Riff."

Callan credited Robbins with providing the education that later gave him a successful movie and television career. "Jerry was a taskmaster, but he had two sides to him," said Callan. "I always liked the man. Even when he yelled at me, I liked the man, because I believed he was doing it for a reason, to make the show the best. I don't know whether he cared about me or the kids . . . the show was the thing with him." Callan recalled, "One time he really reamed my ass. He pulled every rank on me. He said, 'What do I have to do to get through to you?' He says, 'I expect to see you coming out with a tennis racket saying, Tennis anyone? What do I have to do . . . take your Thunderbird away from you?'—because he knew I had this little white T-bird, and that hurt. Every time he'd ask me a question, I'd just say, 'Yes, sir. No, sir.'"

In his unpublished memoir in progress, *Spilling the Beans,* Callan recalled that during this rehearsal session Robbins asked him, "Do you hate me?"

"No, sir," was Callan's reply.

Robbins then suggested, "Well, before you go onstage tonight, I want you to think of something to hate."

Callan remembered, "As the overture began and I was waiting for the curtain to rise, I kept saying to myself over and over, *Jerry Robbins, Jerry Robbins, Jerry Robbins!*"

Robbins was equally demanding of Larry Kert and Carol Lawrence, who played Tony and Maria. Both Kert and Lawrence were stronger singers than dancers. "He had me crying much of the time," said Kert. Lawrence went through numerous auditions before winning the part that would lead her to stardom. She remembered, "We rehearsed with words, without the words, with music, without the music, improvisational. It was endless. In the killer-killer scene where Tony comes through the window, I look in his face and I know that it's true, he has killed my brother. And I run at him and pound on his chest, and I say, 'Killer, killer, killer, killer!' And then I dissolve in a heap of tears on the floor. We were working alone, Jerry, Larry and me, in a room upstairs in the theater. And Jerry took me aside—he always had little things that he would secretly tell the person that you were working with that you never knew—and he would take me aside and he'd say, 'He doesn't feel guilty. Hurt him. Really make him feel guilty. Hit him harder, hit him harder!' Well, we did that for about two and a half hours and we went to dinner. By the end of it, I was really banging on his chest. We were performing at that time, and Larry came to my dressing room, and he was bare to the waist, but he was all taped, his entire chest, with adhesive. I said, 'What happened?' He said, 'I went to the

doctor because I was in so much pain, and he said that you can't hit me any-more because you're loosening the rib cage from my lungs.'

"I started to cry. I couldn't believe it, because I adored Larry. He said, 'I'm just so afraid to tell Jerry. Will you tell him?' So I went to Jerry, and I said, 'I hurt him, and he's all taped up, and I can't hit him in the chest anymore, Jerry, because I'm loosening his lungs from the rib cage.' And he said, without miss-ing a beat, 'Hit him in the head, you won't hurt anything there.' And that's what I had to do for two weeks—I hit him in the head."

Larry Kert died in 1991. William Weslow, a friend of Kert's in later years, recalled that he complained that Robbins had undermined his confidence with a verbal assault on opening night. Referring to Robbins' "cruelty" toward Kert in rehearsals, Weslow claimed, "Larry told me that Robbins called him 'an un-talented faggot.'" Arthur Laurents recollected in his memoir that during a re-hearsal of the rumble scene, Robbins used that epithet repeatedly, out of frustration, to taunt Kert into giving a more emphatically masculine perfor-mance. Kert was openly gay, and Robbins may have resorted to such dis-paragement to try to get what he wanted from the performer. But opinions remain divided over that particular rehearsal episode and whether or not Rob-bins' more scathing personal attacks were justified.

Grover Dale said recently, "During the rumble, I was the person who held on to Tony. That was my job in the rumble. . . . And I do not recall ever hear-ing Jerry use the word 'faggot.' That would have been stupid for him to do be-cause it would have undermined everything he was trying to create offstage as well as onstage. Jerry always protected the protocol of the gangs. . . ." In an-other recent exchange, Michael Callan suggested, "Jerry was tough but never used 'faggot' or any obscenities to my knowledge. . . . If anyone was a whipping boy, it was me, not Larry!" Of course, memories on all sides are fallible and often colored by emotion as events recede into the past. Robbins' alleged use of such language with Kert may seem out of character, as several cast members noted, but might also be seen as an effort, however unsettling, to mimic the sort of abusive slur that was commonplace in the real world of teenage gangs. While unable to recall the incident in question, one of Robbins' loyal assis-tants expressed skepticism yet acknowledged that he could have gone to such an extreme if only as a rehearsal tactic during an improvisation.

Chita Rivera, who was also bound for glory, became one of Robbins' staunchest defenders. She said, "I've always felt—and they can call me Polyanna all they want—but if he hadn't been the way he was, none of those people would have danced the way they did. None of them would have had the careers they had, as far as I'm concerned, because people give up, we all give up, and we give up a lot of times too soon. And dancing isn't easy. And he knew it and he made you do what you were really capable of doing, something you never even dreamed you could possibly do, he made you do. . . . It's deep, I'm sorry. I have no patience with those that down-talk him."

Rivera was one of those who was receptive to the language and images that Robbins employed, and credited him with teaching her how to act. "He gave me such confidence. There was a set of steps at the theater backstage, and we used to sit on that step and . . . just talk about the character. I'd never talked about something I didn't know about before, a person, and he talked in colors and textures, that sort of thing. It was just a fascinating way to dissect a person and why they existed. I've never been one to step outside of myself. . . . He made me aware of myself and my imagination and my voice. I suddenly heard myself, so I was getting these layers of people within myself—which is what we all have—just by listening and trusting him."

Robbins' trouble-shooting assistant, Gerald Freedman, later directed the landmark rock musical *Hair* and worked with Joseph Papp at the New York Shakespeare Festival. Looking back at *West Side Story*, Freedman thought that some of Robbins' methods may have been unnecessary. "It was a bit phony. I know you hear all these stories and they're very colorful. And it worked—he had these kids angry at each other. What Jerry didn't realize was that they were operating out of love, not hate, out of mutual respect for the project . . . *not* I have to hate you when I'm working just as hard as you every day and with you all the time, working on the same project, committed to it in the same way. I don't mean to denigrate it at all, or the vision. [As a director] you do anything to activate an actor's imagination."

From the actor's standpoint, Jay Norman agreed with Freedman. "It *was* a gang war," said Norman. "Jerry tried to create animosity, even backstage. That's true. He tried. But you know what? Thank God none of us was that stupid. That's a place for me where Jerry fell short." Marilyn D'Honau

(Clarice) felt the tactics were excessive because of the horseplay inspired among the young men in the cast. "The only thing I think that it did was . . . a lot of the guys were playing their parts offstage. So I was a little scared . . . they were going to grab you." She added, "Jerry could be very nasty to us. He said, 'You know why? I let it out on you because you're the closest to me—the dancers.' And I think that's true, because he was a dancer. But it's like he got a pleasure out of being vicious."

D'Honau's friend Carole D'Andrea (Velma) saw Robbins as a "shy little child" and recalled, "That was his big downfall, that he would terrorize people. But he came up to me at the end of the first week—it was a brutal day at the end of a brutal week, and it was scary because it was my first Broadway show—he just came over and leaned down and said, 'Carole, I promise I will never put you down.' I turned around and I said, 'You don't have to take care of me. I can take care of myself.' I think that just sealed us forever. He loved that."

Ronnie Lee (Nibbles), who had worked on *The King and I* and *Peter Pan*, was one of those who "was constantly in emotional turmoil" with Robbins. Lee remembered, "It didn't help that I was voted the Equity deputy. . . . When it was time for a five-minute break, no matter where he was at artistically—his intensity was enormous, the genius flowed—I would go to Ruth Mitchell and say, 'It's time for a break,' real cold, and let his artistic juices be damned. It was a constant quiet battle, and he would shout at me occasionally. I'd say he succeeded fairly well in making me feel like shit." Lee added, "I regret that I didn't have the emotional maturity to understand that I was working with . . . one of the unqualified geniuses of the theatrical century and let myself be used like a dancer should be used by that capable a person."

Jay Norman described Robbins succinctly as "a workaholic burning the candle at both ends." The little time that Robbins had for any amorous social life during production was split between actress Lee Becker, who performed the role of Anybody, and Tommy Abbott, who played Gee-Tar. The relationship with Becker was brief, and ended shortly after she began entertaining the notion of marriage, although according to Wilma Curley (Graziella), Becker did manage to convince Robbins to put her into the first-act dance-hall number, "which made no sense at all for her character." The romantic affair with Abbott went on intermittently for some years. One dancer suggested that the relationship was one-sided, that Abbott "serviced" the director at his convenience, placing himself on-call in a sense and often to his chagrin. Still, Robbins remained loyal to his friend and later brought him into City Ballet as a ballet master (Abbott also restaged a number of Robbins' Broadway shows in revival). Looking back, Grover pondered the complexity of Jerry's relationships. "Over the years, I watched him agonize about choosing between men and women a number of times. The man I knew as a friend was a loving one. For reasons of his own, he didn't seem willing to make a lasting commitment with anyone."

The eight weeks of rehearsal in New York culminated on August tenth with a "gypsy run-through" at the Broadway Theatre. In his memoir in progress, Gene Gavin (Anxious), described the scene: "The gypsy show was the first chance the producers had of seeing the show in front of an audience. It was basically a friendly audience, a notice of invitation being posted backstage at all the current shows. The run-through was done in practice clothes, with chairs and benches being placed around the stage as sets, and work lights only; the bare minimum. . . . At the end, the audience sat there stunned. The word was out, we were something to be reckoned with, great, the best, innovative. Everyone said we couldn't miss, that we would be the season's hit. And, I have no idea how many people told me that Lauren Bacall had, at the end of the show, just sat there with tears in her eyes. I began to wonder if anyone had seen the show, or had they only watched Miss Bacall weep."

The show moved to Washington, D.C., on August thirteenth for a three-week tryout at the National Theatre, and at that point the title was changed from *Gangway* to *West Side Story*. Before the opening, Bernstein wrote to his wife, "Everyone's coming, my dear, even Nixon and 35 admirals. Senators abounding, and big Washington-hostessy type party afterwards in Lennuhtt's house. . . . We have a 75 thou. advance, and the town is buzzing. Not bad. I have high hopes." He added, "I tell you this show may yet be worth all the agony."

The gala premiere took place on the evening of August nineteenth, with Robbins insisting on a full "tech" rehearsal that afternoon. The performers made it through on pure adrenaline that night, while further blood was spilled onstage and off, with President Eisenhower's chief of staff, Sherman Adams, in the audience, along with Mr. Robert Kennedy, an army of congressmen and the cream of Washington high society. Bernstein reported that he ran into Justice Felix Frankfurter in tears in the lobby during the intermission.

Of that night, Martin Charnin (Big Deal) recalled, "I got pissed at Jerry particularly. . . . I had to leave the Rumble at the end of the first act by climbing up and over the courtyard, the schoolyard fence. The shop had sent the fence over very late and they neglected to shave off the barbed-wire top. So I ended up with stigmata on opening night. The only fight I ever had was racing over to Jerry at intermission and screaming my lungs out how he had endangered my life. I got an apology, but that was hardly as important as whether or not the light cue went on properly."

Robbins, Bernstein and the cast partied until five in the morning. The reviews were raves. *The Washington Post* called the show "a uniquely cohesive comment on life." Flushed with success, the creators and cast traveled on for another two-week tryout in Philadelphia and enjoyed a similar reception, though Michael Callan recalled, "We got something like seventeen bows in Washington. We got to Philadelphia and we only got twelve curtain calls. I looked at Tony [Mordente] and said, 'What's the matter with the audience?' We didn't know what we had."

The show premiered at the Winter Garden Theatre on September 26, 1957. According to Ronnie Lee, "The opening night in New York, you felt like you were part of Cinderella's entourage." Robbins was mobbed by fans. Bernstein, who conducted that night, later read the reviews aloud to a chic crowd at Sardi's—all raves except for Walter Kerr in the *Herald Tribune,* who complained that the show was "not well sung" and "rushingly acted." Nevertheless, the impact of the musical registered with Kerr, as he started his notice with the memorable line, "The radioactive fallout from *West Side Story* must still be descending on Broadway this morning." Brooks Atkinson praised the show in the *Times* as "profoundly moving . . . as ugly as the city jungles and also pathetic, tender and forgiving." He added, "This is one of those occasions when theater people, engrossed in an original project, are all in top form. . . . The subject is not beautiful, but what *West Side Story* draws out of it is beautiful. For it has a searching point of view."

A Broadway tradition known as the "gypsy robe" was continued with *West Side Story.* This was a robe bestowed for luck on one cast member before opening night. The gesture traced back to Arthur Partington on *Call Me Madam*; and the new recipient was a member of the Sharks whose stage name was Elizabeth Taylor, an ebullient and much-loved dancer who was married at the time to Miles Davis. Davis and his wife, formally Frances E. T. Davis, attended the gala celebration party at the Ambassador Hotel (where celebrants danced to the music of *My Fair Lady* and Robbins wandered in a happy daze) and later threw a cast part of their own, which Jerry attended. The Davis marriage became its own tragic love story, as the jazz great was cruelly abusive. Francis recalled, "Miles didn't like a lot of people. He was basically a recluse, and he didn't like people around me. He was extremely jealous. He thought a woman should be with her man." After six months, Miles forced his wife to withdraw from the show, and later vetoed Robbins' personal invitation (delivered during a run-in at the Copacabana) to allow her to perform in the *West Side Story* movie. Frances Davis eventually fled from her abusive husband and made a new life for herself in Los Angeles.

The show initially ran for almost two years (734 performances), then toured for nearly a year and returned to Broadway in 1960, lasting another 253 performances. Robbins often returned to watch from the wings and would give notes to the cast. The show lost out on a Tony Award that first year to *The Music Man*, but Robbins won as Best Choreographer. Surprisingly, *West Side Story* required time to find its audience, with its place in cultural history secured primarily by the 1961 movie. Columbia released the original cast album, and a successful run in London's West End was launched in December 1958, with Robbins in charge. Stephen Sondheim was modest in his estimation of the show's impact on the future direction of Broadway musicals. "I thought it was unique in its coalescence of words, music and staging, with the accent on the latter. To me a significant show is one that influences shows that follow. Because of its special nature, I don't see *West Side Story* as having done that, simply because no subsequent show had a story and style requiring the kind of blend that *West Side Story* represented."

There would be endless revivals, which Robbins delegated to trusted assistants like Alan Johnson, who started out as a Shark understudy. The original cast was bonded by a kind of familial affection and there were a number of nostalgic reunions over the years. According to Johnson, "Somehow that group became stronger as a family than any other show I've been connected to. The *West Side Story* people have gone on to become writers, directors, producers, teachers, choreographers. I call it the University of *West Side Story.* When you do a production that can teach you about theater—the definitive kind of lessons of what's required of you onstage at every moment, it's really incredible."

Ballerina Muriel Bentley was later sadly miscast in the Chita Rivera role. Tony Mordente said, "I remember even though Jerry hired her [Muriel] because of how close she was to him, he really used to rip her apart. He'd come to rehearsal and in Jerry's fashion . . . just tear her apart. . . . And the funniest thing was one night she said to me—she was really angry—she said, 'That sonofabitch! I was his first fuck. . . . How can he do this to me?' I laughed hysterically. Later we talked about that very thing with Jerry, and Jerry got that real giggle on his face. And she says, 'Oh yeah, you remember on the train. I broke you in, baby.' It was hysterical to see her talk to Jerry outside of rehearsal like that. During rehearsal she would never say anything to Jerry because she knew Jerry as well as anybody else did." Even with Robbins repeatedly abusing her in the theater, Bentley remained an adoring, lifelong friend.

In spite of the show's ultimate success, there was a fallout of bad blood between its creators, although all of them would work together again in the years to come. Robbins' self-aggrandizing credit was one source of conflict. Freedman defended him, saying, "Jerry's vision was very, very clear. I'm not leaving out the fact of his wild energy and ferocious appetite to look the best, but somehow within that he knew where he was heading. And I think 'conceived, choreographed and directed by' is absolutely apt. I don't care what the other guys contributed to it. Jerry was the center of it." When the show opened in Philadelphia, Bernstein wrote to his friend David Diamond and declared that "this show is my baby." Still, during the Washington run, Bernstein was generous enough to bestow sole credit for the lyrics to Sondheim, with whom there had previously been a shared arrangement. That act of generosity registered with Laurents. He felt that Robbins did not deserve the "conceived by" credit as it applied to the gangs concept and tried to persuade him to eliminate the credit for original conception.

Laurents explained the history of the contention as follows: "When it was written, my agent called to tell me Jerry asked for the credit 'conceived by.'

I felt the conception of a contemporary *Romeo* was Jerry's, and so I agreed. When we opened in Washington, two things happened. Steve Sondheim was ignored in the glowing reviews. The lyrics credit was shared by him and Lenny. Lenny had only met Steve on the show, but felt the credit was far more important for Steve and removed his name—one of the most magnanimous gestures anyone has ever made in the theatre. The second event happened on television. Lenny, Jerry and I—Steve was excluded—were given the keys to the city because of what the show did for juvenile delinquency. 'This was your conception, wasn't it, Mr. Robbins?' the presenter asked, and Jerry said, 'Yes.' You don't make a scene on television, but after it, I asked Jerry—my friend for over a decade—to remove the 'conceived by' credit, because it obviously was taken to mean the use of juvenile delinquency and juvenile gangs, which were *not* his idea. He asked to think it over, did so and said I was right, but the credit was too important to him. Which is one reason I say he wasn't evil because he informed, he informed because he was evil."

The HUAC legacy was a source of continuing strife for Robbins, although for the most part it remained buried. It was not something that was discussed by the creators or cast of *West Side Story.* As it happened, the actor who played Doc, Art Smith, had been one of those named by Elia Kazan. In fact, Robbins would cast quite a few blacklisted performers in future shows, which may have been purely by chance or perhaps an indication of his conscience working overtime. Some colleagues with whom Robbins later consulted on casting doubted that he would ever have showed such favoritism; in order to appear in one of his shows, a performer had to have the talent to deliver. Still, many of those who were blacklisted were talented enough to work for Robbins. And one of them would soon become the bane of his existence.

O n January 27, 1958, in the Terrace Room of the Plaza Hotel, Robbins was given *Dance Magazine's* Outstanding Achievement Award. He had received the same award eight years earlier for his performance as a dancer in *Prodigal Son,* and now he was being recognized for his work on *West Side Story.* In his acceptance speech, Robbins expressed gratitude to the show's producers as well as Bernstein, Laurents, Sondheim and Peter Gennaro. The honoree concluded, ". . . the question mark in my mind is this: now that the dancers—who to me are the most progressive and daring and accomplished people in the theater—have learned how to act, have learned how to sing, have combined both the modern and ballet fields, have accepted no barriers—where are they going to go next? That is the question! To them I dedicate the base of this statue."

Robbins was soon invited by Gian Carlo Menotti to bring a group of dancers to the Italian-American Festival of Two Worlds in the Umbrian village of Spoleto. Robbins took advantage of the opportunity to establish a small touring company, Ballets: U.S.A, which also appeared that year at the Brussels World's Fair. He later said, "I didn't decide to form my own company; it just happened." Robbins recruited a dozen dancers for the project, including Wilma Curley, Jay Norman and Tommy Abbott, all three from the cast of *West Side Story.* Todd Bolender and Sondra Lee were also cast in the original troupe, and Maria Karnilova later joined as a guest artist for the company's debut in New York. Robbins brought his ballets, *The Concert* and *Afternoon of a Faun,* into the repertory and choreographed two new works: *New York Export: Opus Jazz* and *3 x 3.* The producer was Leland Hayward, and additional financing was obtained along the way from the eccentric Standard Oil heiress-philanthropist Rebekah Harkness, who entertained deluded fantasies that Robbins would stage a ballet to one of her musical compositions. He was not so inclined and soon barred her from coming to his rehearsals.

Looking back on his four years with Ballets: U.S.A. (the troupe was repeatedly disbanded and reestablished), Robbins said, "I was happiest when I had my own company." Of his first Italian experience, he told *Dance Magazine* in September of 1958, "The countryside is more lovely than can be described. . . . The people are kind, sweet, wonderful. . . . Artists are revered there—no one could do enough for us. . . . We lived in an atmosphere of good living such as most of us had never imagined. . . . found there was a balance between living and working—instead of all work, which seems to be the dancer's lot as we have known it in the States. We performed only two or three times a week. . . . Most of us were housed in spacious villas or were cordially treated in private homes. . . . We quickly learned to accommodate ourselves to four-hour lunch periods and to custom-made, handmade suits, shoes,

sweaters. . . . I know . . . that these are luxuries based on our American standards and wages, and that not too many Italians can live as we did. But that's
the way it was for us, and it was ideal."

Robbins shared a villa with Wilma Curley, Patricia Dunn and his sometime lover, Tommy Abbott, who was now also serving as his assistant. Curley
recalled the domestic scene as one of hilarity and high spirits, with Robbins at
the mercy of their obstreperous Italian maid. "We had a wonderful housekeeper named Albertina. She would hit Jerry. She called him 'Robby.' He
would say something and she'd swat him. He'd say, 'She won't take directions
from me. She won't listen to me.' And she'd say, 'Eh, Robby,' and then whack!
We would all crack up and he would be laughing while he was almost crying
because it was affectionate, what she was doing, but she really smacked him."

Curley continued, "I remember one morning after we had been partying
quite late. And we were all at the breakfast table. It was one of the funniest
groups you would ever want to see. I had this long blond hair and I had on a
crinoline. Pat Dunn had a bikini on and dark glasses, and she always slumped.
Tommy Abbott had a velvet coat on. And Jerry comes down the stairs wearing
a wig and wrapped in a sheet with a candelabra in his hand. We saw him coming and we all said, 'Don't laugh, we're not going to notice.' Then some Italian
count who was trying to date me showed up in the doorway. And while the
guy was talking, Jerry is falling all over himself, trying to get his wig and sheet
off. We just laughed at him.

"Sometimes we would steal his clothes. He had a shirt that he meticu-
lously ironed and cleaned, but it had holes in it. Now, he didn't like people that
dressed improperly. He liked neatly dressed people. He didn't like over-sox
and over-pants. He'd say, 'Get all that crap off.' But then he'd wear this shirt
with holes in it. So we just took it. He spent days looking for it, blaming Albertina, who kept hitting him. Then we took his shoes—these were his magic
shoes that he created with—and we had them bronzed and mounted on two
boomerangs. On opening night, for gifts he gave very wonderful art books
with black orchids on them. Nice presents, and they were personal. So we gave
him his bronze shoes back, and later he hung them on the wall in his office."

Curley's association with Robbins started when she was an eleven-year-
old student at the School of American Ballet and continued for almost fifty

years. She became one of his most trusted assistants, one of the few who were never intimidated by him. She said, "I found Jerry funny. He couldn't get angry at me. I just cracked up every time he said anything nasty. The affection survived because way deep down, Jerry was not a nasty man. If he said something and you didn't laugh, he didn't know how to get out of it, so he would then say something nastier, and then unfortunately the other person always took it personally." Curley recalled that he deliberately terrorized the dancers in the company, except for the chosen few he favored. "Jerry would say, 'They're scared shitless of me,' and then he'd laugh. He did it on purpose, and he got what he wanted out of those people."

Jay Norman was Curley's frequent partner in *Afternoon of a Faun*, and both were cast in *New York Export: Opus Jazz*, an abstract work set to Robert Prince's Jazz Concert. Highly regarded by Robbins, artist Ben Shahn designed an urban rooftop setting. Norman remembered one of the early *Opus Jazz* rehearsals: "I had a tiny solo . . . and then I started dancing with Wilma Curley. I had to blow a kiss and then roll backwards, do a back somersault, and wind up standing up again. He made me do it over and over, the solo and the rollback. Now my spine is starting to hurt. We were in the theater and he finally went way out into the orchestra . . . and he says, 'Do it again.' And he just kept saying, 'Do it again.' What was making me angry was, usually he would say, 'Look, you're terrible, you're not doing this right, I want this,' and he'd be very specific about what he wanted. Well, he wasn't saying anything. Finally, I said, 'What the hell do you want? I've been doing it! You know I can do it.' He said, 'You'll do it because I want you to do it.' That was his big comeback. And then he went further back and said, 'Do it again.' So I did it, if that's going to blow his dress up. That was it. But see, that was mild in comparison to things he did to people."

Dancer James Moore recalled having a lunch with Robbins at the time and feeling comfortable enough to question Jerry about his ultra-draconian methods: "I remember talking to him about the way he would act during rehearsal, how vicious he could be . . . and he said, 'You know, when I'm working, all I can see is the work, for everything else I have blinders on.' Anything else was a distraction, so he just cut or lashed out at anything disturbing him or getting in his way."

Ballerina Erin Martin also danced in *Opus Jazz* and suggested that Robbins' choreographic direction at this point was an aesthetic spillover from *West Side Story*. Martin said, "He was making a formal statement in the balletic vocabulary about popular dance that he had used in *West Side Story*. Not that the vocabulary in *West Side Story* wasn't classic, but he was taking generic forms and putting them into a classical form which really was very unusual." Robbins explained that *Opus Jazz* "tries to express one aspect of the mentality of young people today and their attitude towards the world. As to its form, jazz obviously suggested itself as the only suitable musical language. To show the vitality, the sensibility and the élan of this youth through American youth, it was essential to find a different form based on the movements and rhythms peculiar to dancing and to modern life."

The Spoleto Festival opened on June 8, 1958, and Ballets: U.S.A. created a sensation for the mostly Italian and European audience. Reporting for the *New York Times*, Howard Taubman called it "a rousing success." He identified *New York Export: Opus Jazz* as the highlight of the evening, suggesting that the ballet was "a delightful and searching distillation of our jazz fads and fancies." Taubman followed the troupe to Brussels the following month for the World's Fair and wrote that the ballet had been "refined and is now a taut and tender work of art," evocative of "the young America that has come to be known as the 'beat generation.'"

Robbins' other new work, *3 x 3*, was a less ambitious piece of frivolity set to a woodwind trio by George Auric, with the accompanying musicians stationed on high ladders. The piece involved six dancers with comical hats and a number of floating balloons. In *Dance Magazine*, Doris Hering later observed, "It was one of those childhood fantasies to which Mr. Robbins has returned intermittently throughout the years, and each time with less conviction and more embellishment."

Ballets: U.S.A. was booked for a month on Broadway at the Alvin Theatre. Before the September fourth premiere, Walter Terry announced in the *Herald Tribune* that "New York is a Jerome Robbins Festival." Terry pointed out that Robbins' work would soon be on display at five Broadway theaters, with his choreography featured at the New York City Ballet and American Ballet Theatre, in his two hit shows, *West Side Story* and *Bells Are Ringing*, and with his new company. Expressing his characteristically high-minded aesthetic creed, Robbins stated for the record, "What really interests me is the conduct of man, the rites he performs to face the mysteries of life."

As in Spoleto and Brussels, the Ballets: U.S.A. program included *New York Export: Opus Jazz, 3 x 3, Afternoon of a Faun* and *The Concert.* John Martin characterized the opening as "an amusing evening all around, and an enormously talented one. Mr. Robbins has done himself proud." However, although Robbins and the dancers made a splash in New York, the company was unable to attract audiences elsewhere in America and was forced to cancel the remainder of the tour while still on the road. Robbins disbanded the troupe with the promise of a return engagement the following year. He was once again changing directions.

R obbins described his next musical, *Gypsy,* as "almost the antithesis of *West Side Story.* Where *Story* is told through movement—dance—*Gypsy* does nothing of the sort. Where the earlier show had a cast trained in modern and ballet idioms, *Gypsy* has children and performers trained in tap." Billed as a "musical fable," *Gypsy* also featured striptease routines, which were actually a kind of sophisticated parody of those burlesque acts for which Minsky's was famous. The book recalled the bygone era when vaudeville was dying and being replaced by burlesque houses. Robbins said, "One sure thing . . . the show's not going to start a new trend in dance."

Gypsy originated with the high-powered, pugnacious David Merrick, who wanted to produce a musical based on the memoirs of burlesque queen Gypsy Rose Lee. Lee's book told the story of how she and her sister, actress June Havoc, were pushed into show business as children by their mother, Mama Rose Hovick, who was a ruthless and charming stage mother, hell-bent on achieving fame vicariously through her offspring. Merrick envisioned the role for Ethel Merman, whose last success on Broadway in *Call Me Madam* had come under Robbins' guidance. Merman had recently flopped with *Happy Hunting* in 1956; however, this was her only real failure on stage in almost thirty years. Robbins pushed for Arthur Laurents to write the script despite the history of their troubled collaboration on *West Side Story.* Robbins was also keenly aware of where Laurents stood with regard to those who had named names, but he had complete faith in Laurents' talent. The playwright was uninterested in *Gypsy* until he learned about Mama Rose's lesbianism and alleged homicidal past. Laurents discovered that she had once quarreled with a hotel manager and pushed him out a window to his death. "How can you resist doing a musical based on a woman like that?" said Laurents.

Robbins, of course, had his own stage mother and was intrigued by the character. He later said, "I am fascinated by this theatrical family. Essentially, it is a story about recognition—all kinds of recognition. Not merely the kind that comes with fame, but people recognizing each other and themselves—what they really are. . . . It's about family life—how a mother comes to recognize her daughter, and a daughter learns to know her mother." Robbins was speaking from experience, having witnessed over the years such moments of struggle and recognition between his mother and sister.

Laurents wrote the script in the fall of 1958 while the score was being composed by Jule Styne and Stephen Sondheim. The latter had wanted to do both music and lyrics, but was vetoed by Ethel Merman, who insisted on bringing in a more experienced composer. Sondheim's surrogate father, Oscar Hammerstein II, prevailed upon him to work with Styne and to accept the more limited role of lyricist. Despite their contrasting temperaments and the age difference—Styne was fifty-three and Sondheim twenty-eight—the two hit it off famously and their exchange would lead to one of Broadway's most memorable scores. While Robbins was in England supervising the London production of *West Side Story*, he remained entirely outside the *Gypsy* creative loop of Laurents, Sondheim and Styne.

Later in the year, Laurents and Sondheim met with Robbins in Manchester, England. This was the first time that Robbins heard the famous first-act number, "Everything's Coming Up Roses." After it was played for him, Robbins complained that he didn't understand the title of the song. Sondheim recalled, "And I'm thinking, 'Oh my God, is it too poetic?' Because one of the problems was to come up with a phrase that means, 'things are going to be better than ever,' that isn't flat and yet isn't so poetic that you can't believe that Rose with her street jargon would say it. The point was to find a phrase that sounded as if it had been in the language for years, but was, in fact, invented for that show. I was really proud of finding that phrase. And Jerry says, 'I just don't understand that title.' I say, 'Why not, Jerry?' And he says, 'Everything's coming up Rose's *what?*'" Laurents recalled, "We howl about it to this day."

Sondheim further explained, "Yes, Jerry really did ask that question in Manchester. I don't think it reflects the kind of incomprehension the remark implies, but merely his attempt to take in a new piece of material which he wasn't certain about and therefore didn't quite approve of at the moment."

The show went into rehearsals at the beginning of the year at the New Amsterdam Theater, a rundown house with a huge auditorium called the Roof where Ziegfeld had once held court. Sondheim recalled for Meryle Secrest one of his happier moments working there with Robbins on the crucial second-act number, "Rose's Turn." Robbins had initially planned a dream ballet to reveal the nightmare of Rose's climactic mental crisis, a dance that would draw on earlier scenes from her life. Sondheim said, "Jule Styne was going around with our leading lady Sandra Church [who played Gypsy]. They had a date after rehearsal, so Jerry said to me, 'Why don't you stay and we'll talk about the number.' I decided that what we should do is take all the songs of the show that were connected with . . . Madame Rose, and mash them up, just the way Jerry was going to do with movement. . . .

"It was one of those things you dream of when you're a kid. You write a song with the star, only it was Jerry Robbins as the star. He started moving, performing a strip, sashaying back and forth on the stage, and I started to ad lib at the piano with the tunes that were already written. . . ." The ending of the song went through several revisions, until Oscar Hammerstein advised Sondheim and Styne that it needed a definitive ending that would be a showstopper for the star. Arthur Laurents recalled that Robbins brought a similar improvisational magic to the number "All I Need Is the Girl," "though Jerry approached it as a chore to be done with." In his memoir, Laurents recalled, "Jerry paced, pondered—I could almost see his ideas in the movements of his body so I was ready when he turned to me and said, 'You be the girl [in this number] because you can't dance.' He placed me on a stool which scenically became a garbage can in a theatre alley, mimed doing this, mimed doing that, asked for some lines to get him into the song . . . [and] dance. I gave him some, threw him others as he blocked the dance with an occasional break for a tap combination from his assistant. [Betty Walberg's] piano began to push the action and Jerry drew me into what amounted to an improvisation. He knew where he was going. . . . He gestured to do it next to him; we did it together. Betty played us to a big climax and 'All I Need Is the Girl' was finished. Not complete, not polished, but characters and relationship dramatized, story told through music and movement—a wonder! Only Jerry Robbins."

Both Robbins and Merman were initially surprised by Laurents' script. They had been expecting more of a sentimental gloss on the worlds of vaudeville and burlesque. Robbins had commissioned veteran performers from the era to serve as consultants, but Laurents took the story and the character of Mama Rose in an unusual direction, exaggerating the real-life personage and thereby creating an unforgettably grotesque portrait of a mother who will do anything to see her daughters win fame and fortune. Rose is a beguiling monster ("the very mastodon of stage mothers," according to Walter Kerr) who sacrifices her children to the seamy underside of show business. First, Baby June, Rose's favorite, is dragged into a singing, tap-dancing kiddie show and becomes a child star, rising from tank-town fraternal lodges to the Orpheum Circuit. Meanwhile, her older, less talented sister, Louise, masquerades as a boy in the troupe, which Rose manages with the aid of her kindly boyfriend-agent, Herbie. After June becomes a teenager, she runs off and kills the act, but not her mother's twisted dreams. Rose next sends Louise into the sleazy bump-and-grind of burlesque. After Louise becomes the star stripper Gypsy Rose Lee, she, too, abandons her mother, and even Herbie finally recoils from Rose's demented ambition, all culminating with Merman's eleven-o'-clocker, "Rose's Turn."

Gypsy Rose Lee was content to have the story focus on and distort her mother as long as her name was kept in the title. June Havoc, on the other hand, was outraged by the liberties Laurents and the other collaborators took with the musical. She recently said, "I never met Jerry Robbins in my life. I never met Arthur Laurents. I never met any of these people. They never at any time consulted me. . . . They just made up a story!" In his memoir, Arthur Laurents recalled that in an effort to have Havoc sign a release for her story, he and Leland Hayward met Havoc in Stratford, where she was performing Titania in *A Midsummer Night's Dream*. According to Laurents, Havoc called her sister's book "vulgar" and refused to sign until she saw the show during its Philadelphia tryout. Laurents suggested that the point of contention was that Havoc "demanded that it be stated [in the play] that she was thirteen years old when she ran off and eloped." David Merrick delayed giving anyone on the show contracts until Havoc had signed an agreement giving up the rights to her part in the story. Havoc recalled, "A lawyer stepped in, Louis Nizer, and he said 'No, we can't have this.' But he didn't do the job completely because they still went ahead and did it. I signed a thing saying that no one would represent me on the stage over the age of seven, no matter where or how, and that I wasn't to be mentioned or used after that. So I signed it happily."

The age limit is questionable, as Havoc was portrayed by two older actresses. Jacqueline Mayro was a ten-year-old cast as Baby June, and Lane Bradbury was in fact a sixteen-year-old who played the adolescent June. Bradbury was hired as a last-minute replacement for twenty-one-year-old Carole D'Andrea, who was a favorite of Robbins. He was apparently compelled to fire her by a committee that included Merman and the composers, who wanted a stronger singing voice. Robbins told D'Andrea that she had to be replaced because of the legal action threatened by Havoc regarding the age of the character, but this appears not to have been the case. Havoc denies that she threatened to sue over D'Andrea, and according to Sondheim, the decision to replace D'Andrea "was a group decision made by all of us, not just by Jerry. June Havoc had nothing to do with it, as far as I know. Jerry was fond of Carole, as we all were, and probably told her the June Havoc story so that her feelings would be less hurt. Incidentally, he subsequently made Lane's life as difficult as possible, out of guilt at having fired Carole, going so far as to humiliate her in public on the stage. . . ."

D'Andrea recalled that Robbins was incensed that "David [Merrick] proceeded to hold auditions without Jerry and . . . hired Lane Bradbury. Jerry was in a rage. . . . He says, 'I'll fire her the minute we open the show.' He made her life miserable."

Sandra Church remembered, "All of us [in the cast] were not too nice to her [Lane] at first because we all loved Carole."

Bradbury would never forget the treatment she received from Robbins. "I had to learn the part in three days in New York, and then I went to Philadelphia," said Bradbury. "They threw me into the costumes and pushed me onto the stage. I did manage to learn three songs and twirl batons, and all the dialogue and everything. But then there was this scene where I'm sitting at the table with Rose and Gypsy, and there's a teapot there, and they wanted me to move the teapot just so that Ethel Merman could sweep the silver into her pocketbook. It was just a joke, making it a clean sweep. That was one of the things I forgot to do. I forgot to move the teapot. And then . . . I forgot it again. I got a note about it, and I thought, 'Okay, I've studied in Actors Studio. I'll make this fun. I'll do a sensory thing and I'll make it so that I want tea.' But . . . I forgot to move it again. My sensory work maybe wasn't so good because I didn't move the teapot. I went upstairs to change clothes, and Jerry came into the dressing room. He took a red lipstick and he wrote on the mirror: *Remember to remove the fucking teapot!* That just put the fear of God in me.

"So then my preparation was, *Remember to remove the teapot, remember to remove the teapot, remember to remove the teapot,* and [I was] really uptight about it. Well, I forgot it again. So I hear at the end of the day, when they're calling the rehearsal times for the following day, the [stage manager] said, 'There will be a teapot rehearsal for Lane Bradbury in the lobby from 4:30 until 5:00.' So I went to the lobby, and the stage manager had set up a table, and he put the teapot there. He would say the line and I would move the teapot, and he would move the teapot back. And he would say the line again and I would move the teapot. This went on for a half an hour. Then we went into New York and we had two previews in New York. At the second preview, I started upstairs to change clothes after the scene, and Jerry Robbins was at the top of the stairs, and he screamed down at me: 'You bitch!' I knew I must have forgotten to remove the teapot.

"So I went out and finished the number, and there was a scene where Dainty June goes back and gets her batons off the train, and she twirls them and does a split. . . . And there were always two sets of batons on the train in case some of them fell off. Well, I went back there and there were no batons. All I could do was just put my hands up in the air and do a split, but the joke was lost. So I went to the stage manager and said, 'What happened to my batons? What happened to them!' Jerry Robbins was standing there and he said, 'I took them so that you would remember to remove the teapot.' This was the night before we opened in New York."

Several in the show recalled how Bradbury had been humiliated and was reduced to tears onstage when she was unable to find the batons, her empty hands twirling in the air. Arthur Laurents remembered finding Bradbury in a state of hysteria in her dressing room and later being "shredded" by Robbins over the teapot. At the end of the night, Laurents confronted him about the underhanded mischief of stealing the batons and was told, "What do you care? It wasn't in one of your scenes." From there the scene turned to fierce if petty squabbling over *whose* show it really was. Credit was still a source of contention between the two, and Robbins again had his name in a box, though Laurents had been paid off with an additional percentage from the producers. However, Bradbury did subsequently remember the teapot on opening night and received favorable notices. Robbins was unable to fire her without cause, but according to Bradbury, seven months into the run she was sidelined with a leg injury, and later replaced in the role when Robbins' stage manager advised her to take additional time off, her absence exceeding the union limit. Thus, according to Bradbury, she was tricked out of her role in the show.

Others in the cast fared better with the director. Jack Klugman, who would later be known as half of TV's *The Odd Couple*, was cast as Herbie despite his misgivings about his singing voice. He remembered, "Jerry was very open. We were very friendly, but of course he was very shy. . . . He kept his distance all the time. But I would hug him. 'Hey Jerry!' I would say, and I would hug him, and he would just freeze. He wouldn't know what to do and would get very embarrassed. I would say—and I don't use this word at all with anybody else—he was the only genius I've ever worked with, the only one. . . . Though he's not my kind of director, you understand, in terms of acting. What he knew about acting, I think, you could stuff in a thimble. But he knew what worked. . . . If he told me to jump out a window, I would do it, and it would be good. I knew with him it was right. I saw him work with Ethel. She would do something and then he would say, 'Ethel, try this and that.' And he would give her certain gestures, and he would just transform it into something wonderful to watch."

Sandra Church recalled, "Jerry left Jack and me alone to do our own act-ing. That's the way I felt. And he was very supportive of actors. But he wouldn't deal with the strip number. Just would not deal with it. And out of town in Philadelphia, the audience would get mad because some nights he'd say I would strip and some nights I wouldn't strip, so you know people won-dered what's going on. And it was very funny. But I remember once Ethel de-cided—here I am acting and there was a curtain that kind of beat you in the back—and Ethel decided she wanted to be up behind it the whole time. Of course, I didn't want that to happen. I mean, why, for my big number? So I just did it lousy for two nights while she was walking around."

The strip numbers were deemed so risqué that the children in the show were not allowed to watch the second act. Ballerina Maria Karnilova per-formed as one of the strippers in the number, "You Gotta Have a Gimmick," as did dancer-comedienne Faith Dane, who also had experience with a spe-cialty act in burlesque shows. According to Robbins' assistant, Robert Tucker, Faith Dane was somewhat disgruntled that part of her strip act was used in the show. Tucker recalled, "I auditioned every one [of the strippers], every one in New York. Then Jerry'd sit me down and talk about each strip. They were all the same, except one I saw that was using electric lights, which was very clever. And another, she looked like she'd been a ballerina or something. It went on like that until he got what he wanted. And he took the idea of the electrical one, he liked that. And Faith [Dane] with the bugle—poor thing, that used to be her act. And she tried to sue the producers. It was her act and she tried to get some money for it and nothing ever happened to it. It was the same old thing: 'It's in my show, it's my number now.'"

Jacqueline Mayro stole scenes and became a child star with her perfor-mance of Baby June. Mayro recalled, "You couldn't interrupt Mr. Robbins to say hello to him in the morning. You did not say hello to Jerome Robbins, be-cause Robbins said, 'I don't want my train of thought interrupted, so don't say hello to me.' . . . Robbins had very exacting standards for everybody and he was no different with the children. I don't know why I remember this. I thought it was so very strange that one time he played hide-and-seek with us. We all thought that was very odd, because Robbins wasn't known for his charm and caring. Most of the time he was extremely demanding of all the children, and we were treated in the same way and had the same demands put on us as the adults did. It bothered me . . . that the children—this speaks more to me than Robbins—that the children had to call him Mr. Robbins and the adults could call him Jerry. That came actually from him, too."

Of working with the children on *Gypsy*, Robbins said, "You forget their age if they have discipline. . . . Of course, they find it a little harder to make changes than adults." He added, "I think adults are sometimes just as child-like."

Mayro remembered, "Originally there were two complete sets of Baby June and her Newsboys. Robbins wanted somebody younger than me actually, smaller than me, so originally we were on pink contracts because, literally, as we went into rehearsal there were two sets of Baby June and her Newsboys. We were actually . . . for the first two weeks in competition. It was a little back-stage drama that went on, because the younger Baby June's mother was a real stage mother. . . . When it became clear that Robbins was leaning towards my set . . . the mother of the [other] Baby June started hitting the little [girl]. It was one of those things that you cringe about, that Madame Rose would do."

The rehearsal pianist on *Gypsy* was John Kander, who would later team up with Fred Ebb to write such shows as *Cabaret, Zorba* and *Chicago*. Kander described an early breakthrough in his relationship with Robbins: "Jerry would stay after rehearsal occasionally. We'd just stay and we'd improvise stuff together. One night it had gotten to be about nine o'clock . . . and he was feeling tired. . . . He said, 'Let's quit and go sneak into the movies.' So we went downstairs and we sneaked into the movies. We were sitting in the back, and it was *The House on Haunted Hill,* a Vincent Price horror film. I remember it was filled with skeletons and an acid lake or something like that. At one point, I looked over. I was very tense with him because he was still Jerry Robbins. I noticed his hands were up around his eyes. I thought, 'Oh god, he's got a headache, he's going to be really impossible.' Then I watched as his fingers slowly spread so he could look through them, and I realized he was scared to death from the movie. That was the most humanizing moment. Suddenly, then I saw who he was. We stayed friendly for quite a while after that."

But Kander witnessed the extremes of Robbins' behavior over time. The composer said, "I don't think there was anybody who didn't admire him, even the people who were afraid of him . . . I think he was just sort of crippled in one department, that's all. . . . Jerry outside of rehearsal was just this sweet [and as] lovely a guy as you can meet. Everybody has to work differently. . . . When I was at Columbia, we used to go to the NBC Symphony rehearsals and watch Toscanini over and over again throw these incredible tantrums. And he was a genius, he was a great, great conductor. And then I've gone to rehearsals of many other conductors who didn't behave that way at all and they were great talents and the music came out wonderfully. I think there was at least for a period a kind of mythologizing of that kind of behavior—well, that's called 'artistic temperament.' I call it bad manners. Mr. Abbott could be plenty tough, but I never saw him hurt anybody's feelings except on purpose, if you know what I mean by that, never because of any sort of self-indulgence. That was Jerry, and he had his own demons. But he was a huge talent, and he certainly affected me and I learned from him."

Kander continued, "The interesting thing is when we would talk, sometimes going back and forth to Philadelphia, his two great gods were George Abbott and George Balanchine. With both of those men, there was an ease of creativity that allowed them to produce in a funny way a larger body of work than Jerry did, because Jerry, I think, somehow or other was always looking over his own shoulder—whatever I do has got to be magnificent, perfect. I'm just judging from his conversation, whereas Balanchine would produce five new ballets for a season and four of them would be really mediocre and one of them would be *Firebird*. Same with Mr. Abbott. It was the process of working that I think they enjoyed. I don't know if the process was something Jerry enjoyed."

Kander suggested that Robbins was simply unable to work any other way and pointed out that such conduct is now rare in both the theater and concert hall. "I think it has changed, but I think for a lot of reasons and not because there aren't any Jerry Robbinses around or because people behave differently. I don't think it really has anything to do with that. I think the sadistic dictator choreographer has become unacceptable, in a way that the sadistic dictator conductor of a symphony orchestra is no longer acceptable. Conductors simply do not behave that way anymore, and I assure you they get just as high a standard of playing, if not higher, than they did forty years ago."

Robbins was repeatedly badgered by *Gypsy*'s headstrong and outspoken producer, David Merrick, and eventually appealed for assistance from the show's co-producer, Leland Hayward, who was also Merman's agent. A company meeting was called. According to Merrick's biographer, Howard Kissel, Hayward told Merrick, "I have something to say to you, David. . . . You're being negative. You're disturbing the rehearsals." A master of polite control, Hayward continued bluntly, "Look, David, you got into this show for $10,000. Let's go upstairs and I'll give you a check for $10,000." The upshot was that Merrick stayed on as producer but was barred from attending Robbins' rehearsals.

During the Philadelphia tryout, Robbins tried to cut the song "Little Lamb," which was performed by Sandra Church. Jule Styne, Stephen Sondheim and Arthur Laurents prevailed upon the Dramatists Guild to threaten the producers with an injunction against the show unless the number was restored. All three authors understood the dramatic importance of the song, as it marked the emergence of Louise as the show's heroine. But Robbins insisted on replacing the song in order to give the show a big dance number, which didn't come off because it failed to relate to the characters. According to Sondheim, Robbins balked at restoring "Little Lamb" even with the threat of injunction: "Jerry was furious and wouldn't stage it, so Arthur did."

After the show opened at Philadelphia's Shubert to mixed reviews, gossip columnist Dorothy Kilgallen circulated rumors of "backstage battles" between Merman and Robbins. Merman denied the story in her memoir, *Merman*, and recalled, "Along with Josh Logan and George Abbott, Jerry was one of my favorite directors. I called him 'Teacher.' Learning 'Rose's Turn,' I followed in back of him as he walked through the number, copying his moves and gestures. He also taught me to sit still and get my effects. I'd never been presented to better advantage."

With the innocence of a child's eyes, Jacqueline Mayro saw the Merman-Robbins relationship as a test of wills and occasional "clash of egos." Mayro was onstage when Merman had her first entrance and recalled, "Merman said to [Robbins], 'When I come onstage on opening night, I'm going to get tremendous applause when I make my entrance. So when I come on . . . should I stop and acknowledge the audience, or should I just stay in character and wait for the applause to die down?' He said, 'No, no, no, definitely wait for the applause to die down. Do not acknowledge your audience.' Guess what happened on opening night? Merman turned around and she acknowledged the audience."

Mayro continued, "I loved Ethel Merman . . . because she was so honest. She was who she was. At one point there was a *Gypsy* run-through . . . and I think Jack Benny came to see it and he said, 'Jesus, if they leave the show like it is, they're going to have to call it "Baby June."' Ethel Merman didn't like children on the stage with her because they took away [attention] from her. . . . Children are a threat on a stage, particularly a role like Baby June, which is just one of those roles that people in show business love so much. They kept cutting back my part and cutting back my part and cutting back my part, and that was fine. She did what she needed to do. Her name was Ethel Merman. But she was just great. . . . I'd be waiting or watching in the wings, and she would say, "I had this great meal, and I'm going to tell you about it as soon as I get offstage," and then she just went right on the stage. There was no preparation or anything."

John Kander remembered, "Jerry and I stood in the wings when [Merman] sang 'Everything's Coming Up Roses.' She stood there in the middle of the stage. . . . I remember tears were pouring down her face during this performance. The curtain came down, and she came offstage and caught the two of us. She said, 'See? I'm acting, I'm acting!'"

With sets from Jo Mielziner and costumes by Raoul Pène du Bois, *Gypsy* premiered May 21, 1959, at The Broadway Theatre and received effusive raves from the critics. The most low-key among them, Brooks Atkinson, reported, "Under the genial direction of Jerome Robbins, who is willing to take time to enjoy what he is doing, the performance is entertaining in all the acceptable styles from skulduggery to the anatomy of a termagant." Atkinson called it "a good show in the old tradition of musicals" and noted, "For years Miss Merman has been the queen." Walter Kerr observed, "I'm not sure whether *Gypsy* is new-fashioned, or old-fashioned, or integrated, or non-integrated. The only thing I'm sure of is that it's the best damn musical I've seen in years." The show ran almost two years and spawned successful revivals with Angela Lansbury and Tyne Daly. Hollywood produced a disappointing movie three years later with Rosalind Russell in the starring role (much to Merman's chagrin). Arthur Laurents said, "We can say she [Russell] wore black-and-white pumps and that's about it."

Of the early Broadway run, Jack Klugman remembered, "We had opened and we were an enormous hit, and it was about . . . a week later, and [Jerry] was in the wings looking at the show, and on his face was a sort of questioning look of wonderment. And I knew what he was thinking. I said, 'Jerry, there is no formula.' It was as though he was looking to see, what the hell did I do that I can do the next time to make it easier? I said, 'Jerry, it's just hard work and your gift. It's never going to be easier.' So he kind of was embarrassed and he laughed that I was reading his mind. He knew it was good."

Klugman harbored great affection for Merman and worked with her throughout the run. He said, "She and I got along so well. She said she never had a leading man get along with her that well. But I adored her. I would sit there and she would sing to me, and I would just smile because I had been a fan of hers for years. And we'd come offstage and she'd say, 'Did you pay to get in?' [I said], 'No, baby, but I got the best seat in the house.' She knew I didn't want anything from her and I wasn't going to upstage her or do anything like that, so we had a wonderful relationship."

Sandra Church had her ups and downs with Merman and remembered how the star gradually dropped the character over time and reverted to her stage persona. "It was amazing to watch her after a couple of months slip back and be awful. It just slowly went away. And it was Jerry who had gotten her to act and be this other character. I don't know how he did it really. And when he wasn't around, she lost it."

Four months after the opening, Robbins was back in Europe with his Ballets: U.S.A. troupe, when he received a letter of complaint from Leland Hayward. Rather than address Robbins with the typically endearing "Gypsy" or "Jerry," Hayward's salutation was one of chilly formality: "Dear Jerome." The letter, dated September 23, 1959, stated:

> I fear you have lost your marbles, blown your stack—and are way out, due to taking all those bows all over Europe. This unkind reference to your stability is in connection with the cable I got from you, and

the call from Edith [Weissman] yesterday, about that nasty subject—
the strip in a play called "Gypsy," that you had something to do with.
You forget, dear, the problem. This thing is all right while we're doing
the montage city to city. In other words, red dress, blue dress, etc.,
works and Sandra [Church] actually plays that part of it better than
she used to. Remember, I said better, not great. The catastrophe is
when she comes out at Minsky's, in what I call her Eskimo dress, covered up from tip to toe, or perhaps I should spell it tit to toe. Raoul
Du Bois is in Europe, so I can't get him to do a new costume. The
point of it is simply that the thing has no climax, and no wallop. . . .

If you are too damn lazy to come back and fix it, then drop me
a note and tell me what to do with it. My idea was not to restage it
in its entirety, because it would be too tough to do, but simply to try
to get something to climax the career of this divine woman, by her
triumph at the Minsky burlesque house.

I realize how difficult it is for an artist like you to think about
sordid details of a show that is only doing $82,600.00 per week, out
of which you are receiving a considerable percentage, but I am going
to keep pestering you until you tell me something to do with that
God-damn strip, which is driving me nuts.

It's terribly early in the morning Jerry,—9:30 to be exact, hence
my apparently grouchy condition. Also, the fact that I am going in rehearsal this morning with "Goodbye Charlie" at 10 o'clock, and am
going out of my mind over at "Sound of Music."

Of the costume that was the ostensible point of contention, Sandra
Church recalled, "I started out in a black dress. . . . I was layered in three
dresses. Blue was the second and red was the last. . . . It never changed. Then
the last costume in the last scene was pretty bad. It was a green dress. It was
weird. . . . They kept me wearing that one, too."

Robbins was not about to be distracted from his ballet company (which
Hayward was, after all, producing). There may have been another reason for
the testiness of Hayward's letter—at the time, Robbins was romancing Hayward's wife, Slim. Hayward had become involved with Pamela Churchill, and

recently announced to Slim that he wanted a divorce. Slim recalled, "Everyone in my world knew what was going on." In New York, she received a cable from Robbins, who was in Spoleto. "The cable simply read, 'Move over, Lady Brett. Why don't you come and be with me. Call me.'

"When I called Jerry, he'd heard everything from the usual town criers in New York. He instantly knew what to do with me. 'Tell the concierge at the Ritz to put you on an airplane to Rome, and have him cable me what flight you're on. I'll take care of the rest. Just don't stay by yourself.'

"At this point, I was putty in anyone's hands. I numbly followed Jerry's instructions. And soon found myself in Spoleto, installed in the sweetest little apartment, where you could only take a bath at six o'clock because at five they built the fire under the water tank. 'I have to work all the time,' Jerry said, 'but you can stay in the theater with me, eat every meal with me, and never leave my side. If that's what you want to do.'

"That was just the beginning of his kindness. Once Jerry had finished his work in Spoleto, we rented a car and drove all over northern Italy. We stayed in funny small hotels, stopped at quaint restaurants, looked at beautiful things. We were on a safari to hunt down every Piero della Francesca we could find, and we saw quite a few of them. The trip was a great comfort, as if the world had reached out to put its arms around me.

"It was Jerry's tender and abiding friendship that got me through the most miserable time in my life." Their romantic affair was short-lived, but the friendship flourished. After Slim returned to New York that fall, she started a three-year romance with playboy-gambler Ted Bassett, and in 1962 she married (what Slim described as a "cerebral decision") British aristocrat Sir Kenneth Keith, an arrangement of salon convenience that later ended in divorce. Throughout these years, Slim maintained an unshakeable trust in Robbins. She wrote of him, "Perhaps it is Jerry's obsessive need for privacy that makes me feel so secure. Or his ability to sit quietly and listen to one's troubles and fears and terrors without overreacting or preaching. He's able to hear every word you say, he equates the truth with the condition, and then he comes back with short little bits of advice, without shooting you into a pulp. And his advice is almost always right. He makes astonishingly accurate observations of situations and people. He sees truth, but always with a sort of twinkle which puts pretension right out of business. But better than the advice is the sense of love that he gives, whether you're right or wrong. He loves you for how you are."

Slim's daughter, Kitty Hawks, said, "Mom was Mom. If you wanted a stable family, she was not the crew you signed up for. But I think the friendships were stable." Of Robbins, Kitty recalled, "The thing that . . . I found true of him when I was in my late twenties—I remember Leonard Bernstein as well from when my mother and Leland were married and later, and I never, when I was in his presence, felt that he wasn't aware that he was Leonard Bernstein—with Jerry I didn't feel that. When he was among friends, I never had the sense that he thought of himself as a star. He was just Jerry having a good time. There wasn't that kind of selfish self-conscious remove. It was almost schizophrenic, because I'm sure he'd go to work and be what he was at work. . . . And it's often the other way around, where people in real life can be disgusting and then they can go to work and pretend that they're fabulous. They're not fabulous, but they do a good imitation of fabulous when they're at work. But when they get home, the imitation is over. With Jerry, it was quite the opposite, you know? I think when Jerry got home, the best of him was there when he wasn't being as creative and as intense.

"I can't believe that there's anybody on that level of genius—whether they're painters, or musicians, or choreographers, or architects—who haven't that kind of single-minded and selfish focus when it comes to the work they do. Otherwise they wouldn't be able to do that kind of work. And it doesn't make them popular. . . . I've known fairly creative people—he was one of the few [about whom I can say] I would have no fear in sitting Jerry next to somebody that was a friend of mine from school. He would find out something great and they would have a fabulous time with him. Whether they knew he was Jerome Robbins or not, they would end up with Jerry. That's not true of very many people. . . . It would take him a while to warm up. I can't know that, because I knew him for so long and under circumstances where he was always around people that he loved and felt comfortable with. But I'm sure that if you were meeting him for the first time, he wasn't moving forward into your life, [rather] he had to hang out and wait until he saw that it was okay. . . . All it would take was something to make him laugh and then he'd be fine. Humor was the key."

In Spoleto that year, Robbins offered the same repertory that he had the year before, along with one new ballet, *Moves,* which had its premiere July 3, 1959. This ballet was planned with music from Aaron Copland, a series of waltzes entitled *Dance Panels.* Robbins recalled, "A strange thing happened. I went straight to rehearsal without the music, right after Aaron played it for me. I tried to remember it, but could only recall the counts. When I began working with the company just with counts, I got interested in what they were doing without music. It fascinated me, and [we] continued working that way. It really moved along. I was sorry I wasn't able to do *Dance Panels,* but in a very real way, Aaron's music was the accidental genesis of my ballet without music, *Moves.*"

Without scenery or costumes, the ballet was a plotless exploration comprised of five movements. One of the original cast of twenty, Jay Norman, explained how Robbins created his silent ballet. "What he did was put in, what would you call them, little keys from one dancer to another to let them know tempo. When one dancer would finish this [movement], another dancer would start. . . . Everyone would ask, How did you all stay together? It was easy, absolutely easy, the way he did it. A lot of different little sight cues; audible cues were a stomp on the floor—not hard but just enough to hear. But Aaron Copland was supposed to write music for that. And imagine having the balls, in plain English, to just go ahead, all right, I'll do it without. This was a full piece, this wasn't like a five-minute thing. It was probably seventeen to twenty minutes. . . ."

The ballet was received with wild applause from the audience in Spoleto. One Italian critic wrote, "We do not wish to prophesy that from now on geniuses of the dance will express themselves in absolute silence, putting aside music, which for centuries has been a responsible collaborator with the dance. But without doubt, the day on which Jerome Robbins' *Moves* was premiered on the stage of Teatro Nuevo di Spoleto will become engraved in the history of 20th-Century choreography." Two years later, when *Moves* premiered in New York, John Martin was less enthusiastic about its novelty as a silent ballet, suggesting that "there is little to be said in praise . . . In essence it is a throw-back to . . . German modern dance . . . circa 1930. There, however, the absence of music was more than compensated by the inherent continuity of movement produced by inner muscular motivation. . . . Here the basic technique stems from the ballet classroom, which produces nothing of the sort. Beside the general formlessness that results from Mr. Robbins' venture into abstraction, he has punctuated his style with realistic gesture . . . and given it an air of commonness."

In its four years of existence, Ballets: U.S.A. was far more successful on its international tours than it was at home, especially outside of New York, where Robbins was less of an audience draw. One of the stage managers, Tom Stone, was just out of Yale when Robbins recruited him. Stone was then newly married to ballerina Erin Martin, and he recalled, "We went out on this tour of Europe for the State Department in 1959. It was something like a five-month tour to twenty cities. . . . It was really a baptism of fire for me because we were moving twice a week, and as stage managers we had to stay up all night long to take the sets down and then immediately start to set back up in a new city and reproduce the lighting. It was awful, it was truly, truly awful. Jerry was unremittingly critical and demanding about everything, and all I wanted to do was have a honeymoon, to go out and take in Florence, and of course I couldn't do this.

"But the tour itself was epic and unbelievably beautiful. We went everywhere, and in the middle of it we had a plane crash. . . . I'd dreamed about this and predicted it two months before it was going to happen. My boss, Dick Evans, said, 'Well, it's just wishful thinking.'" In Stone's dream, "all the scenery and costumes were lost," as it happened in reality. Stone said, "As it turned out, when we left Athens, there *was* a terrible storm that came up over the Aegean. We were heading for Edinburgh and the weather forced us down in Rome. When we got to London, we were sitting in the airport in the VIP lounge waiting to go on to Edinburgh, and an official from the airport came and got Jerry . . . and Jeannot Cerrone, the business manager for Rebekah Harkness. . . . They came back absolutely pale green. I said to Dick, 'What's the matter?' He said, 'Remember that dream you had? Well, the plane's gone down, the cargo plane.' As it turned out, the [plane] went down fifty yards offshore of Italy. The pilot swam ashore, but all the scenery and costumes were lost.

"So we went to Edinburgh and they opened up all the stores for us, the department stores, and they bought new costumes and sneakers. [The New York City Ballet] sent us a whole set from City Center, the whole set of *Afternoon of a Faun* . . . while we were performing in Edinburgh before we were due to open in London. . . . This was my first opportunity to run a show. Dick and Jerry and everybody went down to London. They reproduced the scenery for all the other ballets in one week at Covent Garden. And we opened in London."

The London audience demanded fifteen curtain calls, what one critic called "an almost feverish reaction." The company played to capacity houses throughout Europe and the Middle East (including Paris, Monte Carlo, Salzburg, Belgrade, Dubrovnik, Copenhagen, Stockholm, West Berlin, Warsaw, Barcelona, Madrid, Lisbon and Reykjavík). In Tel Aviv, nine performances drew an audience of 30,000 in July and August, with members of the Israeli cabinet in attendance. Robbins was hailed as a "Ballet Ambassador."

Photographer Arnold Newman recalled running into Jerry in Israel. "I went for the first time to Israel in 'fifty-nine, and Jerry was there with his Ballets: U.S.A. So we were all being looked after—in those days, they were trying to build up publicity for Israel, the tourism—and we were taken out to dinner, Jerry and I and about three or four other people by the American-Israel Cultural Foundation. . . . At dinner they asked me what I was doing. I said, 'Tomorrow I'm going down to Eilat,' which was in the south. Today it's a big modern resort; in those days it was just a few houses, practically shacks . . . and it was just across the road from Jordan. You could walk over to Jordan. Jerry started asking me all kinds of questions about my trip. I looked at Jerry and said, 'Sounds like you'd like to go.' He said, 'Frankly, I'd like to.' So I said, 'Look, I'd be delighted to take you along. I've got a big car all to myself with a driver and a guide.' I understand it was the only time he left his group at that time.

"We drove down. At times he would just suddenly curl up and sort of close inward. And later some of our mutual friends said that's the way Jerry was. We got down there . . . and there was an article on Jerry and an article on me in *The Jerusalem Post*, which prints in English. We were rather amused, the two of us sitting on the beach. . . . We made arrangements and bought tickets to fly up to Jerusalem, because on Friday night there was what they call a synagogue tour. . . . We walked from place to place in the religious section. There must have been seven or eight different synagogues. The last one was the Hasidic one. The Hasidic . . . felt that the way to pray to God was through the joy of dance and singing. So while we were sitting there, suddenly a lot of the Hasidic Jews, with the big hats . . . began to dance in the center, singing and clapping their hands. And Jerry got excited. Finally, he jumped out of his seat and ran down and joined them. . . . It was mind-boggling just to see him dancing, this great dancer with these people who had been doing it for centuries. He was clapping his hands, singing with them, singing the prayers with them. . . . And he came back after they stopped—sweating, all excited, flushed—and he said, 'One day I'm going to make a ballet out of that!' And of course it was Tevye, *Fiddler on the Roof.*"

In Paris, Robbins was joined by his father, who had recently remarried. Harry and his wife, Frieda Weiss Robbins, attended one rehearsal during which Jerry was especially demanding of one of his ballerinas. One of Robbins' colleagues remembered, "His own father came into the studio in Paris and he [Jerry] was working with one of the dancers . . . who was one of his dearest, dearest friends there, and he almost crippled her. And his father came and said, 'I can't stand this any longer,' and he walked out. Oh, it was awful!" Such open disputes with his father were rare, though Robbins never forgot Harry's early efforts to thwart his career ambitions. Harry's new wife was graciously accepted by Jerry and was apparently a welcome addition to the family. Jerry's sister recalled, "Frieda was a very good lady. She took very good care of my father, and living with Harry was no joy. He constantly compared her to my mother."

Robbins' father and the rest of the family watched at home when Ballets: U.S.A. appeared on *The Ed Sullivan Show.* Supervising all the dancing and camera work, Robbins presented *New York Export: Opus Jazz* in November 1959 and won Sullivan's invitation for a return engagement in January 1960. Robbins and Sullivan had evidently buried their HUAC hatchet. In fact, several years before, Sullivan had written a column applauding Robbins for his success with *Peter Pan,* and Sullivan was proud to take credit "for those of us who in earlier years fought the Commie invasion of theatre to the best of our ability."

Robbins was deeply skeptical about presenting dance on film and television. He said at the time of his troupe's second appearance on Sullivan's show,

". . . television is a two-dimensional medium. And you never sense in television the limitations of space. You cannot sense, either, the kinetic energy of the dancer nor his dangers, feats and pleasures. . . . Very few, if any, persons have taken advantage of what the camera can do to create dancing for television. Most of them use the stage technique. It really is something else entirely."

Despite his misgivings, Robbins again took up the challenge of translating dance for the camera later in 1960 with the filming of *West Side Story*. The movie was being produced by United Artists with the Mirisch brothers— Harold, Walter and Marvin—in control as a fraternal *éminence grise* behind the scenes. They had originally invited Robert Wise to direct, but Robbins' contract gave him an ironclad right of "first refusal"on making the movie. Robbins wouldn't agree to a limited role as choreographer and threatened to torpedo the movie unless he was hired as director. An uneasy compromise was reached whereby Wise and Robbins would co-direct, while Wise was also billed as one of the producers.

Wise's credits included such films as *The Set-Up, Somebody Up There Likes Me* and *Run Silent, Run Deep* (and later *The Sand Pebbles* and *The Sound of Music*). Recalling his decision to work with Robbins, Wise said, "We had a couple of fairly soul-searching meetings, Jerry and I, one here [in Hollywood] and one in New York, as I recall. We both had our misgivings about how it might work, how it would operate. So finally we came to this arrangement: that he would be in charge of and direct all of the dance numbers and musical numbers. And I would be there as he was shooting those, to give him the thoughts I had about what he was doing, maybe suggest an extra camera on this angle, or change of lens, or something like that, any little thoughts I had. But he was doing [the dance scenes]. And then when I was doing what they call the book part, all the dialogue scenes, I would direct those scenes and he would be there to give me the actions, the way things were going, and suggest little things maybe to improve it. So that's the way we did it. We went back and forth." Wise continued, "I spent almost two years on that picture. We had about six or seven months of pre-production preparation, which included the three months of Jerry to have his dance rehearsals, and then there was the pre-scoring, and then about six months or so of shooting, and about six, seven months . . . of post-production, finishing it up."

Most of the show's original cast was replaced in the movie, which featured Natalie Wood (Maria), Richard Beymer (Tony), Russ Tamblyn (Riff), Rita Moreno (Anita) and George Chakiris (Bernardo). According to Wise, Natalie Wood was discovered unexpectedly. "We were trying to cast the boy, what's-his-name, Tony. . . . Somebody told us that they'd heard there was a very good test at Warner Brothers for Warren Beatty for *Splendor in the Grass,* and maybe he was our Tony. So we went over to see the test, and the test was run, and we were there to see Warren, and who's supporting him but Natalie. We forgot all about Warren. We said, 'My god, there's our Maria right there' . . . so we started negotiations then to sign her. . . . She was down in Atlantic City with Bob Wagner . . . on some kind of holiday I think. So Jerry and I had to fly down to Atlantic City to see her and talk to her about doing *West Side Story.* . . . And we did the pitch and flew back to New York, and the studio started negotiations and wound it up a couple of weeks later."

Wood's assistant on the movie was Mart Crowley, who would later write *The Boys in the Band* (1968) and based the character of Harold on his friend Howard Jeffrey, who served as Robbins' first assistant. Crowley remembered that Robbins' affection for Wood complicated and strained the relationship in the beginning. "I know that he fancied himself in [the] throes of romantic love in a way, he *fell* for her . . . and who wouldn't? She was just so captivating, it was almost impossible not to. But Natalie was very hip, and she knew all about Jerry. Natalie was a girl who liked *men,* heterosexual men. . . . I was her best friend, but there were no bones about what was going on at all. I knew all the men in her life and she knew all the men in my life—far less in mine than in hers. I think [Jerry] kind of frightened her in a way—not frightened her, but she just knew that she had to handle that relationship very, very carefully because she didn't want to humiliate him or alienate him—and she was crazy about him. He was doing nothing but helping her. So it was a very delicate moment, I think. And of course they remained friends until she died."

Robbins did not have control over casting, which was a sore point for him. Carole D'Andrea had played Velma on Broadway and recreated her role in the film. She recalled, "Jerry was merciless to Rita Moreno, merciless! She wasn't Chita. . . . She's a wonderful actress, she did a great job, but she wasn't Chita. It was painful for him not to have everybody that he wanted." Whatever misgivings Robbins may have had about Moreno, she would win an Oscar for her portrayal of Anita and spoke highly of Robbins, saying, "What he did that was so unusual [was] that he choreographed for character. He choreographed the way a writer writes."

By nature and temperament, Wise and Robbins were opposites, as were their approaches to the work. "You get your results in different ways," said Wise. "I'm a very quiet director on the set. I don't raise my voice, or rarely ever raise my voice . . . because you're always answering questions from not only actors but crew members. You don't have to be loud and yelling at all . . . you just have to know what the hell you're doing, that's the main thing." Wise described Robbins as "very demanding, very demanding, very demanding, do it again, do it again, doing it again—he drove the dancers out of their minds sometimes." Wise added, "It was wondrous, exasperating, sometimes maddening but it paid off, and I know I made the right decision when I agreed to go along with him as the co-director. . . . He was a tremendous talent, there's no question about it. . . . We didn't become buddies. I don't think I ever saw Jerry after we worked together. That's not unusual. But there was no big problem between us at all."

The dancers' rigorous daily routine was enforced by Robbins and his assistants, Howard Jeffrey, Margaret Banks, Tommy Abbott (who played Gee Tar as he had on Broadway), and later Tony Mordente (who played Action in the movie after performing A-rab onstage). Russ Tamblyn, whose background was in acrobatics rather than ballet, said, "Every day before rehearsal, even when we were shooting, we would have a two-hour warmup, and the warmup consisted of floor exercises and stretches. Then . . . we would do stuff at the *barre,* and then do running stuff, where they would do *tour jetés.* And it would get out of my league because there was a lot that I couldn't do. But they would do leaps and double-spins and stuff like that."

As with the Broadway show, Robbins tried to incite hostilities among the actors in the rival gangs. "It wasn't a law," said Tamblyn, "but he didn't want us hanging around together. . . . It was a little silly, because when you're in your late twenties to be doing that, I don't think anybody took it too seriously. . . . I think there were a couple of Sharks and Jets that were living together and then at the end of the day would go off together." Tamblyn added, "We had a lot of fun, but there was a lot of pain and a lot of misery, and . . . there was a kind of military attitude . . . a Nazi attitude with Jerry and Howard [Jeffrey] especially. . . . Howard was his lieutenant, or his sergeant, or whatever. Jerry used to come and set the routines and then Howard would make everybody work it out until they got it, and then Jerry would come back in and change everything. That was basically the process."

Dancer Harvey Evans recalled, "After we filmed 'Cool,' for every scene that was filmed after 'Cool,' we had to run to the soundstage and do 'Cool' full out, then run up to where the camera was and do the scene. So when we finally didn't have to do 'Cool' anymore, we burned our kneepads in front of Jerry's office . . . a big bonfire. . . . And we did rain dances to stay in New York and they got mad at us for doing that. It rained a lot. I think we were in New York at least two months. We were prohibited from doing rain dances—that's how silly it became."

Margaret Banks remembered one of the casualties during the filming. "You remember the long opening shot in New York of Eliot Feld [who played Baby John] running against the fence for a couple of blocks? God, you know what the humidity in August is in New York. . . . And Eliot must have run that scene over and over and over—there was a bump in the camera, there was a hair on the lens. He had to do it again and again, until the poor kid—he was only eighteen at the time, he was the youngest in the film—would reach the end and literally throw up. And Jerry would say, 'Sorry, Eliot, we've got to do it again. We didn't get it.'"

The exterior locations in Manhattan included four blocks on the West Side that were about to be torn down during the summer of 1960 to make way for Lincoln Center. Wise explained, "We liked that [area] very much, so we made a deal with the contractor, maybe gave him five or ten thousand dollars, instead of starting on West Sixty-first, to start on Sixty-fourth so we could have that street to use as a real New York street. That was a big set street for us. . . . But we didn't have a playground. The playground in the film is East 110th Street, right in the heart of a Puerto Rican neighborhood. So this is what happens when you shoot films, you make your own turf. So in the film sometimes they'll jump and they're on the West Side and they'll come down on the East Side. When they're on the East Side, they'll jump up and come down on the West Side."

Wise credited Robbins—who initially had wanted to shoot the movie in black-and-white rather than Technicolor—with translating the stylized dancing into the realistic settings of the movie. Wise said, "I fought from the beginning to open the film in New York in its setting, in its background, because we couldn't put stylized sets on movie stages like they had on the theater stage—they don't work in films. . . . Jerry agreed with this, but he said, 'You've given me the most difficult task right off the bat: to make my most stylized dancing in the piece and put it against the most real backgrounds we have in the picture.' " The result was a unique blend of film and dance techniques that opened with dramatic aerial shots and the Prologue street scene. Wise recalled, "What Jerry worked out was this. The kids were walking along the street in tempo with the music, and one of the boys raises his arms up, and they go a few more steps, then two of the guys do that, and a few more steps, all in tempo, they gradually segue right into the dance. Which made it work. Otherwise the rhythm of the dance and the realism of the street wouldn't work like it does on the stage. But Jerry was very, very clever."

Wise recalled that problems arose with the producers due to Robbins' perfectionism and the number of re-takes that he demanded, causing the production to spend additional time on location in New York. "There was a tendency," Wise said, "for him to think, well, we didn't get the number quite right, or this setup quite right today, we'll come back tomorrow and try again. And the more you do that, the further behind schedule you get." Russ Tamblyn remembered the kind of re-shooting that Robbins demanded early in the film. "He didn't do a lot of tantrums, but . . . he did things that were just sort of nuts. When we were dancing in New York, we did one really long sequence down the block, where we danced down the street. They did it all in one take." According to Tamblyn, Wise was satisfied with the scene, but Robbins insisted, " 'I want all you guys to do the same routine, same steps and everything, except I want you to do it on the other foot.' " Tamblyn added, "One of the things that Jerry used to say all the time was, 'Now don't forget, once it's on film it's there forever!' It was really hard for him to print something and move on."

The studio and Mirisch Brothers apparently believed that Robbins was being profligate and fired him without warning in Los Angeles. The "Prologue" and "Cool" numbers had been shot, but the "Dance Hall" and the end of the movie were yet to be filmed. Robbins was barred from the set, although he did return for some of the editing and later attended the Academy Awards. Wise recalled, "It was kind of an unhappy time when he was taken off the film, when we were about sixty percent of the way through shooting. Natalie Wood particularly was upset and I wasn't happy, but I had no control over it. The company was the one that made that decision." The movie's $4.5 million budget eventually rose to $6 million, but Wise suggested that the budget was not substantially affected by Robbins' departure. "I don't think the pace of shooting picked up appreciably after he left," said Wise. "It was just the nature of the beast."

Russ Tamblyn heard news of the firing early from his agent and told some of the others in the cast, expecting them to be relieved that Robbins was gone. "I was surprised that they were devastated by it," said Tamblyn. "They were very disappointed." While Robert Wise went along with the decision to remove Robbins, Natalie Wood threatened to leave the picture until agents from William Morris pressured her into changing her mind. Mart Crowley said, "She threatened to quit and the agents went berserk and said, 'You can't do that!' So she trudged on, but she wanted to quit."

In Robbins' absence, Wood asked for assistance from Tony Mordente in working with Richard Beymer, who many felt had been miscast as her love interest. Mordente recalled, "I did some slight restaging for her and the stuff for Richard Beymer, because neither one of them was getting along very well at all. So it was . . . how to make them look like they *were* dancing. . . . Richard really didn't have any feeling for the role . . . and I think when he was there, he really felt like an outsider. And I think because of that feeling—it's like when an animal gets the instinct of somebody having fear, they attack. And I think it was easier for Natalie to attack than to have to help. He really couldn't help her because he really wasn't right for the role. I think she felt that and I think that's where the defensiveness came in. . . .

"We talked about it at length in some areas, and somebody who is gone now, it's tough to say, but Natalie really didn't have a bad bone in her body.

And I told her a couple of times, 'You know, you really have to do this dance hall with him and you have to be in love with him. I'm not the director of the film,' I said, 'but you have to feel a rapport with this guy, especially in the cha-cha.' And she said, 'You know, I really don't dislike Richard. I just feel like he's not helping me.' And I said, 'But that's not his fault. You can't attack him for that, because it's not his fault. He was cast.' I felt sorry for Richard, because he was really miscast and he really felt ill-at-ease doing the whole movie. And I think it's a period of his life that he'd just as soon forget."

Both Wood and Beymer were dubbed for their singing, with vocals provided by Marni Nixon and Jim Bryant. Likewise Rita Moreno had a vocal stand-in, Betty Wand. The dubbing was rather obvious and awkward, as was later pointed out by critics. According to Crowley, Wood "never forgave" Wise for not informing her beforehand that she was being dubbed. "They wanted vocal perfection," said Crowley. "It was done behind her back."

Noting the higher quality of the early scenes shot by Robbins, Crowley speculated, "What would *West Side Story* have been like if he had not been fired? . . . One of the [things] that always struck me was that Jerry just didn't pay any attention to Bob Wise whatsoever. It was beyond humiliation, it was that he did not exist on the soundstage. Jerry just took the finder and went and set up the shots and didn't refer to him. I suppose they chatted and talked about what pieces of film they needed. But you didn't get the sense that anybody was running the show except Jerry Robbins on the stage. And Bob Wise was just sitting on the sidelines. I thought, how humiliating for him. Who knew that he was just sitting there waiting, waiting, waiting until his moment . . . to lower the boom."

Crowley was one of those who suspected there were longstanding hostilities between Wise and Robbins, even though Wise denied this and insisted that he played no part in the decision to fire Robbins. Crowley pointed out that the two directors failed to acknowledge each other two years later when each received an Oscar for directing (Robbins also received a special Academy Award for choreography). Crowley said, "Listen, I went to the Academy Awards that night, and believe me, there were two camps: there was the Wise camp and there was the Robbins. It was pretty frosty out . . . oh, there was tension."

The movie opened in New York at the Rivoli on October 18, 1961, and went on to become the year's top-grossing film. Critical opinion was divided. Stanley Kauffmann called *West Side Story* "the finest American film musical ever made, which, almost by definition makes it the finest film musical ever made anywhere." He added that Robbins' choreography evoked a "feeling of thrust at the audience, of gliding in and out of reality." On the other hand, Pauline Kael attacked the script (which had been adapted by Ernest Lehman from Laurents' book) as "painfully old-fashioned and mawkish," and she disparaged the dancing, suggesting "it's trying so hard to be great it isn't even good." She dismissed it all as a "piece of cinematic technology." Whatever the unresolved tension between stylization and realism, the dancing in the movie held up for the popular audience and surely did reflect Robbins' direction to the dancers in the early rehearsals: "I want the movements sharp—like a pistol shot."

There is no doubt that being fired was a low blow to Robbins' ego, and a setback for which not even his two Oscars were sufficient compensation (the film garnered ten awards, a record at the time). Before the movie's release, Robbins stated, ". . . I loved the crew and I respected Mr. Wise. I just think I was used as a patsy for some people without enough experience in the problems of filming musicals. But I'm real proud of the picture, and I'll stand by the work I've done, in contrast to the work I didn't do, or did not completely rehearse."

Elsewhere, Robbins said, "I'm in love with the live stage. It's my first and only love. Movies? I'm fascinated by the medium but not by Hollywood." The feelings were mutual: Robbins would never be hired again in Hollywood, although he later engaged in a prolonged flirtation with a film project based on the life of Nijinsky. At the time Robbins made his break with movies, he also issued a somewhat defiant justification of his perfectionist creed to the *New York Times.* He said, "I'm enormously demanding in the theatre. Through this drive to bring a work to as high an artistic level as possible, I feel I have gotten from my collaborators their best work. I ask for a great deal, but no more than I give myself. I am extremely self-demanding. I do ask people to extend themselves as far as they can.

"One thing I have absolutely no patience with in the theatre is anyone who works in it without being a completely dedicated artist and professional in all senses of the word, bringing to the theatre not only his talent but also coming equipped with technique and craft." Robbins added pointedly, "I feel that if someone doesn't have an insane love for the theatre, he shouldn't be in it."

Always a survivor, Robbins put his bittersweet Hollywood adventures behind and soon returned to the theater that was his natural home. In his domestic life, he found time for some leisure activities. He indulged himself by playing piano—"but never except for myself"—and by taking amateur photographs. He sometimes spent hours developing film in his darkroom. His preferred subjects were "mostly faces, only occasionally a scene." He said, "Photography is my antidote to the theatre . . . I work quietly, alone, in the dark, without pressure or time limits." But such diversions were never more than temporary distractions, respites from that "insane love" that was the passion and principle by which he lived.

SEVEN

Fiddler and the
Sacred Vision

Early in 1961, Robbins reassembled his Ballets: U.S.A. troupe for a return to Europe and a New York engagement. At forty-two, he was experimenting with a beard and his hairline was receding. Chronic problems with his Achilles tendons harried him in the studio. If these were signs that age was catching up, his energy and drive were undiminished as far as his dancers were concerned. With support from Leland Hayward and Rebekah Harkness, Robbins had expanded the company to twenty dancers and added *Interplay* and *The Cage* to the repertory. He also staged a new ballet, *Events*, an episodic jazz confection with a score from Robert Prince and scenery from Ben Shahn. A series of vignettes set against a looming backdrop of atomic holocaust, this twenty-five-minute dance explored topical themes and reflected the concerns of a decade marked by unprecedented social change. Robbins wasn't about to allow himself to fall behind the times.

Ballerina Erin Martin described the direction he was now pursuing: "I don't think anybody was really aware enough to sense the potential reverberations of history, but what we did sense was that something new was happening. . . . I think he was trying to find a new form, trying to find how to present in a formal way a lot of the vitality from popular dance and theater dance that

he'd used. That felt very interesting, combined with the fact that we were am-
bassadors at that point. This was during the early sixties, when the United
States Information Service was sending out artists as diplomats to show the
Socialist Republic that America was more than just some kind of adolescent
country. It was part of the Cold War. So wherever we went we created little ex-
plosions [with] what we were doing. We were into the sixties' cultural revolution, and it hadn't progressed yet to the kind of social revolution that it
became at the end of the sixties and into the seventies with the Vietnam War.
But what was happening is that things like social dancing were changing from
very codified partner stuff to things like the twist and Chubby Checker. We
look back on this now and it really seems a hoot . . . really silly and adolescent,
but it was in the air. And there were rumblings of things that would become
the Civil Rights Movement and the Women's Movement.

"I think you could see it in context with what Jerry had been through with
HUAC and the fact that he really was a patriot. And a lot of these ballets were
somewhat shocking in their content, but because they were formalized they
didn't have a kind of critical anti-American atmosphere, the way, for example,
Anna Sokolow's dances were critical of the culture. The closest thing I think
that Jerry ever came to that, was the last ballet he did for the company, *Events.*"

This new work premiered on July twelfth at the Spoleto Festival, and according to Martin, "It was not entirely successful on any level, but I think he
had tried to go farther than he ever had before to make a social statement. It
had a feeling of an alienated society, it had a feeling of brutality and inhumanity. . . . There was a section clearly that Jerry made that was about racism
and it was quite disturbing. The context was something like a party—it had
that feeling—and people getting drunk, and people becoming more and more
bestial, until there was this white woman riding [African-American dancer]
Johnny Jones like a horse. There was another section that had to do with the
toppling of religious idols and a lot of crutches were involved. It was Kay
Mazzo's first stage appearance. [She was] the idol, the Madonna toppling.
And then there was this wonderful . . . very tender duet for two men, and it
was [danced by] Glen Tetley and Eddie Verso. Eddie and I were about the same
size. He was a taller version of me, but we were both kind of skinny kids. . . .

I was the understudy. . . . It was very poignant and it was clearly autobio-graphical. [The ballet] was dependent on a lot of theatrical devices—lights and scene changes, and at the end this big set piece [that] was called the 'falling man.' It was one of those Ben Shahn things with the fist coming down and lit-erally crushing the participants."

The tender male *pas de deux* culminated with unexpected violence. Eddie Verso surmised, "It was a pedophile relationship, I have a feeling. I was the young boy and Glen Tetley the older man. . . . I guess it was a dark time for Jerry because it was a really dark ballet. . . . At that point, I was eighteen years old. I just went and danced and I never thought anything of it. And then all of a sudden, people would say, 'These two *guys*—wait a second now!'"

Verso's partner, Glen Tetley, danced for Martha Graham, Hanya Holm and American Ballet Theatre and would later become a noted choreographer. He recalled that the *pas de deux* in *Events* supposedly "took place in Central Park. Talking with me, Jerry said, 'You are walking in this place and everything you see is beautiful. Everything is wonderful in a sensual marvelous light. There is beauty in everything you see.' What he choreographed was a homo-sexual rape in which I was the aggressor and . . . Eddie was the young street-tough kid who I raped. It was quite powerful choreography. It was stylized, but quite graphic at the same time."

Tetley remembered that Martha Graham was outraged when she attended a performance of *Events* in New York. "Martha walked out of the entire evening. She made a point of being seen walking out." Graham offered no ex-planation that night, but a short time later she saw Tetley again in a perfor-mance of John Butler's *Carmina Burana.* "Martha came to see that," said Tetley, "and this time she came backstage and knocked on my dressing-room door. She struck me in the face as hard as she could, right after the performance. Martha said, '*That's* for Jerry Robbins.' Then she took me in her arms and hugged and kissed me and said, '*This* is for tonight.' I think she always had a chip on her shoulder about Jerry." Tetley suspected that Robbins earned Gra-ham's animosity in earlier years with public statements that she construed as being critical of modern dance. Of her reaction to *Events,* Tetley explained, "I think the reason that she walked out of Jerry's homosexual rape was not the fact of the rape scene, but there was a lack of dignity of the human soul, in a spiritual sense, to the inner core of choreography. Martha would react very strongly when she felt it was not there."

Tetley earlier left the company in Stockholm in a dispute over credit. He had been a featured performer at A.B.T and expected the same treatment from Ballets: U.S.A. But Robbins insisted on billing his dancers alphabetically, imitating the policy that Balanchine had established at City Ballet, where supposedly there were to be no stars that might outshine or distract from the choreography. As Robbins put it, "I think that the time of individual accomplishments has lost its interest. I conceive dance as a group expression, for the most moving questions of today are those which concern human groups." Of course, audiences resisted this sort of anonymity imposed in the theater, as did the performers.

Tetley's contract with the company stipulated separate billing, which he hadn't received on tour, and a tense squabble ensued offstage. "There was a green room and a dart board there," said Tetley. "There were some dancers, and I put this poster up on the dart board . . . I picked up a lot of the darts, and with a dart I went POW at the poster, and there was a silence in the room. And I turned around and there was Jerry. And he said, 'What are you doing?' I said, 'Jerry, I'm throwing darts at your name.' And he said, 'Ahh, okay, I'll help you.' So he picked up darts, and we were throwing darts at . . . Jerome Robbins' Ballets: U.S.A. And he said, 'Okay, now we're going to throw darts at your name.' I said, 'Aha, you're going to have a hard time because it's a very small target on that poster.' And then I said, 'By the way, Jerry, I've had it. I would like to leave the company. I would ask you to release me from the company immediately.' And Jerry said, 'Sure, sure, no problem.'

"So then I get back to New York City, and the company came back. . . . Ballets: U.S.A. was going to have a Broadway season. So Jerry's agent called me up and he said, 'Glen, Jerry is driving himself nuts. Do you think you could come back and dance just this one season with the company because Jerry is crucifying the person that took over your role in *Events*. If you could consider coming back, it would mean a great deal to the rest of us.'

"So I said, 'Okay, but two things: I want twice the money I was getting before and I want the billing that was promised to me from the beginning. I *want* that.' So he said, 'I have to talk to Jerry about that.' I said, 'If you don't call back within four hours, the answer is no, the answer is *no*. I'm not going to hang around.' He called back in two hours and said, 'You've got both. You've got the money and he's agreed to the billing.'

"So I went in and danced *Events*, and that's when Martha Graham came— and she came with [dancer] Bert Ross. They had heard the story about the billing. . . . Martha was dead on about billing. Bert Ross came back and he said, 'I thought Jerry was going to give you billing.' I said, 'He couldn't have!' No billing. I went running around the theater. If I had found Jerry, I think I would have killed him. . . . Why did he have to be so miserably mean? It had been promised."

On a program that included *The Cage, Afternoon of a Faun* and *Interplay*, the American premiere of *Events* took place at New York's ANTA Theatre on October 17, 1961. John Martin didn't mention the rape scene in his *Times* review, but stated that the ballet "is substantially another session with the Jets and Sharks, this time gone completely paranoid, both gangs. They slouch and twitch and roll in morbid self-pity, until at last the atom bomb gets them. . . . It is an ugly work, visually, psychologically and philosophically." Perhaps anticipating the American reaction to the ballet, Robbins told the *Times* the week before, "In Europe they said it was 'engaged' . . . meaning that is was committed to the world around it. 'Events' is about certain aspects of the atmosphere of today, the social world we live in. But it is a fantasy, not realistic."

Avoiding a more explicit discussion of the political, racial and sexual content of the ballet, Robbins warned critics not to ask him to explain the meaning of his work. "I rebel violently," he said, "against being classified and being specific about what my ballets are about. Try to ask a painter what he thought about when he put red in one spot and blue in another. I work for months, days and hours and keep changing until many, many moments come from a deep unconscious stream. Then I work through all the layers until I get to the level I call the key or spine of that work. Once I hit that, the work pours forth. Before that I change, alter, probe, discard, and examine. So you can see that by the time I get to it, I'm hard put to analyze all the stages I've gone through to get there."

On the night that *Events* opened in New York, stage manager Tom Stone became the hunted target of Robbins' wrath when Stone failed to bring the Ben Shahn drop down at the end of the ballet, thereby ruining the climax. The stage manager recalled, "The music is pounding away, jazz music pounding, pounding, pounding away. In those days I put on two warning lights, one right next to the other one. I never made a mistake the entire tour. It's opening night on Broadway, I'm twenty-four years old, and I put on the drop light and the curtain light. And I kept my hand on the curtain light. I pushed it and instead of bringing the drop in, I brought in the house curtain. It was awful, and I couldn't stop it because I was a neophyte. . . . There was an intermission. Jeanie Rosenthal [the lighting designer] appeared before anyone else. She looked at me and said, 'Tom, welcome to the club. We've all done it, honey . . . and don't let anybody else try to tell you any differently. Why don't you go back in the alleyway and we won't let Jerry find you.' He came back looking for me and he couldn't find me. Nobody would tell him anything. And at the end of the show, he came back [again] and Natalie Wood was with him, so he couldn't say anything to me. He just walked by me. We had a three-week run. He glowered at me every time he saw me. He muttered a few things here and there. I figured I was finished as a stage manager.

"Then we had a closing-night party at Sardi's . . . in a private room upstairs. I was sitting at the bar by myself. I was still shriven by this experience. I didn't want to sit with anybody or anything. I didn't want to take a chance I'd see Jerry, so I was off in a corner at the bar. They had a man at Sardi's with an accordion who used to make up songs. People would give this guy money and they'd tell him what the subject was and he would invent a song and start singing it. And I hear this man with the accordion singing a song about *the stage manager who let the curtain in too early.* So I turn around and there's Jerry at the other end of the room, smiling. Everybody's smiling at me. He came over and he hugged me. It was just wonderful. And then the next day he called me and he said, 'Would you be available to be the stage manager of *Oh Dad, Poor Dad?*' So I said, 'Yes, of course.' And I stage-managed that with him. That was another whole story, with Barbara Harris and Austin Pendleton and Jo Van Fleet. As Austin Pendleton says, 'We were the three most neurotic actors in New York at that time of our type, and you had all three of us.'"

Arthur Kopit's avant-garde, absurdist comedy, *Oh Dad, Poor Dad, Momma's*

Hung You in the Closet and I'm Feelin' So Sad, was the first non-musical play directed by Robbins and his first venture Off Broadway. The show was produced by Roger Stevens at the Phoenix Theatre on East Seventy-fourth Street, not far from the brownstone where Robbins was living. When he took on the project, the play had recently flopped in London with Stella Adler in the lead role of Madame Rosepettle. He said at the time, "It's an extremely difficult play to stage. . . . The author was very extravagant in his stage directions. For instance, they call for a piranha fish and a Venus flytrap that grow to huge proportions right onstage." Robbins cast Jo Van Fleet in the lead, and for his carnivorous fish and plant, he recruited set designers William and Jean Eckart.

In Robbins' production, the one-act play *Oh Dad* ran under an hour and a half and was to have been preceded by a curtain-raiser entitled *Sing to Me Through Open Windows,* a half-hour piece also written by Kopit. But the twenty-four-year-old playwright nixed the opening play during rehearsals. Kopit remembered, "It was a magical play and Gerald Hiken was in it, and he did a most exquisite job. . . . The problem was it was very haunting and effective. As a curtain-raiser, you weren't prepared for *Oh Dad,* for a comedy, so it hurt the beginning of *Oh Dad.* It was just that simple, and the producer saw that. Jerry loved the play, and I loved the way it was done. It was never going to be done like that again, but for the evening to work, it had to go."

The actor, Gerald Hiken, respectfully disagreed, saying, "No, that isn't what I got. That's a very sweet way of putting it. It was quite acrimonious. It wasn't a gentle, well-it's-not-a-good-way-to-start-an-evening. It was, 'When are you going to finish the play? When are you going to give us something that makes sense?' So Arthur Kopit's memory would be more flattering. . . . With Jerry Robbins, you didn't get *nice.* It was quite a wonderful play and we worked on it very hard. . . . My exact memory is that it did not have an ending, or the ending that it had seemed very unsatisfying to all of us, and Kopit either refused or . . . couldn't do anything with it. I've even run into people who've performed it since then, and when I tell them what happened they say, 'That's right, the ending . . . doesn't go anywhere.'" Hiken portrayed a magician, and this play told the story of a sensitive boy whose youthful illusions were shattered. As Kopit indicated, the style and mood of the piece did pose a problem as far as setting the stage for the surreal pyrotechnics of *Oh Dad.*

Robbins' assistant Bill Daniels recalled, "I tried very hard with Arthur to keep the play [*Sing to Me Through Open Windows*], but I think Jerry . . . brought Leland Hayward in to look at it. He [Hayward] didn't understand this play . . . which was a kind of very poetic play in which Gerald Hiken was doing a marvelous job. But Arthur Kopit was a young man, and these were his first two pieces that were going to be produced by Jerry Robbins. So when he heard, I think, that Leland Hayward didn't understand this piece, he just wanted to pull it. I remember going to him and saying, 'Believe me, Arthur, this play and the other play together will show the reach of your talents,' and so forth. And he really turned on me and said, 'Just forget it, Billy. Get out of my way, this is gone.' Oddly enough, the play was really Jerry's and my favorite of the two one-actors . . . and of course it was dropped, and Gerald Hiken's wonderful performance was never seen. But that was all Arthur Kopit, it wasn't Jerry Robbins. I'll tell you that for sure."

Kopit acknowledged that it was his decision and pointed out, "It was surprising. I think he [Jerry] was much sorrier to see it go than I who had written it."

Without a curtain-raiser, Robbins had the problem of how to open the evening and prepare the audience for the comic horror show that was to come. He decided on a filmed prologue (provided by graphic artist Fred Mogubgub), an animation reminiscent of the silent-movie style of Georges Méliès. Kopit recalled, "Jerry did a lot of scrambling to try to let the audience know they could laugh, and he did a very brilliant cartoon overture to the play. That was the hardest part . . . how to get the audience to understand the tone. Jo Van Fleet wasn't a natural comic actress so she couldn't just come out and you knew you could laugh. It's a play that you can see as sort of scary and forbidding." Indeed, the title and comic premise derived from Kopit's vision of the monstrous matriarch who keeps her husband's stuffed corpse hanging from a hook in the bedroom closet. The grotesque corpse tumbles out briefly in the middle of a seduction-murder scene between the shy, stammering Momma's boy, played by Austin Pendleton, and the babysitter whom he strangles, portrayed by Barbara Harris. When Momma later enters the scene, she complains to her son in a tone that makes the outlandish nightmare almost plausible, "I've found your dead father on the floor of my bedroom and there

Jerry's sister, Sonia (left), and their parents, Harry and Lena Rabinowitz (above). (*Courtesy Sonia Cullinen, Jean Handy*)

The formidable Rips women: (left to right) Ida, Francis (Fanny), Gertrude (Gert), Jean, Mary, Lena and Anna. (*Courtesy Jackye Lee Maduro*)

Jerry, age sixteen (center, middle row) at Camp Kittatinny. (*Courtesy James Jacobs*)

Jerry's stage debut was a one-line walk-on in the Yiddish Art Theatre's *The Brothers Ashkenazi*, 1937. Here, Albert Einstein (center) visits backstage with Mayor Fiorello LaGuardia (second from right, front row). Jerry is third row back, fourth from left. *(Museum of the City of New York)*

Jerry performing in 1939 with Anita Alvarez at Camp Tamiment in the Poconos, a unique training ground for performing artists. *(Courtesy Anita Alvarez Jacobson)*

With dancer Katie O'Brien (left), Sonia and her husband, George Cullinen, 1941. Jerry's brief affair with O'Brien may have helped draw him to the Left. *(Courtesy Sonia Cullinen)*

With Rose Tobias, 1947. She thought they'd get married—until Monty Clift came knocking. *(Courtesy Rose Tobias Shaw Collection)*

About to testify before HUAC on May 5, 1953: the event that would haunt him for the rest of his life. *(© Bettmann/Corbis)*

On the Town, 1944: Leonard Bernstein, Robbins, Betty Comden and Adolph Green. *(Photofest)*

Robbins and Broadway

Billion Dollar Baby, 1945, with Joan McCracken, who was "madly in love" with Jerry. *(Graphic House/MCNY)*

Nancy Walker in *Look, Ma, I'm Dancin'!*, 1948. *(Photofest)*

Nanette Fabray in *High Button Shoes*, 1947. *(Museum of the City of New York)*

Miss Liberty, 1949: rehearsing Allyn Ann McLerie and Tommy Rall. *(George Karger/MCNY)*

Rehearsing Maria Karnilova (left) and Nora Kaye in *Two's Company*, 1952. Jerry was engaged to Nora—while living with Buzz Miller, also in the cast. *(Museum of the City of New York)*

Yul Brynner and Gertrude Lawrence performing "Shall We Dance?" in *The King and I*, 1951. *(Museum of the City of New York)*

Fancy Free, with Janet Reed, 1944. His first choreography for Ballet Theatre and an instant sensation. *(Kosti Ruohomaa/Black Star)*

Robbins and Ballet

Three Virgins and a Devil, 1941: Jerry's first solo with Ballet Theatre. *(Carl VanVechten/MCNY)*

As Hermes in *Helen of Troy*, 1942, with Michael Kidd and Nana Gollner. *(Kosti Ruohomaa/Black Star)*

In Balanchine's *Prodigal Son*, New York City Ballet, 1950. *(George Platt Lynes)*

Robbins' controversial "predatory" ballet, *The Cage*, with Nora Kaye and Nicholas Magallanes, 1951. (*Walter E. Owen/Photofest*)

In *Tyl Ulenspiegel*, New York City Ballet, 1951. (*Walter E. Owen/Photofest*)

Tanaquil Le Clercq and Todd Bolender in Robbins' "lunatic" comedy, *The Concert*, 1956. That year, Le Clercq would be stricken with polio. (*Sara Leland/Photofest*)

The team behind *West Side Story*, 1957: (left to right) Leonard Bernstein, Arthur Laurents, Robbins, Irene Sharaff, Stephen Sondheim, co-producer Robert Griffith and Sylvia Drulie, who worked with Roger Stevens. (*Martha Swope/TimePix*)

The dance at the gym. (*Museum of the City of New York*)

Rehearsing the movie. ABOVE: Russ Tamblyn and the Jets *(Hulton Getty Collection/Archive Photos)*.
BELOW: Robbins with George Chakiris and two fellow Sharks *(Photofest)*. An uneasy co-director-
ship and charges of profligacy got Robbins fired partway through—but he won two Oscars.

Robbins' groundbreaking ballet *Dances at a Gathering*, 1969, with Edward Villella and Patricia McBride. *(Martha Swope/TimePix)*

Robbins and Ballet

Rehearsing with Rudolf Nureyev for the London *Dances*. *(© Bettmann/Corbis)*

Rehearsing with Villella for *Dances*. *(Martha Swope/TimePix)*

Robbins' Bach marathon, *The Goldberg Variations*, 1971, with Peter Martins (left, in shadow) and Karin von Aroldingen (center). *(Martha Swope/TimePix)*

In 1972, Robbins adapted Stravinsky's *Circus Polka* for himself as Ringmaster and forty-eight students from the School of American Ballet. At the end, they spelled out "I.S." *(Martha Swope/TimePix)*

Peter Pan, with Mary Martin, 1954. *(Photofest)*

Robbins and Broadway

Barbra Streisand rehearsing *Funny Girl* with co-star Sydney Chaplin, 1964. First, great hostility, then "they suddenly became chummy." *(Henry Grossman/Photofest)*

Rehearsing "Mr. Goldstone, I Love You" from *Gypsy*, 1959, with Ethel Merman, Carole D'Andrea (replaced in Philadelphia by Lane Bradbury) and Sandra Church. *(Photofest)* "I don't understand," Robbins complained to Sondheim. "Everything's coming up Rose's *what?*"

Though lingering anger over the HUAC testimony didn't keep Zero Mostel from working with Robbins, he made Jerry's life hell—both on and off the stage. ABOVE: John Carradine, Jack Gilford, David Burns and Mostel in *A Funny Thing Happened on the Way to the Forum,* 1962. *(Photofest)* BELOW: Robbins rehearsing Maria Karnilova and Mostel in *Fiddler on the Roof,* 1964. *(Eileen Darby/MCNY)*

Robbins and Ballet

Balanchine and Robbins rehearsing their collaborative ballet, *Pulcinella*, 1972. (*Martha Swope/TimePix*)

Rehearsing Mikhail Baryshnikov in *Other Dances*, 1976. (*Martha Swope/TimePix*)

Curtain call: The mystical ghost story *Dybbuk* reunited Robbins and Bernstein, first in 1974, then a reworking in 1980. *(Henry Grossman/TimePix)*

Music by Verdi, choreography by Robbins, New York City Ballet's *The Four Seasons,* 1979, was a cavalcade of stars and new faces. Here, Robbins rehearses Suzanne Farrell, Peter Martins, Patricia McBride and Mikhail Baryshnikov. *(Martha Swope/TimePix)*

Jerome Robbins, Fire Island, 1947. *(Courtesy Rose Tobias Shaw Collection)*

Jerome Robbins, 1994. *(Fred R. Conrad/New York Times Co./Archive Photos)*

is a girl in my bed, buried under your stamp and coin collections. She has stopped breathing."

Kopit suggested that Robbins was aware of his limitations when it came to working with the actors. "Jerry was brilliant at casting and finding out what the actors could do and knowing when it was right," said the playwright. "He would have Bill Daniels go and talk to the actors and do a scene, and he [Jerry] would sit out there and he would watch and say . . . that wasn't quite right, do this and this and this, until he felt that it was the way it should be. . . . I remember once Jo Van Fleet was very unhappy. She didn't know something and Jerry knew what it should be. We talked and he said, 'Look, would you have dinner with her, because if I talk to her, I will say the wrong thing. I will talk to her about the effect that I want and I know that's not the way to do it. So just make her feel better.' My marching orders were very clear—don't tell her what to do, but just soothe her, take her to dinner. But Jerry knew that if he went, he could get upset . . . and make things worse."

Kopit noted that Robbins possessed "a remarkable combination of absolute confidence and insecurity. There was no bombast at all. He didn't try to hide it when he didn't quite know how to do something, but you saw that he was completely certain that he would find out how to do it, he would figure it out. I thought this is someone who absolutely loves what he's doing and doesn't necessarily know what he's going to do the next moment, so it was all a process of discovery. . . . I never had anything close to a difficult time with him. Nor did any of the actors that I saw when we finally went into rehearsal. . . . The wild card was Barbara Harris. She really saved us, because Jo was not as adept at creating wonderful [comic] turns. She was fabulous, she was very strong, and she had a scary style, hauteur, and manner; but it really was Austin's vulnerability, his oddity, and Barbara Harris' genius that lifted the play. . . . They had a scene that really worked between them, the bedroom scene, it just came at the right place in the play. That saved our asses because, as wonderful as the production was, Jo couldn't do on her terms what Barbara Harris was able to do, and Jerry didn't know how to get that, and you couldn't. It ended up that Jo was wonderful in it . . . but until it opened, we weren't quite sure what was going to happen with it. It was a little touch-and-go."

The show's costume designer, Patricia Zipprodt, recollected that Robbins gave in to Van Fleet when conflict arose over her wardrobe. "I'd given her a big black evening dress with a big partition in the back with red flowers on it. Jerry and I had gone over eight thousand reds to figure out one that would be right. We got the red picked. Then we spent a fortune doing the inset in handmade roses, the whole thing. And Jo puts it on for dress rehearsal and she doesn't like the color. 'It should have a little more blue in it!' Jerry's met his match, and so have I. So this goes on and on and on. It was one of my very first real shows, so I thought people stuck up for what they wanted. And nobody did. Everybody said, 'Oh, Miss Van Fleet, what do *you* want?' There I am, I fought for this thing, and here we are at one a.m. in the basement of the Phoenix [Theatre] with Jerry, and the costume-shop people, and the producers and the agents. It was this whole thing. And everyone gave way but me. . . . So of course we changed it. Jerry said, 'All right, take it back.' It was just a matter of which red. . . . My rage grew, and everyone went away but Jerry, who was wandering around. All of a sudden he started to go out the basement door out into the alley, and I started after him. I got a hold of him and I shook him till his hat fell off. 'How could you do this! We picked this! We spent hours!' I wouldn't do that today—I've learned. Well, the next day a big box of tulips arrives [for me]. He thought that was the best thing I had done, and he was still laughing about it."

Others in the original cast with small roles included Tony Lo Bianco and Barry Primus. Lo Bianco later appeared in countless movies, including *The French Connection, Body of Evidence* and *The Juror.* In *Oh Dad,* Lo Bianco played the Head Bellboy. "If you're in a Jerome Robbins play, you have to come equipped as an artist to fulfill this man's dreams," said Lo Bianco. "He was always very sweet. From my point of view, with all the stories you hear about his being so tough, he was always very endearing, and I saw his soft side all the time. A very shy individual, and very tortured. In a funny way, he was just tortured by his genius, from his mind working all the time, that inward stuff. When you've got all that cooking, like he does, you tend to go inside to cook. You see things differently than the rest of the world does. A lot of people get a lot of bad raps, but they're not ordinary people." Lo Bianco added, "Jerry was a genius, and like many geniuses he was not a whole package, as far as being warm and friendly and so on and so forth. . . . He would have us move in a certain way, and I didn't have any conflict with him. He never came down on me. He was nothing but a gentleman with me."

Barry Primus later worked extensively as a stage and screen actor and also wrote and directed Robert De Niro's 1992 film *Mistress*. On *Oh Dad*, Primus started as an understudy and over time established a warm friendship with Robbins. "I came in from [working with] Anna Sokolow," said Primus, "and I did a reading for Jerry which he said was the worst reading he'd ever heard for sure. He said, 'You're either very talented or you're an imbecile. . . . Since Anna sent you, I'll assume that you're very talented.' He had no jobs but he liked me. . . . I think he paid me an extra's salary because there was no money in the budget, and then as soon as the show opened he bumped me up to being a regular in the production and having me cover everybody in the show. The only time I ever really yelled at Jerry was the very first time we worked together. . . . I was crossing the stage as one of the bellboys—he had me take some boxes across the stage for Jo Van Fleet. I piled them up so I couldn't see where I was going on purpose, and wandered around stage bumping into things. Jerry yelled, 'What are you doing?' I said, 'I'm trying something, for Chrissake!' I yelled back without thinking. He didn't say anything. And then I think it was the next day Betty Walberg, who was his accompanist, said, 'You know, Jerry thinks you're very talented and he likes you a lot.' . . . That was the end of that."

Primus continued, "Jerry used to drop down and play cards with us all occasionally, once or twice a week. He would appear out of nowhere and scare everybody to death. He would come downstairs with all us guys and he would come into the poker games and play with us. And then afterwards we would go out to a corner bar on Third Avenue. We all would go, three or four of us. . . . I think it was about a month into the run, he took me aside and said, 'You're talented and you can make a lot of yourself, but you gotta work hard.' One of the great things I remember about that show was that Jo Van Fleet . . . had a long, long monologue, and at the end of her monologue at matinees, she sometimes would start the applause for herself by clapping offstage. Jerry happened to be back there one night, and I was standing right offstage, and Jerry was standing offstage also in the same wing where Jo was. And as she started that applause, she looked up and saw Jerry looking at her. All he did was look at her and wave his finger at her: *No, no.* I don't think she did it again."

Tony Lo Bianco described Van Fleet, saying, "Oh, she was magnificent. Jo Van Fleet was a real killer. I mean a killer of star proportions. Grand old dame, very tough woman, but with a softness and tender heart underneath. . . . She used to call me all the time, 'Lo Bianco,'—she used to love to say my name. I remember driving home with her one night and there was a bum on the street, sort of a youngish guy, and she said, '*Oh, what a waste, the absolute waste of man!*' She had a lusty appreciation for masculinity."

Oh Dad opened on February 26, 1962. In the *New York Times,* Howard Taubman wrote, "Jerome Robbins has staged the fruit of Mr. Kopit's curious fancy with a blend of humor and eeriness. Each of the three scenes is prefaced by a bit of film that sets the cockeyed mood. With the help of William and Jean Eckart's tricky sets and with his own relish for fluidity of movement, the director has done his best to keep the piece afloat even when Mr. Kopit's imaginative flights will not soar. . . . As Madame Rosepettle, Jo Van Fleet is sinuous, glamorous and witch-like, moving like a serpent, chuckling like a madwoman and turning a fat acting part into a tour de force." Walter Kerr observed, "In directing the acting company, Mr. Robbins has made slippery, tantalizing monsters out of Miss Van Fleet and baby-doll Barbara Harris."

The role of the ingenue babysitter launched Harris' career, and the production established Robbins' credentials as a director of straight plays. *Oh Dad* ran for well over a year at the Phoenix (454 performances), toured for eleven weeks and then moved to Broadway on August 27, 1963, opening at the Morosco for a limited six-week run. Robbins supervised the new production and cast changes: Van Fleet was replaced by Hermione Gingold, Harris by Alix Elias, and Pendleton by Sam Waterston.

The second round of New York reviews were mostly favorable, although some critics were not as enthusiastic about the new cast, especially the lead. In the *Daily News,* John Chapman contrasted the performances of the two stars: "In the old one, Miss Van Fleet was a good actress acting extravagantly. In the one at the Morosco, Hermione Gingold is an extravagant actress playing herself, and she isn't too amusing." In the *Post,* Richard Watts suggested that by "succumbing" to Gingold's farcical style, Robbins "sacrificed the subtlety of his original staging." As if to settle the dispute, *Times* critic Paul Gardner applauded Robbins and stated categorically, "Everything works perfectly in the larger house. . . ." According to Gardner, "Miss Gingold's interpretation is her own. Whereas her predecessor was more subtle and evil, Miss Gingold's style is broad and ghoulish and consistently comical in the best Gingold tradition. Her fans will be delighted."

Several years later, Barry Primus worked with Robbins again at the American Theatre Laboratory. By that time, Primus had also worked with Elia Kazan at the Lincoln Center Repertory Theatre. He compared the two directors, saying, "My ideal of a director lies somewhere between Jerry and Kazan. Jerry, because his results were spiritual, he was battling back and forth with his perfectionism. Kazan, because he had a lot of patience, he had this perfectionist-compromising quality, which is a very strong position to come from. He knew exactly when to compromise his perfectionism. I remember Jerry saying about Gadge that he was 'the absolute quintessence of electricity.' He [Kazan] still possesses unique energy . . . this incredible power and sexual and violent quality that breaks out. [But] Kazan was someone who could work with you in a non-directed way. Kazan once said to me, 'Barry, there's only two things you gotta know about directing. . . . The only things you've got to remember is when to direct and when not to direct. It takes a lifetime to figure that one out, Barry.' He knew when not to direct, Kazan. I wouldn't say Jerry knew that."

Looking back, Arthur Kopit suggested that Robbins' thoroughgoing perfectionism as a choreographer may have prevented him from fully realizing his vision of the production as director. "I think that he wasn't really sure that he'd brought it off," said Kopit. "I don't know whether it was like that with his ballets. I would think *not* on some level, because he would know that he had gotten what he wanted out of them, I suppose. But maybe he wouldn't know about the effect [of his ballets]. He tried things, he was always stretching himself, so perhaps the anxiety was always there. But in this case, [it was] because he couldn't control the actors the way he could dancers. He couldn't say, 'This is the move I want,' so if the actor wasn't doing that, it wasn't matching his visual image fully. So I suspect he was somewhat dissatisfied by the experience of directing a play."

With regard to Robbins' visionary angst, Kopit continued, "I suspect that was something at his core, that was part of why he was so driven and why the process went so long. . . . He doesn't come in having all the answers. He begins something and he will explore his own psyche, his own emotional baggage. He will take from everything, he will research. And if he does it right, then people will be the instruments of his vision. Then the vision will happen. So you had to be there for him because you *were* him, I think is what it was. He wasn't somebody who blocked it out on a page. He had to get in there and mess around, so you had to listen to him very carefully and do what he wanted, and if you were going to create some noise, it was like a headache to him. It would be a disturbance. That's what I think it was. I think everything was an extension of his own mind and his own vision, and to the degree that you allowed that vision to work, then you were okay." Kopit added, "It was a sacred enterprise."

On the night of April 9, 1962, Robbins collected his two Oscars for *West Side Story* in Los Angeles (Rosalind Russell presented one, saying, "Jerome, I told you") and left immediately for Washington, D.C., at the request of Hal Prince, who had a new show opening for tryouts on April eleventh under the direction of George Abbott. Prince recalled, "When *A Funny Thing Happened on the Way to the Forum* was in Washington, D.C., playing to no audiences, having received the worst reviews (headline in the *Washington Post*: 'MR. ABBOTT: CLOSE IT!'), it became obvious that we needed Jerry to inspire a new opening number and stage it and perhaps tidge up other small moments in the show. . . . I contacted him by phone and he agreed to come right after the awards. I suspect in an effort to distance himself from Robert Wise and the rest of that film's creators and management, when he received his Academy Award [for the direction of *West Side Story*], he took the opportunity to thank Bobby Griffith and Hal Prince. It was stunning. And generous. The next day, he flew to Washington and rolled up his sleeves to work."

As it happened, there was another reason for Robbins to be in Washington: the Shah of Iran was visiting the Kennedy White House, and Robbins' Ballets: U.S.A. had been invited to perform for the occasion. The troupe quickly rehearsed *New York Export: Opus Jazz* and headed to Camelot. Stage manager Tom Stone accompanied Robbins to the performance of *Forum* the night before the White House engagement. "I had to come down early to set up the West Wing of the White House," said Stone. "John-John and Caroline were wandering through the hall with their Secret Service agents. It was just an unbelievably wonderful, idyllic, hopeful time. I set up the stage and then Jerry came in the night before directly from having won the Oscars. I met him at the hotel he was staying at. The two Oscars were on the fireplace. He said, 'Look, we're going to have a quick dinner because we've gotta go over and see this new show of Hal's.'"

Robbins had earlier agreed to direct *Forum*, with music and lyrics from Stephen Sondheim and a book by Larry Gelbart and Burt Shevelove. But while in Europe the year before with Ballets: U.S.A., Robbins had decided to withdraw from the project. Sondheim recalled, "...a letter arrived in the mail. As best I can remember, the letter was saying, 'I'm sorry, I just can't do it.' It was torn in four or eight pieces, and then he'd put it in an envelope. That was to show how tortured he was for having let everybody down." Incensed that Robbins had abandoned the project, co-author Larry Gelbart sent Robbins a telegram that stated in part, "Your cowardly withdrawal is consistent with your well-earned reputation for immorality."

Gelbart was referring to Robbins' HUAC testimony. Now Robbins was being invited back to doctor the show, and there were others involved in the production who felt the same way Gelbart did. Tom Stone remembered Robbins' reaction when he saw the first Washington performance. "So we're sitting there [in the National Theater] and Jerry says, 'Sophomoric.' He's getting blacker and blacker and blacker. He said, 'Stay here. I'll go talk to Hal.' So he comes back . . . [and] we watch the second act. He's now just as black as his suit, you know. He says, 'I'll see you at the White House tomorrow morning. I've got to talk to these people.' It turned out that was the night that he agreed to doctor the show. I don't think he really liked the show, or he didn't want to get into it because of Zero [Mostel]. But of course he adored George Abbott, and so he took it on and walked into that buzzsaw there with Zero."

Mostel, the rotund and irrepressible comic actor, became the star of *Forum* after Phil Silvers rejected an early offer and Milton Berle later backed out. During the McCarthy years, Mostel had been blacklisted, and he was a close friend of Jack Gilford, who was also in the show and whose wife, Madeline, of course, had been named by Robbins. Prince described the political delicacy of the situation: ". . . as Jerry had 'named names,' I felt I could not invite him to Washington without Zero Mostel's permission, as Zero had been named before the [House] Committee. I approached Zero and told him that I thought that Jerry was perhaps the key to putting the show over the top. Zero took a long pause, and then, looking me in the eye, said, 'Well, you haven't asked me to have lunch with him, have you?'"

Mostel offered Prince a bottom-line rationalization for staying with the show and working with Robbins. According to an account published by his wife, Kate Mostel, the actor explained, "Listen, Hal, I'm a professional and Jerry's a professional, and if he can help the show, get him. Besides, we of the left don't blacklist." Jack Gilford also had misgivings about working with Robbins and initially considered leaving the show. But his wife, Madeline, insisted that he stay on and "not blacklist himself." She told him, "Don't be a schmuck—wouldn't you work for Warner Brothers?" The film studio had been one of those enforcing the blacklist in Hollywood, and Jack Gilford's career had unquestionably been damaged during the previous decade when he had been dropped from Fred Allen's popular TV show. Like many on the left, Mostel and Gilford were not willing to forgive those who had informed, and Robbins would not be allowed to forget.

Over the years, social encounters between blacklistees and informants were awkward and often openly hostile. Madeline Gilford had already had an opportunity to remind Robbins of what she saw as his perfidy before HUAC. At a party at the home of Hal and Judy Prince, she confronted Robbins. "I finally told him off," said Gilford. "I was egged on by Gene Saks, Joe Stein and Herb Gardner. Hal and Judy had a house then on Eighty-first Street, where the dining room and garden were in the basement and there was a beautiful winding, central stairway through this old mansion. It was gorgeous. . . . It was New Year's Eve. Hal's parties were very lavish, and I had a darling little white ermine coat—my sister ran a thrift shop. You know that Russian ermine wasn't allowed anymore. Carl Fischer, who was Hal's general manager and George Abbott's nephew . . . was teasing me about my ermine coat. He said, 'How come you have a Russian ermine, Madeline? You have your Party card in your pocket?' I was drinking and had my coat on. I was ready to go. It was very late, and we were the last people at the party. Jack always said I was the last one to leave any party, and it's true. I said to Herb, Gene and Joe, 'I am sick of . . . having to run into him [Jerry] and having to avoid him. . . .' And then I told them the toast I wanted to give, and they said, 'Do it, do it!'

"So I go up the staircase and I waited very discreetly. This main floor divided a large living room and a small library that faced the street, and in this small dark library was where they had set up the bar. And just the bartender was in the corner, he had already put out the lights, and he was putting away the bottles and the glasses. Jerry Robbins was in there and seemed to be alone. So I went over to him and I said, 'Jerry?' He said, 'Yes.' I said, 'I'm Madeline Lee.' He said, 'I know.' I said, 'Well, I have a New Year's toast for us.' I said, '1953 can kiss my ass!' And he went absolutely purple. I said, 'It was 'fifty-three, wasn't it?' He said, 'I don't know.' I said, 'Well, one of us better remember.' And I turned on my heel. I thought it was magnificent. And Herb Gardner, Joe Stein and Gene Saks come upstairs as I'm making my grand exit and they say, 'Did you do it? Did you do it?' Then from out of the shadows in that room comes Ron Field, who was ecstatic. He said, 'What did you say to him?' . . . I didn't know Ron was in the corner there, and I told him what I said." Among the theatrical notables described by Gilford, Ron Field choreographed *Cabaret* on Broadway (before Fosse did the 1972 movie) as well as *Applause*, and Joe Stein wrote *Fiddler on the Roof.* Gene Saks directed many Broadway comedies, notably those by Neil Simon.

During rehearsals for *Forum*, the atmosphere was often tense, but the work at hand usually took precedence over politics and personal grudges. As far as Mostel and Robbins, Hal Prince remembered, "Zero worked with Jerry, ventilating his ill-humor about him only socially, and out of Jerry's earshot." Some of the tension may have been dispelled at their first meeting on the set. Designer Tony Walton recalled Robbins' being introduced to the cast. "Jerry came in and we were all lined up on the stage. He very quietly and shyly and charmingly said hello to all of us . . . and [there was] endless tension as he got down towards Zero. When Jerry came over to him, Zero said, 'Hiya, Loose-lips!' Everybody, even Jerry, cracked up."

Madeline Gilford recalled, "They had done one version in New Haven, they were playing another version in Washington, and they were rehearsing a third version. 'Everybody Ought to Have a Maid' was going in, which was very hard to learn. They were all hoarse. Zero smoked, and Jerry Robbins said something [to him] about smoking. Zero said, 'Mind your own fucking business, we're just working together. Don't get social, we have nothing to do with each other socially.' So that was the relationship. He used to make Jerry Robbins say good morning to everybody, teased him, deviled him, Zero did." Gilford added that Robbins favored her husband as far as utilizing his talent. "Jerry fell in love with Jack, and Jack consequently had the only solo in *Forum* ['I'm Calm']. Zero doesn't even have a solo."

Walton recalled Robbins' speed and ingenuity in restaging in the weeks before the New York previews. "He [Jerry] was astounding because it was as if you had given him an exercise in how to do something with nothing. . . . Of course, he worked right through the show, but the opening number ['Comedy Tonight'], in memory and I hope I'm not exaggerating, he almost fed to Steve [Sondheim], who was pretty much in a state of exhaustion and depression by then and flailing a bit."

Sondheim recounted Robbins' critical assessment of the show in Washington. According to the composer, Robbins told him, "The opening number is killing the show. You open with a charming number ['Love Is in the Air'] and the audience does not know what they're in for, that it's a real farce. You've got to write an opening number that says baggy pants." The result was "Comedy Tonight." Kate Mostel recalled that the number "was sung by Zero as an actor presenting a company of players in a comedy for the enjoyment of the audience. When Zero said, 'I now present the entire company,' each actor entered alone from upstage center, came down to the footlights, formed a straight line and sang a whole chorus ending with 'Tragedy tomorrow, comedy, comedy, comedy, comedy tonight.' After the applause, Zero said, 'One, two, three,' and the lights blacked out, the actors vanished and the play started—at exactly the point it had started in New Haven."

Stephen Sondheim recalled, "He [Jerry] certainly deserves the credit for saving the show with 'Comedy Tonight,' because it told the audience at the top of the piece what kind of evening they were in for. I had attempted to do this earlier, with a song called 'Invocation,' but George Abbott had rejected it because he didn't like the tune. Nevertheless, I think the main reason Jerry agreed to work on the show (although he had always liked the script and score, and he smelled a lot of money to be made) was that he worshiped George Abbott and was grateful to him."

Abbott, who was then seventy-five, had tried to simplify the show. Abbott cut subplots, songs, characters and complications from the wildly complex farce that Gelbart and Shevelove had conceived. The script was inspired by work of the Roman poet-playwright Plautus, who died in 184 B.C. and had ironically written a play entitled *Mostellaria*. The *Forum* book went through at least ten rewrites over a period of five years. The story involves a virgin slave girl (Philia) separated from her true love (Hero) when she is sold to a braggart gladiator (Miles Gloriosus). But the plot is simply a pretext for puns, malaprops, sight gags, slapstick kicks to the rear, double takes, mistaken identities, breakneck swinging doors, and the endless vaudevillian antics that one critic characterized as "healthy vulgarity." Clad in a ludicrous toga, Mostel played the lead role of Pseudolus, the ever-conniving slave, with Gilford as his eunuch foil, Hysterium. Others in the cast included David Burns (Senex), John Carradine (Lycus), Raymond Walburn (Erronius), Preshy Marker (Philia), Ronald Holgate (Gloriosus) and Brian Davies (Hero).

Referring to Robbins' well-known intensity, Tony Walton lightheartedly dubbed him "the nightmare genius." Walton remembered, "While Jerry was creating and choreographing it, he would just say, 'What have you got? Was anything cut from the show?' . . . And he could come up with anything. If there was a spare leg from a gag that had been cut, then he would find a way to use that and build on it and build on it and build on it. [He would] use little pieces of rejected props and costumes. It was really inspirational. I'd had one of my minuscule offerings to the show, which was that when [Zero] said 'Raise the curtain!' it dropped into a little pit and completely disappeared. That was a good laugh. Jerry found a way to use that pit, which was just staggering. He'd hide things in it, have people walking one leg up and one leg in it. . . . I wish I could remember it all now, it was wonderful."

Robbins reportedly told Sondheim before the show arrived in New York, "I could do this so much better if I had more time."

Forum opened at the Alvin Theatre on May 8, 1962. Robbins was not mentioned in the reviews, which were for the most part raves that lauded Mostel's performance in particular. Calling Mostel "a very animated blimp," John McClain noted in the *Journal-American*, "[H]e is quite largely the whole show and he gives warning in the opening number that there will be 'Comedy Tonight.'" Walter Kerr called Mostel "a whole road company all by himself." In the *Times*, Howard Taubman described *Forum* as "noisy, coarse, blue and obvious like the putty nose on a burlesque comedian."

An instant hit, *Forum* ran more than two years (964 performances). Mostel, George Abbott and Harold Prince won Tony Awards, as did the writers, Gelbart and Shevelove. The show spawned a successful Richard Lester movie in 1966 with Mostel, Gilford and Phil Silvers. Taking over the lead in the 1972 stage revival, Silvers won a Tony, and Nathan Lane followed suit in the 1996 revival. (Lane was later replaced by Whoopi Goldberg [in 1997], and while she was not eligible for a Tony, Larry Gelbart noted, " . . . what other performer ever made the choice of a role a standing ovation in itself?") While Robbins was not involved with the movie or revivals, his influence would always be felt in "Comedy Tonight," which he later restaged in a revised form for *Jerome Robbins' Broadway*.

Shortly after the opening of *Forum*, Robbins presented his Ballets: U.S.A. for its swan song performance, which took place at a Democratic Party fund-raising gala at Madison Square Garden. The same troupe that had appeared the month before in the intimate setting of the White House was transported into Manhattan's giant arena, which was packed with an audience of more than fifteen thousand. The dancers were overshadowed by the throng of celebrity entertainers who appeared onstage, including Ella Fitzgerald, Jack Benny, Maria Callas, Harry Belafonte, Jimmy Durante, Mike Nichols, Elaine May and Henry Fonda. Peter Lawford served as master of ceremonies. This was the memorable night that ended with Marilyn Monroe regaling President Kennedy with her famous rendition of "Happy Birthday." Just a few years later at his American Theater Laboratory, Robbins tried to develop a play based on the Kennedy assassination, a subject with which he was fascinated. But that production would remain an unrealized dream.

Another ambitious dream was put on the shelf when Robbins disbanded his ballet company. He had hoped to mount a new version of Stravinsky's *Les Noces* (The Wedding), originally choreographed by Bronislava Nijinska in 1923 for Diaghilev's Ballets Russes. Robbins first planned a production for his troupe's inaugural appearance in Spoleto, but discovered that the Festival lacked the resources required to mount the ballet. After Ballets: U.S.A. folded, Robbins tried to undertake a production for London's Royal Ballet. But that company, too, failed to stage *Les Noces*, ostensibly because of the burden of accommodating the necessary chorus, percussion and, most important, four grand pianos that had to be situated on the stage rather than in the orchestra pit. Such was the story at the time; however, in 1966, the Royal Ballet restaged Nijinska's original version with the full complement of chorus and instruments.

While Robbins continued to cast about for a company to mount the ballet, he turned his sights to directing another show for Broadway, committing himself to Bertolt Brecht's antiwar play, *Mother Courage and Her Children.* Adding another credit to his résumé, Robbins co-produced the show at the Martin Beck Theatre with Actors Studio veteran Cheryl Crawford. The play would rehearse for five weeks and open in New York without the benefit of out-of-town tryouts. The cast featured Anne Bancroft in the lead, with Gene Wilder, Barbara Harris and John Randolph in supporting roles. Ming Cho Lee was recruited for scenery, and Motley for costumes.

Robbins had been fascinated by Brecht's work for many years, and his interest may have betrayed a lingering sympathy for the political left. While Brecht had openly supported the Communist cause, the German playwright was hardly doctrinaire in his views. Testifying before HUAC in 1947, Brecht denied having been a member of the Communist Party, and subsequently fled the country. In East Berlin, he established the Berliner Ensemble with state support to produce his plays and to carry out his radical dramaturgy. *Mother Courage* was one of Brecht's mature works and reflected his didactic credo that drama should provide political instruction as well as entertainment. Written in 1939, the action takes place during the Thirty Years War of the early seventeenth century. Mother Courage is the peasant vivandiere who sees her two sons and daughter destroyed by greed and cowardice as she drags her wagon-canteen through the battlefields and tries to profit from the war's devastation. The tone of the play is relentlessly sardonic and bitter, as in the mother's alarmed complaint, "Don't tell me peace has broken out!" Brecht's comic style, with its harsh Germanic sarcasm, was a far cry from the broad American humor of Robbins' musicals and ballets.

At the time Robbins started to work on *Mother Courage,* he was already involved with early preparations for *Funny Girl* and had Anne Bancroft in mind for the part of Ziegfeld Follies star Fanny Brice. Bancroft had recently won an Oscar for her performance in *The Miracle Worker.* But the thirty-one-year-old actress was thought by some critics to be too young for the role of Mother Courage when Robbins first cast her. He defended his choice and suggested that the characters of Fanny Brice and Mother Courage were actually quite similar. "The two women have a lot in common," said Robbins. "They are both earthy and gutsy, and both of them look at the world through shrewd, tenacious eyes—mother peddlers fighting for survival for themselves and their families. As for Annie's age, she can convey any age she wants to."

Robbins acknowledged the special challenge posed by Brecht's play: "*Mother Courage* is a very unconventional play to produce, not like anything we're used to seeing on Broadway. . . . Brecht, of course, attempted to change the conventional idea of theater. In *Mother Courage* he tells the audience ahead of time what's going to happen in each of the numerous scenes. He isn't interested in creating suspense about what's going to happen. He's interested in showing how and why it happened."

Brecht died in 1956, and his principal American exponent was British-born playwright and critic Eric Bentley, who provided the translation for Robbins' *Mother Courage* production. At the time Bentley became involved, he wasn't aware that Robbins had been a friendly witness in 1953. "I didn't know about Jerry's Communist past at this time," said Bentley. "I'll tell you the great hypocrisy that he pulled on me. When I [later] read his [HUAC] record, I read that he said that Madeline Lee and he had talked about dialectical materialism. . . . Well, do you know in those years before *Mother Courage* when I didn't know about this, he asked me what dialectical materialism was as a person who'd never heard of it, when we were studying Brecht together. That's what a hypocrite that Jerry Robbins was, he completely hoodwinked me—he pretended to be totally ignorant of all things Communist."

Of course, Robbins was not inclined to disclose a political past that remained a prickly source of embarrassment for him. Bentley recalled that one of their earliest meetings did not augur well for the production. "At the beginning of the *Mother Courage* proceedings, just before rehearsal, when Jerry was studying the play and the music and all that, I go over to his apartment on the Upper East Side, and he has an upright piano there. He doesn't play the piano, but he has . . . a young woman there playing the music for him. As I come in with Sandy Matlovsky, who's going to be the music director, the conductor, and had done seven years of *Threepenny Opera* . . . he [Jerry] turns around from his seat . . . by the piano, looks me straight in the face, and says, 'Why do you bring me this shit?' I wait to hear what the shit is. The shit is the music, which is by Paul Dessau, as a favor to Mr. Brecht, and my lyrics, as he [Jerry] goes on to explain. He says, 'The music is shit, the lyrics are shit!' And then he's getting himself more angry by his own words. 'And you want me to get your name up in lights on Broadway and you bring me this?'

"I was so aghast and insulted that I turned right around and walked out. Sandy came after me. . . . He held my arm as we went down the stairs. He said, 'Hey, don't pay any attention. Jerry does this to everybody. He's trying to break you in.' I said, 'Hey, but I don't want to be broken in, thanks very much. And I'm going to go home and resign. He can still use my translation, but I'm not going to work with him.'

"So . . . I wrote a note and sent it special delivery. Well, he was much grander than me. I got a reply by special messenger over in a taxi with his reply all typed out . . . apologizing to me, saying he couldn't remember what he'd said but he would gather from my indignation that it was terrible, and he was sorry that he had, and that it would never recur, and would I please come back. So of course, since he's writing me back and promising not to do it again, I went back. And to be fair to him, he stuck to the agreement as far as I was concerned. He was a realist, and having perceived that I was not one he could break in, he wanted me anyway."

While acknowledging that Robbins possessed "a sensational sense of music," the conductor, Samuel (Sandy) Matlovsky, never forgot Jerry's bullying tactics, saying, "I still after all these years berate myself for not quitting, because I had a reputation of not taking too much shit from people, and at one point I swore that no matter what happened I'm not going to add to that history. And so I took a lot of shit from Jerry, and gritted my teeth. . . ."

Bentley recollected that over time his association with Robbins was invariably strained and awkward. "Jerry was most mistrustful," said Bentley. "In some ways, his communications with others were very bad because he had difficulty in being genuinely warm or open with another human being, I think. I had many sessions with him at his home preparing the production, both in New York and he invited me out to Sneden's Landing, where he was living. I was surprised at the extreme coolness and remoteness between us. For one thing, we were both gay. I didn't want to bring up sex because there was no sex relation between us, but you would have thought there would have been some kind of openness, even gossip and chatting and joking. Absolutely not. I never had a colder weekend than the weekend alone with Jerry Robbins in his home. . . . He never settled down to have a drink and a chat, or became informal. . . . I've never worked with someone so unpleasant to work with, frankly."

Robbins' home in Sneden's Landing was known as the "Ding-Dong House," as its former tenants represented a kind of musical tradition. Aaron Copland once lived there, and Robbins' duo-pianist friends Arthur Gold and Robert Fizdale were later residents. Bentley described the exclusive community where Robbins lived intermittently over the next decade: "I know a good deal about Sneden's Landing because one of my relatives by marriage lives there. . . . It's now the land of television bigshots like Mike Wallace, and it used to be theater bigshots like Katharine Cornell. . . . It has the extraordinary advantage of being handy to New York. . . . It's very aristocratic, you know, very elegant, spaced out. It's not a gay community as such." Over the years that Robbins resided there, Sneden's was still relatively quaint and undiscovered.

During the rehearsal period for *Mother Courage*, Robbins often retreated to his upstate refuge, which he rented but never bought. Bentley recalled, "A young man would show up to drive him to Sneden's Landing. He was a bruiser type. I thought he was probably going to beat Jerry up or something like that."

Like other observers who saw Robbins in the company of young men wearing leather, Bentley speculated, "I interpreted his sex life to be sort of sadomasochistic." Robbins created such impressions, though he remained as guarded about his private life in the 1960s as he had been during earlier decades, even with the birth of the gay rights movement and the so-called Sexual Revolution. Behind the scenes, he continued to pursue both gay and heterosexual relationships. Before rehearsals for the Brecht play began, Robbins was romantically linked to actress Zohra Lampert, who was cast as the mute daughter of Mother Courage.

With regard to Robbins' attitude about his sexuality, his assistant director Bill Daniels recalled, "Jerry, when I knew him, never talked about it much. He was always kind of conflicted about it, as a matter of fact. I remember him dating Zohra Lampert after we first read her for *Oh Dad*. But those were the days when they [gay men] were still in the closet a little bit, I guess."

Work continued to take priority over his personal life. Daniels recalled the intensity of Robbins' research for the Brecht play. "When he was preparing for *Mother Courage*, he had all the Brecht photographs, huge albums he imported at great expense, to look at Brecht's productions of *Mother Courage*. He filled himself in with everything and he went to Europe [to visit Brecht's theater]. He would do anything to have a successful production. That kind of focus and energy is unusual. It's admirable. If he stepped on a few people or me or whoever, it didn't really matter." Daniels, who soon left the production to accept an acting job, added, "He was very meticulous . . . but frankly he was way over his head with *Mother Courage*. I think everybody was over their heads with *Mother Courage*."

Difficulties arose when Robbins tried to wed the methodologies of Brecht and Stanislavski, as their contrasting approaches to acting and directing were not easily compatible. Brecht's so-called theory of alienation deemphasized the individual performer and called for a restrained style of acting. Stanislavski's method was far more emotive and geared to individual interpretation. Gerald Hiken stepped in to assist Robbins after Bill Daniels departed. Hiken said, "He [Jerry] and I worked on any number of things to stimulate the imaginations of the actors and get them to participate in this thing. We threw tennis balls at them unexpectedly so that they would realize that they always had to be on guard against snipers—all that kind of stuff. They didn't take to it at all. It was really dismal."

Matlovksy recalled that Robbins consulted with Method acting guru Lee Strasberg during rehearsals. "There was a grandiose announcement at one point that Strasberg came down from the mountain with a bunch of tablets and announced to everybody that he had in his hand proof that Brecht could be directed in the style of the Actors Studio. Well, in other words, he gave Jerry the blessing that it could be done with the technique of the Actors Studio. And a roundtable discussion centered on that. I'm still rolling my eyes. . . . This was a green light by Strasberg to go ahead. Well, the actors were drowned in Actors Studio technique—terrible, terrible, terrible. Really, it was abysmal. I tried to quit and Cheryl Crawford begged me and I didn't . . . and so the little time that we had before it fell off the cliff, I did stay, but it was a terrible experience in many ways. Jerry just could not handle it." Eric Bentley suggested that Strasberg had earlier encouraged Robbins and Crawford to pursue Marilyn Monroe for the part of Courage's mute daughter, but Monroe was apparently unavailable.

According to one observer who watched Robbins rehearse, "Jerry had Anne Bancroft go down to the Lower East Side to watch a woman selling fish or something. It had nothing to do with Brecht and *Mother Courage.*" The *Times* reported that Bancroft frustrated Robbins when she attempted to carry out his stage directions by imitating him. At one point, the actress explained a flourish she was including in her movement, telling Robbins, "I'm doing it this way because it's the way you did it . . . and I thought if you did it this way, it must be a beautiful movement."

Bruce Glover played the role of the Catholic Sergeant and later became a familiar character actor in movies. Glover recalled that Robbins experimented with having cast members rehearse multiple roles. "Since we're all going to do different roles, they sent us off in committees. We don't start reading. We don't read through the play. We have no rehearsal. We go to groups . . . and they give us all charts. We're supposed to write down the various motivations of the character. So we're going to create roles by committee. . . . It's horrendous. We do this for three weeks in the various roles . . . and they tell us that when we're not in one of these rehearsals—which are not really rehearsals, because we're not even doing the lines—we have to go and play Monopoly. There are card tables set up in the big room down underneath the stage—card tables with Monopoly sets—and we're supposed to go play Monopoly, because the play is about greed. It's an insulting experience and it's anxiety-making."

Gerald Hiken offered an example of the resistance that Robbins encountered from the actors. "Mike Kellin, playing the Cook, never exhibited anything negative with his character. He was always laid back, smiling. He kept saying, 'That's who I am, I can't give you anything else.' So we were playing Monopoly offstage . . . and I was instructed to tell the other people who were playing with Mike to cheat. And we cheated and when he discovered it, his rage was enormous. And Robbins jumped to him and . . . suggested that this was the very kind of thing he wanted to see in the show. And Mike couldn't see the application. He was just angry that he was cheated and didn't think that it had anything to do with acting. It was like that all the time. Jerry had these ideas that got balked by people who had their own ideas."

Glover remembered, "Finally I'm notified that they're going to do the Catholic Sergeant scene. At last I'm going to get on stage with Annie Bancroft. She was rehearsing separately with her sons and daughter. . . . I've got this other actor, one of her sons, I've got him on a rope, and I bring him in, and I throw him down. I pull off my shoes, and I spit on my feet, and wipe them with my socks, and it's interesting. It looks like it's going okay. Then Jerry goes, 'Okay. Let's go through it again. Don't sit down this time.' So then I pull off my shoe and I'm balancing on one foot, and I put the shoe under my arm and I'm cleaning my foot standing up."

Robbins continued to demand changes in the scene until Glover was thoroughly exasperated. "Now I'm standing there, and the first line is, 'Who are you people?' Jerry goes, 'No, no, no, no! *Who are you people?*' It took a long time to get to this place, but now we're finally just standing there and he's giving me my first line . . . and he's not an actor. And at this point I'm not an actor anymore either. I'm now a crazed maniac. And Anne Bancroft is standing there wondering, 'Who is this lousy actor they've gotten playing this role?' None of them know that we have been three weeks sitting around playing Monopoly.

"It might have been the second day I'm doing this stuff and he's still giving me a line reading. I finally blow up and I go, 'Jerry, I don't know where to get on with you, you're like a frigging train.' He turns and walks away from me. I said, 'Don't walk away, you little shit.' And I said, 'Oh, fuck, what did I just do?' And he turns around and he walks back, comes right up close to me, looks me in the face. I say, 'Well, I guess I'm going to get fired.' And he says, 'I'm sorry, I'm sorry,' very charmingly. He says, 'Okay, just go through it.' Next day, the role is taken away from me."

Glover later managed to win back the part. He recalled that Robbins, in trying to incorporate Brecht's ideas on acting, discouraged Gene Wilder from embellishing his role. "Wilder was playing the Chaplain. He got a wonderful idea. He's playing the Chaplain as this embarrassed guy who's supposed to be religious, who's always looking at some girl's crotch or her breasts, and looking away, and getting caught looking. It's wonderful. So Jerry goes to Wilder and says, 'Oh, don't do that!'"

Both Glover and Bentley remembered that Robbins heaped abuse on the actor who played a younger soldier. Glover called him "Emo" and described him as a "sweet guy with kind of a primitive farmboy look about him. And Jerry falls in love with the physicality of that. I think I was one of the guys he liked physically, too, but luckily I had Emo. If Jerry liked you, if he had a sexual urge for you, he was brutal to you . . . so Emo is like just constantly being bombarded by this guy. Not that Jerry makes a pass at anyone. He's a great artist, so he's got some class. He's a classy man."

Bentley confirmed Glover's recollection, saying, "Jerry, as I saw him then, wasn't the kind of director who uses the director's couch. That wasn't going on. He was much too ambitious for the show, to be fooling around like that. But he did something very neurotic that did have to do with his sado-masochistic complex. It was this: There was one small part of an angry soldier who was only in one scene. He had to come on and act a towering rage in a very short period of time. So you'd think Jerry would be very careful casting a young actor in such a small part who can do something as difficult and big as that. Instead, what happened was that Jerry noticed on the street a motorcyclist in a leather jacket whose face and general demeanor seemed suitable. So he called that young guy over and asked him if he was an actor. Of course, he wasn't. He was illiterate. But Jerry gave him the job. I'm sure they never made any sexual contact and I'm not sure the boy was gay. What did happen was that Jerry used him as a punching bag, insulting him through countless rehearsals when he would be shouting from the auditorium of the Martin Beck, 'What the fuck do you think you're doing up on that stage!'

"And then Jerry got his comeuppance, because the end of the story is that on the opening night Jerry came back a half an hour before the show wearing his tuxedo for the party afterwards, and I met him onstage. I was not wearing a tuxedo. The stage manager comes up to us and says, 'I have had to excuse [Emo].' 'Oh,' said Jerry. 'What's the matter, was he drunk?' [The reply was] 'Oh, it's something stronger than alcohol.' In other words, the guy was drugged!"

Glover, who took over the role, remembered the young man was too inebriated to perform. "Emo was gone," said Glover. "He was fired. He had been totally devastated. He had been destroyed by this whole experience."

During the final phase of rehearsals, Robbins called for drastic alterations of the sets, the costumes, the script and the actors' performances. According to Patricia Zipprodt, Ming Cho Lee was reduced to tears when Robbins demanded that Lee's elaborate period sets be replaced by minimalist scenery and a filmed cyclorama projecting images of twentieth-century warfare. Eric Bentley soon found himself hard-pressed to defend the integrity of Brecht's play when Robbins insisted on shortening scenes and cutting dialogue. Bentley recalled, "In the last week before the previews, the last week we were alone with the play, he's worried. He's foreseeing that it isn't going to be a great hit. There's something wrong. . . . It was in the shape he'd given it, but for some reason or another it wasn't exciting. That was true. So he has to think of a remedy and it has to be a remedy he thinks of, carried out to his exact instructions. It devastated me because it was something that's never happened in my experience. I've never heard of it happening in the theater.

"He concludes that the play is too long. He said, 'We're not going to cut out any whole passages; it's just every page has to be shorter, every speech that's more than a few words has to be shorter.' And he wanted that for tomorrow afternoon. . . . I said, 'Even if I was to type all night or have a secretary helping me, I couldn't do all of *Mother Courage* shorter because it has to be done with great judgment and taste.' So he said, 'All right, then, this is how we'll do it. . . . You and I will sit onstage and we'll have the actors do a line rehearsal. We'll go through the play, there'll be a run-through but just sitting down, and you will shorten each speech as we come to it, and you tell the actor the short version.'

"Well, we did it. I don't know to what extent it was ever fully carried out, because I never saw the final stage manager's script. . . . I'm sure it's one of the things that killed the show. Interestingly, on the side, Mel Brooks was not married to Annie Bancroft yet, but he was her boyfriend and he was around a lot. And I think this idea of shortening the play may have come from him. In the middle of the rehearsals, he said to me in his jocular kind of a way, 'Why does Mr. Brecht take a whole paragraph to say anything? Why not just a remark?' And he says, 'Maybe it's just that I don't like Germans.'

"The awful thing was that when Jerry rejected Ming's work, as he kept doing, as he wanted to do with my script also, he didn't do it when it was on paper. He let the whole thing be constructed at enormous expense, which was one reason we couldn't keep the show running. Jerry always spent too much money. He'd then reject it when it's all onstage at the Martin Beck. So Ming was tearing his hair out. . . . Jerry loved to destroy people's work. It couldn't become good until it was remade by him."

Mother Courage opened on March 28, 1963. The play was destined to run only fifty-two performances, closing with a loss of $150,000. Yet most of the reviews were surprisingly favorable. The *Daily News* called it "a visually stunning and imaginatively devised production," and credited Bancroft with "a brilliant portrayal." In the *Times*, Howard Taubman wrote, "*Mother Courage*, praise be, is a different theater experience. In its humor, irony and truth, it is a work to welcome and cherish." Taubman applauded the director: "Mr. Robbins has staged each scene incisively, and they build powerfully." In the *World Telegram and Sun*, Norman Nadel enthused, "Exhilaration is the word for *Mother Courage*. . . . The adaptation by Eric Bentley rolls easily off the actors' tongues without sacrifice of Brecht's Germanic harshness." Nadel concluded that the production "achieved a precise balance between straightforward story-telling and theatrical embellishment."

Despite the reviews and a Tony nomination for the show, Robbins later described it as a ghastly experience. He said, "There I was hoping to produce and direct Bertolt Brecht in New York, and half of Broadway—agents, actors, actresses, you name them, hot on the scent of a fashionable playwright, turned the production into a horse on which they were going to ride to success. It was dreadful." Robbins provided contradictory accounts to Eric Bentley and Gerald Hiken as to why he believed the production failed. Bentley recalled Robbins lamenting that he had tried to follow "the correct Brecht interpretation" too closely, appropriating ideas for his scenes from a videotape of the original German production. Bentley said, "After it was all over, he realized that hadn't been a good idea and said to me, 'If I had just done it the way I do my Broadway musicals, just the best way I know how, and not trying to be like something else, it would have been better.'"

On the other hand, Gerald Hiken remembered Robbins suggesting that he should have utilized an additional feature from Brecht's production. "Jerry said something to me that I thought was profound. He said, 'I made one mistake with this show. I did not use a turntable.' The show was produced with a turntable by Brecht so that Courage could roll her wagon and stay in front of the audience. It made it a very easy show to do, but because Brecht had done it that way, Robbins wouldn't do it that way."

Looking back in 1995, Robbins said that he regretted having undertaken the project and claimed that Cheryl Crawford had talked him into it. Bentley remarked, "The career of Robbins is very extraordinary because he was a success boy, and I think *Mother Courage* had been a great blow, because while it was not a fiasco and didn't close on Saturday night, it was not a Broadway hit and it didn't make money, and he was very interested in hits, not to mention money." Despite the setback, Robbins remained as determined as ever to prove that he could succeed with Brecht and would soon take up the challenge again.

On June 4, 1962, Robbins served as best man for his friend Jule Styne who married Margaret Ann Bissett Brown at Temple Emanuel in Manhattan. Jule Styne's son (Robbins' godson), Norton Styne, recalled, "My father's respect for Jerry Robbins was optimum. He was a guru as far as my father was concerned. I know that there was more than one occasion where my father would talk to Jerry Robbins and had him look something over that my father was going to do. . . . This man [Robbins] was like the ultimate knowledgeable individual, not only on a show, but the man was so bright. The man was the ultimate choreographer-director, but you see, he really knew music so well. . . . All I can tell you is that Jule Styne loved Jerry Robbins."

At the time of the Styne wedding, Robbins and the composer were involved in preparations for *Funny Girl*, which Robbins was slated to direct. Styne was writing the score with lyrics from Bob Merrill. Merrill had taken over from Stephen Sondheim, who had earlier withdrawn when the show was being planned for Mary Martin in the lead. Sondheim didn't think the Brice role was right for Martin, and she later abandoned the project, objecting to the book. Robbins pushed for Anne Bancroft to replace Martin, but after Bancroft heard the Styne-Merrill score, she, too, withdrew from the production. At that point, the hunt for an actress to play Fanny Brice took several turns, with David Merrick and Ray Stark as the show's original producers. Stark was married to Brice's daughter, Fran, and he had championed the project in Hollywood unsuccessfully before turning to Broadway. Robbins and Stark made an overture to Eydie Gorme, but she was turned down when she insisted that her husband, Steve Lawrence, play the part of Brice's gambler-husband, Nicky Arnstein. Robbins then flew to the Midwest to discuss the Brice role with Carol Burnett, who reportedly told him, "I'd love to do it, but what you need is a Jewish girl."

Enter Barbra Steisand, whom David Merrick had originally suggested for the role. Merrick had become a believer in Streisand's talents after being prevailed upon to cast the young, headstrong songstress as Miss Marmelstein in *I Can Get It for You Wholesale*. On that show, Merrick had complained after hearing Steisand's audition, "How many times have I told you I don't want ugly girls in my shows?" Fanny Brice, of course, had been the ugly duckling among Ziegfeld's gorgeous swans, and similarly Streisand was something of a homely underdog in the entertainment world. While her supporting role in *Wholesale* had not qualified her as a Broadway star in 1962, she was already a rising sensation with her singing career. *The Second Barbra Streisand Album* skyrocketed into *Billboard*'s top ten that year, and *The Third Album* would be released during the New York previews of *Funny Girl*. *Cash Box* reported that "the Streisand name could be the biggest to hit show business since Elvis Presley."

After Jule Styne first saw the twenty-one-year-old Streisand perform at the Bon Soir (in fact, Styne attended twenty-seven of twenty-eight shows at the club), he told Robbins, "You've got to see Barbra Streisand. She's Fanny." Styne's opinion carried additional weight because he had known and worked with Fanny Brice in the 1930s. Robbins subsequently caught Streisand's act, as did the Starks. Fran Stark's reaction was "There is no way *she* will play my mother." Brice's daughter was put off by Streisand's quirky, ethnic manner— the real Fanny didn't speak with a Jewish or Brooklyn accent, although she was Jewish, grew up in Brooklyn, and used dialect in her routines. The Starks were justified with their concerns about Streisand filling the role and carrying the show. The actress would face the challenge of playing Fanny Brice both as the young, aspiring performer and as the mature Follies star. The book followed Brice's career from her early days in Keenan's Music Hall to her reign with Ziegfeld, while tracing her ill-fated romance with Nicky Arnstein, who spent eighteen months in prison for embezzlement and finally dumped Brice.

Despite the producers' misgivings, Streisand was invited to audition for a group that included Robbins, Styne, Merrick, the Starks, Isobel Lennart (who wrote the script) and John Patrick (a writer who was serving as a consultant). Recalling the audition, Patrick told Streisand's biographer Anne Edwards, "I can't tell you how horrible she looked. . . . She wore a Cossack uniform kind of thing. She read the scene where Fanny's husband, Nicky Arnstein, has just left her. Tears were called for, and she could not manage it."

Robbins and Styne prevailed upon the Starks to give her another try. Robbins worked with her for nearly an hour, and then she read the scene on-stage with a stage manager. Again there were no tears from the would-be Broadway star. Never one to hide consternation, Robbins chided her, "You're supposed to cry, Barbra."

But Streisand defended herself by blaming the script, saying, "Mr. Robbins, I can't cry with these words."

After an awkward silence, the writer, Isobel Lennart, piped up, saying, "I don't blame you, Miss Streisand. They're terrible words. And they're mine."

Robbins was amused by the exchange. He was also well aware of the problems with Lennart's script.

Streisand was called back seven times to audition in the summer of 1963. She arrived late for the last audition, and Robbins told her, "Forty minutes we've been sitting here waiting for you." He added, "You better be worth it."

Streisand had been working with her acting coach Allan Miller, and that day she delivered a monologue that showed off her ferocious intensity, eliciting laughter and applause from the entire group, including the director. "As far as I'm concerned," Robbins told her, "you *are* Fanny Brice."

Allan Miller recalled that after the audition, Ray Stark told Streisand's agent, Marty Erlichman, "Look, with Bancroft we had a major actress. She can't sing, and she's not funny, and we had a million-dollar advance. With Burnett we had a major star talent. She can sing, and she's funny, but she can't act, and we had a two-million-dollar advance. With this kid, we've got *no* advance. But, she can sing, she can act, she can do the whole thing. And if she makes it for us, she's worth five million. *We go with the kid.*"

Streisand later said, "The show is fate. . . . The play is really about me. It simply happened to happen before to Fanny Brice. . . . I'm so much like the person it's incredible. Little, silly things. We both love the color white. We both grew up in Brooklyn, had typical mothers concerned about food and health and trying to marry us off. The way we work. I choose my music, my clothes, everything. People tell me things. I couldn't listen to anybody. I had to do it myself. And here it is in the play. It's incredible. It's scary." She added with a laugh, "I'm waiting for Nicky Arnstein."

On July 25, 1963, Ray Stark informed the press that Streisand had been cast as Fanny Brice. A short time later, Robbins strongly advised Stark to replace Isobel Lennart as the writer. When Stark refused, Robbins bowed out as director. He was eventually replaced by Bob Fosse, who also quit within a matter of weeks when he heard gossip circulating that Stark didn't have complete faith in him as a director. During their early tenures with the show, Fosse and Robbins both agreed on one point of criticism regarding the score: Neither wanted to include the Styne-Merrill number "People." The two directors felt the song was inappropriate for the character of Fanny Brice. At one point, Styne explained to Fosse, "The reason she is singing this song . . . IS BECAUSE THIS SONG IS GOING TO BE FUCKING NUMBER-ONE ON THE HIT PARADE!" When Fosse exited, he was replaced by Garson

Kanin, who also tried to cut "People." Styne and Merrill prevailed only by having a back-up song ready for the show's Boston tryout early in 1964, with the proviso that if the number didn't stop the show each night, it was out. By that time, thanks to Styne's commercial foresight, the song had already been released as a single, and "People" stayed in the show.

While the score did not include any of Brice's material, Styne and Merrill deftly re-created the style and color of the period, giving Streisand exactly what she needed to display the full range, throb and tremble of her talent. "Sadie, Sadie" was reminiscent of Brice's "Rose of Washington Square," while "The Music That Makes Me Dance" called up her standard, "My Man." Streisand would move with ease (if any performance could ever be described as easy for her) from the bluesy lament of "Who Are You Now?" through the brisk strains of "Don't Rain on My Parade." The show would also offer the quasi-Ziegfeld production number, "Rat-Tat-Tat-Tat," a World War I military drill performed up and down a grand staircase. Streisand would descend the same staircase as a pregnant bride for "His Love Makes Me Beautiful."

If to some degree every show goes through tribulations and revisions out of town, *Funny Girl* had more than its share. By all accounts, there was constant tension and acrimony, and the source was often Streisand, who was intent on making the show into her personal vehicle for capturing glory on the Great White Way. With such grand ambition and her imperious, high-strung temperament, she did little to endear herself with the rest of the cast. Steisand's understudy, Lainie Kazan said, "She was uncomfortable with all the members of the company.... She took herself very seriously, was distant, never able to laugh at herself, relax. Garson exerted great patience explaining where the humor of a scene should come from."

Streisand's relationship with Garson Kanin was frayed during the Boston tryout, and at the same time personal complications arose between her and Sydney Chaplin, who was playing the role of Nicky Arnstein. "There was great hostility in the company," said John Patrick. "Barbra and Sydney Chaplin, her leading man, hated each other. In the scene where she sits on the doorsteps and sings 'People,' he would look up at her adoringly and whisper out of the side of his mouth, 'You're off-key, you bitch!'" Such behavior was apparently only a prelude to romance. Most accounts agree that Streisand and

Chaplin had a brief affair in Boston, as gossip-hound Earl Wilson reported in his column. At the time, Streisand was married to Elliott Gould, and Chaplin was married to dancer Noelle Adams. Kay Medford, who played Fanny Brice's mother, said, "I don't know what happened at this point to change Chaplin's attitude toward Barbra, but about the second week in Boston they suddenly became chummy." The offstage romance may have added some sparks to the love scenes, but the show was still in disarray, running almost four hours.

Six songs were cut by the time *Funny Girl* moved to Philadelphia's Forrest Theatre, where it opened on February 4, 1964. While the *Philadelphia Inquirer* reported it was "a Streisand triumph," the reviews overall were decidedly mixed. As producer David Merrick sold his interest and departed along the way, ultimate control now resided with Ray Stark. At this point, Streisand was disenchanted with Garson Kanin. Jean Stapleton, who played one of the Brices' friendly neighbors, Mrs. Stakosh, explained, "Garson Kanin represented everything golden in the theater to me. He did the Group Theatre and so forth, so I was thrilled that I was going to work with Kanin. And this is no reflection on his talents, but he had not acquired the skill of moving people around the stage, especially in a musical. He just couldn't do it, he didn't do it, and I was stunned. He was at a loss, and this is probably why he was replaced."

Streisand aggressively campaigned for the return of Robbins. Fearing a flop, she told Stark, "I think I'm not being directed enough. I need a lot more direction." Her coach, Allan Miller, said, "Robbins had obviously heard how terrific Barbra was getting to be in the show . . . and was talked into coming to take a look. Later, he admitted to me that if he hadn't seen how much she had done with the part, he wouldn't have come back at all."

Robbins joined the company as "over-all consultant" on February nineteenth, and reportedly commanded a fee of $1,000 per day. When the show opened for previews in New York the next month, he was billed as "production supervisor," with Kanin retaining his director credit. But once Robbins appeared on the scene before the show closed in Philadelphia, Kanin gracefully withdrew. During the next month, *Funny Girl* underwent a transformation. Robbins knew exactly how to show Streisand off to best advantage, which may explain why two such temperamental perfectionists were able to maintain a fruitful creative rapport. When Walter Kerr later called her portrayal of Fanny Brice "a marvel of secure insecurity," the critic might have been speaking of Streisand and Robbins.

Robbins' ex-lover, Buzz Miller, performed a small role in the show and reported to Streisand biographer Randall Riese, "There were rumblings . . . that 'this is working for Barbra. And if it works for her, it works for all of us.' " Miller also said of Robbins, "He tightened the show and cut my number to ribbons. . . . I played in a number called 'Cornet Man,' and he changed it entirely, because it was not good for Barbra. It was completely revised so she didn't look like she was standing there with egg on her face. See, Barbra was not really a dancer. She clapped her hands and stomped her feet. The number was a tour de force for myself, but it was wrong for the show. I understood it, but I hated it."

Royce Wallace, who had danced in *On the Town*, was cast by Robbins in *Funny Girl* as Fanny's maid-dresser. Wallace said, "He [Jerry] reached back and got me, and I had a ball. I loved that show. He was a magnificent person and personality. We had a good time, and we used to have a little taste now and then. He'd say, 'I'm tired. Are you goin' next door?' He didn't like being seen and we'd go out to a little place and I'd buy a drink for him, and he'd buy a drink for me. This man was out of sight. But he could get mad as hell, though, if things weren't going right. He knew what he was doing and he knew what he wanted to see."

Wallace became a supportive confidante for Streisand. "We got along because I played her maid," said Wallace. "And I'd ask her, 'Now what do you want me to do with this [scene], girl?' We got along, 'cause she would say [referring to Robbins], 'Now he's gonna give me a hard time.' And I'd say, 'No, he's not, honey. He's the sweetest man in the world. You're gonna be so pretty when you finish, you're gonna be so pretty doin' whatever he asks you to do . . . and you *do* it.' She was kind of afraid of him . . . and I'd say, 'You were a star in that last show and now you're gonna be a star in this show . . . and you're *what!* What is wrong with you?' "

Some, if not most, of the cast anticipated that contentious fireworks between Streisand and Robbins were inevitable because of their extreme personalities when it came to the work. Wallace said, "She was scared of him, and he was scared of her. But they got along beautifully. And everybody didn't think they would. She would explain what she was doing, and if he felt it wasn't exactly what he wanted or close to it, he would tell her and *show* her why. I could see he loved doing it. He was very good with her. There was no trouble because they both respected each other, and she looked up to him like a father, as little as he was. She didn't know anything about dancing and movement. She'd say, 'Oh, I like that.' And he'd say, 'Okay, do it again.' And she just tried to do everything he wanted, and he was just grinning all the time. And everybody was standing around with their mouths open to see if there was gonna *be* something, you know. But they were marvelous together."

The stage manager, Tom Stone, agreed, saying, "Jerry got along very well with Barbra. He didn't make her a star, because she would have been one anyway, but he certainly shaped the show in such a way to make it possible for her to shine. Between the two of them, there were no threats with one another. They both knew what they wanted. And Jerry liked her a lot. He felt like a father to her in a way. I remember when she got the two movies, *Hello, Dolly!* on top of *Funny Girl,* I saw her in the street at a shoe store, and she really snubbed me. I hadn't seen her in quite a while, and at that point, Jerry had optioned a play that I had written. I had a meeting with him afterwards and told him about her, and he said, 'Look, she's just a young kid, she'll get over it. She's a sweet kid.' Of course, she never did—she got worse."

The show's original choreographer, Carol Haney, was fired soon after Robbins rejoined the production, although she retained her credit. Stone recalled, "Jerry took the show apart and put it back together. He did not treat Carol Haney very well at all. I thought it was awful the way he treated her . . . and she was very sick. He tended to take people who were weakened and get at the weak points. Sometimes this was okay, because it would force them to pick themselves up and get out there and do something; other times it was just pure sadism. He had a lot of dark shadows in his own life and a lot of insecurities and a lot of anger. He was a little Jewish boy from the other side of the river and he was gay and fighting it. But with *Funny Girl* it was an extraordinary experience to see how good he was at what he did right up close. And what he did essentially was he took the show away from Sydney Chaplin and gave it to Barbra. Before that, there had been a terrible imbalance, and Sydney was walking through his role, anyway. He didn't really give a good damn what anybody thought about his effort, just as long as he was collecting his money. He treated Barbra very, very badly . . . Sydney was a monster."

Chaplin lost all of his numbers in the second act and watched helplessly as his part was cut out from under him. His only remaining solo in the first act, "You Are Woman, I Am Man," was a comic seduction scene played in Arnstein's private dining room, and the number wasn't registering with the audience. Robbins told Jule Styne and Bob Merrill, "It won't go over alone for Sydney. Can you write a countermelody to tell us what Fanny is thinking. Use that accompaniment, but write comedy lyrics for it." Styne and Merrill quickly complied. In the theater lobby the next day, Robbins listened to their sixteen-bar countermelody, then added it immediately to the show. Meanwhile, Streisand worked with her acting coach to play the scene with the sort of comedic sophistication that Brice would have gleaned from movie stars of her day like Mae West, Marie Dressler and Greta Garbo. The Styne-Merrill line, "A bit of pâté? I drink it all day" fit Streisand perfectly, and the scene became a highlight in the show, consistently delighting and winning audience laughter. Chaplin, who had almost stolen *Bells Are Ringing* away from Judy Holliday, was here put in his place by Robbins on behalf of Streisand.

"Jerry, of course, saved the show," said Jean Stapleton. "He put in that wonderful number ['You Are Woman'] and he moved scenes around and did a lot of good doctoring. . . . At that time, my children were about six and four. I brought them down to the theater one day. Now Kay Medford had said to me that Jerry was kind to children and animals, period. And it was proven there, because he was so darling to those children, so sweet and happy they were there."

Like a number of others in the cast, Stapleton came down with the flu before the New York premiere. She recollected how gentle and considerate Robbins was when he informed her that she might have to be replaced. "I refused medical examination and assistance because that's not the way I go for healing. I'm a Christian Scientist, I explained, and Jerry was the soul of kindness. He said, 'Well, that's okay.' And Jule Styne was very much knowledgeable about this. He was cute. He said, 'I tried it once for my gambling—it didn't work.' Jerry took me aside, and he said, 'You know what we have to do, we have to audition people for your part.' But he was very, very kind. And in three days I was back, in time for a full weekend of performing. It was that close to the opening, because the next weekend we did the recording of the [cast] album, and I always regret that I didn't sound quite up to par."

The show's opening was postponed five times by Stark, primarily to allow time for Robbins' handiwork. On the day of the last preview, the first and final scenes were still unfinished. Streisand's first sweeping entrance had been planned with two leashed wolfhounds. But crossing the stage with these two less-than-cooperative animals proved more than the actress could handle when she tried to pause center stage. The dogs were summarily cut and the scene was rehearsed the next morning without them. Royce Wallace recalled, "The idea was good, but the dogs didn't know they were supposed to stop when she stopped. They took 'em right out and after that, we said, now let's get on with the show." Streisand's last scene had been rewritten more than fifty times and was finally set and rehearsed three hours before the curtain rose at the Winter Garden Theatre on opening night, March 26, 1964.

For Streisand, it was a night of glittering exultation, perhaps marred only by the hypercritical proclivities that she shared by nature with Robbins. The performance concluded with a standing ovation for the star, and twenty-three curtain calls. The Starks threw a glitzy party at the Rainbow Room, with its window wall sixty-five stories above Manhattan. Ironically, the band played "Hello Dolly" as the first of three hundred guests arrived, including such luminaries as Aristotle Onassis, Senator Jacob Javits, former New York governor Thomas Dewey, Sophie Tucker, Angela Lansbury and Bette Davis. Wearing an elegant black gown, Streisand entered on the arm of Elliott Gould, and the band greeted her with the opener in the show, "I'm the Greatest Star." All of those assembled, including Robbins, rose to their feet and offered Streisand a jubilant ovation.

Most of the reviews the next morning were glowing. In the *Times,* Howard Taubman concluded, "Fanny's personality and style are remarkably evoked by Miss Streisand. Fanny and Barbra make the evening. Who says the past cannot be recaptured?" Walter Kerr complained that the second act was a letdown because of forced sentimentality and Chaplin's undeveloped character. But the critic acknowledged, "Still, it's the star's evening; long may she wave to Mr.

Ziegfeld." The *Journal-American* predicted the show "should be a smash." In fact, *Funny Girl* ran more than three years (1,348 performances), leading to a successful London production (1966) and the movie for which Streisand won the Oscar for best actress (1968, shared with Katharine Hepburn).

Streisand's comments the day after the show opened sound remarkably similar to those made by Robbins after his triumph with *Fancy Free* almost exactly twenty years before. Streisand said, "Now that I'm supposed to be a success, I'm worried about the responsibility. People will no longer be coming to see a talent they've heard about. I now have to live up to their concept of a great success. I'm not the underdog, the homely kid from Brooklyn they can root for anymore. I'm fair game."

The cast album from Capitol Records reached *Billboard*'s Top Forty at the beginning of May and continued to climb, only to be denied the top spot by the arrival of the Beatles in America. *Funny Girl* lost out that year at the Tony Awards to *Hello, Dolly!*, and the star of that show, Carol Channing, prevailed over Streisand as best actress in a musical. As production supervisor, Robbins was without a category. His nearest competition on Broadway, Gower Champion, won the Tonys for direction and choreography on *Hello, Dolly!*, but Robbins was already working on a pet project that would more than settle the score the following year.

Champion, like Robbins, ran into difficulty with straight plays, failing when he tried works by Lillian Hellman and Paul Ford. In *The Season: A Candid Look at Broadway*, William Goldman wondered "why these men [Robbins and Champion], so obviously gifted in one field, should be so disastrously inept in another." Goldman offered an explanation from an unnamed associate in the theater: "In a musical they start with a total picture in their minds and then all they do is put in the puppets. In a play they have to work with actors; they have to draw out, not put in, and neither of them can do that. Only puppetsville."

Robbins acknowledged the difficulty to the press, saying, "The fact that most actors think I'm going to approach a production from the choreographer's point of view is kind of a problem. . . . But I don't approach a straight play that way—at least not consciously. And what most actors don't realize is that even when I do conscious choreography, the movement always is dictated by character, situation and material." This apparent conflict between choreographing and directing would spur and consume him throughout the rest of the decade.

Based on stories by Yiddish author Sholem Aleichem, *Fiddler on the Roof* afforded Robbins the opportunity to come to terms artistically with his family heritage. To some extent (though not entirely), this show would also facilitate a reconciliation with his father. Harry Robbins was invited by his son to participate in researching the show, and there was a coincidental irony to be savored in the fact that Sholem Aleichem's real name was Rabinowitz. The Russian-born writer died in New York in 1916, two years before the birth of Jerome Rabinowitz. Set in the Russian town of Anatevka circa 1905, the show centered on the plight of Tevye the milkman and his family. The musical adaptation began as a collaboration between playwright Joseph Stein, composer Jerry Bock and lyricist Sheldon Harnick. Stein recalled that a number of producers, believing that the ethnic subject matter would limit the show's commercial potential, turned down the project before Robbins tentatively agreed to direct. Even after the show opened, David Merrick declared, "It's a Jewish show. . . . No one will go."

Stein explained that most producers, like Merrick, were reluctant because "they felt that there would be no audience for it, and *we* didn't know that there would be. None of us were at all sure about our project. . . . I think it was a personal project for all of us, including Jerry, because none of us had the remotest idea that this would be very successful. The cliché, it was a labor of love—this one really was."

Harold Prince had been asked to direct *Fiddler* before Robbins became involved. Prince remembered, "Apropos that show, it was brought to me to direct by Bock and Harnick. I told them I did not feel comfortable with the *shtetl* community, that it did not reflect my background and that I felt a bit at a loss to direct those characters. I recommended that they get Jerome Robbins as the only person who *could* give it a universal language. Jerry was not available at the time. Later, he became available and agreed to direct it for Fred Coe, its producer. But then, he [Jerry] insisted that I produce it with Fred. Subsequently, I took it over and Fred stayed on as associate producer. Fred was a man of great taste and acumen, but not particularly equipped to handle a big production. And that's what happened."

The show was to star Zero Mostel as Tevye, the devout father of five daughters (instead of the seven in Aleichem's stories), three of whom confront him with the anguished dilemma of their marrying out of faith. This family crisis takes place at the same time that Czarist pogroms threaten the *shtetl* community, ultimately leading to the eviction and banishment of all of the Jewish peasants from their homes. Over the course of the evening, the audience learns by way of the humor and poignancy to see through Tevye's outbursts of anger and rough exterior to the very heart that bonds him to his family and faith. Tevye's wife, Golde, was played by Maria Karnilova, who remembered the depth of Robbins' personal investment in the show. "It was a very emotional show for Jerry," said Karnilova. "As far as Jerry was concerned, this was *his* family back in Russia."

In this regard, Sheldon Harnick recalled, "Early on when Jerry accepted the show, one of the things he told us was that when he was six he had been taken to Poland by his parents, and he said he never forgot that trip—even at the age of six it was very emotional—to the little village where they came from. . . . What was desperately important to him was that he had gone to Poland, and that village [Rozanka], as many others, had been wiped out during World War II. So he had a mission with *Fiddler*, almost an obsession, and that was to give those *shtetls* that had been wiped out in World War II, to give them another life onstage—he said, 'For maybe twenty-five years.' And of course, it's gone way beyond that now. But that was his goal, and he was going to do it."

Harnick continued, "We started pre-production meetings at least six months before we went into rehearsal. I'd never had that. . . . Robbins worked out of a great knowledge that once you got into rehearsal, you had to have as many things fixed as possible or it was too late. In those six months of pre-production meetings he just asked questions. He was like—I've used this image—he was like an extraordinary district attorney, and he just kept asking us questions. We would give answers. Sometimes they were simplistic. One of the main questions, of course, was, 'What is the show about? What gives these Sholem Aleichem stories their power?' We kept saying, 'Well, it's about this dairyman and his five marriageable daughters.' He'd say, 'No, no, that isn't good enough, that isn't strong enough.' Weeks went by. Finally, at one of the meetings somebody said, 'Oh my God, you know what this is about? It's about the dissolution of a way of life.' And at that point Robbins got so excited, he said, 'That's what it is, it's tradition. And if that's what it is, then we have to have an opening number which will set up some of those traditions so that people can see them break down during the show.' He was just very excited."

The opening number for Tevye and company became the Bock-Harnick gem, "Tradition." The score included such affecting songs as "If I Were a Rich Man," "Sabbath Prayer," "Miracle of Miracles," "Sunrise, Sunset," "Do You Love Me?" and "Matchmaker." All of the numbers were not only entirely integrated into the action but also managed to evoke a way of life. Robbins said, "The real reason I wanted to do the show . . . was to get that concept of tradition onto the stage. Sholem Aleichem may not spell it out line by line but that is the real meaning of his work, the notion that without tradition life can be as shaky as a fiddler on the roof. As first, I was unhappy about the script. I had to discover how the show was going to be different from something called, say 'The Rise of the Goldbergs.' The difference was that fiddler, sawing away on the roof. In a very real sense, that fiddler is my own."

The director also credited his grandmother Ida Rips with being an inspiration for *Fiddler*. Robbins described her as "a tiny little woman, a marvelous woman who never used glasses though she was always poring over the Torah. And evidently a very fierce social worker in lower Jersey City. But she had a beauty in—I don't know what the word is—composure—a kind of Oriental thing. It contained her entire being."

Robbins' research included taking his collaborators, his cast and often his father to Orthodox Jewish services in Brooklyn and Manhattan. In addition, Robbins studied Gorki's films and read books like the sociological study *Life Is with People: The Culture of the Shtetl*, by Mark Zborowski and Elizabeth Herzog. Utilizing the Stanislavski approach again, Robbins tried to impart an appreciation of the relevant history and cultural values to the cast. "I wanted to make a *shtetl* out of *them*," said Robbins, "To make them understand what the community in *Fiddler* was like, I told them to think of the Jews in Anatevka as though they were a theatrical company trying out a new show out of town. Each person was trying to build something in common with his neighbors. In doing it, each person was an outsider to the rest of the world."

There were many non-Jewish performers in *Fiddler,* and Robbins tried to sensitize them to the realities of anti-Semitism and bigotry. Harold Prince wrote, "I remember the first day of rehearsal, the entire company was made to improvise scenes in which one member owned a white bookstore in the South and confronted a black customer, refusing to serve him. I thought it a dubious exercise, but one whole day was given to it. And the next day, the entire company played out what life in a concentration camp would have been like. Again, in view of the fact that *Fiddler* takes place forty years before these events, I question the applicability of such an exercise. Again, on a positive note, the company *was* committed to the project."

Prince also recollected that Robbins had to be prodded into starting rehearsals. "He was afraid to take that first step on the first day's rehearsal and tried to postpone it on the pretense that it wasn't ready. Well, I presumed that *it* was and *he* was and I agreed to the postponement but insisted that he pay me out of pocket rather substantial pre-production expenses. He caved in immediately, almost tearfully, in a phone conversation (how could I do that to him, etc.) but we got over that quickly and he did go into rehearsals on time." Robbins' auditions for *Fiddler,* however, had been interrupted on November 22, 1963, when Broadway, like the rest of the country was shut down by the assassination of President John F. Kennedy. The tragedy in Dallas took place ten months before the show opened. Eight weeks of rehearsals were initially scheduled to begin in January of 1964, but Robbins stalled until Prince finally coerced him to start work the following June.

Robbins' deal on *Fiddler* was potentially lucrative. For directing and choreographing the show, he reportedly received a fee of $10,000, fifteen percent of the profits and three percent of the weekly gross, which turned out to be approximately $75,000 when the house played at capacity. He was already a wealthy man, and this show would make him a multimillionaire many times over. The financial security that he derived from his Broadway shows included additional yearly income generated by the countless revivals and tours.

On *Fiddler,* Robbins once again faced the disconcerting challenge of working with Zero Mostel, who had been Robbins' first choice for the role. According to Sheldon Harnick, "Before Robbins became involved, Joe Stein and Jerry Bock and I all thought that we wanted Howard da Silva. We had seen Howard do *The World of Sholem Aleichem* . . . off-Broadway, and Robbins felt that he wanted somebody who was larger-than-life in the main role, so he wanted Zero. And all of us knew that there'd been political friction between them. But during rehearsal at any rate, what I saw was that Zero knew that Robbins was the right person and, I think, he felt that Robbins was stronger than he was, so that he gave in generally to Robbins. What Robbins wanted, he would do, whereas for the rest of us sometimes, Zero could be extremely difficult."

Others recall that Zero was mercilessly obstreperous with Robbins. "There was always that little problem about the blacklist, because Zero was very aware of it and made everybody aware of it," said Joseph Stein. "There was no love lost between them. As a matter of fact, I sometimes was having to be a go-between. They didn't even remotely socialize. . . . Zero was tough on Jerry. Zero spoke of him occasionally with contempt, and it was uncomfortable. He even talked about his direction very negatively."

Tom Stone attended a dress rehearsal and remembered, "I was standing and I just said, 'This is the best thing Jerry's ever done by far, it's absolutely extraordinary, stunning.' And I went back to tell him that. He said, 'Come on, let's go have some lunch.' So I went out to a little restaurant with him, and in walks Zero . . . and he sits at a table next to us—Jerry and myself and I don't know who else was there, Pat Dunn, maybe. And Zero just sat there and insulted Jerry for forty-five minutes non-stop. All of it was very, very ugly and loud, and Jerry just sat there and took it . . . about him personally, about the Communist business—that's what it was about. That was the core of it all. I was very embarrassed, too. For us younger folks, it didn't mean anything—we hadn't been through it. But Zero was not going to let Jerry off the hook. He was going to beat him and beat him and beat him and be nasty to him and insult him in front of people in the rehearsals, things like that. And Jerry had no choice but to sit there and take it. He loved the material, that's all, and he really wanted to do it. He loved researching about the Jews, he really cared."

Opera singer and actress Julia Migenes performed the part of Tevye's daughter, Hodel (the one who pledges herself to the student revolutionary, Perchik). Of the Mostel-Robbins feud, Migenes said, "They were killing each other. There was the political stuff and also the professional. I'm sitting with Zero, who's sweating like crazy. He was like a father to me. And he was saying, '*Tell* that Jewish fag!' talking about Jerry. He called him 'the Jewish fag.' They had a fight to the finish. . . . Jerry had this thing about trying to be Method, and Zero was this bigger-than-life wild guy. Zero had a game going with the conductor, who he called, 'A live metronome.' He couldn't stand that the guy was a live metronome, so he'd make him watch and try to keep up with him. He'd go too fast, then way too slow, way too fast again, and way too slow again."

Dancer Chuck Rule recounted one of the skirmishes in rehearsal. "Zero once screamed at him, 'If you want that kind of performance, why don't you get Red Buttons!' And stormed off the stage. Jerry screamed after him, 'If I'd wanted Red Buttons, I would have hired Red Buttons!' So then Jerry dismissed us all and said, 'Go home, come back tomorrow.' I understand that he went in and talked to Zero. . . . I always loved Zero, we got along very well. But he had a slightly sadistic streak."

Robbins later told the press, "Mostel likes to test you when you work together. There was a certain amount of squaring off at each other, but I think we both felt some good healthy respect beneath it all." While Mostel bedeviled Robbins during rehearsals and out-of-town tryouts in Detroit and Washington, D.C., the beleaguered director vented some of his frustrations on the rest of the cast. Beatrice Arthur played the role of the matchmaker, Yente. According to several accounts, Robbins was particularly demeaning to her. "He did not want Bea for the part originally," said Joseph Stein. "We auditioned many people. And we auditioned Bea. I know that I liked her and I think that Jerry Bock and Sheldon liked her. [Robbins] was very hesitant, kept looking for other people to do the part. I think his vision was a little Molly Picon-ish woman." Actress Molly Picon played Yente in the 1971 movie. Stein continued, "Of course [Bea] was wonderful in the part, I thought. Jerry took her reluctantly because he never came across anybody that did it as well in auditions. I think he took it out on her in a way. Also he kept asking me to cut her part down. In a sense, her part is not focal, not central to the story. He drove her crazy. I know he drove her crazy."

Chuck Rule remembered that Jerry's unyielding demands drove Bea Arthur to despair. "We had a terrible time with *Fiddler.* As a matter of fact, Bea Arthur was ready to quit. Bea was brilliant in the part, but Jerry wanted the focus on Tevye and his wife, Golde. So he kept cutting [Bea's role] down. There was no way to keep her from being brilliant because she was just fabulous in the show, little Miss Bea. We did have bad times with Jerry. In Detroit, the blackness on the stage was so thick you could cut it with a knife. It was horrible. You remember that cartoon, Al Capp, with the guy who walked around with the thundercloud over his head—that was Jerry there. I was so angry in Washington, D.C.—we were playing the National—and I stormed out of the theater. . . . There's a long alley by the side of the theater at the National. Bea was sitting there smoking a cigarette. I came out and I said, 'Bea, I'm going to rip his cock and balls off and shove 'em down his throat.' And Bea looked at me, she took a puff of her cigarette, and she said, 'What cock? What balls?' And then took another puff. I never forgot that, the timing was superb, naturally. . . . And I called my wife. I said, 'I'm thinking of committing suicide.' She said, 'Shut up, go to mass, and just forget about it.'"

Rule also acknowledged one of Robbins' masterstrokes. "He called us all to the Martha Washington Hotel in Washington, and he had choreographed the finale of the first act, which culminates in the Bottle Dance. He did this, and we just burst into applause. And he was beaming ear to ear, he was just so happy. He had found the finale of the first act. We thought it was wonderful—none of us really hated Jerry, we just hated the way he treated us. So anyway, we gave him a big hand of applause and said it was sensational. He said, 'It goes in tonight!' That was not long before we came to New York."

Chronicling the show in the book *The Making of a Musical,* Robbins' assistant, Richard Altman, explained how the idea for the Bottle Dance was derived from a Hasidic wedding ceremony that he and Robbins attended in Manhattan's Ansonia Hotel. "One evening during the entertainment that followed the wedding ceremony, a Jewish comedian did a funny dance while balancing an empty wine bottle on his head. Jerry said nothing about it at the time, but I remember the rapt smile on his face and his almost hypnotic absorption." The

Bottle Dance called for four villagers to perform a brief but exuberant dance with wine bottles balanced on their heads. According to Altman and stage manager Bob Currie, after trying various devices and gimmicks like morticians' wax to fix the bottles to the dancers' heads, Robbins finally commanded, "Those bottles will damn well stay on their heads or they'll lose their jobs!" Later, Robbins provided staged business to cover for the inevitable eventuality of fallen bottles, and no dancer was fired.

Altman also recalled that *Fiddler* was running too long when it left New York and was cut in Detroit and Washington with decisive encouragement from Hal Prince. Altman wrote, "Some trimming of the first act was done, but most of the cuts—about twenty minutes' worth—eventually came from Act Two, much of it from the 'Chava Ballet.'" The ballet was an elaborate sequence of choreography with which Robbins tried to illuminate Tevye's anguish after learning that his daughter Chava has eloped with a gentile. The dance involved almost the whole company, and Robbins gradually whittled it down effectively.

Collaboration among the principals—Robbins, Bock, Harnick, Stein, Boris Aronson, who created the scenery, and Patricia Zipprodt, who designed the costumes—was contentious, though without the degree of heated, wounding hostilities that erupted on *West Side Story*. For his part, Sheldon Harnick received some wise advice on how to work with Robbins. "Before we went into rehearsal," the lyricist recalled, "I spoke to Sondra Lee, who was a very close friend of Jerry's and was a very close friend of mine. She said, 'Jerry can be difficult, especially as it gets toward opening. But,' she said, 'when he seems unreachable, try humor, because if he's reachable that will do it.' And I found that to be true. Luckily, on occasion I could make him laugh, break the tension. Except that about two weeks, three weeks, before we opened, then I couldn't reach him that way either. Whatever his demons were, they had just taken charge. Nevertheless, for me it was a wonderful experience, and I came out of the experience just loving him. I really loved him."

At the outset, Harnick received a friendly warning about Robbins from Stephen Sondheim. Harnick said, "Steve Sondheim had alerted me to the fact that Robbins was the kind of person who would change your work. If he thought that it should be changed, he would do it and he wouldn't always ask you. We were in Detroit on the road with *Fiddler*, and I came into a matinee, and I heard the song 'Matchmaker.' I think Robbins had spoken to Steve Sondheim about it. I think that's what had happened. Steve certainly didn't want Robbins to change my work without asking me, but that's what he did. He changed a line or two. I was appalled, and I thought how do I deal with this? So I went to the girl who was playing Tzeitel . . . I went to Joanna Merlin and I said, 'This evening, would you change two lines in the song?' I gave her two awful lines. She looked at me and she said, 'You want me to sing *this*?' I said, 'Please.' She said, 'Okay.' So she sang it that night. And after the performance, Robbins came up to me and he was grinning from ear to ear. . . . He said, 'Okay, next time I'll ask.'"

Harnick described Robbins' approach to the set designs devised by Boris Aronson: "Jerry told Boris that he wanted it to have a Chagall-look, and he kept having Boris redo the sketches, until finally what Boris was doing was just Chagall. And he brought in these Chagall sketches, and I remember Robbins laughing and saying, 'Boris, there's got to be Boris Aronson in there, too.'"

Richard Altman recollected that Robbins' "tireless trial-and-error tactics were particularly exasperating to Russian-born set designer Boris Aronson," who was then in his sixties and set in his ways. Aronson started his career on Broadway in 1935 with *Three Men on a Horse*. Altman wrote, "What conflicts arose between them were focused on Jerry's need for more and more space—a traditional source of stress between director and designer—and on the apparent indecisiveness that by then had become Jerry's hallmark." But Altman also recalled watching the first performance of the Bottle Dance in Washington with Robbins and Aronson at the back of the theater. "The applause that erupted at the end was tremendous, and suddenly I felt Boris tugging at my arm. I turned to him and saw that tears were streaming down his cheeks. 'Any man who can do that,' he said, nodding toward Jerry, 'I forgive everything.'"

Patricia Zipprodt remembered the prolonged intensity of the *Fiddler* collaboration. "We were demented because there was no solid ground . . . and then it was like Jerry was exploring. And of course the longer it took to raise the money, the more he explored. I think I spent a year drawing momma and poppas. So we are all going through the same torment. As is he, except that he is electing to do it and we have no choice. His mood was . . . black is my word for it. It was terrible, and it destroys everybody—not destroys them, but everyone is vulnerable, no one escapes. It doesn't matter who the hell you are or how well you know him. You get caught in this deep interior. It ends up being, I think, both stimulating and destructive."

Robbins reached back into his past and hired his early mentor, Gluck Sandor, to perform the role of the Rabbi. Maria Karnilova recalled, "Jerry was indebted to Sandor, because he was so young and learned so much from him. That's why he hired him, and because Sandor was not working. And he was exactly the right type for that role." Sandor later went over the top with his performance, despite Robbins' efforts to tone down his portrayal. Chuck Rule said, "Jerry was in love with him [Gluck] when he was fifteen years old. What Jerry was mad at was he wanted a little bit more dignity, and Gluck was just incapable of giving him what he wanted, because Gluck was just a mime, a comic mime. Jerry got some letters from Jews protesting [Gluck's performance]. Jerry was right. Gluck just didn't understand that he had to reel it in a little bit. . . . We had a big Jewish audience. Later, when we were talking about Gluck in the dressing room, Jerry said, 'Rabbis are just too intelligent, they're too well-educated to act like buffoons.' He was hard on Gluck, but he loved him, and he kept him working. He was not going to fire him."

Dancer Duane Bodin said, "Gluck Sandor was the sweetest old guy . . . and Jerry was very cruel, very cruel in rehearsals to Gluck. I got off easy at corrections, but Gluck was not spared. Just acting-wise, just punch-punch-punch-punch. [Jerry said], 'No, no, that's terrible! What are you *doing*?' And Gluck took it because he was of that age, and it was the last thing that he would do." On the other hand, Joseph Stein suggested that Robbins was generous with Sandor. "Once he put him in the show, he protected him. Like, he gave him a little dance that startled me, because there was no real reason for it, in the middle of the wedding scene, but it was kind of like a gift to him. And that little gift is now in every show all over the world."

Years later, Robbins lauded Sandor's performance, while noting that he and Sandor didn't take time to reminisce during their *Fiddler* reunion, never hinting that there had been any strain between them. Sandor's friend Anzia Kubicek remembered, "I had a very heated discussion with Sandor once after *Fiddler.* I said, 'That's really a work of art.' Oh! He just jumped up and bristled. 'That was not, that was commercial theater.' I said, 'Well, how do you draw the line? It was soulful, it had a message, it got through to people. How do you draw the line between being a work of art and being a commercial piece?' He said, 'When you do it to make money.' So unless you're starving it's not art. He was old-fashioned in some respects. We just don't have that kind of spirit anymore."

Fiddler on the Roof opened September 22, 1964 at the Imperial Theatre. The show had been fine-tuned in Washington and was running well, but before the Broadway premiere, Robbins repeatedly warned the cast, "Washington isn't New York." Advance sales totaled approximately $650,000, which was promising, but less than *The Sound of Music* that topped $1 million in pre-sales. On the afternoon of the premiere, a final rehearsal was scheduled. On his arrival at the theater, Zero Mostel pretended to be drunk, a lark played so effectively that some of his fellow actors were briefly mortified. After rehearsing for about an hour, Robbins simply let the cast go and left the theater, without delivering a final pep talk. The company was on its own. Stein recollected, "I was living at the time in Westchester and I got a room at a hotel across the street from the theater. I remember looking out of the window and seeing the lines all around the block. I couldn't believe my eyes. It extended as far as I could see. I had had three or four hits, but nothing like this. It's rare in the theater to have one show that has as much effect as this has had."

In the audience that night, Robbins' family rejoiced. Several observers described the scene backstage when, after the final curtain, Harry Robbins, with tears in his eyes, asked his son, "How did you *know* all that?" Family friend Dorothy Gilbert said, "I was backstage, too, at *Fiddler.* There was a lot of emotion there. Harry was a little hard of hearing and sometimes his voice was loud. Everyone knew Jerry was his son. He was so thrilled at the attention that he was getting. He was proud to be Jerome Robbins' father, very proud. It's too bad it had to be *Fiddler* that brought the two of them together. It waited such a long time."

Viola Zousmer recalled how deeply Harry was moved by *Fiddler* in later years. "This was the father who was so against his son becoming a dancer. Every time I visited him, he grabbed me and played me the record of *Fiddler on the Roof.* And he'd sit there and cry." But Zousmer was also aware that the wounds from Jerry's youth never completely healed, even with this celebration of the family's roots. "Finally, Harry realized his son had made it," said Zousmer. "But Jerry never really forgave him. It made it tough for him."

Hal Prince threw a party for the company at the Rainbow Room after the *Fiddler* premiere. According to Richard Altman, stage manager Bob Currie said, "Jerry Robbins made a comment to me that night I'll always remember. He said it amazed him to look around and see all those people he'd been working with for so long, because they seemed like human beings having a good time. Until then, he'd thought of them only as obstacles in the way of his work." The good time was interrupted when the first of the reviews came in after midnight. Walter Kerr's review in the *Herald Tribune* cast a pall on the gathering. Kerr called *Fiddler* a "near-miss," lacking sufficient spirit and emotion to do justice to its historical source. Kerr lauded the star but complained that he had been misdirected: "Mad or melting, the actor is a delight, and he could play the Sholom Aleichem bittersweet truths with utter legitimacy if anyone had asked him to." Kerr also suggested that "it might have been an altogether charming musical if only the people of Anatevka did not pause every now and again to give their regards to Broadway. . . ." Jerry Bock later told Richard Altman, "Kerr's review wasn't so much crushing as shocking. I could never have anticipated that kind of accusation, for the notion that we'd made so many concessions to the Broadway stage was beyond my comprehension." The rest of the reviews would more than make up for Kerr, but not before most of the company had left the party mistakenly sensing disaster.

In the *Daily News* the following morning, John Chapman hailed *Fiddler* as "one of the great works of the American musical theatre. It is darling, touching, beautiful, warm, funny and inspiring. It is a work of art." While registering quibbles with regard to the score, Howard Taubman wrote that the show was "filled with laughter and tenderness. It catches the essence of a moment in history with sentiment and radiance." Taubman praised the director, suggesting, "Jerome Robbins has staged 'Fiddler on the Roof' with sensitivity and fire. As his own choreographer, he weaves dance into action with subtlety and flaring theatricalism. The opening dance to a nostalgic song, 'Tradition,' has a ritual sweep. The dances at the wedding burst with vitality. A dream sequence is full of humor. And the choreographed farewells of the Jews leaving their Russian village have a poignancy that adds depth. . . ." In the *Post*, Richard Watts, Jr., credited Zero Mostel with making the show a success, describing his performance as "brilliantly resourceful and intelligent."

Fiddler on the Roof ran almost eight years—a staggering 3,242 performances—and received the Tony Award for best musical in 1965. Robbins won as best director and best choreographer. In their respective categories, Tonys also went to Harold Prince, Joseph Stein, Sheldon Harnick, Jerry Bock, Patricia Zipprodt, Zero Mostel and Maria Karnilova.

Soon after the show opened, Robbins was dismayed to see Mostel improvising, altering his performance with total disregard for Stein's script and Robbins' direction. Stein said, "The key word is he [Zero] was unprofessional, he was really, really totally unprofessional. I don't think he would change the dialogue particularly, but he would ad-lib. Also he would do things like suddenly throw in a Yiddish word. At one point, I had a very bitter argument with Zero because he threw in a couple of Yiddish words and got big laughs. I went back and said, 'What do you think you're doing?' He said, 'These people talked Yiddish, that's their language.' [I explained] when they're talking English, the way I wrote it, they're really talking Yiddish. When you throw in a Yiddish word, it's terribly confusing. We were very careful not to put a single Yiddish word in the script. He was not abashed one bit. He said, 'Listen, when I'm in front of the audience, it's between me and them.'

"It drove all of us crazy. But of course when we first opened, the Mostel performance was one of the great performances of the American theater. I remember even though I was involved with the show, I was awed at how powerful a performance he was giving. But once it was a hit and once he was sure he could relax, he started doing things that were thoroughly unprofessional. The show continued to work despite that, but I'm sure it drove Jerry crazy."

Maria Karnilova confirmed Stein's assessment, saying of Mostel, "He was a monster. He was a sick man, I believe. He was an exhibitionist and he could not take orders. He was a brilliant performer when he was in his right mind, but when he got cut loose, he just didn't know what he was doing. He was *not* professional. He would suddenly stop and talk to the audience and ruin the show. . . . I think Jerry was absolutely shattered that they were permitting this man to destroy his show. That's why he never did another show."

In fact, Robbins eventually became so distraught that he advised friends not to see the musical, and while he did pursue other productions (even casting Mostel again), he would not return to Broadway for years. His disillusionment with the collaboration process had been festering for some time. Sheldon Harnick remembered, "I think it was just before we opened and there was nothing more that Robbins could do, I was walking with him in the street one day and I said, 'What'll be your next musical?' And he said, 'I don't know whether I'll do one again.' I said, 'Why not?' He said, 'Well, I get these images in my mind. I know what it should be, and because I can't put on stage what I think I see in my mind, it gets so frustrating I can't bear it.' I guess it was those feelings of frustration which helped to create such friction between him and the company about two to three weeks before the show opened. When the rehearsals were done, there was nothing more he could do, and he didn't think he'd done his job right."

Similarly, actor Barry Primus recalled visiting Robbins at one of the later *Fiddler* rehearsals. "We sat together," said Primus. "He was always whispering to me, 'Look at Zero. Look at this guy trying to be crazy.' He would laugh, and it was this kind of wonderful laugh like, 'Look, he's going to try to fuck me up now.' But there was a kind of real appreciation. And he said, 'You know why I can't stand the theater? I can't stand *making* people do what I want. I'm sick of it, I'm sick of that. It costs too much to get someone to do it.' And I think he implied he didn't like being disliked for it over and over again either."

Robbins had another chance with *Fiddler* when he oversaw the London production three years later. The role of Tevye was performed by the then-unknown Israeli actor Chaim Topol. The part of Golde was played Miriam Karlin, who recounted how Robbins redirected the role for Topol and molded the actor for the part. "What Jerry did with Chaim Topol was fantastic. He created something so extraordinary. I think that's where he spent most of the time. Because Chaim Topol had already played this in Israel in Hebrew for a very short season, so he had his own way of doing it . . . and it was way, way, way over the top. To watch Jerry working with Chaim, it was like you've got a great big onion, and he took away so many layers of skin until gradually there was this wonderful little core, this jewel in the center. . . . That's what I saw happen, because . . . obviously there was so much talent there, but it was just all over the place and overdone, and it was so overly caricatured Jewish in a way. And he [Topol] eventually gave it such dignity, it was just terrific. And that was Jerry."

Fiddler opened on February 16, 1967, at Her Majesty's Theatre in London and ran for 2,030 performances. Topol virtually made his career out of *Fiddler* revivals and was later nominated for an Oscar for his performance in the film directed by Norman Jewison.

The movie of *Fiddler* was produced by the Mirisch Brothers, the same team responsible for firing Robbins on *West Side Story*. Actor Barry Primus recalled that Robbins engaged in some discussions about directing *Fiddler*, but his ideas apparently fell on deaf ears, if they were ever entertained at all. Primus said, "*Fiddler* fell apart because Jerry wanted to start the script from zero, he wanted to start from nothing. He had this idea which was to start with an album of pictures and then go backwards, an album of people, let's say on West End Avenue, and they go back in time."

Producer Walter Mirisch reported to Richard Altman that Robbins had never been seriously considered as far as directing the movie. "I am aware of the immense contribution Jerry Robbins made to *Fiddler* on the stage," said Mirisch, "but would he have had any more to contribute to it as a film? I never went to him and would not have expected him to move toward me. I feel that Robbins is one of the most brilliant men I've ever dealt with in films, but on *West Side Story* he didn't seem able to pick up the tempo and style of picture-making. Things were just not getting done, and ultimately I had to split with him."

Typically, Robbins was not inclined to repeat himself. Two days after the Broadway opening of *Fiddler*, he met with Adolph Green, Betty Comden and Leonard Bernstein—the *On the Town* team—about a musical adaptation of Thornton Wilder's Pulitzer prize-winning play, *The Skin of Our Teeth*. The four friends had together first attended Elia Kazan's production of the play in

1942, with a cast that included Fredric March and Montgomery Clift. Wilder's satirical comedy relates the adventures of a mythical New Jersey family, the Antrobuses, and their survival (by the skin of their teeth) through every imaginable form of calamity, from pestilence and war to fire, flood, depressions and the Ice Age. Unfortunately, the new collaboration was almost as calamitous for Robbins and his cohorts.

Neither the material nor the personalities gelled and the experience was discouraging for all involved. Leland Hayward was producing the show with a $400,000 investment from the Columbia Broadcasting System, which planned to produce the album. Bernstein reminisced about the project in a poem that appeared in the *New York Times*, October 24, 1965. The composer had taken a sabbatical to work on the musical, and his recollection read in part:

And so a few of us got hold
Of the rights of Wilder's play The Skin of Our Teeth.
This is a play I've often thought was made
For singing; and for dance. It celebrates
The wonder of life, of human survival, told
In pity and terror and mad hilarity.
Six months we labored, June to bleak December.
And bleak was our reward when Christmas came,
To find ourselves uneasy with our work.
We gave it up, and went our several ways,
Still loving friends; but there was the pain
Of seeing six months work go down the drain.

The cancelation was announced to the press on January 5, 1965, and at that time Betty Comden insisted that there was "no estranged relationship," explaining that the collaborators were "having problems solving the adaptation, which had created production difficulties." But Bernstein told his friend David Diamond there had been a bitter dispute that he attributed to personalities. At the time, he called it "a dreadful experience. The wounds are still smarting." Still, the composer would eventually work with Robbins again.

Early in 1965, Robbins turned to Bernstein, Stephen Sondheim and Arthur Laurents—the *West Side Story* veterans. There were discussions between them to try to launch yet another project, but nothing materialized.

Undoubtedly, these failed efforts with "old friends" were a disillusioning blow to Robbins coming on the heels of his bittersweet triumph with *Fiddler*, confirming his decision to abandon Broadway. Yet he recovered some momentum later in the year by returning to Ballet Theatre (now American Ballet Theatre, or ABT), where Lucia Chase had finally agreed to produce *Les Noces*. This supremely elaborate staging of a Russian peasant wedding surely drew on Robbins' recent experience with *Fiddler on the Roof*, but he insisted, "It wasn't a spring-off of *Fiddler*. My conferences with Stravinsky predate all of that." At the time that Robbins undertook *Les Noces*, he had not yet seen Bronislava Nijinska's staging, and he later admitted, "When I saw Nijinska's, I was so deeply impressed and full of admiration for her version that I know if I had seen hers first, it would have been impossible to choreograph my own. I had to have it clean to myself to be able to do it, and if I had seen her version and her solution of things first, I would have had a hard time with my interpretations. In other words, it would have been hard not to have been influenced."

ABT's archivist, Charles Payne, described Robbins' return to the company after nearly a twenty-year absence. "For both parties it was a remarriage of convenience: Ballet Theatre was so eager to obtain a new work from Robbins that it agreed to his terms; on his part, Robbins was so anxious to have the ballet produced that he was prepared to create it on dancers not of his own choosing and to generously forgo a choreographic fee. He also proposed and agreed that his royalty payments should not exceed those accepted by Stravinsky for the music rights, however low they might be." With Stravinsky's specifications that four grand pianos, a singing chorus and four sets of tympani were to be placed onstage, this ballet was enormously expensive and would lose money even when playing to a full house. Payne recalled that Lucia Chase gave in to Robbins' demands that he should be "allotted four hours of rehearsal time on each working day and it was understood that if, at any point, even at the last moment before the premiere, either his creative inspiration flagged or rehearsals did not proceed well and according to schedule, the entire project would have to be canceled."

In an article that appeared in the *New York Times* before the ballet opened, Robbins wrote, "I am deeply grateful to Lucia Chase . . . for the comfort of her company out on a very high limb. I've told her over and over the tree is slippery and the height tremendous, but nothing will avail. 'Forward,' she cries. 'Danger?' yell I. 'Onward,' she prods. So here we go."

Robbins pointed out that Stravinsky described his *Les Noces* as "a dance cantata . . . using ritualistic elements and presenting them through actual wedding material of popular verse: a suite of typical wedding episodes." Robbins explained, "These are not necessarily happy rituals. In a Russian wedding there is as much lamentation, grieving and protestation as there is dancing and drinking. In the first half (the preparations) there is little joy: both bride and groom are constantly and emphatically reassured that it's all for the best while the parents traditionally grieve over losing their children, and the bride over leaving her home and losing her virginity. There are also passionate, almost pagan, invocations of Saints and the Virgin to bless and help the wedding. In the second half, after the offstage church ceremony, the rituals turn to earthy traditions. The drinking makes everyone bawdier, a married couple is selected to warm the bridal bed, and finally the marriage is allowed to be consummated while all sit outside the nuptial chamber."

Noting the "elegant–barbaric" complexities of Stravinsky's score, Robbins acknowledged the special burden placed upon the performers. He wrote, "The dancers must count continuously, unerringly and with unceasing concentration. Their energy in rehearsal has been exhausted as much by using their brains for computers as their muscles for dancing. For once the music starts, nothing can stop it. You push a button and this terrifying machine begins to scream, launches into lamentations and incessant chattering, shocking you with unexpected outbursts and hypnotic murmuring." Meanwhile, the singers create what Robbins called "a montage or Joycean stream, of Russian folk songs and poems, pieces of wedding conversations, toasts, taunts, prayers, ribald folk symbols and fertility images expressed in terms of animals and all nature."

Such was the breadth of vision Robbins brought into each rehearsal, and as usual, he blinded himself to distractions. Ballerina Erin Martin danced the role of the Bride and William Glassman was her Bridegroom. Martin recalled,

"One time when we were rehearsing *Les Noces*, Billy Glassman was dropped on his head. We were in some very weird rehearsal place, it was like an old theater that wasn't being used anymore, very musty. . . . Of course [the fall] brought the rehearsal to a halt." Glassman was unconscious. Martin said, "But in between the time the accident happened and the ambulance got there—because they did take him away, he had a concussion—Jerry didn't know what to do. So he got a few people on the edge of the stage and started rehearsing another little piece of the ballet. That was the way he kept control. It wasn't a maniacal thing, it wasn't that he thought of himself as a martinet or anything like that. I don't think he was. I think that's just the way he got things done." The next day, Robbins sent Glassman a helmet filled with flowers.

"I think all good artists have a vision," Martin continued. "All artists don't necessarily have to be consumed by a vision. I read a little piece in the paper about Sam Shepard. . . . He talks about himself as though he and his art are inseparable, and I'm sure it was that way with Jerry. It's not as if he didn't have another life, but the vision controlled him . . . and in the physical realization of that vision, he did whatever he had to do in order to make it happen. I think that's why there are all these stories about Version 1, Version 2, Version 3, A, B, C—I think that has a lot to do with that vision. The vision is there and sometimes it's not complete, and until it's complete you have to keep going after it."

Robbins was so nervous and uncertain of himself during rehearsals of *Les Noces* that he threatened on occasion to give up on the enterprise. But there was at least one moment of levity described by his rehearsal pianist, Gladys Celeste. "Jerry was coaching a boy. I can't remember who it was, and the rhythm was so difficult, and this boy couldn't get it. So I stood up and I showed him the step in front of Jerry. And I said, 'It's this: 1-2-3-4-5-6, 1-2-3-4-5.' And I demonstrated the step. And I said, 'I've got it, why can't you get it?' Jerry was openmouthed. He loved that."

Oliver Smith designed the scenery, and Patricia Zipprodt created the ballet's stylized peasant garb. Zipprodt recalled fierce arguments with Robbins over the shade of red for one of the Matchmaker's costumes. She managed to prevail upon him for a muted color tone so the minor character wouldn't steal focus from the Bride and Bridegroom during the crucial moments of the wedding festivities. Zipprodt lightheartedly summarized her long working relationship with Robbins as "years of fussing over the damn reds."

Leonard Bernstein conducted the premiere of *Les Noces* at the New York State Theater on March 30, 1965. The ballet was immediately acclaimed by the critics and became the hit that ABT desperately needed at the time. In the *New York Times,* Allen Hughs described the ballet as "an overwhelming fusion of animal energy, ritualistic ardor, and rhythmic attack." In *Dance Magazine,* Doris Hering wrote that the dancers "were drawn into a relentless sea of stamping, jumping, and somersaults. Sometimes there were brief allusions to national style in the use of squared arms or the digging of one heel into the ground and curving the feet outward. Always they seemed to be caught in something jubilant and ominous at the same time."

Robbins' accomplishment was in weaving once again classical, modern, jazz and ethnic social dances into a single idiomatic fabric, and in so doing creating not so much an evening's entertainment as a kind of emphatically elevated theatrical event. This was one wedding that was not meant to be forgotten. Critic Clive Barnes later called Robbins a "compassionate puppetmaster," because of the "life-asserting grace" with which he endowed his wedding couple at the moment of their sexual awakening. As in so many of Robbins' dances, a single moment or the briefest phrase of movement could offer such a revelatory key to the whole.

The choreographer indicated at the time that he wasn't completely satisfied with the results obtained through his first exploration of the material. Robbins wrote, "I have enjoyed doing it immensely, and look forward to the next time I attempt to scale that mountain, for although I have completed the ballet, I haven't finished with it. It is too deep and complex a work not to remain challenging. There may be other routes, and I'll want to try it again if the opportunity comes." The ballet was restaged for the Royal Swedish Ballet (1969, 1980, 1986), the Hamburgisches Staatsopher (1976, 1982), the Teatro alla Scala (1982), the Finnish National Ballet (1989) and the Norwegian National Ballet (1990). Robbins was still revising his choreography when he restaged *Les Noces* for the New York City Ballet just months before his death in 1998.

Late in 1965, Robbins committed himself to direct *The Office*, an offbeat comedy by Maria Irene Fornés. The Cuban-born, avant-garde playwright had recently scored Off-Broadway with *The Successful Life of 3* at the Open Theater. With plans to open *The Office* on Broadway at Henry Miller's Theater, Robbins was set to co-produce with Ivor David Balding and Joseph E. Levine, who invested $150,000 in the project. As director, Robbins was to receive $5,000 plus twenty-five percent of the profits and four percent of the weekly receipts ($40,000 at capacity). The cast of eight included Elaine May as a would-be secretary and Jack Weston as the office manager, Ruth White as the company owner, Doris Roberts as a secretary and Tony Lo Bianco as a salesman.

Lo Bianco recalled the difficult time he had winning an audition because of his earlier success playing poker with Robbins and other cast members during the production of *Oh Dad*. "I'm a good poker player, and so I used to win quite a bit, and quite often. Later on, Jerry's casting *The Office*, and Ivor David Balding is the producer. And I heard about this play and no one called me about this role. So . . . I call Ivor and I say 'I understand there's a terrific role up there for this swashbuckling sort of Italian gentleman that I should be doing.' He said, 'Well, okay, I'll get back to you.' So he calls me back and says, 'Gee, I don't think so.' I said, 'Okay.' And they still haven't cast this part. And I call him back again and I said, 'What the hell do you mean, "I don't think so?" Let me come up and see him [Jerry].' And he said, 'Jerry's a little funny. . . .' I said, 'What do you mean . . . funny about what? I just worked with him on [*Oh Dad*].' He said, 'Well, you know, when you guys played poker, he's a little mad because you won all the time.' I said, 'What the hell does that have to do with my acting or this part! I wasn't cheating, I just won.' So finally, they said, 'Okay.'"

Work on the play was postponed when Robbins was hospitalized for a slipped disc. After several months of convalescence, he started rehearsals on March 17, 1966, at the Ballet Theater School on West Fifty-seventh Street, where designer Ed Wittstein constructed a duplicate of the stage set. The office scenery of the fictional company, Hinch Inc., was entirely realistic, down to the water cooler, steno pads, and official Hinch letterhead. Robbins said at the time, "We were all staggered when we first started. . . . It was like a foreign land. But practically everything is used. If they [the actors] don't know what they're doing, and believe in it, it's not going to work."

Tony Lo Bianco recollected, "The stage at a $75,000 cost then was on hydraulic lifts, so that each scene, the stage would start to tilt up from the back towards the audience. And the audience was actually getting sick, like they were on a boat, they were getting nauseous from it. We would do this thing and nobody knew quite what the hell was going on, and I would come on and do my [Italian] bravado and so on. And he [Jerry] never talked to me, never gave me any notes, never gave me anything more. I would jump on tables, I did every goddamned thing I wanted to do, swirled coats on my entrance, very flamboyant. He just sat there and laughed and enjoyed it. He would have things shooting out of the floor, like cardboard mechanics of Elaine May. He had all this marvelous stuff going on. But Elaine May, we had to shove her out, literally push her out to take her curtain calls. She was petrified, she didn't want to go out. I mean, the booing was so loud it moved the asbestos curtain. I never heard such booing in my life. And she would say, 'No, I'm not going out there!'"

One of the other actors, Bernie Passeltine, recalled, "The play basically took place in an office, and strange things kept happening to the office manager, Jack Weston. As the play went on, stranger and stranger things happened. He tried to get rid of his wife, who you never see, and he has this thing going on with the secretary, who's Elaine May. It's a very fey kind of piece. Originally what they wanted to do was have the whole set tilt as the play got crazier and crazier. And then when we were in previews Jerry was frightened to death at the whole set tilting so that it looked like it was going to go into the first row. So they cut it, and that cost a fortune, of course."

Robbins again had some difficulty getting his vision across to the actors. Passeltine, who later worked for Robbins in a revival of *West Side Story*, said, "It [*The Office*] was a tense set . . . it was really like everybody was walking around like on eggshells. That's my favorite quote—the eggshell production. It was strange, it was tense, and it's very hard to do a fantasy-comedy when everybody is tense. There wasn't any screaming and yelling, except at this poor guy who was the stage manager, who was taking a lot of pills, as I recall. But it was my first Broadway show, and I had a small part. But I have fond memories of Jerry because I was one of the readers—Peg Murray and I were the readers—and we kept reading and reading with actors for months and months. I read with every actress in New York, I think. Jerry had offered it to Zero Mostel, that's who he wanted to do it, and that's why he ended up with Jack Weston, because he wanted that physical type. Gene Wilder came in to read for it and was absolutely stunning. He had done it at the Actors Studio as a workshop or reading. He was charming and he would have been perfect, but he didn't look like Zero—he wasn't fat." Passeltine continued, "With Elaine May doing the role, the focus of the piece seemed to change, and she was pretty charming and funny, although she didn't quite get past the first few rows. She had never really done that kind of thing before."

Bill Daniels joined the cast as a replacement. Of *The Office*, Daniels said simply, "It didn't work; it didn't work for Jerry, anyway." After two weeks of previews, Robbins decided to close the show. "Jerry certainly didn't need the money and he just didn't care," said Passeltine. "I remember our dresser saying, 'I don't understand, we're selling out every night!' We were, but the truth was the play, I think, would have failed . . . the way it was being done and the way it was written. I think it was probably Jerry's fault. I don't think the script was solved, really. I was amazed at how Jerry pulled it apart in a very realistic way, which was quite wonderful early on, but then he never really put it back together again. You can't do a comedy-fantasy that way. I don't care who you are, you have to put it back together, and he never did it. I think part of that was maybe because he never thought that he was going to get to the end of it. . . . We were doing it, and he was right about, say, twenty pages of the play, because at first the audience loved it. Then at the end they didn't know what was going on. I remember at the first preview people were booing—not many, a few. I remember standing next to Elaine at the curtain call and a tear rolling down her cheek. And I thought, 'Boy, this is the beginning of my career.'"

Robbins' assistant on the show was Sheldon Harnick's brother, Jay. Passeltine recalled, "We were still in previews, and in the afternoon we were rehearsing a new scene which I wasn't in. And Jay was out front rehearsing the scene, and all of a sudden Jerry came backstage, pulled up a chair, sat with the bunch of us, and started shmoozing and telling us charming and wonderful stories about the old days when he was a dancer and all this stuff. It was really fun. And then we went to dinner, and we came back, and the notice was up, and we never saw Jerry again. That was it, forget about it. He never came back."

For Robbins, admission of defeat involved an unavoidable anguish when breaking the news to his cast that he was cutting his losses. Lo Bianco recounted his parting with Robbins. "When we closed, Jerry came up to our dressing rooms, each of us, to tell us that we were closing. And he came in his shy way, and he said to me, 'We are closing, and if I had done my job like you did yours, we'd still be running.' This was Jerry Robbins, and for him, that's something else to be said."

Unable to solve the play's ending to his satisfaction and anticipating at best a cool response from the critics, Robbins simply acted on the same instincts that possessed him when he closed his first solo directorial effort, *That's the Ticket*, out of town almost twenty years before. "He did the right thing by closing it," said Lo Bianco. "It was a strange play. I still don't know what the hell it's about, and I don't think anybody does. It was a weird off-the-wall piece. But it was a marvelous experience."

Robbins' rising star over the previous two decades as a Broadway player coincided with the emergence of his attorney, Floria Lasky, as a power within her field, an accomplishment all the more impressive given the male domination of her profession at the time. Lasky, who also represented Elia Kazan, was an aggressive, savvy women who dressed with a touch of show-biz flamboyance and was dominated by Robbins throughout their association. One of her clients, producer Michael Abbott, recalled, "She was only out for Jerry Robbins. They had an extraordinary relationship. I'd be in important meetings with her about a play I was doing or a television show and she would always leave word, 'We don't want to be disturbed except for Mr. Robbins.'" Abbott added, "She became probably the most powerful theatrical lawyer we have in the city. For her clients she's marvelous. She will *kill* for you." Lasky surely contributed to Robbins' Machiavellian command of his legal and financial interests within the commercial domain of the theater. Like his secretary, Edith Weissman, who was by now an indispensable administrative assistant, his lawyer played a constant and well-defined supportive role in his life.

With Lasky and Weissman in his corner, Robbins explored several new projects at the beginning of 1966. Laurence Olivier invited him to direct *The Bacchae* by Euripides at England's National Theatre, an ambitious project that illness later prevented Robbins from undertaking. There were offers in America to direct two more shows: *Come Back! Go Away! I Love You!* with a score from Sheldon Harnick and Jerry Bock that Robbins pursued then bypassed; and an adaptation of Eugene Ionesco's *Exit the King*. Robbins acquired the rights to the Ionesco script and retitled it *Ceremonies*. He said of the play, "It's marvelous theater . . . it celebrates the act of living." But he eventually gave up on the project, after trying unsuccessfully to engage Zero Mostel for the lead role of the doomed king. Mostel was booked elsewhere at the time.

Robbins' home and office were now located at 117 East Eighty-first Street, a four-story townhouse off Park Avenue that he acquired in the fall of 1965. Some years later, he bragged to actor-comedian Alan King that he bought the place for a song; after his death, it sold for approximately three million dollars. Robbins had a dance studio and photographic darkroom constructed in his new home, and his neighbor, globe-trotting socialite Mica Ertegün, later helped him decorate. Mrs. Ertegün and her husband, Ahmet, the Atlantic Records executive, befriended Robbins over the years. Before he moved in, the townhouse underwent months of renovations under Robbins' close supervision—a project that he directed like one of his Broadway shows. While construction was under way during 1966, he maintained a temporary residence two blocks away at the Stanhope Hotel on Fifth Avenue and Eighty-first Street.

Later that year, Robbins was invited to Truman Capote's famously chic Black-and-White Ball, an indication of Robbins' fashionable social coinage at the age of forty-eight. He was much sought after as a prestigious trophy in the Upper East Side salon scene. Although he had recently become romantically involved with aspiring writer Christine Conrad, he attended Capote's ball with Lady Slim Keith, who was a friend of Capote's and deemed a most desirable companion for such a high-profile evening on the town. Photographs were later published of Robbins dancing that night with Slim's longtime friend, Lauren Bacall. Robbins and Bacall were lured onto the dance floor of the Plaza's ballroom when Peter Duchin's band offered the Irving Berlin number "Top Hat." In George Plimpton's oral biography, *Truman Capote*, historian Arthur Schlesinger, Jr., recalled, "I saw Betty Bacall dancing out on the floor. I've known her for years. So I went and started to cut in. She looked at me with considerable scorn and said, 'Don't you see who I'm dancing with?' And I looked, and it turned out to be Jerome Robbins, who I had never met. So I retired crestfallen."

During this period, while continuing to field theatrical offers and explore options, Robbins entertained renewed ambitions to direct his own company, a performance troupe that would be comprised of multitalented dancers, actors and singers. Not long after *Fiddler* first opened, he told the press that he envisioned an experimental theater that might be established outside the commercial confines of Broadway. "No one is going to hand it to me," said Robbins. "Perhaps at some point my daily work will naturally turn into a theater like the one I want. Ballets: USA was a step toward it."

His wish was soon fulfilled, thanks to Roger Stevens, who was one of the original producers of *West Side Story* and was now chairing the National Endowment of the Arts. Shortly after *The Office* closed in the spring of 1966, Robbins received a $300,000 NEA grant for a project he called the American Theater Laboratory. After extensive auditions, Robbins recruited ten performers. The original group included Erin Martin, James Moore, James Dybas, Julia Migenes, Cathryn ("Skipper") Damon, Cliff Gorman, James Mitchell, Gerome Ragni, Leonard Frey and Barry Primus. Primus and later Grover Dale acted as Robbins' assistants. Tom Stone served as stage manager. Robbins shielded the group from the press, and consequently there was an air of secrecy about the work (although members were not sworn to secrecy, as was sometimes reported). In accepting the grant, Robbins stipulated that he was not obligated to mount a production. "His one condition," said James Moore, "was that he did not have to produce anything."

Over the course of two years, the Theater Lab moved from the Ballet Theatre School on West Fifty-seventh Street to Bohemian Hall (formerly Stage 73 on East Seventy-third Street) and finally to what is now the Dance

Theatre Workshop at 219 West Nineteenth Street. Future avant-garde director Robert Wilson was studying architecture at the time and contributed designs, and Tom Stone constructed the Lab's first work space. "I fixed it up by
myself with literally almost no money," said Stone. "I made folding flats and
things that he [Jerry] could do anything he wanted with. I collected all kinds
of props and hung drapes. It was a torturous time for him and an exciting time
because he was dealing with one of his great inadequacies, which was communicating what he wanted to other people, particularly performers. He was
digging, digging, digging, trying to find the key that would show him what he
was going to do with the opportunity, what he was going to do with all these
theatrical techniques." Stone recalled one of the theater exercises Robbins conducted. "We'd do things like play with luminescent paint and big balls. I fixed
up a whole room with black velour and black light, and then I would switch it
on and off and they'd paint each other and paint the ball and bounce the ball
around and try and feel each other in the dark. And then Jerry made me do it.
It was one of the most embarrassing moments of my life."

Erin Martin characterized the Theater Lab, with Robbins as its sole creative fountainhead, in the context of the times, saying, "The two years that we
spent in the lab were a quest for him. It was truly experimental and it was very
much of its time because simultaneously there was Jerzy Grotowski, *Towards a
Poor Theater*, there was The Open Theater, The Living Theater, [Richard] Shechner, [Joseph] Chaikin. People like that were all working, however in a more
egalitarian situation, towards a kind of hybrid form. I know that Jerry had said
that he wanted to see if he could approach theater the way he approached ballet, which was more viscerally. But [his approach] was more personal and specific as the auteur, and that's not what most experimental theater was like. I'm
sure Grotowski was a taskmaster, and probably Shechner and Chaikin. But
[Judith] Malina's and [Julian] Beck's Living Theater . . . was a more egalitarian
kind of situation. And yet we managed to have some of that in the Theater
Lab, and I think it was a learning experience for everybody. The only problem
was that actors are not only used to having more latitude, but they need it.
They need to ask more questions. I remember in the Lab there were times
when Jerry got very squeezed, very uptight about what exactly was coming out,

whether it was good enough. And of course because he didn't have a complete vision, it was very difficult for him."

Robbins later explained, "I wanted to see . . . if I could make theater pieces the way I make ballets. I mean, I'd bring some actors and singers and dancers together and see what would happen. Without time pressures, without *having* to produce; if something comes up, let it develop. What I wanted from the American Theatre Laboratory was the kind of freedom you have in the ballet studio while you're creating. Unknown things come out of you. I have maybe some vague idea of the territory I hope a ballet will land in, but the details of that territory I never know. I really don't."

Without a set goal as far as production, the Lab was a departure into uncharted territory both for its director and for the performers. James Mitchell recalled, "We didn't work on pieces. It was all exercises that Jerry would invent. A lot of it came from Noh Theater. He was interested in masks, he was interested in transferring the actors' intent into a mask so it went from your face, and the audience looked at the face. That's very simplified, but he was interested in that. He just invented reams and reams and reams of exercises." Mitchell continued, "He was very, very careful about expenditure and having a record of the expenditure. Every time the door was locked, the camera was on. Everything was taped, but everything—the breaks, everything. The camera never stopped. There was somebody taking notes, handwritten notes, of exactly what happened. Can I go to the bathroom? It was noted. Everything was noted. Nothing, nothing, nothing was left unrecorded, so that if he was ever called to account—'What did you do with the money?'—he could say, 'Do you want to watch six months of tape?'"

Lab sessions usually ran from ten a.m. until six p.m, often six days a week. "I cannot tell you what a wonderful two years it was," said Barry Primus. "We arrived every morning and we had a dance class, and it was usually Anna Sokolow who taught. Sometimes Jerry taught us. And Jerry would teach me, by the way, during lunch hour sometimes. He was terrifically generous and wonderful that way. . . . He was a great teacher. Once I was lying on the floor relaxing, and Jerry marched into the room, looked around the room, and said, 'Roll over.' And he said, 'Lift your arm, lift your arm. Slowly get up from the floor, slowly get up from the floor. Walk to the window, now walk around the window.' And I did it for a while, everything he was telling me. Then he turned to me and he said, 'You just did the first whole beat of *Afternoon of a Faun.*' It was wonderful—just a friendly way of saying good morning."

Primus also recalled, "I remember one afternoon when Jerry had the company find for themselves an everyday object that would help explain to an archeologist a thousand years from now who we were and how we lived. One by one, carrying our imaginary objects, we entered the space and left our gifts, creating a memorial to our era. This always seemed to me the essence of Jerry Robbins' work: To find a bridge that, like a blessing, can bring the ordinary up to the level of the sacred and sublime."

According to Erin Martin, in this regard, Robbins expressed his admiration for Anna Sokolow's artistry on one occasion, saying simply, "She's the real thing." Other teachers invited to the Lab included Jay Harnick, who coached scenes from Shakespeare's *Macbeth* and *Hamlet*; and Marion Rich, who gave voice lessons. Gerome Ragni utilized his time with the group to write early drafts of the rock musical, *Hair,* which was produced for Joseph Papp's New York Shakespeare Festival in 1967 and opened on Broadway the following year. James Dybas said of Ragni, "I used to see him writing on pieces of paper. I think he wanted Jerry Robbins to think he was participating, but what he was really writing down was *Hair.* I said, 'What are you doing?' He said, 'I'm writing a play.' I said, 'Oh, come on, Raggles.' He said, 'You'll be great in this play,' and he told me what he was calling it—*Hair*—and I howled." Ragni later tried unsuccessfully to interest Robbins in directing the show. Gerald Freedman subsequently took over, and *Hair* became the fourth longest-running musical of the sixties, an early indication of how Broadway was changing in terms of music and spectacle in this Age of Aquarius. Although he played his part in bringing about such changes of fashion and aesthetic, they were not altogether welcomed by Robbins, who represented another age and sensibility.

Robbins recruited Robert Wilson into the Lab to offer a series of specialized therapeutic exercises. Dybas remembered, "Jerry brought Bob in to do a Happening—we had a Happening that Bob did. We put black curtains up and we had Saran wrap and Day-Glo paint and portable radios, and Lenny Bernstein and several others—there was an invited audience—were there watching all of this going on. The ten of us just giggled and laughed because we didn't know what was going on. We went along with it. It was about experimental theater." Wilson cast Robbins, with his bald head, chiseled face and bristly beard, as Sigmund Freud in a 1969 production at the Brooklyn Academy of Music and later collaborated with minimalist composer Philip Glass on *Einstein on the Beach*. Erin Martin said, "Bob Wilson, when he was first in New York studying architecture, he had like a salon, a coterie of people including Jerry and Stephen Sondheim . . . that somehow came into his aura and they all sat around and helped Bob do his architectural models."

Wilson recalled, "I first met Jerry because he had heard of some work that I was doing with children in Brooklyn at that time in order to support myself in getting through school. I had worked with brain-damaged children while I was at Pratt Institute. And so he came out and he saw some of the work I was doing, and then we talked. And a year later or so, we met again and he told me about this Lab that he had going. He was curious about the way I was working. At that time, I had no idea that I would ever work in the theater and wasn't particularly interested in theater. . . . I was studying architecture, but what I was doing was a sort of crossover between architecture and performance, design, and it was a time in the sixties where you had this crossover. Someone like [Robert] Rauschenberg would paint a goat and put it in the middle of the room, so it was painting, or was it a painting or was it a sculpture, sort of coming off the wall and becoming three-dimensional? And some of the work that I was doing with children was free work, and I guess really related to theater.

"I think one of the things he [Jerry] was interested in was how you view something in 360 degrees instead of two dimensions. One of the early conversations I can remember having with him was about this. What he had been doing was in a proscenium arch, so that it had a two-dimensionality to it and one side was always hidden. And I was becoming aware of Merce Cunningham and John Cage, and Merce was performing in gymnasiums so the dancer was orienting in 360 degrees. So this was something that interested Jerry, and he was curious in the work I was doing how the performer would orient himself in a completely different way than in a proscenium theater."

Wilson continued, "The work I was doing was movement-based. At that time, I was working with a woman who had started working with hyperactive brain-damaged children in a movement therapy—I hate the word *therapy*, but that's what it was. And she had a belief that if one doesn't fully develop in the primary stages of physical activity then their mental readiness to learn is hindered. . . . Often they're diagnosed as retarded, but it's maybe just simply a lack of physical activity. Children are put in playpens or live in cramped quarters. . . . In my work, I was going back and exercising with children at the primary stages of physical activity—creeping and crawling, look to your left side, look to your right side, etc. What happened was amazing. Their vocabulary would increase. Jerry asked me to come in and do a workshop with the actors similar to what I was doing with the children. . . . That's how it started."

Through his theatrical foundation, Robbins provided generous financial support for Wilson's early productions and public support for his work. Looking back, Wilson said, "I think the thing that fascinated me about Jerry's work, and still does—I think for me one of his major contributions is that Jerry created a *visual book* of theater. For me one of the dilemmas of Western theater is that we haven't really adequately developed a visual book for theater, that if one wants to study as a designer, you have to go to Yale, or you go to Northwestern—wherever you go—you study theater decoration. Myself, I hate decoration. It's a waste of time. But one should study architecture. . . . In our Western theaters for the most part, what you see is illustrating or decorating what you hear; it's sort of a text. I'm much more interested in Eastern theater. If you look at the Balinese or you look at the Indonesian, or if you look at the theater of India, if you look at the classical theater of Japan, the classical theater of China, African theater, theater of Latin America, in fact the world as a whole . . . first of all, it's a non-realistic theater, it's not a naturalistic theater.

"But more to the point, it has a visual book that is learned, studied, it's part of the tradition, it's passed on, and it's as important as the audio book. So if you're a Noh dancer or performer, you learn how to stand and how to walk, as well as speak an interpretive text. So that your training is in all of the arts. So the visual book—the meaning of gesture or movement or space design or whatever—quite often is as important as what you hear. For me, that was what was very important in what Jerry did, his contribution. If you look at his work, if you look at *West Side Story*, he was a choreographer writing as an author of a work. So the visual book, dance, or whatever was the book."

Robbins was passionate about incorporating such ideas in the Lab. Specialists in Japanese Kabuki and Noh drama introduced the group to traditional tea ceremonies and stylized, masked rituals. The mask work was incorporated by Robbins into rehearsals of Bertolt Brecht's *The Measures Taken*, using Eric Bentley's translation and music from Hans Eisler. A production of the play performed by the entire ensemble was planned for Spoleto in 1967, but the project fell through at the last minute. At least part of Robbins' decision to scuttle the Brecht play derived from his disputes with Eric Bentley over the language. "We were disagreeing vigorously and he's being abusive as usual," said Bentley, "and so he dropped it. . . . I kept a corrected version of *Measures Taken* which has his handwriting on it. Some of his notes are quite interesting and others just show his desire to intrude and have his way. He once told me, standing in the entrance of his apartment on the East Side, that when he directs a show he has to get to the point where it seemed to be coming from his lips and not from Mr. Brecht's or mine. No other directors go to that degree of interference with the writer. But it was his obsessive need to feel on top of the whole thing, the way he was in pure dance."

Bentley described *The Measures Taken* as Brecht's "most outrageous, blatant piece of Stalinist propaganda," and asked, "Why was he [Robbins] so fascinated with that?" The appeal for Robbins was probably more personal and theatrical than political, as he had been so deeply frustrated by his effort with Brecht's *Mother Courage.*

Another ongoing project at the Lab was based on the John F. Kennedy assassination. This experiment started with theater exercises, and later a script that Robbins optioned from Tom Stone for $500, eventually appropriating the idea and passing it on to another playwright. Stone said, "He [Jerry] took the Warren [Commission] Report and he started doing improvisations. . . . I wrote a script, I was in such despair over his despair. He read it and he said, 'Look, I'll option the play, you can help break in a new stage manager for me, and we'll work on the play at the same time.' That was during the summer when we made the move down to West Nineteenth Street. . . . And he couldn't move it. He couldn't make the script go anywhere. We went to Joe Papp, and Joe Papp came over. A lot of people came over to see this very fascinating idea that Jerry was working on, because they had heard about it. But nothing ever got off the ground. I was feeling very dispirited about it. We had a long talk. . . . And then he brought in a more established playwright, John Guare [who had done *House of Blue Leaves*]. . . . My impression was that suddenly I had evaporated as the playwright and it was Jerry's. And he was moving it along and he was going with other playwrights."

Of this project, Grover Dale recalled, "We had learned Japanese Noh techniques and we started to do the Kennedy assassination in that style. It was electrifying. . . . It's just a crime that no one got to see it. Leonard Frey played Jackie Kennedy. And he [Jerry] wouldn't allow anybody to see it." James Dybas said, "I always thought Jerry wanted to solve the Kennedy Assassination. We were working on Lee Harvey Oswald's diary, and we all played all of those characters who were mysteriously murdered, à la Jack Ruby and Dorothy Kilgallen. Men would play women, women would play men—we would just mix everything up. We were instruments. He used all of us that way. Then he would constantly move on to something else."

With regard to the polarities of Robbins' personality, Dybas said, "It was like having an alcoholic parent. You never knew which one he was going to be today. Jerry could be cruel, but it was his way to get out of you what he knew you needed. He knew how to manipulate and control. But he loved to see things coming out of you, unexpected and wonderful things. Ultimately it served everybody very well—Jerry, all of us benefited by the association, and it truly was a family—everybody cared about each other in that group. If somebody was having a bad time or if Jerry was giving somebody a rough time, you can bet your bippy that somebody was around with that person at lunch or someplace else to console the person."

Robbins often socialized with members of the group. "Lots of times in the afternoon, Jerry would hang out with us down below and listen to the Supremes," said Barry Primus. "There was a bar below and Jerry loved to sit in a bar with Erin and me . . . and Gerry Ragni. We would always dance to the

Supremes and Jerry would watch us. And then occasionally he would get up and he would do it. That was our afternoon. Then we would go back upstairs to the Lab."

On one occasion, Robbins' personal explorations during this period led him into some peril. Since Grover Dale's early days with *West Side Story*, he had become a protégé and trusted friend to Robbins. "He had a powerful effect on my life," said Dale. "He was there for me plenty of times, but I was there for him when he took a hallucinogenic on the beach and had a terrible experience. . . . There was . . . myself and Jerry [and one other from the Lab]. He had never done a hallucinogenic. I had, but I decided I'm not going to do it, I'm just going to be there—and I'm so glad I didn't so I could help him through that. It was remarkable when the journey started . . . and then as the thing really took over on him, I was really scared for him, but he weathered it. It was LSD. I've never seen anybody in that amount of anguish."

This misadventure took place on the beach at Watermill on Long Island. Dale suggested that Robbins later used the experience in his work, incorporating images like the long stalks and fronds of dune grass into his 1972 ballet, *Watermill.* The third member of the beach party confirmed Robbins' LSD episode, saying only, "It was a bad trip for him." The trauma occurred when Robbins was almost fifty years old and discouraged him from further experimentation with drugs.

Robbins disbanded the Theater Lab in the spring of 1968, without having mounted any shows. Barry Primus recalled, "I think we became withdrawn and slightly frightened after two years of working and we hadn't shown anything." Primus suggested the process of pure exploration without a goal ultimately compelled Robbins to end the project. "That's what did him in—he might even have said that. Every time he found a way to do something, particularly with the Kennedy thing, we then undid it and went another way. He was haunted by the fact that yet there was another way. . . . I think what happened is he had to get back to really hitting a time period and a limit after these two years because it indulged a part of him that was already scary." Primus added, "It was very painful for him, the end of that company. I came in one day and Jerry was very upset. As a matter of fact, an actor had said he didn't want to work anymore, that we were always changing things, and people didn't understand it. . . . and he [Jerry] cried. He was very, very vulnerable. He felt lost."

Playwright John Guare related his brief involvement with Robbins and the Theater Lab to Sondheim's biographer Meryle Secrest. Of the Kennedy assassination piece, Guare recalled that the work was based on improvised fantasies. "Wonderful, but they were mainly dance," said Guare. "I didn't see how they needed me."

Robbins next tried to adapt Bertolt Brecht's *The Exception and the Rule.* Having been foiled by Brecht twice (*Mother Courage* and *The Measures Taken*), Robbins was desperate to succeed on his third try at adaptation, with John Guare writing the book (rather than Bentley), and with Bernstein and Sondheim composing the score.

At one point, Guare asked Sondheim, "Why haven't you all worked together since *West Side Story*?" Sondheim told him, "You'll see." The group labored for eight months. Guare said, "It was supposed to deal with the idea that in 1968 having 'good intentions' was not enough, and that it was presumptuous and hilarious to expect that *showing* man's inhumanity to man would change anything in the world. I guess we still had illusions. . . . And it was odd, because when we were in the middle of writing it, Bobby Kennedy was killed." At one point, Robbins locked Guare in a room of his Sneden's Landing house and told the writer that he wasn't to come out until he finished the script, instructing Guare to slide his pages under the door as he completed them.

Retitled *A Pray by Blecht, th*e show was budgeted at $600,000 and scheduled to open at the Broadhurst on February 18, 1969, with Stuart Ostrow producing. In his memoir, *A Producer's Broadway Journey,* Ostrow wrote that Brecht's play reflected his "preoccupation with the struggle of the masses. The story was about a merchant and a coolie and how the merchant exploited the lower classes. It was Jerry's and Leonard Bernstein's notion to juxtapose the musical's theme with black and white race relations. I brought in Jerry Leiber to write the lyrics, John Guare to write the book, and Zero Mostel to play the merchant. (Stephen Sondheim was momentarily persuaded to join the project after hearing Guare's idea of turning the musical into a live-on-the-air broadcast.) Possibly due to the 'radical chic' syndrome, as Tom Wolfe labeled it, or the fact that five white middle-class New Yorkers knew little about the suffering of the black man in the sixties, the project bogged down. . . . *A Pray by Blecht* suffered from an excess of self-righteousness and talent."

Playwright Arthur Laurents was briefly consulted and criticized the play as being anti-Semitic. Robbins insisted that it could be fixed with rewriting. But Sondeim remembered that he and Robbins soon gave up on the project: ". . . it seemed clear to us that the show wasn't going to work, but Lenny was insistently determined on going ahead with it." Robbins' withdrawal took place abruptly in the middle of an audition. Guare recalled, "Robbins said, 'Excuse me a moment,' and he left the theatre. Minutes went by and he did not come back. So I went backstage to see what was happening. The doorman told me, 'Oh, he got into a limousine. He was going to Kennedy Airport.' I had a feeling of horror and relief. Lenny burst into tears and said, 'It's over.'"

Robbins headed for Europe. Eighteen years later, he and Bernstein would try to revive the project in a Lincoln Center workshop production with Zero Mostel's son, Josh. In the meantime, Robbins' quest for a theater in which to realize his sacred vision appeared to have been thwarted. A movie based on the life of Nijinsky (later produced by Harry Saltzman) fell through for Robbins; and likewise a production of George Tabori's disturbing concentration camp drama, *The Cannibals*, which had been planned for the American Place Theatre, was shelved. Barry Primus was involved with the latter project and recalled, "Jerry struggled with it. He was fascinated with it. . . . He was again trying to use that work we had done [in the Lab]. How would he do something that pared down and memorialized that period [of the Holocaust]? He went to Sweden, and he sent me a telegram saying, 'I'm getting off it, I can't do it, it's too much.'"

With the decade drawing to a close, Robbins discussed the state of the American commercial theater with the *New York Times*, saying, "I don't like the whole operation as much as I used to—the tremendous pressures on one's work which stands less and less chance of coming to any sort of fruition. Things are getting tighter and tighter. Broadway is becoming more and more formalistic so that the chance of fulfillment is absolutely freakish. . . . Even off-off Broadway you see the big dollar sign of economy—will it work?" Robbins pointed to the need for a subsidized theater, as was the case at least to some extent with ballet, opera and orchestras. He concluded, "What we have now—and I think a spade should be called a spade—is show biz, not art."

Under such adverse commercial and artistic circumstances, Robbins set out to do what he did best: he would reinvent himself once again, returning like a prodigal to the ballet studio and the one theater that offered him a permanent home.

EIGHT

Balanchine's Shadow

For Jerry Robbins at fifty, the pursuit of perfection was as torturous as ever and as inescapable as his past. While the recurrent agonies inherent in his creative process frequently overshadowed the joys, he nevertheless maintained a balance in his personal life that enabled him to work. By the end of the sixties, Robbins was living in a highly compartmentalized social world that included several circles of intimate friends who served as a kind of emotional support system and surrogate family. Robbins had his Manhattan townhouse and getaway rental retreats in Sneden's Landing and Watermill, where he established a number of friendships outside of the theater. These alliances flourished through the years and in many ways sustained him in the daily struggles of life and art.

One of Robbins' early neighbors in Sneden's Landing was Dr. Daniel Stern, a psychiatrist of some renown for his studies of the mother-child relationship. He and his family offered Robbins a welcome refuge from the combat zone of his professional life. Grover Dale remembered festive spaghetti dinners that he attended with Robbins at Dr. Stern's upstate home, where the atmosphere was enlivened by the children amusing Jerry by splattering the walls of the kitchen with pasta and tomato sauce. Dale suggested, "Jerry loved the Sterns. That was the family Jerry had always wanted as his own. I saw the longing in his eyes. Over cups of chamomile tea, I listened to the painful memories of his childhood."

Dr. Stern contributed the title for Robbins' next ballet, *Dances at a Gathering* (which was dedicated to the memory of lighting designer Jean Rosenthal). At the time that Robbins returned to City Ballet to rehearse in 1969, he was passionately involved in a new affair, with a woman named Christine Conrad, whom he had met several years before at a dinner party in Watermill to which she had been taken by friends. Non-Jewish, with Polish ancestry, Conrad was then half his age and employed by producer Kermit Bloomgarden. She later served as New York City Film Commissioner in Mayor Lindsay's administration and became a literary editor, author and screenwriter (her credits include the 1994 Arnold Schwarzenegger/Danny DeVito movie *Junior*). Conrad remembered that Robbins' eyes and demeanor lit up with obvious interest when he first met her. There was an immediate attraction and rapport between the two, and a whirlwind, globe-trotting romance ensued. One year, they traveled together to Europe, visiting Sweden, Finland and the Soviet Union, where Robbins had been invited to judge a Moscow ballet competition.

Robbins' FBI files indicate that his trip abroad was monitored by Hoover's agency and by the CIA. Given the Cold War climate, the Russians, too, were undoubtedly aware of his presence. In Leningrad, Robbins and Conrad sensed that they were being watched, and encountered resistance from the Soviet bureaucracy when they tried to visit the Vaganova Choreographic Institute, the ballet school associated with the Kirov Theatre (originally called the Maryinsky). "So it was quite frustrating to be there," said Conrad, "although we did go to the Hermitage, and we saw a wonderful collection of Impressionist paintings then stacked randomly in the basement. We went to the Summer Palace and I remember we laughed over Catherine the Great's bed. It was quite spectacular."

For Robbins, Leningrad's fabled ballet school was a site of enormous historical interest. This was where generations of legendary Russian ballet stars had been trained, including Nijinsky, Pavlova and later Nureyev, who defected in 1961. Balanchine's roots also traced back to the Maryinsky and the nineteenth-century classical repertory of choreographer Marius Petipa, who created such masterpieces as *Swan Lake* and *The Sleeping Beauty.* The school was named in honor of Agrippina Vaganova, the former Maryinsky soloist and venerated teacher who codified the classical ballet lexicon with her comprehensive system of training. Of course, Robbins was intent on visiting the institute where this Russian dance tradition was preserved. Yet when he met with bureaucratic stonewalling, he avoided confrontation with the authorities and typically, according to Conrad, would not use his celebrity status to gain advantage. "Jerry was too embarrassed to raise a fuss," said Conrad. "He was never someone who would use his name to get into a restaurant. He would never think like that. He would die first." Conrad finally managed to prevail upon the Russian officials on his behalf to allow a visit to the school. Afterward, Robbins was so incensed at the way he had been treated that he withdrew as a judge from the Moscow competition and abruptly left the country.

Conrad remembered that she and Robbins had a more gratifying adventure when they later traveled to Israel where his silent ballet, *Moves,* was to be performed by the Bathsheva Dance Company. "We were both awestruck by the old city of Jerusalem," said Conrad. "I still have things that we bought there— a Bedouin dress and some jewelry and embroidered pillows." Conrad contrasted Robbins' attitude toward Israel with Leonard Bernstein's: "Bernstein had a much more open and direct connection with Israel, based on his many concerts there. Jerry didn't have that direct identification. Later in life he took more of an interest in his Jewishness, but he remained secular, I would say."

Soon after returning from Israel to New York, Conrad moved into Robbins' townhouse, a domestic arrangement that was to last about a year. Kitty Hawks recalled Slim Keith's reaction to this latest Robbins romance, saying, "I remember the way my mother would refer to Chris Conrad. There was always a little tension because I think Mom could be very possessive and jealous, and I don't think she liked it if she didn't think she was the most important one, because I think she probably was at a certain point."

Robbins' longtime pianist friends, Arthur Gold and Robert Fizdale, voiced skepticism concerning the prospects of his affair to Howard Talbott, a French translator and balletomane who met Robbins through Gold and Fizdale in the late sixties. Talbott said, "I have the feeling that Jerry was very interested in emerging from just homosexual relationships and getting hooked up with a woman permanently. Once he brought this very good-looking, young woman to Gold and Fizdale's house when I was there. . . . After she and Jerry left, they [Gold and Fizdale] said, 'Oh well, you see, Jerry's *trying.*'"

Robbins was again considering marriage. "He had given me jewelry and other gifts; and we talked about getting married," said Conrad. "We didn't get formally engaged. People just weren't doing that as much in the sixties." Conrad acknowledged Robbins' desire to have children. She continued, "Had we gotten married, I doubt we could have sustained it. For one thing, I was very, very young. But even from the day I moved out, we never stopped seeing each other as friends. Our relationship just shifted. . . . We never talked about it directly, but we both understood that it would have been very difficult to survive a marriage over time. I had very good feelings for him; I didn't want that to change. I wanted to keep the good part. And that turned out to be the case, because we remained very close over the years."

During the period that she and Robbins were living together, Conrad watched some of his rehearsals for *Dances at a Gathering,* while most of the dancers remained unaware of the ongoing romance. He bought Conrad a green chiffon James Galanos dress to wear to the premiere, which she and Robbins attended together. "It was very exciting for him to do that [ballet] and it was thrilling to be there," said Conrad. Robbins later acknowledged that *Dances at a Gathering* reflected changes in his life during this period of transition and suggested the underlying inspiration was "just a feeling of love and relationships with people." He also said, "Some of it came out of all that hard, congealed work at the American Theater Laboratory. It also came after Leonard Bernstein, John Guare and I had been struggling over a musical [*A Pray by Blecht*] for a year. We couldn't solve the problems. All that frustration, I think, went into *Dances at a Gathering.*"

Robbins had been absent from City Ballet since staging *The Concert* in 1956. At the time that he departed, he was the company's associate director. Balanchine didn't restore that title to Robbins on his return. He was to be a guest choreographer, and Robbins later admitted that he felt slighted by the change of status. He also felt insecure about his creative powers, having been away from ballet since choreographing *Les Noces* four years earlier. He explained, "It's almost like an artist who has not been drawing for a long time. I didn't know how my hand would be."

Balanchine had good reason to welcome Robbins' return. The Russian choreographer was now sixty-five years old and had been almost solely responsible over the years for providing the company's repertory (though there were contributions along the way from Antony Tudor, Frederick Ashton and others). Lincoln Kirstein recalled, "After years of independent labor, he [Robbins] gave evidence of interest in our enterprise. Balanchine has always wished for someone, almost anyone besides himself, to share the pressure of continuous composition and production. Out of any three novelties, only one has much chance of remaining in the repertory after two seasons. His own work dominates almost by default." Kirstein also noted, "Balanchine had long acknowledged Robbins as the native-born choreographer with the strongest structural and musical sense."

At the time of Robbins' return, Balanchine was feeling more than just age and work-related fatigue. His relations with his leading muse, Suzanne Farrell, were strained to the breaking point. In keeping with his habit of cultivating passions for, and often marrying, his ballerinas, Balanchine had become deeply enamored of Farrell, whose exotic sensuality onstage epitomized the image of the Balanchine ballerina of her era. He desperately hoped to marry her, despite their forty-year age difference and the fact that his love was apparently unrequited. Early in 1969, Balanchine obtained a Mexican divorce that ended his sixteen-year marriage to Tanaquil Le Clercq. But Farrell soon married Paul Mejia, a young dancer in the company, and the choreographer fell into a state of brooding melancholy and emotional exhaustion. As it happened, Farrell left the company on the same night that Robbins' new ballet opened, exiling herself in Europe for the next five years to work with Maurice Béjart's Brussels-based troupe. The loss of such an enormously popular attraction was indeed a blow to the City Ballet enterprise, but the acquisition of a choreographer of Robbins' stature to work side by side with Balanchine was to prove a far greater compensation in the long run.

For *Dances at a Gathering*, Robbins again turned to Chopin, but unlike his comic take on the music in *The Concert*, he was now inclined toward a more romantic rendering of the composer. The music called up memories from his earliest days of studying interpretive dance with his sister, and he was drawn into a more sentimental view of past and present. While the work was still in progress, Robbins told Clive Barnes, "I'm doing a fairly classical ballet to very old-fashioned and romantic music; but there is a point to it. In a way it is a re-volt from the faddism of today. In the period since my last ballet, I have been around looking at dance—seeing a lot of the stuff at Judson Church and the rest of the avant garde. And I find myself feeling just what is the matter with connecting, what's the matter with love, what's the matter with celebrating positive things? Why—I asked myself—does everything have to be so sepa-rated and alienated, so that there is this almost constant push to disconnect? The strange thing is that the young people—what you might call and I use it in quotes, the 'hippie' world—is for love. Is this bad?"

Robbins started *Dances at a Gathering* as a *pas de deux* for Patricia McBride and Edward Villella, both of whom had already distinguished themselves in Balanchine's choreography, most recently with the "Divertimento Brillante" movement of *Glinkiana* and in the sprightly "Rubies" variation of *Jewels.* While Robbins was familiar with Villella and McBride as far back as their days at the School of American Ballet, they were part of a new generation of City Ballet dancers with whom the choreographer had not had much contact. A former street kid from Queens, Villella exhibited a tough, often cocky, sense of mas-culinity, and performed with an explosive bravura style that was to make him one of the leading dancers of his era. He had briefly worked with Robbins on *Afternoon of a Faun* in 1957, when the future City Ballet star had first joined the company. His partner for *Dances,* Patricia McBride, was an ebullient, sparrow-like lyricist who projected utterly wholesome, all-American charm. McBride remembered Robbins from the days of *West Side Story,* when he and cast mem-bers from the Sharks and Jets took *adagio* classes at the school. She said, "That was my first view of Jerome Robbins, taking class with him and the guys. I was just a little ballet girl then and he terrified me." McBride joined the company in 1959 and danced in several Robbins ballets then in the repertory (*Interplay, Fanfare, The Cage* and *The Pied Piper*), but her exposure to him had been limited and she had never danced for him before in new work.

Like many in the company, both McBride and Villella were thrilled with the prospect of Robbins rejoining City Ballet. In his memoir, *Prodigal Son*, Villella recalled Robbins entering the studio for the first rehearsal of *Dances*. "The rehearsal of another ballet was finishing up, and I was standing quietly at the barre doing a few simple *battements tendus* when Jerry walked in. His hair had gotten a little gray, but he looked fit and spry as always. But on his face was the most terrified expression I had ever seen on a choreographer. He barely said hello. Nervous tension had stiffened his body, and his eyes were darting around in his head. He went straight to the piano and buried himself in the score. Every now and then, he looked up, but it was as if he were hiding, not daring to come out into the studio. How unusual, I thought, to see the great man of Broadway and ballet, the winner of so many Tony Awards, and an Oscar, one of the world's most acclaimed choreographers, looking so vulnerable and insecure."

Patricia McBride arrived minutes later. She, too, sensed Robbins' nervous apprehension but nevertheless welcomed him with a kiss on the cheek. "It's hard to resist Patty," recalled Villella. "She's so charming and direct, and I could see him [Jerry] relax a little." Once the rehearsal was under way, Robbins was tentative, struggling with himself, progressing through fits and starts until the work began to flow. Villella wrote, "By the time the rehearsal ended, the ice had been broken. It was more than that—we felt we'd accomplished something. Patty and I were both drained and worn out, and we were unsettled because we were both scheduled to dance that evening. Yet it was great to have Jerry back, and we were elated."

For McBride, the *pas de deux* was the beginning of a long association with Robbins that would continue until she retired in 1989, having performed in seventeen of his ballets. With regard to *Dances*, the ballerina recalled, "I loved the experience. I was a little nervous, but he was very gentle. I loved how gentle he was. He was so different from Mr. Balanchine. I guess because at that time Mr. Balanchine was the head of the company, I was not so intimidated by Jerry. I just wanted to get what he had to show me and try to do what he wanted. . . . I always tried to copy what he [demonstrated]—I tried to get inside his body and be him while I was doing it. But of course you're always yourself. . . . I was in awe of the way he showed it. I always thought it was so beautiful . . . the feeling was beautiful, his feeling, and it was understated."

McBride continued, "He [Jerry] didn't explain anything. It was just dancing to piano music. He let me be me and let Eddie be Eddie. It was just learning the choreography and capturing the mood of the piece. I know he was very specific later on in other pieces how he wanted it very natural, the spirit, and not selling it to the audience—'Easy, easy, easy. Nice and easy, nice and easy. Not to sell it.' It was great fun and I loved just being with him in the room." The feeling was transparently mutual, as Robbins later said, "Patty McBride, I just *love* working with her."

The refined French ballerina Violette Verdy was later cast in the ballet and suggested that McBride was unique in her relationship with Robbins. Verdy said, "I'll tell you something about Patty. You know those wonderful representations of a woman holding a lion's mouth open with a smile on her face and no effort? Patty McBride makes me think of that. She disarmed Jerry Robbins. She disarmed him with her innocence, her goodness, and her good will, and he was to her like he was to no one else, because he realized that she was absolutely innocent and fresh and good. It's very, very true. And Patty will have a lot of lovely things to say about Jerry because she saw more of his good sides than we did because she deserved it. We were not as darling as she was."

Robbins rehearsed the ballet at least five hours a day and five days a week for more than three months. He told *Newsweek*, "It all started to pour out, as if some valve inside me had opened up and the purity of working with dancers took over." Without a preconceived plan, Robbins added two more couples, and about two-thirds of the way through the ballet, he received encouragement from Balanchine to expand the piece even further. According to Villella, after watching a rehearsal, Balanchine told Robbins, "Wonderful. . . . Don't stop. Do more. Make it more, make it more." Robbins later remembered Balanchine saying, "Make more. Make it like peanuts." Robbins increased the size of the ensemble to ten dancers—five couples. In addition to McBride, Villella, and Verdy, the final cast also included Allegra Kent, Sara Leland, Kay Mazzo, Anthony Blum, John Clifford, Robert Maiorano and John Prinz.

Dances at a Gathering was a plotless work set to eighteen Chopin piano pieces—mazurkas, etudes, waltes, a nocturne and a scherzo. Typically, Robbins immersed himself in the music. He said, "I listened to a lot of recordings, different people playing the same piece. I used mostly Rubinstein and Novaes and some Brailowsky. I listened to some of the Dinu Lipatti. Then it was enough for me, and after that I knew I would start to get confused." Gordon Boelzner was Robbins' rehearsal pianist and also played in performance. Robbins lauded Boelzner for being attuned to the dancers and playing "it for movement, without those extra questions of pianism." According to Robbins, it was the dancers who were to reveal the subtleties in the music. Robert Maiorano remembered Robbins' direction, "Don't dance to the music. Let it take you." For some observers, *Dances* would call to mind Balanchine's 1960 *Liebeslieder Walzer*, with its simple conceit of dancers dancing, although the latter work differed in its period and ballroom setting, and required much less in the way of mimetic or gestural acting from the dancers.

There was no scenery for *Dances*, but Thomas Skelton's lighting suggested an amorphous outdoor scene, as if the dance were taking place in an open field or meadow. The piece began with a solo for Villella (to *Mazurka, Opus 63, No. 3*), and progressed over the course of an hour through a fluid sequence of duets, trios, quartets and quintets, punctuated by clever, often breathtaking lifts and exits. Until the end, no more than six dancers appeared onstage at one time. Despite the abstract nature of the piece, there was a sustained dramatic intensity in the dancing, Robbins' characteristic signature. Once again, he was blending the classical ballet vocabulary with social and folk idioms. As the festivities of the imaginary gathering unfolded, he defined specific relationships between the participants through a rapturous tapestry of gesture and movement that was rife with metaphor. As one critic noted, "Each variation is a miniature but rich portrait of social behavior."

Near the end of the ballet, Villella touched the ground as the other dancers watched, then all gazed up at the sky, perceiving something unspecified on the horizon that brought the gathering to a close. Referring to the final tableau, ballerina Sara Leland said, "We call it 'the storm' because the music sounds stormy." The mysterious ambiguity of the moment invited any number of critical interpretations, but Robbins would resist being pinned down as to its ultimate meaning. He later said of the ending, "If I had to talk about it all, I would say that they are looking at—all right—clouds on the horizon which possibly could be threatening, but then that's life, so afterwards you just pick up and go right on again. It doesn't destroy them. They don't lament. They accept."

By reentering the ballet world, Robbins had reduced the number of collaborators who might challenge or undermine his vision. With *Dances,* while there was no set designer, Robbins recruited graphic artist Joe Eula to create costumes. Eula had no previous theater experience when Robbins happened to see an invitation that Eula had designed to promote a benefit for Cesar Chavez and the migrant workers movement. Eula remembered, "Jerry called me and said, 'From what I've seen of your drawing, I think you can do costumes. Would you like to do it?' I never did costumes in my life. It's a true story. And I told him I'm not in the union, and he said, 'I don't cotton to any of that shit.' He said, 'Why don't you come and look at rehearsal,' and I did and fell in love with everybody."

Eula quickly learned how to cope with Robbins. The designer recalled, "He was the greatest sadistic person I ever knew. He was so glad to be unhappy. He really was mad, but he was a genius. I got along infamously well with him because I didn't give a shit. Whenever he'd carry on with me, I'd take the scissor and I'd hand it to him point first. Then he'd turn all red, and he was always red anyway. You had to know how to read Jerry from the beginning, and I was always able to read him. What he did was always put you on the defensive. And I used to say, 'Well, what do *you* want, *Sonny?*' And that used to throw him right out of the box. I said, 'In the end, you're the boss, so what are you looking for? I'm here to help you.' And it worked like a dream. I came up with the idea with *Dances at a Gathering,* instead of going formal I went completely informal. The boys with the rolled up shirts and boots and the girls with these one-layered little things. When he saw them in the beginning, I said, 'You told me you didn't want them all gussied up. This is exactly what you wanted. Now if you want to change it, let me know and we'll go gussy.' He'd get so angry and then walk away and say something. But we did get along very well. He liked me."

All of the dancers faced a challenge in adapting to Robbins' theatrical approach. Edward Villella contrasted the working styles of Balanchine and Robbins, explaining, "Balanchine usually chose a dancer for a new role because that dancer epitomized an idea that he had in relation to the music; he was going to showcase that dancer's unique qualities and abilities, his technical talents, his musicality, his temperament. . . . Mr. B was satisfied if the dancer was able to pick up what he wanted. But if a dancer couldn't, that was fine, too. He'd change it. Jerry didn't work this way at all. He might have been choreo-

graphing with a specific dancer in mind, but he tried to bend t
vision."

Villella continued, "Jerry's background as a theatrical dir
large part in the way he used dancers. He was far more detailed i
tions than Balanchine. . . . He imposed his vision on us, but he v
ing himself to see what he could come up with. He talked very
about what he wanted, and in great detail. He'd dissect the moveme
us images to work with. . . . Balanchine believed that if what he ha
graphed didn't feel natural, he was at fault, not the dancer. With Jei
dancer didn't do exactly what he wanted, he tended to hold the d
sponsible. Jerry had difficulty instilling confidence in people because
could never entirely please him: it was never 'right' enough. And if the
ment he gave us didn't feel natural, he didn't concern himself. The dance
to adjust."

The required adjustments were burdensome for a company accustc
to Balanchine's flexibility and accommodating style. With Robbins,
dancers often learned multiple roles and were played off against each otl
kept in suspense about the final casting while being subjected to the ent
array of rehearsal techniques that he had accumulated over the past thirt
years. His directorial tactics, with emphasis on Stanislavski methods like sense
memory, were alien to dancers who had not been trained as actors. Resent-
ments were inevitable, as he brought his Broadway style into the ballet studio
and demanded a standard of performance virtuosity that was daunting and at
times punishing to many City Ballet dancers.

Yet those demands would yield results and distinguish him stylistically
from Balanchine, however deeply he felt the influence of the Russian master.
To those who believed in Robbins, the genius behind the apparent cruelty created highly dramatic, individual performances that the dancers would not otherwise have been capable of delivering. Both Villella and McBride credited
Robbins with bringing out unique qualities in their dancing that had not been
tapped previously. With regard to his opening solo, Villella recalled Robbins
telling him, "I feel that there's a romantic side to you that people don't see because they don't look beyond your pyrotechnical ability, the physical, athletic
feats you do. . . ." McBride said, "I feel that Jerry found a different side of

ddie, like I feel he saw a different side than Mr. B saw in me. It was very spe-
al to have that side, to work like that. . . . I got to be much more lyrical,
hich I loved. I didn't have to be so technical [and] fast." McBride described
er persona onstage as "much more womanly than my normal self."

Violette Verdy had only a brief, piquant solo in *Dances*, but felt so over-
taxed by Robbins that she tried to withdraw from the ballet before it opened.
Yet Robbins prevailed upon her to perform. Verdy recalled, "I was afraid of
Jerry in some ways. I was a little bit afraid of the impossible-to-satisfy desire
for perfection. . . . I adored it and admired it and was pleased it was there and
that he was really a great director in that sense, but I also needed, of course, to
protect myself. Because I already have a personal drive in that direction, but
not to the point of going insane. I could not take as much as he seemed to be
able to take. My capacity for pushing was not the same because I always feel
that you must do as much as you can and then there's a certain quantity that
must come from somewhere else, and that also needs to not be imposed. The
minute it became too much of an imposition and something that was not natural or healthy, I became self-protective in a way. And it was a deep, deep subject in that it was a physical need, it was a need for avoiding something, and it
was almost like I was in danger of maybe even some form of a little nervous
breakdown. Really, seriously, because my personal drive and my personal undertakings were . . . taxing me to such a degree that to have that much of an
imposition besides was beyond the natural order of things."

Verdy suggested that, because of his background, Robbins was initially
somewhat insecure in his command of the classical form in contrast to Balanchine, who was more firmly rooted in European tradition even as he redefined
it to suit his own ends. "When Jerry came to the New York City Ballet, he
would always say to us in rehearsal, 'Can you do that step on pointe?' And we'd
say, 'Of course, no problem,' and we would say, 'Well, it's not the usual way of
getting there, but we can do it.' He was not as secure about all that, because by
then, my god, Balanchine had made pointe work go to such places with so
much use of it and invention and daring adaptations of other steps that were
more like jazz or tap or Broadway. Balanchine had done it, but in a very clever,
knowledgeable way. He knew pointe work as well as women did . . . and that
is what makes a great ballet master . . . when they know that idiom fully. But

Jerry developed into it slowly. Because of the kind of movement he needed, he would *croon*—it was a crooning . . . rather than opera singing. Let's say Balanchine would sing opera and Jerry would croon, you see what I mean? It's a different way of using it [the form], for different reasons, different effect, and different purpose."

The range of opinion about Robbins among the cast members of *Dancers* was a microcosm of the way that Robbins divided each new cast and each new generation of City Ballet dancers. John Clifford was nineteen at the time, and was not only dancing but had been encouraged by Balanchine to become a choreographer (at the time Jacques d'Amboise and John Taras were also staging ballets for the company). Clifford said of Robbins, "He was tragic because his great talent was offset by his insecurity, which manifested in sheer tyranny. . . . You couldn't breathe in Jerry's ballets. If you did it the way he wanted in rehearsal, if you actually performed it like that, there was no you there. I don't mean it egotistically, but there just was no you. You were really just in a shell doing exactly not only Jerry's steps but Jerry's memory, Jerry's this, Jerry's that; so it was really pretty joyless."

By contrast, John Prinz said, "It was wonderful to work with Jerry. With *Dances at a Gathering* . . . each one of us did each other's parts, and you really didn't know which one you were going to end up with at the last minute. . . . I did this one movement with Allegra Kent—it was called the "Wind Waltz"— it was something he understood, he sensed in me, he sensed my essence of what I am as a dancer and as a person because it really suited me. That was a period, too, he got into that hippie-type thing, a very earthy thing, and a little bit of folk kind of dancing, and it was just perfect for the time." Prinz also remembered, "Jerry was one of these people you shook in your boots a little bit when you knew you had to go to a rehearsal with him."

Allegra Kent had worked with Robbins the decade before as a teenager on *The Concert*. Like Violette Verdy, Kent tried to withdraw from *Dances*. In her memoir, *Once a Dancer . . .* , she explained that Robbins was typically experimenting with his cast and demanding too much rehearsal time from principal dancers in supporting roles. She also anticipated reprising her part in a planned revival of Balanchine's *The Seven Deadly Sins* that season, "so I bowed out of *Dances*. I quit by telegram. I envisioned someone in a Philip Morris costume with shiny buttons and a pillbox hat delivering the telegram to Jerry in the main rehearsal hall. It said, 'I love what you're doing, but I think I'd rather sit in the audience than appear in your work as a secondary player. Much love as always." Subsequently, *Seven Deadly Sins* was canceled, and ". . . Jerry convinced me to rejoin the cast of *Dances at a Gathering*. I had met him in the hall. Staring into my eyes, he had said, 'I know you're disappointed about *The Seven Deadly Sins*. But I want you back in *Dances*. Let's work together again.' He was honest, and I felt he had reassessed me as a dancer. I said yes and was very happy about returning."

Billed as a "preview," the ballet was first offered on May 8, 1969, at the Twenty-fifth Anniversary City Center Gala (with an official premiere scheduled to take place on May 22 at the New York State Theater). Recalling the night of the first performance in his memoir, Villella wrote, "Jerry had been backstage before the curtain went up. He was dressed in dinner clothes, his face was flushed, and he was wishing everyone *merde*. It means shit, which is how French performers wish each other luck. Then he went outside to watch from the audience. Excitement was building backstage, and presumably out front. I collected myself, continued to warm up and focus my concentration. The curtain rose, I walked out onstage and danced the first variation. I felt that I had never done it as well and came offstage in a little bit of a daze. I could hear the applause in the wings. Backstage everything was spinning. People were clustering around congratulating me, but I wasn't even aware whom I was talking to. Suddenly an image floated before my eyes, a head, a man's bearded face. It looked like Jerry, but it couldn't be. He was out front. I tried to blink the image away, but it wouldn't move. Then my hand was being grasped and I was startled to see it *was* Jerry. His eyes were open wide and he was breathless."

According to Villella, Robbins bestowed an extraordinarily rare compliment at that moment, saying, "I've never done this before. I never left the audience while a ballet was going on in the middle of a premiere, but I had to come back and tell you. You danced so beautifully. I was so impressed that I couldn't wait in my seat. I had to come back to see you now."

The ballet became an enormous, instant hit with the audience, probably the greatest single success that City Ballet had experienced up until that point. Robbins and the dancers won standing ovations and riotous cheers of "Bravo" during the curtain calls. The reception was reminiscent of that which Robbins had achieved with *Fancy Free* twenty-five years before. John Clifford, however, suggested that the triumph did not inspire universal jubilation among the dancers. "At the premiere of *Dances*, or the preview—umpteen curtain calls and a major success—none of us was happy. We were exhausted. Not one of us had the feeling that you normally do after a premiere. . . . Jerry's only comment that I saw was that he went up to, I think it was Kay [Mazzo], and he said, 'That bow in your hair is all wrong, the bow doesn't look good.'" Clifford added, "He got great things out of people the hard way."

The ballet received euphoric rave notices after its official opening at the State Theater and generated a bonanza of publicity over the years as a mainstay in the repertory. Clive Barnes wrote, "It is as honest as breathing, as graceful as larksong, and in some very special way more a thing to be experienced than merely just another ballet to be seen. It is also one of the most significant evenings in the American theater since O'Neill. . . . Chopin is all daggers and poet, all poet and peasant. This Robbins has accepted. And then Chopin's feel for place, his need for belonging, for that peasant assurance of the earth beneath him and the sky above. This Robbins has captured." Barnes was already touting Robbins as the logical successor to Balanchine as the company's director, but Balanchine would continue to serve in that capacity for the next fourteen years.

Robbins later recalled of Balanchine, "I got a kiss from him for *Dances at a Gathering*." Balanchine was apparently delighted but also somewhat bemused and mystified by the popularity of the ballet. Patricia McBride remembered hearing Balanchine's reaction to *Dances*, saying, "Mr. B loved the ballet, he loved it— and he said, 'You know why I brought Jerry to the company to do this ballet?' I said, 'Why?' He said, 'Because Jerry's good. He's good, he's a good choreographer.' He [Balanchine] believed in him. Mr. B used to watch every performance from the wings. I'd come on in that first wing on stage right in the front and he'd be there watching every performance." McBride speculated about the impact of the ballet on Robbins, saying, "When he [Jerry] had that big success, I think he was always afraid that it would be lost and that the feeling had to keep growing. So he was there to protect it, to keep it going. He was always very gentle with that ballet."

Robbins was also fiercely protective of the choreography, especially as new casts took over the roles. Bruce Wells danced in the ballet during its first season and referred to himself as "the whipping boy during *Dances at a Gathering*." Recalling one of his performances, Wells said, "This one night, I left out a hop. I was dancing with Kay Mazzo, and . . . I had to skip around Kay, and I skipped one skip. And he [Jerry] came backstage and into my dressing room, in front of the other dancers, shaking just like he was in convulsions, and pointing at me and screaming, 'I'm going to take you out of all of my ballets! How dare you leave out that hop! You're trying to sabotage me, my entire career.' I'm just standing there. I'm all of twenty-one at this point. And I'm thinking, 'This is the great Jerry Robbins. This is the great Jerry Robbins and obviously one hop is not going to change your career. My career apparently is over, but your career is not.' And I somehow felt that it was so out of proportion, his reaction. He took it so personally."

City Ballet Manager Betty Cage observed, "I know he liked the dancers and I know he liked working with them and I know he felt it was his company. But if you saw him screaming at somebody, you would think, 'Why doesn't he get some dancers that he likes?'"

Robbins granted an interview on *Dances* to critic Edwin Denby that appeared in *Dance Magazine.* The critic suggested that during the last moments of the ballet, when the dancers look at the sky, "It is like looking at an airplane, I think of missiles and war." Robbins was dismayed by such ominous images, and after the interview wrote Denby a letter of concern from Stockholm (where Robbins was rehearsing *Les Noces* for the Royal Swedish Ballet). Robbins insisted that the ballet had nothing to do with airplanes or atomic bombs, but rather that he was thinking of clouds and birds.

Undoubtedly, the choreographer's sense of the meaning of the ballet changed over time. He was more and more disposed toward a Balanchine-like formulation, insisting that the dancers were simply dancing with each other to the music, thus minimizing the dramatic elements, which he had in fact communicated to the dancers all along. Edward Villella remembered being directed by Robbins through the opening solo of the ballet and being told, "It's as if it's the last time you'll ever dance in this theater, in this space. And this is your home, the place you know. It's familiar, and I don't want to overstate it, but it's almost as if the atom bomb is going to fall. Everything is going to change."

The next year, Robbins followed up *Dances* with another Chopin exposition, *In the Night*, which Patricia McBride described simply as "a continuation in the same vein." The ballet opened on January twenty-ninth. All nocturnes and *pas de deux*, the atmosphere of the piece was less rustic and expansive than *Dances*, more urban ballroom and aristocratic. The cast featured McBride, Violette Verdy, Kay Mazzo, Francisco Moncion, Anthony Blum and Peter Martins, the Danish-trained premier danseur who was then twenty-five years old and would one day take command of the company. As a dancer, Martins sensed that Robbins was "almost (but not absolutely) impossible to please" and called him "a man of courage and impeccable artistic taste" for choosing "to place his work next to Balanchine's."

If Robbins was to some degree overshadowed by Balanchine and suffered by comparison, he was also inspired by his example. Violette Verdy saw a kind of artistic theft in Robbins' effort to emulate Mr. B. "As we always say, if you're going to steal, steal from the best. Sure, he stole . . . everybody steals. Jerry stole—not commercialized, not vulgarized, those two words are too strong—but he adapted to public absorption, digestion and understanding, to the public's comfort. He made Balanchine absorbable through his work. . . . The more noble aspect of Jerry was, I am convinced, that for all his demons, his fears, his anxieties, his perpetual dissatisfaction and fantastic sense of perfection, the only man that could represent anything important was George Balanchine. And the serenity that Balanchine had about his own perfection was extraordinary to witness for Jerry, who had the other kind of perfection, which is the relentless drive without ever thinking that perfection has been attained. . . . Balanchine was beyond greed and effort. And Jerry wanted to be with Balanchine because he thought if there was anybody greater than him, Balanchine was the only one. And Balanchine also represented something that he had not yet achieved, which is the calm and the serenity, because Balanchine was unpossessive, and Jerry was possessive. And Jerry felt, what is it about Balanchine that he's so unpossessive and so calm, when perfection drives me to the greatest pains and the greatest desire and the greatest dissatisfaction?"

Verdy continued, "I thought, why does Balanchine so admire Jerry? Because Balanchine had a tremendous admiration for Jerry. And very often, probably, had a little tang of thinking that Jerry was more gifted than he was, because the comparison that Balanchine made was at the level of judging himself as only a craftsman. Balanchine never admitted the idea that he might have genius, he never thought of it, would never want to consider such a huge statement, because he thought da Vinci was a genius, Michelangelo was a genius, Shakespeare was the guru and the genius; but he never thought he was that. He thought he was a tremendously good craftsman. And he looked at Jerry, who was not as good a craftsman, yet with wonder and admiration he felt Jerry was even more gifted than him. I could tell that. Isn't that amazing? And he would watch Jerry with tenderness and emotion, like a son who was more gifted than the father."

Robbins received his share of approbation. Reviewing *In the Night,* Walter Terry placed him in the historical lineage of eighteenth-century ballet master Jean-Georges Noverre, who believed that dance should "speak to the heart" through a synthesis of stage action, movement and drama. Terry wrote, "Noverre, choreographer, innovator, reformer, set out to restore meaningfulness, expressivity, even truth to an art that had become almost acrobatic. . . . Today Noverre would be awed by the fireworks of ballet technique, but he also would have been amazed at the emergence of a theater dance that would 'speak to the heart.' Perhaps *In the Night* would have affected him most, even more than modern dance masterpieces, for he would see a vocabulary of movement rooted in his own classical traditions, and he would experience physical fireworks used to illumine the fires of the heart."

Critic Arlene Croce suggested that Robbins' plotless treatment of Chopin was reminiscent of Michel Fokine's classic *Les Sylphides,* but that Robbins had created more of "the effect of a dramatic web and a continuous dramatic action behind the scenes." Interviewed by Croce, Robbins denied that this was his conscious intention, saying, "I had no idea about some drama happening offstage and I'm not even sure Fokine invented it. What would we know if we found out he had? It's not such a new idea anymore. Think of the second movement of Balanchine's *Serenade* or *Symphony in C.* Those girls who come on are certainly coming from somewhere." With Balanchine, however, the dancers were rarely given dramatic motivation and subtext. With Robbins, they were typically supplied with the kind of direction that actors might receive when working on a scene. Like a magician whose tricks are revealed to the audience, Robbins was not pleased when his hidden agenda was pinpointed and exposed, either by critics or by his dancers. In this regard, Robbins said, "The trouble with interviews is that they pin you down to verbal formulations when what really matters is on the stage."

With Robbins' return to City Ballet, he and Balanchine shared an office at the State Theater on the fourth floor, an arrangement that continued until Mr. B's death in 1983. Actor Barry Primus remembered visiting Robbins at his City Ballet home. "I consider this my premier moment, my premier story about Jerry," said Primus. "We went upstairs and he opens the door and there's his office. . . . He said, 'Look at that, look over there. Look, look.' He says, 'There's Balanchine's part of the room.' And Balanchine's part of the room had a piano and a shawl draped on it, music falling on the floor, his hat was on the ground, lots of coats and papers. Sloppy, creatively sloppy, very romantic. And then Jerry's area had a piano, his sailor cap, his pea jacket, his scarf, and his little music folded in half, and nothing else. He said, 'God, I wish I could be like him.' That tells it."

In the spring of 1970, Robbins collaborated with Balanchine on a revival of Stravinsky's *Firebird.* Balanchine's 1949 version (after Fokine) was originally danced by Maria Tallchief and Francisco Moncione and was now to be restaged for a teenage Gelsey Kirkland and City Ballet stalwart Jacques d'Amboise. The new production restored Marc Chagall's original designs. Robbins' contribution was primarily limited to directing the comic monsters in the Danse Infernale. At its premiere on May 28, 1970, *The Firebird* was unveiled with great fanfare. Lincoln Kirstein masterminded the gala event as a publicity spectacle that landed Kirkland and Balanchine a spread in *Life* magazine. For Robbins, this ballet was a case of honorable mention, while his contribution blended seamlessly with Balanchine's distillation of the Russian fairy tale.

As Balanchine's new "baby ballerina," Kirkland was by now also performing in *Dances at a Gathering*, for which she had been initially drafted as an understudy. Of the Balanchine-Robbins relationship, Kirkland recalled that "their egos always seemed to mesh" because of "the contrast of their concerns and preferences." Many, though not all, City Ballet dancers in Kirkland's generation were under the impression that Robbins was gay. As Bruce Wells recalled, "He was never openly gay. He was one of those stuffed shirts. But there was always a boy." Robbins' apparent sexual preference seemed to explain why he and Balanchine never clashed over the affections of a ballerina. But the actual reasons for their compatibility in all spheres probably had more to do with their mutual respect and the deference that Robbins repeatedly paid to the acknowledged master. Looking back, Bruce Wells speculated about sexuality serving as a creative catalyst for choreographers like Balanchine, Robbins, Antony Tudor and Frederick Ashton (the latter two were both gay), saying, "It was the friction that they needed to create the spark to do what they did. Jerry definitely did it with both men and women. He almost would design the sandpaper of his life to irritate him to keep the creative spark alive."

Wisely perhaps, Balanchine chose to cast a blind eye to Robbins' behavior in the theater. John Clifford saw himself as a Balanchine protégé and recalled the advice that he received from Mr. B regarding Robbins. "Mr. B was very careful with Jerry and he understood Jerry's demons," said Clifford. "One day I was over at O'Neal's across the street [from the theater] and I was practically crying. I was mentally drained. And Mr. B walked in and sat with me at the bar and said, 'What's the matter?' I knew Balanchine very well at that point, and Mr. B's habit was, if you badmouthed or if you were negative about anybody else in the company, Mr. B would make it your problem. So it was better with Balanchine never to say anything negative about anybody else. But finally Mr. B said, 'What's wrong? If you're unhappy we're all in trouble.' I said, 'Mr. B, I don't know what to do about Jerry.' And he said, 'You know, dear, he will teach you how not to treat people.'

"A month later, I was at a small party, maybe during *Goldberg* or something. Jerry had gotten us all to the point where we didn't know if we were coming or going. Balanchine said, 'If you had no hair on your head and a big grey beard, you'd be unhappy too.' Mr. B and I would go out to dinner a lot, and he adored Jerry, but he understood Jerry's flaws. Mr. B smoothed the way. And Jerry was very aware of it—he told me that once in Paris twenty years later. He knew that Mr. B was facilitating his idiosyncrasies and calming the waters."

On July fourth of 1970, during the company's annual Saratoga season, Robbins staged an open working rehearsal to preview his new ballet, *The Goldberg Variations*. Bach's famous musical antidote for insomnia represented for Robbins a weighty, almost insurmountable choreographic problem. The structural complexity of the baroque composition, published in 1742, with its thirty variations in the same key, would not easily lend itself to dance, and Robbins was characteristically indecisive about how finally to treat the work. Nearly an hour and a half in length, this was a massive undertaking that initially required thirteen principal dancers, five soloists, and a corps of twenty-three. Patricia McBride recalled, "I know Jerry drove a lot of people crazy, like with *Goldberg* he couldn't decide whether he wanted the piano or the harpsichord. We actually premiered it as a work in progress. It was a monumental work and Jerry never felt that comfortable working with large groups. If you notice his ballets, a lot of them are small groups, the bulk of his work. In *Goldberg* it got to be really big at the end. Till the last day, they could not say whether it was the harpsichord."

Robbins used the harpsichord for the Saratoga preview, but later decided that the instrument didn't carry sufficient sound in the theater. He explained his personal take on the music, saying, "I guess, after the Chopin, I just wanted to get away from romantic music. I wanted to see what would happen if I got hold of something that didn't give me any easy finger ledge to climb. It seemed to me that in *The Goldberg Variations* Bach was describing something very big and architectural, and so I thought I'd try that and see how I could do. The piece was really spread over a long period, which in a way I'm grateful for because it gave me time to think. It was like approaching a beautiful marble wall. I could get no toehold, no leverage to get inside that building. The first weeks of rehearsal were as if I were hitting it and falling down, having to start over."

Robbins progressed slowly, at one point conducting rehearsals from a wheelchair with his ankle in a cast, having snapped an Achilles tendon in the studio. According to John Clifford, one dancer suggested afterward, "Oh, so he was finally struck down!" Robert Maiorano said, "He was able to do a double pirouette in his wheelchair—you see, that's him in the theater, you deal with what you got." Bruce Wells recalled the delays with *Goldberg*, saying, "Jerry was piddling around, and it was supposed to premiere soon, and of course it was not ready . . . and we're rehearsing and rehearsing and rehearsing, and it's supposed to premiere in Saratoga, but it's not getting ready at all, and there was this big joke about how they were going to bring us back after twenty years: *Goldberg Variations in Rehearsal for Twenty Years, Together Again As You've Always Loved Them*. It was going to be this retrospective of our whole careers, because he wouldn't make any decisions.

"But we did have a very exciting night in Saratoga Springs, where he had to produce something. We went out there in our practice clothes, he stood on the side of the stage and he described what he was working on to the audience. And I do remember that being an incandescent night, because it was filled with raw, creative energy in a performance space, and the man was now saying things of course we had never heard. That was a thrilling, thrilling night. John Clifford and I did a duet. I remember we brought the house down, and we were not really aware of the little jewel that we had until that happened. That was very exciting."

Gordon Boelzner was the accompanist for *Goldberg*, and Joe Eula designed the costumes. Reviewing the Saratoga preview, Walter Terry wrote that "total enchantment prevailed." But completion of the work was postponed that summer. Robbins traveled to London later in the year at the invitation of Frederick Ashton to stage *Dances at a Gathering* for the Royal Ballet. Sara Leland was enlisted to serve as his assistant in London. During the decade, she and Wilma Curley were Robbins' most trusted ballet mistresses. They supported him in the studio and were charged with coaching and preparing new casts for his ballets. According to Curley, she did much of the casting under Robbins' supervision. While he would polish the work during later rehearsals, she served as an intermediary and buffer with the dancers, introducing his ballets to companies like the Joffrey Ballet, which performed *Moves* (1967), *Interplay* (1972) and *New York Export: Opus Jazz* (1974). Tommy Abbott performed similar duties for Robbins both on Broadway and at City Ballet.

Betty Cage remarked, "I think Jerry was hardest on his assistants, his ballet masters and mistresses, because they were torn to shreds by the time they had the courage to leave him."

Bruce Wells was close to Tommy Abbott during the latter's tenure at City Ballet, and described the pitfalls of working as Robbins' assistant while at the same time carrying on an intermittent affair. "I think ultimately, at least in Jerry's male relationships, if you hung on long enough, Jerry would love you for that, but ultimately Jerry needed to break it off. There was a control factor. Tommy Abbott, who unfortunately you cannot speak to because he passed away, was Jerry's very close confidant and lover, stage manager, dancer in *West Side Story*—he did the whole thing, and he came into City Ballet at a time when Jerry didn't trust any of the City Ballet ballet masters. We quite frankly didn't have as many as they have today, unbelievably it was less. But Tommy and I would room on tour . . . and he had unbelievable stories. His one comment [was] that he did everything on *Fiddler on the Roof* except perform. When Jerry would fire the stage manager, Tommy would go on. When Jerry would fire the dance master, Tommy would go in. Whatever, whoever somebody was firing, Tommy would always go in because Jerry could rely on Tommy to be his right-hand man. On the other hand, eventually he did the same thing to Tommy and it broke Tommy's heart."

Edward Bigelow remembered another side of the story, saying, "Tommy Abbott got to be in a mess, I guess it was alcoholism or whatever else, I don't know. And Jerry really looked after him, although there was really no necessity. However intimate life may be in a ballet company, and it can be quite intimate, one doesn't necessarily know about a lot of things. People have a lot of sides."

Robbins' engagement with the Royal Ballet put him in the studio for the first time with Rudolf Nureyev, who had already established his celebrated stage partnership with British prima ballerina Margot Fonteyn. The thirty-one-year-old Russian star was well-known for his tempestuous nature and commanding artistry. Nureyev had been a fan of Robbins since seeing a production of *West Side Story* in Paris while touring with the Kirov before his defection. *Dances at a Gathering* was scheduled to premiere at Covent Garden's Royal Opera House on October 19, 1970. Robbins arrived in London on September sixth and commenced rehearsals—four hours a day, five and sometimes six days a week. He put Nureyev and the Royal Ballet dancers through the same rigors and multiple casting that he enforced at City Ballet. Ballerina Lynn Seymour was in the original British cast of *Dances* and described the relationship between Nureyev and Robbins, saying, "They really, really admired one another. It was terribly respectful and cautious, I would say, from both of them, treading carefully."

Monica Mason, who eventually danced the role originated by Violette Verdy, remembered, "You worked until you dropped. Until you actually couldn't do another step. And then he [Robbins] still asked you to do it again. And it was punishing. But you felt that you were learning so much in the process." Another British cast member, Michael Coleman, said, "He shamed you into working because he could do everything better than you."

Given their more traditional classical training, the dancers at the Royal Ballet possessed a very different sense of musicality and style—more restrained and aristocratic—than the Balanchine-oriented City Ballet dancers on whom Robbins had first set *Dances.* The same was true of Nureyev, who was a sensation dancing in the classical repertoire, stamping each role with his own highly individual interpretation. For him, Robbins' ballets represented new territory to conquer, and he was anxious to prove himself. Anthony Dowell was also cast in *Dances* at the Royal and recalled, "I think Rudolf was always hungry at that stage to work with anyone, and he knew Jerry was someone whom he could learn from or take from. And in the studio, that was that. Rudolf was a great worker, the ego didn't get in the way when he knew something was good or someone was going to give him something. It was a good relationship."

Nureyev would eventually step into Edward Villella's role. For Robbins, the primacy of the choreography had to be asserted, and he soon put Nureyev in his place. Costume designer Joe Eula attended some of the rehearsals in London and remembered that on Nureyev's first entrance for his solo, "Jerry told Nureyev, 'I don't want the audience to know who you are until you're off the stage.'" Monica Mason commented, "Isn't that wonderful? Wonderful. Yes. He [Robbins] didn't want you to bring who you thought you were. . . . He just wanted you to serve his work. And I think it was an extraordinary way of working, and brilliant. I wouldn't have missed it for the world. I treasure it. Every second." Mason continued, "It wasn't about the emergence of the individual as a star. I remember the way he used to correct Rudolf, you know, and Rudolf would take it from him. Jerry would say, 'No, not like that. No, you turned the corner too soon.' And Rudolf would look at him, and Jerry would say, 'I mean it. You turned the corner too soon. You don't turn it until you are on that foot and then it's that angle and it's that way,' and sort of like that. And you know, Rudolf would do it!"

Joe Eula recounted one last-minute contention between Robbins and Nureyev. "Jerry almost lost it opening night with Nureyev. Nureyev refused to wear the dark color tights. He wanted light tights, right up until the end, he was rehearsing in light tights, so you could see the veins in his cock and the cheeks of his ass better with white. The shirt he didn't mind. But the earth color was the whole point—the guy was part of the earth. Dress rehearsal in the afternoon opening night, Jerry said to me, 'Go and have a set [of brown tights] made . . . and make sure they're perfect. And just give them to me.' And he went to the dressing room before curtain and, whatever transpired, Mr. Nureyev came out in the brown tights."

By the time the ballet opened in London, Robbins was suffering from hepatitis and returned to New York immediately after the premiere. One British critic wrote, "A creation so moving could only come out of deep personal feeling. . . . The solos are inventive, the double work sparklingly original and places fiendishly difficult, but all so finely wrought that one was only aware of move and effect. The choreography for the men is particularly notable, as he [Robbins] has completely broken away from the very limited range of steps men are usually given. . . . The quietly serious ending, after so much gaiety and freshness, leaves one with the curious, inexplicable, theatrical emotion. I make no apologies for saying that it made me want to cry."

Robbins maintained a cordial relationship with the Royal Ballet over the years, surpassed among foreign companies only by his later association with the Paris Opéra, which was to embrace him more wholeheartedly and with a deeper pocketbook. Still, the Royal brought *Afternoon of a Faun* into its repertory the following year (for Dowell and Antoinette Sibley), and soon added *Requiem Canticles* (1972), *In the Night* (1973), and *The Concert* (1975). Anthony Dowell became the company's artistic director in 1986 and explained that the Royal Ballet was less able to afford the fees, royalties, rehearsal time and the sort of hospitality that Robbins demanded. "It was always a big consideration," said Dowell, "if you were going to have a Robbins work . . . of the financial implications—his coming over, and where he would stay, and all that. . . . The contract was always brought up if we weren't giving him what was in the contract in lighting time and stage time. Of course, at the Opera House in those days it was everything getting on just by the skin of its teeth, it was really very difficult. As I say, I think that's why I regret that in my time as director that his work disappeared a bit. But Paris with its very large company, they just gave over so much time to him. There was no way I could have done that."

Robbins surely sacrificed substantial income by turning his back to Broadway and making what was to be a long-term commitment to highbrow dance. Shortly after his return to City Ballet, he said, "Lately I've been struck by the fact that at the end of the year when the income tax man comes round and they sort of organize my earnings, my earnings in ballet come to maybe a couple of thousand dollars a year. Now I'm so curious to see whether I could make my living just at ballet, without having to become an organizational man like George [Balanchine], but just on my own."

Betty Cage described the early financial arrangements established by City Ballet, saying, "When we started Ballet Society we had a one-page deal, and when we used guest choreographers, everybody got a $25 performance royalty, and I think maybe they got something like $200 to $300 for a fee, or $500 maximum. Then after a bit we stopped using that, but I don't think we ever paid more than $2,000 to $3,000 as a fee. We probably paid Jerry more, we probably paid him around $5,000. And at that time Jerry was probably getting $30,000 as a guest elsewhere, at least $20,000, and that was some years ago. Balanchine wasn't getting a fee. You see, what Balanchine did, he looked on it as such a luxury to have a company that he didn't care whether it paid his salary, because if he ran out of money, he'd go do a Broadway show or something. He never cared about money anyway, and if he had money he would take everybody to dinner. He didn't want money in his pocket. But Jerry felt very insecure and he wanted money."

Cage recalled that, early on, Robbins pressed for a contract. "Jerry came in one day and said, 'My lawyer says we should have a contract.' I said, 'Oh? Well, all right, why not?' Nobody had a contract—Balanchine didn't have a contract, I didn't have a contract, our conductors didn't have a contract. But Jerry's lawyers wanted a contract. Anyway, they started negotiating, and this went on, I think, over a period of maybe eight months. They kept asking for more, and this should be written down. I said, 'Well, we can't do that. I know you have this contract with Broadway, but we're not Broadway and we can't do this. We can't even meet these fees that you have in here.'

"So I said to Jerry one day, 'You know, we're really getting nowhere with this contract. I don't see why it's so important. Nobody else has a contract.' He said, 'Well, I have a contract for everything.' I said, 'I know you do, but you also charge other people more than you charge us, and your lawyers assume that this is just like you are doing a Broadway show and it isn't. We can't operate this way. Look, if you get mad at us and you don't want us to do your ballets anymore, we don't want to do them. If you don't want us to do them, tell us and we'll stop doing them all whenever you want it. Why don't we just have a letter between us saying how your ballets can be done by us as long as you want them to, and if at any time you want to take them away, you'll take them away.' He said, 'Well, all right.' That's what we ended up doing. I think we're the only people he ever dealt with without a contract. You don't want to work with people who don't want to work with you."

During the early 1970s, Lincoln Kirstein organized a new board of directors for the company and recruited Knopf editor Robert Gottlieb as one of its members. Gottlieb described the board as "a rubber stamp for Balanchine" and remembered, "The board didn't need to exercise strict financial controls, since that role had been filled from the beginning by the company's formidable manager, Betty Cage, whose powerful nature and gimlet eye were directed at saving money. . . ." Gottlieb assisted Cage with the hairy logistics of programming each season according to the wishes of the two choreographers and input from the general manager, Kirstein. According to Gottlieb, "Balanchine liked a rousing closer, with the whole corps de ballet whipping up a storm. Jerry Robbins had very definite ideas about when and how often his ballets should be scheduled."

The company thrived over the decade that many consider its Golden Age with three disparate personalities—Kirstein, Balanchine and Robbins—exerting varying degrees of control. A key figure in the administration, Edward Bigelow said, "How those two characters [Kirstein and Balanchine], the irresistible force and immovable object, ever associated from 1934 until they each died, I don't know. I have no idea. But when you have three forces, when you add Jerry to Kirstein and Balanchine, it's fascinating. There were no contracts but somehow it worked. But Jerry was mostly right about the necessity for certain types of protocols and duties to be recognized and put down on paper. He was annoyed because here was the great Balanchine saying, 'I don't care about that.' But he didn't have to. And he would say in his grand manner, 'I don't have to.' In spite of all that, it didn't interfere with how they operated with the company and with each other. The point is not so much what didn't happen, but what did happen. Nobody remembers, now that everybody is famous, that it took twenty-five years for these things to become masterpieces."

Robbins' Bach marathon, *The Goldberg Variations,* finally premiered at the State Theater on May 27, 1971, with a cast that included Renee Estopinal and Michael Steele (in the *Theme*); Gelsey Kirkland, Sara Leland, John Clifford, Robert Maiorano, Robert Weiss, Bruce Wells (all with *Variations* in Part I); Karin von Aroldingen, Peter Martins, Susan Hendl, Anthony Blum, Patricia McBride and Helgi Tomasson (with *Variations* in Part II). Robbins opened the ballet with a statement of the theme, a stately sarabande for two dancers in eighteenth-century period costumes. Framing the piece and lending at least some slight sense of continuity, they returned at the end of the night dressed informally while dancing in the same courtly style. Robbins later said in passing that Balanchine had offered him a suggestion for the ending that didn't mesh with his own vision.

For the bulk of the variations, Robbins devised a two-part structure that in the first half involved playful children's games, frolics and flirtations, with the dancers dressed in leotards and rehearsal clothes. The second half presented a more mature and refined technical display, with the dancers in period costumes. The stylistic flourishes of the piece ranged from baroque to ballroom and even Broadway. *Goldberg* was seen as a kind of extravagant dance manual, which was to some observers excessive and overwrought. Again, Robbins avoided literal narrative but etched relationships, however fleeting, and a continuous thread of gestural hints that placed the work outside the realm of Balanchine's pure neo-classicism.

While *Goldberg* may have been uneven and overly long, it was an ambitious undertaking and predictably elicited a wide range of criticism. Music critic Alan Rich hailed it as a "masterpiece" comparable to Bach's music, and Clive Barnes suggested that it was "a work of such amplitude and grandeur that it can make you fall in love with the human body all over again." In the *Village Voice*, Deborah Jowitt, a loyal Robbins partisan, called it "a sumptuous banquet." In *Newsweek*, Hubert Saal was put off by the work and complained, "Robbins has not heard the passion in Johann Sebastian Bach."

In *Ballet Review*, Arlene Croce observed, "Robbins, working without recourse to story, scenery, and orchestra, and working, moreover, with one of the most exacting and complicated scores in the keyboard repertory, is Robbins working under great and obvious strain." Faulting Robbins for apparently having no subject other than the music, Croce added, "The trouble with *Goldberg* is that it doesn't exist as a ballet. When Robbins has wrestled every last musical repeat to the mat, we don't come away with a theatrical experience but with an impression of endless ingenious musical visualizations. . . ."

Croce, who joined the *New Yorker* in 1973, was to become an almost constant thorn in Robbins' side for the rest of his life, as she repeatedly voiced her preference for his Broadway shows like *Gypsy* and his lighter ballets like *Fancy Free* and *Afternoon of a Faun*. Her views were in some ways shared by dancers from earlier generations. Many of them, however, were simply dismayed to see Robbins attempting to style his work along the formal lines of Balanchine. Maria Karnilova said, "I was completely disappointed that he [Robbins] became so influenced by Balanchine. Oh God, yes, because to this day I consider that Balanchine was not the icon that they make him out to be. He was a brilliant choreographer, but he choreographed in one style and the whole of American ballet became that style." Similarly, Janet Reed said, "I was really sorry to see the later things he did for New York City Ballet. I felt he was going too far over to the abstract style."

Richard Thomas was more vehement, saying, "It was unfortunate . . . that he ever, ever took on the position he did as second banana to George Balanchine. That, as far as I'm concerned, is the real tragedy of Jerry's life, because as a young choreographer starting out in Ballet Theatre . . . he was as gifted as any young choreographer that has ever come along. He proved it time and time again. I think he was equally talented as Balanchine. Balanchine did more good ballets than anybody else in the world, but he also did more bad ballets than anybody else in the world. So consequently you're talking about a man who just did more ballets than anybody in the world. But it didn't make him the alpha and omega of all choreographers—not so—because there were many great choreographers. Jerry was a true American product, and he should have held on to that. I think the earlier work with City Ballet was much better than the latter works, when he just became so influenced with this sort of gala situation that they had going there. . . . He became less and less Robbins. I think *Age of Anxiety* was wonderful. It was marvelous to do, and it was a wonderful ballet, and it was a Jerome Robbins ballet. It may not have pleased a lot of people, but critics aren't someone you want to please anyway—they're the last people you want to please. To thine own self be true. I think Jerry got misled in a lot of directions."

Alicia Alonso discussed this artistic issue with Robbins and recalled, "He spoke to me about Balanchine. I said, 'Jerry, you have a style. You're working with Balanchine, what's gonna happen?' He said, 'No, no, I respect him, and I will always respect him. He [Balanchine] has an idea and a way of working. I will try not to be too different. I will try with his artistic line to introduce my artistic line, but without shocking.' That's what he did with all the ballets he did with Balanchine with the New York City Ballet. He was not imitating Balanchine. He was himself. He did not go to the extreme [of Balanchine]. I think that helped him to be so classical with his [later] work, more sublime."

Unquestionably, in his own mind, Robbins was in some fashion reaching for the sublime. He appears to have seen Balanchine as the perfect mirror and vehicle through which to define himself and perhaps to achieve a measure of spiritual redemption. Immediately after the opening of his next ballet, *Watermill*, which was an autobiographical effort that bore little if any resemblance to anything in Balanchine's repertory, or to any other ballet for that matter, Robbins remembered Balanchine coming backstage and telling him, "We [choreographers] dare to go into the world where there are no names for anything . . . we get our hands into that world just a little bit." Such was the elusive looking glass through which Robbins would attempt to step during his remaining years.

For *Watermill*, Robbins again utilized his experience at the American Theater Laboratory with Kabuki and Noh Theater. Critics pointed out the similarities between this ballet and the vast, slow-motion, theatrical collages of Robert Wilson. Of course, the two were dipping into the same Eastern theatrical sources. Robbins steeped himself in a heady mixture of ideas from Zen Buddhism and Taoism. His alter-ego in the piece, Edward Villella, was portrayed as a kind of Zen Everyman at midlife, who stripped down to his dance belt and contemplated his past against a dreamlike landscape of changing seasons and phases of the moon, natural cycles that defined the passage of time as the subject of nostalgic meditation. Working against audience expectations of Villella's usual virtuoso feats, Robbins gave him almost no dancing. Villella explained, "I had to control the stage, rivet the audience's attention by barely moving at all. . . ." What movement there was, Robbins slowed down to the point of deliberate tedium, challenging the attention span of the audience for more than an hour. Lincoln Kirstein aptly described the piece as "a race against anxiety which endurance temporarily wins." Robbins later said of the gestation of *Watermill*, "It certainly was a healing period. What I was healing from I don't know. It was a reevaluation. Or some sort of contemplative, internalized reassessment that came out after I had done *Dances at a Gathering* and *Goldberg Variations*."

Watermill was more theatrical event and ritualistic spectacle than ballet in the conventional sense. Clive Barnes suggested, "It is a ballet that attempts to question the art of ballet and, indeed, our concept of the theater." The scenery—like an exquisite Eastern painting with its three huge sheaves of wheat blooming against the sky—was designed by Robbins and David Reppa. Japanese composer Teiji Ito attended rehearsals and created much of the score while work was in progress. Flutes and percussion were augmented by natural sounds—dogs barking, crickets, and a passing airplane. Patricia Zipprodt designed costumes that combined silky Orientalism with dancers' rehearsal attire. All in all, the piece was an attempt at cultural transposition, a contrived artifice into which Robbins projected scenes from a personal past filtered through fantasy and imagination.

Beyond the various harvest and picnic scenes, the staged memories were at times discordant and unsettling, as when the subject of sexuality was raised through several heavy-handed vignettes. A romantic *pas de deux* of recollected youth for Penelope Dudleston and Hermes Condé was delineated in slow motion and led to a cold, anal copulation, resurrecting an attitude seen before in *The Cage.* Similarly, the depiction of a homosexual rape and castration was carried out as a clinical display, which troubled Arlene Croce, who saw it as Robbins stooping to gratuitous "shock theatre."

Penelope Dudleston recalled the personal nature of Robbins' work, saying, "He got the inspiration from his home in Watermill that was right there on the ocean. And he used to go out and do his *t'ai chi* and meditate and all this stuff watching the waves. He did a lot of walking. It was a very rejuvenating place for him, and he got the idea for the ballet from where he lived. I understood it to be more of a story about his life. I think that's where he found himself and he reflected on his life, everything from his sexual preference to his inspiration happens in this ballet." Dudleston believed that her *pas de deux* was a reflection of Robbins' earlier relationships with women like Nora Kaye, saying, "That was a very emasculating period for him from which *Cage* came out of . . . and from whatever happened there, then he went very gay."

Onstage, Dudleston played a beach scene during which she slowly combed her long blond hair as a prelude to the *pas de deux.* She remembered rehearsing the day before the premiere: "I'm brushing my hair and I'm supposed to be doing this in slow motion, and you have everybody in the company watching, and for some reason I did something that pissed him off. He just grabbed the hairbrush and hit me over the head with it and said, 'Use your head!' That was embarrassing. I mean, it hurt. I really didn't know what I had done wrong. He kept telling me I was supposed to act like I was stoned and I was a very hyper-energetic person. I'm sure that was the problem. But then he sends me two dozen long-stemmed red roses. That's how he was. Yeah, he lost his temper, yes, he hit me over the head, but oh well, it happened."

The collaboration with Patricia Zipprodt on costumes became so contentious by the time the ballet opened that she was ready to call it quits and made her feelings known to Kirstein and Balanchine. "The endless *Watermill*," said Zipprodt. "I just got to the point one day where I said, 'I can't stand it anymore, I've got to go away for a while.' And we were at the New York State Theater for dress rehearsal, and all of a sudden the elevator door opened and I just jumped in . . . and the only other occupant in the elevator was Lincoln Kirstein. He said, 'Ho!' I said, 'Oh, Lincoln, I just can't do anymore! I think I'm going to have to quit.' He looks at me and he turns absolutely white, and he says, 'Please don't leave. If you leave, I'll leave.' It went as far as Lincoln. Yeah. And Balanchine was in a cab riding from Karinska's costume shop back to the theater. [When he arrived], he said to me, 'Don't worry. It is his problem. You have to understand, it's *his* problem.' It kind of kept me going for a while, because the source of the problem was Jerry and I shouldn't take it personally and lose my perspective. But we all just went through it."

Watermill opened at the State Theater on February 3, 1972. Edward Villella remembered, "When the curtain came down, there were shouts of approval, but there were also boos and hisses. I knew the piece was very different from what anyone expected from the New York City Ballet, that this Eastern heartbeat was not necessarily compatible with our Western attitudes. I had anticipated a certain amount of surprise, maybe even controversy, but I didn't expect the amount of disapproval. I had expected audiences at least to respect it for its originality. There were those who were entranced by it. The audience seemed equally divided. I think Jerry was shocked by the reception. When he came onstage for his bow, his eyes were wide open, but he wasn't seeing."

Robbins later said, "I must admit I was a little thrown by the reception. . . . I was sitting next to a friend on opening night, and about halfway through, when people started to giggle, I whispered, 'They're going to boo at the end,' but then I was surprised when they *did.*"

There were critics who applauded the work. Clive Barnes called it "a fantastic ballet," enthusing that *Watermill* "embraces a concept of humanity that cannot be constrained by national or ethnic boundaries." The *Daily News* deemed it "a towering achievement." In *Dance Magazine,* Doris Hering saw it as a work of "tender majesty," citing the famous line from Emily Dickinson and crediting Robbins with having "absorbed the essence of oriental thought." Deborah Jowitt lauded "the cohesive beauty of its images." In *Dance News,* Nancy Goldner wrote that "it is one of the most perfect productions I have seen," while Patricia Barnes noted, "no one seeing it can remain untouched in some way by it."

Other notices were less than kind. The most scathing attack came from Arlene Croce, who denounced the work as "tedious hokum . . . a glib, trendy picture puzzle." She opened her diatribe in an explicitly personal vein, suggesting, "if it really is the personal testament that its admirers take it for—personal in the sense of autobiographical—then it is even worse than I think it is." Croce concluded, "After *Watermill,* it is a question of just who Jerome Robbins is. I believe that he is fatally attracted to pretentious undertakings. . . . The man is like a Houdini of stagecraft, and he seems to have grown tired of his magic, tired or afraid. In the sense that his technique is a part of him, as much a part of his being as his central nervous system, he has grown tired—or afraid—of himself. Perhaps he hoped that by entertaining stasis as a serious theatrical proposition he could construct something utterly unlike himself. A new Robbins, perhaps, would emerge."

Such hostilities were readily apparent on the night of the premiere, and Robbins was deeply affected. Dudleston remembered that, after the performance, she attended a party given by Robbins at his townhouse. "I was with Jerry and Leonard Bernstein after *Watermill* (and after a couple other things) and it was always Jerry just furious because the audience didn't understand, they didn't relate to it, the reviewers. And it was, 'Why was Balanchine always the best?' When would he be the best? I really think Balanchine, with his prolific choreography, kept Jerry going because Jerry was competitive. And I think even maybe without even knowing it, he was competing with Mr. B."

An unusual friendship developed between Robbins and Dudleston that continued long after she left the company in 1975. "I loved Jerry very, very intensely, which was unusual for City Ballet, because most people were only into Balanchine," said Dudleston. "And we would go out for drinks or lunch or something. We were very good friends. I socialized with Jerry. He *asked* me, 'Do you want to go to lunch?'" She added, "I did not just love him. He could be very cruel, physically and mentally. One time I trimmed my hair and he lost his head. [He said] 'How dare you cut your hair!' He could really push you, but if you put your foot down and stood up for yourself, he also respected that. I found that after I left the company and we wrote and called each other at different times, kept in touch, I got to know him much better. . . . I never saw Jerry being any kind of a bad guy or evil. I was always very grateful that I had the opportunity to work with him and that later we could become such good friends. He was always there for me when I needed him."

Robbins offered Dudleston emotional support and counsel when she went through a series of personal crises. "He communicated with me—even when I was in the New York City Ballet and he was away, he would send me postcards and stuff. But when I moved away, and then when I had my breakdown, he was there for me. And when I had my back surgery, he was there for me. He was always on the phone, sending flowers, sending cards, saying, 'Please call me; let me know if you're okay.' You know, that kind of thing. I mean genuine concern. I remember things he said, like, 'The most precious thing in your life is your moments of serenity. And you need to seek those at this time.' He gave me guidance that way. And I'd tell him about all the negatives, and the narrow-mindedness. I'd go on and on, and he would calmly say, 'The world is difficult everywhere. Calm down. Center yourself.' I was up living up at this ballet camp up in the woods. He said, 'Go out on the deck. Look at the mountains. Watch the sunset. Take your diary. Analyze what you're thinking. Put it down. Look at it. Decide if it's important to you.' You know, those kinds of things. He didn't say go to see this doctor or try this drug or anything like that."

Dudleston continued, "I think he was fairly psychic, personally. He definitely saw things that weren't there, things that the rest of us can't see. He heard things that weren't there. When I was hospitalized, I talked to Jerry, and he did tell me that he heard me and saw me in his dreams. . . . Often he would have dreams about the pieces [ballets] because he was so involved in them. And then he would go into the studio and expect to see happen what happened in that dream. And that was not possible. Because we're not weightless. I mean we are connected to the ground. I really experienced this with him. Because we could never—being human—we could never really do what he visualized. We could to a point, but human people could not do what he wanted."

In the spring of 1972, Robbins demonstrated the depth of his commitment to Balanchine and the City Ballet enterprise with his participation in Balanchine's Stravinsky Festival, an extravagant celebration dedicated to the composer who had died the year before. Balanchine billed the Festival as a "Presentation of Thirty-one Ballets to Music by Stravinsky, Twenty-one Made for the Occasion." Robbins admitted his initial apprehension on being asked by Balanchine to contribute five ballets in a single season. The sheer enormity of the undertaking was daunting for everyone (other choreographers included John Taras, Todd Bolender, John Clifford and Lorca Massine). Kirstein noted, "Balanchine insisted on the imploded fusion of one big bang."

Betty Cage recalled, "Of course, we all thought Balanchine was crazy when he said he was going to do it. And I said, 'What, a whole week of dark house for rehearsals? You're mad!' He said, 'Well, it's the only way we can do it.' The amazing thing was it was the same audience every night for two weeks, one week of rehearsal and then the real thing. And people came from all over the world, and they were there every single night. There were so many new ballets. I think everybody was practically dead when it was over. It was impossible, you couldn't do a thing like that, but they did it. The stage managers, the crew, the dancers—everybody. It was unbelievable. I can't imagine any theatrical event in my lifetime that is comparable."

Robbins displayed characteristic stylistic range in mounting *Scherzo Fantastique, Circus Polka, Dumbarton Oaks, Requiem Canticles* and *Pulcinella* (co-choreographed with Balanchine). Each of these works struck its own distinctive mood and tone through the dancing. *Scherzo* was a breathlessly ebullient and often air-borne crowd-pleaser that featured Gelsey Kirkland and Bart Cook, who was to become a favored Robbins dancer and one of his longtime ballet masters. The ballet was set to Stravinsky's sprightly sixteen-minute *Opus 3* (with its 1909 echoes of Rimsky-Korsakov and Debussy). The skimming dance elicited a compliment for Robbins from Clive Barnes, who wrote, "Mr. Robbins is adept at seeing the skeleton beneath the skin of Stravinsky's music." *Dumbarton Oaks* (set to a 1938 Stravinsky concerto for small orchestra) was a 1920s tennis party parody, a lighthearted romp for Allegra Kent and Anthony Blum (restaged in 1986 as *Piccolo Balleto*). While it was well received ("a total charmer," according to Clive Barnes), Allegra Kent said of the piece, "I couldn't find anything to latch on to, and I suspect Jerry couldn't, either."

On the other end of the stylistic spectrum was *Requiem Canticles*, a plangent choral work which Stravinsky's original program note called "a celebration of death" (composed five years before his own) and which Robbins abstracted into a starkly agonized clenching and unclenching of hands and mimed vocalizations of grief. Balanchine had employed the same score in 1968 to commemorate the death of Martin Luther King, Jr. As another "serious" work from Robbins, the ballet was naturally divisive for critics. Hubert Saal pegged it as "a masterpiece, the finest work he has ever done," while Nancy Goldner described *Requiem* as "mannered and manipulative . . . and ever so corny." The ballet would not be one of Robbins' more memorable creations. Some clunkers, of course, were inevitable, given the rushed circumstances and prolific output that the Festival demanded. In this Balanchine-Robbins competition, the Russian master would retain his title, widely credited with three masterworks—*Symphony in Three Movements, Violin Concerto* and *Duo Concertant* —out of seven new ballets. Still, Robbins had a significant audience following who preferred his more romantic aesthetic, even with his lapses into sentimentality and pretense, to Balanchine's more emotionally austere technical craftsmanship.

Stravinsky's four-minute novelty, *Circus Polka*, was first composed in 1942 on a commission from the Ringling Brothers Circus for a Balanchine "ballet" performed by elephants. For the 1972 Festival, Robbins adapted the piece for forty-eight aspiring ballerinas from the School of American Ballet. Cavorting merrily in tutus, the children spun around the stage in three concentric circles with Robbins costumed as ringmaster—donning top hat and tailcoat for the occasion—and brandishing a whip. At the end, while giving the impression of benevolent father, Robbins directed his charges to spell out the initials I. S. The enthusiastic audience for the premiere immediately demanded an encore. Edward Bigelow remembered that in subsequent performances, Robbins had the children spell out Lincoln Kirstein's monogram as well as his own.

Robbins made another stage appearance in the raucous Italian commedia piece *Pulcinella* (after the 1920 Massine-Picasso ballet), on which he collaborated under Balanchine, as it were. Robbins said, "The story is mostly George's. His Pulcinella combines the traditional commedia dell'arte with Goethe's *Faust*. He's a terrible, stupid man with a marvelous voracity for life. He steals and gives his loot away. He beats up people and becomes a victim. He has a great instinct for survival." Robbins also stated, "Every ballet I do with George is essentially George's conception. I am really more of an assistant than a co-choreographer. . . . When I work with him, I try absolutely to understand what it is he wants and what he's after and to do that. I only try to fulfill myself as an extension of him."

According to Edward Villella, who performed the title role, Robbins handled the crowd scenes and deferred to Balanchine on the specifics of characterization, as the latter was more familiar with the stylistic requirements of what was essentially a pantomime ballet (Balanchine had previously utilized commedia figures in *Harlequinade*). The collaboration between Robbins and Balanchine, with the two occasionally directing rehearsals together, harked back to their work on *Tyl Ulenspiegel*; and *Pulcinella* possessed much of the same raffish buffoonery as the earlier work. Pulcinella's episodic adventures began at his funeral, when a pact with the devil brought him back for a visit to a brothel and a riotous spaghetti dinner, which was a Balanchine idea staged by Robbins. The decor was designed by Eugene Berman, who was Balanchine's choice. Before the ballet premiered, Balanchine likened the experience to "working on a Broadway show," and with typically glib humor and nasal intonations, pointed out the advantage of collaboration under such time pressures, saying, "Two people work faster than one."

While in so much of his work Balanchine turned away from drama and discouraged dancers from emoting, he was a gifted performer of mime and characterization (having started his career as a dancer at the Maryinsky). Violette Verdy, who danced the role of Pulcinella's girl, recalled the magic of watching Balanchine demonstrate in the studio for Villella. "One day I was there watching with Lincoln Kirstein," said Verdy. "We turned to each other practically with tears in our eyes because it was so touching. I said, 'It's incredible—it's everything that one knows about theater.' And Lincoln said, 'Yes, it's not only the commedia dell'arte that you see there, it's also the French theater and the early modern Russian theater.' All this—everything—went into *Pulcinella*."

Penelope Dudleston remembered one of the rehearsals when both choreographers were present: "That was a real bad scene. I don't know what was going on, but Jerry ended up hitting me. He strikes me in the face saying, 'Use your head,' over this stupid thing where I was supposed to be pantomiming that somebody stole my pearls. I'm going on, trying to get it right, not knowing what I'm doing wrong. He says, 'You've got to make them believe it!' and I'm just not getting it. And Mr. B was there and saw this, and the two of them went marching off. Needless to say, he did not hit me again."

One of the highlights of the ballet was a short duel between two outlandish, ragtag beggars played by the two choreographers. Robbins credited Balanchine with choreographing the scene, though both undoubtedly contributed and were themselves merrily delighted to return to the stage. Dudleston recalled, "I watched them [rehearse]. They set everything that was going to happen. Jerry would do this and that. And then opening night Mr. B just ad-libbed on him. It got carried away with them hitting each other with canes. It was so funny, I thought I would die." Neither landed any blows, of course, which was the premise for the hilarity. The company and the audience rejoiced in the hijinks of these two natural hams. Their shared curtain calls brought roars of approval from spectators who sensed an almost familial bond with the company. Most critics applauded *Pulcinella*, while noting that it was still in need of revision, which Balanchine later undertook on his own but never completed to his satisfaction.

In the fall of 1972, the two choreographers showcased their work during City Ballet's extended tour of Russia and Poland. The ballets first had to be

screened for official Soviet approval during this era of Nixon's détente poli-
cies. The Robbins repertory finally included *Dances at a Gathering, In the Night, The
Goldberg Variations* and *Scherzo Fantastique,* all of which found favor with audiences
behind the Iron Curtain (while the official Marxist critics were predictably
cool with their reception). Among those in the admiring Leningrad audience
who would dance for both Robbins and Balanchine before the end of the
decade was the Kirov's young rising star, Mikhail Baryshnikov.

An Evening's Waltzes was a pure dance invention that Robbins set to
Prokofiev's 1946 *Suite of Waltzes* (waltzes from *Cinderella, War and Peace* and
Lermontov). There were eight couples in the cast that featured Patricia McBride
and her future husband, Jean-Pierre Bonnefoux, Christine Redpath (a newly
emerging Robbins favorite who replaced an injured Gelsey Kirkland), John
Clifford, Sara Leland and Bart Cook. This ballet was a technical experiment
that fell flat with most critics. For the McBride-Bonnefoux *pas de deux,* Robbins
had the dancers search to find each other across the ballroom and then execute
a series of unconventional turns and lifts (with McBride at one point supported over her partner's head like a flying angel). Robbins was set in his ways
by now, as far as method and manner in the studio. Bonnefoux, a French-
trained classical dancer, recalled, "The work [with Jerry] was just very challenging. It was that the man had so many ideas in his head and was just so brilliant.
You always felt you were trying to catch up with what he was telling you."

An Evening's Waltzes, with scenery and costumes from Rouben Ter-Arutunian,
opened at the State Theater on May 24, 1973. Clive Barnes called it "bland,"
noting that it lacked the "dazzling quality" of *Scherzo Fanastique.* Sounding almost apologetic, Robbins recalled being pushed into *Waltzes* by Balanchine,
saying, "The Company needed a new ballet. That's what happens in a repertory. Balanchine always says, 'Just keep working, keep doing things. Some of
them are bound to be good.' But it's a hard thing to do—to keep plunging
ahead when your instinct is to polish and hone. It's hard to live with the reactions. . . . Because some of the works are masterpieces, the audience expects all
works to be masterpieces."

Later that spring, Robbins spent ten days in Moscow as a judge for the Soviets' International Ballet Competition, and then traveled on to Italy to stage a special event at Gian Carlo Menotti's sixteenth Spoleto Festival. Robbins' *Celebration: The Art of the Pas de Deux* brought together a group of ten dancers—five couples representing five nationalities—Americans Patricia McBride and the elegant Helgi Tomasson (a longtime Robbins favorite, originally from Iceland), Violette Verdy and Jean-Pierre Bonnefoux from France, Anthony Dowell and Antoinette Sibley from Britain, Carla Fracci and Paolo Bortoluzzi of Italy, and Bolshoi soloists Melika Sabirova and Mozafer Bourkhanov of Russia. The program included various classic and romantic *pas de deux* (from *Don Quixote, La Sylphide, Coppélia, Sleeping Beauty* and *Le Corsaire*) as well as Balanchine's *Tchaikovsky Pas de Deux,* Frederick Ashton's *Thais,* Victor Gsovsky's *Grand Pas Classique,* and Robbins' *Afternoon of a Faun.* Robbins also introduced his new *Bagatelle* to Beethoven (later evolving into *Four Bagatelles* that premiered for City Ballet the following year with Gelsey Kirkland and Jean-Pierre Bonnefoux). Framing the evening, Robbins opened with an elegant waltz to music from *Swan Lake* and crafted an adagio finale for five Swan Queens and their Princes.

Violette Verdy remembered, "He [Robbins] organized the evening but he allowed us to choose the *pas de deux* we would do." The Spoleto audiences adored Robbins almost as much as their national heroine, Carla Fracci; and while in Italy, he was pleased to be greeted on the street as "Maestro." *Celebration* proved even more popular that year than Luchino Visconti's staging of Puccini's *Manon Lescaut.* Patricia McBride remembered, "We [dancers] would go out with Jerry and it was fun. He loved it there. It was a wonderful great place. I think Aidan Mooney was with him on that trip."

Aidan Mooney worked for *Newsweek*'s research library and was a deeply impassioned balletomane and Balanchine aficionado. John Clifford remembered introducing Mooney to Robbins several years before. "Aidan was a fan of mine and started coming around to my rehearsals," said Clifford. "I brought them [Mooney and Robbins] together." Over the course of the decade, Mooney was a constant presence at City Ballet, although he had no formal association with the company. Betty Cage said, "Oh goodness, Aidan was always floating around. He was in and out of the office and the theater, and he was also a friend of Lincoln's."

Edward Bigelow surmised, "I would say Aidan was a spy for Jerry, and I know that he did go to performances and he did tell him what he saw. And Jerry respected his opinion." Mooney quickly became a mainstay in Robbins' life. One of Mooney's friends recalled, "Jerry let Aidan take care of his house when he was away. There was a huge rapport. They were both a bit dominating as personalities. When they were together, Aidan was a stronger personality than Jerry was. Aidan was very much an intellectual ally, and Jerry had a very intellectual side to him. . . . Sometimes you get annoyed with Aidan because he's extremely opinionated, but he's a fascinating person. Aidan argues with anybody about anything. . . . Aidan's passionate about Balanchine and Robbins. He loves, absolutely adores them. He's a person who will actually groan out loud with pleasure when he watches a ballet."

Later, Mooney's friend William Earle, a philosophy professor at Baruch College, also became part of this fraternal clique. Robbins' friend Michael Koessel characterized the intellectual sparring in the Robbins-Mooney friendship, saying, "They were very funny together. I have to admit, it was harder for me to disagree with Jerry, although he was pretty respectful, actually. The thing [was] that Aidan could disagree with him. . . . I think part of it was Jerry was amused. Aidan gets very passionate about things that most people don't have strong opinions about. There's an enormous amount of hyperbole [on Aidan's part]. . . . I have a great picture of Jerry holding his two fingers up behind Aidan's head as Aidan posed for a picture with a surfboard he had just purchased. Because Aidan was all of a sudden . . . interested in surfboards, and he went out and bought one of these huge used surfboards to hang in his apartment. He saw them as art objects. That's an example of the kind of passion he felt towards things that most people are completely indifferent towards. . . . Aidan is a real culture vulture. There's nobody in New York quite like Aidan, I think. He sees everything five times and knows exactly what he thinks of it and can go on and on. I think part of it was amusement, but Jerry would argue back with him. . . . For what it's worth, Aidan has actually very conservative political views. Jerry, I would say, [was] kind of a left-leaning liberal in his politics. Not a socialist . . . not very far to the left, but obviously other people's politics didn't bother him."

Robbins' political past was a lingering stigma. For friends like Arthur Gold and Robert Fizdale, Robbins' artistry exonerated him. In his memoir, *Original Story*, Arthur Laurents wrote of Gold and Fizdale, "The boys, as Jerry called them, were also acolytes of Balanchine. Whether he or Jerry was the greatest choreographer of the century depended, I supposed, on which was in earshot." Harold Talbott recalled, "Gold and Fizdale would whisper to me about Jerry, that there were loads and loads of people who, when he was in public, would turn their backs on him and never speak to him. And they would whisper there was this terrible thing that Jerry was capable of doing because of his [political] past. And of course little did they know that I was a raging rightist. I thought, good for Jerry. He went way up in my estimation. They felt that he was a person who had really suffered from what he decided to do to save his skin."

Talbott described Robbins' status in the salon scene, saying, "He became this immensely desirable social figure. I think that although he hung out with the likes of Mica Ertegün and Lady Keith, I think he must have felt a tiny bit of insecurity because of his origins. When I knew him, I got a distinct feeling that he instantly related to me as a society boy and that was not negative for him, but it just was that he knew he wasn't of that world. He said to my friend Bobby Fizdale, 'Oh, I like your tennis player,' you see, because I was tall and thin and part of the whole *Philadelphia Story* world. I think that Jerry was immensely sought after in those circles and an extremely desirable escort for women. . . . People were very jealous. Jerry was immensely coveted. To have him at your table meant that women were making endless efforts to shine, everyone was thrilled—oh, Jerry's in the room!—I can't tell you. I can't tell you what a sought-after person he was."

As a young man, future Hollywood producer Howard Rosenman had a brief affair with Leonard Bernstein in the late 1960s and later came to know Robbins and Stephen Sondheim. Rosenman became romantically involved with Slim Keith's daughter, Kitty Hawks, and entered Robbins' social orbit during the early seventies. A medical-school dropout from an Orthodox Jewish family on Long Island, Rosenman was one of those who was contemptuous of Robbins' political past. Rosenman recalled, "Of course, I was very, very quiet about it. I always felt like saying to him, but I never did, 'You going to rat me out, boy?' That's the way I felt about him and I was in constant turmoil whenever I was with Jerry. He kind of knew the way I felt. . . . He knew why I didn't admire him. So there was always that *entente cordiale.* When we were thrown together in family situations for a period of about four or five years, every Thanksgiving and every Christmas, anniversaries, birthdays—usually it was just me and Slim and Jerry and Kitty. And they loved him. . . . He was so refined finally, his taste was so pure and so chic, and he would always have the chicest people around, and refined in an aesthetic way, too. Normally, I kind of loved that, but because it was splashed with the politics of infamy, to me it was like being in a concentration camp.

"He had major energy, and he was open. He was very humble. I always attributed that humility to paranoia, guilt. But you know people that were not politically sophisticated and didn't know about it thought that he was truly humble and that he was a great guy. Occasionally, he'd catch my eye—because I was so fascinated by this, by this dichotomy and his duality, I was so into it, this dialectic, as it were—that he would occasionally catch my eye and I would always know that he knew what I was thinking. . . .

"He lost a lot of friends. Did he care? I guess he did care. He never recovered, from my point of view. He had to deal with that his whole life. I was in a restaurant once when Lillian Hellman saw Jerry Robbins and walked out of the restaurant. Can you imagine being branded like that? How do you go anywhere? He was always uncomfortable in a room. You'd see Jerry in rooms of people, he was never comfortable in his own skin. He was most comfortable with groups of boys or with Slim and Kitty in an environment that he could control. . . . But Jerry had the affect of a Zen master, which I think he cultivated. He had that ascetic, grand, majestic look. But it was haunted. It wasn't the satisfied, open look of a Buddha. He was a betrayer, literally so. I wouldn't know how to live with myself. I suppose my judgment is harsh. I'm certainly no genius; Jerry was a genius. So don't geniuses get away with everything? But I know, and the people that really knew him know, and they knew that. I don't think people who had really a lot of integrity forgave him. . . . I think Lenny really had contempt, because Lenny felt so passionately about certain things."

Early in 1974, Robbins and Leonard Bernstein reunited for *Dybbuk* (later called *The Dybbuk Variations*). This ballet was inspired by S. Ansky's 1920 Yiddish play *The Dybbuk*, which Robbins and Bernstein first discussed adapting as early as 1944. Their new effort was difficult from the beginning. In February, Bernstein's friend Helen Coates wrote, "Lenny is depressed because Jerry can't make up his mind how the ballet should go. So Lenny is at a standstill with it." Robbins later said, "I think Lenny and I had different ideas. He took the dramatic side. I took the abstract. They're two parallel paths that don't converge."

The cast featured Patricia McBride and Helgi Tomasson as the ill-fated lovers, Leah and Chanon. McBride recalled, "*Dybbuk* was a great ballet. I think I loved doing that ballet more than any other. I just loved the feeling of it. He [Jerry] gave Helgi and me books of the story. You wanted to devour this book and to learn about what he wanted there. Seeing him and Leonard Bernstein together, it just was fantastic. Leonard Bernstein was such a flamboyant character. He'd come in the studio, you'd get a big hug and a kiss."

Wilma Curley remembered disputes between the two creators over the concept of the dance and cuts that Robbins demanded in the score. At one point, Robbins summarily ejected Bernstein from a rehearsal. "We were watching the *Dybbuk* rehearsal," said Curley, "and Lenny was sitting two rows down from us. And Jerry yells at him, 'Get out of here!' And not a peep out of Lenny. Jerry threw Bernstein out of the theater. I loved watching it."

Robbins prevailed in having the dance make only passing, episodic allusions to its narrative source. Drawing from the Jewish mystical tradition of the Kabbalah, the Ansky play told the story of a young couple, Leah and Chanon, who were pledged to each other by their fathers and later fell in love, only to be separated when the girl's father arranged for her to marry a wealthy suitor. According to Bernstein's program notes, "Chanon [an impoverished rabbinical student], desperately turns to the Kabbalah to help him win Leah for himself, and as a last resort, he invokes the powerful but dangerous other-worldly formulae of ancient usage. At the supreme moment of discovering the secret words that unleash the dark forces, he is overwhelmed by the fierce ecstasy of the enlightenment and dies. At Leah's wedding, Chanon returns as a dybbuk [supernatural spirit] and, claiming her as his rightful bride, clings ferociously to his beloved." After the dybbuk is exorcized by the elders, "Leah, unable to exist without her predestined bridegroom, leaves her life to join him in oblivion." Robbins later removed the play's synopsis from the ballet program notes, believing that knowledge of the story caused confusion and was unnecessary for the audience to appreciate the dance.

Bernstein's score, with its intricate lyricism and sudden rhythmic surges, was suggestive of Hasidic ritual ecstasies. While much of the score was tonal, the composer included serial passages and utilized an obscure system of numerology derived from his studies of the Kabbalah. He later wrote, "It was the integer 2 that particularly fascinated me, since Ansky's *Dybbuk* is really a drama about dualisms—Good and Evil, Ends and Means, Male and Female, Justice and Necessity, Self and Society . . . and especially the duality of the so-called True World as opposed to *this* world in which we seem to reside."

Robbins initially divided the fifty-minute ballet into eleven sections. The piece opened with a ceremonial Hasidic interlude ("In the Holy Place"), setting the scene with line formations for seven young holy men in hats. The pledge made by the lovers' fathers was depicted by an emphatic clasping of hands, and the subsequent arranged marriage for Leah was symbolized by her rejection of a bridal veil. A series of love duets for McBride and Tomasson— both costumed in Patricia Zipprodt's flowing white caftans—took the form of passionate running leaps. Mysterious, other-worldly messengers came onstage to witness the proceedings, and a series of stylized male solos led to the ecstatic climax achieved by Tomasson's Chanon. Evoking love, possession and exorcism against an oppressive backdrop of social, religious and paternal authority, the work was thematically reminiscent of *The Guests*, with its non-specific treatment of *Romeo and Juliet*. But with *Dybbuk*, Robbins was determined to transcend the literal specifics of the ghost story, venturing further into Balanchine's realm of pure dance abstraction. Strangely enough, there were repeated incongruous echoes from *West Side Story*—at the beginning of a section called "Maiden's Dance," four women were seen kneeling behind Leah, swaying and snapping their fingers.

The ballet first appeared at a gala preview on May 15, 1974, and premiered the next day, with Bernstein conducting both performances. *Newsweek* praised *Dybbuk* as "the loving handiwork of inspired men" and applauded its "spine-tingling climax." Clive Barnes credited Robbins with having "caught the intense spiritual incandescence of both his leading dancers." Offering more mood than substance, the ballet was a letdown for other critics. Nancy Goldner wrote, "Robbins' decision to treat the play as abstract fantasy is legitimate, but what is so disappointing is the absence of abstract emotion, idea, or even point of view." The *New Republic* characterized the undertaking as "a pretentious botch of a good opportunity, all windup and no delivery."

Robbins was never satisfied with the ballet and revised it in 1980 under the title *A Suite of Dances,* excerpting eight episodes, eliminating Rouben Ter-Arutunian's scenery and attempting to achieve even greater distance from the ballet's narrative roots. Croce dismissed the effort, writing, "In Robbins's case, I can't help thinking that there must be a personal dybbuk involved who saps his energy and turns him to the pursuit of cosmic bellyaches in dance." In the *New York Times,* Anna Kisselgoff wrote, "Oddly, the work is now too dramatic to be fully satisfying as a plotless ballet." Such was the slippery middle ground that Robbins occupied as he continued to bring his dramatic sensibility into Balanchine's rarefied domain.

In the spring of 1975, City Ballet's Ravel Festival posed another speed and endurance contest for its choreographers. With scores from Maurice Ravel, Robbins would mount five ballets and Balanchine six in a period of three weeks. The Festival's gala opening night on May fifteenth drew such notables as Andy Warhol, Pat Kennedy Lawford, Sargent Shriver, Happy Rockefeller and France's First Lady Anne-Aymone Giscard d'Estaing. Onstage that night, Balanchine (already a Kennedy Center Award Honoree) received the French Legion of Honor award and quipped in appreciation, "We owe a lot to France. La France gave us La Dance—and it's why I'm still alive today. It's the wine."

Balanchine provided the Festival's artsy highlight with his ensemble work *Le Tombeau de Couperin,* and the conversation piece *Tzigane,* which was the first ballet that he choreographed for Suzanne Farrell after her welcome return to the company in January. Robbins also cast Farrell in *Concerto in G* (later called *In G Major*), pairing her with Peter Martins. In her memoir, *Holding On to the Air*, Farrell recalled, "He [Robbins] designed the ballet's central *pas de deux* on Sara Leland and Bart Cook, and only later asked Peter and me to learn it and dance the premiere. This method was unfamiliar to me—Balanchine never changed his casting once he began a ballet, unless injury forced him to—and I did not particularly like the audition atmosphere that was sure to encourage insecurity all around. But Jerry was polite, helpful, and accommodating, and he had created a very beautiful, languid *pas de deux* that I enjoyed dancing. The ballet was an enormous success and became one of the few from the festival that had a future life."

As a kind of professional courtesy extended to established stars, Robbins donned kid gloves for his work in the studio with Farrell and Martins, as he would later do with Baryshnikov and Natalia Makarova. Regarding *Concerto in G*, Martins remembered that Robbins "constantly made clear how interested he was in us as dancers, and that he had no ideal notion of what this piece absolutely must be like. He asked us what we thought, and he used some of our ideas." In later years, the Robbins-Martins relationship was destined to be strained and tested, with nothing less than the fate of the company hanging in the balance.

With its French-flavored, jazzy score, *Concerto in G* opened on May fifteenth. City Ballet press officer Leslie Bailey was in the audience and recalled, "After the adagio in the second act, there was a moment of silence. I was standing in the first ring and Jerry was sitting nearby and I looked at him, and the *shock*—it was his usual insecurity. Because the shocked look on his face was, *oh my God, they hate it.* But it wasn't that anyone hated it, it was that it was so staggeringly gorgeous, these two blonde gods onstage, that the audience was stunned. And then they started to scream. And Robert [Irving, the conductor] immediately struck up that music which is very bright and bouncy, and you couldn't hear it because the audience was yelling. They had just been stunned because they were so beautiful. And then I looked at Jerry again and he had sat back, he was relaxed now that he knew they liked it. He always had that feeling—*will they like it?*"

Clive Barnes termed the central *pas de deux* "a lovely, bluesy duet," while pointing out that the "sportive choreography" was for Robbins a return to the familiar children's games of *Interplay*. This was relatively safe territory for Robbins that he exploited again with *Ma Mère l'Oye*, with an ensemble of dancers acting out fairy tales. Following a scenario for the dance specified by Ravel, Robbins' ballet portrays a Sleeping Beauty who falls asleep for a hundred years and dreams of other fairy tales like *Beauty and the Beast* and *Hop o' My Thumb* acted out by dancers in practice clothes. While received favorably by most critics, some reacted to the element of caricature in the work. Robbins said defensively, "I love *Sleeping Beauty* and all the fairy tales presented there. Some people said my treatment wasn't worthy of Ravel, but I followed his libretto exactly." The ballet was later successfully revived as *Mother Goose (Fairy Tales for Dancers)*.

Robbins' other contributions to the Festival—*Introduction and Allegro for Harp, Chansons Madécasses* and *Un Barque Sur l'Océan*—were uneven and less consequential, as though he were spreading himself too thin and, like the audience after three weeks, was surfeited as far as Ravel was concerned. With its exoticism and French art songs (based on poems by Evariste Parmey), the score of *Chansons Madécasses* drew Robbins into the area where he was most vulnerable to critical accusations of frivolous pretense, even with gifted performers like Patricia McBride and Helgi Tomasson dutifully committed to carrying out his vision. In this case, working with two couples—one light-skinned and one dark-skinned (Debra Austin and Hermes Condé)—Robbins was trying to acknowledge a less than significant racial theme in Ravel's source material. Meanwhile, Robbins limited the dancers to floor work without the athletic excitement and emotional expressiveness of jumps and lifts, at times calling for long moments of watchful stillness. Croce complained, "The only reason one can't formulate a meaning for what he has put on the stage is that there isn't any."

Robbins was taking strident heat not only from some of the Balanchine-oriented dance critics, but also from Broadway pundits who were wondering in print why he had chosen to exile himself from musical comedy. In the *Post*, Martin Gottfried wrote, "He hasn't done a Broadway show in twelve years—since *Fiddler on the Roof*. He has abandoned the collaborative give and go of the musical for the absolute control of the ballet choreographer. Though he has a right to that choice, frankly I think he is denying himself the exercise of a prodigious personal talent." The following year, Gottfried taunted him, suggesting, "Today he is a god and it may well be the very deification that is keeping him away from the theater. Glorification appeals to hammy impulses and why risk a fall? How can he compete with his own reputation that by now has reached supernatural proportions?" The critic concluded, "Successful people in high or low entertainment tend to mistake the adulation they receive for true value. This self-importance can become foolish and it would be even more foolish if Robbins spent a lifetime playing a Sardi's ascetic, only to find at the end that it had cost him the use of a joyous part of his abilities and very soul."

In fact, Robbins continued to field Broadway offers, but the music and style of the musical were changing, with shows like *Applause, A Chorus Line, Company, Follies, The Wiz, Dancin'* and *Sweeney Todd.* Ironically, Robbins had helped usher in the new era that seemed to exclude him. *Evita* won the Tony for Best Musical in 1980, and *West Side Story* was revived that same year. At the time, Robbins said, "There are very few shows over the years that I wish I'd done. I know the story is that I never wanted to do musicals again. But it isn't true."

Yet he acknowledged that he had turned to ballet to avoid the pressures and compromises of Broadway while pursuing his own artistic goals. "I felt that as a director, and sometimes as choreographer, I was always serving other people's material. I also wanted to try to create theater pieces the way I create ballets, not necessarily with a fixed script. I had done a lot of musicals and I was interested in other things. But I never made a definite statement about never going back to Broadway again. . . . What I love about working in a ballet company is that your life doesn't depend on one project. In a Broadway show, everyone—the dancers, composer, orchestra, stagehands, sound man, lighting person, all are there to get across the high wire. The chances of making it are very rare, as you can see from the percentages. If you don't make it, you have to start again from scratch. That's a terrifying price to pay."

On April 27, 1976, Robbins received the Capezio Award "for bringing a new classicism and daring innovation, profundity and hilarity to the world of ballet. . . ." The award ceremony took place at the Pierre Hotel, with Patricia McBride and Edward Villella serving as presenters. In his remarks,

Robbins credited them with inspiring his return to ballet in 1969 after watching them rehearse *Afternoon of a Faun*. He said, "It was through Patty and Eddie that I returned to the world I've been in for seven years and very happily so." Robbins donated his $1,000 award to the School of American Ballet.

That spring, Robbins again turned to Chopin, choreographing *Other Dances* for "The Star Spangled Gala" to benefit the Library of Performing Arts at Lincoln Center. Robbins had previously donated three-quarters of one percent of his profits from *Fiddler on the Roof* to the library's Dance Collection. This was a substantial sum that started at about $500 per week and continued to climb with revivals. The new ballet was a wedding gift financed by Léonide Massine's ex-wife, Eugenia Doll (Mrs. Henri), for Natalia Makarova, the Kirov star who defected in 1970 and joined American Ballet Theatre. Her partner for *Other Dances* was Mikhail (Misha) Baryshnikov. Both Russians fared well with Robbins in the studio, though their classical training didn't necessarily predispose them to the idiosyncrasies of his musical phrasing and choreographic style.

The ballet consisted of four mazurkas and a waltz (the latter also used by Fokine in *Les Sylphides*). In *Baryshnikov at Work*, the dancer recollected, "I think the most difficult thing for Jerry was to find the form—the structure—of the ballet. He approached each section as a musical whole, and then had to work out the sequence in a way that was theatrically sound. It is my feeling that the dances could have been placed in any order, even though the way it evolved resulted in what is very much a classical pas de deux structure: pas de deux, variations, variations, coda. He didn't use many verbal or psychological descriptions to elicit from us what he wanted. Sometimes he would say something as brief as, 'This is a military variation,' or 'This pose is like a late nineteenth-century photograph; try and get that feeling.' But basically the whole ballet is just a *musical idea*. It was born of and lives inside the music. Jerry understands it that way."

Natalia Makarova articulated her understanding of the ballet and Robbins' intentions in a slightly different way than Baryshnikov, placing a more explicit emphasis on the dramatic subtext of the movement. In her memoir, *A Dance Autobiography*, Makarova wrote, "In *Other Dances*, the body seems to be weaving a shawl of Velenciennes lace, the choreographic design is the fabric of the lace, and the space between the threads is filled with the pauses, the hesitations, the subtle nuances, that fine understatement of movement that for me is the most precious feature of the romantic—and, for that matter, of any—ballet. For me, Jerry Robbins is the most romantic of all the neo-classical choreographers. On the surface he is like Balanchine, working primarily in the genre of the plotless ballet, but the degree of abstraction is not as great with Robbins. He is less geometric and for me he is more poetic, because in his choreography there is always room for self-expression. I do not feel I am a mere instrument following precisely the prescribed design. Besides, though Jerry's ballets do not have traditional plots, they always have something reminiscent of one, which is hard to articulate in a logical way. When I perform *Other Dances* with Misha, we always try to convey a certain dramatic message to the audience."

Baryshnikov recalled that during some rehearsals, Robbins would simply demonstrate the entire dance as a point of departure. Describing Robbins' characteristic style, Baryshnikov noted that "he would show me one of those combinations that are so *his,* and so beautiful—the twists of the shoulder, the open relaxed steps gradually changing into smaller, more delicate movements." In a statement indicative of their rapport, Baryshnikov later said lightheartedly, "Sometimes I think Jerry's inspiration comes out of his beard."

The costume designer on *Other Dances,* Santo Loquasto, observed, "Jerry admired Misha, so he was on his best behavior." During subsequent ballets for Baryshnikov, Robbins often created the choreography with other dancers beforehand, thus easing the burden on the Russian star (and avoiding any potential conflicts). Robbins utilized Christopher d'Amboise in such a capacity as early as *Watermill,* when he (the son of City Ballet veterans Jacques d'Amboise and Carolyn George) was an eleven-year-old student at the School of American Ballet. At that time, Robbins staged some of Edward Villella's role with the young dancer acting as a kind of stand-in. D'Amboise recalled, "He [Jerry] began using me—a double-edged sword—*using* me is what people called it. But I would go in and work with him for hours, working on choreography that I would then teach to Misha, or then teach to Peter Martins, or then teach to somebody else. He liked to work with me. All these ballets that

other people ended up premiering . . . he worked out on me. Which of course
was fantastic, because you learned so much. And then also I did the roles
[later] anyway."

D'Amboise suggested that Robbins was frustrated whenever he departed
from his instinctive dramatic orientation, saying, "He had a hard time choreographing ballets that didn't have a motivation. When you think of his great
ballets—*Fancy Free, Interplay, The Cage, The Concert*—they're all theatrical, they're
all motivated by character. And even *Dances at a Gathering*. . . . He didn't really
know what to do choreographically when he didn't have that."

While *Other Dances* didn't evoke a veiled story with multiple characters like
Dances at a Gathering, the new ballet did eloquently exploit the dramatic subtext
and motivation intrinsic to the romantic *pas de deux*. Describing a lesson that
he attributed to Balanchine, Robbins pinpointed the essential "drama" or romantic conceit of two dancers onstage, saying, "A girl puts up her arm; a boy
raises his arm; they walk toward each other and touch. That's enough." Of
course, such a simple scenario could be treated in any number of ways, and in
the hands of lesser artists would most likely lack interest and meaning. Where
Balanchine found an austere, geometrical beauty in partnering and utilized the
men primarily as supportive cavaliers, Robbins injected a passionate intensity
and often tilted the balance between the sexes, where the man or woman might
be seen as the object of aggression. In those ballets in which he was not in-
dulging his penchant for children's larks, there were at times thrilling elements
of physical danger that increased the emotional tension and raised the stakes
of the partnering. Under Chopin's protective wing, *Other Dances* relied more on
graceful subtleties, blending earthy folk movement with the airy élan of classical dancing.

Clive Barnes instantly declared *Other Dances* a masterpiece and observed
that it "could fit into *Dances at a Gathering* without a shudder of notice. It has
precisely the original ballet's sense of place and style, of Slavic forms growing
in an alien soil of transposed dance images, character motions and national
glints, into an oddly pure form of classical dance. There is no choreography—
with its mixture of character fervor and classic grace—quite like it anywhere."
The gala premiere took place on May ninth at the Metropolitan Opera House,

and on the same night, Mayor Abraham Beame presented Robbins with the city's Handel Medallion for lifetime achievement. *Other Dances* subsequently entered the repertories of both American Ballet Theatre and the New York City Ballet.

Later that year, Robbins' personal life took another turn into romance by way of a chance encounter with Jesse Gerstein, who was then a nineteen-year-old aspiring photographer. Michael Koessel met Robbins during the next decade through Gerstein and recalled, "They met on the street [in Manhattan]. I know that Jerry had the feeling that he was just a boy who needed to be looked after. I don't know any of the sexual details, although I think that even when they were living together they had separate rooms. I think there was something of a father-son-type relationship between them to a certain extent. . . . At least initially my impression is that Jerry felt this was someone who needs to be taken care of."

Gerstein went to work for Robbins' longtime friend Richard Avedon, and eventually established himself as a commercial artist. According to Koessel, Robbins "also respected Jesse enormously, because I think he thought of Jesse as being very talented. He *was* very talented, and in particular Jesse was enormously graceful socially. That's something I've heard other people who've gone out with Jerry comment on . . . that they could never compete with Jesse at a social level. Jesse fit into crowds that few of Jerry's other friends could move in quite so easily—the Mica Ertegün crowd. . . . Jesse could move through pretty comfortably. The rest of us felt a little more awkward when we got in those situations. Jerry had what we would refer to as his society friends and his friends, mostly men, that he'd hang out with at the beach, take vacations with, that kind of thing. . . . And he very seldom would mix the two. Only on special events like at opening dinners, or when someone was throwing him a birthday party, or he got an award, or something like that, would the two crowds mix."

Though not a monogamous relationship, Robbins and Gerstein lived together until the early 1980s and maintained a close friendship after the breakup. Gerstein's friend Lisa Stevens recalled, "Jerry loved Jesse like a friend, lover, son, etc. Even though each had other relationships after they parted, their connection remained firmly intact and probably stronger than when they were together." Mike Koessel remembered, "One of the reasons, he [Jerry] told me, that he and Jesse broke up eventually was that their age difference led to a huge power difference, and it was something that Jerry said he wasn't crazy about. . . . He said he felt like he did all the planning, he did all the work, and that Jesse just followed along. He said one night Jesse was going to take control of the evening, he was going to pick which movie they went to or where they went to eat or what they were going to do. And he said that just didn't work. But he said he really wanted that to work. So I don't think that he wanted to be a dictator, at least not in all aspects of his life."

Robbins later had a brief affair with independent filmmaker Warren Sonbert, whose avant-garde movies included *Rude Awakening* (1972), *Divided Loyalties* (1978) and *Friendly Witness*, which played at the 1989 New York Film Festival. Sonbert died of AIDS in 1996. His friend and fellow filmmaker Nathaniel Dorsky remembered a week-long visit from Robbins and Sonbert in San Francisco during the late seventies (when the San Francisco Ballet staged several Robbins ballets). "Warren was a person who had a very definite sense of what was legitimate entertainment, so to speak, in terms of opera and so forth, and was very strict about it and very dedicated to going to things constantly," said Dorsky. "And I do remember Warren talking about them struggling to see eye to eye and getting into conflicts because Jerry wouldn't hop on his wagon. . . . They had different aesthetics. I think Warren's aesthetic taste was more toward the classical in terms of cinema, even traditional Hollywood cinema or Mozartian opera and so forth, where Jerry was more of a blood-and-guts content kind of guy. He wanted to feel things. That was another area of eventual aesthetic conflict they had, where Jerry would like some silly things, like Bergman or something. And I remember he was a little afraid of drugs, because he had had some kind of very bad experience. There was a Chabrol film that Warren took him to—we all went to it—it had some depiction of an LSD trip in it, which we as filmmakers found just sort of silly because all they did was put different color gels over the camera and had some balloons and images out-of-focus. This terrified Jerry—Jerry actually got horrified like it was going to bring on a relapse."

Dorsky also recollected attending a picnic and Fourth of July fireworks display with Robbins and Sonbert. "It was really like a friend of yours was dating someone who was visiting from New York. . . . And yes, you could ask this person questions about the New York City Ballet and about various dancers and about Balanchine. It wasn't hard to come up with topics for conversation. Jerry was completely unassuming. There was no air whatsoever of this person being of a world-renowned stature. He wasn't even like someone playing modest, he was just a person."

Late in 1976, a revival of *Fiddler on the Roof* brought Robbins briefly back to Broadway. The production was staged by Ruth Mitchell and Tommy Abbott. The star was again Zero Mostel, who was fresh from his success that year in *The Front*, Martin Ritt's movie about the blacklist that starred Woody Allen. Before *Fiddler* closed its out-of-town run in Boston, Robbins exercised his contractual right to take over and direct the musical a week prior to its Broadway opening at the Winter Garden in late December. The Mostel-Robbins feud continued where it left off twelve years before. According to Mostel biographer Jared Brown, when Robbins tried to offer Mostel direction, the actor repeatedly scoffed and put him off with the line, "We'll talk about it later."

Gerald Schoenfeld of the Shubert group recalled, "Zero Mostel hated him for naming names, loathed him. But he nevertheless respected him. Zero told us, because we did the revival of *Fiddler* with [him], 'Can you imagine that little sonofabitch came to my dressing room?' Because he had the right to direct the last week of the show. That was in Boston. So Zero said, 'I let him come in my dressing room, but I'll tell you something, I never shook his hand.' Now of course what he was saying was, he was really very happy that he came, but he would never yield to the situation."

Audiences and critics enthusiastically welcomed Mostel's return to the role of Tevye. In the *Times*, Mel Gussow hailed Mostel's opening night performance, declaring, "the king returns to his throne." Martin Gottfried agreed with that sentiment in the *Post*; but later in the run, when Mostel again turned to ad-libbing, Gottfried condemned his behavior as "disdainful of theatre; inconsiderate of the company; contemptuous of the audience." To no avail, the critic accused Mostel of "making a fool of himself."

Thelma Lee, who played Golde, was unperturbed by Mostel's improvised antics. "It didn't bother me, because I was a stand-up comic," said Lee, "and I could deal with anything that Zero did. I actually liked it; it was interesting. . . . In the dream sequence one night, he ripped my nightgown off. But I just finished the number in a blanket. And the audience just screamed. Then afterwards they built me another nightgown underneath the nightgown, so that if he pulled one off, the other one stayed."

During another performance, Mostel played the number "Do You Love Me?" with a bucket on his head. Such irreverent liberties were hardly appreciated by the show's director. After putting up much resistance, Robbins finally allowed a performance of *Fiddler* to be filmed on March 23, 1977, by Amran Nowak Associates. The film became part of the collection of the Theatre on Film and Tape Archive at Lincoln Center. But Robbins was so dismayed by Mostel's performance that he refused to allow anyone to view it over the years, other than cast members of future revivals where there was an interest in preserving his choreography.

At the beginning of the year, Robbins wrote to his friend Penelope Dudleston, and chronicled recent events and frustrations in his life. While he had seen Harold Pinter's *No Man's Land* (with John Gielgud and Ralph Richardson) three times and lauded the play, he complained that he was slowing down and that his work was now impeded by knee problems and the strike by musicians. He expressed concern for the dancers who were out of work, and only drawing partial salary thanks to the filming of two Balanchine ballets. Robbins also reported that he had become a local hero when, despite his abject terror, he managed to scare off a mugger who was attacking one of his neighbors on Eighty-first Street. But his tone implied that his inspiration was flagging, that age was catching up, though he retained a wry sense of gallows humor. He was relieved to have weathered the holidays without emotional trauma and recounted how he had tried to cook a New Year's pudding and ended up spattering his kitchen ceiling with rum and eggs, much to the tolerant dismay of his Chilean cook.

In 1977, the ballet boom was in full swing. The art form was enjoying unprecedented popularity, with audience numbers across the country rivaling even those in professional sports. The movie *The Turning Point*, a sophisticated ballet soap opera, cashed in at the box office that fall, with Oscar-nominated performances from Anne Bancroft, Shirley MacLaine and Mikhail Baryshnikov. Herbert Ross directed and co-produced with his wife Nora Kaye. Arthur Laurents wrote the screenplay based on two ballerinas (played by MacLaine and Bancroft), one of whom gave up her career for marriage and family, while the other established herself as the company's prima ballerina. To some degree, their story mirrored that of Nora Kaye and Isabel Brown (whose daughter Leslie danced with ABT and played the role of the young ballerina-starlet in the film). While Robbins wasn't directly involved with the movie, the ballet company in Laurents' screenplay was a fictional Ballet Theatre, and actor James Mitchell played a secondary character loosely based on both Robbins and Oliver Smith.

Mitchell recalled, "I played the artistic director of the company, that was the idea. They asked me to grow a white beard, because I was supposed to be a combination of Oliver Smith and Jerry. Hey. Anyway, the first time I saw Jerry after that, and he'd seen it, the first thing he said to me was in the street—he said not hello, he said, 'Give me back my beard.' That was it. I didn't write it. Oh lord. He could always very quickly turn anything into something very sharp."

Laurents remembered that he had tried to write a gay subplot into the script, but that his efforts were sabotaged by Herb Ross, with tacit support from his wife. Their marriage of twenty-five years had flourished, and undoubtedly, the sexual issues and wounds of the past were not something they wanted to see dredged up in the movie. Ross reportedly told Laurents, "Nobody in the ballet is gay anymore." Laurents' sanitized rendering of the story earned him one of the movie's eleven Academy Awards nominations.

Meanwhile, at City Ballet, Robbins was planning a full-length, three-act ballet, *The Arts of the Gentleman*, based on the courtly initiation of young men into fencing, horsemanship and ballroom etiquette. Robbins worked on the fencing with a Hungarian master swordsman who served as armorer at the Metropolitan Opera Association. Lincoln Kirstein called the early work on the fencing "a tour de force of brilliance" and remembered, "Robbins had been seriously ill, nor had his recovery been quick. He had apparently abandoned *The Arts of the Gentleman,* only the introduction of which he had been able to sketch." In fact, Robbins was hospitalized for surgical treatment of diverticulitis, and would not resume work on the ballet until the spring of the following year. His physical condition required a colostomy, about which he was typically stoical. He later told his friends, Ninette Charisse and Bobby Tucker, when the subject of colostomy came up, "Oh, that's nothing. I've got one."

Leslie Bailey was one of City Ballet's press agents at the time of Robbins' hospitalization. Bailey recalled that there were suspicions at the *New York Times* that the choreographer might be terminally ill. Bailey said, "One night [dance critic] Jennifer Dunning is working at the *Times,* and one of the editors, Seymour Topping, a cultural editor . . . was walking by and he sees Jennifer working on [updating] Jerome Robbins' obituary. So this clicks with something in his head, which is Jerome Robbins happens to be in the hospital. He had a bout of diverticulitis, which of course was no big thing. I would say at eleven or maybe twelve o'clock at night, I get a call at home from this editor, and he's in quite a perturbed state. He says, 'You have to tell me, is Jerry Robbins dying? Shall I tell them they have to hold a spot on the front page?' So I explained to him about no, no, it's true he is in the hospital, but it's not serious at all. What I always thought was so wonderful about it, and I did eventually tell Jerry, was we don't always know how we're going to be treated [after we die], but we knew Jerry would be on the front page."

While Robbins was still dealing with his own health problems at the end of 1977, his father died at the age of eighty-nine. Harry and his wife had been living in a Florida retirement community, where Robbins had helped them to relocate some years before. The funeral took place at the family plot in Saddle Brook, New Jersey. "There was no family gathering," Sonia Cullinen recalled. "I went down to Florida when Harry was dying. And I had to pick out a casket for him, and it had to be a special shape because of the size of the plot. And he came up [by train] and the hearse picked up the body. We had the ceremony at the back of the hearse. Jerry was there and the Masons, and he was buried. The sisters, of course, and the family were there, but it was just at the hearse. I went down and stayed with him until he died. I don't think he was too long in the hospital. Jerry never came down. I think Harry died of old age.

He was fragile and had gotten old. I don't think there was a diagnosis of any illness. I remember the back of the hearse, because they opened the back and then these Masons came with their white aprons.

"Jerry took care of Harry and Frieda. In fact, he took care of them too well. He took my mother and father out of business, and this was very bad thing for these two people, I mean they had nothing to do. He retired them. And they had the house down at the beach, but Harry didn't know what to do with himself. He played pinochle, cards, and he took care of my kids during the summer when I was working. Harry was a very creative man, and nobody knows anything about that. He worked in the [corset] factory, but he made all kinds of inventions. He had all kinds of ideas. He was always working with something, always finding another way of doing it, of making something work. This turned over into baking bread. He had to do things. He was very frustrated with his life—work, work, work. He used to say, 'It feels so wonderful but it comes out so terrible.'"

Robbins weathered yet another scrape with adversity the following year when his dog, Nick, a black terrier-like mutt, went missing. Robbins had acquired Nick as a birthday present several years before from Aidan Mooney and another friend. While running an errand in Robbins' Upper East Side neighborhood, his housekeeper tied Nick outside a store, and the dog subsequently disappeared. Robbins initiated an all-out, city-wide search, with a newspaper ad, posters, and a TV appeal. "It got enough publicity," recalled Leslie Bailey. "You would have thought it was the Lindbergh baby." The search efforts eventually led to a seedy drifter known as "One-Eyed Joe," who had apparently absconded with the beloved pet. Robbins said, "I swapped some dough for the dog, he gave me the dog and split."

R obbins eased back into the ballet studio during the spring of 1978, first contributing a short Chopin piece for a televised tribute to Israel, celebrating thirty years of statehood in May of that year. The Robbins segment featured the partnership of Mikhail Baryshnikov and Gelsey Kirkland, who were both dancing at American Ballet Theatre at the time. Robbins' choreography for the evening wasn't new. Kirkland described the piece as "solos and *pas de deux* from *Dances at a Gathering* and *Other Dances.*" Not long after the program aired, Baryshnikov shocked the ballet world by announcing that he was leaving ABT to join City Ballet. The Russian phenomenon was determined to make the stylistic transition from the classical repertoire in which he had soared to superstardom to Balanchine's modern aesthetic.

Prior to Baryshnikov's entry into the company, Robbins presented his "Marche de la Garde Républicaine," which was the third section of a hybrid ballet called *Tricolore,* with a Georges Auric score and decor from Rouben Ter-Arutunian. The other two sections were choreographed by Peter Martins and Jean-Pierre Bonnefoux. Premiering on May 18, 1978, the ballet was conceived by Balanchine, who became ill and passed on the assignment to Robbins and the others, with the idea of creating a French flag-waving number as a counterpart in spirit to *Stars and Stripes* and *Union Jack.* "It's a job," said Robbins at the time. "I've been given a certain number of people to use, and I've been told how to use them." Robbins later admitted that he was not inspired by the Auric score. Drawing stylistically from the French military honor guard and the Can-Can, Robbins started with a ceremonial presentation of twenty women and twenty men in plumed helmets, then turned to nine "Majorettes" with eye-catching leg garters (led by Karin von Aroldingen). Ballerina Nina Fedorova entered on high with a French flag for the finale, which was a less than rousing apotheosis. Anna Kisselgoff wrote, "Unfortunately, she was not Liberty leading the People, but like the ballet in which she appeared, somewhat behind expectations."

The following month, Robbins unveiled *The Arts of the Gentleman* as part of a works-in-progress presentation called *A Sketch Book,* which included a *pas de deux* staged by Peter Martins and three parts of the projected Robbins ballet. The three segments consisted of *Fencing Dances and Exercises* (to music from George Frideric Handel and Heinrich von Biber), *Solo* (to Georg Philipp Telemann) and *Verdi Variations* (to Giuseppe Verdi). Robbins never completed the projected work as conceived, but the Verdi piece—a classical, pure dance exercise utilizing music from *I Vespri Siciliani* and *I Lombardi*—found its way into the repertory (incorporated into the Spring section of *The Four Seasons*). Peter Martins danced the premiere with Kyra Nichols, who Robbins recruited from the corps and who was something of a discovery. Lincoln Kirstein noted that

Nichols "was revealed as a ballerina of considerable potential—noble, steady, assured, with a security and holding power much past her eighteen years." The Martins role was originally created for, and later taken over by, Daniel Duell, whom Robbins would cast frequently in the years ahead, along with his brother Joseph. In the fencing-class segment, the Duell brothers wielded foils and danced a spinning, swashbuckling duet.

Robbins was continually talent-hunting in the ever-youthful company. Jean-Pierre Frohlich also performed in the fencing piece and would one day serve as the handpicked ballet master entrusted with preserving the Robbins repertory for posterity. Janet Reed recalled, "Frohlich was a little boy in *Nutcracker* when I was ballet mistress. I can just see Jerry looking at him and thinking, That's me again. Because Frohlich was a skinny little kid, and he came from a musical family. So I can see Jerry thinking of him as a son."

Robbins turned sixty in October and told *The Washington Post*, "It was traumatic for few days. It was hard to think of myself as 60 . . . but I did it! I once asked Mr. Balanchine how he felt about being over 70, and he told me, 'I always wondered about what it was like on the other side of 70, and you know what, it's the same thing.' The hardest part for me is still having to do the same grinding barren work every day—that's the most depressing part."

Robbins suggested that his Verdi work-in-progress was "like a tryout." The following year, with renewed determination, he expanded on the idea, creating *The Four Seasons*, a half-hour ballet that utilized additional ballet divertissement from Verdi's operas while following the composer's scenario for *Sicilian Vespers* (originally produced at the Paris Opéra in 1855). The new work required forty-nine dancers, a cavalcade of stars and new faces that effectively measured the company's capabilities at the time. This was the first premiere danced by Baryshnikov at City Ballet. He partnered Patricia McBride in the Autumn bacchanal portion of the ballet. Baryshnikov and McBride later alternated with Suzanne Farrell and Peter Martins, with Robbins altering his choreography to suit each of the four stars. Others in the cast included Joseph Duell, Heather Watts and Peter Frame (Winter); Kyra Nichols, Daniel Duell (Spring); Stephanie Saland, Bart Cook (Summer); and Jean-Pierre Frohlich appearing as Pan in the Autumn piece with both casts of stars.

The ballet premiered on January 18, 1979, with decor by Santo Loquasto. With its two star casts, *The Four Seasons* became a hot ticket that season. Robbins called it his "happy ballet," explaining that he hoped to "evoke the sweetness of the old opera-ballets." He appears to have most delighted in the camp revelry and technical extravagance of the Autumn piece. The variations for Baryshnikov and later Martins were precisely tailored to their talents, with the Russian offering up explosive leaps and seemingly every acrobatic feat imaginable. Martins, on the other hand, with his more reserved Danish style, was a gallant yet lighter weight bacchant, concentrating on beats and turns. Likewise, the ballerinas offered a stylistic contrast. Farrell was all speed and dazzle, while McBride exhibited a more restrained approach. The two ballerinas possessed a different sense of musicality and attack with regard to the movement, and in fact performed different steps in the same role (technically, for example, where Farrell executed double *soutenu* turns, McBride was given *chaînés* turns).

Robbins was quite deliberate about enforcing this contrast. McBride recalled, "I remember once I was very upset with him [Jerry] . . . during *The Four Seasons*. I was having so much fun with that variation. I loved it. And I was carrying on. And he told me, 'It looks like you're making fun. Don't have so much fun. Don't play with it. Just simple.' So I thought, He doesn't want me to have a good time. This is all that's going to make that variation for me. It was a very Russian variation. And then I saw Suzanne doing it—she could do all that. Anybody else who did it was able to do that and then he's telling me not to do it. So I had to do it the way he wanted it, just straight and simple and subdued. I felt like I was dying to really carry on because it was so camp. . . . But I wanted to please him basically, nobody else but him in his ballets, so of course I would try to get as close as I could to what his idea was of the piece."

The Four Seasons stayed in the repertory and Robbins was as always the vigilant caretaker and guardian when it came to maintaining performance standards. Gen Horiuchi later danced Frohlich's role in the Autumn piece and recalled, "Actually, that was my favorite role and Jerry enjoyed casting me in it. But then there was one point that I really enjoyed too much in it, and I got a lot of applause. Every time I'd go on, I brought down the house. But then next season, *Four Seasons* was in rep again and Jerry didn't cast me. It's very him, isn't it? It tells me that one role shouldn't be bigger than the piece itself. After that season, he started casting me again."

In February, Baryshnikov was invited to perform at the White House by President Carter. Robbins accompanied the Russian dancer, as did Misha's partners for the occasion, Patricia McBride and Heather Watts. The minuscule stage in the East Room of the White House was hardly sufficient, and its low-hanging chandeliers put a lid on Baryshnikov's leaps. In addition, there was no stage crew provided. "I felt sorry for him—he had no one," Robbins later recalled. "So I became a kind of stage manager and kept my eye on everything—sound, costumes and all." Baryshnikov performed four dances, including a Chopin *pièce d'occasion* that Robbins cobbled together for him and McBride. The opening *pas de deux* was from *Other Dances,* followed by a solo from *Dances at a Gathering* and a newly choreographed solo and *pas de deux.*

Back at City Ballet, Balanchine was again in ill health, suffering angina attacks. He asked Robbins and Peter Martins to help finish staging *Le Bourgeois Gentilhomme,* based on Molière's play with music by Richard Strauss. This was Balanchine's third attempt at this ballet, which he had previously staged in 1932 and 1944. The cast included Rudolf Nureyev, Patricia McBride and Jean-Pierre Bonnefoux and twelve School of American Ballet students. Rehearsals were just under way when Balanchine bowed out, after staging a *pas de sept* and starting some of the character scenes. Nureyev was cast as Cléonte, the prankster who assumes a series of disguises to win his beloved Lucille (McBride) away from her unyielding father, Monsieur Jourdain (Bonnefoux). This was the first time that Balanchine and Nureyev worked together, an unlikely arrangement, as Balanchine was rather dismissive of the flamboyant Russian star. Nureyev, however, was an impassioned admirer of Balanchine and was less than pleased to have to work with his replacements—even with Robbins, who was, after all, not Balanchine as far as Nureyev was concerned. Nureyev's lover and longtime friend Robert Tracy was one of the students in the cast, and he recalled, "I don't think Rudolf and Jerry had such a good relationship at that time. They were very tense with each other. He [Jerry] was more interested in doing things for Baryshnikov."

In the end, Robbins contributed the banquet scene and Balanchine returned to make some final revisions. The ballet premiered on April eighth at the New York City Opera (with scenery and costumes from Rouben Ter-Arutunian) and was an immediate dud with the audience and critics, due to uninspired choreography and an equally uninspired performance by Nureyev. Anna Kisselgoff wrote, "It was disappointing, but not surprising to see Rudolf Nureyev playing Rudolf Nureyev. . . ."

Robbins fared much better the following month when he presented Baryshnikov, Martins and Frohlich as the three sailors on shore leave from *Fancy Free*. The three male solos were performed at a benefit performance for the School of American Ballet, and *Fancy Free* entered City Ballet's repertory the following year. There was friction between Martins and the choreographer, as the dancer tried to re-create the role originally danced by Robbins. Martins wrote, "The rehearsals nearly drove me out of my mind, for Jerry's way is to teach the material (the steps) and the interpretation at the same time, where I prefer to learn the material and then interpret (if it needs interpretation) once the material is second nature." Robbins apparently had a much easier rapport with Baryshnikov and applauded his interpretation of the bravura role.

In June of 1979, Robbins staged *Opus 19 / The Dreamer*, set to Prokofiev's *Violin Concerto No. 1 in D*. The cast featured Baryshnikov and McBride with an ensemble of ten other dancers. McBride recalled that Robbins and Baryshnikov "got along very, very well, really well. I think it's everyone's dream to have a ballet done on you. That's better than diamonds. It's such a gift."

Opus was one of Robbins' angst-driven ballets set against a deep-blue backdrop (lit by Ronald Bates) with all the dancers in Ben Benson's blue practice outfits except for Baryshnikov, who stood out in beige and ostensibly took the part of Robbins' heroic alter-ego. While Robbins was again tapping into his "unconscious stream" and referencing past ballets like *Dybbuk*, he was also testing Baryshnikov's unique instrumentality, providing him with challenging, idiosyncratic movement that drew from the folk, modern and classical idioms. As Anna Kisselgoff observed, Baryshnikov spent "a great deal of time in ballet's fourth position with his arms at chest level." Rather than the flying Misha, the audience was treated to extended floor work, with the dancer crouching, bouncing and turning, and endlessly traveling around the stage, ever in pursuit—a formula for anxiety.

The plotless romantic premise was established in the first encounter between the principals and in their *pas de deux*, with the ensemble at times concealing McBride, creating the impression of the hero finding and losing love in the passing crowd. With its star attractions, the ballet became immensely popular. Kisselgoff aptly suggested, "To be dramatic without disclosing what there is to be dramatic about is no small accomplishment." This was to be the last work created by Robbins for Baryshnikov at City Ballet, as the dancer left the company that fall and became artistic director of American Ballet Theatre the following year. Most observers agreed that he had distinguished himself with Robbins' choreography while never quite finding a home in the Balanchine repertory.

In the late 1970s, while he was still living with Jesse Gerstein, Robbins employed Aidan Mooney's friend Peter Schabel to conduct private, therapeutic morning workout sessions at his Manhattan home. Schabel had trained at SAB and danced for the Houston Ballet and Maurice Béjart. "He wanted to do a very short ballet barre, so that's what I did with him," said Schabel. "I'd give him floor exercises and go through them with him, stretch him a little bit, and we'd do a little ballet barre. He had this studio on the top floor in his townhouse. He was always very tense when we worked, very stiff, very tight in his upper body. I would pull his shoulders back and open up his chest. I used to put his back on my knees and take his arms and pull them over my knees to stretch his upper back. He was very tight . . . and it was mostly from tension. Maybe when he was younger, he'd been flexible. . . . He was very coordinated, I still remember that, and very musical. We would just do little things at the barre, and he still worked everything very well even at that point. But there was no flexibility and there was no flexibility in him as a person, like his body was becoming his personality, which happens, I think, to most people."

Schabel continued, "He took me to the ballet one night, and unfortunately I told him what I thought. We went to City Ballet and it was a revival of *Sonatine*, a Balanchine ballet, and he asked me my opinion, and I liked it. And he hated it. He said, 'It's the worst piece of shit I've ever seen, Balanchine knows it's shit, I don't know why he revived it,' and on and on and on. He asked me what I thought when it had originally been done for Violette Verdy, and I said, 'Well, I liked it when Violette did it very much.' And this was a revival for Suzanne and Peter, after Suzanne came back to the company. So I said, 'It's even more interesting, I think, in some ways now with Suzanne because she adds a lot of—'And he just went off on a tirade about how the ballet was terrible. He was foaming at the mouth because he was so upset that I liked it. At that point, I was a kid. I was completely unimportant, and I don't know why my opinion would really mean that much to him.

"He was discussing something with Ethel Merman when I came in one day. She'd wanted him to do a show for her . . . but he didn't want to work with her. He thought she was too old, and this and this, and said, 'I don't want to get involved in Broadway anymore,' so he was putting her off politely. And [afterward] he told me something like, 'You can't ever tell people what you hear when you're here.' So it's been a while since I've told anybody, almost twenty years. He wanted me to do some filing for him, too. He was cataloguing music, and he had a library in his house, and he wanted me to help with that. So I did it with him one day . . . and I corrected him on something, and that was a big mistake. He said something like Hayden wrote this [piece of music]. So I said, "That's not Hayden, that's Handel." He became incensed at that. But I was right. . . . He was a very bright man, so he didn't make mistakes very often, and he knew music very well. But he certainly didn't like to be caught in a mistake."

In the summer of 1980, with considerable misgivings, Robbins again turned to television. The occasion was a ninety-minute broadcast on the NBC series, *Live from Studio 8H*. The program would include *Afternoon of a Faun*, *The Cage* and excerpts from *Fancy Free*, *The Concert* and *Dances at a Gathering*. The cast of dancers featured Patricia McBride, Bart Cook, Helgi Tomasson, Ib Andersen, Sara Leland, Heather Watts, Stephanie Saland, Jean-Pierre Frohlich, Christopher d'Amboise and Robert Maioranco. Robbins had recently expressed his reservations about televising dance, saying, " . . . the art of photographing dance for television hasn't improved much in the last twenty years, it seems to me. One just hopes the work comes out not slaughtered. Certainly one doesn't expect it to be enhanced, and you're grateful if the result can at least be representative of the basic patterns of the ballet. There's no way on TV of giving the thrill, the excitement, the tension of a live performance, in a three-dimensional, fixed space."

While the program was ultimately well-received, for Robbins it was a debacle. Bart Cook recalled assisting him on the TV show by necessity and later stepping into the role of ballet master. "I think that [*Studio 8H*] was a great project," said Cook, "but he and the director [Rodney Greenberg] fought, naturally. According to his history just like with *West Side Story*, they booted him off the screen. So I was appointed [to take over] because I was in the program. Suddenly I was dancing and then going into the camera booth to look at the angles and then calling Jerry on the phone, smoothing out the kinks so that the show could get on in forty-eight hours. And it did. It was not too long after that, Tommy Abbott decided to leave the company, and Sarah Leland was cracking [as Robbins' ballet mistress]." Cook served as Robbins' ballet master for the next fifteen years. "Throughout my life with Jerry, we went up and down at least six times. I was on the outs and then I was back on the ins. I was his right arm for a long time. Basically, it was Mr. Balanchine who assigned me to help Jerry out. He actually said to me, 'It will be a great learning experience for you and I need you to do this.'

"Of course, you know Jerry had a very set idea about how things should be done. Well, I was ballsy enough to try it a different way or two. I could bring him to great gales of laughter sometimes, and he did enjoy that. But of course then he would say, 'You can't do that.' Jerry was a problematic soul, I think, in a lot of ways. He had a hard life. He was always second fiddle to Mr. Balanchine. I think that was really a thorn in his side. And Mr. Balanchine would stand in the wings in awe [watching Robbins' work], and he would say, 'I don't understand.' I would hear him say that."

Robbins later suggested that Balanchine had wisely tried to discourage him from doing the *Live from Studio 8H* broadcast and that he regretted not having taken the advice. Even with his reticent attitude about television, Robbins would allow several of his ballets to be televised on the PBS *Dance in America* series. That same year, Baryshnikov and Makarova performed *Other Dances* for the cameras; and Robbins also allowed *Antique Epigraphs, Fancy Free* and *In Memory Of* to be filmed for broadcast in 1986 and 1987.

In the fall of 1980, Robbins staged a minor work, *Rondo,* to Mozart's Rondo in A Minor for Piano. The *pas de deux* for two ballerinas in practice clothes was a passing novelty danced by Kyra Nichols and Stephanie Saland, who gently mirrored and mimicked each other executing classroom steps. Robbins gave himself to a more ambitious undertaking the following spring with the third of Balanchine's gala composer festivals, this one dedicated to Tchaikovsky. "Two months before the Tchaikovsky Festival, I thought, I don't like Tchaikovsky," said Robbins. "Why should I do Tchaikovsky? Because Mr. Balanchine wants me to do Tchaikovsky? But you don't necessarily have to enjoy doing something for it to be good."

Robbins choreographed three ballets: *Pas de Deux* (later called *Andantino*), *Piano Pieces* and *Allegro Con Gracia.* He also contributed an incidental piece to *Tempo di Valse,* which was a collection of waltzes that included Balanchine's "Garland Dance" from *The Sleeping Beauty* and the "Waltz of the Flowers" from *The Nutcracker.* Robbins later admitted that the placement of his ballet *Andantino* on the opening-night program occasioned the only serious clash of temper he ever experienced with Balanchine. Robbins recollected that Balanchine had yelled at him in such a pique for his complaining about being slighted that he became concerned for Balanchine's heart (Mr. B had already had a triple-bypass operation). The day after the squabble, Balanchine offered an apology for raising his voice.

While Robbins had little experience with Tchaikovsky other than the *Swan Lake* frame of his Spoleto *Celebration,* the major hit of the Festival (and the company's subsequent Saratoga season) was Robbins' *Piano Pieces,* which premiered at the State Theater on June 12, 1981. Among those in the cast were Ib Andersen, Kyra Nichols, Daniel Duell, Maria Calegari, Joseph Duell, Bart Cook and Heather Watts. A small part was also danced by Stacy Caddell. Her comments about Robbins echoed those of previous generations. "When we did *Piano Pieces,* it was hard, because Jerry would come in with Version A, B, C, D, E, F, G, up to J—like cut-and-paste. That used to really scare me. I didn't see that one was necessarily better than the other. I think Mr. B was very supportive of Jerry in saying, 'Don't worry, it'll be fine.' But I don't think Jerry ever felt that way."

Piano Pieces received glowing notices. Even Arlene Croce acknowledged that "you see the dancers' individual qualities and sense Robbins's delight in them." While Croce admired the ballet's unpretentious simplicity, Anna Kisselgoff called *Piano Pieces* "a brilliant step forward in the art of the *pas de deux*." Robbins' palette for the piece ranged wide from classical to ethnic, folk, modern and Broadway. He again demonstrated his ability to uniquely capture the subtle and not-so-subtle qualities of individual dancers in the manner of *Dances at a Gathering.* The three leading ballerinas—Maria Calegari, with her pliant hyper-extensions; Kyra Nichols, with her elegant bravura; and Heather Watts, with a careless assurance at times reminiscent of Suzanne Farrell—all made distinctive and contrasting marks that enthralled the public and led to cheering ovations at the opening.

Robbins, of course, was never secure with public approbation and constantly concerned that any dancer might undermine the work. Gen Horiuchi danced in the ballet later and recalled, "I was cast to do *Piano Pieces* in London in 1983 and I was seventeen or eighteen years old. It was one of my worst performances ever. After the show, Jerry came backstage, and as soon as he spotted me, he said, 'You! You ruined my ballet. You'll never ever get to do this ballet again!' No matter how old you are or how long you've been in the company, he doesn't take anyone for granted. In a way, of course, he lied, because he cast me again later on."

In the fall of 1981, Robbins added final touches to another revival of *Fiddler on the Roof,* with Herschel Bernardi as Tevye and Maria Karnilova recreating her performance as Golde. "Jerry invented the concept of the show. He knows what it's about," said Bernardi, who described the direction he received for Tevye's soliloquy addressing God. "I'd always just used my hands . . . I was doing it Germanically. Mickey Mouse! I'd look at one hand and then at the other. But Jerry had Jay Fox, who plays the Fiddler, stand next to me when I did the speeches. 'Enough,' he finally said, and moved Jay offstage. Then he said, 'Jay is inside of you. Internalize.' It's so effective now. I am now talking to my essence—my own tradition, not my own hands. And that's what those kids and their marriages are breaking up—my essence and tradition."

In September, Robbins took a group of fifteen City Ballet dancers to the People's Republic of China, touring Peking, Shanghai and Canton for three weeks. The repertory included *Interplay, Afternoon of a Faun,* Spring from *The Four Seasons, Fancy Free,* the *pas de deux* from *In G Major, Andantino,* and various Balanchine excerpts. Robbins said at the time, "I'm going to China with a small group of dancers and give some lectures on how you make a ballet. It's made me think about how so much of it is outside of craft. So much of it has nothing to do with steps. I don't know why things click sometimes and not other times, or why I'm free enough sometimes and not other times." The tour came about at the invitation of International Communication Agency, and Robbins later explained that Balanchine had first received the invitation and declined because he wasn't interested in touring with a small company.

Bart Cook served as ballet master on the China tour. Cook recalled accompanying Robbins to Washington, D.C., later in the year when Robbins became a Kennedy Center Honoree. "I went on a plane with the Ertegüns to D.C. when Jerry received his honors. . . . And I went along to help, and it was mostly to make sure that Misha [Baryshnikov] knew what he was doing. He hadn't danced for a while. The Ertegüns hired their private jet, and we all hopped on board and went down." At the Kennedy Center celebration, Baryshnikov paid verbal tribute to Robbins and danced in an excerpt from *Fancy Free* along with a cast of ABT and City Ballet performers. Robbins' friend, Christine Conrad, recalled that Robbins had first asked Stephen Sondheim to present him with the award, but Sondheim had declined. The other honorees that year were Cary Grant, Helen Hayes, Count Basie and Rudolf Serkin. For the ceremony, President Reagan and Nancy Reagan were of course seated in the center box, flanked by Robbins and his fellow honorees in plush red seats. The only *faux pas* of the glittering occasion came during the gala reception, when President Reagan addressed Robbins as "Jerome Roberts" and was quickly prompted to correct himself.

The Kennedy Center award was indeed a pinnacle of recognition. At this point, Robbins' Broadway career still outshone his achievements in ballet, at least as far as the mass audience was concerned. Bart Cook remembered,

"When we were in Washington, we were in a cab and the cab driver knew who Jerry was from *West Side Story*. And he was completely hats off. 'What an honor to have you in my cab.' When we got out of the cab, Jerry muttered something like, 'He doesn't know I'm a classical ballet choreographer.'"

By now Robbins had choreographed almost fifty ballets and had been involved in fifteen Broadway musicals (not counting those he had doctored). But his work in the theater was still far from over. On December sixth, the day that he received his Kennedy Center award, he told Alan Kriegsman of *The Washington Post* that he was working on a new ballet to Gershwin's music. He also revealed that he was planning another ambitious production that was too close to the heart to discuss in detail. "The one [project] I care about the most is the hardest for me to talk about," said Robbins. "It's very, very personal, a theater piece that I've been trying to push around—no, that's not right—I've been trying to solve it, for years. It involves most of what I know about the performing arts. Maybe it will just stay on paper, and end up a posthumous 'writing,' or maybe I'll find a way of getting it on. What I need is workshop time, and not having to worry about getting it produced. It would be somewhat autobiographical, but not in a realistic way; I'd call it a dream or fantasy relating to events or feelings in my life. On second thought, it would be misleading to call it autobiographical—it would deal more with phantasmagorical reactions to developments in my world."

NINE

Demons and Angels

Robbins postponed his autobiographical project for almost ten years and likewise put off a return to Broadway, though he was considering a retrospective production for which he planned to restage song and dance numbers from his hit musicals. He later suggested to Allyn Ann McLerie and other performers from his early shows that he wanted "to leave behind something more than a reputation." For a choreographer, the dances created over a lifetime represent a uniquely fragile and precarious bequest to posterity. Even when notated or recorded on film, each dance inevitably passes beyond the pale of collective memory without the enduring blueprint of a playwright's script or composer's score. As Robbins continued to devote himself to staging new ballets, he was keenly aware of his own mortality and increasingly concerned about the ultimate preservation of his work.

While living with photographer Jesse Gerstein, Robbins relocated his beach retreat from the Watermill area to nearby Bridgehampton, where he eventually bought a waterfront home and became a part-time resident for the rest of his life. His social circle at the beach continued to widen. In 1982, Robbins' friends Arthur Gold and Bobby Fizdale introduced him to novelist-lawyer Louis Begley and his wife, biographer Anka Muhlstein, who were neighbors in Manhattan as well as Long Island. Begley and Muhlstein became steadfast allies. They met Robbins at a time when he was first reading Proust and they later offered their assessment of Robbins' theatrical vision. Writing together, the two authors suggested that genius was "the power of those who have it to revolutionize our perceptions, to fit us, as Proust would have it, with a new pair of glasses. We put them on and get used to the new prescription; they slide to the tip of our nose; *presto* the world changes. . . . Jerry Robbins has accomplished just such a miracle." Of that perceived miracle, Begley and Muhlstein also noted, "In Robbins's world everything is possible and yet uncertain and perhaps foredoomed."

There was nothing to suggest such an ominous aspect when Robbins blithely described his contentment with life at Balanchine's City Ballet, saying, "George is alive. I'm happy to be here." Such felicity was evident in his next ballet, *Gershwin Concerto*, which opened at the State Theater on February 4, 1982. This work was a return to that refuge of childhood innocence first seen in *Interplay*, but there was also a definite hint of doom and Lost Generation angst (Robbins said that he meant the ending to appear "almost disastrous, with everyone orbiting in all directions"). The score was Gershwin's 1925 Piano Concerto in F, with its three-part symphonic structure and jazzy, rapid-fire changes of tempo and mood. Robbins had first conceived the ballet thirty-five years before as a vehicle for Nora Kaye. Referring to the Kaye role, he said, "I always knew the girl in the ballet was a loner. That plaintive music she has, has a touching quality." When Robbins finally staged the piece, the role of the loner was danced by Maria Calegari. Others in the cast of twenty-four included Christopher d'Amboise, Darci Kistler and Mel Tomlinson.

D'Amboise recalled a game that he devised with Robbins that allowed the work in the studio to gel. "What I began to play with him—and this is really how I learned how to choreograph to a great degree—was what I called the Next Step Game. He'd say, 'Okay, here's kind of a movement.' And I'd do the movement and one more. So he would have an idea for the step and then I'd do that and the next. So that would give him an idea of where to go with it. . . . Even in partnering the *pas de deux*, working on the *Gershwin Concerto*, a lot of that happened. He did that for Darci and me. Constantly I would go home and listen to the music and I'd know it, I'd know the crescendo's coming here, and I would start to just second guess what he would want. Because his basic vocabulary was actually fairly limited that he used in most of his pieces. . . . So we played this game a lot and I think that's why he liked using me. Because if he didn't know where to go, I would give him something to lead him on."

D'Amboise also recollected, "Mostly he treated me like shit. He believed, I think, that the best way to get performances, at least when I was working with him, was to push you in a negative way. One of his favorite games was to pit friends against each other. Joseph Duell and I were contemporaries, we were both soloists, and he would have Joe understudy me for the *Gershwin Concerto*. And then he'd get furious one day at something and he'd say, 'Chris, get out. Joe, come on.' He always had an attitude, and I don't know where it came from, that made you feel like he believed you were trying to pull something on him, that you would cheat him, that you were somehow manipulating behind his back and he caught you. And you always had this sense, *what is that?* Of course you're killing yourself for him and he's treating you like you've robbed him somehow or he was afraid you were about to.

"On the good side, there's no one that made you care more about what you were doing than Jerry. It may not have always been pleasant and often it worked against your ability to really put yourself joyfully into the work and really be your best, but your standards were so high with him. What always amazed me that I admire about Jerry more than anything is that he could walk into a rehearsal of a ballet he did forty years before and *care* about every little thing. I can't do that about a ballet I did last year. It's extraordinary to me and that showed in every performance you saw."

Robbins recalled that he was initially frustrated by the central blues section of *Gershwin Concerto*. "I have so much gratitude to the dancers for their patience until I got it right," said Robbins. The ballet evoked an elegantly hedonistic Jazz Age as seen through distinctly modern eyes. While conjuring the bygone era, Robbins couldn't resist including a few references as homage to Balanchine's 1970 Gershwin ballet, *Who Cares.* Santo Loquasto created a blue backdrop with asymmetrical Art Deco effects appropriate for the sleek, urban asymmetries Robbins brought into his ensemble. The female corps was at times a stationary audience watching the principals as if they were in the studio rather than onstage. On the surface, *Gershwin Concerto* was another plotless work ostensibly about dancers, but Robbins was also engaging in a kind of ongoing commentary on Balanchine's company, its personalities and neo-classical style. In a sense, he was placing his own indelible signature and theatrical imprint on each cast of dancers.

Mel Tomlinson came to City Ballet by way of Dance Theatre of Harlem and was cast after Robbins saw his performance in Balanchine's *Agon*. "I really had to work hard to earn Jerry's respect," said Tomlinson. "I was a challenge for him because what can you do with someone like Mel Tomlinson? He's not classical. He's not modern. He's tall. And really for the first time, here's a black dancer in the company. People think of Arthur Mitchell, but Arthur Mitchell was in such a wonderful place where he could pass for anything. I couldn't pass. So it was, what am I going to do with you besides put you in a white costume? All of my costumes for the most part were white, and I said, 'Why?' And Jerry said, 'I want you to pull up hard so everything can be seen, because you're dancing with some of the best dancers we have and you didn't go to the School of American Ballet.' So I had to get over that and let him know that my inspiration came from a different source, from the heart, and I didn't know whether he knew what a heart was."

Tomlinson continued, "He taught me how to be able to be ready to go on. Because he had about fourteen versions and didn't decide which one until the last moment before the curtain. Then it was, 'Oh, my God!' He was demanding and it had to be the same way each time. He would push people to such an edge that they would just scream. I'm talking about the soloists and corps—the principals he treated like gold, I think, because he knew what they could do. . . . He was omnipotent. It was like puppeteer and puppet. He could make you shake. He could intimidate you. When you knew you had a rehearsal the next day you had to prepare at home to go in there and be there *on time*. . . . Once he'd get going, he was fine, but when he couldn't figure something out, he was terror. . . . I told somebody, 'Well, if I do go to hell, I will not be afraid of the devil.' He said, 'Why?' I said, 'Because I have worked with Jerome Robbins.' "

Gershwin Concerto was a sensational hit with the audience and most critics. Tomlinson partnered both Maria Calegari and Darci Kistler (the last of Balanchine's chosen muses). His performance in the bluesy central *pas de deux* with

Kistler was called "marvelously swaggering" by Anna Kisselgoff. The critic added, "By contrast, Mr. Tomlinson's next duet with Miss Calegari has a quieter passion, with its tight embraces and forward swoons." While Kisselgoff deemed the ballet "a masterpiece" worthy of Gershwin, Croce complained, "It's like most Robbins ballets—its only subject is New York City Ballet." As usual, Robbins refused to pin down his subject, saying, "I would always be more interested in a thing that evokes many responses rather than one that gives you only the responses that are not conditioned by imposed specifics. That's what dance is about."

For many, if not most, City Ballet dancers, the attitude persisted that Balanchine was god and Robbins was either demigod (at best) or devil. Likewise, the audience was to some extent divided in affection between the two choreographers. Against this backdrop of split allegiances, a traumatic rite of passage commenced when Balanchine's failing health forced him to be hospitalized in November of 1982. At seventy-eight, Balanchine was suffering from a rare viral infection called Creutzfeldt-Jakob disease, which was determined only after his death. He spent his last five months at Roosevelt Hospital. As it became evident that he would not resume his duties at City Ballet, the question of his successor became a matter of pressing concern to the dancers, the audience, and the company's board of directors.

Robbins had long been touted as the logical choice to take over as director, even though he appeared to have little interest in the day-to-day responsibilities of running a company. Wilma Curley remembered, "I know that Jerry did not want to be the director, because that's why he stopped Ballets: U.S.A. Jerry never wanted to be the boss of anything. To take over full directorship, he would have to do all the shit things. When Ballets: U.S.A. went beyond fourteen dancers, Jerry stopped showing up. He really wanted no part of administration." Like others, Curley recollected that Balanchine was resignedly pessimistic about the survival of the company and his work. "He wanted the company to die after he was gone," said Curley. "He said he didn't care if his ballets ever went on, he couldn't care less. He knew they would never be the same without him."

In mid-March 1983, the company named Robbins and Peter Martins co-ballet masters in chief, with primary administrative duties assigned to the latter along with the mandate for preserving Balanchine's repertory. Robbins was now sixty-four, and the board was obviously thinking long-term in turning to Martins, while recognizing that Robbins' inclusion as an advisor was a tacit stamp of approval and an indication of the continued creative vitality of the company. Martins had strong support among board members, and it appeared to some that Balanchine had been grooming him as future director. With Balanchine's encouragement, Martins had choreographed seventeen ballets, albeit without great success. Balanchine named him ballet master in 1981, and Martins had been teaching company class and assisting with casting and repertory. While there were other candidates who at times appeared to have won Balanchine's favor as designated heir, Martins prevailed in the end, thanks to the board. According to Balanchine biographer Bernard Taper, Martins visited Balanchine in the hospital seeking his "official blessing as successor," but "Balanchine would not give him that assurance. 'Look,' Balanchine said, 'nobody is going to hand it to you. You're going to have to take it, you're going to have to fight for it.'"

Of this period of uncertainty, City Ballet manager Betty Cage recalled, "That was a very difficult time because we had this stupid board, and while Balanchine was still in the hospital, the board decided that they were going to put Peter in charge of the company. And the dumb chairman of the board, Orville Schell—who since has died, so I can say anything I want about him—somehow leaked to the *Times* that Peter was being put into this position and Balanchine had been made *emeritus*. We started getting calls from all over the world, how can you do this to Balanchine? It was the most embarrassing thing, it was awful. So we had a meeting with Orville Schell and a few of the staff members. We told him, 'How could you do this? You're out of your mind?' At that meeting, Orville Schell said, 'Well, we know how Balanchine ran this company, and it's not going to be like that anymore.' We couldn't believe it. All these years we had been thinking really we're so lucky—all the other ballet companies have to scrounge around for choreographers and we've got Balanchine. And there's the board saying they can't wait till he dies. In the leak to the *Times*, Orville Schell said, of course, we offered it [the directorship] to

Jerry Robbins, who refused. Of course they hadn't offered it to Jerry. And Jerry comes in and walks in to Orville, and says, 'What do you mean, you offered it to me? Who offered it to me? When did you offer it to me? When did I refuse?'

"So after that meeting, Orville came into my office and said, 'Oh, what I've just been through [with Jerry].' I said, 'You deserve it, how dare you do that!' He said, 'I came to you for comfort.' I said, 'Well, you're not getting it.' He didn't know what he had done. Those are board members. Jerry probably wouldn't have been interested [in directing], but on the other hand he didn't want to be reading in the papers that he had refused it. That was awful. Frankly, I don't think Jerry did want it. But he would have liked to have been offered, and if he had refused, it would have been his decision."

Edward Bigelow agreed in part with Cage's assessment, saying, "Jerry was very upset about that. He would have liked the courtesy. He would have liked to say no."

The planted story was confirmed by City Ballet press officer Leslie Bailey, who said, "I do remember that thing about Jerry being asked and turning it down. It seems to me I was very involved in that little deception. Quite honestly, I think it was put together to make things look good. . . . I think it was sort of thrown around and it was more or less decided that if we were to say that they had made an overture to Jerry and he had indicated that he wasn't interested in that kind of administrative situation, that this would sound good."

The *Times* article indicated that Robbins had no desire to direct and that Martins was Balanchine's heir apparent. Yet Betty Cage later insisted, "The myth of Balanchine having chosen Peter came from the board. Balanchine never chose Peter for anything. Never. The last thing Balanchine did, the last time he was on stage was that last festival we had [the 1982 Stravinsky Centennial Celebration], and he asked John Taras to do one thing for him, he asked Jacques [d'Amboise] to do one thing for him; he didn't ask Peter to do anything. He had no idea of appointing Peter. I think all of us who were there knew that Balanchine had never chosen anybody.

"Balanchine used to say from time to time, 'Oh, Diana Adams, she's wonderful, she could carry on.' Or, 'Oh, Jacques [d'Amboise], he knows, he could do.' Or, 'Suki [Schorer], such a good teacher, she could do.' He said these things all the time. And Jerry knew what we all knew. Jerry was at those meetings when we were telling them off. . . . The board wouldn't have known whether Peter was competent or not. They thought he looked like a god, a good-looking hunk of something, mainly chin. They were seduced by him. I know the president of the board thought he was God's gift to womanhood. I suppose all boards are like this. But it's a great misfortune that ballet companies have to have boards made up of business people. They don't know what they're doing."

Former City Ballet board member Robert Gottlieb specifically denied Cage's allegation with regard to Balanchine's intentions. Gottlieb wrote, "That Martins was the legitimate heir was as clear to me as to everyone else. Not only Kirstein but Balanchine had told me so, twice. The more memorable instance came one evening when we were standing silently in the wings, watching Martins and Farrell in 'Diamonds.' Suddenly he [Balanchine] said, 'It has to be Peter. He understands what a ballerina needs,' and receded into silence." Yet Gottlieb also admitted that "whether Balanchine was referring to more than his [Martins'] partnering technique, I have no way of knowing."

John Clifford shared Betty Cage's point of view, saying, "You know what Lincoln [Kirstein] said—and this I think is the truest of all—that Mr. B wanted everybody to fight for it. Mr. B *really* didn't care." Edward Bigelow pointed out that neither Balanchine nor Kirstein was consistent on the issue. "George or Lincoln might say something one day and something else another day and they'd both be right," said Bigelow. In this regard, Shaun O'Brien speculated, "Lincoln saw to it that Balanchine wouldn't name anybody. Lincoln is the one who would really inherit the company, in a sense, as the crown prince blessed by the Pope. Balanchine would say nothing. Balanchine was very Russian."

Balanchine died on April 30, finally succumbing to pneumonia. City Ballet carried on its performances that day. In her memoir, *Dancing for Balanchine,* Merrill Ashley recalled, "I was not scheduled to perform that day, but, like everyone else, I needed to be with Balanchine's 'family,' the other Company members. As I entered the theater, I met Jerry Robbins, who embraced me wordlessly, his arms trembling." Lincoln Kirstein addressed the matinee audience, saying, "I don't have to tell you that Mr. B is with Mozart and

Tchaikovsky and Stravinsky. I do want to tell you how much he valued this audience, which is like a big family that has kept us going for fifty years and will keep us going for another fifty."

Robbins joined more than twelve hundred mourners who turned out for the first of two requiems at the Cathedral of our Lady of the Sign. Balanchine's body was on view in an open coffin. Allegra Kent recalled the Russian Orthodox service: "Countless mourners were standing in the sanctuary. The air was thick and heavy with the scent of burning incense and candles. Jerry, the first person I saw, beckoned to me and I hurried over to him. We embraced with feeling, and as we separated, he took my hand and held it for a long moment. . . . Jerry was giving me a gift of strength and courage through this gesture. All present stood the entire length of the service, which was three hours or longer. Unseen choruses sang and chanted in beautiful voices. Many older women fainted from lack of oxygen. . . . In this ancient Russian ritual, every sense was invaded with grief. I stood among my friends, the people who loved George Balanchine the most, and we united in a single purpose. This requiem service felt like an extension of Jerry's masterpiece, *Dances at a Gathering*—the undanced portion when Edward Villella touched the ground toward the end of the ballet."

According to insiders, the arrangement that ensued with Robbins and Martins sharing power was often contentious. Wilma Curley said, "I know Jerry was quite satisfied with that title, co-ballet master. But at the same time, you have to understand, you want to talk *co*, there ain't no *co* with Jerry. So whenever you hear co-whatever, you know it never happened. Peter had to ask if he could go to the bathroom. I don't think Jerry cared what Peter did. When Jerry wasn't interested in someone, he almost didn't exist." Edward Bigelow explained, "The thing about Jerry was he wanted to run everything, but he didn't want to have to take responsibility, although he wanted everything to go his way. As far as the company was concerned, he didn't want to be in there and have to put up with it, but he wanted to make sure everybody did what he wanted. That's on the managerial side. He wanted his finger right there."

Robbins later said, "I collaborate with Peter on all the major and important decisions that have to be made." Yet Robbins apparently held Martins in rather low esteem and a few years later refused to support Martins' American

Music Festival. Designer Joe Eula said, "They made Peter the doorman—Jerry and I used to call him that. He [Peter] was always so fucking stiff. Jerry'd say, 'He's the doorman.'" Many City Ballet insiders recalled clashes of temperament between Robbins and Martins, although the latter would later say, "People think we didn't get along. I thought we got along." Shaun O'Brien said, "Jerry and Peter tried to cooperate, but there were a lot of slamming doors—it was a bad scene." Likewise, John Clifford recalled, "It was horrible, their relationship, the two of them, nothing but animosity. Peter was telling me horrible things about Jerry. And the dancers were coming up to me and saying, 'Oh we're so glad Jerry's here, because even though he's impossible at least we know he knows what he's doing.' After Balanchine's death, Jerry, more than before, took on the mantle of the real artistic figurehead of the company. . . . I said to Jerry one time, 'Do you like his [Peter's] lights?' Jerry said, 'No, they're fucking awful. He's ruining all of Balanchine's ballets.'" Clifford added that Robbins ultimately avoided confrontation with Martins over the staging of Balanchine's works. "Jerry's thing was, 'I've tried, but you know I'm not going to fight with him.'"

For the rest of the decade, Martins drew fire from critics, who complained, often bitterly, about the direction in which he was taking the company, the quality of performances and the status of the Balanchine repertory. In Martins' defense, Edward Bigelow said, "The thing is Balanchine didn't like the way things were going through the last few years [of his life], and Peter was the only obvious one to take over. A good ballet master is more than a choreographer. It's a rarer animal, rarer species. When I look at Ballet Theatre, Joffrey, Paul Taylor, the Royal Ballet, I think the New York City Ballet is very lucky. Somebody who can occupy that place and keep something going like this is very extraordinary. And Peter manages. People talk about him, these intellectual reviewers, and they're just full of shit. They don't know what they're looking at. They're looking at what they thought they saw when Balanchine was running it, and nobody remembers the criticism that he kept getting over the years."

Robert Gottlieb sympathized with Martins' unenviable position and recently wrote, "How *can* Martins—how could anyone—emerge easily from under the tremendous weight of Balanchine? Twyla Tharp, hardly the most effusive admirer of other choreographers, once said to me, 'George Balanchine is God.' No one can be expected to replace God successfully, but Martins *has* succeeded in keeping this going, which means making a future possible."

By assuming an apparently subordinate role in the enterprise, Robbins avoided much of the fallout. By all accounts, he was deeply affected by Balanchine's passing and tried to bolster morale among the dancers by making his continued presence felt. Although teaching was not his forte, on one occasion he made a point of conducting company class. "Jerry pulled the whole company together and he said that he was there for us," said Jerri Kumery, "and whatever time of the day or night, call him, please don't keep it inside if you're having trouble. You would expect that from Peter but not from Jerry. All of a sudden he [Jerry] came in and he taught company class, which I'd never seen in my life. It was fun because he didn't know the terminology, but he wanted to be with family. He'd say, 'Now we're going to do six big squats, and we're going to do eight more big kicks here.' It was adorable. But he had to be with us, he didn't just disappear."

Later in the year, as a kind of symbolic gesture, Robbins returned to the stage in the role of Herr Drosselmeyer, which was originally performed by Balanchine in his version of *The Nutcracker,* the company's classic holiday spectacle. This was to be its one thousandth performance since Balanchine first staged the ballet in 1954. Unfortunately, Robbins' appearance as the mysterious figure bearing the gift of the magical Nutcracker unexpectedly fizzled. "I did Jerry a disservice," confessed Edward Bigelow. "He wanted to have his own bag of tricks when he did Drosselmeyer, and there was this wand. When we did *Tyl* [*Ulenspiegel*] thousands of years ago, we had these wands that you put some paper in and they would flame like Roman candles. I found these things at a magic shop down on Ninth Avenue. So when Jerry decided he wanted to do a performance of Drosselmeyer, he thought of that and he wanted one. So I went out and got him one, and the paper you put in it."

Near the end of the first act, Robbins had his big moment when Drosselmeyer positioned himself above the clock, flapping his arms with wand in hand to initiate Clara's wondrous journey. Bigelow continued, "And Jerry was waving it [the wand] onstage and pressed the little button and it didn't go off. I had practiced with the thing. You had only one chance—if it didn't work, it didn't work. And it would have been absolutely wonderful. I was always embarrassed and chagrined. It was one of the things that Drosselmeyer did to amuse the children, but goddamn it didn't work, and Ed Koch was Mayor and he was in the audience."

Robbins took over the role that night from a disgruntled Shaun O'Brien, who had regularly performed Drosselmeyer for many years. O'Brien recalled, "I was appalled when Jerry came on, I really felt sorry for him. He was wearing this black satin coat which was way too long for him. He had glasses on. He looked like Woody Allen in a raincoat, and he just wandered around as Drosselmeyer."

The following year during a *Times* interview, Robbins' eyes filled with tears when he was asked about the changes at City Ballet after Balanchine's death. He said, "I thought it was business as usual, but there is something more here, a feeling of community and love we're not always aware of, that's very moving."

According to the provisions of Balanchine's will, 113 of his ballets were distributed among fourteen legatees. Robbins inherited both *Pulcinella* and *Firebird*. The disposition of the Balanchine estate raised issues of intellectual property with regard to choreography and set precedents that later influenced Robbins when it came to drawing up his own will. Balanchine's executor, Barbara Horgan, when first filing the estate tax, pointed out that "there has been no recorded case in which a choreographer's right to control his work, and thus, its value, has been protected by the law of copyright." The valuation of the works was problematic, but a formula based on anticipated income was hammered out with the IRS. Because Balanchine chose not to leave his works to City Ballet, the board was naturally concerned about losing the Balanchine repertory. The Balanchine Trust was set up by several beneficiaries, including Barbara Horgan, to oversee and administer most of the ballets. After the board threatened legal action against the trust, the company was granted licensing agreements for the ballets and the exclusive right to use Balanchine's name in fund-raising. Robbins and his attorney, Floria Lasky, later took precautions against such potential disputes. Rather than divide his works, Robbins would leave them all under the control of his estate and a handpicked group of advisors.

At the onset of the post-Balanchine era, it was Robbins who provided the first clear signs that the company was indeed alive and well. His ballet *Glass Pieces* premiered less than two weeks after Balanchine's death and quickly established that City Ballet was not going to become a mere Balanchine museum. Like *Watermill*, the new work was another avant-garde departure for Robbins with his choice of a minimalist score from composer Philip Glass. The cast of thirty-six included Maria Calegari, Bart Cook, Helene Alexopoulos, Peter Frame, Lourdes Lopez, Joseph Duell, Lisa Hess and Victor Castelli.

Robbins later recalled that he considered directing the Philip Glass opera, *Akhnaten*, before hitting upon the idea of using its opening instrumental sequence in the ballet. While the opera excerpt served as the final movment in *Glass Pieces*, Robbins used selections from the composer's CBS recording, *Glassworks* ("Rubric" and "Facades"), for the first two sections. Modern dance choreographers like Lucinda Childs had previously set compositions to Glass' austere, trance-inducing music, but Robbins was the first to wed minimalism to pointe work and the conventional ballet syntax (two years later, and less successfully, Robbins would repeat the experiment with composer Steve Reich). Robbins recruited his Upper East Side neighbor and friend Fran Lebowitz as a consultant on *Glass Pieces*, describing the role of the arch literary humorist as "a weird piece of litmus paper" for his ideas. Lebowitz said of her brief venture into choreography, "It's the only art where the elements of the art are unfortunately alive. All I remember is the dancers sitting on the floor glaring at him [Jerry] through a haze of cigarette smoke." Speaking as a writer, she observed, "It's as if all the words in the dictionary glared at me while I was trying to put them together."

In addition to dancing in the ballet, Bart Cook served as ballet master and provided Robbins with a crucial idea for the set design carried out by Ronald Bates. Cook said, "The *Glass Pieces* backdrop was my notes. I had to use a big piece of graph paper and it wasn't big enough, so I hooked four or more together, and drew columns, and put the counts on them for the girls in the back. I came to rehearsal, rolled it out on the stage, and said, 'I think we should project this up on the back so the girls can see their counts.' So Jerry went over and grabbed Ronnie Bates and used it. I also do stained glass and have done my whole life in New York. I had taken some slides to Jerry's Hampton house. He invited me to dinner to show him some slides of my work. We started talking about glass pieces and Philip Glass. *Akhnaten* had just premiered at the State Theater. Next thing we knew, we were doing a ballet called *Glass Pieces.*"

Cook continued, "Artists throughout the ages have always absorbed what's around them for sure, just like a sponge, and Jerry had that definite ability. . . . I know for *Glass Pieces* that Jerry was very interested in all the downtown dance events, and I think he got many of his germ ideas for the movements from the different people that were choreographing at the time. But his major talent was capturing the period—as was Mr. Balanchine's, you know? All great artists absorb what's going on and distill it. And voilà, a statement of the times."

In *Glass Pieces*, Robbins' style was sci-fi cinema with a touch of Chaplin's *Modern Times.* He deployed his ensemble in the systematic fashion of an efficiency expert, using the corps dancers as so many modular set pieces, capturing the insidious pace and pulsing electronic anonymity of the computer age. The dancers were costumed in Ben Benson's glistening unitards. Performed against the graph-paper grid backdrop, the movement was stripped down to the simplest vocabulary, rendering a visible counterpoint to the incessant repetitions of the music. The heartfelt human note was struck emphatically in the central "Facades" duet danced by Bart Cook and Maria Calegari, transforming the piece into a kind of Orwellian romantic metaphor. Croce described it as "a hypnotic spectacle." Kisselgoff declared, "Mr. Robbins succeeded in taking ballet into a brave new world."

As if to demonstrate his versatility once again, Robbins next unveiled a ravishing paean of sentimentality, *I'm Old Fashioned (The Astaire Variations).* George Balanchine once called Fred Astaire "the greatest dancer in the world," and offered his own Astaire tribute with *Who Cares?* Robbins wrote a fan letter to Astaire in June of 1974, praising him for his work since *Flying Down to Rio* and thanking Astaire on behalf of millions of admirers.

Ten years later, Robbins would base his thirty-five-minute ballet homage on a film clip from the 1942 Astaire–Rita Hayworth movie *You Were Never*

Lovelier, excerpting the dance sequence to Jerome Kern's "I'm Old Fashioned" (the lyrics by Johnny Mercer actually preceded the dancing). Robbins studied the film for some twelve hours, trying to analyze the elusive magic of Astaire's musicality. Using the song as the springboard theme, Morton Gould provided a symphonic score tinctured appropriately with Latin rhythms, as the movie followed Astaire's escapades as a nightclub dancer in Buenos Aires. Robbins cast three principal couples—Kyra Nichols and Sean Lavery, Heather Watts and Bart Cook, Judith Fugate and Joseph Duell—and an ensemble of eighteen dancers from the corps.

The dancers and their world were again the focus, this time filtered through the lens of Astaire and embellished with multiple layers of personal reference and association. The vintage film clip included one of those charming throwaway moments when Astaire and Hayworth bumped into one another, then bowed in mock courtesy and exited through French doors. For Robbins, the bump and bow became a motif, and he threw in a few gratuitous rumba thigh slaps for Bart Cook that served to remind the audience of Astaire's solo as well as the sailors in *Fancy Free* and Robbins' own creative roots, which of course traced back to the same glamorous era.

Weaving a series of classical variations based on the Astaire-Hayworth theme, Robbins put the emphasis on partnering yet avoided presenting superficial Astaire imitations, even in the finale when the entire cast appeared as Astaire-Hayworth lookalikes (in tuxedos and black gowns) and danced before the projected film. With the orchestra taking over the sound track and the dancers relating to the giant screen, the dazzling theatrical effect was something akin to interactive video on a grand scale. The ballet premiered on June 16, 1983. Leslie Bailey recalled, "The morning of the gala of *I'm Old Fashioned*, which was a big society gala, I walked into the theater—it was a little after ten—and no one was there but Jerry. Jerry was on the stage and he was tap dancing in his sneakers and he was marking out the ballet. He tapped up those stairs and down the stairs, just the way the dancers do, tapping sideways in pointe shoes to do those steps they do. And Jerry was tapping up and down the stairs, and I just looked and thought, This is what they should be paying for—those society ladies wouldn't care about Kyra and Maria and Heather if they saw this. This is what they'd be giving $10,000 a table for, because it was priceless and it's still in my mind. I can still see him there tapping in sneakers." After the performance that night, Robbins and his dancers were rewarded with a standing ovation, and two years later, Robbins received the Astaire Award for lifetime achievement in dance.

Kyra Nichols absorbed an essential approach to performance from Robbins and later said, "Jerry definitely knew what he wanted. He really had an influence on me, in terms of my presence on stage, being able to be myself, to create an atmosphere around me. Most of his ballets are like that: you're dancing for an audience, but you're really in your own world."

Early in 1984, Robbins cast Nichols, along with Stephanie Saland, Maria Calegari and five other ballerinas, in *Antique Epigraphs*. Here Robbins conjured a world that stretched between his dancers and Greek antiquity, with suggestions as well of Isadora Duncan's Greece. For this ballet, Robbins chose the same Debussy music (*Six Epigraphes Antiques* and the *Syrinx* flute solo) that he had used in *Ballade* more than thirty years before, but this time he reversed the order of the pieces and pursued a more ethereal direction. Dancer Jerri Kumery recalled the subtext that Robbins brought into the work. "I remember him telling us it was about statues, women's statues that he was just so empowered by, and their eyes, how all the story and the power came through the eyes. There were five of us that were supporting the three principals. I remember it being about a spell and telling secrets. We all had knowledge that he'd given us, knowledge and experiences and mysteries that we were telling stories about. I think that it originated with Bart Cook. Bart went to Europe and he saw these statues in a museum in Naples [the National Archeological Museum], and they came from Greece. Bart saw them and he brought a book back for Jerry, and they were in this book. And Jerry was just blown away with the power and the look of these women. I think then Jerry went to see them."

Occupying a single room in the Naples museum, the statues are bronze and possess haunting enamel eyes. Robbins recalled his visit to the statuary, saying, "It was like walking into the center of a dance by Martha Graham."

Still another level of meaning of *Antique Epigraphs* undoubtedly derived from the music and may explain in part why Robbins chose an all-female cast (aside from some temporary adherence to Balanchine's credo that "ballet is woman"). In his program notes, Robbins pointed out, "Like the *Epigraphs* and

Afternoon of a Faun, Syrinx was inspired by French poetry about life and myths of Greek antiquity." In fact, Debussy's *Epigraphs* were conceived as a setting for Pierre Louÿs' collection of pastoral prose poems entitled *Les Chansons de Bilitis.* The poems were actually a case of nineteenth-century literary fraud, as they were at first falsely ascribed by Louÿs to one of Sappho's group of lesbian lovers.

With such ghostly nymphs and classical statuary in the back of his mind, Robbins crafted a beautifully sensual mood piece of utmost simplicity and stillness. In the final *Syrinx* section, the ballerinas, costumed in Florence Klotz's flowing pastel gowns, assumed various stylized positions and poses in tableau, appearing as motionless as figures on a Grecian urn. These prolonged moments of stasis were most appropriate, as Debussy's flute solo was based on the mythic tale of Pan's pursuit of Syrinx, the nymph who, as a means of escape, was turned into a reed and thus immobilized by her fellow nymphs. Clive Barnes applauded Robbins' treatment of the material, observing that "all eight women have acquired the still secret of poetry."

Robbins showed no sign of mellowing. To achieve his results, he was as demanding and detail-driven as ever. Kumery remembered, "We were doing the little *pas de trois,* Maria [Calegari] and Vicki [Hall] and I. There was a lot of partnering; we kept changing hands and intertwining and stuff. At that point, I was married and I had a marquis diamond ring on—not big, but it was marquis. We were trying to do something very fluid, and Jerry grabbed my hand and he caught the ring. And he looked at me and said, 'Don't you *ever* wear that ring in my rehearsal ever again!' So the rehearsal ended and we ended up walking down the corridor, the main hall, together, and we were shoulder-to-shoulder. It just kind of happened that way. And he turned to me and he goes, 'Jerri, you're really dancing beautifully.' With me, he would bite but then he would give you an honest nice thing like that at the end. I know it wasn't because he was trying to make up. I felt that I was finally at an artistically high level with him. I wasn't holding back and I wasn't scared anymore. It was a real genuine moment. But boy, when something got in his head, he would say it. I couldn't believe the ring pissed him off. And I never wore the ring ever again."

In the spring of 1984, Robbins undertook a collaboration at City Ballet with the iconoclastic modern dance choreographer Twyla Tharp, whom Robbins had known since 1969 and supported financially with his foundation (as he did for Paul Taylor and others). The Robbins-Tharp project had been approved by Balanchine shortly before his death. The title of the piece, *Brahms / Handel*, referred to its score, which was an orchestrated version of Brahms' twenty-five variations and fugue on a theme by Handel. Tharp's status with the company was that of guest artist, and Robbins later said, "I don't think Lincoln [Kirstein] and Peter [Martins] liked the idea of Twyla coming in very much." In retrospect, Kirstein said, "The kids liked Twyla's energy. At a certain point, muscle takes over from mind. I don't think we will work with her again, though you never can tell."

From the outset, the ballet was an uneasy marriage of styles. While the two choreographers to some degree spurred and edited each other's work, they divided the cast between them *à la* Jets and Sharks, setting up a kind of friendly, all-around competition. In her memoir, *Push Comes to Shove,* Tharp wrote, "Jerry had the notion of dividing the company into two camps, the blues and the greens. He wanted the blues. 'Of course, Jerry, you know green is a lousy color,' I said. We began by alternating variations, although each of us could add anything or bring our group through the other sections at any time so no one would be sure who had done what."

Apparently, both choreographers relished the who-did-what guessing game for the audience, made all the more slippery with each alluding to Balanchine. Even with Robbins' modern background, his neo-classical formalism (and that of the company's dancers) was a sharp contrast to the trademark lunges, flexed feet and flicking hands that Tharp brought into her work. Robbins' cool, low-key sensibility was somewhat overshadowed by Tharp's extravagant acrobatic stunts, as when she dragged her ballerinas in splits across the stage or hoisted them into cartwheels in the air. Yet, where Tharp offered razzmatazz kitsch and breakneck speed, Robbins provided the decorum that finally grounded the ballet despite its stylistic incongruities.

While the dancers may have been caught between two abrasive fountainheads, Robbins and Tharp worked together without conflict, though early on Robbins said lightheartedly, "We are beginning to discover why painters don't collaborate on the same painting." Tharp later recalled, "There actually never were any harsh moments between us. Jerry went out of his way to be encouraging as he passed through a rehearsal, and he remembers that one day, when he was boggled, I came into our dressing room and told him to take a bite out of whatever was bothering him most. We each tried to watch videotape to keep up with all the rehearsals and be as organized as possible, but the opportunities in this kind of situation are endless, and we were running out of time. One day Jerry and I both decided we could not have the ballet ready for its premiere. . . ."

Recollecting that decision, Robbins said, "I went to Lincoln and said that I didn't think it was going to come off. He said, 'We're not afraid of failure. Keep going. Work for another week and see what happens.'"

Without postponement, the ballet opened on June 7, 1984. The cast included two principal couples, Merrill Ashley and Ib Andersen, Maria Calegari and Bart Cook. The clashing blue and green costumes were simple Oscar de la Renta designs. Jennifer Tipton devised a complementary blue-and-green lighting scheme that changed colors according to the ever-shifting balance between the two groups onstage. Jerri Kumery remembered the opening night, saying, "They [Robbins and Tharp] were very in control and reserved, but you could feel the tension. There was one point on opening night when the ballet was finished that there was—not a fight, but a little altercation about who would go out first in front of the curtain. And they went back and forth before somebody would walk out and take the first bow. It must have been Twyla. I just remember we were all standing there and the curtain was pulled, and it seemed like hours."

The audience was delighted, and if nothing else, the ballet was an innovative novelty for the company. Robbins later said, "Twyla and I were surprised, but the critics loved it." The love wasn't unqualified, but most of the reviews were indeed favorable. In the *Times*, Anna Kisselgoff wrote that the ballet was "really something new—radical in its break with rules of genteel ballet sensibility, as exciting as it is flawed. Everyone should see it." Arlene Croce called it "a wonder of a new ballet," and surmised, "These are all happy dancers, and this is choreography they cherish."

Robbins realized as much as anyone that the latest generation of City Ballet was technically and talent-wise very different from those that came before. Comparing the company's dancers in 1984 with those who performed at City Ballet during its first twenty years, Robbins said, "The level of [technical] training is so immense that most of our corps girls today can do what our principals did then." On the other hand, Robbins explained, "Before, there were people who were capable of dramatic presence as well as classical beauty—a dancer like Tanny [Le Clercq]. Over the years, George developed more and more toward a classically aimed company. Now I find that dancers are embarrassed if asked to act. It is hard to get them to relate to each other, let alone act. Our ballerinas today have other qualities. . . . And with all our vast admiration for our ballerinas, they don't have the complexity that Allegra Kent brought to anything, even to walking across the stage."

The idea that the training at the School of American Ballet would emphasize athleticism and technique rather than dramatics and acting was entirely consistent with Balanchine's neo-classical credo. Robbins was evidently content to work with what he saw as a deficiency on the part of the dancers in terms of their dramatic abilities, with technical prowess as compensation. At the same time, he lamented that his ballets like *Dances at a Gathering* and *Watermill* were no longer performed as they had been by their original casts. Still, a year later, he praised recent performances of *Moves* and *Antique Epigraphs*, gushing that "the New York City Ballet is an extraordinary instrument to create on. It always has been, and it remains so now."

In this regard, Wilma Curley sensed an inconsistency in Robbins that she attributed to his somewhat misplaced regard for Balanchine. "It was like a father thing. After George died, Jerry always wanted to do what George would do. He tried to do a white ballet and started trying to use dancers he thought George would use, dancers that Jerry would *never* have cast in his ballets before. I'd say, 'Why are you using that person?' And he'd say, 'Oh, I like her, I like her.' And he really didn't like her. But he got into George's yak about his image—the small head, the long neck, the whole thing—but that was a crock. So I think he was sort of trying to fulfill old George's mission somehow and not being as true to himself. And I don't think that the youngest dancers, even right when George was alive, were taught to respect anybody else. And once he died, 'Eh, who the hell is Jerry?' And Jerry tried to make what he thought George would like. George always absolutely trusted what Jerry did. It was that simple, but so few people got to hear him [Balanchine]. That's the horrible thing. That dancers were taught by the school, by the management and so forth that George was everything and that's the way they treated him. The awful thing is that as much as George knew that, he never corrected it. George would glib you to death and say whatever you wanted him to say at the moment. The same with the school. George hated the school. He wouldn't go there. And every time I hear that quote, 'First a school,' I want to throw up. He hated the school."

Robbins expressed his feelings with regard to his mentor in somewhat oblique fashion with his 1985 ballet, *In Memory Of . . .* , which was set to Alban Berg's *Violin Concerto.* The music, with all its dissonant turmoil, was originally inspired by the death in 1935 of Berg's young family friend, Manon Gropius (daughter of architect Walter Gropius and singer Alma Mahler). *In Memory Of . . .* was surely a meditation on life, love and death, and that the ballet's central role was danced by Balanchine-muse Suzanne Farrell caused it to be seen as a Robbins elegy for Mr. B. Jerri Kumery recalled, "We knew that the music was written for that girl that died [Manon Gropius], the eighteen-year-old who died; but everybody knew that it was about Mr. B. It was very understood; but it was never said, never spoken of."

Crediting Robbins with "true Balanchinian wisdom," Farrell noted in her memoir that "although the final version depicted a life, death, and resurrection, Jerry never said there was any specific story." When the piece was later broadcast on PBS, Robbins cautioned against a specific interpretation while acknowledging that the ballet was about "the sense of losing people, and the struggles they go through when they're ill and die—and hopefully arrive at peace for themselves." The dance portrayed Farrell and Joseph Duell as young lovers separated by the figure Death (Adam Lüders). The ending was a mystical apotheosis that placed a transfigured Farrell among the angels. The ballerina remembered, "I enjoyed dancing the evolution of my role from a young woman in love with a young man to a highly dramatic *pas de deux* with Death to a resurrection supported by both figures. In the aftermath of Balanchine, *In*

Memory Of . . . was a ballet of welcome substance." Robbins would restage the ballet the following year for the Paris Opéra, which was then under the direction of Rudolf Nureyev.

Another wrenching tragedy befell Robbins and his New York City Ballet family in February of 1986, when Joseph Duell jumped from a window to his death at the age of twenty-nine. Previously hospitalized for treatment of depression, the troubled dancer had been torn between the advice of his therapists and a female psychic, who was a kind of New Age spiritual advisor for a small group of City Ballet dancers. Christopher d'Amboise recalled, "God, it's weird talking about Joe. Lincoln Kirstein, who was also very involved with Joe Duell, left me some things after he died. When I went to pick them up, I got a couple of paintings. Everything was packed in Lincoln's apartment. And there was this wooden carved cat. I thought, That's odd, I don't really remember that in his apartment. And I turned it over and it had: 'To Lincoln from Joe.' And it killed me, because Joe's death really affected me a lot. I do remember seeing Joe dancing at a Robbins ballet, I forget which one it was, and I'll never forget the look of misery on Joe's face as he was performing it. And of course after he died, I remembered it, and thought, Why didn't I offer some help? But Joe had so many things going on that were personal and tortured. I think Joe had tried to kill himself already when he was younger. There were so many things. God, I heard stories of Joe on stage having an exorcism."

Others heard the same tale, but the company's management was apparently unaware of Duell's unstable condition. Robbins had encouraged the young dancer's career and was hit hard by the news of the suicide (which came two days after the premiere of his second minimalist ballet, *Eight Lines*). In the spring, Robbins staged *Quiet City* in memory of Joseph Duell, setting the ballet to Copland's incidental music for Irwin Shaw's play *The Quiet City*. Robbins cast three men, Robert La Fosse, Peter Boal and Damian Woetzel. In his memoir, *Nothing to Hide*, La Fosse wrote that at the start Robbins "had them [Boal and Woetzel] come on one at a time from the corner and do very godlike movements. At a certain point in the music trumpets called out, and he told me to run, jump and fly in the air as they lifted me even higher. At the moment, I thought this was going to be Jerome Robbins' version of *Apollo*. From the first step, I felt this was a ballet about the heavens, something spiritual. I understood what he was after, even though Jerry doesn't ever really say what he's doing." Bart Cook was serving as Robbins' ballet master and remembered that all were aware that the ballet was a tribute to Duell. Cook said, "I don't think that anyone ever spoke about it, but I believe that everyone knew. It was a difficult time for everyone."

Early in 1987, Robbins flew to Los Angeles to visit Nora Kaye, who had been hospitalized and was dying of cancer. Kaye was initially reluctant to see him. Her longtime friend, Isabel Brown, recalled, "It isn't that Nora didn't want to see him, but she was so sick she didn't want to see anybody. I think that was the main reason. At that point she just wanted to let go. He was coming really toward the very end. She'd gotten over everything a long time ago. I don't think she could bear the thought of all that, and so she just voiced this opinion, but she did let him come in and see her and they did say good-bye. I was there. Actually, I was the only one allowed in there with Herbert [Kaye's husband] and the nurse. I think at that point she wasn't too aware."

Nora Kaye died on February twenty-eighth. Robbins stepped in to offer his support to a grief-stricken Herbert Ross and the following year eulogized Kaye at a memorial service at New York's City Center. Speaking with obvious emotion, Robbins characterized her as a great dramatic performer not because of her flamboyance but because of her enormous intensity and economy of gesture. He closed with a recollection of his visit to Spoleto after her death. He said that he had been sitting on the town square after breakfast and was feeling a sense of tranquility when he was possessed by visions of "people that I loved from the past." These passing phantoms included his secretary, Edith Weissman, and Tommy Abbott and Nora Kaye in her cork-wedge shoes. "And she [Nora] saw me," said Robbins. "She caught my eye and she came over and she said, 'I see you.' And she looked at me and she went on. And there was nothing more than that, nothing deeper than that, except that she said, 'It's all right. I'll see you again.'" Robbins added poignantly, "And I hope so."

In the spring of 1987, Robbins returned to musical theater with a re-newed effort to adapt Brecht's *The Exception and the Rule*, formerly called *A Pray by Blecht* and now retitled *Race to Urga*. The show was being produced by Gregory Mosher as a Lincoln Center workshop. John Guare set about rewriting the script, and Leonard Bernstein reworked the score for three months. Robbins cast the show and went into rehearsals during April, with several open rehearsal-previews in May at the Mitzi Newhouse Theater. In place of Zero Mostel, who'd died in 1977, Robbins cast Mostel's son, Josh, who stepped into his father's role as the capitalist merchant racing across the desert with his coolie to a fictional Urga. The show's original producer in 1968, Stuart Ostrow, said of the new staging, "I wasn't involved, but Jerry asked me to watch a run-through, and I told him it still suffered from an excess of self-righteousness and talent. He really wanted to please Bernstein—Lenny had the score recorded—but Jerry's heart wasn't in it."

According to Bernstein biographer Humphrey Burton, Bernstein wrote a memo to Robbins and his colleagues describing the new script as "straight and strong and funny and hard-hitting, especially with its Prologue and Epilogue and the few message songs in between; but apparently that's not enough to justify our efforts morally; we are ethically bound to reach an affluent public at all costs and by all means." In a letter to Burton, Robbins suggested that Bernstein's support had been "grudging." In addition, Stephen Sondheim refused to contribute his lyrics to the project. Robbins vented his frustrations on the cast, in particular on Josh Mostel. Mostel was born in 1946 and grew up hearing his father's stories about Robbins. In retrospect, the young Mostel said, "I think Zero would give him shit and they would give each other shit, but I think that was sort of par for the course with both of them."

As his father's son and as the show's union representative, Josh Mostel was not likely to win Robbins' affection. Mostel recalled, "I was the Equity deputy. Somebody had to do it. You know, we'd get these ten-minute breaks that we'd long for, and we'd go off. We were in this little green room where everyone was smoking, and I wasn't a smoker. I would go into this room just to be away from it. So we'd get in there, and I look at my watch. And then the stage manager comes in and says, 'Okay, we're back.' I said, 'No, we're not back, it's eight minutes.' He said, 'Well, Jerry wants you back.' I said, 'Well, fuck Jerry. Equity says you have ten minutes.' He says, 'What am I gonna do? He's yelling at me.' I said, 'That doesn't mean you can yell at us.' And then we have this discussion. He says, 'Okay, it's ten minutes now.' Oh, it was a form of torture."

Mostel continued, "Jerry was quite the case. And we would have these long marching rehearsals where we're marching hopelessly in the desert and we'd go twenty-nine steps. He'd say, 'Try twenty-nine steps stage left, and then fourteen steps down.' Then he'd say, 'All right, try thirty-two steps to the left, nineteen down, and twenty-four to the right.' And we're just trudging. It was like trudge rehearsal, it was so particular and it was so picky. . . . Oh man, he could be a real prick. He'd just get you. He once kicked Greg Mosher out of rehearsal. We were rehearsing, Greg Mosher walks in, and Jerry all of a sudden gets uptight, and after about a minute turns and says, 'Look, Greg, I'm a little stuck now, and just to have another director around, it makes me nervous.' So Greg left. Jerry would give me shit, he'd give the company shit, and he'd give John Guare shit. He was an equal opportunity shit-slinger. And he wouldn't tell us what time the performances were. And so before the performances, we'd say, 'What's the schedule this week?' He'd say, 'Well, you know, I don't want word to get out.' "

Robbins abruptly abandoned the production as he had eighteen years before. That same month, the New York Public Library named its collection of dance film and videotape in his honor—the Jerome Robbins Archive of Recorded Moving Image. The library hosted a reception and opened a tribute exhibition of posters, photographs and costume designs that surveyed Robbins' career. He noted, "That this archive is funded through *Fiddler* makes a nice circle." Mikhail Baryshnikov and a host of dance luminaries turned out to celebrate the occasion. Robbins recalled being taken as a young boy by his parents to listen to stories in the children's room of the Forty-second Street library. He said, "Yet the most exciting things were these walls of books. And inside them were adventures, strange knowledge and new people."

In the fall, Robbins was moved by the AIDS crisis to devote himself to public activism, serving as artistic coordinator for a benefit called, "Dancing for Life." The gala event drew support from the New York City Ballet, American Ballet Theatre, the Joffrey, Dance Theatre of Harlem, and other companies, including those of Merce Cunningham, Paul Taylor, Twyla Tharp, Elliot Feld, Mark Morris and Lar Lubovich, who first proposed the idea to Robbins. At the time, Robbins said, "The whole world should be concerned about this plague. If a benefit like this focuses more attention on it, that's all to the good. . . . I'm tired of people thinking that AIDS equals only homosexuality and the arts as if the disease could be contained within those communities. That's shortsightedness." Robbins added, "AIDS is not the wages of sin. It's a disease that gets started anywhere."

The beneficiaries of the fund-raising gala included the American Foundation for AIDS Research, the Gay Men's Health Crisis, and the National AIDS Network. After taking this public stand with regard to the disease, Robbins was approached by a number of gay rights organizations soliciting his support, but he was still closeted regarding his personal lifestyle and reluctant to come out as a gay activist. While he continued his efforts on behalf of AIDS research, his experience with lending his name to political causes in the forties still called up painful memories. Moreover, as he approached his sixty-ninth birthday, Robbins undertook what may have been the most ambitious theatrical project of his life. He once said, "Doing a show is like being on a subway for three months"; however, in this case the ride would require almost three years.

J*erome Robbins' Broadway* (originally entitled *Jerome Robbins's Broadway Dances*) started as a monumental research project aimed at reconstructing numbers from *On the Town, Billion Dollar Baby, High Button Shoes, The King and I, Peter Pan, Call Me Madam, West Side Story, Gypsy, A Funny Thing Happened on the Way to the Forum* and *Fiddler on the Roof.* The project had been under consideration for ten years when Robbins shifted into high gear in 1987. With memories of the shows of that Golden Era fading, Robbins felt an increasing sense of urgency about accomplishing the restoration. He explained, "I hated the idea that they were just disappearing and became more things that people talked about in the past. I felt it more important now than ever before, because those kinds of shows are no longer being done. This is not a concert. I want to do the numbers as they were done on Broadway in the original shows. I want to give the feeling of the times, what musicals were like at those times." Lamenting the changes he had witnessed on Broadway in more recent years, Robbins said, "I'm not crazy about what happened since they took the New Testament and made a musical out of it."

He assembled an all-star team of collaborators, including many from his past who served as consultants. This group included Leonard Bernstein, Jerry Bock, Betty Comden, Adolph Green, Stephen Sondheim, Sheldon Harnick, Joseph Stein and Jule Styne. Fifteen original numbers were eventually revived. Grover Dale was recruited to co-direct. Robin Wagner coordinated the recreation of scenery from designers such as Oliver Smith, Boris Aronson, Jo Mielziner and Tony Walton. Joseph Aulisi eventually played a similar supervising role with the costume designers, including Alvin Colt, Irene Sharaff, Patricia Zipprodt, Miles White and Raoul Pène du Bois. The producers of *Jerome Robbins' Broadway* were the Shubert Organization, Japan's Suntory International Corporation, Roger Berlind, Byron Goldman and Emanuel Azenberg.

Gerald Schoenfeld, the head of the Shubert group, explained that the production was initiated with an overture from Robbins' attorney. "Floria Lasky came to see us and asked if we would support what she called 'a reconstruction of Jerry's works,' without any assurance whatsoever that he would go further with it," said Schoenfeld. "And that was going to cost a million dollars because he didn't really recall the staging and he needed to get assistance. Because of who he was, he received special consideration from the Lincoln Center archive, to get access to his own material and to take it out under the most stringent conditions regarding its return so he could work on it. And he interviewed people who worked on his shows with him for their recollections, and it really came together to the point that he said he would like to produce the show. . . . Well, we immediately agreed. I guess we agreed for two reasons: we had already invested a million dollars in it, and the other reason was the opportunity to be associated with anything that Jerome Robbins would be doing.

"So then began a very torturous negotiation because he insisted on getting fifty percent of all royalties and he insisted on twenty-three weeks of rehearsal. And of course the other parties were not very happy about giving him that amount, but he insisted. And this dragged on for a long time. And finally I went to a meeting, and I said to the others, 'Either you want to do it or you don't want to do it. I'm finished with this procrastination and disagreements.' And Leonard Bernstein told the rest of them that he's a genius, and no matter what we feel, we have to cater to genius. So we all went along." Schoenfeld explained that a formula was devised to allocate the other fifty percent of the royalties. "We set aside a certain percentage for the designers and the royalty holders, based on the number of minutes that their song or their bit was in the show. And that was accepted."

Schoenfeld also recollected the difficulties for producers working on a day-to-day basis with Robbins. "It became a situation where if we would have meetings, his technique was to put you immediately on the defensive. I don't know whether he was frightened, whatever, but his personality was such that he would get into a defensive mode, like a porcupine, and you had to evade the barbs that he would throw. And Manny Azenberg was our manager. I think he drove Manny to the point almost of a nervous breakdown, where Manny could not even deal with him. So I had to step in and deal with him. Manny wouldn't even come to meetings."

With the assistance of a casting agent, Robbins combed the country to find performers from his early shows who could help him with the task of recreating the long-lost production numbers, most of which were staged at a time before the dances in Broadway musicals were routinely notated or recorded on film. Robbins said, "I'm going to have to do some fiddling because I don't have any notes, tapes or anything recorded of the early works." He recounted how he began the complex curatorial process, saying, "I picked out one show to see what I could do to research it. I tracked down some of the original dancers in *High Button Shoes* and one of those dancers said, 'Oh, I've got a silent film of the Bathing Beauty ballet.' 'Great,' I thought. I saw it. It lacked a middle section. I had to find out what happened in the middle. And forty-one years after the show was done, I track down one dancer, and she says, 'Oh, so-and-so knows that ballet very well. Call him. He was in that number.'"

With *High Button Shoes,* the trail eventually led to Kevin Jo Johnson, who was in the road company and had taken several pages of notes on the sequence. Robbins' detective work led to a number of heartfelt reunions with former cast members. Johnson and several others from *High Button Shoes* met with Robbins one morning at the studio in his townhouse. Robbins said, "So first I played the ballet score, and I told them what I thought happened. And then we got to the music of the part that was missing in the movie, and we all looked at each other blankly. Kevin Jo Johnson said, 'Oh, I know what went on there.' He opened up his attaché case and brought out three or four mimeographed sheets. He had the dance counts for the whole ballet. Not the steps, but the action and on what counts it happened. Counts for the seven bathing beauties, the three crooks, the five cops, the two con men, the two sets of identical twins, the lifeguard, the boyfriends, the gorilla. He had noted who went in which of the seven bathhouse doors and who came out where and when. As soon as we read the notes, we all shouted, 'Oh yes! Now I remember! You did so-and-so and the money was in the skirts and the con men would do that!' So it all came back. It was a wonderful day—the reunion with the dancers and the work."

The idea was to open the production in time for Robbins' seventieth birthday in October of 1988, but he was sidetracked early in the year with a new ballet, *Ives, Songs*, and consequently rehearsals for the musical were delayed until the end of the summer. *Ives, Songs* was an ambitious undertaking, a forty-minute ballet with a score comprised of vintage songs of early twentieth-century Americana by Charles Ives. At the time Robbins started rehearsals during City Ballet's winter season, many observers, including Lincoln Kirstein, thought this would be his last major work, though Robbins said at the time, "Sure, I'm not as agile as I was at twenty-five, but I still get around. If Martha Graham can do *Rite of Spring* at ninety, and Balanchine could work up until a year before his death—then I'll go as far as I can go, and when I can't go, I'll stop."

Robbins described *Ives, Songs* as "an album, filled with mementos, photographs, postcards, memos and journal notes—like turning the pages of a picture book." The diversity of tone and subject matter in the songs posed a considerable challenge for the choreographer, who catalogued and reviewed more than one hundred Ives compositions before selecting eighteen for inclusion in the ballet. He said, "There are some that have to do with religion, some that have to do with bands, some that have to do with dying. There are ones about children, ones about eccentric people, ones that are political diatribes, ones about war. There's a vast amount of material to make your way through and to try to make sense of. . . . When I first started to examine the songs, I felt that if you went down them chronologically, you'd more or less get a picture of Ives himself and his reflections of the world around him." Yet typically, Robbins warned, "I don't want to be held to the idea that this is going to be the story of Ives' life as seen through his songs. The things I say are side references; and not statements about content. A ballet is too complex for any of those definitions. I prefer people to come and not look for things that they've read about."

As Clive Barnes pointed out, there was a kind of spiritual affinity between Robbins and Ives. Both were commentators on the American scene and times, both mixed elitism and populism, and both rebeled early in their careers against European domination of their respective art forms (for Robbins, it was the Russian hegemony in ballet, while Ives reacted to the prevalent German influence in classical music). In his ballet, Robbins pursued a course of free-association, superimposing his own memories and impressions over those suggested by the songs, bucking if not quite transcending the cliché of having the somber figure of Charles Ives wandering through the action onstage at the outset and conclusion. Anna Kisselgoff called the ballet "pure Robbins at his best," and observed that its Proustian atmosphere of remembrance was akin to that seen in the works of Antony Tudor, who had died the year before. Clive Barnes later saw in the work "a Prospero-like air of farewell," and though the assessment was premature, Robbins' mature command of the stage did possess a certain Shakespearean majesty.

The cast of forty included Helène Alexopoulos, Alexandre Proia, Stephanie Saland and Jeppe Mydtskov. Of her work with Robbins, Saland recalled, "God knows, Jerry made me cry, but I loved him so much, and not because I felt like an abused person but because I really got what he was doing. I really understood his pain with it. I feel so blessed and fortunate having had that experience. There's nothing that replaces it." Dancer Stacy Caddell agreed and remembered Robbins offering his support to her during this time. "*Ives, Songs* was interesting, and at that point I felt more comfortable with him. He was very demanding in certain respects, but it was great to watch him do things—his musicality and his phrasing. . . . When I would have a problem or something, Jerry was one person that I went to and would talk to about things in the company. So for me Jerry was like a really big figure. There was a time when I didn't want to dance, and Jerry said, 'If it matters to you, *I* want you here.' He was just incredibly supportive and very, very sweet. He really took time out of his schedule, his Broadway schedule, which was insane, and talked to me for quite a while. It meant a lot to me."

The rehearsal period for *Jerome Robbins' Broadway* was the longest in Broadway history. Gerald Schoenfeld recalled that Robbins offered a small, begrudging compromise. "He called me one day and asked if he could come over and see me. I was visiting in East Hampton, I very seldom go there. So he drove over from Bridgehampton, and he said, 'I have a deal.' 'What's that?' I say. He'll give me twenty-two weeks if I'll give him one extra week of previews. So I said fine. Everything was really an obstacle to overcome with him. But let me tell you, when I was in the theater and I looked at the work evolving, I could look at the stage and he could look at it with one turn of his head, and he would take in more than I would take in if I spent the entire day. He was leaping, pirouetting, *grand jétéing*, like he was a young boy with his cast. He would reduce people in the company to absolute tears with his vicious sarcasm. And then when he would praise them, they would absolutely think that God had bestowed his hand on them. So it was staggering."

As co-director, Grover Dale voiced early concerns about Robbins' approach to the show. "I wasn't his 'yes man.' Maybe that's why he wanted me there. After months of painstaking work reconstructing those glorious dances, he actually turned to me one night and said, 'Okay, Grove, what do you think this show should look like?' The shock of being asked my opinion blinded me temporarily to the exercise in futility I was about to undertake. I talked for hours, trying to convince him that this work did not need the adornment of costumes and sets. 'Just show the purity of the dances. Let them slide onstage from the wings. Let them pass through each other. Let the audience discover them in a fresh way, yada yada yada.' Jerry liked opening new doors, so he let me continue. There were always doors to be opened. Behind them, there were always twelve more doors to be opened as well. The exploring usually brought him full circle back to his first choice. That's what happened with the show. We constructed duplications of what was done originally. Months later, we took the company up to Purchase and tried it out in front of an audience for two nights without any sets, lighting or costumes. It was fantastic! That's the one and only time he said, 'Grove, I think you were right, but I can't go back on it now. We've spent hundreds of thousands of dollars on wigs and costumes that are already being built.' Maybe he said that for my benefit, I don't know. If he really believed he had just seen the right way to do the show, he wouldn't have cared about how much money was spent, he would have served his choreography.

"He lost a lot of sleep over the show. The stakes were enormous. It wasn't like he was worried about one show, he was worried about eighteen of them rolled into one." Dale believed that the production suffered from being over-rehearsed, saying, "Eight weeks into the rehearsal period was when we should have opened. That's when the love and respect for the man and his work peaked. There were no wounded bodies around."

Robbins later referred to the "enormous toll" that the rehearsal process exacted from him. The burden of his workload caused episodes of instability and paranoia. As he pushed himself and his performers to the limit, his behavior became erratic. According to some of those who worked in his home-office, he believed at times that someone was trying to poison him and limited his diet in the theater to Snickers candy bars and soda. He was especially hard on his domestic staff (one assistant called him "Attila the Hitler"). He would later cancel the retirement benefits of his domestic staff, though he did provide for a number of employees in his will and most remained devoted to him. Whatever personal excesses he was exhibiting, the quality of the work in rehearsals was never compromised.

While there were no longer Broadway stars to compare with the Ethel Mermans and Zero Mostels, the cast of more than sixty performers featured Jason Alexander, Faith Prince, Charlotte d'Amboise, Debbie Shapiro, Scott Wise and Robert La Fosse. Dancer Mark Esposito appeared in numbers from *On the Town, West Side Story, The King and I* and *Fiddler on the Roof.* He remembered Robbins' concern with the show's basic concept torn between past and present. "Jerry was really worried about it all just being a carbon copy. He wanted it to be seen again for *the first time.* That was the pressure that he was under, whether he was going to be able to produce that with the contemporary dancers he had. Because dancers over the years have become much more technically proficient, but I think what's happened with a lot of them is that they've lost the acting in the dancing. Jerry was never a technical dancer, by no means—it was all about acting. He never approached me as a dancer, he always treated me as an actor. It was always about his choreography and making it as brilliant as it is, but it always came from the actor's point of view. I remember when we were rehearsing the *The King and I* section, it was always about the intensity in your face, even though you were wearing a mask. He always told me it just comes through, it just filters through. It was the same thing with the Bottle Dance [in *Fiddler on the Roof*]. Even though there were technical and balancing acts, it was more about the dramatic intention with him."

Actor Jason Alexander, later known for his *Seinfeld* TV role, performed the pivotal part of the scene-setting emcee as well as leading roles in the excerpts. He also wrote the connecting scenes in the script that linked the numbers. Of working with Robbins on the book, Alexander recalled, "He didn't know what made it an evening. And I kept saying, 'What makes it an evening? What do you want to share? Do you want to share your process of creation? Do you want to share the moment of inspiration for how to crack each show?' I kept saying it could really be a kind of wonderful exploration into how an artist creates. So I'd go off and I'd write a monologue where I played him and all the dancers were coming out of my head. He'd go, 'Naah, naaah, I don't like it, it's too much about me, it's too much about me.' Of course he wanted everything to be about him, but not that openly.

"Then he would say, 'Maybe we could just tell them something about the shows so that they understand the number better.' So I'd go off and write something like that. It was a very hit-and-miss, trial-and-error, and he never really knew. As we were getting closer and closer, I said, 'Look, Jerry, why don't we just tell them what they need to know about the shows and we'll try to do it in an interesting way and I'll be a character for the shows.' He got to a point with me where there was enough trust that he went, 'Okay, I've got other things to do.' I think at that point he was too overwhelmed to be concerned about it, he had so many other things on his plate."

Alexander continued, "Jerry never really directed me as an actor. I'll tell you a funny story: There was one time when we were working through the *Fiddler* section and I had based my Tevye on a Topol-esque approach, a very gravelly Russian voice. There was a small opening monologue and Jerry said, 'You know what I'd like you to try? Come out and do the first line as Tevye, then do these two lines as you, then do these two lines as Tevye, these three lines as you, then go into the song.' I said, 'Wait a minute, you want me to come out with the beard, and the outfit, and the voice, drop it, pick it back up, drop it, then pick it up again?' He said, 'Yeah.' I said, 'Why would I do that?' He said, 'I think it will be dazzling.' I said, 'I think it'll be confusing and stupid—it'll look like I can't sustain the character.' We got into this long conversation about it, and he finally said, 'Would you do me a favor? Would you just show it to me once so that I can see it.' I took a minute to think about it and I finally said to him, 'You know what? I can't do that, Jerry, because there's a possibility you might like it, and I'm telling you I'm not going to do it for you eight times a week.' So I never did it. And he deferred.

"I also became one of the Equity deputies on the show and I had to go up against him quite a bit, and I think I was the only person in the show who really didn't give a rat's ass whether I opened in it or not—I didn't think it was going to do anything for me. I was really there just to learn a little bit about directing, which is the reason I took the show, so I didn't care. They would send me oftentimes in to see if I could shake him loose from something he was holding to. On many occasions it worked, and on a couple it didn't. But that was the reason the producers, all the producers, were just going up the wall. He would say blue on Monday and they would buy blue, and then he'd say red on Tuesday, and they'd go, 'But you said blue. Where are we going to get this from?' They really had very little recourse.

"Nobody could talk to him with very few exceptions. He had a lot of trust in Lenny Bernstein and a couple of the other collaborators he really believed in. But he was paranoid or seemingly paranoid to listen to most people. He thought that in some ways they were the enemy." Alexander added, "The experience in general was very positive, despite the nightmarish episodes. There were extraordinary things that happened during the course of rehearsals. They were profound for me and I wasn't involved in the productions the first time. But some of the meetings between the original cast and our cast were heartbreaking, they were just amazing exchanges, and he was the orchestrator of all this."

Actress and dancer Charlotte d'Amboise, sister of Christopher d'Amboise, was cast as Anita for the *West Side Story* segment and as Peter Pan. She also performed "Dreams Come True" from *Billion Dollar Baby*, though the number was cut before the show opened. "The main thing Jerry taught—which was unbelievable to watch—was the way he focused every scene," said d'Amboise. "And he was all about that, and that's where his brilliance lies. Because so much of theater is where your eyes are looking, what you watch and what the audience sees. Everything was all about who or what we were watching. Everything had a focus. It was a huge lesson to me. And I have to say most directors nowadays do not know how to do that in musical theater or in straight theater."

Nancy Hess performed in sequences from *On the Town*, *West Side Story*, *High Button Shoes*, *Fiddler on the Roof* and *The King and I*. She recalled, "You knew that regardless of what a monster he could be that you would never be monstrously exposed onstage. You would always be taken care of onstage because of his artistic integrity. It was a very difficult experience, it was actually a very unhappy time for almost the entire *Robbins* cast, I would say, physically and emotionally. However, I wouldn't change that experience, I wouldn't wish my life without that experience—in a million years I wouldn't, because I feel like it enriched me in many ways. Subsequent experiences have made me appreciate him, even though he was maniacal at times—and the ultimate control freak. He was protecting himself, his own best interests, by controlling everything. But, at the same time, you knew you were never going to go out there and fall on your face."

Later nominated for a Tony Award, Charlotte d'Amboise also had complete faith in Robbins' shaping her performance. She said, "I remember thinking to myself, You know what? Whatever he [Jerry] does with me, I know that I'll be great. I know that he would never put me onstage and allow anything that wasn't up to a certain level. I have never had that with a director, really. I trusted him completely. You completely trusted him, and he completely takes you there, and orchestrates you. It's great to have that much attention put on you as a performer. You're being watched and taken care of, ultimately. And he would get a great performance out of everyone. When we did *West Side Story*, we learned it the first week and we did it for six months every day in rehearsal. What he would do is find it right away, and then he would spend six months changing it. He explored everything, and there was not a thing unexplored, and then he was happy. I don't know if he was ever really happy, but ultimately he would know, 'Okay, I'm safe, this is the best that I can do.' He was a perfectionist like I've never seen."

Before the show opened, Robbins vehemently defended his uncompromising approach during a *Times* interview, saying, "I am a perfectionist. I wear that badge proudly. I think that's what art is about—trying to make it as good as you possibly can." He added, "People gripe. They gripe. I can't help what they say. I don't think it's anybody's business how I work. I'm not in the profession to show people how I work."

Of course, he preferred to be judged by results rather than methods. D'Amboise noted, "People used to sometimes say that he wants to dim you, *not* bring out the performance in you, because he had to control everything you do. But ultimately he loved that [way of working] and that's why the performers he really loved, as far as theater [goes], were really big personalities. Also, he played every role. He was a great actor and a great pantomime. Truly great. Tevye? No one did it better than him. Every role in *Jerome Robbins' Broadway*, the women and the men, he did better than anyone."

In this regard, Jason Alexander recalled a moment of truth with Robbins. "I really adored him, and I saw him be evil. But, ultimately, I think I was always able to understand. I said to him one time, 'I know why you have a demon.' He said, 'Yeah, why?' I said, 'Well, the fact of the matter is that you can dance anything you create better than anybody you give it to, but you can't dance it all at the same time, and so it's never going to be exactly what you see in your head and I bet it drives you insane.' He said, 'You've nailed my life.'"

While still in the midst of rehearsals in October of 1998, Robbins celebrated his seventieth birthday with a glitzy, star-studded bash thrown for him by Mica and Ahmet Ertegün at Maxim's. More than a hundred guests were seated at banquet tables appointed with pink roses and pink lamps. There were overlapping circles of friends from all the worlds he had conquered. His sister, Sonia, and her family attended. And there were personal friends like Lady Slim Keith, who reportedly "swept in wearing black velvet and a jeweled top." Slim's circle included her daughter, Kitty Hawks, as well as Lauren Bacall and Claudette Colbert. From the theater came Robbins' collaborators like Jule Styne, Stephen Sondheim, Sheldon Harnick, Jerry Bock, Oliver Smith, John Guare, Arthur Laurents and Adolph Green. Betty Comden offered a heartfelt rendition of "Broadway Blossom," and Nancy Walker belted out "And I Can Cook Too." The ballet world was represented by Mikhail Baryshnikov, Peter Martins, Patricia McBride, Tanaquil Le Clercq, Maria Calegari and Heather Watts. Others on hand for the chocolate cake rituals included Arthur Gold, Robert Fizdale, Eugenia Doll, Bill Paley, Kiki and Jerzy Kosinski, Fran Lebowitz, Bill Blass, Oscar de la Renta, Jerry Zipkin, Rosamund Bernier, Mary and Swifty Lazar, Brooke Hayward, Peter Duchin and Irene Selznick. In a brief birthday speech, Robbins professed his love for everyone in the room, and by the end of the evening there were many in the crowd with tears in their eyes.

Out of that throng of well-wishers, Robbins was destined to lose one of his dearest friends. When he returned to rehearsals, he had a bitter falling out with designer Oliver Smith over the color of a backdrop. Smith's friend Richard D'Arcy said, "Jerry called Oliver on stage in front of the cast and ridiculed him about the work. And Oliver just said, 'I do not have to take this anymore. From now on, you speak to me through my agent or the Shuberts.' Because Oliver is a big Shubert fan, and he was their shining light—they were very fond of him. Oliver stopped talking to him, he would not speak to Jerry. I think that hurt Oliver a great deal, he was just very, very hurt by that."

Jerome Robbins' Broadway premiered at the Imperial Theatre on February 27, 1989. That night Robbins gave each member of the cast an autographed photograph taken during the rehearsal period. Alexander said, "I remember on opening night he was wandering around before the show and visiting everybody. And I was downstairs and I was getting dressed, and he came down, gave me a hug, and he was crying. I said, 'My god, Jerry, I hope these are tears of happiness.' And he said, 'No, no, I don't want this to end.' He was so loving the process of revisiting these moments. He wasn't always able to show it, but boy, when he was kind there was nobody like him. He could be the most lovely and charming man on the planet, especially when children were around. He loved children. And despite his cruelty at times, I think he had tremendous affection for everybody in the show."

Of the opening night, Charlotte d'Amboise said, "I remember at the beginning of the show we all go up and then we bow, and then everybody goes and does their own thing. But at the very beginning of the show, we're all in our costumes, and I'll never forget, the audience stood and applauded for us, and I started crying because it was such a relief. Now, I thought, I can leave now, it's done. It felt like closing night, not opening night. And some people did give their notice that day. You were so sick of the material, I can't tell you. So, yes, in a sense [the show was overrehearsed] because the passion of it was gone, but I have to tell you, he got his reviews and he got the show that he wanted."

Frank Rich enthused, "While *Jerome Robbins' Broadway* may celebrate a vanished musical theater, it does so with such youthful exuberance that nostalgia finally gives way to a giddy, perhaps not even foolish dream that a new generation of Broadway babies may yet be born. . . . Audiences inured to the hydraulic scenic gizmos, formless acrobatics, deafening amplification and emotional vacuity of this decade's Broadway spectaculars will find Mr. Robbins's musical theater a revelation." Rich also pointed out that as a loosely woven anthology the show was necessarily limited in comparison to the more integrated works from which its numbers were drawn, those musicals that demonstrated Robbins' "gift for relentless theatrical flow."

In the *Daily News*, Howard Kissel wrote that he was unable to be "entirely objective" about *Jerome Robbins' Broadway* because "as certain numbers began I choked back tears remembering the first time I heard the cast albums, the first time I saw the shows." Kissel added, "The evening pays tribute to an ego that is apparently as huge as the talent behind it, but what was great about the period it covers is that Broadway was genuinely a community." Clive Barnes saluted the show as "the kind of Broadway you give your regards and heart to." Jack Kroll of *Newsweek* observed, "The special force of this brilliant, poignant and proud show is that it's both a celebration and an elegy." Indeed, the outpouring of nostalgia was for a Broadway and an America that no longer existed. Writing for the *Times* Op/Ed page, Jay H. Lefkowitz saw *Jerome Robbins' Broadway* as a "history lesson" and a gauge for lost cultural values. Lefkowitz reported, "I was mortified to discover a few things about the audiences. There were youngsters in their twenties who didn't even know who Zero Mostel was. There was laughter and tittering during 'The Small House of Uncle Thomas,' particularly in the pantomime of Eliza crossing the river."

Grover Dale, who was married to Anita Morris at the time, recalled his mixed feelings after the premiere. Their young son, James, had given Robbins a glass marble for good luck at the first reconstruction rehearsal, "and thirteen months later, the show opened. I was relieved to go home to my family in California and remove myself from the tension surrounding the production. With packed bags waiting at the door, I was tempted to head to the airport without calling Robbins. I reconsidered and picked up the phone. We talked briefly, acknowledged our differences, and what needed to be done to maintain the show. As we were about to say goodbye, he asked me to give James a message. 'Of course, Jerry, what is it?' He said, 'Tell James his marble worked.' After thirteen months of hell, he remembered the damn marble! He knew how to melt your heart, whether you were an audience or a friend. An amazing man."

Like its *On the Town* finale backdrop of lighted Broadway marquees tracing the hit parade of Robbins' musicals, the show was more a sentimental reminder of the past than a faithful recreation, especially for some of those veteran performers who had been in the original Robbins productions. Some of the excerpted numbers proved to be irretrievable, and Robbins had been compelled to substitute new material. Nanette Fabray recalled assisting Robbins with the restoration of the soft-shoe number, "I Still Get Jealous Over You," which was danced by Jason Alexander and Faith Prince. Fabray said, "Jerry asked if I would come in and help him with the number, which in the show with Jack McCauley and me, was a momma and poppa, older people who loved each other very much. I was able to remember some of the steps, and I was able to remember the attitude, which during the morning I was there, I kept talking about—'It must be gentle, it must be sweet, it must be a love dance, it must be soft.' And I would do soft steps. And when he invited me to come and see the show, it was completely changed. I don't know whether he did it or the people that he had doing it, but the attitude was wrong. It was a hotshot kind of a straw hat, strutting number. It wasn't what it was originally supposed to be, and I don't know how Jerry let that happen."

Wilma Curley, one of the original Jet girls, was similarly disappointed in the suite of dances from *West Side Story* that closed the first act. "It was just wrong," said Curley. "The steps were wrong. The emphases were all in the wrong places. Tony was Robby La Fosse, who personally I really like, but he's not Tony. Jerry had all these boring, blue-eyed Jets. The Jets' character was the fact that they were so typical New York-American—all sizes, all shapes, all intensities—whatever. Now they're all blond, blue-eyed lovelies. The Sharks should eat them."

Helen Gallagher, an original in *High Button Shoes*, saw the same sort of disparity in the restaging of the Mack Sennett ballet. "What we did was very different from what they ended up doing [in *Jerome Robbins' Broadway*]. It was really interesting, because he called us all in one day, all the oldies, to watch the young people do the numbers. I know I particularly watched the Mack Sennett, which I [had been] only very peripherally in, because I was a character and I couldn't be in it, which was what broke my heart in that show. . . . Jerry said, 'Well, what do you think?' I said, 'There's something missing, but I think it's the way the kids are trained today.' He says, 'Yeah, that's it.' I said, 'They're so facile.' Their legs went up higher than ours did, but we had a tension behind it that they don't have because it's so easy for them. . . . They were like empty zeroes. It used to be that in the chorus there was somebody from Minnesota and there was somebody from Texas and there was somebody from North Carolina— and we all came together and we all had different cultures, and now everybody's raised on the same thing. It's all homogenized. It's television. It's so sad, it's the passing of an era. But hopefully at some point the aliens will arrive and there will be something very new. It'll come around again, it always does."

Even with glowing reviews and a half dozen Tony Awards—including Best Musical and Best Director for Robbins—and even with advance sales of almost $8 million (with an unprecedented top ticket price of $55), *Jerome Robbins' Broadway* lost money for its investors, with the initial production budget ballooning to $8.7 million. According to Gerald Schoenfeld, the Shubert group lost approximately $2 million in the final tally. At the time the show opened, *Gypsy* was a hit revival and another national tour of *Fiddler* was under way, all of which put Robbins' weekly combined royalty income at an estimated $48,000. Still, as a matter of pride and ego, the fact that his retrospective was losing money was a source of prickly consternation for him.

After the opening, Grover Dale assisted Robbins on the Tony Awards broadcast and on restaging the show for its subsequent run in Los Angeles. Dale had idolized Robbins for years, but the relationship had been put to the test. Dale said, "I get this call, 'Come in and help me do the Tony Awards.' So

I go in, spend two days, and come back. I didn't stay for the show, I just flew back here [to Los Angeles]. I got a Tony Award, too, because my name was on there as co-director, but I knew this was his show, he was the real, true director of it. So he gets up and he thanks the stage manager [Beverley Randolph]. He calls me at four in the morning in tears, weeping because he couldn't remember my name. . . . He said he was so nervous he couldn't think of anybody's name except Beverley's. It may be true. I'll give him the benefit of the doubt.

"Our friendship got breached over a political issue. When the road company was done, my job was essentially to put it on its feet and he would come in for the last week out here [in LA]. So he came out. I remember one day he was giving notes, he had a long list of notes. There was a black girl, an African-American girl in *The King and I* ballet, and I heard him say something—because he was so dedicated to the replication, exactly the way it was, and he went into this discussion of why it was important to see this material in the context in which it was originally presented. And at that time there were no black people in the ballet. And it bothered him that of all the dancers' arms that were showing, hers were black, and would she mind whitening up. She wept and ran out of the room. I saw the union representative go after her. I thought, Uh-oh. I knew the union representative—I can't speak for him—but I sensed that there would be no remorse at calling the union on this one. So I went to Jerry and I said, 'Jerry, go to that girl and apologize to her—now!' Well, we got into it, big time. Major accusations. He did go and he did make the apology. But boy, that was it.

"But with hindsight, he gave me the greatest gift I have ever gotten from anybody—that experience [with *Jerome Robbins' Broadway*]. I wanted his approval. I saw that and I knew that I wasn't going to get it. And for that to surface into my conscious mind, I went home every night directly from rehearsal, and I worked on that. I said, I've got to find what it is that *I* approve of. So out of all of that time alone I got to what it was that I approve of, and it wasn't being around him or the theater. I changed my whole life. I came home and I had a new purpose in my life, which served me well, because it got me through tragedies that were yet to unfold in my life. Fortunately for me, I got to address that through him. . . . Looking back, I can see how all those events stacked up into growth opportunities, even the terrifying parts. He had a powerful effect on my life."

Gerald Schoenfeld recalled that Robbins blamed the Shuberts for the show's failure at the box office. "We had great trouble marketing the show because we didn't know what to call it. We didn't want to call it excerpts or a revival or whatever. And then of course with the poster it was difficult also to use that, and in view of the size of his name that he insisted on, we really weren't able to convey very much about the show with the poster. And then we learned really very few people remembered Jerome Robbins. Even if you mentioned *West Side Story* or some of the other plays, they were out of the memory of a great many people in the American population. With the logo of the show, of course he wanted his name big. Big! So we did that big J, and we tried to make it into some kind of a dance silhouette. And he finally approved it, and then later of course blamed us for doing a lousy poster, because the show didn't do as well as he thought it would. I said, 'You wanted your name that way and you approved it.' He said, 'Not at all, I didn't care what you did with my name.' He would alter the past to suit the occasion."

In April of 1989, Robbins announced that he was taking a leave of absence from the New York City Ballet. Asked by Anna Kisselgoff if he was in ill health, Robbins replied, "Absolutely not. I'm tired and I want a complete rest with no problems. I hope to spend some time at the beach." Robbins was feeling the strain and the years. He was losing his hearing and had difficulty distinguishing voices in groups. Many of his friends and colleagues had already passed away. He told *Newsweek*, "George Balanchine, Bob Fosse, Antony Tudor, Freddy Ashton, Gower Champion, Michael Bennett—that's a lot in five years. It makes one think a little."

On June eighth, the New York City Ballet billed its Spring Gala as "A Salute to Jerome Robbins in his 70th Birthday Year." With an obviously delighted Robbins seated in the first balcony, the company performed *Glass Pieces*, *Afternoon of a Faun* and *The Concert* (which, as a surprise for the occasion, featured principal dancers in the corps roles of "The Mistake Waltz"). The evening finished with the Robbins-Stravinsky bauble, *Circus Polka*, and on this occasion the children arranged themselves to spell out the monogram JR. Gerald Schoenfeld recalled his encounters with Robbins on such occasions, saying, "I would see him at a gala at the ballet when they were honoring him. I would go over to him and I would rub his bald head from behind and he would turn around, and he would say, 'Hello, baby.' That was his most endearing term."

Schoenfeld later invited Robbins to visit Tokyo on behalf of the Suntory International Corporation, which had the performance rights for a Japanese run of *Jerome Robbins' Broadway.* "The Suntory people wanted him to go to Japan, and asked me, 'Would I talk to him,'" recalled Schoenfeld. "I said, 'Fine, I would.' Jerry said, 'Absolutely not!' So I told them no. One day I was up at Lincoln Center, and he wanted to see me. And he said, 'About that trip to Japan, ask them if they'll give me round-trip first-class transportation. I want to stay in a two-bedroom suite at the Okura Hotel. I want to have somebody assigned to take me around Tokyo. I want to see the Kabuki and the Theatre Noh. I want to go to Kyoto for a week, and I want my guide to accompany me there. I want a car at my disposal at all times. So let me know, and then maybe I might go.'

"So I put it to the Suntory people and they said they would take care of everything. So off we go. And he had a friend, a gay man, a young man [Jesse Gerstein], who was really dying of AIDS. I never saw more tenderness from anyone than he exhibited to Jesse. I said to him when we were there, Suntory invited you to have lunch as the guest of honor at the chairman's house. Now the chairman of Suntory was one of the great industrialists of Japan, really one of the ruling clique, the businessmen who are in that position are really the leaders of the country. But *he's* not going. 'What do you mean you're not going?' He said, 'I'm not going.' I said, 'I really think you're ungrateful as hell. They've done everything for you. And now they ask you to go to a luncheon in your honor, and you're telling them no? That's really not acceptable.' So he agreed to go.

"Well, they gave him a gift at that luncheon, and he was overwhelmed. It was one of these screens, portraits. As I recall, it was a painting of a rare screen. Oh, he was touched. And then they wanted to take pictures and so on. He said, 'I'm not interested.' So I had to go through the whole thing all over again with him. I said, 'You're the honored guest. What's the matter with you?' Well, by then, against his own inclinations, he warmed up to me. And we flew back to New York together with Jesse."

Michael Koessel was a graduate student in philosophy when his friend Jesse Gerstein first introduced him to Robbins on New Year's Eve of 1987. Koessel recalled how Robbins' relationship with Gerstein was altered when the latter was diagnosed with AIDS. "Jesse had his tests in January of 'eighty-nine. I remember when he went in for it and when he came out. He lied to everybody but two people, Jerry and Lisa Stevens, and told me that he had tested negative." Lisa Stevens was an aspiring filmmaker who was romantically involved with Gerstein at the time. Koessel continued, "He didn't want sympathy, he didn't want people to know. Apparently, he was already showing signs of illness. I didn't see any of these at all. Maybe if I'd been a little more astute, I would have. Jerry's relationship with Jesse had been, I felt in the last year, growing increasingly distant, and when those results came back, Jerry just completely devoted himself to Jesse.

"I didn't know that at the time. I only found out in retrospect. It was about a year later. I used to take care of Jesse's dog and I used to take care of Jerry's dogs. He had a much nicer apartment than I had as a graduate student and I had keys and everything. I spent a fair amount of time in their apartments and stuff. One night at about four in the morning, Jerry called me and told me I had to go down to Jesse's and do this, that, and the other thing, a bunch of stuff that needed to get done. I was like, 'Why? This is crazy.' He said, 'Jesse's stuck.' It turned out later that Jesse was in the hospital, he'd been admitted to the hospital quite suddenly and needed help, but that was explained a bit later. . . . Jesse's getting sick really solidified the relationship. . . . Jerry was amazing around sick friends. If I was sick, he would send me chicken soup and almost insist that I come over and stay in the back bedroom to be taken care of."

Koessel recounted the evolution of his relationship with Robbins, saying, "The summer of 'eighty-eight, I probably spent every weekend out at the beach with him—I kind of became the favorite new friend. The friendship continued into the fall and into the winter, and then the next summer we went off to Turkey. After that, it was like we were old friends. It's obviously not one of his older friendships but it was very intense for a period of time. Then it kind of relaxed into a nice friendship, where we would call each other regularly and get together, and sometimes spent holidays together. It's interesting, we spent Christmas together quite frequently, actually. When I was in the City, we would choose to have Christmas dinner together. . . . And I went to a number of plays with him when they were being done in New York—*The Bacchae* was one. . . . At one point, the country house, the beach house, and his home in New York had like twenty copies of *The Bacchae* kicking around, along with tons of secondary literature on Greek drama and that sort of thing, just because of the interest in that play. A few things that he talked about almost incessantly: Proust, Chekhov, *The Bacchae*."

Architect D.D. Allen entered Robbins' life at about the same time. She recalled, "I must have met him in 'eighty-eight. I met him through Jesse. Jerry and I were both reading *War and Peace* at the same time. I was living at the American Hotel in Sag Harbor at the time, and Jerry's house became my home-away hotel. We just became really close friends. . . . Jesse was at Jerry's, so we all just hung out that summer as much as we could. We just couldn't get enough of each other, it was great."

Allen worked with Robbins on an addition to his beach house. She said, "I did a little project with him. I built a little shack with him under his house and we went through a kind of creative nightmare together. I've worked with a lot of creative people and a lot of people in his business, and there are different ways of getting people to do their best work. Someone like Tommy Tune, for example, gets work out of people by encouraging and positive reinforcement, and . . . Jerry was the complete opposite. He just broke you down, but there was something about him that made you want to go back and try again. . . . Jerry was not an easy man and he was often not a very nice man. He had a warm and tender side, but he made me cry a number of times; he caused me a lot of unhappiness, but he was also extremely generous and very loving.

"The beach was really where you saw Jerry at his most relaxed and most warm and easy to be with. He had a way of giving wonderful lunches. It just seemed like he threw together the old sorrel soup. He cooked on a stove that had been around since the beginning of time. Everything was kind of old and original and worn, and the whole house just had a spectacular patina. Everything was very carefully selected, but it all looked like it had been there forever and just landed out there. You didn't have any sense of it being decorated or arranged. It was just everywhere your eye landed was something special to look at, but it was not self-conscious at all."

Michael Koessel recalled a telling moment at the beach. "That summer he was a little bit infatuated with me," said Koessel, "but he didn't push boundaries at all, he was not pushy in any way. But he also met D.D. Allen the same summer. At one point, the four of us—Jesse, Jerry, D.D. and I—were walking along the beach. We were kind of swapping partners, so that there were only two of us talking with each other at a given point in time. I think it started out with maybe Jesse and me, and then D.D. and me, and then finally Jerry and me, and the other two with each other. And we were walking along there, and Jerry turned to me and he said something like, 'You know, if I had met you and D.D. four years ago, it would have solved a lot of my problems in life.' I think he thought that the ideal was to have two kind of intelligent, WASPy—one male, one female—partners."

Koessel described Robbins as "an incredibly conflicted person over lots of things. . . . He certainly was moody, but at a personal level he could be—he wasn't always—but he could be enormously, enormously generous. He could be very loving, very affectionate, very warm. He had the capacity to just sit there and hold your hand, believe it or not. There were a lot of very, very human qualities that a lot of people who worked with him probably were unaware of. He really was, probably of all my friends, the only person who would actually take my hand and just hold it, which is very, very nice."

In the fall of 1989, Robbins spent a month in Paris rehearsing dancers at the Paris Opéra for his ballet *In the Night*. He announced in November that he was resigning his position as co-ballet master in chief at the New York City Ballet, and explained, "It's important at my age to do other things." He said that he planned to devote time to his memoirs and to his autobiographical theater project. Before the end of the year, Robbins and Gerstein rented an apartment in Paris. Gerstein's friend Lisa Stevens recalled, "Jesse found the apartment in Paris. . . . He had just been diagnosed as HIV-positive and decided that he always wanted to live in Paris, so he got the apartment and began looking for work so he could stay. He ended up coming back and forth to

New York a lot, as he still had a [photographic] studio there and all his major clients were there. Jerry helped him secure the tenancy agreement, but it was primarily Jesse's place. The building was on Boulevard Raspail and Cherche Midi, 58 Boulevard Raspail to be exact—on the Left Bank."

Paris Opéra ballerina Ghislaine Thesmar danced in *Afternoon of a Faun* and *In G Major* during the early 1970s and later became a social friend to Robbins after she retired from the stage and became a teacher at the Paris Opéra. She recalled his life in Paris, saying, "I went many times to Boulevard Raspail, which was a very pleasant, bourgeois apartment with just essential furniture— nothing chichi or very elaborate. It had lovely, lovely draperies, I remember. Later I got the washing machine and many things that he didn't want to keep when he left, and a few *tableaux*. He gave some of the things to the church, you know, the American church. . . . I was very privileged in the end because I belonged to the bunch of friends that were free, and he could share a huge free affection that had nothing to do with ballet, really wonderful freedom and great fun. We happened to become very good friends. I really adored this man who was an *eternal jeune homme*—so young in the head and so curious of everything, a greediness for life and for everything that is interesting. The man in life was absolutely phenomenal.

"It's very strange because, my first rapport being purely professional, we were each at our place and that was it, *en equilibre* for what it should be. But then when we became real friends he used to come to my home and crawl on the floor with all my dogs, and we used to have wonderful dinners. . . . The Jerry that I met in Paris was cheerful, full of *joie de vivre*. He used to bring us to wonderful restaurants. L'escargot *qui'il aimait beaucoup* behind Montparnasse, he used to bring us there. Otherwise, I know he came many times to my house just in total simplicity. We had little picnics at my house in the Marais. He was incredible. I think he felt very free here. He would come back from the plane and ask, 'Well, what's on in Paris? Did you see such-and-such exposition and film of late?' And I felt like an idiot because I'd only heard about half of what he was talking about. When all the people of my generation, like Chris Redpath, Susie Hendl, and Aidan [Mooney], and everybody came around, we used to go out together; but he also had maybe a group of men that I didn't know especially. They were more the intellectual group, you see, because we were more the group for good food and play and fun. He really had to see everything, know about everything, and he had this hunger at seventy, seventy-four—it's amazing, the hunger of life he had. This man has been a real lesson of youth for me, I must say."

The following year, Robbins would attend the funeral services for Leonard Bernstein, Arthur Gold and Lady Keith, among others. Slim's daughter, Kitty Hawks, recalled, "After my mother died, I found, going through all of her stuff in detail, all of the boxes of music, a cassette that was labeled 'Slim.' I put it in the machine and it was Jerry walking along the beach in Watermill. She was in the hospital I think at the time. And it was just Jerry walking along the beach, describing what he saw, what he was thinking about her. You could hear the ocean in the background. It was indicative of a remarkable friendship and a remarkable man. He was so visually acute and so sensually sophisticated, as was she. It was as if she'd lost her sight, but she was simply confined for a while and feeling like hell, and this was his way of giving her a gift that had to be, because she loved him so much, and she got to hear his voice. And he giggled a couple of times on it. As you know, he had the best laugh in the whole world."

Robbins became the target of an anonymous personal attack after Lady Keith's death. At the time, Sara Corrin was working as an assistant in his home office. She said, "When Lady Keith died, we were all really sad. Mr. Robbins was really depressed so we stayed as far away from him as we could. But a few weeks or a month after she died, we got this delivery one day of Vidalia onions from a fancy gourmet kitchen someplace in Maryland or somewhere, and it was addressed that it was from her. We didn't open it. You could see that it was from her on the top of the package, and around the whole side of the box it said, 'You never miss them until they're gone.' And we just flipped because she had just died, and we knew that he was going to have a heart attack. So we went and put the box out on his entranceway hall outside of the office and shut the door. We knew he was going to have a fit, and when he found it, it was like, 'Who did this!' We never found out how that happened or who did it."

During the same period, Arthur Laurents organized a Memorial Tribute to Leonard Bernstein at the Majestic Theatre and used the occasion to publicly remind Jerry of their shared past. Putting the needle in and causing quite a stir, Laurents introduced Robbins to the audience by saying, "There were only two things Lenny Bernstein feared: God and Jerome Robbins."

During the spring of 1990, Robbins suffered a serious bicycle accident. Michael Koessel remembered, "It was the last time he ever rode a bike. We went biking in Central Park, and we went down to the left from where the Metropolitan Museum of Art is, and it winds down, it goes under a bridge. And before you get to that bridge, you can turn on a path and go up at the higher level that the bridge is at. And Jerry saw that path at the last minute and thought he would try to take it . . . but in order to do it, he had to jump a curb, and he jumped it at an angle, and his bike went right out from underneath him, and he went right down and was knocked completely unconscious. And when I got to him—I was just behind him—his eyes were wide open and he was kind of frothing at the mouth a little bit. It was incredibly scary. Fortunately, it was in the park, [and] it was a sunny Sunday or Saturday afternoon, late morning, something like that, and there were a lot of people around, and they got him to a hospital immediately.

"I took the bike home for him, took the dogs for a walk, and then went over and met him at the hospital. He was just starting to recover there, and it was pretty clear that things were going to be all right, although there was something going on with the brain. But I remember the first thing he said when I got there and he was conscious, and he was aware, the first two things he mentioned: One was, 'You'll take care of the dogs.' I said, 'Of course.' It was a time when I spent a lot of time in his house taking care of the dogs. And number two, he said, 'This is why my mother always told me to wear underwear, you never know what might happen.' And it turns out that he didn't have underwear on and he was at the hospital. That was the most endearing thing he ever said about his mother."

The bicycle accident took place while Robbins was rehearsing at City Ballet for a two-week retrospective of his ballets. "A Festival of Jerome Robbins's Ballets" opened June 5, 1990, and presented twenty-eight works, including all those in the company's active repertory since Robbins' return in 1969, with American Ballet Theatre dancers performing an excerpt from *Les Noces*. Robbins had intended to present two new short pieces set to Charles Ives' songs, "Charlie Rutledge" and "Three-Page Sonata," both of which had been cut from *Ives, Songs.* But the bicycle accident prevented Robbins from rehearsing them adequately for the festival, and consequently no new ballets were premiered.

During the festival's planning stage, Robbins telephoned Edward Villella and invited him to reprise his role in *Watermill.* Villella, then fifty-three years old and director of the Miami City Ballet, initially balked at the idea of a return to the stage. He told Robbins, "Let me consult my body and think about it for a while." The next day, Robbins simply announced to the *Times* that Villella had agreed to perform. In his memoir, Villella wrote, "Typical Jerry move; he doesn't take no for an answer. I was half mad at him, but knew I would have done it anyway. And I realized he knew me well enough to know that." Villella had never had a formal farewell performance to mark his retirement from City Ballet, and his return to *Watermill* served as the appropriate swan song. Doris Hering wrote of his performance, "If anything, Villella was more profound than before. . . ."

Running from *Fancy Free* through *Ives, Songs,* the festival provided a grand summation of Robbins' ballet career in the same way that *Jerome Robbins' Broadway* recapitulated his years on Broadway. On the closing night at the New York State Theater, six dancers from the Paris Opéra (Isabelle Guérin, Jean Guizerix, Fanny Faida, Manuel Legris, Elisabeth Platel and Laurent Hilaire) appeared as the three couples in *In the Night.* While struggling with the nuances of the partnering, they brought a stylish formalism into the work that harked back to the more dramatic dancers of Robbins' youth at Ballet Theatre. The following year, Jean Guizerix danced as a guest at City Ballet and distinguished himself in the Villella role in *Watermill.* Ghislaine Thesmar said of the Paris Opéra dancers, "Our education is much closer to all the girls of the ABT period, absolutely. Nora Kaye and all these, much closer to them. With us, Jerry had his classical ballets done in a more earthy way, you see, and I think he liked that in a way. He was afraid, of course, of a little point of French vulgarity, and yet he was very happy."

The closing night of the festival ended with a sentimental farewell ceremony. After the curtain came down on *The Four Seasons,* the last ballet of the program, Robbins appeared onstage alone. Then, the company's dancers, most outfitted in costumes from various Robbins ballets, entered one at a time or in small groups to present him with single white roses. They were joined in the flower tribute by Lincoln Kirstein, Peter Martins and Edward Villella. Robbins laughed delightedly when a dancer costumed as the Ringmaster from *Circus Polka* cracked a whip in his direction. The curtain fell to thunderous applause and after the audience departed, a private champagne celebration took place on the stage. In a short speech, Robbins thanked the company and management, and the dancers gave him an autographed group picture. Robbins told them that he had come to the realization during rehearsals that affection would not allow him to abandon City Ballet "cold turkey, like when I stopped smoking."

He was not about to rest on his laurels. One of his assistants recalled, "He used to make himself notes that he put up in his bedroom. And the one that was most important to me, and it was up there for a long, long time, which is why I actually thought it was a permanent fixture—on a piece of paper he took a crayon and in big blue letters . . . he wrote, DON'T STEW. And in really big red letters . . . he wrote, DO. I thought, That's my motto. That is the single most important thing I learned from him—Don't Stew, Do. And he certainly did."

With his ballet and Broadway retrospectives behind him, Robbins turned his attention to his "phantasmagorical" autobiographical project. On February 15, 1991, the *New York Times* carried an announcement that Jerome Robbins was planning a new stage production at Lincoln Center that was to be "based on his own life." In reality, he had been trying to tell his personal story for more than twenty years, and had made sporadic efforts at writing his memoirs. One of his earliest efforts involved a short soliloquy he had composed at the American Theater Laboratory. Actor Barry Primus remembered, "I was always tracking that piece. It was called *My Name Is Rabinowitz.* I think that came out of the mask work we were doing at the time. We were doing monologues in connection with the masks and Japanese Noh drama, and I think Jerry thought he would do a piece too. It was a single monologue that he wrote. He actually wrote it—'I am Rabinowitz, and I did this . . .'— and I played the guy. I played that part."

Having given up his efforts to write a conventional memoir, Robbins decided to adapt what he saw as the defining moments of his life into an experimental work of musical theater. He was by nature inclined to turn his life into drama, distilled to some essential truth that he could shape and embellish. Most important, he would be the one to decide what to tell and what not to tell. He had his assistants assemble all of his personal files, which included years of production notes, journals and news-clippings, as well as his own sketches and drawings. The files were organized over a period of several months in the office at his townhouse. At one point, cartons and boxes filled with memorabilia were moved to a large studio space on the top floor. Here the pages of the script in progress were spread out on a Ping-Pong table. A computer was installed and a typist was hired. As usual, Robbins' research blurred the thin line between devotion and obsession.

Before bringing in a writer to assist him, Robbins himself wrote and rewrote a number of scenes that recalled his early years growing up between New York and New Jersey. Robbins once expressed his insecurity as a writer, saying, "I don't know how to write. What I would be able to say in a hundred scribblings can be summed up in one word—WORK." He retitled the project *The Poppa Piece,* as the story focused more and more on his troubled relationship with his father. As Robbins revised and edited, he encouraged his office staff to read the script and related materials, which included journals, scrapbooks and correspondence. Robbins constructed a collage of his life. One of his administrative assistants who initially catalogued and organized the project recalled, "I actually had mixed feelings about everything because that's when I got to see all these things . . . that I really wish I had not seen. . . . Honestly, I was horrified by a great deal of his life, the things that I learned about him. I thought a number of cruel things had happened to him as a child, and I thought he was enormously sensitive. But I think it produced an unbelievably cruel streak in him, which was definitely there, no question. I don't think he was ever purposefully cruel, but I think it came natural to him sometimes."

Another assistant, Megan Raddant, who typed much of this personal material, compared his fantasies to those of Proust and the Marquis de Sade. Raddant, who was in her twenties at the time, said, "The things that he made me type, and he would stand behind me while I'm typing them and tell me to type faster while I'd be typing his torture visions. . . . He would make you type something so many times, and then he would tell you that you had the wrong version, and he would scream and scream. He liked to yell at me a lot, and I really tried my best. I really worked very hard and I didn't make very many mistakes, and he would still yell at me. It was just hard, so after a while, I quit. . . . And I went to Mexico for a long time, and I never spoke to him again, but he gave me a thousand dollars for the trip, which was very nice."

Raddant recalled an incident that took place prior to her departure. "One time his lawyer calls me," said Raddant. "She says, 'Megan, we're filing a lawsuit against you and a police report.' I start laughing and say, 'What for?' And they were totally serious. This is Floria [Lasky], who I had a good relationship with. She said, 'You've stolen the doggie raincoats, the Persian rug and the vacuum cleaners.' So I had to pay somebody to go out to his house out in the Hamptons and get these things out of the house and bring them back so that I wouldn't be prosecuted. Doggie raincoats. And I had two days in the office of him screaming at me because he thought I had stolen them. And the rug was rolled up in his bedroom closet in Manhattan."

Another of Robbins' former assistants, Sara Corrin, confirmed Raddant's version of the story and explained that a maid had misplaced the items in question. Corrin said, "Everybody has certain people that they like, and the thing with Mr. Robbins was that if you had whatever those qualities were, then everything was peachy, and if you weren't particularly to his taste, then he could be really horrible. Or if you were basically fine, he tries so hard to be nice, and then after a certain point he just can't do it anymore. And then he turns. And it was really true. He was trying so hard to be a nice person, and then he just lost it. And he did that with so many people. And he did that pretty much with almost everybody in the office. . . . I think it was like being in an abusive relationship if you stayed with him. You became like a victim of domestic violence because that's what it was like in the office. I know that he could be really difficult elsewhere, but I think there are more people who have nice things to say about him in the theater than people that worked with him administratively. Because the end product was so amazing—the breadth and style of his dance was just so incredible."

With *The Poppa Piece* script still unfinished, a workshop production was planned for the spring in association with producer Gregory Mosher. Robbins recruited a team of collaborators, including director Gerald Freedman, who went as far back as *Bells Are Ringing.* "He invited me to his cottage in the Hamptons," Freedman recalled. "He brought out a large suitcase crammed with hundreds of pieces of paper. There were articles, scenes written and rewritten, fragments of ideas, magazine images and photographs. It represented the accumulation of years of thought and creative wrestling with his relationship to his world of father, family, work, and his Jewishness. We spent a week working through all of it; long walks on the beach, hours of writing, chatting while cooking, talking incessantly, probing, sifting, poking at the material."

Freedman was disarmed by Robbins' candor in discussing the intimate details of his life and surmised that his openness derived from their shared heritage. "It seemed he had nothing to hide. . . . I had a relationship with Joe Papp and Jerry that I think had a lot to do with my Jewishness. I was a cantor for a while, and I came from a Hasidic family, so they both reacted to me in a similar way, which was hanging on to that part of me as some kind of comfort and corroboration of their own Jewishness."

With the Jewish theme in mind, Robbins turned to *Fiddler* lyricist Sheldon Harnick, who recalled, "What he was doing was chilling work. It was just extraordinary work." But Harnick explained that difficulties arose from the nature of the material itself. "I had meetings with Robbins where he would tell me about the way he grew up and this sad, bitter relationship with his father. But I think I was the wrong lyricist. I think it should have been maybe Stephen Sondheim, somebody who writes with more edge than I do. I think I had three tries on this one lyric, and I kept getting closer but I wasn't getting it. In fact, the first time I came in and read him the lyric, there was a long pause. He looked at me and then he said to my surprise, 'You could talk to your father, couldn't you?' I said, 'Yeah, I could.' He said, 'I can tell from the lyric. . . . I couldn't [talk with my father]—that's the difference.'"

While Harnick took up the challenge to try to make the lyrics "harder and more bitter," Robbins commissioned playwright John Weidman to write additional scenes and dialogue for the piece. The score was being composed by Douglas Wieselman, a member of the Kamikaze Ground Crew, whose music reflected a variety of influences, from the circus to the traditional Jewish Klezmer of Eastern Europe.

Without a finished script or score, auditions were held at Lincoln Center during the winter and early spring, and rehearsals started at the beginning of June. John Weidman had worked with composer Stephen Sondheim and contributed the book for the musical *Assassins* the year before at Playwrights Horizons. The playwright sensed what he and Robbins' other collaborators were up against on this latest project: "My own feeling was that ultimately Jerry was going to have to create the whole thing himself or it wasn't going to get done. It was so deeply personal that there really wasn't a role in it for Sheldon or for me or for anybody else. . . . Jerry was dealing with the kind of material that you could deal with in therapy in the theater. . . . That's what it always felt like."

To portray himself as a young man, Robbins cast an up-and-coming actor, Jace Alexander (not to be confused with Jason Alexander), who had delivered a compelling performance of Lee Harvey Oswald in *Assassins*. Of *The Poppa Piece*, Alexander said, "I have no idea why I was cast, except I think that what Jerry saw in me was—I was a very angry young man."

Robbins had been impressed some years before with Ron Rifkin's performance as a tormented Holocaust survivor in *The Substance of Fire*, a play by Jon Robin Baitz. Rifkin was now invited to portray Robbins' father in the piece. In keeping with his habit of multiple casting, Robbins also recruited Jewish actor-comedian Alan King for the same role. Actors and dancers of varied theatrical backgrounds were chosen to fill out the ensemble. With the writing still under way and the director struggling to come to terms with his past, scenes were rehearsed out of order. The performers were called in as they were needed and without knowing what scenes they were going to rehearse on any given day.

According to Ron Rifkin, Robbins was in top form during rehearsals. "He was in incredible shape. He was wearing T-shirts and jeans and sneakers. He was fit, he was showing ballet steps. His arms were moving. His legs were moving beautifully. He was really fit and handsome."

Jace Alexander, at twenty-eight, was struck by the irony of the role he was playing. He later became a director and looked back on the experience of working with Robbins as an extraordinary episode. "I was a young actor who had some dance experience only in as much as I had studied dance in college. I was a decent dancer, not like a trained dancer, but just somebody who could move his body. And here I was playing Jerome Robbins and being taught steps by Jerome Robbins, and it was this weird fantasy down in the basement of Lincoln Center. Now, you have to get this picture in your head of me and Ron Rifkin, who is basically an older version of me, a guy who had danced in his life but was never really a dancer . . . and Michael Richie, who was the stage manager. Here's the three of us on a line doing steps with Jerome Robbins choreographing us. It was a really bizarre scene. It was out of *Saturday Night Live.* We just had to laugh at ourselves. . . . We were having a great time, and we were looking goofy, and I don't know what Jerry was getting out of it."

Both Alexander and Rifkin were surprised by how patient and unassuming Robbins was during rehearsals, in light of his reputation. There was no sign of the famous temper, no venomous outbursts directed at the actors. Asked to account for Robbins' apparently angelic behavior, Rifkin said, "Obviously, his demons tortured him. He was obviously tortured because I'm telling you he was really sweet, and I know that was not what people thought of him. People did not think of him as a sweet person."

Robbins charmed the actors as he plunged deeper and deeper into his troubled psyche. Alan King, who had been acquainted with Robbins for years and considered himself a fan, was also fascinated by Robbins' anguished effort to subdue his demons: "After a while I felt like it was sort of an exorcism, and it got weirder and weirder. . . . The more he talked about his father the more I felt his father needed defending. I became so emotionally involved in this *Poppa Piece.* I told him, 'You're trying to make your father look like some kind of putz. I'm going to challenge you. I'm going to fight for your father.' "

Robbins seemed to appreciate the challenge and encouraged King to pursue his contentious interpretation of the role. The director was undoubtedly intrigued to see what King might come up with in contrast to Rifkin's portrayal, which may have been closer to Robbins' intentions. "What I remember most," said Jace Alexander, "was Ron Rifkin playing this really sweet, pathetic man who was unable to truly communicate with his son or anybody. He was like a Jewish, Lower East Side Willy Loman. . . . It was almost like he couldn't get through the day, and the day was just basically what he knew, which was selling and making. Jerry's relationship with his father seemed that he loved him dearly, that he was embarrassed by him at the same time." Alexander added, "Jerry was always less than what his father hoped he would be."

The idea of *The Poppa Piece,* as Robbins developed the story line, was to use his father and Jewish upbringing to explain, if not to justify, his decision to act as a cooperative witness before HUAC. This premise may have been a case of creative myth-making, but it was also confessional, albeit a fantastic rationalization which Robbins had come to believe and wanted others to believe. One insider recalled that Robbins "described his life being like a tent that was supported by two posts in the middle. . . . One of those posts was his bar mitzvah, and the other post was HUAC."

This view of the story was consistent with what Robbins communicated to John Weidman during the writing process. Weidman suggested, "You could say that the problems that he had with McCarthyism were grounded in the unresolved problems that he had with his father." That Robbins was still haunted by his father was made clear in the first scene, which, according to the playwright, opened with the image of the dead father on a hospital gurney. "What I remember was a dance which developed out of the idea that his father was dead but sort of arose from the dead and draped himself [over his son]. It was somebody literally dealing in choreographic terms with the oppressive presence of his dead father. In another choreographer's hands, it might have seemed like a Freudian cliché, but in Jerry's hands it was brilliant."

For Robbins, love and hate for his father were hopelessly tangled with memories of a son's failure to win approval and a father's inability to express affection. Consequently, his father would take much of the blame for Robbins' actions during the HUAC ordeal. His sense of having been a victim of persecution pervaded his memories of the HUAC experience and those of his bar mitzvah, with the two events linked inextricably in his mind to his father. The traditional rite of passage into manhood for most Jewish boys was, for Robbins, a trauma in 1931 that still tormented him, although his sister had no recollection of his actual bar mitzvah being as melodramatic as Robbins portrayed it. Sonia suggested that he was "inclined to turn his life into drama and fantasy."

Dancer Mark Esposito recalled that the bar mitzvah scene began with a thirteen-year-old Jerry (called "Jacov" in the piece) wearing knickers and bicycling with some young, non-Jewish friends. "There were bicycles on stage and it was like a bicycle ballet that Jerry created. It was just incredible. There were four of us. It was beautiful, it was so circular, so moving. . . ." This was a game of follow-the-leader on bikes, and Esposito saw Robbins "being an outcast in that situation . . . surrounded by these spokes and wheels. I just remember how beautiful they were, as well as how spooky they could be. [He was] being engulfed by all these kids."

Rifkin and Alexander, as father and son, were positioned at the side of the stage during most of this sequence, watching the action unfold and reacting. For Rifkin, the scene was unforgettable. "Maybe it was a romantic notion on my part, but I felt that could have been, in terms of musical theater, his most important work, because there was something so profoundly personal about it."

The bicycle ballet led to a scene in the dining room of young Jerry's home, where a wizened mentor, the Tzaddik, tutored the boy for his bar mitzvah. The ancient man was armed with props that Robbins presented as icons of the faith—a yellow star, a hooked nose and raggedy beard. While the tutor instructed him with lessons from the Torah, chanted and sang, the bicyclists circled ominously outside the window, taunting and mocking those inside. Finally, one of the cyclists burst through the window, an unexpected invasion that Robbins, as stage magician, exploited to the hilt, illuminating the grotesque, anti-Semitic furies of his youth.

Young Jerry chased the invaders away, and the scene shifted to a Jewish community center where his bar mitzvah took place. Robbins dramatized this lavish ritual with exquisite, painstaking attention to detail. The elders of the synagogue dressed the boy in traditional vestments, yarmulke and prayer shawl. Then Robbins dramatized the ecstatic devotions of the ceremony, compressing his recollected experience to the moment of trial and performance. When the boy's caterwauling voice was unable to do justice to the sacred text of the Torah, he broke down into anguished sobs. After being consoled by his mother, who was never more than a shadowy figure in the piece, the boy delivered his obligatory closing speech, thanking his rabbi, teachers and family for helping him to take his place in the community. *Adon Alom* was sung by all. The boy received gifts and handed out candy to the younger children, still inwardly writhing over his failed performance. Left alone at the end of the scene, the boy was furious as he ripped off his yarmulke and prayer shawl, only to be spotted by his father standing in a doorway. The confrontation was suddenly revealing and poignant. The boy thumbed his nose at his father and mocked him with a Bronx cheer, then ran offstage in brazen defiance—all according to Robbins' explicit direction.

Even with this climactic break, Robbins had not yet made the case against his father. Weidman recalled another scene written by Robbins and revised ten times. It involved young Jerry "being brought into a steam room by his father. . . . The room is full of old, kind of saggy, vulgar Jews farting and belching, but their qualities, including their vulgarity, are clearly meant to be, and are, appealing and manly and sort of heroic. And the little boy is frightened that he won't be able to measure up. And his father is in a cheerful way saying, 'Come on. What's the matter with you!' And the guys are kidding him about his son."

In an early version of the scene, the boy had been shamed about his physical endowments, an explicit reference to his sexuality that Robbins later omitted. One of his assistants said, "I guess by the time it got to the full script stage, not all the details were in it anymore. He had been laughed at by many men in this bathhouse . . . because of how small he was. And teased about never amounting to anything."

Robbins depicted his father singing a boisterous song with a thick Yiddish accent, then shoving the scrawny boy into a raucous celebration. Half-naked revelers surrounded and taunted him while holding on to each other's shoulders in a circle. This dance was called the "Matzo Ball Ballet," as huge tubs of chicken soup arrived and the celebrants immersed themselves in the steaming broth, cavorting and singing, conjuring the Old World that Robbins' father had known. With a stroke of stage magic, the scene moved from the steam room to the locker room of a high school athletic team. The sport was never specified, but Jerry was a cheerleader and mascot, goaded by a reveling pack of teenagers into leading the team cheer. Robbins indicated that the boy was aware of being patronized by his non-Jewish peers even as they tossed him about in a backslapping, orgiastic frenzy of male bonding.

Here Robbins turned dream swiftly into nightmare, with the shrieks of the team transporting the boy into the exterminating room of a concentration camp. This final tableau faded quickly as the doors to the gas chamber opened and he suddenly found himself the object of unhealthy fascination on the part of a crowd of adolescent, hometown jocks. One of the dancers, Joey Mc-Kneely, thought the staging of the locker-room scene represented Robbins' "awakening, in a way, to his sexual identity, because that's what it seemed like with all of these guys jumping on each other and congratulating each other. It was like homoerotic, but very straight. It was very bizarre."

It was at this time that Robbins told Sheldon Harnick the story about his father humiliating him as a boy by dressing up as Santa Claus and taking away his toy train. There was more to it, though, than just a child's shame. "One of the things he wanted to do in this theater piece was to try and convey what he felt when he went up before the House Un-American Activities Committee," said Harnick, and Robbins intended the Christmas anecdote to show how his father had instilled in him the fear that because he was Jewish, "everything was going to be taken away from him." That was the nightmarish horror that HUAC represented to Robbins. But in rewriting his history, he omitted any reference to his fear of being exposed as homosexual. He apparently included that scenario only in his earliest notes and drafts and later altered the story. Megan Raddant recalled, "I saw a couple of versions, but in the one that he edited when I was there, he admitted that he was afraid that it would expose him, and that's why he gave the names, because it would ruin him and he would not ever be able to be a choreographer in New York . . . and he wasn't willing to be ruined."

Regarding Robbins' multiple versions of the story, another assistant, Fay Greenbaum, speculated, "He did everything to prove that he deserved to exist on the planet. He hated himself. And in a weird way, I could see him denying that he was ever pressured [with exposure] as part of this self-hatred, part of his, 'Oh, I wasn't really pressured . . . I did it.' Because he did absolutely take responsibility for his actions. He never shirked responsibility for any action, however small, that he ever did in his life."

Robbins' father may have been the ultimate villain in his son's eyes, as if there were a history of abuse, and yet in *The Poppa Piece* script he appears to be guilty of nothing more than being insensitive to the needs of a confused, gifted boy. The actual source of the rancor, which again Robbins omitted, was the fact that his disapproving father, Harry Rabinowitz, tried to prevent him from becoming a dancer. Rather than dramatize that struggle, Robbins appears to have been using his art to create a scapegoat, distorting the reality of HUAC and avoiding deeper conflicts in his psyche. Weidman surmised, "The image of his father was like a canvas on which Jerry painted a picture that haunted him." Curiously for a man steeped in Freudian analysis, his picture all but ignored his mother, Lena, and his sister, Sonia, who were, of course, enormously influential in his life.

Robbins shared an anecdote with several associates about how as a young boy he walked in on his parents having sex, and had been horrified thinking that his father was killing his mother. This episode did not make it into the script, which was purged of virtually all sexual references. As confusing as this early incident may have been for him at a time when sexual matters were not discussed with children, it now communicated something that he chose not to reveal. The episode was one that Robbins repeated to his analysts and recorded in his notes, and according to one associate, "He could never stop thinking about that scene with his parents his whole life. That's all his therapy was about. All the time. He never got over that. He would talk about his fantasies while he was having sex with men. He couldn't get off . . . unless he was imagining that he was killing the person. And so he would write the elaborate fantasies that he would have while he was having sex that would allow him to finally find his ecstatic moment."

John Weidman speculated that the parental scene may have been "less idiosyncratic and interesting" than others he intended to include, as Robbins had his own agenda he was seeking to capture in the drama. As relentless as he was in this self-exploration, he was evidently not prepared to relate the whole truth of his past, especially those details of his personal dilemma with HUAC that would raise the issue of his sexual identity.

The HUAC scenes took several forms, as the painful memories were transfigured in Robbins' imagination. "Over a period of time," recalled Gerald Freedman, "he did it as a burlesque sketch, he did it as a quiz show, he did it as a clown piece, he did it, I think, as something personal with a lot of microphones, like a genre news piece. He could never leave it alone. . . . But my feeling is he never felt he got it right. . . . My sense was it was still troubling to Jerry, no matter how he thought it through."

In one version, his father appeared in the courtroom costumed as a Pagliacci clown, heckling and ridiculing his son. But even this self-flagellation failed to satisfy Robbins, who seemed unable to decide whether to indict himself or his father. Fictionalizing the scene, playwright Weidman had young Jerry take the stand and name "Rabinowitz" as the first of the eight ill-fated names on his list. But this ironic meddling with the story line also fell short of winning Robbins' approval. Was his conscience still bleeding when he thought of those he named who became victims of the blacklist? No one knew better than Robbins how and why his life had gone out of control in 1953 in ways so destructive to those on his course.

The workshop continued into the fall, but Robbins would prevent the curtain from ever rising on his *Poppa Piece.* Without any formal announcement, he gave up on the project. Rehearsals ceased, and everyone involved with the piece returned to their lives, disappointed and somewhat mystified that there would be no performance. In retrospect, John Weidman admired Robbins' courage for undertaking such an ambitious, if impossible, mission. "The honesty in the materials . . . the size of the emotional issues . . . and that he was attempting to work them out in his art really seemed almost heroic to me."

Sheldon Harnick knew of another reason aside from the unresolved script issues that prevented Robbins from following through on the project. "As I understand it, some very dear friend of his was dying of AIDS. Jerry took him into his home to care for him, and I think for about two months he cared for him, and then he died. When that happened, I found myself thinking, what a compassionate thing to do. How can Robbins go from the compassion that he's displayed . . . back to his very bitter piece about his father? I'll be surprised if he can. I never heard from him again about it. I ran into

John Weidman on the street one day and I said, 'Has Jerry called you? Are you working on *The Poppa Piece* again?' And he said, 'No, I never heard from him.'"

Jesse Gerstein died on October 14, 1991. For several months, Robbins had taken him in and provided care for him with the help of his domestic staff. Michael Koessel recalled, "He [Jesse] died at the townhouse. I think there was a nurse. And the last six months of Jesse's life were very, very bad. He was very, very thin. And he was a kind of a dashing man who lost all of his hair and had lesions. And also Jesse never ever once mentioned that he was dying. He never once suggested that he might be dying, he always talked about the future."

Sono Osato and her husband, Victor Elmaleh, had a home near Robbins' Bridgehampton beach house, and she said, "We knew Jesse. He was a very nice, talented photographer, young. In a way, he could have been Jerry's son. He had dark hair, he looked something like him, he was much taller. And I think that his death must have been absolutely horrible for Jerry. . . . He really had a very, very bad time. That requires a great deal of strength, because it must be terrible to watch."

Robbins' sister recalled, "When Jesse was dying, Jerry called his mother and father and they were with him when he died." Gerstein's friend Lisa Stevens remembered, "Jerry nursed Jesse and stayed by his side until the end. I was there for the last three months, every day after my work day until about midnight, and weekends to give Jerry a break." In his remaining years, Robbins would have several male lovers, but according to those who were close to him, no other relationship carried such heartfelt significance. Stevens explained, "My relationship to Jerry was part of a triangle with Jesse. I knew Jerry through Jesse, and after Jesse died, Jerry and I saw each other only occasionally. We both loved Jesse so much. The morning after he died, Jerry and I asked each other, 'Did Jesse ever talk about me to you?' It was a slightly complicated triangle. Jesse's death really broke Jerry. He was not the same after that. He told me that morning that he felt like a hinge that was missing its door, and he demonstrated by holding his upper arm out straight from his shoulder, then letting his forearm drop down to dangle loose and limp, as if it were broken . . . he [later] had his ashes scattered in the same spot as Jesse's out at the beach."

TEN

A Twilight of Legacies

A month after Jesse Gerstein's death, Robbins was back to work with the Paris Opéra, then under the direction of Patrick Dupond. Robbins' *Concerto in G*, known in Paris as *En Sol*, was revived, and *Dances at a Gathering* and *Glass Pieces* were premiered. French *étoiles* Isabelle Guérin, Manuel Legris, Laurent Hilaire and Monique Loudieres led the cast of *Dances at a Gathering*. One critic wrote, "After lengthy negotiations, Robbins succeeded in imposing his stringent rehearsal requirements; observing the magnificent results made one meditate on the enormous value of the choreographer's presence, particularly now that so few truly great practitioners are still with us."

One of the reasons for Robbins' affection for Paris over the years was the fact that French critics and audiences generally held him in higher regard than they did Balanchine. Robbins' ballet master, Bart Cook, suggested, "Paris adores Jerry more than Balanchine. He could do no wrong. At one point, he had *West Side Story* going, and the New York City Ballet and the Paris Opéra dancing his repertory. To them, Jerry's dancing was freedom. To many New York City Ballet dancers, it was regimented."

During the same period, John Clifford staged some of Balanchine's works at the Paris Opéra and credited Robbins with modernizing the company. "At the Paris Opéra, the dancers are much more trained to be slaves. . . . It's a very hierarchical system there. So when Jerry would have his temper tantrums, they were much more used to that kind of autocratic royal behavior, and they didn't have the adjustment process that Americans did and definitely Balanchine dancers did. . . . So Jerry, in working with them, they all adored him right off the bat—*and* they were terrified of him. I remember when I was there staging *Serenade* and *Prodigal Son,* and he was in the theater staging *In the Night* . . . the pianist would come down during the break in tears and hysterical—the man was about ready to commit suicide. He came up to me one day and said, 'How did you live with it in New York?' The dancers were all hysterical, too, but less so than in New York. And this was all despite the fact that even though he was Jerry when he was there, he was a mellower Jerry. He was less temperamental, but he was still intense.

"The thing about Jerry was, more than anybody, he has brought the Paris Opéra Ballet into the twentieth century. Nureyev started it, but Jerry did it. That company changed so drastically. The way they approach dancing is more professional, more Americanized now."

Jean-Pierre Bonnefoux, who had trained at the Paris Opéra and danced with City Ballet, agreed with John Clifford's assessment. He recalled seeing Robbins in Paris and said, "He seemed so happy, and he had an apartment, and they gave him anything he wanted. You know, he really appreciated the dancers also, which was so nice. He seemed very, very comfortable. It seemed to be good for his life at that time at the Paris Opéra. That's really a place that's so complicated with unions and this and that, but they seemed to have given him whatever he wanted, and that was also one of the reasons for his happiness, because he knew that nobody else could work that way in Paris. There was nobody else but Jerry who could have all his own way. I think he could really appreciate it. You know, when you go to New York maybe sometimes people will compare him to Balanchine or other people, but I think in Paris he was the king, that was him. He was the greatest man. Balanchine was not around anymore. There was that sense that he [Robbins] was the king, and he could do whatever he wanted.

"I think what was extraordinary was for him to Americanize the way of working [at the Paris Opéra]. They really changed their mentality, the dancers, in order to work that way. They had some status symbol, or star thing, or whatever you call that—they thought it should be done the way *they* wanted it to be done. And then when Robbins came, they realized that to really work with him, they had to change. They react to what they have learned, and the discipline was there when I was a little boy. So you understand discipline and you understand to accept it also. I think that he was so good that they really were lucky to work with him."

Early in 1992, Robbins decided to learn to speak Russian, as he was about to stage *In the Night* for the Kirov in St. Petersburg. Robbins had long been enamored with Russian culture. On the ground floor of his townhouse, he kept pictures of Tolstoy and Chekhov. His assistant, Fay Greenbaum, was later recruited to tutor him in the language. "I started teaching him Russian," said Greenbaum. "I'd worked with him all this time, knew all the phenomenal things he did . . . and this was the first time I really thought, My God, this man truly is a genius. It was awesome. . . . Russian works extremely differently from English or French. . . . The whole structure of the language, the way you have to think about the world and organize it is different. And he just got it. . . . Of course he was enormously frustrated. He felt like he wasn't getting it, because he couldn't speak it in two days. . . . He also started to cry in the lessons, because it wasn't happening fast enough. He wanted to do it and it was really hard and he wasn't going to have time."

For Greenbaum, who worked for Robbins intermittently for more than ten years, Tolstoy provided a clue to Robbins' character. She said, "The first Christmas I worked for him [in 1985], I gave him . . . a postcard—it was just pictures from Tolstoy's estate. . . . [Robbins] was the sort of person you did not give gifts. He didn't want them, certainly not from his staff. Then he didn't quite know what to do because I'd given him a gift, even though it was just a postcard, and one day . . . he walked by and he said, 'Well, Tolstoy must have been very difficult to live with.' I said, 'Yeah, because he had all these high principles, and then he had this enormous creative urge that made him break all of his principles, so he was totally miserable.' And Robbins went, 'Oh, yeah, yeah.' Afterwards I thought about it for a minute, and I said, Oh, that's why he likes Tolstoy so much, because he's the same way. . . . He has all these ideals of how he's supposed to be and he's not that way at all. . . . By the time I knew him I think perfection was his only ideal. But I think when he was younger he had all these ideals about justice, that sort of thing, that we all have when we're younger, and about being fair. I think it's one of the reasons that the McCarthy thing was so difficult for him, because I think it absolutely went against his ideals to do what he did. But his drive was much stronger than his ideals."

Robbins' assistant, Victor Castelli, preceded him to St. Petersburg to teach the ballet to the Kirov dancers. *In the Night* had its Russian premiere on March eighteenth. The three couples were performed by Altynai Asylmuratova, Konstantin Zaklinsky, Olga Chenchikova, Murat Vaziev, Yulia Makhalina and Alexander Kurkov. According to critic Igor Stupnikov, "The dancers coped with technical difficulties, but to my mind the ballet is still slightly under-rehearsed." Still, at the age of seventy-three, Robbins was able to add yet another international triumph to his résumé.

That same year Robbins made a bid to direct the television movie of *Gypsy*, starring Bette Midler. Craig Zadan (who first met Robbins in the early seventies while writing a biography of Stephen Sondheim) was one of the production's executive producers. Zadan recalled, "We proceeded with the negotiation on the rights, which took about a year and was very contentious and very difficult, and I never really believed the deal would be closed. It was Shirley Bernstein [Leonard Bernstein's sister] representing Arthur Laurents at the time, and it was Flora Roberts, who was representing Steve Sondheim, and it was Floria Lasky, who represented Jerry and Jule Styne. It was beyond belief, the negotiations. They were all real big screamers.

"One of the issues was about who's going to direct it. I got a call one day and it was Jerry Robbins. . . . He said, 'I really would like to direct this.' By that time . . . he was in his seventies. And it wasn't just that he was that old, but he was wearing hearing aids, he didn't hear that well, and he was a little off. Also, the last thing he did in Hollywood was *West Side Story*, and everybody knows the stories about what happened, about how he's incapable of keeping to a schedule and he's incapable of doing rehearsals within any amount of time. You go bankrupt, you can't possibly do a TV thing on that kind of schedule. But I said to him, 'Let's just talk about the project. Bette Midler was going to be in New York and I was going to be in New York, and he said, 'Why don't we have lunch?' So Jerry, Bette, Neil [Meron, also an executive producer], and myself went to lunch with him. He was as charming as could be. Bette knew him because she had been in [a revival of] *Fiddler.* She loved him, and she thought he was the greatest thing ever. It was really strange, because at the lunch all he did was make excuses of why he was fired on *West Side Story.* It was really embarrassing, because he was half apologizing and half making excuses and half defending himself. Finally, we said, 'Look, we'd love to have you involved, but we need somebody who is going to take responsibility.'"

Zadan continued, "There was a coincidence that happened. He had worked with somebody on *Great Performances*—a *Dance in America* program—named Emile Ardolino. And we had picked Emile Ardolino as the guy that we wanted to direct this. So it just turned out that we picked the same person. He [Robbins] said, 'I would love for Emile to do this.' The next thing we know, he decides he wants to co-direct with Emile. So Emile goes, 'I'm not doing this. I love Jerry, I idolize him, I worship him, but there can't be two directors.' So Jerry would start calling me . . . saying, 'I want to co-direct this with Emile.' I can't say to him, 'Emile doesn't want you.' So I had to say the network will only invest this kind of money if there's one person calling the shots and it has to be Emile. Then he would blow up and he'd start screaming at me at the top of his lungs, and he'd hang up. And then two minutes later, the phone would ring and he'd call back and apologize, and the cycle would continue.

"Eventually, we made it very clear the way it was going to work—that he could have all the input he wanted, but that Emile was going to direct it. So then he kept calling me and again making excuses. Then he started calling Emile and he started calling Bette. They didn't return his calls, because they knew about all the violent phone calls I was getting from him. The more they didn't call back, he kept calling me and getting more and more violent on the phone and nastier and nastier, like it was my fault. It just became this really difficult experience. . . . It was like this borderline personality kind of thing, where it always started with sugar and spice and it always ended with violence and an explosion of his vitriol, and he would always end up hanging up on me. This went on during the whole production of the movie."

Gypsy aired on CBS in 1993, and both Bette Midler and Emile Ardolino won Emmy Awards, as did the film's producers for Outstanding Made for TV

Movie. Ardolino died of AIDS before the broadcast. Of the skirmishes with Robbins, Zadan added, "The recurring thing was always his obsession with his being fired from *West Side Story*. Every phone conversation went back to that. . . . Winning the Oscar, it made it worse for him—how could you win an Oscar for something you got fired off of? . . . I think that all the people who worked with him became the equivalent of abused children. I see this community of kids that looked at him as a father figure, and it's exactly the same psychological damage that happens between, let's say, an abusive father and son, or an abusive father and a daughter. And you almost never recover, no matter how much therapy you have. . . . Is it necessary to live a life like that, to hurt people as deeply as he did, in order to be talented and in order to achieve a career of brilliance? . . . He was not at home in his skin. He was not at home being Jewish, or gay, or in the theater."

Zadan also compared Robbins with other "directors and choreographers on Broadway and their relationship to Hollywood. If you examine it, there's Tommy Tune, who never wanted to do a movie; Michael Bennett, who never wanted to do a movie, would have nothing to do with Hollywood; Bob Fosse was enamored of Hollywood and became a great film director. It's really interesting to go back and look at all of these guys and see which of them stayed in the theater and never ventured into the movie business. . . . Jerry really wanted it [Hollywood], but he got fired. Jerry's one that wanted it as much as Fosse wanted it. It was not that he had a passion to direct the movie of *Gypsy*; it was all about showing Hollywood that he could do it, and I think that's the most interesting aspect of the whole story."

Later in 1992, Robbins restaged *The Concert* at the Paris Opéra to much acclaim, and by the end of his life, that company's repertory would include twelve of his ballets. On May 4, 1993, Robbins was named a chevalier of the French Legion of Honor. The ceremonies took place in New York at the French Embassy on Fifth Avenue, and the award was bestowed by the French ambassador, Jacques Andreani. Mica Ertegün later gave a small party for Robbins. Michael Koessel recalled, "He invited me to come to a dinner at Mica's when he got the Legion of Honor award . . . and he invited me to bring a guest. I told him I'd like to bring [a friend], Rick. But there was some problem. Mica wanted to have boy-girl-boy-girl seating and there were too many men. He said he would speak to her about it. Then he called me back, and he said, 'You know, I really can't, she's doing me this favor, I just can't. I'll speak to Rick. Give him my apologies, but I just can't intrude there. This is the way she wants to have it. It's really her party, not mine.' I think he felt conflicted."

Later that year, Robbins staged *Moves* for the Paris Opéra and also *New York Export: Opus Jazz* for the Alvin Ailey American Dance Theatre. Wilma Curley and Edward Verso, both veterans of Ballets: U.S.A., assisted Robbins during his brief guest tenure with the Alvin Ailey troupe. Curley recalled, "The last thing we worked together on was *Opus Jazz*. We took a car out to New Jersey to see the company. The nicest part about it was after we went through the [Lincoln] tunnel, he was saying, 'That's where I was born, that's where I was raised—Weehawken, all through there. That street used to have snow on it, we could sled straight through.' And I was so glad he was in a good mood, because I really was not in the mood to be in a car with him for two hours. He was in a marvelous mood recalling his youth in Weehawken."

Both Curley and Verso remembered that the work did not go well for Robbins, who was by now unable to discern voices clearly in the rehearsal studio even when wearing a hearing aid. At a disadvantage, Robbins sometimes became the object of mockery by the dancers. Verso said, "That was the worst experience I had with him choreographing. There was total disrespect from them to him, it was incredible. They would not do anything he wanted. I think they've heard too many things, and they weren't going to take this from him."

Ailey dancer Sarita Allen explained, "A lot of it I can attribute to a generational thing just in terms of his language. He would call us 'little girls.' Maybe he did that with other companies, too. I think it was just his language. He would go, 'Little girl,' and 'Fella,' and 'Boy,' and 'You people'—like we had never set foot onstage. I think the biggest challenge for us, which was not bad, it's just that the Ailey style, when Alvin was around, it was the complete opposite of his [Robbins'] style. Where Alvin would always say, 'Do more, more, more,' our challenge was to do less, even though his style of jazz was so totally, totally different in his thinking. He'd keep saying, 'Easy, easy, fella!' In fact, to this day, when those of us who were in the cast look at each other, we just laugh and we say his lines all the time. . . . It wasn't a bad thing, it was just, again, a challenge because it was a total opposite style than what we were used to. Everything felt like we were almost marking. That was the style that he was after. We figured out that it wasn't discrimination, but I guess that's just the natural kind of sensing that most black people have. Automatically when a white person comes in and they're being nasty to everybody, we just automatically assume—it's wrong and it's always a cliché, but I think it's just something that's inbred.

"After a while, we were laughing because he was so funny. I'll never forget this one time, he lined us all up. Actually, that was the first day. And he stood in front of each person and looked nose to nose, looked dead in their face for a long time. And then he'd go, 'You!' And then he told the people where to go. This is another joke that we all still have. There were three of us he looked extra long and hard and said, 'You wait and *you* wait.' We all still laugh about this to this day."

The ballet, with its finger-snapping jazz style from an earlier era, opened at New York's City Center in December. Anna Kisselgoff wrote of the Ailey dancers, "If anything, they approach the choreography here too carefully and too reverently. They strive for the precision that Mr. Robbins demands, but do not quite achieve the freedom that experienced ballet dancers would find more easily, especially in the partnered lifts. . . . Undoubtedly, the Ailey Company will eventually let loose with characteristic exuberance."

Encouraged by Mikhail Baryshnikov, Robbins created a new work early in 1994, his first in five years. *A Suite of Dances* was set to Bach's *Suite for Solo Cello.* In a way, Robbins was mining a musical vein with Bach, continuing from where he left off with *The Goldberg Variations,* as he had done with Chopin and the spinoff works that followed *Dances at a Gathering.* The new ballet, however, with its simple vocabulary of skips and turns and arm swings, bore little resemblance to his earlier ensemble piece. *A Suite of Dances* was a solo for Baryshnikov staged under the auspices of the White Oak Project, a hybrid modern troupe that the dancer founded with choreographer Mark Morris. Baryshnikov said of the dance, "I think it's all about Jerry—a man leaning on one leg and listening, wondering, 'Okay, what's next?' There's irony and urgency and also a bittersweet quality. This is a man of intelligence, a thinking man."

Robbins returned the compliment, saying, "For a while, I didn't feel in condition; I couldn't feel my body. But Misha wanted to try something, and I want to work with smaller forces now. I started listening to the music. It began to open up. It's given me a real booster. I can't think of anyone better to work with. If I think it's too dark, he lightens it—and vice versa. A great, great artist." Robbins later told *Time* that the ballet "was a real do-or-die thing for me."

A Suite of Dances premiered at the New York State Theater on March 3, 1994, with cellist Wendy Sutter providing the accompaniment onstage. In May, the ballet entered the New York City Ballet repertory with Baryshnikov appearing as a guest. Of that performance, Jack Anderson observed, "The sounds of Bach set Mr. Baryshnikov into motion. The steps he danced looked casual, yet elegant. Mr. Robbins turned Mr. Baryshnikov into the best sort of aristocrat, one so cultivated and at ease that he does not need to be ostentatious." The dancer was outfitted in pink ballet slippers and a simple two-tone red costume from Santo Loquasto. Looking back on his ballet collaborations with Robbins, Loquasto said, "He had his own vision that he wanted you to interpret. And his vision was always clouded—he had a difficult time communicating, not that he wasn't articulate. He was never really interested in collaboration."

In March, Robbins commenced a long series of rehearsals with students at the School of American Ballet for a ballet entitled, *2 & 3 Part Inventions*, set to Bach's piano studies. One of the SAB students, Kristina Fernandez, later described Robbins' effort to exercise restraint during his work with these fledgling dancers. Writing for *Ballet Review*, Fernandez recalled, "He never lost his temper with me, but he did with other people in the studio. One day, a girl we were working with started crying. After that, every time Jerry would start to get mad, he would just walk out of the room or he'd sit there and stamp his feet a little bit and let it go. And then he would proceed very calmly. I think he understood this was our first time working with a choreographer. It was interesting to see him actually trying to hold that back after a certain point. I believe that when he saw her crying, it made him think about it."

Robbins said at the time, "I can't work as fast as I used to." At seventy-five, he also admitted, "One has a feeling about mortality at odd moments." Not surprisingly, the youth of the cast led him into one of his sprightly *Interplay* moods. Divided into twelve sections and providing a clever visual counterpoint to the music throughout, the ballet premiered with matinee and evening performances at Lincoln Center's Juilliard Theater on June fourth. *2 & 3 Part Inventions* entered the City Ballet repertory on January nineteenth of the following year. Of its first school performances, Anna Kisselgoff wrote, "For all his concern with form and structure, this is Mr. Robbins at his most relaxed, giving the lie to those who say classical choreography is dead."

At the invitation of his cousin Viola Zousmer, Robbins spent Thanksgiving that year with her and her brother, Perry. Zousmer and Robbins were the same age and had not seen each other in years. Early in November, she wrote him a letter, saying, "I think and drift back and remember our youth and what good times we enjoyed together with our families. . . . Maybe I'm a little maudlin, but somehow the years seem to be flying by too quickly. If at all possible, I'd love to be with you."

Robbins flew to West Palm Beach on November twenty-third and spent three days with his cousins in a small retirement community in nearby Lake Worth. Viola Zousmer remembered, "He did come in his old dirty hat and brought his old luggage. It was tough to break the ice, but once we did we had a fantastic time—we had laughs, we had jokes, we got down to basics. We didn't put on airs with each other. His one problem was that he got so into ballet that he lost his perspective on everything else. So he came here and he couldn't believe it. I live in Florida with older people, Jerry's age, and he saw a different part of life. He would get up in the morning and look around and look out and was just so thrilled and amazed with seeing ordinary people. This was part of life he missed out on. Every time I was in the room with him, he was looking out the window at the back. I remember he sat in the living room meditating while I was making a meal for him. And I went in and said, 'Jerry, I want to say something—do you realize you're a genius?' He said, 'What are you talking about?' I said, 'The world thinks of you as a genius. What do you think of yourself?' He said, 'I think of myself as doing things that make people happy.'"

Viola Zousmer also recalled that the one subject Robbins would not discuss was his father. "I said, 'Jerry, your dad was great.' He said, 'I don't want to discuss him.' I said, 'Why? We loved Uncle Harry. He was great.' He said, 'I don't want to talk about him. He was so against what I was doing, he almost turned me off.' And when he left, we took him to the airport, and he sat in the front with my brother, and I sat in the back with my sister-in-law, and he turned around and said, 'I want to thank you for the best Thanksgiving I ever had,' and he went out of the car, crying. That was the last I saw of Jerry."

In the spring of 1995, Robbins returned to City Ballet and created *West Side Story Suite*, for which he utilized his six excerpt scenes from *Jerome Robbins' Broadway*, with the addition of "Something's Coming." As in the show, Robert La Fosse performed the role of Tony, with Elena Diner as Maria, Jock Soto as Bernardo, Nancy Ticotin as Anita, Nikolaj Hübbe as Riff, and Natalie Toro as Rosalia. Some of the dancers sang numbers while others were performed by singers in the pit. Danish dancer Nikolaj Hübbe performed the vocals for "Cool" without ever having singing lessons. All of the dancers were called upon by Robbins to write biographies for their characters and to fulfill the basics of acting, which was unfamiliar territory, as these ballet dancers were not Broadway gypsies. Robbins later said that the City Ballet dancers "were holding back, and I had to say, 'Look, each of you has your own story. You can't be just nice people and then scream and yell.'" Robbins also recalled that he had once approached Balanchine about adapting *West Side Story* at City Ballet after he had received such an offer from the rival American Ballet Theatre. Mr. B reportedly told him, "That's good. You should do it, because our boys don't fight."

Barry Primus visited Robbins during rehearsals and recalled, "When he was redoing *West Side Story*, I went to see him at Lincoln Center Annex. He said, 'Jesus, I'm getting old. I'm choreographing from a chair at times.' It was the first time he said that."

As a nostalgia piece, the ballet was well-received by audiences and by most critics, though some notices faulted the classical dancers for falling short of the gritty, action-packed original show. In *Dance Magazine*, Lynn Garafola applauded the adaptation, writing, "With their clear lines and exploding masses, dynamic rhythms and gestures that even today retain the power of the vernacular, the dances—especially those for the men—seem fresher and more exhilarating than ever." Anna Kisselgoff's headline in the *Times* read, A CLASSIC

DISTILLED TO A PURE ESSENCE. At the time, Robbins wrote a letter to former City Ballet ballerina Penelope Dudleston and boasted that nine performances of *West Side Story Suite* had sold out in June, including the Sunday matinees. He also told Dudleston that he was looking forward to an upcoming trip to Paris and hoped to choreograph another new ballet on his return. But Robbins expressed doubts that his aging body would allow him to work again.

Robbins did begin rehearsals for a ballet that winter, but the work was abruptly postponed. In December, Robbins underwent surgery to replace a heart valve. Michael Koessel said, "I thought the decline became most noticeable after he had his heart operation. I thought after that his mental health suffered. He became very forgetful. There were times when he was very coherent and alert and other times when he wasn't at all."

Koessel recalled introducing Robbins to a special friend during this period. "There's . . . a friend of mine, who's an eighty-six-year-old woman. Her name is Mary Wood Lawrence. She's actually a remarkable woman and Jerry was quite fascinated with her. . . . She was the wife of my mentor as an undergrad, I went to college up in Williamstown, Mass. . . . When he had his heart operation, she came down and we went over to the hospital and visited him. They're kind of the yin and yang of growing older. Jerry, I think, grew older with great, great difficulty. He used to say, 'There's nothing good about growing old, there's just nothing good about it at all.' I would say something like, 'Well, don't you get wiser?' And Mary has taken just the opposite attitude towards life, which is that every new day is this rich, wonderful experience, and getting older is part of that experience. It's not a continual decline, it's a continually new experience. I think he was fascinated by her because of this contrasting attitude and wanted to be like that. I don't think he could quite figure it out. I remember the first time she met him, she said you could tell by looking into his eyes—I wish I could remember the exact words—that there are real demons in there, that he's terribly tortured. And I think that's absolutely true. I remember following up on this conversation with her. She said to me, 'You know, he'll never be happy, will he?'"

Koessel continued, "Every morning he would wake up and talk about his dreams, and they were always terrible dreams. Obviously, on the other hand, he had enormous success and clear moments of happiness. And everyone has pointed out what a great sense of humor he had and he could find some of the simplest things—like a girl jumping rope, or something like that—he could find them incredibly amusing and just fixate completely, just stand there and laugh and smile."

In the months after his heart surgery, Robbins began to exhibit the physical and mental symptoms of Parkinson's disease. Still, he refused any form of special assistance and returned to the ballet studio the following year. He continued to walk his dogs in the neighborhood, to travel on his own to the theater and restaurants. For relaxation he played computer games and watched *Jeopardy* on television most evenings. There were signs he was mellowing at last. Bart Cook remembered, "Poor Jerry had to wear the wires for his heart. The doctors actually told him he couldn't get angry or lose his temper. I think I was helpful in having him see another way of working. I was able to say to him, 'Jerry, don't you think you could get more out of these people if you treated them a little differently?' He actually sat there one day—I can remember, it was in Robert Denver's old studio—and said, 'You know, you're probably right, I ought to try that.' And I believe he started trying. I don't know if would actually choose consciously how to try to pursue the work differently, but I wouldn't put it past him."

When he returned to the beach during the summer, Sono Osato witnessed his decline but she also sensed Robbins' indomitable spirit. She said, "He would come for dinner or lunch or whatever, and we would laugh a lot. We would reminisce and laugh a lot. Then sometimes I saw him deteriorate and I realized that there was something very much the matter with him. He took very tiny steps. I think he was beginning to get Parkinson's. I'm sure it was after-effects of the heart attack. He was frail. Going upstairs was not easy. But I must say that he was very brave in a sense that he never talked about how he felt, whether it was bad or better, he didn't discuss his health at all. And he never lost his sense of humor, never. We used to roar. We'd be sitting there reminiscing and roaring. . . . But for him to lose his body, so to speak, for a choreographer it's as bad as it is for a dancer, because they can't show anymore. When their body is stiff, they can't really demonstrate, and that's the way the choreography is made, through demonstration. They can't talk the steps, they have to show the dancer what to do and how to do it."

Early in 1996, corps ballerina Kristina Fernandez was hampered by an injury and suffering personal distress. She informed Robbins that she had decided to take a leave of absence and return to her home in Arizona to recuperate. Robbins asked her to write to him, and she later sent him a letter, describing the beauty of the desert and its sunsets. Robbins wrote her a reply, telling her about rehearsals and saying how pleased he was to hear from her. "It was as if we'd been friends for years," said Fernandez. "He said he had never been to that part of the country, but would love to see the sunsets. And he told me to keep those things with me always." She took his advice to heart as a reminder to maintain balance in her life.

Fay Greenbaum remembered Robbins telephoning her for assistance in December of 1996. She said, "I was on my way out the door to meet somebody. The phone rang and I just let the machine answer, and I heard it was him. So I grabbed it. . . . I said, 'Mr. Robbins, are you okay?' He said, 'I don't know, I'm a little shaky.' My heart started racing, I thought, Oh my God, I'm going to have to take him to the hospital, he's going to die on me. I said, 'What is it?' He said, 'Well, you know, I called Chris [Pennington], I called Cat [Catherine Anderson]'—those were his two personal assistants at the time—'and neither one's home, and I didn't know what to do, so I called you. Could you come over?' I thought, Oh my God, this is really the end. I said, 'Well, I was actually just on my way out the door to meet somebody. They're coming from New Jersey so I'm sure they're already gone, but let me see if there's something I can do.' After making arrangements I jumped in a cab and I ran over. He said, 'Could you send two faxes for me?'

"In all fairness to him, it was the day of the Kennedy Center honors and he was supposed to be there, he was supposed to be having lunch with the President. He was there for Lauren Bacall, which amazed me since Eddie Villella was getting one that day. He didn't feel well enough to go. And I was horrified when I saw him. I hadn't seen him in a while, maybe close to a year, and he had become so drawn, he had aged, and he had this shuffling gait. I knew something was not going well. . . . I asked [his assistant] Chris afterwards, I said, 'Does he have Parkinson's disease?' Because that's what it looked like to me. He had the tremor in his hand and that shuffling gait. And Chris said, 'Oh, he's fine, he's fine.' Anyway, he had to find a way to fax the President to tell him he wasn't going to be there for their lunch date and to fax Betty Bacall to say he wasn't going to be there. That's the last thing I ever did for him."

Robbins felt strong enough at the beginning of 1997 to mount a major new ballet, the work that he had started rehearsing at City Ballet before having his heart surgery and continued to develop intermittently during the previous year. This was to be his last ballet. *Brandenburg* was set to four of Bach's six *Brandenburg Concertos*. Robbins' ballet master, Jean-Pierre Frohlich told the *Times*, "Whenever Jerry concentrated on it, the steps just flowed. He'd come into rehearsals with a basic idea of how he wanted a scene to look. Yet, as he watched the dancers, his initial idea might develop in unexpected ways." Frohlich was as evasive as Robbins in describing the ballet, saying, "It's a plotless piece in which the steps create the mood."

Brandenburg was much more than that, as Robbins at seventy-eight demonstrated again his uncanny ability to reinvent himself. He later spoke of his regard for the music, saying, "I find the richness [of Bach] very, very exciting, thrilling, and disturbing in a way. . . . It doesn't seem like something by an old man. . . . He's taking strange journeys while searching out all the things he wants to find out." Nor did Robbins' ballet with its youthful enthusiasm, speed and visual complexity seem like something created by an old man.

Like the music, the ballet was full of strange journeys and sublime surprises, with numerous references to Robbins' past dances going back to his cartwheeling *Fancy Free* sailors and the childhood romps of *Interplay*. He was emphatically recapitulating himself with this farewell gesture, yet continually surpassing audience expectations in typical Robbins fashion through unlikely combinations of the classic and vernacular. It was as if he were out to explain once and for all what he meant when he once said of his choice of form: "I think that the classical style is the one which provides the best basis, owing to its restrictions. But whereas its discipline interests me as a point of departure, I cannot bring myself to accept the limitations it imposes, the narrowness of the combinations it offers. The possibilities of the human body are endless. Why not use them all?"

The ballet premiered on January twenty-second, which was also remembered at the State Theater that night as Balanchine's birthday. The two principal couples were Wendy Whelan and Peter Boal, and Lourdes Lopez and

Nikolaj Hübbe, who were joined by an ensemble of sixteen. With the dancers in stylish peasant outfits by Holly Hynes, the ballet began with a festive folk dance, and from there the dancing alternated between duets for the principals and group formations for the rest of the communal gathering. The configurations were often quite intricate and marked by lightning-fast transformations. Anna Kisselgoff wrote, "Within seconds, *Brandenburg* takes off on its own into a kaleidoscope of changing patters, of energy made visible. Never has Mr. Robbins moved bodies in space with such dazzling speed and density. Choreographically, he has outdone himself here." At the end of the premiere, Robbins acknowledged the ovation by taking a single, lone curtain call.

In *Commentary*, Terry Teachout described *Brandenburg* as a kind of bittersweet pinnacle in Robbins' effort to emulate Balanchine. The critic wrote, "No more a direct dance statement than *Dances at a Gathering*, *Brandenburg* is a theatricalized portrayal of neoclassicism, and one which, for all the fetching grace and fluidities of its complex ensembles, is to George Balanchine's *Symphony in C* as *West Side Story* is to *Romeo and Juliet*." While acknowledging that Robbins had distinguished himself as an artist comparable in stature to Leonard Bernstein, Teachout argued that the choreographer was entrapped by his romantic, self-conscious nature, and hence, forever barred from Balanchine's realm of "wholly natural genius."

At this stage, with his mental awareness diminished, Robbins was unperturbed by critical judgments. *West Side Story* veteran Gene Gavin recollected that Robbins attended a performance of *Brandenburg* with Buzz Miller. Robbins and Miller had long since reconciled after their romantic breakup of the fifties and were now dear friends. As Miller related the story to Gavin, after the curtain came down on his ballet that night, Robbins turned to him and said, "I don't know how I do it."

Many of Robbins' longtime friends from the theater would visit and pay their respects during the last year of his life. Barry Primus remembered, "The last time I was with him, I suggested that we go out to [Jackson] Pollock's house. He had never been out there in all the years he'd been out on the Island. I was surprised. So we met about five days later in front of the bank in East Hampton. I drove up and we met by the movie theater, and his assistant drove the car and Jerry went with me. We went out there and it was a beautiful day. We saw the house and we saw the yard. Jerry I noticed was, like always, most interested in the surroundings. He was fascinated just by the beauty of the day. Taking a walk was always special with him. I think out of his shyness came tremendous observations. So we were there, and I said, 'Well, what do you think?' He said to me under his breath, 'I really don't like this art.' Then we drove back and we had lunch and talked. He was silent, I remember, during the conversation. Jerry would sometimes get these—I don't know what to say—it was like a panic attack. After he had his heart attack, he had a lot of problems. He would say, 'It takes me two hours a day to get started.' He said, 'I should have worked out more.' So afterwards coming outside, he met the most wonderful dog and everything just went completely gay and happy. It was a little puppy and he just couldn't take his eyes off this white, fluffy puppy. Then like always he settled down to say goodbye in a very serious way. When I called him since then, I would say, 'How are you?' and he'd say, 'Not too good.'"

Gerald Freedman called Robbins in December of 1997 to arrange a visit. "I said, 'Jerry, I just have to see you. I'm going to be in New York, let's get together, I just want to talk,'" recalled Freedman. "He said, 'Fine.' God knows I didn't expect him to die six months later." Robbins invited him to brunch at his townhouse around Christmas. Freedman remembered, "He had his old dog with him, and our conversation was constantly interrupted by his talking with his dog. So it was just filled with a wonderful intimacy that was very nice and important to me at that time. I was shocked because he was physically much feebler than I had remembered him. He told me a terrible story about his actually falling down in the street. And again I marveled at how frank and open Jerry was. It was a horrible story. With me it was like there was nothing to hide. And yet we know there was a lot to hide and he hid it a long time."

Robbins sounded a poignant note when he complained to his former protégé, "No one is calling me. And all I want to do is work." Recalling that moment, Freedman said, "It was very plaintive, I can tell you. I thought, I don't believe what I'm hearing. Here's this great theater genius sitting across from me, and he just wanted to work again."

During the same holiday season, Robbins was visited by Gina Trikonis, who had been a replacement in the *West Side Story* Broadway cast and appeared in the movie. She credited Robbins with giving her a career in the theater and in Hollywood, where she later became a costume designer. Trikonis hadn't seen Robbins in thirty-seven years, and she later composed a reminiscence about meeting him again for a Sunday tea in the office at his townhouse. While noting that Robbins was now "frail, vulnerable and smaller" than she remembered, Trikonis wrote, "Yet, when our eyes met, that invisible connection I sensed as a young girl was still there. 'I'm shrinking,' he said, bursting into peals of laughter. 'I keep shrinking and I don't hear so well,' he laughed, putting his hand up to his ear. . . . What I remember most about that afternoon was the laughter. Jerry loved to laugh. 'I came because I wanted to see your face,' I told him. 'I came because I needed to give you a hug, and to say thank you. Thank you for recognizing my talent and for choosing me and giving me the life I now own.' 'Well, you did it,' he said. 'Yes,' I replied, 'but you gave it to me and I ran with it. I never would have gone to LA had you not sent for me to do the movie. My children are here now, because that's where I met their father. So they thank you as well. We profoundly impact lives all the time, and we don't even know it. . . . We are the pebble the ripples form around. I came because I wanted you to know I hold you close and think of you often,' I concluded. 'It's nice to know I'm being thought of,' he replied.

"I admired his city garden. 'Come back in the spring,' he said, 'and see it when it's all in bloom. It's quite extraordinary. It feels like you're not even in the city. It's lovely.' He shared how he found his dog at the Metropolitan Museum of Art. How a crowd had gathered around a lost dog and when he entered the circle, she attached herself to him becoming his shadow. 'I just couldn't leave her there,' he said. 'So I brought her home and she's been my shadow ever since,' he laughed."

During their visit, Robbins told Trikonis, "I'll keep working for as long as they'll let me." Early in 1998, he returned to City Ballet to restage his 1965 ballet *Les Noces*, which was originally done for ABT. Robbins brought back his original costume designer, Patricia Zipprodt, who recalled, "So thirty-three years later, there we are. I tell you! We're much older. He's almost eighty, I'm almost seventy-four, and we're still fussing with the damn reds. Well, I kind of gingerly went up to him. I really didn't want to tangle. I wanted to do it and go home. There's one character in the ballet called the Matchmaker. And all these colors were earthy and muted. So it's like the domino theory, with all the costumes tied to that one. The New York City Ballet costume staff went out and bought to match the exact swatch of the first production—I had copies of the dyed swatches—they went out and bought the whole show. Oh, we were so happy! Jerry comes up one day and he's sort of dark, and he looks at me and says, 'Well, Patty, I've been thinking about the Matchmaker. As I'm rehearsing it now, we're in a much bigger theater, a much bigger stage, and I think that we need to pull this character into a little more prominence, a little more red.'

"I knew what he meant and I thought, Oh no! First of all we'd spent a lot of money, and now that little minor character will probably be the star. So we start doing the reds and the whole process repeats itself exactly as it had thirty-three years ago when we hadn't done it already and we were young and still exploring reds. So there we were doing it again. We had to reset the entire thing. Start with white and dye it all until we got to just the right red. There were two reds that came in that almost made it. One I thought was just right and the other Jerry thought was just right. And the one he had chosen was too bright, I thought, because even in the wedding scene, I saw the Matchmaker rather than the bride. But I figured maybe his vision was dulling a few years ahead of me. So there it is. Later, I read—they sent it to me down in Virginia, I think it was *People Magazine*—a notice about his death and how his sister had decided that he should be buried in one of the red shirts from *Les Noces,* and I thought, There he is in his grave with the *wrong shirt!* Haaa!"

Sono Osato recalled Robbins' headstrong decision to restage the production, saying, "By doing *Les Noces,* he strained himself even more, but I think he wanted to do that. I don't think he wanted to sit around and do nothing. I think he just threw himself into that willy-nilly, no matter what was going to happen."

Kristina Fernandez described the work on *Les Noces,* saying, "Jerry taught us the original steps and then ran the ballet every day. And he started perfecting, began to change things: entrances, what the arms were doing. Some of the things were subtle. . . . There is a part where the Bride is balancing in a grand *plié* and the girls around her are doing poses with their hands on their head, their hands on their hip. Jerry said, 'You're telling her what a hard life she's going to have now. Now that she's married she's going to be doing all the work and it's not easy, it's not all fun and games anymore. . . .' When they run off at the end of that dance, Jerry said, 'Run off like you're going to the church. You live in a little town. Everyone knows where the church is. So go there.' . . . Jerry gives everyone a sense of the entire community: you live in this little town, you walk everywhere, and everyone knows everyone else. It's a whole picture. Everything means something. Jerry helps you be clear about it."

In a written interview at the time, Robbins described the type of dancers he favored, saying, "I guess what I like is a dancer that goes after every performance and gives me more than just a *technically* complete performance—a dancer who fills it with all sorts of surrounding attitudes that seem to bubble from the insides of a person."

The revival of *Les Noces* opened at the State Theater on May 20, 1998, during City Ballet's fiftieth anniversary year. The Bride and Groom were performed by Alexandra Ansanelli and Robert Wersinger. Robbins abandoned the original stage plan that called for having the four grand pianos and singers onstage. Instead, a recording of the score by the Dmitri Pokrovsky Ensemble was employed. The ballet suffered without live accompaniment, and its stylized wedding festivities were dwarfed in the larger, less intimate theater. Anna Kisselgoff wrote, ". . . this is a *Noces* that has lost some of its ritualistic essence. It has shrunk. Nevertheless, it is still Robbins. . . ."

By this time, Robbins' physical fragility was apparent to all. His Chilean cook, Alicia Aedo, remembered, "I was very afraid, because after the show they have a big dinner, gala dinner and Mr. Robbins doesn't recognize so many people, and you know he have a very good memory. The next day he went for a checkup and stay about ten days at the hospital, and then he come home and he was really sick. He was with nurse, night and day, and I didn't like it, because I feel like he's going down the hill. And he never want anybody to take care of him, to be over him. And I was even fighting with everybody, 'Leave the guy alone.' Because he liked to be himself and doesn't want to feel like he was dependent."

Later in the spring, Aedo had a premonition that the end was near. She recalled that during the time that Jesse Gerstein was being cared for at the townhouse, "Mr. Robbins got a gardenia and bring it to Jesse upstairs in a little glass of water. You could see through the [office] window, there was just one gardenia in the plant. That's what was in my mind, it's always in my mind, I don't know why. Then one day I see Mr. Robbins in the office. He was sitting there back to the window, and I was sitting in front. And it was so scary for me and I feel so sad. I see through the window there is just one gardenia, one flower in the plant . . . reminding me when Jesse die, and I was thinking, Mr. Robbins not going to live for a long time. I look at him, and he just look at me and smile.

"Mr. Robbins could not have a continued conversation. He was like in and out. He was very, very confused. And later I was very upset because I saw him look at me, look at everything, but he wasn't there, wasn't really there. And then when Twyla [Tharp] came to see him, I said, 'Look, Mr. Robbins is not okay.' And she was very upset, she was crying with me. We both started to cry because, you know, she said when she was there before when Mr. Robbins wasn't sick, they were talking and talking and talking and laughing and everything. But that day I said to Twyla, 'Keep talking.'"

Tharp later recalled Robbins' state of confusion. He told her that he was planning to revive one of his early works, and she realized that he was referring to *Les Noces*, the revival which he had already accomplished.

Michael Koessel also saw Robbins near the end. "I saw him twice that spring at dinner parties that I had. He came over. They were small dinner parties, no background noise, and he was very alert both times, and I thought he was doing better. But when I would talk to other people, they would say, 'No, you've just seen him at times when he's flourishing, but on the whole he's in a continual state of decline.' I actually saw him the night before he had his stroke. I saw him that Thursday night. . . . We had dinner with him that night, and he wasn't himself at all that night. My partner Rick, it wasn't even clear that he recognized Rick."

In a memorial service eulogy, Robbins' friend Dr. Daniel Stern described his final days. After suffering a severe stroke, Robbins spent three days in the hospital with his sister and friends constantly at his bedside. Sonia Cullinen said of Dr. Stern, "Dan was very supportive, all through his marriages with his first wife, Anne, and second wife, Nadia. Nadia is a beautiful lady, and she's a doctor, and so she was very helpful when Jerry was dying. They were very caring towards me."

Dr. Stern's wife, Nadia, was responsible for Robbins' living will, and she decided to remove him from the hospital so that he might die at home. Sonia and her husband, George Cullinen, stayed until the end. She remembered, "At the house when Jerry was dying, it was just unbelievable. They did not let my kids come in, and we were stuck down in the office. I handled it because I had to. I was so upset. It took me a year to struggle through and let go, to find closure."

Robbins never recovered consciousness. On the second morning that he was home, Alicia Aedo was in the kitchen with the dog. "Tess was smelling death," said Aedo, "and she started running upstairs to Mr. Robbins. And I said, 'That's it.' I said goodbye to him once he was unconscious. I don't want to see him like that. He was so brilliant a man. I feel like I was not part of the family, but it was very touching for my life, Mr. Robbins."

Dr. Stern recalled that Robbins' dog jumped on the bed to be with his master. When the end came, Sonia and the same group of friends were standing in a hushed semi-circle around the bed, overcome with emotion. Before his breath ran out, Robbins moved his head from the pillow and opened his eyes, electrifying those in the room almost as if it had been a performance.

Robbins died on July 29, 1998. Several weeks later, his sister and her family and a group of friends gathered at his beach house and spread his ashes on the dunes. Sonia recalled, "Jerry asked for them to read Kaddish after he died. In the ceremony out at the beach, they had a rabbi come, and I thought it was rather interesting because the rabbi had to be paid off because it's against the religion to be cremated. Floria [Lasky] organized the whole thing."

With Lasky's assistance, Robbins had revised his will many times over the years, and his lawyer was named as one of his estate's executors, along with his accountant, Allen Greenberg. The estate was valued at more than $30 million, and Robbins was quite generous in making a number of personal bequests to more than twenty friends. Michael Koessel and Christine Conrad each received $50,000. Aidan Mooney and William Earle each received $80,000. Choreographer Anna Sokolow received $50,000. Robbins also provided most of his household staff and administrative assistants with sizable bequests and distributed personal mementos to many friends and colleagues.

Robbins gave $20,000 to the School of American Ballet and an equal amount to the Dancers' Emergency Fund, which he had helped to establish with Betty Cage. Jean-Pierre Frohlich inherited $60,000. Susan Hendl, Victor Castelli and Christine Redpath each received $50,000. Robbins provided for a trust to oversee his legacy. In addition, a small group, including his sister and Daniel Stern, were named as beneficiaries, receiving a percentage of the future earnings generated by Robbins' shows and ballets and a percentage of the overall estate. With regard to his choreography, Robbins appointed Jean-Pierre Frohlich, Victor Castelli, Susan Hendl, Ellen Sorrin, Aidan Mooney and William Earle to an advisory committee accountable to the estate's executors and trustees. Most significant perhaps, in terms of his legacy to future generations of dancers and scholars, Robbins provided substantial support to the New York Public Library's Dance Collection (named in his honor). He also donated his personal papers, journals, correspondence, drawings, videotapes and so forth to the library, although access to some of the collection would be restricted for a period of thirteen years after his death.

Two memorial services were held in New York, and a gala tribute was staged by the Paris Opéra. The first event in New York took place at the State Theater on November 16, 1998, and was mainly attended by the ballet community. Peter Martins was a genial host. Robbins was eulogized and the evening was interspersed with videotapes of the choreographer being interviewed about his experiences with George Balanchine and the New York City Ballet. The most poignant moment came when Daniel Stern offered reflections on Robbins as a friend and related the scene of his death in considerable detail. The evening closed with a City Ballet performance of *Dances at a Gathering.* Those in the audience from the older generations, such as Janet Reed, Wilma Curley and some from the original cast, thought the dancing that night made clear just how difficult, if not impossible, the task will be to recreate and preserve the more subtle, evanescent qualities of Robbins' choreography.

In April of the following year, the Broadway community offered its own tribute, organized by Donald Saddler, at the Majestic Theatre. There was a certain tension in the air at both New York memorials as speakers in various ways sought to reconcile Robbins' Broadway and ballet legacies with his well-known reputation.

Grover Dale was one of those who saw the light and the darkness in the man. Dale spoke at the Broadway memorial and later confided, "I've never known a more restless man. Watching Jerry soften at the sight of a playful dog on the beach became a lot more comforting than watching him gain strength by pointing out the weaknesses of others during rehearsals. I often wondered what the work would have been like had he been as sweet to his dancers as he had been to his dogs. Perhaps 'contentment' and 'being a genius' don't mix very well."

Dale added, "If work reveals the man, Jerry showed the world who he was and what he aspired to. It's all in there. It's no accident that his signature work (*West Side Story*) was based on 'the futility of intolerance.' Perhaps that was the important lesson he himself was supposed to learn? Whether he learned it or not is not for any of us to say. But, thanks to his creations, the lesson about intolerance will continue to touch our lives as long as there are stages and screens to show *West Side Story*. Frankly, I think I'm due for another visit."

Robbins' memory was honored and his imperfections acknowledged by those whose lives he touched. Sono Osato privately summed up the man she had known since their early days at Ballet Theatre, saying, "I think on the whole Jerry had a very good life, and I think that he must have been quite thrilled by his success. He would have to be very dumb if he didn't, at some point in between his periods of insecurity, if he didn't appreciate what he was doing and enjoy it. . . . It's hard for dancers when the business is not right, do it again, do it again, and do it again, but the results—if the ballet is good or the show is good—the results! It's worthwhile, all the effort and all the rehearsing, constant fixing. Nothing is achieved without trying, without the effort. He was an absolute master. His work stands as his life's achievement. Those shows and ballets will be done over and over again through the years—probably not the way he would want them done—but they're there for all."

Acknowledgments

As a biography dependent on both anecdotal and archival materials, this book could not have been written without the support of hundreds of individuals whose lives were affected one way or another by Jerome Robbins. Those whom I wish to thank first are the members of his family who were generously forthcoming with their recollections, even regarding episodes of his life that remain painful in memory years after the event. Jerome Robbins' sister, Sonia Robbins Cullinen, and his cousin Bob Silverman read the manuscript in progress, provided letters and photographs, and offered invaluable insights concerning Robbins' background, character and artistry. I also turned to his cousins Saul Silverman, Jean Handy, Jack Davenport, Jackye Lee Maduro, Viola Zousmer Balash, Steven Zousmer, and to his brother-in-law, George Cullinen—all of whom gave me their time and encouragement, sharing family lore and treasured mementos.

I am deeply grateful to all who contributed to the book by way of interviews, discourse, advice and guidance. Some of the people who spoke with me did so off the record, but this is not to diminish their contribution and the debt of gratitude I owe them. Among the many whose kind assistance I wish to acknowledge on the record include the following, in alphabetical order: Michael Abbott, Alicia Aedo, Eddie Albert, Cris Alexander, Jason Alexander, D.D. Allen, Sarita Allen, Alicia Alonso, Anita Alvarez-Jacobson, Peter Anastos, Sonia Arova, Leslie Bailey, Kaye Ballard, Margaret Banks, Robert Barnett, Richard Beard, Sonia Berman, Edward Bigelow, Patricia Birch, Hubert Bland, Duane Bodin, Saul Bolasni, Todd Bolender, Jean-Pierre Bonnefoux, Ruthanna Boris, Patricia Bosworth, Lane Bradbury, Isabel Brown, Vida Brown, Perry Bruskin, Rock Brynner, Stacy Caddell, Paul Cadmus, Betty Cage, Maria Calegari, Michael Callan, Gladys Celeste, Ninette Charisse, Zan Charisse-Guest, Martin Charnin, Jerome Chodorov, Sandra Church, John Clifford, Michael Coleman, Jeremy Collins, Alvin Colt, Betty Comden, Christine Conrad, Bart Cook, Sara Corrin, Peter Crehan, Mart Crowley, Judith Cruickshank, Wilma Curley, Grover Dale, Charlotte d'Amboise, Christopher d'Amboise, Carole D'Andrea, Richard D'Arcy, Marilyn D'Honau, Bill Daniels, Danny Daniels, Jules Dassin, Frances Elizabeth Taylor Davis, Merle Debusky, Nathaniel Dorsky, Anthony Dowell, Penny Dudleston-McKay, James Dybas, Ahmet Ertegün, Mark Esposito, Joe Eula, Harvey Evans, Alex Ewing, Nanette Fabray, Betty Farrell, Sarah Felcher, Sally Fishko, Horton Foote, Frederic Franklin, Gerald Freedman, Leon Friedman, Elizabeth Fuchs, Helen Gallagher, Gene Gavin, George Gaynes, Carolyn George, Virginia Gibson, Sal Giglio, Dorothy Gilbert, Madeline Gilford, Bruce Glover, Miriam Golden, Mimi Gomber-Friedman, Dody Goodman, Robert Gottlieb, Ellen Graff, Dick Grayson, Stephen Greco, Adolph Green, Fay Greenbaum, Tamara Halperin, Ann Hamilton, Ellen Hanley, Sheldon Harnick, Maria Harriton, Kitty Carlisle Hart, June Havoc, Kitty Hawks, Doris Hering, Nancy Hess, Gerald Hiken, Christian Holder, Gen Horiuchi, David Howard, Kirsten Hughes, Mary Hunter-Wolf, George Irving, Jean-Claude van Itallie, James Jacobs, Joe James, Jillana (Zimmerman), Alan Johnson, Louis Johnson, Amanda Jones, Gerald Kabat, Charles Kaiser, John Kander, Miriam Karlin, Maria Karnilova, Bill Katheis, Allegra Kent, Michael Kidd, Susan Kikuchi, Yuriko Kikuchi, Alan King, James King, Christopher Kirkland, Jack Klugman, Michael Koessel, Ruth Ann Koesun, Arthur Kopit, Anzia Kubicek, Jerri

Kumery, Ina Kurland-Phillips, Vivian Kurz, Joana Lanza, Philip Lanza Sandor, Gemze de Lappe, Ring Lardner Jr., Arthur Laurents, Carol Lawrence, Eddie Lawrence, Ronnie Lee, Sondra Lee, Daniel Levans, Robert Lindgren, Ralph and Judy Linn, Paula Lloyd, Tony Lo Bianco, Santo Loquasto, Steve Lowe, Annabelle Lyon-Borah, Tim Lyons, Robert Maiorano, Edward Maisel, Dina Makarova, Natalia Makarova, Joe Marshall, Erin Martin, George Martin, Monica Mason, Samuel Matlovsky, Edith Mayro, Jacqueline Mayro, Patricia McBride, Kevin McCormick, Patrick McGilligan, Allyn Ann McLerie, Joey McKneely, Dorothy McNichols-Miller, Allen Midgette, Julia Migenes, Sara Miot, James Mitchell, James Moore, Tony Mordente, Josh Mostel, Fernand Nault, Patricia Neal, Chris Nelson, Augusta and Arnold Newman, David Nillo, Duncan Noble, Jay Norman, Shaun OBrien, Rosalie O'Connor, Sono Osato, Rhoda Oster, Stuart Ostrow, Dame Merle Park, Arthur Partington, Bernie Passeltine, John Percival, Matt Piers, Frank Pietri, Rebecca Pike, David Pressman, Barry Primus, Harold Prince, John Prinz, James Proser, Marilyn Putnam, Megan Raddant, John Randolph, Janet Reed, Ron Rifkin, Chita Rivera, Jaime Rogers, Howard Rosenman, Pat Ross, Mira Rostova, Ian Ruddle, Chuck Rule, Donald Saddler, Stephanie Saland, Peter Schabel, Gerald Schoenfeld, Lynn Seymour, Elizabeth Shub, Stanley Siegel, Michael Smuin, Lois Wheeler Snow, Zachary Solov, Stephen Sondheim, Jean Stapleton, Maureen Stapleton, Joseph Stein, Rebecca Lee Stein, Lisa Stevens, Haila Stoddard, Tom Stone, Norton Styne, Norma Sullivan, Carol Sumner, Martha Swope, Harold Talbott, Maria Tallchief, Russ Tamblyn, John Taras, Glen Tetley, Joan Tewkesbury, Ghislaine Thesmar, Richard Thomas, Ella Thompson, Sylvia Thompson, Rose Tobias-Shaw, Mel Tomlinson, Robert Tracy, Gina Trikonis, Gus Trikonis, Robert Tucker, Norman Twain, Kirsten Valbor-Linhard, Gwen Verdon, Violette Verdy, Edward Verso, Gore Vidal, Edward Villella, Anne Waldman, Royce Wallace, Constance Walter-Weaver, Arnold Walton, Tony Walton, John Weidman, Robert Weiss, Bruce Wells, William Weslow, Lawrence White, Miles White, Karen Whittaker, Patricia Wilde, Robert Wilson, Robert Wise, Rebecca Wright, Craig Zadan, Paul Zilard and Patricia Zipprodt.

I am indebted to my research assistants, Deane Rink of the American Museum of Natural History, and Joel Simon, whose investigative efforts and book in progress, *The Story of Weehawken, New Jersey*, led me to the Rabinowitz and Rips families.

I thank Victor Navasky for sharing with me his research files and interview tapes for his book *Naming Names*. Eric Bentley offered me the benefit of his research on the McCarthy period as well as his personal experiences with Jerome Robbins and Bertolt Brecht. I am also grateful to other writers— Howard Kissel, Larry Warren, Donna Perlmutter and Lynn Garafola—who reviewed the manuscript and offered assistance in piecing together this portrait. Susan Ray provided monumental support and critical perspicacity all along.

I owe special thanks to Gelsey Kirkland, Bonnie Egan, Peter Stelzer, Merle Hubbard, James Adams, Lisa Filloramo, Shaye Areheart, David Fallon, Rudolph Wurlitzer, Patrick McCormick, Julie Cencebaugh, Sandrine Dumas, Yamit Ben-Hamo, Martha Madison, Sarita Morse, Tamie Lynn, Mindy Aloff, Terri Bastedo, Liora Tzur, Greta Nicholas, Dorota Koczewska, Lauren Charlip, Claire Winecoff, Shirley Arden, Cayman and Victoria Abbott, Don Kaltenbach, Vanessa Rohrbach, Carmel Rose, Warren Eydeler, Allison Lee, Fred Cavallaro, Dean Willis, Bert Fink, Ted Chapin, Jonathan Prude, Stephen Davis, Christopher Davis and Brooke Hayward.

My agent, Peter Sawyer, repeatedly went beyond the call of duty in shepherding this project and interceded on my behalf to obtain crucial documents. With regard to representation, I also wish to acknowledge Fifi Oscard's gracious encouragement.

Finally, I commend my judicious editor and publisher, Neil Nyren, and Penguin Putnam's President and CEO, Phyllis Grann, for their vision, forbearance and generous support throughout the journey.

Notes

EPIGRAPH:

xi—Author's interview with Mel Tomlinson, April 9, 1999.

PREFACE:

xiii—"paced with an American tempo": Jerome Robbins, "The Ballet Puts on Dunga-rees," *New York Times Magazine*, October 14, 1945, p. 19.

xiii—His reputation: Jerome Robbins' FBI file, Freedom of Information-Privacy Act, Department of Justice, Memo from FBI agent Edward Scheidt to J. Edgar Hoover, April 27, 1950.

xiv—"Jerry said . . . on him": Author's interview with Bob Silverman, June 7, 1999.

xiv—"He was . . . didn't know?" Author's interview with James Mitchell, April 9, 1999.

xv—"His father . . . worst nightmare": Author's interview with Sheldon Harnick, Jan-uary 27, 1999.

xv—"My son's . . . to him?" Author's interview with Bob Silverman, August 10, 1999.

xv—"Nobody said . . . he went": Author's interview with James Mitchell, April 9, 1999.

xv—"It won't be . . . a shit": Arthur Laurents in Charles Kaiser, *The Gay Metropolis*, Boston: Houghton Mifflin, 1997, p. 73.

xvi—*The Poppa Piece*: the working title at Lincoln Center was later shortened to *Poppa Piece*, though Robbins continued to use the longer title, with that three-word formulation ap-pearing in his will.

xvi—"As we began . . . would change": Author's interview with Jace Alexander, May 24, 1999.

xvi—"I think it . . . for him": Author's interview with Ron Rifkin, March 29, 1999.

xvi—"He would have . . . to see": Author's interview with Joey McKneely, July 1, 1999.

CHAPTER ONE:

1—According to his sister: Author's inteview with Sonia Robbins Cullinen, October 5, 1999.

1—Harry (originally Chane) Rabinowitz: According to his application for a Social Security card in 1936, Harry Rabinowitz was born September 11, 1888. His age on his marriage certificate and in the 1920 census suggest that he was born in 1887. But his gravestone at the Riverside Cemetery in Saddle Brook, New Jersey, indicates that his death occurred December 16, 1977, at the age of eighty-nine.

2—"managed to escape . . . been drafted": Letter to the author from Sonia Robbins Cullinen, July 13, 1999.

2—"If God lived . . . be broken": Howard Kissel, *David Merrick: The Abominable Showman*, New York: Applause Books, 1993, p. 30.

2—"Uncle Harry used to . . . very organized": Letter to the author from Jack Davenport, May 30, 1999.

2—More than fifty other families: 1920 Census.

3—"Lena was . . . first cousins": Author's interview with Viola Zousmer Balash, August 6, 1999.

3—The Rips clan had immigrated: According to Aaron Rips' citizenship papers, he arrived in the United States "on or about" July 24, 1891, a date not supported by evidence in any New York passenger arrival lists, though he may have arrived under a different surname. However, the 1900 Census indicates that the entire family immigrated in 1893. The 1920 Census, recorded when memories may have dimmed, shows Aaron arriving in 1890 and Ida in 1894. The 1920 Census also gives Lena's arrival date as 1895. Further uncertainty arises from daughter Mary's statement on Ida's 1941 death certificate that she had been living in the U.S. for "50 years." It seems likely that either the whole family arrived about July 24, 1891, or that Aaron led the way on that date and sent for Ida and the children in 1893. This last scenario may well come closer to the truth, as Mary's birth in Europe occurred in September of 1891.

3—"was one of the driving forces . . . in Jersey City": Letter to the author from Jack Davenport, May 30, 1999.

4—"Grandma was a great influence . . . from Jerry too": Author's interview with Jean Handy, May 31, 1999.

4—"As a child . . . to the whole business": in Robert Kotlowitz, "Corsets, Corned Beef and Choreography," *Show*, December 1964, p. 91.

4—Mocking his Hebrew tutor: included in the bar mitzvah scene of *The Poppa Piece* as presented to the author by playwright John Weidman, June 1, 1999.

4—Julius went on to head: Letter to the author from Sonia Robbins Cullinen, July 13, 1999.

4—Harry moved his family . . . by way of Jersey City: The 1922 Jersey City Directory indicates that Harry and Lena were residing at 108 Boraem Avenue, only about seven blocks from Aaron and Ida Rips, who were then residing at 406 Palisade Avenue. Sonia Robbins Cullinen, who was about ten years old at the time, has little recollection of this early period of the family relocating.

5—"about three blocks . . . and uninspiring": Jerome Robbins in "Young Man from a Sad Generation," *Junior Bazaar,* April, 1947, p. 136.

5—"We were the same . . . a daredevil": Author's interview with Viola Zousmer Balash, August 6, 1999.

5—"When we were taken . . . of your fingers": Letter to the author from Jack Davenport, May 30, 1999.

6—"None of them . . . all about this stuff": Author's interview with Bob Silverman, June 7, 1999.

6—Sonia suggested . . . be strong . . .": Letter to the author from Sonia Robbins Cullinen, October 15, 1999.

6—"Jerry often talked . . . during those years": Author's interview with Bob Silverman, June 7, 1999.

6–7—"My father . . . this stuff": Author's interview with Bob Silverman, June 7, 1999.

7—Another show-business connection: Letter to the author from Jack Davenport, May 30, 1999.

7–8—"Their concern . . . waiting for me": "Corsets, Corned Beef and Choreography," *Show,* December 1964, p. 39.

8—"Mother told me . . . very well": Eleanor Roberts, "Ballet Brings Fame to Ex-Chorus Boy," *Boston Post Magazine,* May 9, 1948, p. 15.

8—"like a squirrel hoarding nuts": "Young Man from a Sad Generation," *Junior Bazaar,* April 1947, p. 136.

8—"She had this great . . . by ear": Author's inteview with Sonia Robbins Cullinen, October 5, 1999. Composer-publisher Bob Silverman offered a clarification: "Sonia's probably thinking of the circle of fifths. I probably know about as much as anyone about the various methods for teaching harmony since I was the major domo, director of publications of three of the largest music publishing companies. As you may know, the only difference between a major and minor chord is the handling of the third note in the scale. As to augmented chords, there is no formula. There are augmented jazz chords and the famous augmented chords of Scriabin and Wagner, but that's about it." Letter by e-mail to the author from Bob Silverman, October 11, 1999.

8—"My parents' home . . . forget it": Author's interview with Dorothy Gilbert, October 4, 1999.

8—"I painted . . . the way they were": "Corsets, Corned Beef and Choreography," *Show,* December 1964, p. 39.

9—"Both Jerry and I . . . wanted to do": Author's inteview with Sonia Robbins Cullinen, October 5, 1999.

9—"a man of humor . . . practical jokes": Letter to the author from Sonia Robbins Cullinen, July 13, 1999.

9—"Jerry's father was a . . . from his father": Author's interview with Bob Silverman, June 13, 1999.

9–10—"Harry was sarcastic . . . Harry's vision": Author's interview with Bob Silverman, August 10, 1999.

10—"We had fights . . . saying that": Author's inteview with Sonia Robbins Cullinen, October 5, 1999.

10—"To his father . . . come into this": Author's interview with Viola Zousmer Balash, August 10, 1999.

10—"What I remember . . . bad relationship": Author's interview with Sheldon Harnick, January 27, 1999. While Robbins' sister has no specific recollection of their father ever dressing up as Santa Claus, Jerry did indeed receive a toy train as a gift, lending credence to the anecdote. A *Junior Bazaar* celebrity portrait reported that "Robbins still remembers with some pride that he was the first child among his acquaintances to boast an electric train." From "Young Man from a Sad Generation," *Junior Bazaar*, April 1947, p. 136.

11—"You have to . . . took courage": Author's interview with Viola Zousmer Balash, August 10, 1999.

11—"I think it was . . . strong, powerful women": Author's interview with Fay Greenbaum, June 13,1999.

11—"When I was five . . . years a scar": Letter to the author from Sonia Robbins Cullinen, July 13, 1999.

12—"As I grew up . . . my mother": Letter to the author from Sonia Robbins Cullinen, July 13, 1999.

12—"That music I feel . . . in there": Robbins interviewed by Edwin Denby, *Dance Magazine*, May 1969. Quoted in George Balanchine and Francis Mason, *101 Stories of the Great Ballets*, New York: Doubleday, 1975, p. 107.

12–13—"Sonia showed the . . . to be rivalry": Author's interview with Bob Silverman, August 10, 1999.

13—"Disagreeing with her . . . me to learn": Author's interview with Sonia Robbins Cullinen, October 5, 1999, and letter to the author from SRC, October 15, 1999.

13—He credited his . . ."cut his imagination loose": *New Jersey Observer*, August 28, 1946.

14—"Jerry had a . . . a deep secret": Author's interview with James D. Jacobs, April 6, 1999.

14–15—"I was a . . . living with them": Author's interview with Dorothy Gilbert, October 4, 1999.

15—"Jerry never liked me . . . rest of his life": Author's interview with Arnold Walton, April 15, 1999.

15—"Jerry gave an . . . things you keep": Author's interview with Jean Handy, May 31, 1999.

15—"We were in . . . hasn't got it' ": Author's interview with Viola Zousmer Balash, August 10, 1999.

15—Having first taken classes . . . Carnegie Hall. Ruthanna Boris, a Balanchine-trained dancer and choreographer, described Alyce Bentley as "the Madwoman of Carnegie Hall . . . a Duncan air about her . . . the original female revolutionary . . . and lots of wild hair. . . . We all used to run away from Balanchine from time to time and then go fly, sometimes taking interpretive classes. They were all offshoots of Duncan.": Author's interview with Ruthanna Boris, March 1, 1999.

17—"He will undoubtedly . . . he is unique": John Martin, *America Dancing: The Background and Personalities of the Modern Dance*, Brooklyn, NY: Dance Horizons, 1968 (first published in 1938), p. 259.

17—This was the singular artist . . . "guru": *Bessie: A Portrait of Bessie Schoenberg*, documentary, Pennebaker Hegedus Films, Inc., 1998.

18—"We dancers were taught . . . of an actor": Jerome Robbins in "Robbins Thinks Big About Dances," *New York Times*, May 29, 1983.

18—"He was a dynamo . . . there was magic": Lynn Garafola (ed.), *José Limón, An Unfinished Memoir*, Middletown, CT: Wesleyan University Press, 1999, p. 47.

19—Another dancer recalled . . ."very young teenagers": Author's interview with Anzia Kubicek, March 28, 1999.

19—"This adaptability . . . great affection": Author's interview with Ghislaine Thesmar, October 11, 1999.

20—Dressed in coat and tie: Oral History Project, Dance Collection, NYPL, Jerome Robbins interviewed by Ellen Sorrin, November 28, 1995.

21—"Jerry would . . . very busy'": Author's interview with Philip Lanza Sandor, February 27, 1999.

21—"He had what you call . . . plunged into it": Senia Gluck Sandor in Emily Coleman, "From Tutus to T-Shirts," *New York Times Magazine*, October 8, 1961, pp. 30, 32.

21—Prophetically, Sandor advised: "Robbins Weighs the Future: Ballet or Broadway?" *New York Times*, Arts and Leisure, July 12, 1981, p. 20.

21—"I took his advice . . . understand it then": "Robbins Thinks Big About Dances," *New York Times*, May 29, 1983.

21—"I pushed . . . to the barre'": Author's inteview with Sonia Robbins Cullinen, October 5, 1999.

21—"It was like . . . on with it'": *Bessie: A Portrait of Bessie Schoenberg*, documentary, Pennebaker Hegedus Films, Inc., 1998.

21–22—"I used to . . . better than ballet": "Dancing Through Life," *Newsweek*, March 6, 1989, p. 56.

22—The New Dance Group: Ellen Graff, *Stepping Left: Dance and Politics in New York City, 1828–1942*, Durham, N.C: Duke University Press, 1997, pp. 6–9, 160.

22—Acting on Sandor's . . ."big someday": Author's interview with Philip Lanza Sandor, February 27, 1999.

22—Jerry's sister remembered dancing with her brother: The original program of *The Brothers Ashkenazi* (in the Theater Collection of The Museum of the City of New York) does not include Sonia's stage name (Sonya Robyns), but later programs do. It is likely that she would have joined the cast later in the run.

23—"Because I looked . . . yes, Father'": "Jerome Robbins at 60: Some Vital Reflections," *Washington Post*, Calendar, March 18, 1979, p. 70.

23—The two words: Sol Hurok Attractions, publicity biography of Jerome Robbins, circa 1942, Dance Collection, New York Public Library.

23—"The whole thing . . . made it fifteen dollars": *Washington Post*, Calendar, March 18, 1979, p. 70.

23—"Others outstanding . . . Jerome Robbins": in Doris Hering, "Jerry's Legacy," *Dance Magazine*, April, 1989.

23—"Next day when . . . muttered around": Sol Hurok Attractions, publicity biography of Jerome Robbins, circa 1944, Dance Collection, New York Public Library.

23–24—"He was . . . anybody": Author's interview with Sonia Robbins Cullinen, October 5, 1999.

24—"There was a . . . total obsession": Author's interview with Elizabeth Shub, June 7, 1999.

24—"Robbins' partnering . . . helps the performance:": Anatole Chujoy in *Dance*, January 1938.

24—His sister remembered . . . that show": Letter to the author from Sonia Robbins Cullinen, October 15, 1999.

25—"Jerry said . . . after that'": Author's interview with Barry Primus, May 6, 1999.

25—Robbins later recalled—Oral History Project, Dance Collection, NYPL, Jerome Robbins interviewed by Ellen Sorrin, November 28, 1995.

26—"I used to come . . . be back tomorrow'": *Entertainment Weekly*, August 14, 1998, p. 70.

26—If there was any disappointment: Author's interview with Anzia Kubicek, March 28, 1999. Kubicek recalled, "I went to the opening night of *Fancy Free*. I said, 'Sandor, you should go, why are you not going?' And he said, No, no, no, he wouldn't go. So I called him up during intermission and raved about everything from the Met. . . . At that time they were apparently not on the best of terms. Let it go at that." Philip Lanza Sandor said, "Jerry was in love with Sandor the way that Bernstein was in love with Koussevitsky." Both Sandor and Bernstein's mentor, Serge Koussevitsky, were uncompromising in their principles and highly skeptical of commercial art.

CHAPTER TWO:

27—Not long after . . . yet to be decided: Humphrey Burton, *Leonard Bernstein*, New York: Anchor Books, 1994, pp. 41–43.

28—"It was a rough period . . . in every way": "Corsets, Corned Beef and Choreography," *Show*, December 1964, p. 39.

28—"As I remember her . . . morally loose": Author's interview with Bob Silverman, July 7, 1999.

28—"the stereotype . . . not least": Letter from Sonia Robbins Cullinen to the author, November 29, 1999.

28—"rock-ribbed Republican": Author's interview with Bob Silverman, July 7, 1999.

28—"Everybody in the family . . . wasn't verbal": Author's interview with Bob Silverman, June 23, 1999.

29—"His enthusiasm . . . theater and dance": Author's interview with Saul Silverman, June 20, 1999.

29—"I cannot recall . . . conversational topic": Author's interview with Bob Silverman, August 18, 1999.

29—"It was . . . you have!": Author's interview with Sonia Robbins Cullinen, October 5, 1999.

29—"I think that . . . get married": Author's interview with Bob Silverman, June 13, 1999.

29—"I knew him . . . on a girl": Author's interview with Viola Zousmer, August 6, 1999.

29–30—Given the widespread . . . into the sixties: Kaiser, *The Gay Metropolis*, pp. 22–30.

30—"He would say . . . to choreograph": Author's interview with Alicia Alonso, September 14, 1999.

30—Unfortunately for Jerry . . . into the wings: Sol Hurok Attractions, publicity biography of Jerome Robbins, circa 1944, Dance Collection, New York Public Library.

31—"Let's throw all . . . and movies": Bob Thomas, *I Got Rhythm!: The Ethel Merman Story*, New York: G. P. Putnam's Sons, 1985, p. 63.

31—"Stars in Your Eyes . . . named Jerome Robbins": Joshua Logan, *Josh: My Up and Down, In and Out Life*, New York: Delacorte Press, 1976, pp. 142–143.

31—"Musicals tend . . . be done": *Boston Post Magazine*, May 9, 1948.

31—"During the . . . Jerome Robbins": Logan, *Josh: My Up and Down, In and Out Life*, p. 143.

32—"He was the boy . . . girls' beds": Author's interview with Ruthanna Boris, February 8, 1999.

32—"I was part . . . choreographic sketches": *New York Times*, February 4, 1974, p. 6.

32—Talent for Tamiment's Theater: Martha Schmoyer LoMonaco, *Every Week, A Broadway Revue: The Tamiment Playhouse, 1921–1960*, New York Greenwood Press, Contribution in Drama and Dance Studies, Number 45, pp. 2–7.

32—"Ziegfeld of television": Doris Hering, "Conversation with Max Leibman," *Dance Magazine*, March 1955.

32—A Balanchine-trained dancer: Author's interview with Ruthanna Boris, February 8, 1999.

33—"Danny wanted . . . didn't fight me": Author's interview with Ruthanna Boris, February 8, 1999.

33—Boris also . . . mile away": Author's interview with Ruthanna Boris, March 14, 1999.

33—"young man with laughing eyes": *Ballet Review*, Summer 1988, p. 15.

33—"Mr. Happy": LoMonaco, *Every Week, A Broadway Revue*, p. 60.

33–34—"As the summer . . . into *On the Town*": Dorothy Bird, *Bird's Eye View: Dancing with Martha Graham and on Broadway*, Pittsburgh: University of Pittsburgh Press, 1997, pp. 155–156. Robbins' 1947 résumé (Dance Collection, New York Public Library) indicates that during the summer of 1939 he choreographed solos in *A Sailors' Hornpipe* and in *A Sword Dance*.

34—"He was very . . . a ballet dancer": Author's interview with Anita Alvarez, June 17, 1999.

34–35—"In the middle . . . a masterpiece": Bird, *Bird's Eye View*, p. 156.

35—Robbins received a . . . investigation: Joan Peyser, *Bernstein: A Biography*, New York: Billboard Books, 1998, p. 229. According to Peyser, "Robbins even sent a letter thanking her [Ocko] for the boost to his career." Ocko apparently traveled in related circles as she had helped to find an apartment for Leonard Bernstein and Adolph Green in the summer of 1939, although Robbins had not yet met either Bernstein or Green.

35—"laughed at all . . . minutes long": "The ballet really comes to town," Sunday Magazine Section of *PM*, undated, circa 1944, Dance Collection, New York Public Library.

35—In 1939, he created: The program for the show dated July 22, 1939, in the Tamiment Library at New York University indicates that Robbins' first individual choreographic credit at Tamiment was for *Death of a Loyalist*.

35—Five years later: *New York Times*, March 3, 1945, cited in a letter to FBI Director J. Edgar Hoover from agent Edward Scheidt, dated April 27, 1950, obtained through a Freedom of Information-Privacy Act request.

36—While at Tamiment: The program for a 1941 show in the Tamiment Library indicates that Robbins' contribution was entitled *Lazy Boy*, which was part of a Max Leibman evening called *You Can't Get Away from It All*. Robbins performed the role of Tom, presumably Tom Sawyer.

36—"He was mysteriously . . . my shell": Bird, *Bird's Eye View*, pp. 154–159.

37—"In personal . . . goes way back": Author's interview with Anita Alvarez, June 17, 1999.

37—Tamiment led . . . for material": LoMonaco, *Every Week, A Broadway Revue*, pp. 68–78.

37—"It was pretty . . . a show": LoMonaco, *Every Week, A Broadway Revue*, p. 92.

38—"I could not . . . me to be": Bird, *Bird's Eye View*, p. 159.

39—"such a god . . . own identity": P. W. Manchester, "Jerome Robbins—Theater Man," *Ballet Annual*, New York: MacMillan, 1961, pp. 114–115.

39—"Balanchine came . . . José Limón": *New York Times*, May 21, 1984, Section C, p. 11.

39–40—"trying to conceal . . . empty and meaningless": Garafola (ed.), *José Limón: An Unfinished Memoir*, pp. 93–94.

40—An asthmatic condition: Robbins' FBI file, Freedom of Information-Privacy Act, Department of Justice.

40—"I was not . . . somewhere else": *New York Times*, May 29, 1994, II 20:1.

40—"World War II . . . New York": Ibid.

40—"a dismal . . . behind him": Garafola (ed.), *José Limón: An Unfinished Memoir*, p. 94.

41—Over the years Chase: Donna Perlmutter, *Shadowplay: The Life of Antony Tudor*, New York: Viking, 1991, p. 126.

41—"international in . . . in spirit": Richard Pleasant in Walter Terry, *Alicia and her Ballet Nacional de Cuba*, New York: Anchor Books, 1981, p. 15.

41—"I felt sorry . . . robbing him": Perlmutter, *Shadowplay: The Life of Antony Tudor*, p. 109.

42—Balanchine turned down: Richard Buckle and John Taras, *George Balanchine: Ballet Master*, New York, Random House, 1988, pp. 122–123.

42—"The Greatest . . . Ballet History: Clive Barnes, *Inside American Ballet Theatre*, New York: Hawthorne Books, 1977, p. 3.

42—The expensive overhead: Richard Buckle and John Taras, *George Balanchine: Ballet Master*, New York: Random House, 1988, p. 123.

42—"We were . . . after a while": Author's interview with David Nillo, December 13, 1998.

43—"He didn't . . . his family": Author's interview with Viola Zousmer Balash, August 10, 1999.

43—"We auditioned . . . usually am": Anton Dolin in Terry, *Alicia and Her Ballet Nacional*, p. 17.

43—"We were so . . . the company": Alicia Alonso in Terry, *Alicia and Her Ballet Nacional*, p. 17.

43–44—"All I can . . . imagine?": Author's interview with Miriam Golden, August 30, 1999.

44—"He spoke . . . the union": Author's interview with Alicia Alonso, September 14, 1999.

44—"We were . . . their ballets": Miriam Golden in Perlmutter, *Shadowplay: The Life of Antony Tudor*, p. 112.

44—"We did . . . act and dance": Author's interview with Sono Osato, May 3, 1999.

45—"We didn't . . . out asleep": Author's interview with Michael Kidd, March 28, 1999.

45—"There were times . . . the company": Author's interview with John Taras, March 31, 1999.

45–46—"In those days . . . for one": Jerome Robbins in Tobi Tobias, "Bringing Back Robbins's Fancy Free," *Dance Magazine*, January, 1980, p. 72.

46—"a lighthearted little ballet": John Martin, *New York Times*, August 2, 1940.

46—"We knew . . . for him": Author's interview with Donald Saddler, September 10, 1999.

46—"hanging around . . . Tudor Ballet": Jerome Robbins, Tudor memorial, Juilliard, June 9, 1987.

47—"I think . . . very much": Author's interview with Alicia Alonso, September 14, 1999.

47—"When Tudor . . . she was": *New York Times*, June 8, 1977.

47—"Jerry was . . . Tudor and Hugh": Author's interview with Mimi Gomber-Friedman, September 10, 1999.

48—"I remember . . . to berth": Author's interview with Mimi Gomber-Friedman, September 10, 1999.

48—"Jerry and I. . . . at rehearsals": Author's interview with John Taras, March 31, 1999.

48—"I remember . . . to leave": Author's interview with Janet Reed, May 16, 1999.

48—"You get closer . . . deserved it": *Ballet Review*, Summer 1988, p. 19.

48–49—"He was innocent . . . as such": Author's interview with Maria Karnilova, September 10, 1999.

49–50—"Jerry was . . . with anybody": Author's interview with Mimi Gomber-Friedman, September 10, 1999.

50—"he withdrew . . . contemplate": Author's interview with Janet Reed, August 2, 1999.

50—"Jerry was . . . about dancing": Author's interview with Alicia Alonso, September 14, 1999.

50—"He really . . . came out": Author's interview with Mimi Gomber-Friedman, September 10, 1999.

50—"He used to . . . take off": Author's interview with Hubert Bland, April 21, 1999.

50—"little satire . . . virginal vanity": Edwin Denby, *New York Herald Tribune,* June 28, 1943.

51—"I wanted . . . the show": *Dance Magazine,* March 1958, p. 69.

51—"He was . . . for it": Author's interview with Annabelle Lyon, March 13, 1999.

51—"Offstage he . . . with glee": Sono Osato, *Distant Dances,* New York: Alfred A. Knopf, 1980, p. 229.

51—"laughing out loud": Author's interview with Sono Osato, May 3, 1999.

51—"high praise": John Martin, *New York Times,* February 12, 1941, 24:1.

51—Robbins provided: Sol Hurok Attractions, publicity biography of Jerome Robbins, circa 1944, Dance Collection, NYPL.

52—"I met . . . in touch": Author's interview with Horton Foote, April 18, 1999.

52—"We were . . . his work": Author's interview with Mary Hunter Wolf, April 11, 1999.

52–53—"There was . . . his mind": Author's interview with Janet Reed, February 24, 1999.

53—"Jerry was . . . choreographer himself": Author's interview with Maria Karnilova, September 10, 1999.

53—"It was . . . and that": *Newsweek,* March 6, 1989, p. 56.

53—"does it . . . nice joke": Edwin Denby, *New York Herald Tribune,* October 18, 1943.

53–54—"Jerry had . . . he looked": Author's interview with Richard Thomas, April 27, 1999.

54—"He was . . . at them": Author's interview with Alicia Alonso, September 14, 1999.

54—"Jerry, of course . . . did it": Author's interview with Annabelle Lyon, March 13, 1999.

54—"We were . . . was heaven": Author's interview with Maria Karnilova, September 10, 1999.

54—When he first arrived: Letter from Jerome Robbins to Jean Handy, 1942.

54–55—"We had . . . by them": Author's interview with Maria Karnilova, September 10, 1999.

55—"I looked . . . those days!": Barnes, *Inside American Ballet Theatre,* p. 94.

55—"Fokine encouraged . . . work with": Barnes, *Inside American Ballet Theatre,* p. 94.

55—"No one . . . forty years": Clive Barnes, *Dance Magazine,* August 1990, p. 82.

55—"Dancing is . . . their ground": *The Theatre,* July 1960, p. 46. Originally appeared in *PM,* October 24, 1946.

56—"The Greatest . . . Ballet Theater": cited in Perlmutter, *Shadowplay: The Life of Antony Tudor,* p. 126.

56—"I was in . . . babushkas and boots": *New York Post,* September 18, 1958.

56—Robbins' rebellion: Jerome Robbins' FBI file, Freedom of Information-Privacy Act, Department of Justice.

56—"several instances . . . their causes": *Eric Bentley, Thirty Years of Treason: Excerpts from Hearings Before the House Committee on Un-American Activities, 1938–1968,* New York: Viking Press, 1971, p. 630.

56—Reputedly anti-Semitic: Perlmutter, *Shadowplay: The Life of Antony Tudor,* p. 127. Also, Charles Payne, *American Ballet Theatre,* New York: Knopf, 1978, pp. 109–120.

56–57—"I remember . . . the word": Author's interview with Mary Hunter Wolf, April 11, 1999.

57—According to playwright Arthur Laurents: Letter to the author from Arthur Laurents, May 18, 1999.

57—"At one point . . . go along": Author's interview with Kirsten Valbor, June 9, 1999.

57–59—"Lois and I . . . irate and left": Author's interview with Madeline Gilford, December 4, 1998.

59—"I had been . . . few people": Barnes, *Inside American Ballet Theatre*, p. 94.

59—"She suggested . . . an idea": Jerome Robbins in *New York Times*, February 4, 1974, p. 18.

59—The 1934 painting: For an account of the Cadmus exhibition and controversy, see David Leddick, *Intimate Companions: A Triography of George Platt Lynes, Paul Cadmus, Lincoln Kirstein, and Their Circle*, New York: St. Martin's Press, 2000, pp. 47–49.

59—"I was . . . used it": Author's interview with Mary Hunter Wolf, April 11, 1999.

60—"I would see . . . about it": Author's interview with Paul Cadmus, March 2, 1999.

60—"After seeing . . . about them": *Christian Science Monitor*, May 13, 1944.

60—"At that time . . . dancing then": Tobi Tobias, "Bringing Back Robbins's Fancy Free," *Dance Magazine*, January 1980, p. 69.

61—"We were . . . the choreography": Author's interview with Janet Reed, August 2, 1999.

61—"I remember . . . for sets": *Theatre Arts*, December 1957, p. 80.

61—So began a warm friendship: Author's interview with Richard D'Arcy, July 28, 1999.

62—"He had been . . . suggested Lenny": Peyser, *Bernstein*, p. 136.

62—"I went . . . we did": Tobi Tobias, "Bringing Back Robbins's Fancy Free," *Dance Magazine*, January 1980, p. 70.

62—"Funny you . . . was born": Burton, *Leonard Bernstein*, pp. 126–127.

62–63—"If I had . . . New York": Tobi Tobias, "Bringing Back Robbins's Fancy Free," *Dance Magazine*, January 1980, p. 70.

63—"They went . . . being written": Author's interview with Richard D'Arcy, July 28, 1999.

63—"When Bernstein . . . *Fancy Free*": Letter to the author from Gore Vidal, March 16, 1999.

63—Vidal told: Gore Vidal, *Palimpsest: A Memoir*, New York: Random House, 1995, pp. 127– 132.

63—"He meant the men": Author's interview with Janet Reed, May 16, 1999.

64—"They were . . . other's way": Author's interview with Janet Reed, May 16, 1999.

64—"Johnny Kriza . . . from him": Author's interview with Janet Reed, August 17, 1999.

64—"The real love . . . loved Johnny": Author's interview with Shaun O'Brien, May 18, 1999.

64—"He and Jerry . . . *Fancy Free*": Letter to the author from Arthur Laurents, June 28, 1999.

64–65—"Jerry really . . . like him": Tobi Tobias, "Bringing Back Robbins's Fancy Free,"*Dance Magazine,* January 1980, p. 71.

65—"Muriel told . . . Jerome Robbins": Author's interview with Betty Farrell, May 9, 1999.

65—"patent leather . . . the point": *New York Times,* November 2, 1997.

65–66—"It was just . . . meant to do": Tobi Tobias, "Bringing Back Robbins's Fancy Free," *Dance Magazine,* January, 1980, p. 72.

66—"had to be exact": Ibid.

66—"He took . . . personalities": *New York Times,* November 2, 1997.

66—The time: George Amberg, *Ballet in America,* New York: Duell, Sloan & Pearce, 1949.

66—"The curtain rises . . . the ballet": Burton, *Leonard Bernstein,* pp. 126–127.

67—"sudden hysteria": Betty Comden in Peyser, *Bernstein,* p. 138.

67—"I rushed . . . performance": Author's interview with Adolph Green, July 26, 1999.

67—There was yet another: *Theatre Arts,* July 1950, p. 48.

67–68—"While the audience . . . the theatre": Agnes de Mille, *And Promenade Home,* London: Virgin Books, 1989, p. 175.

68—"louder and funnier": *Cue,* May 1944.

68—"To come . . . the theater": John Martin, *New York Times,* April 19, 1944.

68—"It is really . . . on it": "The ballet really comes to town," Sunday Magazine Section of *PM,* undated, circa 1944, Dance Collection, NYPL.

68—That first night Jerry attended: Author's interview with Betty Comden and Adolph Green, July 26, 1999. Comden and Green recollected Robbins reading John Martin's review aloud at the opening night party. Green recalled, "There was a look on his face, it wasn't joyous, it was a grim, almost unhappy look. Do you remember that, Betty?" Comden said, "I remember that moment absolutely. Yeah, it was kind of a frozen look and a little forbidding."

68–69—"The doors . . . and peace": de Mille, *And Promenade Home, p.* 176.

69—"I was lying . . . changed my life'": Author's interview with Bob Silverman, June 7, 1999.

69—"It was a . . . inside of myself": Jerome Robbins in Tobi Tobias, "Bringing Back Robbins's Fancy Free," *Dance Magazine,* January 1980, p. 76.

69—In the next year: *New York Times,* February 19, 1989.

70—"They wanted . . . 'Let's go'": Peyser, *Bernstein,* p. 143.

70—"I didn't realize . . . arms flailing": "Young Man from a Sad Generation," *Junior Bazaar,* April 1947, p. 138.

70—"Heavens knows . . . all right": *The Theatre,* July 1960, p. 46.

CHAPTER THREE:

71—Epigraph: Betty Comden and Adolph Green, *On the Town*

71—"We were all . . . package together": *Reaching for the Note,* PBS documentary on Bernstein.

71—"We wrote . . . any better": *Newsweek,* March 6, 1989, p. 56.

72—"With *On the Town* . . . his shoulders": Author's interview with Sono Osato, May 3, 1999.

72—"There was not . . . New York, period": Dramatists Guild Round Table, 1981.

73—"roaring egos": *New York Times,* January 8, 1945.

73—"Your assistant, Abbott": *Cue,* February 14, 1948, p. 13.

73—"Leonard Bernstein . . . same doctor": *New York Post,* June 13, 1944.

73—"He may be . . . a pain": in John Richmond, "A Silhouette of Leonard Bernstein," *Tomorrow,* March 19, 1945.

73—"dream . . . villa": Cited in Humphrey Burton, *Leonard Bernstein,* New York: Doubleday, Anchor Books, Bantam, p. 131.

73—"Jerry had . . . at that time": Author's interview with Todd Bolender, April 23, 1999.

73–74—"Nancy went . . . other up": Author's interview with Cris Alexander, May 20, 1999.

74—"Hollywood is . . . to juggle": Cited in Burton, *Leonard Bernstein,* p. 131.

74—"The main thing . . . war brings": *New York Times,* January 8, 1945.

75—"There'd never . . . *On the Town*": Author's interview with Alvin Colt, July 26, 1999.

75—"that Prokofyef stuff": Cited in Ethan Mordden, *Beautiful Mornin': The Broadway Musical in the 1940s,* New York: Oxford University Press, 1999, p. 125.

75—"that made . . . classical": Sono Osato, *Distant Dances,* New York: Alfred A. Knopf, 1980, p. 240.

75—"I believe this . . . these dances": Program, San Francisco Symphony Orchestra, February 12, 1946.

76—"Jerry's choreography . . . never sleeps": Osato, *Distant Dances,* p. 241.

76—"I remember . . . wasn't me": Author's interview with Allyn Ann McLerie, February 2, 1999.

76—"During . . . the time": Author's interview with Cris Alexander, May 18, 1999.

76—"He was . . . trigger it": Author's interview with Sono Osato, May 3, 1999.

76—"Jerry had . . . one person": Author's interview with Mary Hunter Wolf, April 11, 1999.

77—"driving fear . . . him angry": Author's interview with Janet Reed, November 1, 1999.

77—"I know . . . he wanted": Author's interview with Jean Handy, May 31, 1999.

77—"You didn't . . . phobia in you": Author's interview with Royce Wallace, June 4, 1999.

78—"He was intense . . . all the time": Author's interview with Dorothy McNichols, June 3, 1999.

78—"As far as . . . was right": Author's interview with Richard D'Arcy, March 9, 1999.

78—"I thought . . . about then": *Newsweek,* March 6, 1989, p. 56.

79—"I liked . . . and decisive": "Ballet, Broadway and a Birthday," Jerome Robbins interviewed by Clive Barnes, *Dance and Dancers,* June 1989, p. 16.

79—"They had . . . whole thing": Author's interview with Saul Silverman, June 20, 1999.

79–80—"I liked . . . properly hung": George Abbott, *Mister Abbott,* New York: Random House, 1963, p. 200.

80—"It was . . . him back": Author's interview with Richard D'Arcy, March 9, 1999.

80—"Jerry went . . . analyst": Author's interview with Duncan Noble: March 28, 1999.

80—Hunter said . . . acquainted": Author's interview with Mary Hunter Wolf, April 11, 1999.

80—"a neurotic condition": Robbins' FBI file, Freedom of Information-Privacy Act, Department of Justice, Memo from FBI agent Edward Scheidt to J. Edgar Hoover, April 27, 1950. As far as neuroses in the theater, George Abbott wrote in *Mister Abbott*, "Everybody in the creative side of theater is neurotic. The reason is obvious. A child who has a happy, care-free extroverted childhood does not turn his thoughts inward, does not stimulate his imagination with another world in order to escape from this one. It is the boy or girl with troubles who is thrown back upon himself, who lives in a fantasy world, who develops an ability and talent for the make-believe. Generally, however, the neuroses are under control and a certain objectivity is in command until the production is launched."

80–81—"About Jerry's . . . the time": Author's interview with Lois Wheeler Snow, May 17, 1999.

81—"Homosexuality . . . illness": Sigmund Freud, reprinted in Ronald Bayer, *Homosexuality and American Psychiatry*, Princeton: Princeton University Press, 1987, p. 27.

81—"That was . . . cause": Author's interview with Mary Hunter Wolf, April 11, 1999.

81—"He must . . . at all": Author's interview with Sono Osato, May 3, 1999.

81—"could develop . . . here": *Variety*, December 20, 1944.

82—"Maybe it . . . all time": Letter from Leonard Bernstein to Aaron Copland, September, 1944, reprinted in Burton, *Leonard Bernstein*, p. 133.

82—"Standing in . . . of nature": Osato, *Distant Dances*, p. 242.

82—"the freshest . . . Oklahoma": *New York Times*, December 29, 1944.

82—"a reviewer . . . superlatives": Associated Press, December 29, 1944.

82—"Mr. Robbins' . . . its place": *PM*, December 29, 1944.

83—"the ballet revolution . . . all three": Jerome Robbins, "Ballet Puts on Dungarees," *New York Times Magazine*, October 14, 1945, pp. 18–19.

83–84—"Jerry and Lenny . . . of mind": Cited in Joan Peyser, *Bernstein: A Biography*, New York: Billboard Books, 1998, p. 137.

84—"It was . . . racial prejudice": Osato, *Distant Dances*, p. 243.

84—"We had . . . prejudices": Author's interview with Dorothy McNichols, June 3, 1999.

85—"That's . . . *my* show": Author's interview with Royce Wallace, June 4, 1999.

85—"He lives . . . relationships": Emily Coleman, "From Tutus to T-Shirts," *New York Times Magazine*, October 8, 1961, p. 32.

85—"It was . . . hide it": Author's interview with Richard D'Arcy, March 9, 1999.

85—"you knew . . . the edge": *New York Blade News*, March 12, 1999.

85—"in a sense . . . audience": Author's interview with Jean-Claude van Itallie, October 11, 1999.

86—"One reason . . . convictions": Charles Kaiser, *The Gay Metropolis*, Boston: Houghton Mifflin Company, 1997, p. 89.

86—"They were . . . Communists": Author's interview with Harold Talbott, January 10, 1999.

86—"Oliver lived . . . the times": Author's interview with Richard D'Arcy, March 9, 1999.

87—"I was invited . . . sense": Jerome Robbins in Robert Kotlowitz, "Corsets, Corned Beef and Choreography," *Show*, December, 1964, p. 91.

87—"I think that . . . not help that": Author's interview with Sono Osato, May 3, 1999.

87—"The idea . . . like that": Stephen Sondheim in Kaiser, *The Gay Metropolis*, p. 89.

87—"I think . . . the analyst": Letter to the author from Arthur Laurents, April 25, 1999.

88—"I came out . . . a facade": Author's interview with Bob Silverman, June 7, 1999.

88–89—"I auditioned . . . for me": Author's interview with Ina Kurland, March 13, 1999.

90—A practice that continued during the 1940s until the unions finally imposed stricter rules: Changes in union policy for dancers, actors and musicians in the theater were more or less ignored by Robbins. As his longtime assistant, Robert Tucker, put it, "Jerry broke every rule in Equity that there ever was." Author's interview with Robert Tucker, May 12, 1999.

90—"He had . . . loved him": Author's interview with Helen Gallagher, April 13, 1999.

91—"that the system . . . motive')": Charles Payne, *American Ballet Theatre*, New York: Alfred A. Knopf, 1978, p. 152.

91—"I saw . . . his way": Author's interview with Alex Ewing, March 11, 1999.

91—Ninette Charisse: Of Robbins taking her ballet class, Charisse recalled, "We used to call him the 'little Graham dancer,'" referring to Robbins' early modern training. Author's interview with Ninette Charisse, May 12, 1999.

91—"The moment . . . taking class": Author's interview with Glen Tetley, January 20, 1999.

92—"Jerry would . . . that person?'": Author's interview with Robert Tucker, May 12, 1999.

92—According to many observers: Among them, Richard Altman, who later worked as Robbins' assistant on *Fiddler on the Roof*, wrote, "I watched the way Edith worked with Jerry and realized that she was his machinery, swift and efficient, and much of the time his memory as well. She would keep track of things he said he wanted and sometimes forgot to do, and whenever he appeared by her desk she was ready for him . . . Because she was such a gifted administrator and his affairs were so capably managed, Jerry was free to function creatively in his own higgledy-piggledy way." Altman recalled Weissman saying, "When Jerry asks for something, he doesn't want it today or tomorrow, he wants it yesterday." Richard Altman with Mervyn Kaufman, *The Making of a Musical: Fiddler on the Roof*, New York: Crown Publishers, 1971, p. 87.

92—"suave . . . dresser": Author's interview with Janet Reed, February 28, 1999.

92—"Dorso was . . . Hills": Letter to the author from Arthur Laurents, May 21, 1999.

92—"At one point . . . the score": Paul Bowles, *Without Stopping: An Autobiography*, New York: Ecco Press, 1972, p. 273.

93—"'Interplay' looks . . . of passion": *New York Herald Tribune*, November 4, 1945.

93—"contemporary idiom . . . composition": *PM*, undated article circa 1945, Ballet Theatre Scrapbook, Dance Collection, NYPL.

93—"I think . . . about dance": in P. W. Manchester, "Jerome Robbins—Theatre Man," *Ballet Annual*, 1961, New York: MacMillan, 1960, p. 115. Robbins described the same encounter to Clive Barnes and suggested the trip was made by "boat": Clive Barnes, *Inside American Ballet Theater*, New York: Hawthorne Books, 1977, p. 93.

93—"Balanchine liked . . . tour de force": Author's interview with Janet Reed, November 1, 1999.

94—"I'm so . . . could desire," *New York Daily News*, May 25, 1945.

94–95—"the DAILY WORKER . . . a sponsor": Robbins' FBI file, Freedom of Information-Privacy Act, Department of Justice, Memo from FBI agent Edward Scheidt to J. Edgar Hoover, April 27, 1950.

95–96—"We talked . . . for sale": Author's interview with Bob Silverman, June 7, 1999.

97—"Jerry had . . . between us": Author's interview with Bob Silverman, June 7, 1999.

97—"stunty . . . melodic": *New York World-Telegram*, December 22, 1945.

97—"We could . . . for satire": *New York Herald Tribune*, May 19, 1946.

98—"Integration . . . the house": *New York Herald Tribune*, May 19, 1946.

98—"That show . . . typical character": Author's interview with Virginia Gibson, May 3, 1999.

99—"but I don't . . . affectionately": Letter from Agnes de Mille to Jerome Robbins, October 24, 1945, Dance Collection, NYPL, reprinted in part in Carol Easton, *No Intermissions: The Life and Times of Agnes de Mille*, New York: Little, Brown & Company, 1996, p. 377.

99—"Jerry couldn't . . . with you'": Author's interview with James Mitchell, April 9, 1999.

99—"Miss McCracken . . . in herself": *New York Times*, December 22, 1945.

100—"I could see . . . self-tormented": Interview with Trude Rittmann, December 9, 1976, Oral History Project, Dance Collection, NYPL.

100—"I learned . . . of humor": Author's interview with Anita Alvarez, June 17, 1999.

100—"I had . . . Charleston ballet": Interview with Danny Daniels, February 18, 1999. Daniels also said, "You know, the dancers were all bitching because he was so demanding. I know that he wanted to have a ballet class, and some of the dancers said, 'He just wants to try out some ideas.' They were so contemptuous of him. . . . He was very good to me. Everybody was bitching about him and I didn't know what they were bitching about, because it wasn't happening to me, but I wasn't working that close with him. But you know, my experience, and from what people have told me, that he'd be rather sadistic on the ones that he knew wouldn't fight back, that didn't have enough gumption or backbone to stand up to him. If he thought you were going to stand up to him he would leave you alone. Or if you did stand up to him, then he'd back off. I don't know why he felt that he had to treat his dancers that way, that always bothered me, because I didn't think it was necessary to do what he did. . . . Abbott was very stern, though, you know. I remember very vividly, I went to the first day of rehearsals, and we sat down around a table to read the script. I had a part, so I was part of the whole acting group. The woman that played the mother came in late that first morning. Abbott looked at his watch and said, 'You're late; don't be late again.' The next day she came in late, and he said, 'You're fired.' But you don't have to be beating people. That was Jerry's *modus operandi*. But he was just as hard on himself."

100–101—"We were . . . his head": Author's interview with Maria Harriton, April 20, 1995.

101—"It is not . . . quite a while": Author's interview with James Mitchell, April 9, 1999.

101—Arthur Partington was: Author's interview with Arthur Partington, April 28, 1999.

101—"Everybody tells . . . happened": Author's interview with Helen Gallagher, April 13, 1999.

101—"I think . . . particularly": Author's interview with Betty Comden, July 26, 1999.

102—"That happened . . . once": Author's interview with Jason Alexander, May 14, 1999.

102—"the hero . . . evening": *PM*, December 23, 1945.

102—"is by . . . it go": *New York Sun*, December 22, 1945.

102—"a passable . . . act drag": Abbott, *Mister Abbott*, p. 209.

103—"I was . . . of acting": *New York Times*, June 8, 1977.

103—She had . . . he practiced": Vidal, *Palimpsest*, p. 129.

103—"Like most ballerinas . . . for luck": Arthur Laurents, *Original Story By: A Memoir of Broadway and Hollywood*, New York: Alfred A. Knopf, 2000, pp. 43–44.

103—"The dancers . . . luxury cruise": Payne, *American Ballet Theatre*, p. 143.

104—"though acclaimed . . . 'music hall'": Payne, *American Ballet Theatre*, p. 144.

104—"tasted the . . . second week": P. W. Manchester, "Jerome Robbins—Theatre Man," *Ballet Annual*, 1961, New York: MacMillan, 1960, p. 112.

104—"Small inward . . . of society": Reprinted in Clive Barnes, *Inside American Ballet Theatre*, New York: Hawthorne Books, 1977, p. 95.

104—"the somewhat . . . Martha Graham": Burton, *Leonard Bernstein*, p. 153.

104—Robbins social . . . his apartment: "Young Man from a Sad Generation," *Junior Bazaar*, April 1947, p. 138.

105—"came out . . . of it": *New York Times*, June 3, 1990.

105—"He was . . . right there": Author's interview with Janet Reed, August 2, 1999.

105—"Not since . . . by a horn": Payne, *American Ballet Theatre*, pp. 145, 152.

105–6—"The inspiration . . . and motionless": Reprinted in Burton, *Leonard Bernstein*, p. 153.

106—"a lonely place": *Time*, November 4, 1946.

106—"in fright . . . or not": *PM*, October 24, 1946.

106—"Jerome Robbins . . . new creation": *New York Herald Tribune*, October 25, 1946.

106—"Of Robbins's . . . no doubt": Reprinted in *Musical America*, November 1990, p. 13.

106—"worthy of . . . the cuticle": *New York Times*, November 3, 1946.

106–7—"To a frantic . . . needed saying": *Time*, November 4, 1946.

107—"Robbins kisses . . . kisses Robbins": *New York World-Telegram*, October 25, 1946.

107—"So, it . . . Nora's fault": Author's inteview with Sonia Robbins Cullinen, October 5, 1999.

107—"It was . . . complex person": Author's interview with Ruth Ann Koesun, April 27, 1999.

107—"a demon . . . for less?": Nora Kaye in Robert Kotlowitz, "Corsets, Corned Beef and Choreography," *Show*, December, 1964, p. 91.

107—"less sardonic . . . satirical": Cited in Peyser, *Bernstein*, p. 173.

108—"a witty . . . single turn": *New York Times*, March 28, 1947.

108—"the most . . . ribbing": *New York Times*, December 3, 1947.

108–9—"I liked . . . enriching time": Author's interview with Ruth Ann Koesun, April 27, 1999.

109—"an exuberant . . . man": Phil Silvers, *The Laugh Is On Me: The Phil Silvers Story*, Englewood, N.J.: Prentice Hall, 1973, p. 163.

109—"very colorful . . . whatever downtown": Author's interview with Nanette Fabray, February 2, 1999.

109–10—"One of my . . . in the show": Author's interview with Nanette Fabray, February 2, 1999.

110—"Jerry said . . . young dance-maker: Author's interview with Philip Lanza Sandor, February 26, 1999.

110–11—Robbins started . . . contract was": Author's interview with Mary Hunter Wolf, April 11, 1999.

111—"With Mr. Abbott . . . co-producer . . .": Silvers, *The Laugh Is On Me*, p. 163.

111—Part of the play . . . Mack Sennett Ballet": Mary Jean Kemper, "Little Wonder Boy," *Vogue*, February 15, 1948.

112—"He was just . . . was happening": Author's interview with Helen Gallagher, April 13, 1999.

112—"I asked Jule . . . in mind": Jerome Robbins in Theodore Taylor, *Jule: The Story of Composer Jule Styne*, New York: Random House, 1979, p. 118.

112–13—"Phil learned . . . it down . . .": Author's interview with Nanette Fabray, February 2, 1999.

113—"Poor Joe . . . his results": Author's interview with Virginia Gibson, May 3, 1999.

113—"Jerry's forte . . . dance-wise": Author's interview with Ralph Linn, February 23, 1999.

113—"He would . . . beautiful number": Author's interview with Nanette Fabray, February 2, 1999.

113–14—"First I had . . . a point": *PM*, December 1947, Jerome Robbins Scrapbook, Dance Collection, NYPL.

114—"a terror . . . just hell": Author's interview with Miles White, March 28, 1999.

114–16—"The thing . . . another chorus": Author's interview with Nanette Fabray, February 2, 1999.

116—"Not so . . . single look": Jule Styne in Taylor, *Jule: The Story of Composer Jule Styne*, p. 118.

116—"Jerry wasn't . . . the decisions": Author's interview with Helen Gallagher, April 13, 1999.

116—"Substitution of . . . the need": Reprinted in Silvers, *The Laugh Is On Me*, p. 164.

116—"The word . . . the scenes": Reprinted in Silvers, *The Laugh Is On Me*, p. 165.

116–17—"They just . . . town with": Author's interview with Arthur Partington, February 14, 1999.

117—"I hasten . . . the pirouette . . ." *New York Post*, October 10, 1947.

117—"It is . . . Robbins night": *Daily News*, October 10, 1947.

117—"a masterpiece . . . pandemonium": Reported in Taylor, *Jule: The Story of Composer Jule Styne*, p. 122.

117—"one of . . . worth seeing": *PM*, October 12, 1947.

117—"We got . . . big hit": Author's interview with Nanette Fabray, February 2, 1999.

117–18—"Everyone has . . . has meaning": *Boston Post Magazine*, May 9, 1948, pp. 4, 15.

118—"I haven't . . . Not me": Jerome Robbins in *Cue*, February 14, 1948, p. 13.

CHAPTER FOUR:

119—He decorated: "Young Man from a Sad Generation," *Junior Bazaar*, April 1947, p. 138.

119—"Jerry was . . . dog-lover": Author's interview with Bob Silverman, December 2, 1999.

119—baby grand piano: *Boston Post Magazine*, May 9, 1948, p. 4.

119—a cream-colored 1947 Dodge: *PM*, December 21, 1947.

119—"He was . . . the music": Author's interview with Robert Tucker, May 12, 1999.

120—Clift's acting coach . . . they were": Author's interview with Mira Rostova, January 23, 1999.

120—"He didn't . . . at all": Author's interview with Patricia Bosworth, January 15, 1999.

120—"For Monty . . . their affair": Bosworth, *Montgomery Clift: A Biography*, New York: Harcourt Brace Jovanovich, Inc., 1978 (Limelight Editions, 1996), p. 154.

120—With a . . . Jerry's apartment: Author's interview with Mira Rostova, January 23, 1999.

120–21—"Mira Rostova . . . both invited": Bosworth, *Montgomery Clift*, p. 136.

121—"kept their . . . American theater": Robert La Gaurdia, *Monty: A Biography*, New York: Avon Books, 1977, p. 64.

121—"Gadget concentrated . . . staged them": Robert Lewis, *Slings and Arrows: Theater in My Life*, New York: Stein and Day, 1984, p. 185.

122—"Jerry's performing . . . bit awkward": Lewis, *Slings and Arrows*, p. 185–186.

122—"I do remember . . . quite remarkable": Author's interview with David Pressman, June 29, 1999.

122—Like others: Author's interview with Patricia Neal, June 29, 1999. Author's interview with Maureen Stapleton, June 30, 1999.

122—Monty's longtime . . . years: Milt Machlin, *Libby*, New York: Tower Books, 1980, p. 305.

122—Brando stated . . . and drugs: Marlon Brando with Robert Lindsey, *Brando: Songs My Mother Taught Me*, New York: Random House, 1994, p. 157.

123—Cris Alexander once: Author's interview with Cris Alexander, May 18, 1999.

123—"It got . . . dark areas": Author's interview with Richard D'Arcy, March 9, 1999.

123—"Monty was . . . a tragedy": Author's interview with Richard D'Arcy, March 9, 1999.

124—"Monty acted . . . stand him": Oliver Smith in Machlin, *Libby*, p. 329.

124—"I love . . . love women": Montgomery Clift in Machlin, *Libby*, p. 336.

124—"Monty was . . . unable to": Mira Rostova in Bosworth, *Montgomery Clift*, p. 165.

124—"The Monty . . . Clift": Author's interview with Ina Kurland, March 13, 1999.

124—"Jerry looked like Montgomery Clift . . . more than coincidental: Author's interview with Bob Silverman, August 18, 1999.

124–25—"It began because . . . Puerto Ricans on the West Side": *Times* (London), June 30, 1984.

125—"I was . . . with gangs": Author's interview with Russ Tamblyn, March 20, 1999.

125—"As far . . . to Hamlet": Author's interview with Mira Rostova, October 11, 1999.

125—Likewise, David Pressman: Author's interview with David Pressman, June 29, 1999.

125—"Robbins' idea . . . contemporary way": Burton, *Leonard Bernstein*, p. 187.

125—Sonia recalled: Author's interview with Sonia Robbins Cullinen, October 5, 1999.

126—"just came . . . of boyfriend": Author's interview with Gerald Kabat, February 14, 1999.

126—"He was . . . he didn't": Author's interview with Arthur Partington, February 14, 1999.

126—According to Sonia: Author's interview with Sonia Robbins Cullinen, October 5, 1999.

126—"The sexuality . . . give more": Author's interview with Mimi Gomber Friedman, September 10, 1999.

126—Later in the year: Author's interview with Arnold and Augusta Newman, May 3, 1999.

127—"One night . . . first love": Letter from Rose Tobias Shaw, September 11, 1998.

127—"My impression . . . that point": Author's interview with Arnold Newman, May 3, 1999.

127—"Lucky as . . . a bachelor!": *Boston Post Magazine*, May 9, 1948, p. 15.

127—The romance . . . for Robbins: Brooks Clift in Bosworth, *Montgomery Clift*, p. 154.

128—Robinson noted . . . and human": *PM*, December 21, 1947.

129—Although the book was written by Jerome Lawrence and Robert E. Lee: Arthur Laurents recalled in *Original Story By* that he had written a "detailed outline" of *Look, Ma, I'm Dancin'!* for Robbins, but withdrew from the project on advice from his psychiatrist, Theodor Reik. Laurents wrote, "Jerry blew up, but collected himself long enough to get me to sign away my rights to everything for nothing. Since I thought I had indeed behaved badly, I signed Jerry's quitclaim. To no avail: he stayed angry and there was a long caesura before he called me 'baby' again." "Baby" was a term of endearment Robbins often used for friends. Arthur Laurents, *Original Story By: A Memoir of Broadway and Hollywood*, New York: Alfred A. Knopf, 2000, p. 72.

129—"This is . . . for it": "Young Man from a Sad Generation," *Junior Bazaar*, April, 1947, p. 136.

129–30—"Jerry started . . . a trance": George Abbott, *Mister Abbott*, New York: Random House, 1963, p. 221.

130—"We used . . . Crow's Nest tonight": Author's interview with Richard D'Arcy, March 9, 1999.

130—"You know . . . the sign": Author's interview with Ninette Charisse, May 12, 1999.

130—According to . . . "The Crow Flies!": Author's interview with Dody Goodman, May 14, 1999.

130–31—"He went . . . each other": Author's interview with Richard D'Arcy, March 9, 1999.

131—"Jerry was . . . did it": Author's interview with Ninette Charisse, May 12, 1999.

131—"And down . . . very tired": Author's interview with Robert Tucker, May 12, 1999.

131—"I picked . . . close then": Author's interview with Richard D'Arcy, March 9, 1999.

131—"I was not . . . of working": Author's interview with Janet Reed, February 28, 1999.

131—"a good . . . comedy": *New York Times,* January 30, 1948.

132—"a fine . . . good show": *PM,* January 30, 1948.

132—"They don't . . . to me": *Cue,* February, 1948, p. 12.

132—"dansical": *PM,* December 21, 1947.

132—"It was . . . offstage right": Abbott, *Mister Abbott,* p. 221–222.

132—"He had . . . operation, yes": Author's interview with Richard D'Arcy, March 9, 1999.

132–33—"They must . . . so upset": Author's interview with Ina Kurland, March 13, 1999.

133—"He sent . . . hated it": Author's interview with Richard D'Arcy, March 9, 1999.

133—In April: *Daily Worker,* April 5, 1948.

134—"That was . . . a genius": Author's interview with Kaye Ballard, April 8, 1999.

134—"People liked . . . him finish": Author's interview with George Irving, April 20, 1999.

135—"There was . . . ever been": Author's interview with Miles White, March 28, 1999.

135—"probably looked . . . Paul Godkin": *Philadelphia Inquirer,* September 25, 1948.

135—"I was . . . nixed it": Author's interview with Isabel Brown, April 19, 1999.

135—"first goof . . . too soon": Jerome Robbins in Emily Coleman, "The Dance Man Leaps to the Top," *Ballet Annual,* New York: MacMillan, 1959, p. 69.

135–36—"I saw . . . 'Come on'": Jerome Robbins interview with Deborah Jowitt, Kennedy Center Honors Oral History Program, July 1995, as cited in program notes for Jerome Robbins Memorial, Lincoln Center, November 17, 1998. Balanchine's *Symphony in C* had its first New York performance on March 22, 1948.

136—"He made me . . . a masterpiece'": Jerome Robbins in Bernard Taper, *Balanchine: A Biography,* Los Angeles: University of California Press, 1996 (first published by Times Books, 1984), p. 230.

137—"You see . . . long shot": Author's interview with Janet Reed, February 28, 1999.

137—"Balanchine gave . . . wanted to": Author's interview with Janet Reed, November 1, 1999.

137—"Sometimes . . . stage manager": Jerome Robbins in Taper, *Balanchine,* p. 228.

137–38—"It was ... should be": Author's interview with Maria Tallchief, May 3, 1999.

138–39—"The treatment ... articulated publicly": Eric A. Gordon, *Mark the Music: The Life and Work of Marc Blitzstein*, New York: St. Martin's Press, 1989, p. 323.

139—"Lo and ... *West Side Story*": Interview with Rita Carlin Brandt, November 23, 1998, Oral History Project, Dance Collection, NYPL.

139—"a very neatly ... disappointing work": *New York Times*, January 21, 1949.

139—"It is ... classic dance": *New York Herald Tribune*, January 21, 1949.

139—"can turn ... of bebop": *New York Daily News*, January 21, 1949.

140—"The ballet ... didn't exist": Gordon, *Mark the Music*, p. 323–324.

140—"We were at ... him unfortunately": Author's interview with Maria Tallchief, May 3, 1999.

141—"he had. ... SHOSTAKOVICH": Robbins' FBI file, Freedom of Information-Privacy Act, Department of Justice, Memo from FBI agent Edward Scheidt to J. Edgar Hoover, April 27, 1950.

141—Jerry dated ... and forth": Jerome Robbins' FBI file, Freedom of Information-Privacy Act, Department of Justice, including Memo from FBI agent Edward Scheidt to J. Edgar Hoover, April 27, 1950.

141–42—According to ... being false": Eric Bentley (ed.), *Thirty Years of Treason: Excerpts from Hearings Before the House Committee on Un-American Activities, 1939–1968*, New York: Viking Press, 1971, p. 628.

142—"I attended ... seemingly praised": Bentley (ed.), *Thirty Years of Treason*, p. 628–629.

142—When asked ... that way": Bentley (ed.), *Thirty Years of Treason*, p. 630.

142–43—"The reason ... and patriotism": Jacob Weisberg, "The Rehabilitation of Joe McCarthy," *New York Times Magazine*, November 28, 1999, p. 122.

143—Robbins testified ... frantic group": Bentley (ed.), *Thirty Years of Treason*, p. 631.

143—"a disorganized ... introverts": Jerome Robbins' FBI file, Freedom of Information-Privacy Act, Department of Justice, Memo dated December 6, 1954 (NY 100-104408).

143—"In 1948 ... blacklisting": Nora Sayre, *Previous Convictions: A Journey Through the 1950s*, New Brunswick, N.J.: Rutgers University Press, 1995, p. 275.

143–44—According to ... to Jews": R. Lawrence Siegel interviewed by Victor Navasky, June 1976.

144—Robbins later told ... blot out": Jerome Robbins' FBI file, Freedom of Information-Privacy Act, Department of Justice, Memo dated September 22, 1954 (LA 100-32184).

144—"As a rule ... lifelong hangover": Arthur Koestler, *The God That Failed*, pp. 55–56, cited in Victor Navasky, *Naming Names*, New York: Viking, 1980, p. 334.

144—"pointed out ... that line": Jerome Robbins' FBI file, Freedom of Information-Privacy Act, Memo from FBI agent Edward Scheidt to J. Edgar Hoover, April 27, 1950.

145—"The Communist ... suspected Communists": Kaiser, *The Gay Metropolis*, p. 69. In addition, Nora Sayre wrote that by 1953 "more than four hundred and twenty-five people had been discharged from the State Department alone because of their [gay] 'proclivities' and the pace of the dismissals accelerated." Sayre, *Previous Convictions*, pp. 274–275.

145—"I heard . . . be flops": *New York Times,* July 12, 1981.

145—"how five . . . one turkey": Author's interview with Allyn Ann McLerie/George Gaynes, February 2, 1999.

145–46—"But the payoff . . . a choreographer?": *New York World-Telegram,* July 25, 1949.

146–47—"The play was . . . would care": Author's interview with Eddie Albert, February 2, 1999.

147—"I don't think . . . us adrift": Author's interview with Allyn Ann McLerie/George Gaynes, February 2, 1999.

148—"Moss said . . . him enormously": Author's interview with Kitty Carlisle Hart, August 3, 1999.

148—"got reviews . . . standards": Mary Ellin Barrett in Myrna Katz Frommer and Harvey Frommer, *It Happened on Broadway,* New York: Harcourt Brace and Company, 1998, p. 94.

148—"a disappointing . . . for the second . . .": *New York Times,* July 16, 1949.

148—"gravely disappointing . . . of them": *New York Sun,* July 16, 1949.

148–49—"At this time . . . its level": Ethan Mordden, *Beautiful Mornin': The Broadway Musical in the 1940s,* New York: Oxford University Press, 1999, p. 199.

149—"Janet Reed did . . . he danced . . .": Todd Bolender in *Ballet Review,* Summer 1988, p. 21.

149—"There is . . . each other": *New York Times,* December 2, 1949.

149—"I think . . . No": Author's interview with Janet Reed, February 28, 1999.

149–50—Le Clercq had . . . teeth out": Tanaquil Le Clercq with Rick Whitaker, "Jerome Robbins," *Ballet Review,* Summer, 1998, p. 13.

150—"nothing short . . . of *Troy*": *New York Herald Tribune,* December 2, 1949.

150—"irresistibly funny": *New York Times,* December 2, 1949.

150—"The trouble . . . the dance": Maria Tallchief with Larry Kaplan, *America's Prima Ballerina,* New York: Henry Holt and Company, 1997, p. 136.

151—"I watched . . . Mozart-Balanchine *Caracole* . . .": Francis Mason, *Ballet Review,* Summer 1988, pp. 13–14. Balanchine restaged *Caracole* as *Divertimento No. 15,* first in 1956 and again in 1966.

151—"Balanchine was . . . in it": Author's interview with Maria Tallchief, May 3, 1999.

151—"One evening . . . slippers too'": Tallchief, *America's Prima Ballerina,* p. 170.

151—"That was . . . of role": Author's interview with Maria Tallchief, May 3, 1999.

151—"Opening night . . . a dancer": Author's interview with Ruthanna Boris, February 13, 1999.

152—"We rehearsed . . . those stairs!": Tanaquil Le Clercq with Rick Whitaker, "Jerome Robbins," *Ballet Review,* Summer 1998, p. 13.

152—"Those were . . . his version": Author's interview with Todd Bolender, May 6, 1999.

152—"probably not . . . *Fancy Free*": *Newsweek,* March 6, 1950.

152—"took Bernstein's . . . at all": Lincoln Kirstein, *Thirty Years: Lincoln Kirstein's The New York City Ballet,* New York: Alfred A. Knopf, 1978, p. 107.

152—According to Eric Bentley: Author's interview with Eric Bentley, April 10, 2000. According to Philip Lanza Sandor: Author's interview with Philip Lanza Sandor, February 26, 1999.

153—"I would . . . so complex": Jerome Robbins in *Theatre Arts*, July 1950, p. 49.

153—"a tiresomely . . . claptrap": *New York Daily News*, February 27, 1950.

153—"In the . . . and separate": *New York Times*, February 27, 1950.

153—"There can . . . major artists": *New York Times*, March 12, 1950.

153—"The work . . . somewhat overwrought . . .": *New York Times*, January 16, 1954.

153—"though he . . . Balanchine's heart": Taper, *Balanchine*, p. 230.

154—"suffered a . . . 'Sunday'": *Theatre Arts*, July 1950, p. 48.

154—"The scherzo . . . those days": Tanaquil Le Clercq with Rick Whitaker, "Jerome Robbins," *Ballet Review*, Summer 1998, p. 13.

154—"By its . . . good spirits": *New York Herald Tribune*, March 10, 1950.

155—"a piece . . . its content . . .": *New York Times*, March 10, 1950.

155—"Mass entertainment . . . United States": Kaiser, *The Gay Metropolis*, p. 66.

155—remembered by Janet Reed: Author's interview with Janet Reed, May 17, 1999.

155—The contract had: Jerome Robbins' FBI file, Freedom of Information-Privacy Act, Memo from FBI agent Edward Scheidt to J. Edgar Hoover, April 27, 1950.

156—According to her biographer: James Haskins with Kathleen Benson, *Lena: A Personal and Professional Biography of Lena Horne*, New York: Stein and Day, 1984, p. 138–139.

156—In his book *Naming Names* . . . entertain Americans . . .": Victor Navasky, *Naming Names*, New York: Viking, 1980, p. 192. The statement by Horne's manager, Robert Harris, appeared in *The Daily Compass*, New York, October 9, 1951.

157—"One day . . . they did": Author's interview with Bob Silverman, June 13, 1999.

157—"I've said . . . caved in": Author's interview with Bob Silverman, June 7, 1999.

157—"I found . . . to people": Author's interview with Saul Silverman, June 20, 1999.

157—"Jerry talked . . . of history": Author's interview with Sonia Robbins Cullinen, October 5, 1999.

158—Robbins' meeting . . . as 'COUNTERATTACK' ": Jerome Robbins' FBI file, Freedom of Information-Privacy Act, Department of Justice, Memo from FBI agent Edward Scheidt to J. Edgar Hoover, April 27, 1950.

158—"As a result . . . such excuse": Jerome Robbins' FBI file, Freedom of Information-Privacy Act, Department of Justice, Memo from FBI agent Edward Scheidt to J. Edgar Hoover, April 27, 1950.

158—"admitting . . . affiliations": Jerome Robbins' FBI file, Freedom of Information-Privacy Act, Memo from FBI agent Edward Scheidt to J. Edgar Hoover, April 27, 1950.

158–59—"Kirkpatrick had . . . rounded up": Jerome Robbins' FBI file, Freedom of Information-Privacy Act, Department of Justice, Memo from FBI agent Edward Scheidt to J. Edgar Hoover, April 27, 1950.

159—"The interviewing agents . . . Communist cause": Jerome Robbins' FBI file, Freedom of Information-Privacy Act, Department of Justice, Memo from FBI agent Edward Scheidt to J. Edgar Hoover, April 27, 1950.

159—"that in . . . anti-Semitism . . .": Jerome Robbins' FBI file, Freedom of Information-Privacy Act, Department of Justice, Memo from FBI agent Edward Scheidt to J. Edgar Hoover, April 27, 1950.

159—"Jerry's connection . . . Communists": Author's interview with Richard D'Arcy, March 9, 1999.

159–60—"I question . . . the story": Letter to the author from Arthur Laurents, May 18, 1999.

161—"Jerry admired . . . sign": Letter to the author from Harold Prince, June 11, 1999.

162—"As was . . . of songs": Abbott, *Mister Abbott*, p. 227.

162—"During the . . . every night": Abbott, *Mister Abbott*, pp. 227–228.

162–63—"Jerry was . . . Oh my!": Author's interview with Kirsten Valbor, June 9, 1999.

163–64—"He should . . . loved that": Author's interview with William Weslow, February 22, 1999.

164—"Paul Lukas . . . were lovers: Author's interview with Arthur Partington, February 14, 1999.

164—"When [Jerry] . . . for him": Author's interview with Ralph Linn, February 23, 1999.

164—"Jerry is . . . gets obstreperous": Leland Hayward in Emily Coleman, "From Tutus to T-shirts," *New York Times Magazine*, October 8, 1961.

165—"Quite an . . . festive ballets": *New York Times*, October 13, 1950.

165—"it richly deserves . . . Merman?": *New York Post*, October 13, 1950.

165—"A fetching . . . jamboree": *New York Herald Tribune*, October 13, 1950.

165—"Ethel Merman . . . the difference": Abbott, *Mister Abbott*, p. 228.

166—"I would prefer . . . For what purpose?": Larry Parks in Navasky, *Naming Names*, p. viii–ix.

166—As Victor Navasky pointed out . . . no hope": Navasky, *Naming Names*, pp. x–xii.

166—"as a Jew . . . sacred ground": Navasky, *Naming Names*, p. vii.

166—Victor Navasky argued persuasively: Navasky, *Naming Names*, p. ix.

166—"How can . . . know them?": Congressman Francis E. Walter in Navasky, *Naming Names*, p. viii.

167—"the Committee . . . were absent . . .": Navasky, *Naming Names*, pp. ix and xiv.

167–69—"Tip to . . . Russian guns": *Philadelphia Inquirer*, March 24, 1951.

170—"Famed Dancer Shuns Hollywood": *New York World-Telegram*, July 25, 1949.

170—"I first . . . followed him": Author's interview with Jerome Chodorov, January 13, 1999.

170—"When Jerry . . . you want": *New York Times*, March 14, 1999.

170—"Bill Fitelson . . . own feelings": Author's interview with Mary Hunter Wolf, April 11, 1999.

170–71—"I had . . . to be": Elia Kazan, *A Life*, New York: Alfred A. Knopf, 1988, p. 457.

171—"Hoover's lawyer": Navasky, *Naming Names*, p. 51.

171—"It was . . . Ernst's lap": Author's interview with Sonia Robbins Cullinen, October 5, 1999.

171—At this time: Author's interview with Mary Hunter Wolf, April 11, 1999.

171–72—"What are . . . goddamned Committee": Dalton Trumbo in Navasky, *Naming Names*, p. 392.

CHAPTER FIVE:

173—"I suppose . . . Nora Kaye": *New York Times Magazine,* January 3, 1999, p. 18. According to Miller's friend Gene Gavin, Miller was most displeased when Anna Kisselgoff printed this line quote from Robbins, seeing it as irreverent in light of the choreographer's death the previous year. Author's interview with Gene Gavin, November 15, 1999.

173–74—"Jerry was . . . bothered her": Author's interview with Isabel Brown, April 8, 1999.

174—"Though he . . . he is": Nora Kaye in Emily Coleman, "From Tutus to T-Shirts," *New York Times Magazine,* October 8, 1961, p. 37.

174—"Jerry's mother . . . back unengaged": Author's interview with Dorothy Gilbert, October 4, 1999.

174—"Jerome Robbins . . . know American": Charles Payne, *American Ballet Theatre,* New York: Alfred A. Knopf, 1978, p. 198.

174–75—"At that point . . . married anymore": Author's interview with Allyn Ann McLerie, February 2, 1999.

175—"I think . . . could offer": Author's interview with Isabel Brown, April 8, 1999.

175—"Jerry came . . . deep emotion": Author's interview with James Mitchell, April 9, 1999.

176—"I don't . . . a second": Author's interview with James Mitchell, April 9, 1999.

176—"I shudder . . . married Nora": Author's interview with Janet Reed, August 2, 1999.

176—"They were . . . very devoted": Author's interview with William Weslow, February 22, 1999.

176—"They were . . . Jerry loved": Author's interview with Lynn Seymour, May 14, 1999.

176—Shortly before . . . : Author's interview with Stanley Siegel, November 26, 1999. Stanley Siegel's account of the Robbins-Miller breakup is consistent with that of Arthur Laurents, who remembered that Robbins never allowed Miller to meet Leland and Slim Hayward, attempting to conceal his gay lover. Laurents wrote, "Eventually, Buzz refused to remain hidden and left Jerry." Laurents, *Original Story,* p. 376. Miller apparently remained embittered for some years after the romance soured. Dancer-choreographer Glen Tetley remembered an incident when he and Miller ran into Robbins a few years later in Spoleto at the time Jerry was in Italy with his Ballets: U.S.A. troupe. Tetley said, "I knew Buzz very well because Buzz and I were in John Butler's company. We were the competition in the Spoleto Festival, and Buzz not hated, *loathed* Jerry Robbins, *loathed* him. Anyway, Buzz and I were coming up the hill one day on a scooter. I was driving the scooter and he was on the back of my scooter. We saw Ballets: U.S.A. unload from the bus in front of Teatro Nuovo. Jerry Robbins was standing there and all of the Ballets: U.S.A. dancers who knew us were waving at us. Buzz said, 'If you stop this scooter, I will kill you, I will kill you on the spot.' So I went through all of these dancers like they were bowling pins, all of them looking after us. But Buzz was just violent about it. He said so many nasty horrible things about Jerry." Author's interview with Glen Tetley, January 20, 1999. As a gay man, Miller would later "come out" and remain in a committed relationship for more than thirty years (with Alan Groh, who started his career as a dealer in New York's art world at the Stable Gallery in the late fifties).

In 1998, shortly before his death, Miller said, "I can't relate to closeted types. I can't imagine being so out of tune with who you really are." Buzz Miller in Mimi Swartz, "Buzz and Alan," *New Yorker*, August 24 & 31, 1998.

177—"The first time . . . very careful": Author's interview with Gene Gavin, January 9, 1999.

177—"He loved . . . a child": Author's interview with Ninette Charisse, May 12, 1999.

177—"Everybody cried . . . protect myself": Author's interview with Yuriko, December 16, 1998.

178—"They just meshed": Author's interview with Yuriko, December 16, 1998.

178—Robbins was . . . : Rock Brynner, *Yul: The Man Who Would Be King*, New York: Simon and Schuster, 1989, p. 53.

178—Once the show opened: *Variety*, November 7, 1951. *Variety* also reported that at the time Robbins was earning $85 to $100 per week as a dancer at City Ballet.

179—"to kidnap . . . better king": Sheridan Morley, *Gertrude Lawrence*, New York: McGraw-Hill, 1981, p. 189.

179—Early on: William G. Hyland, *Richard Rodgers*, New Haven, CT: Yale University Press, 1998, p. 194–198.

180—"Gradually, he . . . his cock'": Brynner, *Yul: The Man Who Would Be King*, p. 54.

180—"The story is . . . electrifying element": Susan L. Schulman cited in Mary Ellin Barrett in Myrna Katz Frommer and Harvey Frommer, *It Happened on Broadway*, New York: Harcourt Brace and Company, 1998, p. 108.

180—"The strength . . . a marriage": Richard Rodgers and Oscar Hammerstein, "About the King and I," *New York Times*, March 23, 1951.

180–81—"Those who . . . psychosomatic collapses": Morley, *Gertrude Lawrence*, pp. 191–192.

181—"Rodgers had . . . Dorothy Sarnoff": Morley, *Gertrude Lawrence* p. 190.

181—"sang flat . . . father crazy": Mary Rodgers cited in Mary Ellin Barrett in Frommer, *It Happened on Broadway*, p. 108.

181—As the musical: Hyland, *Richard Rodgers*, p. 197.

181—This was the critical scene . . . : Hammerstein Collection, Library of Congress, Letter to R.J. Kaplan, *The King and I* file. Hammerstein wrote, "When they dance the polka, they come closest to feeling and show this desire."

181—Rodgers encouraged: Hyland, *Richard Rodgers*, p. 197.

182—"Use the . . . to it": Author's interview with Yuriko, December 16, 1998.

182—"Without missing . . . true magician": Yuriko Kikuchi, "How He Got What He Wanted," *The Journal for Stage Directors & Choreographers*, Fall/Winter 1998, p. 37.

182—The action in the second act . . . : Brynner, *Yul: The Man Who Would Be King*, p. 57.

182—"In the . . . hysterical laughter": Ronnie Lee cited in Mary Ellin Barrett in Frommer, *It Happened on Broadway*, p. 111.

183—"worked like . . . [and] painful": Author's interview with Gemze de Lappe, April 23, 1999.

183—"There was . . . the other": Interview with Trude Rittmann, December 9, 1976, Oral History Project, Dance Collection, NYPL.

183—"When Jerry . . . his mind": Author's interview with Yuriko, December 16, 1998.

183—"There was . . . of her": Author's interview with Yuriko, December 16, 1998.

183—"I worked . . . whole life": Author's interview with Susan Kikuchi, May 17, 1999.

184—During its out-of-town: Brynner, *Yul: The Man Who Would Be King*, p. 56.

184—Leland Hayward, who had invested: Brynner, *Yul: The Man Who Would Be King*, p. 55.

184—Frank Sinatra was: Brynner, *Yul: The Man Who Would Be King*, p. 57.

184—The premiere took place: Hyland, *Richard Rodgers*, p. 201.

184—As was now customary: In this regard Sonia recalled, "Jerry arranged for his mother, father, sister and her husband to attend all the opening[s]. It was always a great evening. . . . He was also a generous Uncle to my kids and shopping sprees to F.A.O. Schwartz happened many times." Letter to the author from Sonia Robbins Cullinen, March 11, 2000.

185—"Strictly on . . . American humor": *New York Times*, March 30, 1951.

185—"nothing could . . . to dance": *New York Post*, March 30, 1951.

185—"the visual . . . highlight": *New York Daily News*, March 30, 1951.

185—In failing health: Hyland, *Richard Rodgers*, p. 203.

186—"spilled over into": Jerome Robbins in John Guare, "Robbins: Back to Broadway," *New York Times Magazine*, September 11, 1989.

186—"a phenomenon of nature": Jerome Robbins in Robert Sabin, "The Creative Evolution of The Cage," *Dance Magazine*, August 1955, p. 23.

186—"What a dramatic . . . to you": Ibid., pp. 22 and 59.

186–87—"It's about . . . tribal instinct": Ibid., p. 22.

187—"I did not . . . feelers": Ibid., p. 23.

187—"It's basically . . . unrequited love": Author's interview with Isabel Brown, April 8, 1999.

187—There was tension between Robbins and Kaye: In his memoir, *Original Story By*, Arthur Laurents recalled that it was Kaye who prevailed upon Robbins to give up the idea of portraying the women as Amazons. According to Laurents, she told him, "If you don't want to get stoned, you better change them to bugs." Laurents also credited Kaye with bringing a note of humanity into the ballet and thereby willfully rebelling against Robbins. Laurents wrote that " . . . he wanted those females to be ice, inhuman. Nora didn't and added choreography. After the first vivid castration gesture, she clutched her belly in a piercing image of remorse. Jerry was ready to kill her, and he ordered her to omit it. She didn't and after the reviews, he didn't press the point. . . . She always weathered her disputes with Jerry; sometimes they could be mirror images of each other." Arthur Laurents, *Original Story By*, p. 331.

187—"Jerry was . . . you stink!'": Author's interview with Ruthanna Boris, February 21, 1999.

188—"We were there . . . visibly upset": Author's interview with Dorothy Gilbert, October 4, 1999.

188—"It is . . . upon it": *New York Times*, June 15, 1951.

188—"has created . . . coldly feral": *New York Herald Tribune*, June 15, 1951.

188—"a repulsive . . . genius": Clive Barnes cited in Nancy Reynolds, *Repertory in Review: 40 Years of the New York City Ballet*, New York: Dial Press, 1977, p. 123.

188—"a manifesto . . . la lettre . . .": Lincoln Kirstein, *Thirty Years: Lincoln Kirstein's New York City Ballet*, New York: Alfred A. Knopf, 1978, p. 118.

188—"so literally . . . in offices": Edwin Denby, *Dance Writings and Poetry*, New Haven, CT: Yale University Press, 1998, p. 228.

188—"I don't . . . contemporary visualization": Jerome Robbins in Reynolds, *Repertory in Review*, p. 123.

188—Though he later explained: *New York Times*, January 14, 1979.

189—"Keep it antiseptic": Taper, *Balanchine*, p. 230.

189—"While it . . . for shock": Kirstein, *Thirty Years: Kirstein's New York City Ballet*, p. 198.

189—"pornographic": cited in Kirstein, *Thirty Years: Lincoln Kirstein's New York City Ballet*, p. 128.

189–90—"Outside of . . . fun together": Author's interview with Adolph Green, July 26, 1999.

190—At one . . . of laughter": recounted by Howard Kissel, *New York Daily News*, August 2, 1998.

190—"he was . . . the Yemenites": *New York World-Telegram*, November 12, 1951.

190—"traveled to . . . is concerned": Eric Bentley (ed.), *Thirty Years of Treason: Excerpts from Hearings Before the House Committee on Un-American Activities, 1939–1968*, New York: Viking Press, 1971, p. 630.

190—In fact, he had been engaged: Larry Warren, *Anna Sokolow: The Rebellious Spirit*, Amsterdam: Harwood Academic Publishers, 1998, p. 104.

190—"As a dancer . . . in rehearsal": Taper, *Balanchine*, p. 19.

191—"warm and . . . one-man show": *New York Times*, November 15, 1951.

191—"Jerome Robbins . . . had dimension": *New York Herald Tribune*, November 15, 1951.

191—"a fun . . . the stage": Tanaquil Le Clercq with Rick Whitaker, "Jerome Robbins," *Ballet Review*, Summer 1998, p. 15.

191—"Roy Tobias . . . very upbeat": Letter to the author from Jillana (Zimmermann), February 21, 2000.

191—"mild madhouse": *New York Times*, December 5, 1951.

191—"joyous . . . ballet": *New York Herald Tribune*, December 5, 1951.

191–92—"Mr. Balanchine . . . the pit": Letter to the author from Jillana (Zimmermann), February 21, 2000.

192—"Jerry is . . . funny ballet": Author's interview with Edward Bigelow, June 7, 1999.

192—"His great . . . world over": Agnes de Mille cited in *New York Times*, August 16, 1998.

192—"The jokes . . . kinetic pantomime": *New York Herald Tribune*, December 5, 1951.

192—"It was . . . easy laughter": *New York Times*, August 9, 1998.

192—"Janet Reed and Roy Tobias . . . my neck": Tanaquil Le Clercq with Rick Whitaker, "Jerome Robbins," *Ballet Review*, Summer 1998, p. 15.

193—"a very . . . a downer": Janet Reed in *Ballet Review*, Summer 1988, p. 20.

193—"I think . . . one season": Author's interview with Robert Barnett, February 15, 1999.

193—"I was doing . . . the room": Author's interview with Todd Bolender, May 6, 1999.

193—"politics" and "I loved Jerry . . . doing a part": Author's interview with Louis Johnson, February 22, 1999.

194—"sweet and . . . theatrical rouser": *New York Herald Tribune*, February 15, 1952.

194—"It was pretty bad" and "thunderous applause": *New York Times*, February 15, 1952.

194—Le Clercq recalled: Tanaquil Le Clercq with Rick Whitaker, "Jerome Robbins," *Ballet Review*, Summer 1998, p. 17.

194—"found himself . . . of 34?'": Robert Kotlowitz, "Corsets, Corned Beef and Choreography," *Show*, December 1964.

194—In 1995 he said: Jerome Robbins interview with Deborah Jowitt, Kennedy Center Honors Oral History Program, July 1995.

194—"I heard that . . . me that'": *New York Times*, July 12, 1981.

194—"a very . . . love-hate": Author's interview with Jules Dassin, November 24, 1998.

195—"started out . . . business meeting": Author's interview with Miles White, March 28, 1999.

195—"I dropped . . . in this": Author's interview with Sheldon Harnick, January 27, 1999. Perry Bruskin offered another Robbins tale from the show. "In *Two's Company* I was an assistant stage manager and understudy, and my very good friend, named Bill Ross, was the production stage manager, the boss stage manager. I think just before we went to Detroit to try it out, one night Jerry came running over to Bill and started to give him an order or something like that. And my friend Bill was close to six foot tall, and Jerry of course was not. And Bill stood up at his full height, and he turned to Jerry and says, 'Get out of my backstage. Not during a show, you don't tell me anything.' And Jerry meekly, tail between his legs, walked off." Author's interview with Perry Bruskin, February 12, 1999.

195—"Jerry was . . . gay man": Author's interview with Saul Bolasni, April 27, 1999.

196—"Betty told . . . everybody else": Author's interview with Miles White, March 28, 1999.

196—"Well, just think . . . *42nd Street*": "A Celebration in Memory of Nora Kaye," 1987, Dance Collection, NYPL.

196—"so risqué . . . of danced": *New York Post*, January 20, 1953.

196—Throughout the tryouts: Lawrence J. Quirk, *Fasten Your Seat Belts: The Passionate Life of Bette Davis*, New York: Signet, 1990, pp. 376–377.

196–97—"She passed . . . five minutes": Author's interview with George Irving, April 20, 1999.

197—"The show started . . . Bea Lillie might": Joshua Logan, *Movie Stars, Real People, and Me*, New York: Delacorte Press, 1978, pp. 269.

197—Davis refused any assistance: Arthur Laurents was also called in for rewrites and contributed a scene of self-parody, but Davis demanded that the scene be rewritten so the object of teasing ridicule was Tallulah Bankhead. Laurents, *Original Story By*, p. 333.

197—"Jerry said . . . the screen": Author's interview with Shaun O'Brien, May 18, 1999.

197—"We were . . . to cry": Author's interview with Ralph Linn, February 23, 1999.

198—"Colorless and monotonous": *New York Times*, December 16, 1952.

198—"Every now . . . revue art": Ibid.

198—"shoots off . . . in charge": *New York Herald Tribune*, December 16, 1952.

198—"There was . . . involved with": Abbott, *Mister Abbott*, p. 233.

198—"Jerry was . . . to offer": Author's interview with Betty Comden, July 26, 1999.

199—"acrobatic production . . . Neighbor Policy": *New York Times,* February 22, 1953.

199—"I don't know . . . like that": Author's interview with Kirsten Valbor, June 9, 1999.

199–200—"Jerry came . . . hurt himself": Author's interview with Jerome Chodorov, January 13, 1999.

200—"You told him . . . the agony": Laurents, *Original Story By,* p. 331.

200—"I fought . . . about that": Author's interview with Sonia Robbins Cullinen, October 5, 1999.

200—"The last time . . . for him": Letter to the author from Lois Wheeler Snow, January 14, 2000.

201—"the lights . . . an American": Bentley, *Thirty Years of Treason,* pp. 625, 633, 634.

201—"demeanor before . . . social blackmail": Navasky, *Naming Names,* p. 75.

201–2—"In Jerry's . . . to hear": Walter Bernstein in Patrick McGilligan and Paul Buhle, *Tender Comrades: A Backstory of the Hollywood Blacklist,* New York: St. Martin's Griffin, 1999.

202—"I am . . . can appropriately": Bentley, *Thirty Years of Treason,* pp. 633–634.

202—When asked about the profession of Edna Ocko: Robbins may or may not have been aware that Ocko had left the dance profession entirely and was studying psychology. Being named as a Communist would have prevented Ocko from teaching in the public school system.

203—"They were . . . they operated": Author's interview with Jerome Chodorov, January 13, 1999.

203—"We were . . . to order": Author's interview with Madeline Gilford, December 4, 1998. Robbins' sister opined in this regard, "I believe the names named were already on the lists and not any revelations. They wanted collaboration." Letter to the author from Sonia Robbins Cullinen, March 11, 2000.

203—"dialectical materialism . . . *Fancy Free*": Bentley, *Thirty Years of Treason,* p. 627.

203—"The only thing . . . Lindy hop": Author's interview with Madeline Gilford, January 8, 1999.

203—"Stabbed by . . . wicked fairy": Author's interview with Jerome Chodorov, February 9, 1999.

203—Eric Bentley, the editor . . . : Author's interview with Eric Bentley, June 9, 1999.

204—"It was . . . they've done": Author's interview with Norma Sullivan, February 15, 1999.

204—"miserably revolting": Marc Blitzstein to Mina Curtiss, May 7, 1953. Cited in Gordon, *Mark the Music,* p. 343.

204—"never mentioned . . . be questioned": Letter to the author from Arthur Laurents, April 25, 1999.

204—Lardner admitted . . . : Author's interview with Ring Lardner, Jr., November 24, 1998.

205—"Jerry's ambition . . . he did": Letter to the author from Arthur Laurents, April 25, 1999.

205—"He was . . . you're evil'": *New York Times,* May 14, 1999.

205—"I don't think . . . respected it": Author's interview with Eric Bentley, June 9, 1999.

205—"Not that . . . real reason": Laurents, *Original Story By*, p. 332.

205—he was actually able to make more money: Robbins told Frances Herridge of the *Post*, "I like working for live audiences. . . . And although film money looks big, you can actually make more on Broadway if you have a hit." *New York Post*, January 6, 1958.

206—With Ford Motors . . . by HUAC: Mark Goodson in Griffin Fariello, *Red Scare: Memories of the American Inquisition*, New York: W. W. Norton & Company, 1995, p. 325.

206—"We had . . . of explosion": Author's interview with Lawrence White, January 21, 2000.

206—"He kicked . . . to trick": Letter to the author from Arthur Laurents, April 25, 1999.

207—"Jerry and I . . . was understandable": Author's interview with Sonia Robbins Cullinen, October 5, 1999.

207—"It was . . . cover this": Author's interview with Dorothy Gilbert, October 4, 1999.

207—Arthur Laurents recalled: Panel discussion, "Naming Names," George Street Theatre, New Brunswick, N.J., March 21, 1999.

207—But in the early seventies: Navasky, *Naming Names*, p. 223.

208—"The theme . . . towards you": Letter from Victor Navasky to Jerome Robbins, December 26, 1979.

208—Navasky had interviewed: R. Lawrence Siegel interviewed by Victor Navasky, June 1976. The official archive of the Committee Chairman (the Harold H. Velde Collection at the Dirksen Congressional Center) contains no record of the protest filed by Siegel, though the records in the archive are incomplete.

208—Robbins offered: Letter from Jerome Robbins to Victor Navasky, January 4, 1980.

209—"I was . . . on him": R. Lawrence Siegel interviewed by Victor Navasky, June 1976.

209—"HUAC told . . . him socially": R. Lawrence Siegel interviewed by Victor Navasky, June 1976.

209—"I just let . . . did ultimately": Author's interview with Michael Koessel, April 28, 1999.

210—"implied that . . . plagued him": Author's interview with Michael Koessel, April 28, 1999.

210—"Nora was . . . about that": Author's interview with Isabel Brown, April 19, 1999. Arthur Laurents also noted, "Neither Nora nor I approved or condoned but we both worked with Jerry anyway." Laurents, *Original Story By*, p. 332.

210—"From 1953 . . . the theater": Author's interview with Todd Bolender, May 6, 1999.

210—In fact, at the end of 1953: Jerome Robbins' FBI file, Freedom of Information-Privacy Act, Department of Justice, Memo from SAC, New York (100–104408) to the Director, December 15, 1953.

210–11—"you are . . . the Bureau": Jerome Robbins' FBI file, Freedom of Information-Privacy Act, Memo from the Director (100–369307) to SAC, New York, January 7, 1954.

211—"In conducting . . . most discreet . . .": Jerome Robbins' FBI file, Freedom of Information-Privacy Act, Department of Justice, Memo from J. Edgar Hoover (100–369307–12) to SAC, New York, October 22, 1954.

211—Robbins was: Jerome Robbins' FBI file, Freedom of Information-Privacy Act, Department of Justice, multiple memos.

211—"I was . . . the company": Author's interview with Louis Johnson, April 30, 1999.

211–12—"I learned . . . the ballet": Edward Villella, *Prodigal Son: Dancing for Balanchine in a World of Pain and Magic,* Pittsburgh: University of Pittsburgh Press, 1998 (first published by Simon and Schuster, 1992), pp. 47–48.

212—"animalistic": Jerome Robbins in Reynolds, *Repertory in Review,* p. 147.

212—"The mirror . . . work tool": *New York Times,* May 14, 1978.

212—Tanaquil Le Clercq recalled . . . it in": Tanaquil Le Clercq with Rich Whitaker, *Ballet Review,* Summer 1998, p. 18.

212—"She understood . . . faint perfume": *New York Times,* May 14, 1978.

213—"Jerry had . . . humid afternoon": Frank Moncion cited in Reynolds, *Repertory in Review,* p. 148.

213—"She made . . . the paper": *New York Times,* May 14, 1978.

213—"Things that . . . them before": *New York Times,* July 31, 1998.

213—"Not many . . . with himself": *New York Herald Tribune,* May 15, 1953.

213–14—"People said . . . the audience": Jerome Robbins in "The Evolution of the Modern Ballet," *World Theatre,* Vol. 8, No. 4, Winter 1959–60, p. 316.

214—"a combination . . . *the Wolf* : *New York Times,* June 3, 1953.

214—"a gay and . . . tuba": *New York Herald Tribune,* June 3, 1953.

214—"Balanchine didn't . . . tell Jerry": Author's interview with Edward Bigelow, June 7, 1999.

215—"From the . . . a trend": Mary Martin, *My Heart Belongs,* New York: William Morrow and Company, 1976, pp. 198–199.

215—"Oh, they . . . understand this": Author's interview with Lawrence White, January 21, 2000.

216—"Everything went . . . our stools": Martin, *My Heart Belongs,* p. 201.

216—"I certainly . . . of view": Larry Warren, *Anna Sokolow: The Rebellious Spirit,* Amsterdam: Harwood Academic Publishers, 1998, p. 105.

216—"As I . . . the ballet": Jerome Robbins in Reynolds, *Repertory in Review,* p. 161.

217—"I knew . . . quite pleasant": Author's interview with Patricia Wilde, May 15, 1999.

217—"We rehearsed . . . he wanted": Author's interview with Richard Thomas, April 27, 1999.

217—"We had . . . a flood": Author's interview with Patricia Wilde, May 15, 1999.

217—"charmingly composed . . . ensemble formations": John Martin in Reynolds, *Repertory in Review,* p. 161.

217—"non-nervous . . . is serenity": Reynolds, *Repertory in Review,* p. 161.

218—"The most . . . innocent people": Erik Johns in Aaron Copland and Vivian Perlis, *Copland: Since 1943,* New York: St. Martin's Griffin, 1989, p. 219.

218—"degradation ceremony": Navasky, *Naming Names,* p. 319.

218—"Jerry Robbins . . . have time!": Copland and Perlis, *Copland,* p. 211.

218—"inconclusive and . . . usually effective": *New York Times,* April 2, 1954.

218—"That was . . . very difficult": Author's interview with Mary Hunter Wolf, April 11, 1999.

219—"Jerry was . . . breast amputations": Author's interview with Sonia Robbins Cullinen, October 5, 1999.

219—"I wrote to Jerry . . . that situation." Letter to the author from Sonia Robbins Cullinen, March 11, 2000.

219—"Jerry, after . . . Jerry's character": Author's interview with Dorothy Gilbert, October 4, 1999.

220—"I don't mean . . . in it": Buzz Miller in Kevin Boyd Grubb, *Razzle Dazzle: The Life and Work of Bob Fosse,* New York: St. Martin's Press, 1989, p. 41.

220—"Jerry felt . . . a future": Author's interview with Gwen Verdon, June 24, 1999.

220—"I remember . . . successful show": Letter to the author from Harold Prince, June 11, 1999.

220—*"Romeo and Juliet* in the Midwest": Harold Prince in Foster Hirsch, *Harold Prince and the American Musical Theatre,* Cambridge: Cambridge University Press, 1989, p. 28.

221—"an amateur . . . its meeting": George Abbott in Gottfried, *All His Jazz: The Life and Death of Bob Fosse,* New York: Da Capo Press, 1990, p. 77.

221—"Look, the . . . it out": Jerome Robbins in Gottfried, *All His Jazz,* p. 79.

221—"It isn't . . . nobody else's": Jerome Robbins in Gottfried, *All His Jazz,* p. 81.

221–22—"I do not . . . the show": Letter to the author from Harold Prince, June 11, 1999.

222—"There was . . . cuff links": Author's interview with Gwen Verdon, June 24, 1999.

222—"bright, brassy . . . sassy": *New York Herald Tribune,* May 14, 1954.

222—"The last . . . the best": *New York Times,* May 14, 1954.

222—"This is . . . anybody's auditorium": *New York Herald Tribune,* May 14, 1954.

222—"Of course . . . no tomorrow": Buzz Miller in Grubb, *Razzle Dazzle,* p. 45.

222—"Somehow I . . . went on": Shirley MacLaine in Grubb, *Razzle Dazzle,* p. 45–46.

223—"According to . . . theater folklore": Buzz Miller in Grubb, *Razzle Dazzle,* p. 46.

223—"When Jerry . . . and Jerry": Author's interview with Gwen Verdon, June 24, 1999.

223—"[Robbins] talks . . . to lunch": Bob Fosse in Grubb, *Razzle Dazzle,* p. 75.

224—"Jerry's creativity . . . creative": Author's interview with Mary Hunter Wolf, April 11, 1999.

224—"You depend . . . no good": Jerome Robbins in "On Till Morning: The Creation of *Peter Pan,*" *The Journal for Stage Directors & Choreographers,* Fall/Winter 1998, p. 50 (excerpted from panel discussion, Marymount Manhattan Theater, February 23, 1982).

224—"I really had . . . rotten summer": Author's interview with Mary Hunter Wolf, April 11, 1999.

224—"Of the scripts . . . too much": Jerome Robbins in *The New Yorker,* December 11, 1954.

225—"Peter comes . . . in a way": Jerome Robbins in "On Till Morning: The Creation of *Peter Pan,*" *The Journal for Stage Directors & Choreographers,* Fall/Winter 1998, p. 48 (excerpted from panel discussion, Marymount Manhattan Theater, February 23, 1982).

225—"When I was . . . the show": Ibid., p. 50.

225—"It was . . . whole show": Author's interview with Mary Hunter Wolf, April 11, 1999.

225—"He gave . . . at all": Author's interview with Robert Tucker, May 12, 1999.

226—"You've got . . . appalling": Jule Styne in Theodore Taylor, *Jule: The Story of Composer Jule Styne,* New York: Random House, 1979, p. 5.

226—"We wrote . . . hadn't been": Author's interview with Adolph Green, July 26, 1999.

226—"That's when . . . show together": Author's interview with Betty Comden, July 26, 1999.

226—"Jerry did . . . beside himself": Interview with Trude Rittmann, December 9, 1976, Oral History Project, Dance Collection, NYPL.

226—"It was . . . to New York": Mary Hunter Wolf in "On Till Morning: The Creation of *Peter Pan,*" *The Journal for Stage Directors & Choreographers,* Fall/Winter 1998, p. 55 (excerpted from panel discussion, Marymount Manhattan Theater, February 23, 1982).

226–27—"was determined . . . for me": Martin, *My Heart Belongs,* pp. 203–205.

227—"The audience . . . stop flying": Ibid., p. 208.

227—"There's a . . . find them": Jerome Robbins in *The New Yorker,* December 11, 1954.

227—"We had . . . number work": Jerome Robbins in "On Till Morning: The Creation of *Peter Pan,*" *The Journal for Stage Directors & Choreographers,* Fall/Winter 1998, p. 53 (excerpted from panel discussion, Marymount Manhattan Theater, February 23, 1982).

227—"There wasn't . . . of doing": Ibid., p. 54.

227—The sets, created by Peter Larkin: Larkin subsequently broke with Robbins and refused to collaborate on restaging numbers for *Jerome Robbins' Broadway* in 1989.

228–29—"I went to . . . to create": Author's interview with Joan Tewkesbury, March 20, 1999.

229—"vastly amusing . . . delight": *New York Times,* October 21, 1954.

229—"It's the . . . happy disbelief": *New York Herald Tribune,* October 21, 1954.

229—"I made a . . . gold stars": Martin, *My Heart Belongs,* pp. 213–214.

229–30—"We performed . . . do it": Jerome Robbins in "On Till Morning: The Creation of *Peter Pan,*" *The Journal for Stage Directors & Choreographers,* Fall/Winter 1998, p. 54 (excerpted from panel discussion, Marymount Manhattan Theater, February 23, 1982).

230—"perhaps television's happiest hour": *New York Times,* March 6, 1955.

CHAPTER SIX:

231—"If a show . . . good shows": Jerome Robbins in *The Theatre Magazine,* July 1960.

231–32—"Jerry R. called. . . . just right": Leonard Bernstein, *Findings,* New York: Simon & Schuster, 1982, p. 144, reprint from *Playbill,* September 1957.

232—"The production . . . some time": *New York Herald Tribune,* January 27, 1949.

232—"the dance . . . come down": Nora Kaye in Keith Garebian, *The Making of West Side Story,* Buffalo, N.Y.: Mosaic Press, 1995, p. 31.

232—"fell apart . . . show anyway": Letter to the author from Arthur Laurents, May 12, 1999.

232—"our gang . . . bless us!": Bernstein, *Findings,* p. 144, reprint from *Playbill,* September 1957.

233—"When he . . . and pronto": Yuriko Kikuchi, "How He Got What He Wanted," *The Journal for Stage Directors & Choreographers,* Fall/Winter 1998, pp. 37–38.

233—"He didn't hate . . . humiliate her": Author's interview with Yuriko Kikuchi, December 16, 1998.

234—"Jerry was . . . down, down, down": Yuriko Kikuchi, "How He Got What He Wanted," *The Journal for Stage Directors & Choreographers,* Fall/Winter 1998, pp. 37–38.

234—"where there . . . you're doing": Jerome Robbins, The Kennedy Center Honors Oral History Program, interviewed by Deborah Jowitt, July 11, 1995.

234—While recovering: *New York Post,* September 18, 1958.

235—"That was . . . the time": Author's interview with Richard Thomas, April 27, 1999.

235—"I did . . . was marvelous": Author's interview with Vida Brown.

236—"It's not . . . to it": Author's interview with Robert Barnett, February 15, 1999.

236—"There were . . . stabbed myself": Author's interview with Todd Bolender, May 16, 1999.

236—"Sometimes, as . . . it later": Jerome Robbins in *Dance Magazine,* December 1959.

236—"a completely . . . are corny": *New York Times,* March 7, 1956.

236—"in spite . . . of dance": *New York Herald Tribune,* March 7, 1956.

236–37—"*The Concert* . . . to decide": Jerome Robbins, "The Evolution of the Modern Ballet," *World Theatre,* Winter 1959–60, p. 319.

237—He wrote several letters: Undated letters from Jerome Robbins to Slim Hayward, Leland Hayward Collection, Dance Collection, NYPL, #MGZMD46, Correspondence Folder # 1.

237—"saw a lot . . . the earth": Slim Keith with Annette Tapert, *Slim: Memories of a Rich and Imperfect Life,* New York: Simon & Schuster, 1990, pp. 172–173.

237–38—"I was two . . . firm bond": Author's interview with Kitty Hawks, May 15, 1999.

238—Writing to Slim: Leland Hayward Collection, Dance Collection, NYPL, #MGZMD46, Correspondence Folder # 1.

238—"tradition-bound . . . his potential": Jerome Robbins, "Reflections on the Royal Danish Ballet," *Theatre Arts,* September 1956.

238—"an omen": George Balanchine cited in Taper, *Balanchine,* p. 240.

238–39—"That so . . . for everyone": Robert Gottlieb, "Balanchine's Dream," *Vanity Fair,* December 1998.

239–40—"Jerry called . . . so unreasonable": Author's interview with Betty Cage, March 10, 1999. Company manager Edward Bigelow confirmed that Balanchine had requested that Robbins run the company after Le Clercq was stricken. Bigelow said, "That's true. I can't remember what Jerry was doing at that time. There were times when he was quite debilitated. . . . I can only think that he must have been very ill, because it's something he would have done if he could. In Betty's way of thinking he had to do it, but in his way of thinking, he couldn't. She wouldn't have seen it that way." Author's interview with Edward Bigelow, June 7, 1999.

240—"He loved . . . white wine": Tanaquil Le Clercq with Rick Whitaker, "Jerome Robbins," *Ballet Review,* Summer 1998.

240—Jerry remained a loyal and devoted friend: In this regard, Edward Bigelow recalled, "Jerry and Tanny always got along, but especially after Balanchine died, he [Jerry] took care of her. If she wanted to go here or wanted to go there, he would make sure that [his friend] Aidan [Mooney] or somebody took her. Jerry was marvelous, always took care of her, always. One year before Tanny's mother died, he gave a big birthday party for her mother at his house. Taking care of her was just something he always did. He didn't ask anything in return and saw to it that things were done. But there was nothing overt about it." Author's interview with Edward Bigelow, June 7, 1999.

240—"bosom pals": Jerome Robbins, The Kennedy Center Honors Oral History Program, interviewed by Deborah Jowitt, July 11, 1995.

241—Conflicts first erupted: Taylor, *Jule: The Story of Composer Jule Styne*, pp. 9–10.

241—"I'm locking . . . each day": Jerome Robbins in Taylor, *Jule: The Story of Composer Jule Styne*, p. 10.

241—"We had . . . the show": Author's interview with Betty Comden, July 26, 1999.

241—"inscrutable . . . more darkly": Author's interview with Jean Stapleton, April 26, 1999.

241–42—"I went . . . or relationship": Author's interview with Gerald Freedman, March 4, 1999.

242—"The variety . . . and direction": Jerome Robbins in *Dance Magazine*, December 1956.

242—"Jerry set . . . the theater": Gerald Freedman, "From *Bells Are Ringing* to *The Poppa Piece*," *The Journal for Stage Directors & Choreographers*, Fall/Winter 1998, p. 34.

242—"He [Jerry] turned . . . perfection": Author's interview with Gerald Freedman, March 4, 1999.

242—"Jerry gave . . . at him": Author's interview with Eddie Lawrence, January 15, 1999.

243—"Listen to . . . Don't stop!' ": Taylor, *Jule: The Story of Composer Jule Styne*, p. 10.

243—"We had . . . his lap": *New York Daily News*, August 2, 1998.

243—"Bobby was . . . didn't work": Author's interview with Frank Derbas, February 17, 1999.

243—"The redoubtable . . . Astonishing!": Author's interview with George Irving, April 20, 1999.

243–44—"Bobby had . . . very funny": Author's interview with Frank Derbas, February 17, 1999.

244—The New Haven run: Taylor, *Jule: The Story of Composer Jule Styne*, p. 14.

244—"disenchantment . . . a subway": *New York Times*, November 30, 1956.

244—"a sweetheart of a show": *New York Herald Tribune*, November 30, 1956.

244—"The whole . . . Jerome Robbins": *New York Journal-American*, November 30, 1956.

244–245—"Jerry didn't . . . very honest": Author's interview with Jean Stapleton, April 26, 1999.

245—"I am . . . to choreograph": Jerome Robbins in *Dance Magazine*, December, 1956.

245—"The aim . . . major thrust": Jerome Robbins, BBC-TV Obituary Tribute, October 19, 1990.

245—"the futility of intolerance": Author's interview with Grover Dale, March 17, 1999.

246—"a gossamer . . . own world": Arthur Laurents in Garebian, *The Making of West Side Story*, p. 31.

246—"womb . . . to worm": Arthur Laurents, *West Side Story*, in Stanley Richards (ed)., *Great Musicals of the American Theatre*, Vol. I, Radnor, Pennsylvania: Chilton, 1973.

246—"too strong . . . for love": Arthur Laurents, *Original Story By: A Memoir of Broadway and Hollywood*, New York: Alfred A. Knopf, 2000, p. 349.

247—"to bring . . . real simplicity": Stephen Sondheim cited in Humphrey Burton, *Leonard Bernstein*, New York: Anchor Books, 1994, p. 274.

247—"in that . . . three notes": Leonard Bernstein in Burton, *Leonard Bernstein*, p. 274.

247—"We raped . . . a song": Leonard Bernstein, Dramatists Guild Round Table, Fall 1985.

247–48—"I think . . . Jerry off": Letter to the author from Stephen Sondheim, April 9, 1999.

248—He repeatedly acquiesced: Burton, *Leonard Bernstein*, p. 275.

248—"Jerry continues . . . very talented": Leonard Bernstein to Felicia Montealegre, July 19, 1957, cited in Burton, *Leonard Bernstein*, p. 270.

248—"I know . . . I am": Sid Ramin in Burton, *Leonard Bernstein*, p. 275.

248—"I remember . . . that's it!'": Leonard Bernstein, Dramatists Guild Round Table, Fall 1985.

248—"The continual . . . excitement": Jerome Robbins, Dramatists Guild Round Table, Fall 1985.

248—"Kazan said. . . . this context": Author's interview with Gerald Freedman, March 4, 1999.

249—"Bobby Griffith . . . it presented": Letter to the author from Harold Prince, June 11, 1999.

249—"My understanding . . . special": Author's interview with Gerald Freedman, March 5, 1999.

249—"They're all . . . with pride": Leonard Bernstein to Felicia Montealegre, July 1957, cited in Burton, *Leonard Bernstein*, p. 271.

249–50—"About a . . . that cool": Stephen Sondheim in Meryle Secrest, *Stephen Sondheim: A Life*, New York: Alfred A. Knopf, 1998, p. 122.

250—"Certainly, Jerry . . . emphasize directing": Letter to the author from Harold Prince, June 11, 1999.

250—"Peter Gennaro . . . master artist": Stephen Sondheim in Secrest, *Stephen Sondheim*, p. 122.

250–51—" . . . of course . . . a project": Letter to the author from Harold Prince, June 11, 1999.

251—"We were . . . a father": Author's interview with Chita Rivera, April 30, 1999.

251—"We did . . . loved it": Author's interview with Grover Dale, March 17, 1999.

251—"I started . . . each gang": Author's interview with Tony Mordente, April 16, 1999.

252—"I must . . . for Mordente": Author's interview with Chita Rivera, April 30, 1999.

252—"Jerry not . . . his lumps": Author's interview with Tony Mordente, April 16, 1999.

252—"I was . . . a Riff": Author's interview with Jay Norman, March 1, 1999.

252–53—"Jerry was . . . No, sir'": Author's interview with Michael Callan, February 3, 1999.

253—"Do you hate . . . *Jerry Robbins*": Michael Callan, *Spilling the Beans*, memoir in progress.

253—"He had . . . the time": Larry Kert in Peyser, *Bernstein*, p. 275.

253–54—"We rehearsed . . . head": Author's interview with Carol Lawrence, February 4, 1999.

254—"cruelty . . . untalented faggot'": Author's interview with William Weslow, December 27, 2000.

254—Arthur Laurents recollected: Arthur Laurents, *Original Story By*, p. 358.

254—"During the rumble . . . of the gangs . . .": Author's interview with Grover Dale, May 2, 2000.

254—"Jerry was . . . not Larry!!!": Letter by e-mail from Michael Callan, May 10, 2000.

255—"I've always . . . trusting him": Author's interview with Chita Rivera, April 30, 1999.

255—"It was . . . imagination": Author's interview with Gerald Freedman, March 5, 1999.

255—"It *was* . . . fell short": Author's interview with Jay Norman, March 1, 1999.

256—"The only . . . being vicious": Author's interview with Marilyn D'Honou, May 13, 1999.

256—"That was . . . loved that": Author's interview with Carole D'Andrea, March 21, 1999.

256—"was constantly . . . a person": Author's interview with Ronnie Lee, June 16, 1999.

256—"a workaholic . . . both ends": Author's interview with Jay Norman, March 1, 1999.

256—"which made . . . her character": Author's interview with Wilma Curley, May 28, 1999.

257—"Over the years . . . with anyone": Author's interview with Grover Dale, March 17, 1999.

257—"The gypsy . . . Bacall weep": Gene Gavin, *B.C. to BDWY: The Memoir of a Broadway Gypsy*, memoir in progress.

257—"Everyone's coming . . . the agony": Leonard Bernstein to Felicia Montealegre, August 15, 1957, cited in Burton, *Leonard Bernstein*, p. 272.

258—"I got . . . on properly": Author's interview with Martin Charnin, July 8, 1999.

258—"a uniquely . . . on life": *Washington Post*, August 20, 1957.

258—"We got . . . we had": Author's interview with Michael Callan, February 3, 1999.

258—"The opening . . . entourage": Author's interview with Ronnie Lee, June 16, 1999.

258—"not well . . . this morning": *New York Herald Tribune,* September 27, 1957.

258—"profoundly moving . . . of view": *New York Times,* September 27, 1957.

259—"Miles didn't . . . her man": Author's interview with Frances E. T. Davis, March 22, 1999.

259—"I thought . . . represented": Letter to the author from Stephen Sondheim, March 1, 1999.

259–60—"Somehow that . . . really incredible": Author's interview with Alan Johnson, May 17, 1999.

260—"I remember . . . else did": Author's interview with Tony Mordente, April 16, 1999.

260—"Jerry's vision . . . of it": Author's interview with Gerald Freedman, March 5, 1999.

260—"this show is my baby": Leonard Bernstein letter to David Diamond cited in Burton, *Leonard Bernstein,* pp. 275–276.

260–61—"When it . . . was evil": Letter to the author from Arthur Laurents, May 12, 1999.

261—Some colleagues with whom Robbins later consulted: Author's interview with Bill Daniels, March 18, 1999. Author's interview with Gerald Hiken, June 1, 1999.

262—" . . . the question . . . this statue": Jerome Robbins in *Dance Magazine,* March 1958.

262—"I didn't . . . just happened": *New York Times,* June 3, 1990.

262—"I was . . . own company": *New York Times,* July 12, 1981.

262–63—"The countryside . . . was ideal": Jerome Robbins in *Dance Magazine,* September 1958.

263–64—"We had . . . those people": Author's interview with Wilma Curley, June 23, 1999.

264—"I had . . . to people": Author's interview with Jay Norman, March 1, 1999.

264—"I remember . . . his way": Author's interview with James Moore, April 15, 1999.

265—"He was . . . very unusual": Author's interview with Erin Martin, April 18, 1999.

265—"tries to . . . modern life": Jerome Robbins, "The Evolution of the Modern Ballet," *World Theatre,* Winter 1959–60, p. 320.

265—"a rousing . . . and fancies": *New York Times,* June 9, 1958.

265—"refined and . . . 'beat generation'": *New York Times,* July 17, 1958.

265—"It was . . . more embellishment": *Dance Magazine,* October 1958.

265—"New York . . . Robbins Festival": *New York Herald Tribune,* August 31, 1958.

266—"What really . . . of life": Ibid.

266—"an amusing . . . himself proud": *New York Times,* September 5, 1958.

266—"almost the . . . in dance": Jerome Robbins in *Dance Magazine,* May 1959.

267—"How can . . . like that": Arthur Laurents in Secrest, *Stephen Sondheim,* p. 133.

267—"I am . . . her mother": Jerome Robbins in *Dance Magazine,* May 1959.

267—While Robbins was: Secrest, *Stephen Sondheim*, p. 135.

267–68—"And I'm . . . Rose's *what?*": Stephen Sondheim in Secrest, *Stephen Sondheim*, p. 136.

268—"We howl . . . this day": Arthur Laurents in Secrest, *Stephen Sondheim*, p. 135.

268—"Yes, Jerry . . . the moment": Letter to the author from Stephen Sondheim, March 1, 1999.

268—"Jule Styne was . . . already written": Stephen Sondheim in Secrest, *Stephen Sondheim*, p. 138.

268–69—"though Jerry . . . Only Jerry Robbins": Laurents, *Original Story By*, p. 391.

269—Both Robbins and Merman: Howard Kissel, *David Merrick: The Abominable Showman*, New York: Applause, 1993, p. 162.

269—"the very . . . stage mothers": *New York Herald Tribune*, May 22, 1959.

269—Rose next sends Louise: Arthur Laurents identified "the need for recognition" as the central theme of the play. "Rose needed it in lights; Louise needed it from her mother. Parents who live their children's lives, children who grow up to be their parents—these are the stories of Rose and Louise in *Gypsy*, these are themes in *Gypsy*. But the theme that drives all the characters and the whole show is that need for recognition, a need everyone has in one way or another." Laurents, *Original Story By*, p. 382.

269—"I never . . . a story!": Author's interview with June Havoc, April 23, 1999.

269—"In his memoir . . . and eloped": Laurents, *Original Story By*, pp. 388–389.

270—"A lawyer . . . it happily": Author's interview with June Havoc, April 23, 1999.

270—Robbins told D'Andrea: Author's interview with Carole D'Andrea, March 21, 1999. According to Howard Kissel, when he was researching his David Merrick biography, Havoc told him that her reservations about the script concerned the way it belittled her. After all, she had been a major vaudeville star. Havoc signed the *Gypsy* release, according to Kissel, "because she knew how much the show meant to her sister." Note from Howard Kissel to the author, September 28, 2000.

270—"was a . . . the stage . . .": Letter to the author from Stephen Sondheim, April 9, 1999.

270—"David [Merrick] . . . life miserable": Author's interview with Carole D'Andrea, March 21, 1999.

270—"All of us . . . loved Carole": Author's interview with Sandra Church, June 30, 1999.

270–72—"I had to . . . in New York": Author's interview with Lane Bradbury, March 31, 1999.

272—Arthur Laurents remembered . . . from the producers: Laurents, *Original Story By*, p. 398.

272—Thus, according to Bradbury: As Arthur Laurents remembered it, "Six months later, while Lane Bradbury was in the hospital with a damaged hamstring, Jerry and Ethel had her fired. That night, Ethel presented Lane's understudy with a bouquet of flowers onstage." Laurents, *Orginal Story By*, p. 398.

272—"Jerry was . . . to watch": Author's interview with Jack Klugman, December 8, 1998.

273—"Jerry left . . . walking around": Author's interview with Sandra Church, June

30, 1999. Arthur Laurents recalled that Sandra Church won the role over Suzanne Pleshette and claimed that Robbins was never satisfied with her performance in the second-act strip. Laurents wrote, "Jerry lost patience and asked me to rehearse Sandra's scenes in the ladies' lounge. . . . Very little of whatever progress Sandra made in the ladies' lounge remained the moment she went back to rehearse onstage with Jerry. Her terror blocked her and, in turn, when they got to the strip, blocked him from inventing." Arthur Laurents, *Orginal Story By*, pp. 391–392.

273—"I auditioned . . . number now": Author's interview with Robert Tucker, May 12, 1999.

273–74—"You couldn't . . . him, too": Author's interview with Jacqueline Mayro, January 10, 1999.

274—"You forget . . . as childlike": Jerome Robbins in *Dance Magazine*, May 1959.

274—"Originally there . . . would do": Author's interview with Jacqueline Mayro, January 10, 1999.

274–75—"Jerry would. . . . forty years ago": Author's interview with John Kander, March 8, 1999.

276—"I have . . . for $10,000": Kissel, *David Merrick*, p. 168.

276—During the Philadelphia . . . so Arthur did": Letter to the author from Stephen Sondheim, December 13, 2000.

276—"Along with . . . better advantage": Ethel Merman with George Eells, *Merman: An Autobiography*, New York: Simon & Schuster, 1978, p. 204.

276–77—"clash of . . . or anything": Author's interview with Jacqueline Mayro, January 10, 1999.

277—"Jerry and I . . . I'm acting!'": Author's interview with John Kander, March 8, 1999.

277—"Under the . . . the queen": *New York Times*, May 22, 1959.

277—"I'm not . . . in years": *New York Herald Tribune*, May 22, 1959.

278—"We can . . . about it": Arthur Laurents in Secrest, *Stephen Sondheim*, pp. 140–141.

278—"We had . . . wonderful relationship": Author's interview with Jack Klugman, December 8, 1998.

278—"It was . . . lost it": Author's interview with Sandra Church, June 30, 1999.

278–79—Dear Jerome . . . of Music": Letter from Leland Hayward to Jerome Robbins, September 23, 1959, Leland Hayward Collection, correspondence folder, Dance Collection, NYPL.

279—"I started . . . one too": Author's interview with Sandra Church, June 30, 1999.

280—"Everyone in . . . my life": Keith with Tapert, *Slim: Memories of a Rich and Imperfect Life*, pp. 258–259.

280—"cerebral decision": Ibid., p. 266.

280–81—"Perhaps it . . . you are": Ibid., pp. 173–174.

281—"Mom was . . . the key": Author's interview with Kitty Hawks, May 15, 1999.

282—"A strange . . . music, *Moves*": Jerome Robbins interview with Vivian Perlis approved by him for a published response to Jack Anderson, *New York Times*, November 19, 1987.

282—"What he . . . 20 minutes": Author's interview with Jay Norman, March 1, 1999.

282—"We do . . . 20th-Century choreography": Giovanni Carendente, "Ballet at the Spoleto Festival," *Dance Magazine*, October 1959.

282–83—"there is . . . of commonness": *New York Times*, October 9, 1961.

283–84—"We went . . . in London": Author's interview with Tom Stone, March 22, 1999.

284—"an almost feverish reaction": Alexander Bland in *The Observer*, undated clipping, Dance Collection, NYPL.

284—"Ballet Ambassador": *New York Herald Tribune*, September 20, 1959.

284–85—"I went . . . the Roof": Author's interview with Arnold Newman, May 3, 1999.

285—"His own . . . was awful!": Anecdote confirmed by author's interview with assistant stage mananger Joe James, April 29, 1999.

285—"Frieda was . . . my mother": Author's interview with Sonia Robbins Cullinen, October 5, 1999.

285—"for those . . . our ability": *New York Daily News*, March 30, 1955.

286—" . . . television is . . . else entirely": *New York Times*, January 10, 1960.

286—"We had . . . it up": Author's interview with Robert Wise, February 4, 1999.

287—"We were . . . weeks later": Author's interview with Robert Wise, February 4, 1999.

287—"I know . . . she died": Author's interview with Mart Crowley, May 5, 1999.

287—"Jerry was . . . he wanted": Author's interview with Carole D'Andrea, March 21, 1999.

288—"What he . . . writer writes": Rita Moreno interview, National Public Radio, *Weekend Edition*, Sunday, November 7, 1999.

288—"You get . . . at all": Author's interview with Robert Wise, February 4, 1999.

288–89—"Every day . . . the process": Author's interview with Russ Tamblyn, March 20, 1999.

289—"After we . . . it became": Author's interview with Harvey Evans, May 7, 1999.

289—"You remember . . . get it'": Author's interview with Margaret Banks, June 11, 1999.

289–90—"We liked . . . West Side": Author's interview with Robert Wise, February 4, 1999.

290—"I fought . . . the picture'": Robert Wise, American Film Institute Seminars, October 1980 and May 1975.

290—"What Jerry . . . very clever": Author's interview with Robert Wise, February 4, 1999.

290—"There was . . . you get": Author's interview with Russ Tamblyn, March 20, 1999.

290—"He didn't . . . move on": Author's interview with Russ Tamblyn, March 20, 1999.

291—The "Prologue" and "Cool" numbers had been shot: In the end, Robbins claimed responsibility for about forty minutes of the movie. *New York Times*, December 11, 1960. After he left the film, another of Robbins' Broadway efforts quickly fizzled when he teamed up with producers Roger Stevens and Leland Hayward on Patricia Kip Millstein's unwieldy dramatization of Nabokov's *Invitation to a Beheading*.

291—"It was . . . the beast": Author's interview with Robert Wise, February 4, 1999.

291—"I was . . . very disappointed": Author's interview with Russ Tamblyn, March 20, 1999.

291—"She threatened . . . to quit": Author's interview with Mart Crowley, May 5, 1999.

291–92—"I did . . . soon forget": Author's interview with Tony Mordente, April 16, 1999.

292—"never forgave . . . was tension": Author's interview with Mart Crowley, May 5, 1999. Crowley's views were shared to some extent by Allen Midgette, who had auditioned for the role of Tony and ended up with a bit part in the film. Midgette also appeared in films by Bernardo Bertolucci and Andy Warhol, and impersonated Warhol at the artist's request on the lecture circuit in 1967. Allen Midgette maintained a lifelong friendship with Robbins, who looked with some amusement at Midgette's activities in the avant-garde world. Assessing Robbins' artistry, Midgette said, "Jerry was one of the few true artists who dedicated his life to his art. I think you can judge him by the fact that he did direct one movie, and he did win two Oscars, and he never made another movie. I think that means a great deal, more than people want to deal with. He expected others to give what he gave. You know, it's like if you go to a Tibetan monastery, you don't expect to be treated like a baby." Author's interview with Allen Midgette, June 15, 2000.

293—"the finest . . . of reality": Stanley Kauffman, *Dance Magazine*, October 1961.

293—"painfully old-fashioned . . . cinematic technology": Pauline Kael, *I Lost It at the Movies*, New York: Bantam, 1966.

293—"I want . . . pistol shot": *New York Times*, July 3, 1960.

293—"I loved . . . completely rehearse": Robbins in Emily Coleman, "From Tutus to T-Shirts," *New York Times Magazine*, October 8, 1961, p. 32.

293—"I'm in . . . by Hollywood": *New York Herald Tribune*, October 8, 1961.

293–94—"I'm enormously . . . in it . . . occasionally a scene": Robbins in Emily Coleman, "From Tutus to T-Shirts," *New York Times Magazine*, October 8, 1961, pp. 32, 37.

294—"Photography is . . . time limits": Jerome Robbins in *The Theatre Magazine*, July 1960.

CHAPTER SEVEN:

295–97—"I don't think anybody . . . the participants": Author's interview with Erin Martin, April 18, 1999.

297—"It was a . . . second now!'": Author's interview with Edward Verso, April 16, 1999.

297–99—"took place . . . been promised": Author's interview with Glen Tetley, January 20, 1999.

299—"is substantially . . . and philosophically": *New York Times*, October 18, 1961.

299—"In Europe they . . . to get there": Robbins in Emily Coleman, "From Tutus to T-Shirts," *New York Times Magazine*, October 8, 1961, pp. 20, 30.

300—"The music is . . . three of us'": Author's interview with Tom Stone, March 22, 1999.

301—"It's an extremely . . . right onstage": *New York World Telegram and Sun*, February 23, 1962.

301—"It was a . . . had to go": Author's interview with Arthur Kopit, April 3, 1999.

301—"No, that isn't . . . go anywhere": Author's interview with Gerald Hiken, June 1, 1999.

302—"I tried very . . . for sure": Author's interview with Bill Daniels, March 18, 1999.

302–3—"It was suprising . . . touch-and-go": Author's interview with Arthur Kopit, April 3, 1999.

304—"I'd given her . . . laughing about it": Author's interview with Patricia Zipprodt, February 24, 1999.

304–5—"If you're in . . . with me": Author's interview with Tony Lo Bianco, May 5, 2000.

305–6—"I came in . . . she did it again": Author's interview with Barry Primus, May 6, 1999.

306—"Oh, she . . . for masculinity": Author's interview with Tony Lo Bianco, May 5, 2000.

306—"Jerome Robbins has . . . tour de force": *New York Times*, February 27, 1962.

306—"In directing . . . Barbara Harris": *New York Herald Tribune*, February 27, 1962.

306—"In the old one . . . too amusing": *New York Daily News*, August 28, 1963.

306–7—"succumbing . . . original staging": *New York Post*, August 28, 1963.

307—"Everything works . . . be delighted": *New York Times*, August 28, 1963.

307—"My ideal of . . . knew that": Author's interview with Barry Primus, May 6, 1999.

307–8—"I don't know . . . sacred enterprise": Author's interview with Arthur Kopit, April 3, 1999.

308—"When *A Funny Thing* . . . to work": Letter to the author from Harold Prince, June 11, 1999.

309—"I had to . . . of Hal's'": Author's interview with Tom Stone, March 22, 1999.

309—"a letter arrived . . . everybody down": Stephen Sondheim in Meryle Secrest, *Stephen Sondheim: A Life*, New York: Alfred A. Knopf, 1998, p. 149.

309—"Your cowardly . . . for immorality": Larry Gelbart, *Laughing Matters: On Writing M*A*S*H, Tootsie, Oh, God!, And a Few Other Funny Things*, New York: Random House, 1998, p. 214.

309—"So we're . . . with Zero": Author's interview with Tom Stone, March 22, 1999.

310—" . . . as Jerry . . . have you?'": Letter to the author from Harold Prince, June 11, 1999.

310—"Listen, Hal . . . don't blacklist": Zero Mostel in Kate Mostel and Madeline Gilford with Jack Gilford and Zero Mostel, *170 Years of Show Business*, New York: Random House, 1978, p. 8.

310—"not blacklist himself . . . Warner Brothers?": Madeline Gilford in Mostel and Gilford, *170 Years of Show Business*, p. 9.

310–11—"I finally told . . . what I said": Author's interview with Madeline Gilford, January 8, 1999.

311—"Zero worked . . . earshot": Letter to the author from Harold Prince, June 11, 1999.

311—"Jerry came in . . . cracked up": Author's interview with Tony Walton, February 24, 1999.

311–12—"They had done . . . have a solo": Author's interview with Madeline Gilford, December 4, 1998.

312—"He [Jerry] was . . . flailing a bit": Author's interview with Tony Walton, February 24, 1999.

312—"The opening number . . . baggy pants": Jerry Robbins as quoted by Stephen Sondheim in Secrest, *Stephen Sondheim*, p. 154.

312—"was sung by Zero . . . in New Haven": Kate Mostel in Mostel and Gilford, *170 Years of Show Business*, p. 10.

312–13—"He [Jerry] certainly . . . to him": Letter to the author from Stephen Sondheim, March 1, 1999.

313—"the nightmare . . . was wonderful": Author's interview with Tony Walton, February 24, 1999.

313—"I could . . . more time": Jerry Robbins as quoted by Stephen Sondheim in Secrest, *Stephen Sondheim*, p. 154.

314—"a very animated . . . 'Comedy Tonight'": *New York Journal-American*, May 9, 1962.

314—"a whole road . . . by himself": *New York Herald Tribune*, May 9, 1962.

314—"noisy, coarse . . . burlesque comedian": *New York Times*, May 9, 1962.

314—" . . . what other . . . in itself?": Gelbart, *Laughing Matters*, p. 215.

316—"The two women . . . why it happened": *New York Times*, April 28, 1963.

316–17—"I didn't know . . . me anyway": Author's interview with Eric Bentley, June 9, 1999.

317–18—"a sensational sense . . . my teeth": Author's interview with Samuel Matlovsky, June 15, 1999.

318–19—"Jerry was . . . community as such . . . sort of sado-masochistic": Author's interview with Eric Bentley, June 9, 1999.

319—"Jerry, when . . . with *Mother Courage*": Author's interview with Bill Daniels, March 18, 1999.

319–20—"He [Jerry] . . . really dismal": Author's interview with Gerald Hiken, June 1, 1999.

320—"There was a . . . not handle it": Author's interview with Samuel Matlovsky, June 15, 1999.

320—"Jerry had . . . *Mother Courage*": Author's interview with Eddie Lawrence, January 15, 1999.

320—The *Times* reported . . . beautiful movement": *New York Times*, April 28, 1963.

320–21—"Since we're . . . anxiety-making": Author's interview with Bruce Glover, February 5, 1999.

321—"Mike Kellin . . . own ideas": Author's interview with Gerald Hiken, June 1, 1999.

321–22—"Finally I'm . . . from me . . . classy man": Author's interview with Bruce Glover, February 5, 1999.

322–23—"Jerry, as I saw . . . was drugged!": Author's interview with Eric Bentley, June 9, 1999.

323—"Emo was . . . whole experience": Author's interview with Bruce Glover, February 5, 1999.

323—According to Patricia Zipprodt: Author's interview with Patricia Zipprodt, February 24, 1999.

323–24—"In the last week . . . by him": Author's interview with Eric Bentley, June 9, 1999.

324—"a visually . . . brilliant portrayal": *New York Daily News,* April 1, 1963.

324—"'Mother Courage' . . . build powerfully": *New York Times,* April 1, 1963.

324—"Exhilaration is . . . theatrical embellishment": *New York World Telegram and Sun,* April 1, 1963.

324–25—"There I was . . . was dreadful": Jerome Robbins in Robert Kotlowitz, "Corsets, Corned Beef and Choreography," *Show,* December 1964.

325—"the correct . . . been better": Author's interview with Eric Bentley, June 9, 1999.

325—"Jerry had . . . that way": Author's interview with Gerald Hiken, June 1, 1999.

325—Looking back in 1995: Jerome Robbins, The Kennedy Center Honors Oral History Program, interviewed by Deborah Jowitt, July 11, 1995.

325—"The career . . . mention money": Author's interview with Eric Bentley, June 9, 1999.

325—On June 4th, 1962: Theodore Taylor, *Jule: The Story of Composer Jule Styne,* New York: Random House, 1979, p. 234.

325–26—"My father's . . . Jerry Robbins": Author's interview with Norton Styne, February 9, 1999.

326—"I'd love . . . Jewish girl": Carol Burnett in Taylor, *Jule: The Story of Composer Jule Styne,* p. 236.

326—"How many . . . my shows?": David Merrick in Howard Kissel, *David Merrick: The Abominable Showman,* New York: Applause Books, 1993, p. 239.

326—"the Streisand name . . . Elvis Presley": cited by Randall Riese in *Her Name Is Barbra: An Intimate Portrait of the Real Barbra Streisand,* New York: Carol Publishing Group, 1993, p. 153.

327—Styne attended twenty-seven: Anne Edwards, *Streisand: A Biography,* New York: Berkley Boulevard Books, 1998 (first published by Little, Brown & Company, 1997), p. 163.

327—"You've got . . . She's Fanny": Jule Styne in Taylor, *Jule: The Story of Composer Jule Styne,* p. 236.

327—"There is . . . my mother": Fran Stark in Riese, *Her Name Is Barbra,* pp. 147–148.

327—the real Fanny: Edwards, *Streisand,* p. 164.

327—"I can't . . . manage it": John Patrick in Edwards, *Streisand,* p. 165.

327—"You're supposed. . . . they're mine": Exchange cited in Taylor, *Jule: The Story of Composer Jule Styne,* pp. 236–237.

328—"Forty minutes . . . Fanny Brice": Jerome Robbins in Riese, *Her Name Is Barbra,* p. 149.

328—"Look, comma . . . *the kid*": Allan Miller in Riese, *Her Name Is Barbra,* p. 149.

328—"The show is . . . Nicky Arnstein": William Glover, Associated Press, 1964, cited in Riese, *Her Name Is Barbra,* p. 173.

328—"The reason . . . HIT PARADE!": Bob Fosse in Martin Gottfried, *All His Jazz: The Life and Death of Bob Fosse,* New York: Da Capo Press, 1990, p. 162.

329—"She was . . . come from": Lanie Kazan in Edwards, *Streisand,* p. 174.

329—"There was . . . you bitch!": John Patrick in Edwards, *Streisand*, p. 178.

330—as gossip-hound Earl Wilson reported: cited in Edwards, *Streisand*, p. 189.

330—"I don't know . . . became chummy": Kay Medford in Edwards, *Streisand*, p. 188.

330—Six songs were cut: Edwards, *Streisand*, p. 190.

330—"a Streisand triumph": *Philadelphia Inquirer,* February 5, 1964, cited in Edwards, *Streisand*, p. 164.

330—"Garson Kanin . . . was replaced": Author's interview with Jean Stapleton, April 26, 1999.

330—"I think . . . more direction": Barbra Streisand in Edwards, *Streisand*, p. 191.

330—"Robbins had . . . at all": Allan Miller in Riese, *Her Name Is Barbra*, p. 171.

330—Robbins joined . . . "over-all consultant": *New York Herald Tribune*, March 18, 1964.

331—"a marvel . . . insecurity": *New York Herald Tribune*, March 27, 1964.

331—"There were . . . hated it": Buzz Miller in Riese, *Her Name Is Barbra*, pp. 172–173.

331–32—"He [Jerry] reached . . . marvelous together": Author's interview with Royce Wallace, April 26, 2000.

332–33—"Jerry got along . . . a monster": Author's interview with Tom Stone, March 22, 1999.

333—"It won't . . . for it": Jerome Robbins in Taylor, *Jule: The Story of Composer Jule Styne*, p. 247.

333–34—"Jerry, of course . . . to par": Author's interview with Jean Stapleton, April 26, 1999.

334—"The idea . . . the show": Author's interview with Royce Wallace, April 26, 2000.

334—"Fanny's personality . . . be recaptured?": *New York Times*, March 27, 1964.

334–35—Walter Kerr . . . Mr. Ziegfeld": *New York Herald Tribune*, March 27, 1964.

335—"should . . . smash": *New York Journal-American*, March 27, 1964.

335—"Now . . . fair game": Barbra Streisand in Riese, *Her Name Is Barbra*, p. 180.

335—"why these . . . Only puppetsville": William Goldman, *The Season: A Candid Look at Broadway*, New York: Limelight, 1984 (first published by Harcourt, Brace & World, 1969), p. 272.

335–36—"The fact . . . and material": *New York Times*, April 28, 1963.

336—Stein recalled: Author's interview with Joseph Stein, October 4, 1999.

336—"It a . . . will go": David Merrick in Kissel, *David Merrick*, p. 30.

336—"they felt . . . really was": Author's interview with Joseph Stein, October 4, 1999.

336–37—"Apropos . . . what happened": Letter to the author from Harold Prince, June 11, 1999.

337—"It was . . . in Russia": Author's interview with Maria Karnilova, June 16, 1999.

337–38—"Early on . . . very excited": Author's interview with Sheldon Harnick, January 27, 1999. In fact, the village of Rozanka was occupied by the Nazis in 1942 and the Jewish population met with the same tragic fate as so many others: forced relocation, internment, unspeakable atrocities, ghettoization and extermination. The town survives to this day, but there are no longer any Jewish inhabitants.

338—"The real reason . . . my own": Jerome Robbins in Robert Kotlowitz, "Corsets, Corned Beef and Choreography," *Show*, December 1964.

338—"a tiny . . . entire being": *New York Post*, December 13, 1964.

338—In addition, Robbins studied: Robbins' assistant, Tommy Abbott, recalled watching several films with Robbins at his home along with designers Boris Aronson and Patricia Zipprodt. "One film was about Chagall; the other was *Through Laughter and Tears*, and I had to run that one again so a photographer who had come could shoot stills of whatever Jerry found particularly interesting—costumes of the period of our show, houses, a broken-down fence, old wooden stairs. These things fascinated Jerry." Abbott also observed that Robbins made use of the symbol of the circle in the designs and choreography throughout the show, culminating with the final exodus from the shtetl, when the circle of community was broken. Tommy Abbott in Richard Altman with Mervyn Kaufman, *The Making of a Musical: Fiddler on the Roof,* New York: Crown Publishers, 1971, p. 90.

338–39—"I wanted to . . . the world": Jerome Robbins in Robert Kotlowitz, "Corsets, Corned Beef and Choreography," *Show*, December 1964.

339—"I remember . . . on time": Letter to the author from Harold Prince, June 11, 1999.

339—Robbins' auditions for *Fiddler: The Making of a Musical*, p. 96. Altman also remembered one day early in the rehearsal period when "I found Jerry in an exceptionally good mood. 'How do you think it's going?' I asked. 'Oh, I don't know,' he said. 'I don't think I'm doing anything good at all.' Then he sort of chuckled. 'Maybe this is the show where they'll find me out.'" Altman, *The Making of a Musical*, p. 95.

339—For directing and choreographing: Robert Kotlowitz, "Corsets, Corned Beef and Choreography," *Show*, December 1964.

340—"Before Robbins . . . extremely difficult": Author's interview with Sheldon Harnick, January 27, 1999.

340—"There was . . . very negatively": Author's interview with Joseph Stein, October 4, 1999.

340—"I was standing . . . really cared": Author's interview with Tom Stone, March 22, 1999.

341—"They were . . . slow again": Author's interview with Julia Migenes, September 11, 1999.

341—"Zero once . . . sadistic streak": Author's interview with Chuck Rule, April 6, 1999.

341—"Mostel likes . . . it all": Jerome Robbins in Robtert Kotlowitz, "Corsets, Corned Beef and Choreography," *Show*, December 1964.

341–42—"He did not . . . her crazy": Author's interview with Joseph Stein, October 4, 1999.

342—"We had a . . . to New York": Author's interview with Chuck Rule, April 6, 1999. Part of the reason for the low company morale in Detroit was a sour review in *Variety*, which indicated that the show was at least a half hour too long and had limited potential. At the time of the Detroit run (July 27 to August 22), the city's newspapers were on strike, and the *Variety* piece was the only notice at that point. Altman, *The Making of a Musical*, pp. 9–11.

342–43—"One evening during . . . their jobs!": Altman, *The Making of a Musical*, pp. 67–68.

343—"Some trimming . . . 'Chava Ballet'": Altman, *The Making of a Musical*, p. 14.

343–44—"Before we . . . there, too": Author's interview with Sheldon Harnick, January 27, 1999. Harnick also noted the frustration the collaborators experienced when they tried to band together against Robbins: "Jerry's only weapon, if we all ganged up on him and disagreed at a certain point, was to say, 'Okay, do it your way. Get a different director'— which was maddening, and yet we had to trust him because he had total vision." Sheldon Harnick in Altman, *The Making of a Musical*, p. 32. Joseph Stein recalled how Robbins' lawyer, Floria Lasky, guarded his interests. "She protected him violently to the point where it irritated the hell out of me in terms of the project. As far she was concerned, don't you dare touch anything that Jerry touched. She's very protective, even as of today." Author's interview with Joseph Stein, October 4, 1999.

344—"tireless trial-and-error . . . forgive everything' ": Altman, *The Making of a Musical*, pp. 46, 47, 68.

344–45—"We were demented . . . and destructive": Author's interview with Patricia Zipprodt, February 24, 1999.

345—"Jerry was . . . that role": Author's interview with Maria Karnilova, September 10, 1999.

345—"Jerry was in love . . . fire him": Author's interview with Chuck Rule, April 6, 1999.

345—"Gluck Sandor was . . . would do": Author's interview with Duane Bodin, March 31, 1999.

345—"Once he . . . the world": Author's interview with Joseph Stein, October 4, 1999.

345—Years later, Robbins lauded: Jerome Robbins, Oral History Project, Dance Collection, NYPL, interview by Ellen Sorrin, November 28, 1995.

346—"I had a very . . . spirit anymore": Author's interview with Anzia Kubicek, March 28, 1999.

346—"Washington isn't . . . New York": Jerome Robbins in Altman, *The Making of a Musical*, p. 63.

346—On the afternoon of the premiere: Altman, *The Making of a Musical*, pp. 104–105.

346—"I was living . . . has had": Author's interview with Joseph Stein, October 4, 1999.

346—"I was backstage . . . long time": Author's interview with Dorothy Gilbert, October 4, 1999.

346–47—"This was . . . for him": Author's interview with Viola Zousmer, August 6, 1999.

347—"Jerry Robbins . . . the gathering: Altman, *The Making of a Musical*, pp. 105–106.

347—"Mad or melting . . . Broadway . . .": *New York Herald Tribune*, September 23, 1964.

347—"Kerr's review . . . comprehension": Jerry Bock in Altman, *The Making of a Musical*, pp. 106–107.

347—"one of . . . of art": *New York Daily News*, September 23, 1964.

347–48—"filled with . . . adds depth . . .": *New York Times*, September 23, 1964.

348—"brilliantly . . . intelligent": *New York Post*, September 23, 1964.

348—"The key word . . . Jerry crazy": Author's interview with Joseph Stein, October 4, 1999.

348–49—"He was a monster . . . another show": Author's interview with Maria Karnilova, June 16, 1999. Mostel stayed with the show for nine months, when his contract was up and the producers replaced him with Luther Adler. Tommy Abbott recalled that Robbins stayed away from *Fiddler* after the opening with Mostel. Altman, *The Making of a Musical,* p. 119.

349—"I think it . . . job right": Author's interview with Sheldon Harnick, January 27, 1999.

349—"We sat together . . . again either": Author's interview with Barry Primus, May 6, 1999.

349–50—"What Jerry . . . was Jerry": Author's interview with Miriam Karlin, December 26, 1998.

350—"*Fiddler* fell . . . in time": Author's interview with Barry Primus, May 6, 1999.

350—"I am aware . . . split with him": Walter Mirisch in Altman, *The Making of a Musical,* p. 182.

351—"And so a . . . the drain": *New York Times,* October 24, 1965.

351—"no estranged . . . difficulties": *New York Times,* January 5, 1965.

351—"a dreadful . . . smarting": Leonard Bernstein letter to David Diamond cited in Humphrey Burton, *Leonard Bernstein,* New York: Anchor Books, 1994, p. 347.

352—Early in 1965: Burton, *Leonard Bernstein,* p. 347.

352—"It wasn't . . . been influenced": Jerome Robbins in Clive Barnes, *Inside American Ballet Theatre,* New York: Hawthorne Books, Inc., 1977, p. 95.

352—"For both . . . be canceled": Charles Payne, *American Ballet Theatre,* New York: Alfred A. Knopf, 1978, pp. 211, 236.

353—"I am deeply . . . and all nature": *New York Times,* March 28, 1965.

354—"One time . . . after it": Author's interview with Erin Martin, April 18, 1999.

354—"Jerry was . . . loved that": Author's interview with Gladys Celeste, April 23, 1999.

355—"years of . . . damn reds": Author's interview with Patricia Zipprodt, February 24, 1999.

355—"an overwhelming . . . attack": *New York Times,* March 31, 1965.

355—"were drawn . . . same time": Doris Hering cited in George Balanchine and Francis Mason, *101 Stories of the Great Ballets,* New York: Anchor Books, 1989, p. 276.

355—"compassionate . . . grace": *New York Times,* February 6, 1966.

355—"I have enjoyed . . . opportunity comes": *New York Times,* March 28, 1965.

356—With plans to open: *New York Times,* April 5, 1966.

356—"I'm a good . . . said, 'Okay'": Author's interview with Tony Lo Bianco, May 5, 2000.

357—"We were . . . to work": *New York Herald Tribune,* March 30, 1966.

357—"The stage at . . . out there!'": Author's interview with Tony Lo Bianco, May 5, 2000.

357–58—"The play basically . . . thing before": Author's interview with Bernie Passeltine, April 14, 1999.

358—"It didn't . . . Jerry anyway": Author's interview with Bill Daniels, March 18, 1999.

358–59—"Jerry certainly . . . came back": Author's interview with Bernie Passeltine, April 14, 1999.

359—"When we closed . . . marvelous experience": Author's interview with Tony Lo Bianco, May 5, 2000.

359—"She was . . . for you": Author's interview with Michael Abbott, May 22, 1999.

360—"It's marvelous . . . of living": *New York Times*, March 13, 1966.

360—Mica Ertegün, later helped him decorate: Author's interview with Ahmet Ertegün, June 2, 1999. Ertegün said, "Mica kind of organized his house. He lived one house away from us, and she organized him in the country a little bit. You know she's a professional decorator."

360—he attended Capote's ball with Lady Slim Keith: Slim would later break with Capote over his 1975 Esquire story, "La Côte Basque," which was conceived as part of his scandalous book, *Answered Prayers*. A roman à clef, the story offered a thinly veiled portrait of Keith and her friend Ann Woodward, who committed suicide after its publication. Keith wrote, "I met Truman in the early 1950s at Diana Vreeland's house at dinner. . . . Truman had become the darling of New York society and a frequent fixture in the salons of the Upper East Side." The public scandal of "La Côte Basque" finally caused Lady Keith and others in their circle to recoil from Capote's "lying, gossiping, and trouble-making." Slim Keith with Annette Tapert, *Slim: Memories of a Rich and Imperfect Life*, New York: Simon and Schuster, 1990, pp. 218, 236.

361—"I saw Betty . . . crestfallen": Arthur Schlesinger, Jr., in George Plimpton, *Truman Capote: In Which Various Friends, Enemies, Acquaintances, and Detractors Recall His Turbulent Career*, New York: Doubleday, 1997, p. 264.

361—"No one is . . . toward it": Jerome Robbins in Robert Kotlowitz, "Corsets, Corned Beef and Choreography," *Show*, December, 1964.

361—"His one . . . produce anything": Author's interview with James Moore, April 15, 1999.

362—"I fixed it . . . my life": Author's interview with Tom Stone, March 22, 1999.

362–63—"The two years . . . for him": Author's interview with Erin Martin, April 18, 1999.

363—"I wanted to . . . really don't": Jerome Robbins in Deborah Jowitt, "Back, again, to ballet," *New York Times Magazine*, December 8, 1974, pp. 96–97.

363—"We didn't work . . . of tape?": Author's interview with James Mitchell, April 9, 1999.

363–64—"I cannot tell . . . good morning": Author's interview with Barry Primus, May 6, 1999.

364—"I remember . . . and sublime": Barry Primus, "The Sacred and the Sublime," *The Journal for Stage Directors and Choreographers*, Fall/Winter 1998, p. 43.

364—"She's the real thing": Author's interview with Erin Martin, April 18, 1999.

364–65—"I used to . . . I howled . . . experimental theater": Author's interview with James Dybas, May 4, 2000.

365—"Bob Wilson . . . architectural models": Author's interview with Erin Martin, April 18, 1999.

365–67—"I first met . . . the book": Author's interview with Robert Wilson, August 22, 1999.

367—"We were disagreeing . . . pure dance": Author's interview with Eric Bentley, June 9, 1999.

367–68—"He [Jerry] . . . other playwrights": Author's interview with Tom Stone, March 22, 1999.

368—"We had learned . . . something else": Author's interview with Grover Dale, March 17, 1999.

368—"It was like . . . the person": Author's interview with James Dybas, May 4, 2000.

368—"Lots of times . . . the Lab": Author's interview with Barry Primus, May 6, 1999.

369—"He had a . . . of anguish": Author's interview with Grover Dale, March 17, 1999.

369–70—"I think we . . . felt lost": Author's interview with Barry Primus, May 6, 1999.

370—"Wonderful, but . . . needed me": John Guare in Secrest, *Stephen Sondheim*, p. 188.

370—"Why haven't . . . completed them: Secrest, *Stephen Sondheim*, pp. 188–189.

370—Retitled *A Pray by Blecht: New York Times*, October 10, 1968.

370–71—"preoccupation with . . . and talent": Stuart Ostrow, *A Producer's Broadway Journey*, Westport, Connecticut: Praeger Publishers, 1999, pp. 37–38. In a letter to the author dated April 30, 1999, Stuart Ostrow wrote of the American Theater Lab: "It was Jerry's apotheosis; working on a dozen projects at the same time with no commercial deadline; committed to exploring the most fundamental areas of knowledge and artistic creation, areas where there is little expectation of immediate outcomes or striking applications. I remember seeing the first act of a musical about the Kennedy [assassination], a ballet-in-progress, a play about racism, with Billy Dee Williams and Ron Leibman, and much more. Ostensibly, it was my job to *produce* these works for Broadway; to force Jerry to make up his mind, to get on with it. . . . On reflection, I think it was Jerry's farewell to Broadway; he never directed any other musical. . . ."

371—". . . it seemed . . . with it": Letter to the author from Stephen Sondheim, March 1, 1999.

371—"Robbins said . . . It's over' ": John Guare in Secrest, *Stephen Sondheim*, pp. 188–189.

371—"Jerry struggled . . . too much'": Author's interview with Barry Primus, May 6, 1999.

371–72—"I don't like . . . not art": *New York Times*, April 25, 1969.

CHAPTER EIGHT:

373–74—"Jerry loved. . . . his childhood": Author's interview with Grover Dale, March 17, 1999.

374—Conrad remembered that Robbins' eyes: Author's interview with Christine Conrad, October 7, 1999.

374—"So it was . . . quite spectacular": Author's interview with Christine Conrad, October 7, 1999.

375—"Jerry was too . . . die first": Author's interview with Christine Conrad, October 7, 1999.

375—"We were both awestruck . . . I would say": Author's interview with Christine Conrad, October 7, 1999.

375—"I remember . . . certain point": Author's interview with Kitty Hawks, May 15, 1999.

375–76—"I have . . . Jerry's *trying*": Author's interview with Harold Talbott, January 10, 1999.

376—"He had given . . . over the years": Author's interview with Christine Conrad, October 7, 1999. During the time they lived together, Conrad did manage to prevail upon Robbins to give up his old Carmen Ghia for a powder-blue Mercedes that he kept the rest of his life.

376—"It was . . . that [ballet]": Author's interview with Christine Conrad, October 7, 1999.

376—"just a feeling . . . with people": *New York Times*, June 3, 1990.

376—"Some of it . . . *a Gathering*'": Jerome Robbins, *New York Times*, July 12, 1981.

376—Balanchine didn't restore: Jerome Robbins, Oral History Project, Dance Collection, NYPL, interview by Ellen Sorrin, November 28, 1995.

377—"It's almost . . . would be": Jerome Robbins interviewed by Edwin Denby in *Dance Magazine*, June 1969.

377—"After years . . . musical sense": Lincoln Kirstein, *Thirty Years: Lincoln Kirstein's New York City Ballet*, New York: Alfred A. Knopf, 1978, p. 195.

378—"I'm doing . . . this bad?": Jerome Robbins interviewed by Clive Barnes, *New York Times*, April 25, 1969.

378—"That was . . . terrified me": Author's interview with Patricia McBride, March 6, 1999.

379—"The rehearsal . . . were elated": Edward Villella with Larry Kaplan, *Prodigal Son: Dancing for Balanchine in a World of Pain and Magic*, Pittsburgh: University of Pittsburgh Press, 1998, pp. 214–215.

379–80—"I loved the . . . the room": Author's interview with Patricia McBride, March 6, 1999.

380—"Patty McBride . . . with her": Jerome Robbins interviewed by Edwin Denby in *Dance Magazine*, June 1969.

380—"I'll tell you . . . she was": Author's interview with Violette Verdy, January 17, 1999.

380—"It all . . . took over": *Newsweek*, June 2, 1969.

380—"Wonderful . . . more": Villella, *Prodigal Son*, p. 217.

380—"Make more . . . like peanuts": *New York Times*, December 8, 1974. When he related the same anecdote in later years, Robbins sometimes substituted the image of popcorn for peanuts.

380–81—"I listened . . . of pianism": Jerome Robbins interviewed by Edwin Denby in *Dance Magazine*, June 1969.

381—"Don't dance . . . take you": Author's interview with Robert Maiorano, May 26, 1999.

381—"Each variation . . . social behavior": Nancy Goldner, *Christian Science Monitor*, May 23, 1969.

381—"We call . . . sounds stormy": Sara Leland in *Ballet Review*, Vol. III, No. 5, 1971.

381—"If I had . . . They accept": Jerome Robbins interviewed by Edwin Denby in *Dance Magazine*, June 1969.

382—"Jerry called . . . He liked me": Author's interview with Joe Eula, May 16, 2000.

382–83—"Balanchine usually . . . to adjust": Villella, *Prodigal Son*, pp. 216–217.

383—"I feel . . . you do . . . ": Villella, *Prodigal Son*, p. 218.

383–84—"I feel . . . normal self": Author's interview with Patricia McBride, March 6, 1999.

384–85—"I was afraid . . . different purpose": Author's interview with Violette Verdy, January 17, 1999.

385—"He was tragic . . . pretty joyless": Author's interview with John Clifford, March 30, 1999.

385—"It was wonderful . . . with him": Author's interview with John Prinz, May 29, 1999.

385–86—In her memoir . . . about returning": Allegra Kent, *Once a Dancer . . .*, New York: St. Martin's Press, 1997, pp. 213–14.

386—"Jerry had . . . you now": Villella, *Prodigal Son*, p. 222.

387—"At the premiere . . . hard way": Author's interview with John Clifford, March 30, 1999.

387—"It is . . . has captured": *New York Times*, May 23, 1969.

387—"I got a kiss . . . *Gathering'*": *New York Times*, June 3, 1990.

387—"Mr. B loved . . . every performance": Author's interview with Patricia McBride, March 6, 1999.

388—"the whipping . . . so personally": Author's interview with Bruce Wells, May 12, 1999.

388—"I know he . . . he likes?'": Author's interview with Betty Cage, March 10, 1999.

388—"It is like . . . and war": Edwin Denby in *Dance Magazine*, June 1969.

388—Robbins was dismayed: Letter from Jerome Robbins to Edwin Denby, May 27, 1969, reprinted in George Balanchine and Francis Mason, *101 Stories of the Great Ballets*, New York: Doubleday (Anchor Edition), 1989, p. 109.

388—A Balanchine-like formulation: Where Balanchine characterized himself variously with self-effacing descriptions like "gardener" or "chef," Robbins later said, "I don't want to fall into profundities and artistry and surround everything with whipped cream. I work, only instead of being a plumber, I'm a choreographer. I like my job." *New York Times*, December 8, 1974.

389—"It's as if . . . to change": Villella, *Prodigal Son*, p. 218.

389—"a continuation . . . same vein": Author's interview with Patricia McBride, March 6, 1999.

389—"a man . . . to Balanchine's": Peter Martins, *Far from Denmark*, Boston/Toronto: Little, Brown and Company, 1982, p. 110.

389–90—"As we always . . . the father": Author's interview with Violette Verdy, January 17, 1999.

390—"Noverre, choreographer . . . the heart": Walter Terry in *Saturday Review*, February 21, 1970.

390–91—"the effect . . . from somewhere": *Albany Times Union*, 1971 (cited in Reynolds, *Repertory in Review*, p. 267).

391—"The trouble . . . the stage": *Albany Times Union*, 1971 (cited in Reynolds, *Repertory in Review*, p. 266).

391—"I consider . . . tells it": Author's interview with Barry Primus, May 6, 1999.

392—"their egos . . . preferences": Gelsey Kirkland with Greg Lawrence, *Dancing on My Grave*, New York: Doubleday, 1986, p. 63.

392—"He was . . . a boy": Author's interview with Bruce Wells, May 12, 1999.

392—"It was the friction . . . creative spark alive": Author's interview with Bruce Wells, May 12, 1999.

392–93—"Mr. B was . . . calming the waters": Author's interview with John Clifford, March 30, 1999.

393—"I know Jerry . . . the harpsichord": Author's interview with Patricia McBride, March 6, 1999.

393—"I guess . . . start over": *The New Yorker*, June 19, 1971.

394—"Oh, so . . . down!": Author's interview with John Clifford, March 29, 1999.

394—"He was able . . . what you got": Author's interview with Robert Maiorano, May 26, 1999.

394—"Jerry was . . . very exciting": Author's interview with Bruce Wells, May 12, 1999.

394—"total . . . prevailed": *Saturday Review*, August 15, 1970.

395—"I think . . . leave him": Author's interview with Betty Cage, March 10, 1999.

395—"I think . . . Tommy's heart": Author's interview with Bruce Wells, May 12, 1999.

395—"Tommy Abbott . . . of sides": Author's interview with Edward Bigelow, June 7, 1999.

396—Nureyev had been a fan: Diane Solway, *Nureyev: His Life*, New York: William Morrow and Company, 1998, pp. 135–136.

396—"They really . . . treading carefully": Author's interview with Lynn Seymour, May 14, 1999.

396—"You worked . . . the process": Author's interview with Monica Mason, June 1, 1999.

396—"He shamed . . . than you": Author's interview with Michael Coleman, June 7, 1999.

396—"I think . . . good relationship": Author's interview with Anthony Dowell, January 4, 1999.

396–97—"Jerry told . . . the stage'": Author's interview with Joe Eula, May 16, 2000.

397—"Isn't that . . . do it!": Author's interview with Monica Mason, June 1, 1999.

397—"Jerry almost . . . brown tights": Author's interview with Joe Eula, May 16, 2000.

397—"A creation . . . to cry": *Dancing Times*, September 1969.

398—"It was . . . done that": Author's interview with Anthony Dowell, January 4, 1999.

398—"Lately, I've . . . my own": *New York Times*, April 25, 1969.

398–99—"When we . . . with you": Author's interview with Betty Cage, March 10, 1999.

399–400—"a rubber . . . be scheduled": Robert Gottlieb "Balanchine's Dream," *Vanity Fair*, December 1998.

400—"How those . . . become masterpieces": Author's interview with Edward Bigelow, June 7, 1999.

400—Robbins later said: Jerome Robbins interviewed by Ellen Sorrin, New York City Ballet Guild Seminar, March 8, 1993, Dance Collection, NYPL.

401—"masterpiece": *New York Magazine*, July 5, 1971.

401—"a work . . . over again": *New York Times*, May 29, 1971.

401—"a sumptuous banquet": *Village Voice*, June 10, 1971.

401—"Robbins has . . . Bach": *Newsweek*, June 7, 1971.

401—"Robbins working . . . musical visualizations": *Ballet Review*, Spring 1972, Vol. 4, No. 2.

401–2—"I was . . . that style": Author's interview with Maria Karnilova, September 10, 1999.

402—"I was . . . abstract style": Author's interview with Janet Reed, May 17, 1999.

402—"It was . . . of directions": Author's interview with Richard Thomas, April 27, 1999.

402—"He spoke . . . more sublime": Author's interview with Alicia Alonso, September 14, 1999.

403—"We [choreographers] . . . little bit": *New York Times*, December 8, 1974. The context of the Balanchine quotation was subsequently identified during Robbins' interview for the Kennedy Center Oral History Program, July 11, 1995.

403—"I had to . . . at all . . .": Villella, *Prodigal Son*, p. 233.

403—"a race . . . temporarily wins": Kirstein, *Thirty Years*, p. 214.

403—"It certainly . . . *Variations*": *New York Times*, June 3, 1990.

404—"It is . . . the theater": *New York Times*, February 4, 1972.

404—"shock theater": *Ballet Review*, Spring 1972, Vol. 4, No. 2.

404–5—"He got . . . it happened": Author's interview with Penelope Dudleston McKay, May 3, 1999.

405—"The endless . . . through it": Author's interview with Patricia Zipprodt, February 24, 1999.

405—"When the . . . wasn't seeing": Villella, *Prodigal Son*, p. 235.

406—"I must . . . they *did*": Jerome Robbins in Reynolds, *Repertory in Review*, p. 285.

406—"a fantastic . . . ethnic boundaries": *New York Times*, February 4, 1972.

406—"a towering achievement": *New York Daily News*, February 5, 1972.

406—"tender majesty . . . oriental thought": *Dance Magazine*, April 1972.

406—"the cohesive . . . images": *New York Times*, December 8, 1974.

406—"it is . . . have seen": Nancy Goldner cited in Balanchine and Mason, *101 Stories of the Great Ballets*, p. 516.

406—"no one . . . by it": Patricia Barnes cited in Balanchine and Mason, *101 Stories of the Great Ballets*, p. 518.

406—"tedious hokum . . . would emerge": *Ballet Review*, Spring 1972, Vol. 4, No. 2.

406–8—"I was with . . . what he wanted": Author's interviews with Penelope Dudleston McKay, May 3 and June 22, 1999.

408—"Balanchine insisted . . . big bang": Kirstein, *Thirty Years*, p. 214.

408—"Of course . . . is comparable": Author's interview with Betty Cage, March 10, 1999.

409—"Mr. Robbins . . . Stravinsky's music": *New York Times*, June 19, 1972.

409—"a celebration of death": cited in *New York Times*, June 22, 1972.

409—"a masterpiece . . . ever done": *Newsweek*, July 3, 1972.

409—"mannered . . . so corny": *The Nation*, July 10, 1972.

410—Edward Bigelow remembered: Author's interview with Edward Bigelow, June 7, 1999.

410—"The story . . . for survival": Jerome Robbins cited in Villella, *Prodigal Son*, p. 239.

410—"Every ballet . . . of him": Jerome Robbins in Reynolds, *Repertory in Review*, p. 303.

410—"working on . . . than one": *New York Times*, June 23, 1972.

411—"One day . . . into *Pulcinella*": Violette Verdy in Reynolds, *Repertory in Review*, p. 304.

411—"That was . . . I would die": Author's interview with Penelope Dudleston McKay, May 3, 1999.

412—"The work . . . telling you": Author's interview with Jean-Pierre Bonnefoux, May 27, 1999.

412—"bland . . . quality": *New York Times*, May 26, 1973.

412—"The Company . . . be masterpieces": Jerome Robbins cited in Reynolds, *Repertory in Review*, p. 308

413—"He [Robbins] . . . would do": Author's interview with Violette Verdy, January 17, 1999.

413—"We [dancers] . . . that trip": Author's interview with Patricia McBride, March 6, 1999. Glen Tetley also had a recollection of Robbins in Spoleto that year. Tetley recalled, "Jerry loved Spoleto and I loved it, too. I had returned with other companies, doing my choreography, and I decided to buy a house in Spoleto, outside of Spoleto. In 1969, I bought a sixteenth-century tower that was on the mountain outside of Spoleto. It was my passion. I had no money, but I bought it. Over three years, everything I made I poured into it. I had to restore it, it was a ruin completely, but I did a beautiful restoration on it. Quite remote, with eighteen acres, 540 olive trees, a pine forest—just everything, a paradise.

"I was working as a choreographer, doing a ballet [outside the country in 1973]. Of course, when I leave I close the place up tightly with big wooden storm doors and shutters and things. Scott [Douglas] had been with me and we had driven from Amsterdam back. The Spoleto Festival was just about over, and we came up a country road—it's a white road, a gravel road—parked the car, and I opened the gate and I came down to open the house. With the Italian locks, you have to turn them five times until the bolt moves. I turned it once and it opened, the door opened like that. I went in and I realized instantly somebody had been inside the place, that things were in a different place. I looked at the refrigerator and I realized there was food in it, that the freezer door was partly open and there was frost all over it. I ran out and I said, 'Somebody's been in the house, I don't believe this.' I went up to the second floor and I sat down—there's a library—I sat down in shock and I heard footsteps coming from above. I turned around and Jerry Robbins comes down the stairs of my house. He said, 'Hi, I've been waiting for you.' I was in shock. 'Jerry!' He said, 'I have a little something for you because we drank some of your wine and I wanted to give you this to make up.' It was not a quart, but a pint of Dewar's whiskey in a brown paper bag, like a tramp has in his back pocket on the street.

"I said, 'Jerry, what are you doing here?' He said, 'I can't thank you enough. It's been so wonderful to stay here.' I said, 'What!' He said, 'I hope you don't mind, but it was noisy in town, and everyone told me you had this beautiful place here. I spoke with the [Festival] secretary, and she said she didn't have keys but that she thought your neighbors, the farmer neighbors, had keys.' I was in shock. Without informing me or asking me anything he took it upon himself to move into my house. They stayed there three weeks—he had twenty-two people with him. There were no other keys, so they left all the doors and windows open twenty-four hours a day for three weeks. They broke the freezer and refrigerator, which are huge. They had never been closed properly. . . . I had to replace them. I had beautiful solid chestnut butcher-block counters and they had left wet things on them so the wood had split. They had used every piece of linen in the house—you can imagine twenty-two people. . . . Actually I had two maids who used to come and they would come weekly, check on the place. They came and they found all these people there. They quit, they wouldn't come back. Also they didn't know what to do with the garbage. . . . They threw it down in the garden, in the forest. It was disgusting. The worst part [is] he had some of his assistants living there, too, and they had brought up—there were functioning male prostitutes in Spoleto—and they had brought them up there, they had gotten to know the place, and the following year was the first time I had a major break-in with people. They obviously knew how to open the bottom door and broke in and were looking for mainly drugs, which I didn't have. It really was unpardonable and I didn't know, I just can't imagine anyone doing that. For years people would say, 'Oh, I know your house, I've been there.' The big party for the Celebration he gave at my house. I was furious.

"When he finally came down the steps, he said, 'I don't know whose room that is up on the top, but I really loved it, it was so calm and peaceful.' My room, my desk, my letters, with my contracts, with my bank statements, everything on it. Anyway, the next year he had the chutzpah to call me up, and he said, 'I think I'm going back to Spoleto and I'd like to talk to you about renting your place again.' I mean he never rented it in the beginning. I said, 'Jerry, it's just not available. It's not available and in fact it's inhabitable because I'm reconstructing the whole place.' And then he said the most curious thing. He said, 'It was so great staying there, and I want to offer you the same thing. Any time you come to New York, I have a beautiful house here and I have a maid all the time, and there's a number of bedrooms, and you're perfectly welcome to come and stay here.' I said, 'Jerry, I have an apartment in New York, I don't need your house.'

"Later, he felt guilty, and he called me and he said, 'Would you and Scott come up and have dinner with me one night?' So we went up and had dinner, just the three of us, and it was not a relaxed evening at all, but he was trying to be very, very nice. At the end of it, we were leaving and he took me down into his studio—his office was on the first floor. He said, 'I really owe you something for being in your house.' He took an icon, a small icon of St. Sebastian, off the wall. He said, 'Would you take this?' I said, 'Thank you, thank you, Jerry.' So I took it. But it was just a very, very strange thing."

413—"Aidan was . . . together": Author's interview with John Clifford, March 29, 1999.

413–14—"Oh goodness . . . Lincoln's": Author's interview with Betty Cage, March 10, 1999.

414—"I would say . . . his opinion": Author's interview with Edward Bigelow, June 7, 1999.

414—"Jerry let Aidan . . . a ballet": Author's interview with Peter Schabel, December 3, 1998.

414–15—"They were . . . bother him": Author's interview with Michael Koessel, April 28, 1999.

415—"The boys . . . in earshot": Arthur Laurents, *Original Story By: A Memoir of Broadway and Hollywood*, New York: Alfred A. Knopf, 2000, p. 330.

415—"Gold and . . . he was": Author's interview with Harold Talbott, January 10, 1999.

416–17—"Of course, I was . . . certain things": Author's interview with Howard Rosenman, February 3, 1999.

417—"Lenny is . . . with it": Letter from Helen Coates to Alan Fluck, February 24, 1974, cited in Humphrey Burton, *Leonard Bernstein*, New York: Anchor Books, 1994, p. 422.

417—"I think . . . don't converge": Jerome Robbins cited in Reynolds, *Repertory in Review*, p. 313.

417—*"Dybbuk* was . . . a kiss": Author's interview with Patricia McBride, March 6, 1999.

417—"We were . . . watching it": Author's interview with Wilma Curley, May 28, 1999.

417–18—"Chanon . . . in oblivion": Program note, New York Philharmonic, New Zealand–Australia tour, August 1974, cited in Burton, *Leonard Bernstein*, pp. 422–423.

418—"It was the integer . . . to reside": Program note, New York Philharmonic, April 3, 1975, cited in Burton, *Leonard Bernstein*, p. 423.

419—"the loving . . . climax," *Newsweek*, May 27, 1974.

419—"caught the . . . leading dancers": *New York Times*, May 17, 1974.

419—"Robbins' decision . . . of view": *Christian Science Monitor*, May 24, 1974.

419—"a pretentious . . . no delivery": *The New Republic*, July 20, 1974.

419—"In Robbins's case . . . in dance": *New Yorker*, February 11, 1980.

419—"Oddly, the . . . plotless ballet": *New York Times*, January 19, 1980.

419—"We owe . . . the wine": *New York Daily News*, May 16, 1975.

420—"He [Robbins] . . . future life": Suzanne Farrell with Toni Bentley, *Holding on to the Air*, New York: Summit Books, 1990, p. 224.

420—"constantly made . . . our ideas": Martins, *Far from Denmark*, p. 110.

420—"After the adagio . . . *like it?*": Author's interview with Leslie Bailey, February 22, 1999.

421—"a lovely . . . sportive choreography": *New York Times*, May 16, 1975.

421—"I love . . . libretto exactly": Jerome Robbins cited in Reynolds, *Repertory in Review*, p. 322.

421—"The only . . . isn't any": *The New Yorker*, June 16, 1975.

421–22—"He hasn't . . . personal talent": *New York Post*, May 24, 1975.

422—"Today he is . . . very soul": *New York Post*, January 24, 1976.

422—"There are . . . to pay": *New York Times*, February 10, 1980.

422–23—"for bringing . . . happily so": *New York Times*, April 27, 1976.

423—Robbins had previously donated: *New York Times*, December 8, 1974.

423—"I think the most . . . that way": Mikhail Baryshnikov with Charles France, *Baryshnikov at Work*, New York: Alfred A. Knopf, 1978, pp. 195–197.

423–24—"In *Other Dances* . . . audience": Natalia Makarova, *A Dance Biography*, New York: Alfred A. Knopf, 1979, p. 156.

424—"he would . . . delicate movements": Baryshnikov, *Baryshnikov at Work*, pp. 195–197.

424—"Sometimes I think . . . his beard": *Time*, March 14, 1994.

424—"Jerry admired . . . behavior": Author's interview with Santo Loquasto, August 25, 1999.

424–25—"He [Jerry] . . . have that": Author's interview with Christopher d'Amboise, May 10, 1999.

425—"A girl . . . enough": Jerome Robbins interviewed by Deborah Jowitt, Kennedy Center Honors Oral History Program, July 11, 1995.

425—"could fit . . . it anywhere": *New York Times*, May 11, 1976.

426—"They met . . . crowds mix": Author's interview with Michael Koessel, April 28, 1999.

426—"Jerry loved . . . were together": E-mail letter from Lisa Stevens to the author, May 1, 1999.

426–27—"One of the . . . his life": Author's interview with Michael Koessel, April 28, 1999.

427–28—"Warren was . . . a person": Author's interview with Nathaniel Dorsky, December 9, 1998.

428—"We'll talk . . . later": Jerome Robbins in Jared Brown, *Zero Mostel: A Biography*, New York: Atheneum, 1989, p. 294.

428—"Zero Mostel hated . . . the situation": Author's interview with Gerald Schoenfeld, October 14, 1999.

428—"the king . . . his throne": *New York Times*, December 30, 1976.

428—"disdainful of . . . of himself": *New York Post*, cited in Brown, *Zero Mostel*, p. 295.

429—"It didn't . . . one stayed": Thelma Lee in Brown, *Zero Mostel*, p. 296.

429—At the beginning of the year . . . Chilean cook: letter from Jerome Robbins to Penelope Dudleston, January 5, 1977, and author's interview with Penelope Dudleston McKay, May 3, 1999.

430—"I played . . . very sharp": Author's interview with James Mitchell, April 9, 1999.

430—"Nobody . . . gay anymore": Jerome Robbins in Arthur Laurents, *Original Story By: A Memoir of Broadway and Hollywood*, New York: Alfred A. Knopf, 2000, p. 48.

430–31—"a tour . . . to sketch": Kirstein, *Thirty Years: Lincoln Kirstein's New York City Ballet*, p. 327.

431—"Oh, that's . . . got one": Author's interview with Ninette Charisse, May 12, 1999.

431—"One night . . . front page": Author's interview with Leslie Bailey, February 22, 1999.

431–32—"There was . . . so terrible'": Author's interview with Sonia Cullinen Robbins, May 12, 2000.

433—"It got . . . Lindbergh baby": Author's interview with Leslie Bailey, February 22, 1999.

433—"I swapped . . . and split": *New York Times*, July 2, 1978.

432–33—"solos and . . . *Other Dances*": Author's interview with Gelsey Kirkland, December 29, 1999.

433—"It's a . . . use them": *New York Times,* May 14, 1978.

433—Robbins later admitted: Jerome Robbins, interviewed by Ellen Sorrin, New York City Ballet Guild Seminar, March 8, 1993, Dance Collection, NYPL.

433—"Unfortunately, she . . . behind expectations": *New York Times,* May 19, 1978.

434—"was revealed . . . eighteen years": Kirstein, *Thirty Years: Lincoln Kirstein's New York City Ballet,* p. 328.

434—"Frohlich was . . . a son": Author's interview with Janet Reed, February 24, 1999.

434—"It was . . . depressing part": *Washington Post,* March 18, 1979.

434—"like a try-out": *New York Times,* January 14, 1979.

435—"happy ballet . . . opera ballets": *New York Times,* January 14, 1979.

435—"I remember . . . the piece": Author's interview with Patricia McBride, March 6, 1999.

435–36—"Actually, that . . . me again": Author's interview with Gen Horiuchi, June 22, 1999.

436—"I felt sorry . . . and all": *Time,* March 14, 1994.

436—"I don't . . . for Baryshnikov": Author's interview with Robert Tracy, May 25, 1999.

437—"It was . . . Rudolf Nureyev": *New York Times,* April 9, 1979.

437—"The rehearsals . . . second nature": Martins, *Far from Denmark,* p. 110.

437—"got along . . . a gift": Author's interview with Patricia McBride, March 6, 1999.

437—"a great deal . . . chest level": *New York Times,* June 16, 1979.

438—"To be . . . small accomplishment": *New York Times,* June 16, 1979.

438–39—"He wanted . . . a mistake": Author's interview with Peter Schabel, December 3, 1998.

439–40—" . . . the art of . . . fixed space": *Washington Post,* March 18, 1979.

440—"I think that . . . say that": Author's interview with Bart Cook, June 27, 1999.

441—"Two months . . . be good": *New York Times,* July 12, 1981.

441—Robbins later admitted . . . his voice: Jerome Robbins, interviewed by Ellen Sorrin, New York City Ballet Guild Seminar, March 8, 1993, Dance Collection, NYPL.

441–42—"When we . . . that way": Author's interview with Stacy Caddell, May 23, 1999.

442—"you see . . . in them": *The New Yorker,* August 10, 1981.

442—"a brilliant step . . . *pas de deux*": *New York Times,* June 13, 1981.

442—"I was cast . . . later on": Author's interview with Gen Horiuchi, June 22, 1999.

442—In early April of 1981: *New York Post,* April 8, 1981.

442—"Jerry came . . . any expense": Author's interview with Ahmet Ertegün, June 2, 1999.

442–43—"Jerry invented . . . and tradition": *New York Times,* July 20, 1981.

443—"I'm going. . . . other times": *New York Times,* July 12, 1981.

443—Robbins later admitted: Jerome Robbins, interviewed by Ellen Sorrin, New York City Ballet Guild Seminar, March 8, 1993, Dance Collection, NYPL.

443—"I went on . . . went down": Author's interview with Bart Cook, June 27, 1999.

443—The only *faux pas*: *Washington Post,* December 7, 1981.

444—"When we . . . ballet choreographer": Author's interview with Bart Cook, June 27, 1999.

460—"Jerry definitely . . . own world": *Stagebill*, February 1999.

460—"I remember him . . . see them": Author's interview with Jerri Kumery, June 27, 1999.

460—"It was like . . . Martha Graham": *New York Times*, February 10, 1985.

460–61—"Like the 'Epigraphs' . . . Greek antiquity": cited in the *New York Times*, February 12, 1984.

461—"all eight . . . of poetry": *New York Post*, February 6, 1984.

461—"We were doing . . . ever again": Author's interview with Jerri Kumery, June 27, 1999.

462—"I don't think . . . very much": *New York Times*, November 11, 1984.

462—"The kids . . . can tell": *New York Times*, November 11, 1984.

462—"Jerry had . . . done what": Twyla Tharp, *Push Comes to Shove*, New York: Bantam Books, 1992, p. 294.

462–63—"We are . . . same painting": *New York Times*, May 21, 1984.

463—"There actually . . . its premiere . . .": Tharp, *Push Comes to Shove*, p. 294.

463—"I went to . . . what happens'": *New York Times*, November 11, 1984.

463—"They [Robbins . . . like hours": Author's interview with Jerri Kumery, June 27, 1999.

463—"Twyla and I . . . loved it": *New York Times*, November 11, 1984.

463—"really something . . . see it": *New York Times*, June 9, 1984.

463—"These are . . . they cherish": *The New Yorker*, July 2, 1984.

464—"The level of . . . across the stage": *New York Times*, May 21, 1984.

464—"the New York . . . so now": *New York Times*, February 10, 1985.

464–65—"It was like a . . . the school": Author's interview with Wilma Curley, May 28, 1999.

465—"We knew that . . . spoken of": Author's interview with Jerri Kumery, June 27, 1999.

465—"true Balanchinian . . . specific story": Suzanne Farrell with Toni Bentley, *Holding on to the Air*, New York: Summit Books / Simon & Schuster Inc., 1990, p. 276.

465—"the sense . . . for themselves": cited in *Dance Magazine*, May 1987.

465–66—"I enjoyed . . . welcome substance": Farrell, *Holding on to the Air*, p. 276.

466—"God, it's weird . . . an exorcism": Author's interview with Christopher d'Amboise, May 10, 1999.

466–67—"had them . . . he's doing": Robert La Fosse with Andrew Mark Wentink, *Nothing to Hide: A Dancer's Life*, New York: Donald I. Fine, 1987, p. 232.

467—"I don't think . . . for everyone": Author's interview with Bart Cook, June 27, 1999.

467—"It isn't that . . . too aware": Author's interview with Isabel Brown, April 8, 1999.

467—"She caught . . . hope so": Jerome Robbins, Nora Kaye memorial, New York City Center, January 4, 1988.

468—"I wasn't . . . in it": Letter to the author from Stuart Ostrow, April 30, 1999.

468—"straight and strong . . . all means": cited in Humphrey Burton, *Leonard Bernstein*, New York: Anchor Books, 1994, pp. 489–490.

468—"grudging": Burton, *Leonard Bernstein*, p. 490.

468–69—"I think Zero . . . get out'": Author's interview with Josh Mostel, June 22, 1999.

469—Robbins abruptly abandoned: according to Eric Bentley, Brecht's son, Stefan, attended a preview and refused to grant his approval for the adaptation.

469—"That this . . . nice circle": *Los Angeles Times,* June 3, 1987.

469—"Yet the most . . . new people": *New York Times,* June 2, 1987.

469–70—"The whole world . . . started anywhere": *New York Times,* October 5, 1987.

470—Robbins was approached: Author's interview with Leslie Bailey, February 22, 1999.

470—"Doing a show . . . three months": *New York Times,* July 12, 1981.

470—"I hated . . . out of it": *New York Times,* December 2, 1987.

471–72—"Floria Lasky came . . . come to meetings": Author's interview with Gerald Schoenfeld, October 14, 1999.

472–73—"I'm going to . . . that number' . . . the dancers and the work": Jerome Robbins interviewed by John Guare, *New York Times Magazine,* September 11, 1988.

473–74—"Sure, I'm . . . I'll stop . . . read about": *New York Times,* January 31, 1988.

474—As Clive Barnes pointed out: *New York Post,* February 5, 1988.

474—"pure Robbins at his best": *New York Times,* February 6, 1988.

474—"a Prospero-like . . . farewell": *New York Post,* January 22, 1994.

474—"God knows . . . replaces it": Author's interview with Stephanie Saland, April 5, 1999.

474—"*Ives, Songs* was . . . to me": Author's interview with Stacy Caddell, May 23, 1999.

475—"He called me . . . was staggering": Author's interview with Gerald Schoenfeld, October 14, 1999.

475–76—"I wasn't . . . bodies around": Author's interview with Grover Dale, March 17, 1999.

476—"enormous toll": *New York Times,* April 27, 1989.

476–77—"Jerry was . . . intention with him": Author's interview with Mark Esposito, March 10, 1999.

477–78—"He didn't . . . his plate . . . he deferred . . . little recourse . . . orchestrator of all this": Author's interview with Jason Alexander, May 14, 1999.

479—"The main thing . . . straight theater": Author's interview with Charlotte d'Amboise, May 10, 1999.

479—"You knew . . . your face": Author's interview with Nancy Hess, April 14, 1999.

479–80—"I remember . . . never seen": Author's interview with Charlotte d'Amboise, May 10, 1999.

480—"I am a perfectionist . . . how I work": *New York Times,* February 19, 1989.

480—"People used . . . than anyone": Author's interview with Charlotte d'Amboise, May 10, 1999.

480—"I really adored . . . nailed my life": Author's interview with Jason Alexander, May 14, 1999.

480—"swept in . . . jeweled top": *New York Post,* October 13, 1988.

481—"Jerry called . . . hurt by that": Author's interview with Richard D'Arcy, March 9, 1999.

481—"I remember . . . in the show": Author's interview with Jason Alexander, May 14, 1999.

481–82—"I remember . . . he wanted": Author's interview with Charlotte d'Amboise, May 10, 1999.

482—"While 'Jerome Robbins' . . . theatrical flow": *New York Times*, February 27, 1989.

482—"entirely objective . . . a community": *New York Daily News*, February 27, 1989.

482—"the kind of . . . heart to": *New York Post*, February 27, 1989.

482—"The special . . . an elegy": *Newsweek*, March 6, 1989.

482—"history lesson . . . the river": *New York Times*, March 12, 1989.

483—"and thirteen . . . An amazing man": Grover Dale in *The Journal for Stage Directors & Choreographers*, Fall/Winter 1998, p. 32, originally published by *Dance & Fitness*, Issue 41. Revised by Grover Dale in a letter to the author, October 10, 2000.

483—"Jerry asked . . . that happen": Author's interview with Nanette Fabray, February 2, 1999.

483–84—"It was just . . . eat them": Author's interview with Wilma Curley, May 28, 1999.

484—"What we did . . . always does": Author's interview with Helen Gallagher, April 13, 1999.

484—Robbins' weekly combined royalty income: *Variety*, December 20, 1989.

484–86—"I get this call . . . on my life": Author's interview with Grover Dale, March 17, 1999.

486—"We had . . . the occasion": Author's interview with Gerald Schoenfeld, October 14, 1999.

486—"Absolutely not . . . the beach": *New York Times*, April 27, 1989.

486—"George Balanchine . . . a little": *Newsweek*, March 6, 1989.

487—"I would . . . endearing term": Author's interview with Gerald Schoenfeld, October 14, 1999.

487–88—"The Suntory . . . with Jesse": Author's interview with Gerald Schoenfeld, October 14, 1999.

488–89—"Jesse had . . . *The Bacchae*": Author's interview with Michael Koessel, April 28, 1999. Koessel also described a subsequent trip to the Middle East that he undertook with Robbins, Lisa Stevens and Jesse Gerstein: "Lisa, Jesse, Jerry, and I went to Turkey for five weeks in 1989. We went and stayed at the Erteguns' house in Bodrum and then they lent us their boat and we toured along the coast. We all ended up in Anatalia and then we all got terribly sick."

489–90—"I must have . . . self-conscious at all": Author's interview with D.D. Allen, May 21, 1999.

490—"That summer he . . . very, very nice": Author's interview with Michael Koessel, April 28, 1999.

490—"It's important . . . other things": *New York Times*, November 6, 1989.

490–91—"Jesse found . . . Left Bank": E-mail letter to the author from Lisa Stevens, May 4, 1999.

491–92—"I went many . . . I must say": Author's interview with Ghislaine Thesmar, October 11, 1999.

492—"After my mother . . . whole world": Author's interview with Kitty Hawks, May 15, 1999.

492—"When Lady Keith . . . who did it": Author's interview with Sara Corrin, October 25, 1999.

493—"It was the last . . . about his mother": Author's interview with Michael Koessel, April 28, 1999.

494—"Let me consult . . . know that": Edward Villella with Larry Kaplan, *Prodigal Son: Dancing for Balanchine in a World of Pain and Magic,* Pittsburgh: University of Pittsburgh Press, 1998, p. 10.

494—"If anything . . . than before . . ." Doris Hering, *Dance Magazine,* October 1990.

494—"Our education . . . very happy": Author's interview with Ghislaine Thesmar, October 11, 1999.

495—"cold turkey . . . stopped smoking": *New Yorker,* July 9, 1990.

495—"He used to . . . certainly did": Author's interview with Fay Greenbaum, June 13, 1999.

495—"based on . . . own life": *New York Times,* February 15, 1991.

495—"I was always . . . that part": Author's interview with Barry Primus: May 6, 1999.

496—"I don't know . . . word—WORK": *Dance Magazine,* December 1959.

496—"I actually had mixed feelings . . . to him sometimes": Author's interview with Fay Greenbaum, June 13, 1999.

496–97—"The things that . . . closet in Manhattan": Author's interview with Megan Raddant, October 18, 1999.

497—"Everybody has . . . so incredible": Author's interview with Sara Corrin, October 25, 1999.

498—"He invited me . . . poking at the material": "Jerry and the Other One," *The Journal for Directors and Choreographers,* Fall/Winter 1998, pp. 34–35.

498—"It seemed he . . . own Jewishness": Author's interview with Gerald Freedman, March 4, 1999.

498—"What he was . . . the difference'": Author's interview with Sheldon Harnick, January 27, 1999.

499—"My own feeling . . . felt like": Author's interview with John Weidman, May 6, 1999.

499—"I have no idea . . . angry young man": Author's interview with Jace Alexander, May 24, 1999.

499—"He was in . . . and handsome": Author's interview with Ron Rifkin, March 29, 1999.

500—"I was a young . . . out of it": Author's interview with Jace Alexander, May 24, 1999.

500—"Obviously, his demons . . . sweet person": Author's interview with Ron Rifkin, March 29, 1999.

500—"After a while . . . your father": Author's interview with Alan King, April 10, 1999. Curiously, years before Robbins employed a similar choice of words when he wrote that "a ballet is a ritual of *exorcism.*" From Robbins' Preface to *Ballet Panorama,* Photographs by Serge Lido, 1961.

500–01—"What I remember . . . would be": Author's interview with Jace Alexander, May 24, 1999.

501—"described his life . . . was HUAC": Author's interview with Fay Greenbaum, June 13, 1999.

501—"You could say . . . was brilliant": Author's interview with John Weidman, August 10, 1999.

502—"inclined to . . . and fantasy": Letter to the author from Sonia Robbins Cullinen, July 18, 2000.

502—"There were bicycles . . . these kids": Author's interview with Mark Esposito, March 10, 1999.

502—"Maybe it was . . . about it": Author's interview with Ron Rifkin, March 29, 1999.

503—"being brought . . . his son": Author's interview with John Weidman, July 3, 1999.

503—"I guess by . . . to anything": Author's interview with Fay Greenbaum, June 13, 1999.

504—"awakening, in . . . very bizarre": Author's interview with Joey McKneely, July 1, 1999.

504—"One of the things . . . Activities Committee": Author's interview with Sheldon Harnick, January 27, 1999.

504—"everything was . . . from him": Author's interview with Sheldon Harnick, January 27, 1999.

504—"I saw . . . be ruined": Author's interview with Megan Raddant, October 18, 1999.

504–5—"He did everything . . . his life": Author's interview with Fay Greenbaum, June 13, 1999.

505—"The image . . . haunted him": Author's interview with John Weidman, August 10, 1999.

505—"less idiosyncratic and interesting": Author's interview with John Weidman, August 10, 1999.

506—"Over a period . . . it through": Author's interview with Gerald Freedman, March 4, 1999.

506—"The honesty in . . . heroic to me": Author's interview with John Weidman, May 25, 1999.

506–7—"As I understand it . . . heard from him'": Author's interview with Sheldon Harnick, January 27, 1999.

507—"He [Jesse] . . . the future": Author's interview with Michael Koessel, April 28, 1999.

507—"We knew Jesse . . . terrible to watch": Author's interview with Sono Osato, May 3, 1999.

507—"When Jesse . . . when he died": Letter to the author from Sonia Robbins Cullinen, July 18, 2000.

507—"Jerry nursed . . . a break": E-mail letter to the author from Lisa Stevens, May 1, 1999.

507—"My relationship . . . at the beach": E-mail letter to the author from Lisa Stevens, April 29, 1999.

CHAPTER TEN:

508—"After lengthy . . . with us": *The Dancing Times*, March 1992.

508—"Paris adores . . . was regimented": Author's interview with Bart Cook, June 27, 1999.

508–9—"At the Paris . . . Americanized now": Author's interview with John Clifford, March 29, 1999.

509–10—"He seemed so . . . work with him": Author's interview with Jean-Pierre Bonnefoux, May 27, 1999.

510–11—"I started teaching . . . his ideals": Author's interview with Fay Greenbaum, June 13, 1999.

511—"The dancers coped . . . under-rehearsed": *Dancer and Dancers*, July 1992.

511–13—"We proceeded . . . the whole story": Author's interview with Craig Zadan, March 22, 1999.

513–14—"He invited me . . . felt conflicted": Author's interview with Michael Koessel, April 28, 1999.

514—"The last thing . . . in Weehawken": Author's interview with Wilma Curley, May 28, 1999.

514—"That was the . . . from him": Author's interview with Edward Verso, April 16, 1999.

514–15—"A lot of it . . . to this day": Author's interview with Sarita Allen, April 23, 1999.

515—"If anything . . . characteristic exuberance": *New York Times*, December 20, 1993.

515—"I think . . . thinking man": Mikhail Baryshnikov in *Time*, March 14, 1994.

515–16—"For a while . . . thing for me": Jerome Robbins in *Time*, March 14, 1994.

516—"The sounds of . . . be ostentatious": *New York Times*, May 12, 1994.

516—"He had his . . . in collaboration": Author's interview with Santo Loquasto, August 25, 1999.

516—"He never lost . . . think about it": Kristina Fernandez with Rick Whitaker, *Ballet Review*, Summer 1998.

516—"I can't work . . . odd moments": *New York Times*, May 29, 1994.

517—"For all his . . . is dead": *New York Times*, June 6, 1994.

517—"I think . . . with you": Letter from Viola Zousmer Balash to Jerome Robbins, November 4, 1994.

517–18—"He did come . . . saw of Jerry": Author's interview with Viola Zousmer Balash, August 6, 1999.

518—"were holding . . . and yell'": *Dance Magazine*, September 1997.

518—"That's good . . . don't fight": *New York Times*, May 14, 1995.

518—"When he . . . said that": Author's interview with Barry Primus, May 6, 1999.

518—"With their . . . than ever": *Dance Magazine*, September 1995.

518–19—A CLASSIC . . . PURE ESSENCE: *New York Times*, June 20, 1995.

519—Robbins wrote a letter: Letter from Jerome Robbins to Penelope Dudleston McKay, August 20, 1995.

519–20—"I thought the decline . . . laugh and smile": Author's interview with Michael Koessel, April 28, 1999.

520—"Poor Jerry . . . past him": Author's interview with Bart Cook, June 27, 1999.

520—"He would come . . . to do it": Author's interview with Sono Osato, May 3, 1999.

521—"It was as if . . . with me always": *New York Times*, January 23, 1998.

521–22—"I was on . . . did for him": Author's interview with Fay Greenbaum, June 13, 1999.

522—"Whenever Jerry . . . the mood": *New York Times*, January 19, 1997.

522—"I find the . . . find out": *Dance Magazine*, September 1997.

522—"I think that . . . use them all?" Jerome Robbins in *World Theatre*, Vol. 8, No. 4, Winter 1959–1960.

523—"Within seconds . . . himself here": *New York Times*, January 24, 1997.

523—"No more a . . . natural genius": *Commentary*, April 1997.

523—"I don't . . . do it": Author's interview with Gene Gavin, January 9, 1999.

523–24—"The last time . . . too good' ": Author's interview with Barry Primus, May 6, 1999.

524—"I said . . . work again": Author's interview with Gerald Freedman, March 4, 1999.

525—"frail, vulnerable . . . they'll let me": Gina Trikonis, "Sunday Afternoon with Big Daddy," *Dance & Fitness Magazine*, September-October 1998.

525–26—"So thirty-three . . . *shirt*! Haaa!": Author's interview with Patricia Zipprodt, February 24, 1999.

526—"By doing . . . to happen": Author's interview with Sono Osato, May 3, 1999.

526–27—"Jerry taught . . . about it": Kristina Fernandez with Rick Whitaker, *Ballet Review*, Summer 1998.

527—"I guess what . . . of a person": *New York Times*, January 23, 1998.

527—"this is . . . still Robbins . . .": *New York Times*, May 22, 1998.

527–28—"I was very . . . Keep talking' ": Author's interview with Alicia Aedo, June 15, 1999.

528—Tharp later recalled: Twyla Tharp, Jerome Robbins Memorial, November 16, 1998, reprinted in *Ballet Review*, Summer 1999.

528—"I saw him . . . recognized Rick": Author's interview with Michael Koessel, April 28, 1999.

528—In a memorial service eulogy: Dr. Daniel Stern, Jerome Robbins Memorial, November 16, 1998, reprinted in *Ballet Review*, Summer 1999.

528–29—"Dan was . . . find closure": Author's interview with Sonia Cullinen Robbins, October 5, 1999.

529—"Tess was . . . Mr. Robbins": Author's interview with Alicia Aedo, June 15, 1999.

529—Dr. Stern recalled that: Dr. Daniel Stern, Jerome Robbins Memorial, November 16, 1998, reprinted in *Ballet Review*, Summer 1999.

529—"Jerry asked . . . whole thing": Author's interview with Sonia Cullinen Robbins, October 5, 1999.

531—"I've never known . . . another visit": Author's interview with Grover Dale, March 17, 1999.

531—"I think on . . . for all": Author's interview with Sono Osato, May 3, 1999.

Index